Europe and America

The Western World in Modern Times

EUROPE

Solomon F. Bloom

Brooklyn College

AND AMERICA

The Western World in Modern Times

Harcourt, Brace & World, Inc.   *New York • Burlingame*

Maps by Vaughn Gray

Library of Congress Catalog Card Number: 61-8982

Printed in the United States of America

[a.2.61]

To Olga

FOREWORD

Our generation has lived through great and tragic events that have changed the face of the earth. Two world wars followed by vast social convulsions, colonial revolts in Asia and Africa, and civil wars in many countries have set in motion a revolution on a world-wide scale — the first such revolution in history. Great empires and ancient dynasties have collapsed; economic systems and traditional cultures that have stood for centuries, indeed for thousands of years, are disintegrating; new nations and economies are taking their place; and new ideas are forcing people to reexamine their customary moral and aesthetic values.

The revolution of the twentieth century has cost millions of lives. Its end is not yet in sight, but it has already transformed the relationships among the various continents. For five centuries the history of the West had been written as the history of the whole world. A great superiority of material, intellectual, and military resources made Western influence irresistible everywhere. However, since the end of the Second World War, a general reaction against the political domination of the West has set in. The peoples of Asia and Africa are demanding equality with those of the West.

At the same time, the relations among the regions of the Western world itself have been transformed. Western domination meant the domination of Europe, but there have been two Europes — Eastern and Western — significantly distinguished by culture, economic organization, and political institutions. The countries of Western Europe were wealthier, more highly developed technically, and more cultivated and powerful; it was principally these countries that founded empires and new nations overseas and exercised over them a cultural and economic influence long after they had lost political control.

How changed is the scene! The broad band in the center of the Continent, where once the influences of Western and Eastern Europe met and sometimes blended, has become a barrier. On one side, the Soviet Union, much expanded, dominates a group of dictatorial Communist states. On the other side are the democratic states of Western Europe, with varying mixtures of private and public economies.

Eastern Europe now threatens to overwhelm the countries of Western Europe, which have met this threat by drawing closer to each other and closer to the United States. The rapprochement with the United States actually began earlier: twice in one generation the Republic has abandoned her traditional isolation and sent armies to fight beside those of Western Europe in world wars. A North Atlantic community of interests seems to be emerging, and may become a new and enlarged center of Western civilization. In the world at large, the United States and the Soviet Union have become the leading protagonists of rival systems.

Changes of such magnitude are seldom sudden or spontaneous. They are usually the result of tendencies that have germinated for a long time. What are these tendencies, what was their origin, and what has been their course? What, in particular, has been the interaction of Europe and the United States since the Republic was born and what has been its effect upon Western civilization and upon the rest of the world?

Such questions show that it is necessary to study the history of Europe and America as a single whole. This cannot be done merely by tracing their diplomatic and military involvements—for these involvements often arise out of more deep-seated interests and attitudes. It is necessary also to examine and compare the domestic histories of the various European countries and the United States: their political development, intellectual experience, and economic evolution.

That is what *Europe and America* tries to do. It takes its departure from the great movements and events, the ideas and tendencies, that have shaped the course of Western civilization in modern times. It then describes, relates, and contrasts the various national histories and examines their relevance to one another. This is done not only in times of war or revolution, when transatlantic intercourse and influences are most evident, but in those periods when Europe and America went their separate ways.

Thus Europe and America confront each other at every step of their history: their differences and similarities, and their dramatic life together, emerge in full relief. Europeans and Americans have been bound not only by material and cultural ties, but they have shown strong feelings in dealing with each other: love and aversion, imitation and renunciation, identification and misunderstanding. They have had conflicts and reconciliations. There have always been Europeans who regarded America as the hope of the future and others who recoiled from her as an omen of evil things to come. In every age, some Americans have dismissed Europe as old-fashioned and played-out and others have turned to her as the great repository of the values of Western civilization. Americans have displayed a self-conscious Americanism and Europeans a mixture of condescension, resentment, and admiration. Like estranged relatives they have sometimes turned their backs on each other even when they were engaged on similar enterprises.

The drama of Europe and America has so far been a drama in three acts.

In the years when the United States was established and the whole North Atlantic world was in revolutionary turmoil, there were powerful transatlantic bonds: the Enlightenment, a cultural force on both sides of the ocean; the common ideals of the American and French revolutionists; and the involvement of the United States in the struggle between Napoleonic France and the old monarchies of Europe. Although the phrase was not then in common use, the Atlantic world was already a fact.

Then the Atlantic Ocean became wider. America became more broadly democratic and Europe more traditionalist. While America was turning away from Europe to subdue and settle her vast interior spaces, many continental monarchies concentrated their energies at home in an effort to arrest the liberalism they had defeated, but not destroyed, on the battlefield. Of this liberalism America remained the chief embodiment; and now that democracy was added to it and demands for democracy were rising in the Old World itself, the threat to conservatism was redoubled. European conservatives became deeply anti-American, all the more so because liberals drew inspiration from the American example. Both worlds became more conscious of their differences: the dominant public opinion of Europe regarded the United States as a provincial country and the Republic became isolationist, in cultural matters as well as in foreign relations.

The third act opened toward the turn of the twentieth century. The growth of urban life, the conflict between capital and labor, and the imperialistic expansion overseas presented all industrial countries with similar problems and opportunities. Both ethnic and political relations grew closer. The United States became increasingly involved with conditions in Central and Eastern Europe, since a large part of the migrations from the 1880's onward came from those regions. America had always drawn her population mainly from Western Europe, and particularly the British Isles; she now received immigrants from the rest of the Continent: all its parts were represented in her population. At the same time, the old bonds with Western Europe became strong again. The advance of liberalism and democracy during the second half of the nineteenth century had gradually made Western Europe more like America. Later, the common struggle against imperial and Nazi Germany brought Western Europe and America still closer together. And most recently their common interest in defending the democratic order, and the values of Western civilization, against dictatorial Communism has made them allies.

These reunions and separations do not complete the drama. Europe and America have always responded similarly to the secular movements of modern times. They have both had to forge modern states and great markets out of the provincial units of the past. They have had to face the issues raised by scientific, technological, and cultural changes. And even when their political and cultural ties grew slack, their ethnic and economic bonds multiplied.

All along, however, there have been persistent, irreducible differences. Sometimes even the same movements or ideas assumed different, even contrary, aspects on the two sides of the ocean. National groups which were at each other's throats in the Old World have lived side by side without violence or even much strain in the New World. Americans have always hoped to improve on Europe by creating a new and better type of society. Thomas Jefferson believed that it was the destiny and the privilege of America to give substance to the ideals that Europeans had conceived but could not realize at home.

Yet—and this is the crux of our paradox—America has been by no means all new and Europe all old. Religious sects, cultural tendencies, and social habits that could not survive in the tight Old World have flourished in the freer atmosphere of America. That atmosphere has turned out to be a preservative of many a European tradition, while Europe herself has experimented with new cultural and social forms.

So rich and suggestive—and in the end somewhat mysterious—is the relationship between Europe and America, which, though still worlds apart, are parts of the same world.

As I lay down my pen after a dozen years and more of life with this absorbing theme, my thoughts—my warm and grateful thoughts—are with a host of friends and scholars who have read and criticized one or another part of the manuscript. If they are a fair sample, I commend mankind to the affection of the reader. I cannot here mention all of them, but there are a number who have given me the benefit of their special knowledge and of their counsel:

Richard A. Barker, Jesse D. Clarkson, Richard O. Cummings, Robert A. East, Abraham S. Eisenstadt, John Hope Franklin, Daniel Gasman, Dolores Greenberg, Samuel J. Hurwitz, Gerald Krefetz, Hyman Kublin, Robert S. Lopez, Benjamin N. Nelson, Morris Roberts, and Joseph I. Shulim. One friend in particular has stood by throughout. Professor Joseph Dorfman of Columbia University has read and reread successive drafts of the manuscript. He has always been ready to pause in his constant labors to lend a hand in mine. I have drawn heavily upon his learning, of which the five volumes of *The Economic Mind in American Civilization* are a massive monument.

Solomon F. Bloom

NEW YORK
DECEMBER *19, 1960*

CONTENTS

II *The Revolutionary Alternatives*

III   The European and American Solutions

IV *The Liberal World*

V *Steel, Socialism, and Empire*

VI *War and Revolution*

VII   *The Ordeal of Liberty*

Europe and America

The Western World in Modern Times

1 *The Failure of the*

A soiree at one of the most famous French salons of the mid-eighteenth century, that of Mme Marie Thérèse Geoffrin (1699-1777), the cultivated wife of a wealthy manufacturer. The distinguished assembly is listening to the reading of a play by Voltaire, who lived in semi-exile abroad and whose bust presides over the gathering as befits the sovereignty he exercised over the world of letters. The artist, A. C. G. Lemonnier (1743-1824), has portrayed the most brilliant figures of the French Enlightenment. Jean Jacques Rousseau, Turgot, Diderot, Quesnay, and Montesquieu are all present. These men and women and their contemporaries elsewhere in Western Europe, particularly in Britain, and in the American colonies subjected the old order to comprehensive criticism, worked out an equally comprehensive program of rational reform, intellectual freedom, and responsible government, and laid down the basic principles of modern liberalism. The influence of the Enlightenment spread far and wide on both sides of the Atlantic.

Old Regime

1. *Tradition and the Modern Spirit*

Civilization is man's greatest achievement. It is his way of ordering his purposes and needs and of giving direction to his life. But civilization is manifold, for man has devised alternative ways of ordering his life. Among the most enduring of these productions of the human spirit are Western civilization and the Eastern civilization of China and India. Both are ancient, and both spread from their original sources until they encompassed hundreds of millions of people. They are distinguished from each other by their images of the meaning of human existence, and they have produced, in effect, different types of men: the Westerner, enterprising and individualistic; the Easterner, stylized and community-minded. Much of the story of man on this planet is written in the contributions and the relations of these great civilizations.

The Energy of Western Civilization

Western civilization arose in the Near East and spread eventually to America and other continents. For two thousand years, however, it has been intimately associated with Europe. A mere peninsula of Asia, Europe is, except for Australia, the smallest of the continents. Its population, even counting offshoots overseas, has never been more than a minority of mankind. Yet it has played a towering role in the world. The extraordinary length and irregularity of its coastline—a veritable lacework of bays, inlets, channels, and internal seas—and a rich system of riverways brought Europeans close to one another and gave them access to the rest of the world. Although it is situated in the same latitudes as Canada, Europe has a moderate climate and a fairly regular rainfall. The resources of the continent are sufficiently modest to exact effort and forethought and sufficiently ample to reward them. They have neither the luxuriance that makes man lazy and improvident nor the barrenness that makes him niggardly and takes away his hope.

Nature gave Europe a kindred partner. The Atlantic coast of North America with its hinterland is the mirror image of Europe. It has the same riches of bays, inner seas, ports, and islands, and south of Canada its climate and rainfall are moderate.

If nature made Western civilization possible, it was man who created it by a diversified agriculture, proliferating crafts, adventurous trade, and vibrant social and intellectual exchange. The free farmer, the independent craftsman, and the enterprising sailor are the archetypal heroes of the West and the precursors of the inventor, the scientist, the economic organizer, and the political thinker and manager. Intellectual energy and discipline, operating in a favoring environment, produced the characteristically dynamic character of Western civilization.

That civilization was slow in gathering momentum. For a long time, Europe was overshadowed by the riches and refinement of the East. The very word "Oriental" connoted, as it still does, luxury, brilliance, and a subtle wisdom. But by the mid-eighteenth century, when our story opens, Europe not only vied with the Oriental societies in wealth and learning but much exceeded them in the capacity to grow.

Europe was all motion, while the other continents seemed inert, defensive, and self-absorbed by comparison. There were no ships from Asia or Africa in European or North American waters. In the interior of Europe, there were few travelers from the Far East. How different was the scene overseas! The inhabitants of Europe were roaming the world. There was hardly a coast, a sizable island, or a busy bay where European sailors and traders, pirates and soldiers, had not called, by design or inadvertence. European ships brought back precious merchandise from the Far East, Africa, and America. No African or Asian state had possessions in Europe, but a half dozen European states occupied and governed areas several times their size in other continents. They held the coasts of the Western hemisphere and numberless islands, ports, and strips of coast around Africa, the subcontinent of India, and Indonesia.

Nor was the busy enterprise showing signs of faltering. On the contrary. Even while quarreling with one another, European states pressed their opportunities in all the directions of the compass. Two trading groups, the English and the French East India Companies, supported by their governments, vied for the riches of the many provinces into which India was divided. The Empire of China, then as now the largest country in the world, and the neighboring Empire of Japan were closed to foreign traders, but persistent European shippers and agents were trying to pry them open. Europeans ventured into the waters and ports of the South Pacific Ocean, the South Atlantic, and the Indian Ocean. At the extreme ends of the European world two movements of trappers and colonists fanned out like great wings. The Russians, having established a chain of forts across Siberia, sailed to Alaska and explored the American coast to the south. In America, French, Spanish, and English agents and colonists moved westward from the Atlantic coast.

At home, Europe was no less energetic. Intellectual, political, and economic life was vibrant, and great changes were in the offing. There was friction as well as mutual stimulation between what might be called the two societies of the eighteenth century. The traditional society was hierarchical, land-minded, clerical, and legalistic. It favored custom and precedent. A succession of classes, estates, and corporations, defined and distinguished in law, culminated in a nobility endowed with generous privileges. Alongside this society, another order—secular, rational, and capitalistic—had been growing for a long time. Princes and noblemen confronted men who placed enterprise above tradition and capacity above birth. The new order held out the hope of fulfilling human abilities and ambitions and exploiting fruitfully the resources of nature. It drew its inspiration from the contemporary culture—called the Enlightenment—which laid great stress upon the free play of thought and on rationality in public affairs and in practical matters generally. By evoking rational ideals and the hope of progress, the Enlightenment captivated men of influence and cultivation with the vision of a fairer and more creative life.

The modern and the traditional elements of Western society were highly intermixed and seemed to complement each other. For a long time, indeed, the Western world achieved an equipoise of aristocratic grace and rational purpose that was the chief charm of eighteenth-century culture. In the later part of the century, however, the balance became disturbed. As the second half of the century unfolded, there were accumulated differences—and hints of conflict—in every aspect of life, between aristocratic landlordism and independent and capitalistic farming, religious orthodoxy and rational philosophy, provincialism and centralized government, mercantilist regulation and free enterprise, absolutism and representative government, dynastic imperialism and national autonomy. It was the depth of these differences and their resolution that distinguished the great regions of the Western world.

Nobles and Farmers in Europe and America

If a society as complex and differentiated as eighteenth-century society can be said to embody a principle, that principle was aristocracy. Noblemen were always entitled to superior treatment. Public functions and favors, exemptions and privileges, were theirs by right of birth. It seemed natural that only noblemen should hold high office in the administration, the army, the navy, diplomacy, the colonies, and sometimes even in the Church. Human frailty itself seemed becoming in a nobleman. When he failed in his duties and his functions, when he ran into debt or succumbed to vice, he found a broad-minded understanding among his fellow men.

The customary basis of caste was land. A nobleman without land seemed a contradiction in terms. In the countryside landholding on a large scale was the rule. The nobleman was not, of course, the only landowner; behind him was ranged a considerable body of gentry and lesser owners. But the greatest landowners were usually noblemen. There was a psychological as well as an economic association between nobility and land. People of wealth, whether noble or not, usually owned land, which was the principal source of investment and the kind of property most productive of prestige.

The power of the landowner might be qualified by the survival of village communities with substantial rights to use the "commons," pasture, and woodland or to allocate the soil among the cultivators. But in many countries the landowner still derived a handsome return from his peasants, ranging from their labor and fees to a share in their crops. Happy was the peasant who paid only in kind or cash. Besides this, on the Continent the lord often enjoyed the perquisites of local justice, influenced the appointment of village priests, and generally possessed the exclusive right to fish and to raise birds and beasts that fed on his peasants' crops. No one but he could ride to hounds across their fields. His abuses, even more than his rights, became the badge of his order.

Yet, while nobility everywhere enjoyed a formal superiority, its position in the European village and in society generally varied over a wide range from one region to another. Eastern Europe was its paradise. There the nobleman was the dictator of the countryside. His hegemony over the cultivator had been growing for some time. For a century more and more peasants had been dropping into servile status in eastern Germany, Poland, and Russia. Sometimes the landlord could sell his serfs without the land, like slaves. When new lands were opened the noble landlord claimed the lion's share. For example, during a century or more, when peasants from Russia and Poland were moving into the Ukraine (which means "frontier"), noblemen pressed serfdom upon the settlers with the help of the state and of the Cossacks, the freebooters of the frontier.

While their control was all but absolute, Eastern noblemen and landlords did little to advance the cultivation of the soil. There were a few areas, such as Prussia, where landlords improved production and organized their estates on a commercial basis to supply a market. But, generally speaking, Eastern agriculture was primitive as well as seignorial.

In continental Western Europe there was far more progress in agriculture, but there the noble landlord was no longer the organizer and manager of production, as he had been centuries earlier, in the heyday of the manorial system. He had become usually a mere rent collector and consumer of the fees, services, and gifts inherited from feudal days. Nor was the peasant typically a serf. There were some areas, indeed, notably in the Iberian peninsula and southern Italy, where rural conditions were similar to those in Eastern Europe. But northern Italy and England had been free of serfs for centuries. Only one million Frenchmen out of a population of nearly twenty-five million were still serfs, and they were concentrated in the northeastern districts acquired since the preceding century from German princes.

Between the old extremes of serfdom and aristocratic landlordism there had arisen a considerable agrarian middle class, consisting of independent farmers, free tenants, and substantial entrepreneurs. It was to this class that the noble landlord was losing the race of enterprise. Individual cultivation on compact farms was supplanting the old system of dividing the arable land into three fields,

7

one of which lay fallow every year to recover its fertility; of planting uniform crops and using the same methods of tillage everywhere; and of assigning the peasants a number of small strips scattered over the three fields. Individual cultivation enabled the more prosperous farmer to improve his position and rise above his fellows. The steady growth of towns swelled the demand for food and the improvement of roads facilitated its supply. Rich peasants and burghers with ready cash bought land, invested capital to improve cultivation, and sold their produce, thereby making money by feeding the urban population. The poorer peasants, however, for whom the communal features of the old system provided minimal guarantees of subsistence, often became still poorer.

In England these changes amounted to a veritable revolution. Parliament contained many urban representatives in the eighteenth century, but it was controlled by the great and middling landed proprietors, who also dominated the countryside. This control was used to promote large agrarian enterprises. By legislation, purchase, persuasion, and even intimidation, landlords prevailed upon farmers to substitute compact farms for the old system of scattered strips in open fields. They extended their own holdings by buying new farms and by fencing in, for their own profit, common fields which had been used by the villagers for ages. During the eighteenth century Parliament passed some sixteen hundred bills enclosing commons. A sizable number of owners and tenants improved their acres scientifically, rotating crops, experimenting with fertilizer, breeding better cattle, and producing for distant markets on an enlarged scale. They reduced their expenses in order to accumulate surpluses. They then invested these surpluses, reckoned rates of interest and profit, and became at once financiers, enterprisers, and managers. For the poorer peasants, however, the result of the process of enclosure and the growth of commercial agriculture was tragic. They were often virtually dispossessed and lost their footing on the soil. Many of them became wage-earners and gang laborers on the large estates. They eked out a living by doing "cottage work" — processing raw materials, notably textiles, at home. Some of the richer farmers sold their land in the rising market and invested the proceeds in such domestic industries, again notably in textile manufacturing. Thus, as many a landlord supplemented his traditional fixed income with flexible capitalist profits, an agrarian revolution merged into an industrial one.

Like Eastern Europe, Western Europe and England had a frontier. That frontier was overseas. North America was a creation not of Europe as a whole but almost exclusively of Western and Northern Europe, particularly the countries bordering or near the Atlantic Ocean. The population of the British colonies which eventually formed the United States came largely from the British Isles, western Germany, France, Holland, and Scandinavia, with a sprinkling from Switzerland and northern Italy. The northern neighbor was French Canada; neighbors to the south and east were possessions of Spain, France, Denmark, and Holland. Very few immigrants came from Eastern Europe.

The American colonies reflected the difference between traditional and modern agriculture. In Central and South America Spanish and Portuguese grandees obtained huge grants of land and established servile estates. In the West Indies, rich with sugar, powerful and favored landlords carved out plantations which they worked with slaves, first native Indians and then Negroes from Africa. The British colonies on the mainland, however, avoided the extremes of the seignorial and servile system. Most of her farmers were middling people—small but often substantial owners. Although planters and other men of influence established great estates on the newly opened lands of the frontier, there was always room for the small freeholder. The imperial British government favored the large and noble landowner, but its center of power was three thousand miles away. No military force hovered on the edge of the settlement, as in autocratic Russia. Frontiersmen, together with agents of land companies, fought Indians to bring safety to the small settler as well as to the great owner.

The colonies had no native landed nobility, although in the Southern settlements some of the large planters sought to perpetuate the aristocratic practices of primogeniture and entail of property. By virtue of extraordinary grants from the King of Great Britain, a few proprietors tried to exact from farmers a small annual quit rent in the place of feudal services performed of old in Europe. But quit rents were collected with difficulty; and in general such remnants of feudal custom were seldom effectively transferred to the colonies.

By European standards, the American farm was fabulously large. A farm of two hundred acres was not unusual in New England, and it was common in the South and West. The European farmer was happy if he could work a dozen acres. Small wonder that many a Western European farmer who had the resources to do so made his way to the open lands of America. So did ambitious young men of country or town, who indentured themselves as servants, had their passage to America paid by ship captains or by masters, and worked for several years to buy back their freedom.

One great difficulty attended this migration to utopia. In Europe labor was cheap and easily available; there were poor tenants, sharecroppers, hired laborers, or, in Eastern Europe, serfs. In the New World labor was more scarce. The wage-earning class was relatively small, partly because unoccupied land could be obtained at a moderate price. On the other hand, agriculture required much preparatory toil. Land had to be cleared of forest, and roads and barns had to be built. Agriculture involved more sacrifice and loneliness than in the Old World.

Nobles and Businessmen

In towns and cities the European nobility encountered more powerful rivals than in the countryside. Although nine tenths of the 150 million Europeans in the eighteenth century were countrymen, urban society was growing rapidly. This, however, was more true in Western than in Eastern Europe, where urban capitalism was little developed and towns were small and few. In the East, urban traders, craftsmen, and professional men were a drop in the peasant sea. Often, also, the townsmen were separated from the peasantry and nobility by religion and language. As one traveled from Eastern to Western Europe, however, the roads improved and the number and size of towns increased. Cities of millions of people were still a thing of the future, but capitals such as Paris and London, with more than a half million inhabitants each, were worlds in themselves, rich, stirring, and vigorous. Except for Constantinople, there was not a city in Eastern Europe even half their size.

This difference in urban life reflected a difference in the importance of commerce and industry, for the mercantile, shipping, and manufacturing classes played the chief role in the cities. In Western Europe urban wealth was already substantial and was growing apace, particularly in England, France, and the Netherlands. There, as in the East, the accumulations of landed property were large as compared with money capital, but the latter could be transferred more easily from one enterprise to another, from commerce to industry, from finance to commerce. With a little luck it multiplied steadily. Money markets thrived in several centers where investors, enterprisers, and speculators met and speeded the flow of capital. And these urban occupations bred many more new fortunes than did agriculture.

Between the burghers and the nobility there were strong traditional bonds. Business was bound to the aristocratic society by interest and emulation. Wealthy noblemen, as well as high ecclesiastics and princes, borrowed heavily and made the fortune of money-lenders. Liberal spenders and lavish consumers, they enriched the importers of tropical goods and the manufacturers of luxury products. The urban rich accepted the hierarchical scheme of European society. They were as careful to distinguish themselves from the propertyless masses as the nobles were to distinguish themselves from the burghers, no matter how rich or able. In most cities and ports there grew up "aristocracies" of wealthy and powerful families which exercised a monopolistic and hereditary control over politics. In past centuries, the burghers had aligned themselves with the monarchy in its conflict with great noblemen over political power. The influence of centralized monarchy and that of the urban middle and professional classes had grown simultaneously, particularly in Western Europe. In an effort to reduce the power of the aristocrats, the absolute monarchs of the seventeenth century had recruited their administrators, bureaucrats, and judges from among the middle classes. Since offices were traditionally associated with rank, it was only natural that the monarchs should reward those who performed these services with lifetime or hereditary titles. They sometimes sold offices or judgeships as a means of raising revenue, and thereby in effect sold noble dignities. In some countries, the purchase of an estate carried with it the right to give oneself the place names and prefixes that were the badges of nobility. In such ways, the nobility of many a country had become both diluted and enriched. Alongside the men of historic lineage and land there had arisen a new nobility of service or money, called the *noblesse de robe*. The old noblemen, *nobles d'épée*, revenged themselves by snubbing the intruders, who themselves became tenacious defenders of the common citadel of exclusivism.

In the eighteenth century, however, an "aristocratic" or "feudal" reaction set in. The old nobility and the new closed ranks. Monarchs increasingly appointed their officials from titled families. Because urban wealth was overtaking landed wealth, the landed nobility became concerned over its economic position and all the more determined to cling to its privileges. The oligarchies that controlled the towns became equally rigid and exclusive. In the countries of Central and Eastern Europe the privileges of the nobility, especially the great noblemen, were enlarged.

Under the circumstances, European society became more rather than less aristocratic as the century advanced. Among the broad urban classes and the unprivileged generally, there developed in consequence an increasing opposition to the "feudal reaction." This opposition, which was often called "democratic," was strengthened by the feeling of a good many burghers that their class was morally superior to others. When commerce was not speculative and its stakes were modest, it bred thrift, caution, and diligence, and businessmen came to think of these as the peculiar virtues of their class. They looked upon aristocrats as vain, frivolous, and wasteful and upon the lower classes as incompetent and improvident. When Robinson Crusoe's father tried to dissuade him from going to sea, he extolled "the middle station of life" as "the best state in the world, the most suited to human happiness, not exposed to the miseries and hardships, the labor and sufferings of the mechanic part of mankind, and not embarrassed with the pride, luxury, ambition, and envy of the upper part of mankind." According to the elder Crusoe, "peace and plenty were the handmaids of a middle fortune; . . . temperance, moderation, quietness, health, society, all agreeable diversions, and all desirable pleasures were the blessings attending the middle station of life." This was the ideal, but what appeared to the businessman as worldly wisdom appeared to others—above or below him—as narrow calculation. If "aristocratic" connoted open-handedness, "bourgeois" often connoted niggardliness. In France, for example, the latter term suggested parsimony, a dull family life, and a lack of public spirit and refinement.

The evolution of the spirit of independence and self-assertion among the middle classes was marked in the towns of Western Europe and, especially, in the British colonies on the American mainland. In their commercial character these colonies bore a strong resemblance to Western Europe, but their middle classes had the field rather more to themselves than their counterparts in the Old World. Few noblemen went to the colonies, except as transient imperial or military officials. Europe was the splendid metropolis, the seat of authority and fashion, and no highly successful man, noble or not, would exchange it for the colonial hinterland. It was the restless younger sons of the rich and noble, their footloose cousins and poorer relations, and the unfortunates of society, orphans or people at odds with the law, who tried their luck overseas.

As colonial society lacked the aristocratic top, so it had a smaller and less solid "bottom" than the Old World. About one third of the population of the colonies consisted of Negro slaves and indentured servants. But servants and other poor immigrants frequently established an independent, if not always a comfortable, existence, with a farm, a business, or an artisan's shop. The true "middle class" of the colonies was composed of farmers, small tradesmen, artisans, and seamen. Above it rose an "upper class" which consisted of three groups of shifting composition: Southern planters—in effect rural capitalists—who produced crops, principally tobacco, rice, and indigo, for export; the rich merchants, shipowners, and manufacturers of Pennsylvania, New York, and New England; and, throughout the colonies, the professional classes—clergymen, lawyers, physicians—who shared the prestige of landed and moneyed men. These three groups supplied the local and provincial officials, legislators, and judges.

The American upper class was more open and fluid than its counterpart in Europe, for its status did not rest on law. It was, indeed, a "middle class" as this term was understood in the Old World—that is, a class of untitled but substantial propertied persons. Among the prejudices and habits that the immigrants brought with them was class-mindedness. Only members of the upper groups rated the title "Gentleman," "Esquire," or "Mister." Small farmers and shopkeepers had to be content with "Goodman" and laborers with their Christian or family names. Worshipers in churches were seated according to rank and college registers were drawn up in the same way. Even in America, the idea of hierarchy died hard.

Religion, Law, and Administration

All the regions of the Western world reflected the differences between the traditional and the modern in religious and legal life. There were official churches everywhere in Europe in the mid-eighteenth century and in many of the American colonies. Like the nobility, the clergy had special legal immunities and fiscal privileges. In Europe the established churches owned considerable property in country and town, tithed the produce of the farmer, supervised education and a few social services, watched over private conduct, and censored publications. Even in countries which tolerated heterodox faiths, dissenters suffered a variety of financial, legal, and political disabilities.

The established churches, and the dissenting ones too, rested, of course, on religious doctrine supported by authority, and this authority was supposed to be the Old and New Testaments, supplemented in some churches by episcopal direction. There was, however, a current of thought which ran counter to orthodoxy. Greek and Roman literature had long been the mainstay of education and constituted the reading of educated people, and ancient stoicism and paganism had weakened the hold of Christian dogma. A controversy about the validity of this dogma and the authenticity of Biblical texts had been developing among scholars since the Renaissance. The rapid development of physical science since the seventeenth century demonstrated the power and increased the prestige of reason. It suggested that the universe was a rational and harmonious creation, built on grand and simple lines and governed by laws that could be discovered by free inquiry.

If the orthodoxy of religion in the eighteenth century was Christian dogma, the orthodoxy of law was prescription. Any right or property, any immunity or privilege, was deemed valid, no matter how it had been acquired, provided that it was not challenged within a certain period of time. After that, the longer it lasted, the more valid it was. Custom was the real god of the old order. In his classic *Commentaries on the Laws of England* (1765), Sir William Blackstone (1723-80) laid down the rule that the law ought always to follow precedents "unless flatly absurd or unjust; for though their reasons be not obvious at first view, yet we owe such a deference to former times as not to suppose they acted wholly without consideration." Jonathan Swift (1667-1745) observed satirically that "it is a maxim among lawyers that whatever has been done before may legally be done again." Charters, grants, patents, and treaty agreements, no matter how old or how incongruous in the light of new conditions, were presumed to have permanent validity. The privileges that towns or guilds had obtained from the king, the exemptions that noblemen had successfully asserted for a long period, the jurisdictions that churches and religious orders had long exercised by written consent or public allowance, the tolls that a lord had been used to collect at a ford or crossroads—all these and many of the same kind were presumed to be permanent. They were looked upon as "contracts" which could not be changed without the consent of the descendants of both parties.

Since special rights and usages were often shared by whole groups or organizations, society took on the appearance of a collection of communities or corporations. This was notably true of the territorial components of states. Provincialism flourished. Most states consisted of provinces separated by tariffs, legal privileges, and taxes. When a ruler conquered, inherited, or "married" a new territory, he attached it to his former dominions without assimilating it to their laws. This explains why it made no difference whether his holdings were contiguous or scattered and his state compact or sprawling. Germany, with approximately three hundred virtually independent states and statelets, was the paradise of provincialism. Many of its states were made up of pieces scattered over the map. Whole empires could be assembled or dismantled simply by re-shuffling provinces, and without affecting local life or administration. At the beginning of the eighteenth century, Poland was, next to Russia, the largest state in Europe; at the end it had disappeared without a trace into the maws of its neighbors. The international system of provincialism allowed free movement from one territory to another and may be contrasted with the exclusivism of later national borders. Roads, town gates, and river fords were watched, but patrolling on both sides along the whole length of frontiers was virtually unknown.

It was the very stability of custom that gave flexibility to political geography. Custom also preserved local peculiarities, differences, and loyalties in the face of a growing need for uniformity. Traders and manufacturers craved larger markets than the provinces afforded and an easier exchange of goods; rulers wanted the taxes that a richer trade would yield. Under the old rules, a property right, especially if it applied to land, was likely to be a cluster of overlapping rights of several persons or even groups, including unborn heirs. Often land could not be broken up, sold, or mortgaged for credit. The great need of the trader, on the other hand, was to turn property into usable capital. There was a growing conviction among enlightened men that law should not only sanction prevailing usage but also create new rights and relations as circumstances changed, even if it had to destroy old rights to do so. From the sixteenth century on, Roman law, which vested ownership in a single person and suggested the desirability of integrating all laws into a single code, was increasingly adopted in Western Europe.

The vehicle of change was the most flexible of traditional institutions, the monarchy. Noblemen represented provincial and parochial interests, while the monarch's interests extended over all his domains. For several centuries energetic rulers had been gradually expanding their jurisdictions, taking over functions formerly performed by the nobility and the clergy. Military power had passed wholly into royal hands, and the nobleman had lost his right to fortify his castle and maintain a private armed force. In many countries, particularly in Western Europe, he had lost the privilege to gather with his peers to lay down the law to king and country. Thus the increase of royal authority and modernization marched together. By the eighteenth century, absolute monarchy had become the rule in most Continental countries.

Whether absolute or not, all the monarchs needed money. They had to hire professional soldiers, maintain expensive courts, dispense favors to noblemen, patronize the arts, and, above all, support bureaucracies to administer the increasing functions of the state. Money could be obtained from traders, manufacturers, and shippers more easily than from landowners, whose income tended to be fixed, and who were in a better position to resist taxation. Only a permanent and constant increase in the movable wealth of the country could assure a reliable and rising income to the monarch. Since it was commonly assumed that the wealth of the world was on the whole static, it was taken for granted that one of the best ways of getting a larger share of it was to diminish the share of other countries. The interests of power, prestige, and conquest merged with those of commerce in the practices of mercantilism, which had developed, particularly during the seventeenth century, into a systematic policy. In order to prevent the flow of money outward, monarchs discouraged the importation of finished and expensive goods by high tariffs or outright prohibition. They stimulated the development of industries for export by encouraging the importation of raw materials and granting subsidies and monopolies to producers of goods for distant and foreign markets. They often forbade the emigration of skilled craftsmen and invited skilled foreigners to settle in their countries, even if their religious affiliation was heterodox. By keeping wages low and encouraging the employment of children, they assured a cheap labor supply. Their efforts to combat provincialism coincided with the interest of large-scale business to secure free trade and to ease exchange within the country as a whole. Monarchs reduced internal customs and removed river and road tolls, superseded local guild controls by country-wide regulations, and attempted to standardize the number and variety of weights, measures, and coins. They insisted that their colonies purchase manufactures from the mother country and use her trading and shipping services. There was great rivalry for colonies producing tropical goods, such as sugar, coffee, tobacco, and spices, which were in demand all over Europe.

Mercantilism promoted the easier circulation of goods and money within a country and stimulated new enterprise. Yet it fitted into the prevailing system of privilege. Favored groups in the business community obtained monopolies, subsidies, tariff protection, and charters to form trading companies with limited liability. These companies were sometimes vested with the right to exercise political, judicial, and military functions overseas. For their part, monarchs, courtiers, and noblemen enjoyed special opportunities for investment and honorific and well-paying positions in the enterprises they favored or protected. Privileged groups were touched by the spirit of business even as business was touched by the spirit of privilege.

As commerce and industry developed, there arose, particularly in the Western countries, a large group of enterprisers who pressed to enter the fields reserved to old corporations or chartered companies, manufacturers of new products, and "outsiders" and "interlopers" jealous of the special position of privileged traders and shippers. Merchants and manufacturers could not all be privileged, and the hope of the outsiders lay in breaking the combination of economic and political power that lay at the heart of mercantilism. This hope was particularly evident in the American colonies.

Antimercantilist interest was reinforced by the emergence of a huge new market for staple products and necessaries. The growth of towns, the introduction of new industrial techniques, and the improvement of transportation stimulated the growth of this market. The older commerce and industry had exploited the tastes and the fashions of aristocratic and rich consumers; thus they had a strong stake in the preservation of the prevailing society. The new economy catered to the needs of the larger bodies of modest consumers. The new market was indefinitely extensible, provided that increasing layers of the population could rise to the position of buyers. The future of the new economy lay in the improvement of the standard of life of the ordinary man.

Absolutism and Representative Government

Monarchy and nobility prevailed everywhere in the Western world, but their relations to each other and to other institutions varied from country to country and from region to region.

In the absence of a substantial middle and professional class, absolute monarchs and noblemen in Eastern Europe had a virtual political monopoly.

Most of the Eastern monarchies were highly despotic at the center of government, but they all left local administration and contacts with the agrarian masses to the landed nobility, which often overshadowed the townsmen. Some of the Eastern countries strove to adopt modern policies and bureaucratic techniques, but their success was limited. They introduced slowly the methods of shipping and manufacture, particularly the manufacture of military weapons and supplies, from Western Europe. They encouraged foreign trade, but in the East it was often in the hands of great noblemen and landlords rather than the urban middle classes, for exports were usually the products of the soil rather than of manufacture. It was the noble landlord and his agent who were often the capitalists of the region.

In Russia the nobility had been so integrated into the state that the empire could rely upon its cooperation. The old independent feudal nobility had been cowed in previous centuries. Hereditary noblemen had been compelled to serve in the Czar's army and administration. A host of new officials and retainers of the Czar received estates, which were eventually made hereditary, again on condition of further service to the state. In the eighteenth century the state extended the power of the landlords over the countryside and bound the peasantry to the land. The power of the Czar over the nobles and that of the nobles over the peasants grew at the same time. But the peasants could not shift the burden, and autocracy rested finally on serfdom.

There were some Eastern countries where the power of the nobility vied with that of the monarchy and entirely overshadowed the small middle classes. Hungary, although formally under the rule of the Hapsburg monarchs, was in effect managed by a proud and rich aristocracy. Poland was an aristocratic republic in which a feudal parliament, dominated by the greatest landowners, elected the king—usually a foreigner, most often a Saxon prince—and passed the laws. The vote of a single member of this body—in effect the vote of any of the few princely families which held the reins of power—was sufficient to prevent either legislation or the royal election. At every election, the magnates made conditions which enfeebled the monarchy and extended their own control over the countryside. They were the virtual autocrats of their provinces.

Prussia, lying between East and West, was a special case. Her Hohenzollern rulers, obsessed with military power and ambition, had bent all their energies to the accumulation of treasure for the building of an army out of all proportion to the resources, population, and needs of the country. They nurtured those economic enterprises that provided immediate cash for the state war chest. It was a saying in the eighteenth century that Prussia was not a country which had an army but an army which had a country.

The most bizarre absolutism of all was the Ottoman Empire. An all-powerful sultan recruited his army and bureaucracy from among prisoners of war, slaves, and captured young Christians converted to Mohammedanism. The Turks were the privileged nation, exempted from taxation. Since the Mohammedans regarded all Christians as infidels, they did not find their dogmatic differences interesting, with the result that many a heterodox sect persecuted in

Christian Europe was tolerated in the Ottoman Empire. Although the Empire was officially Mohammedan, the sultans recognized the Greek Orthodox Patriarch of Constantinople and compelled their Christian subjects to pay ecclesiastical taxes and accept without demur his Greek appointees to the higher posts in their churches. Trade was largely in the hands of Greeks and Armenians and of foreigners, notably Frenchmen, who enjoyed commercial privileges and extraterritorial judicial rights.

To the despotisms of Eastern Europe, the countries of the Atlantic opposed a closer association between the monarchy and the middle classes, more compact and articulated states, and an alternative to absolute government.

Since the seventeenth century, France had been the model of absolute monarchy in Western continental Europe. The political power of the monarchy had grown at the expense of that of the privileged classes and provinces. The king no longer convened the old parliament, the Estates General. However, the special social and fiscal status of the nobility was preserved. The king had gathered the principal noblemen around his court to keep an eye on them, and he rewarded their obeisance with honorific positions, sinecures, and gifts. At the same time, his administration promoted the interests of the middle classes. The unquestioned royal power kept all these elements in their place. Under the reign of Louis XV (1715-74), however, the prestige and influence of the monarchy waned, both at home and abroad. There was increasing friction between reforming ministers and the privileged classes. The new *noblesse de robe*, which had originally been recruited from the middle classes and was superior in wealth and ability to the *noblesse d'épée*, assumed leadership in the defense of the system of privilege. The traditional association of monarchy, nobility, and urban society was weakening.

The Netherlands and Great Britain, as well as a host of Swiss and German city-states, had representative institutions. They lacked the powerful bureaucracies of the absolute monarchies. The Netherlands was quasi-monarchical in form and had great landed noblemen, but it was effectively controlled by the merchants, insurance men, bankers, and shippers of the great ports, above all of Amsterdam. The cosmopolitan spirit of these ports was reflected in a policy of toleration. In the seventeenth and eighteenth centuries, Holland, though not entirely free, was the freest country in Europe for the expression of opinion.

In England two revolutions in the seventeenth century had resulted in a compromise under which the mercantile classes, the landed classes, and the monarchy shared power in a ratio which fluctuated with circumstances. The power of the monarchy was still ample—at the beginning of the eighteenth century Queen Anne was still vetoing acts of Parliament—but the ruler could not collect taxes or control the army without parliamentary consent. Nor could he suspend laws. Under the common law, the state had to defend the validity of its acts in courts. The nobility and gentry continued to control the countryside while the trading and shipping classes helped to shape economic and colonial policy.

The English peerage was a unique institution. On the Continent, nobility was a matter of family and blood. In many countries all the members of noble houses carried titles and shared in the privileges, exemptions, and favors of their rank. In England, only the current head of the family enjoyed special privileges; the other members sometimes carried courtesy titles but were legally indistinguishable from commoners. The peerage was thus small. It counted its numbers in the hundreds—only about 200 in the mid-century—while in the larger countries of the Continent there were thousands, even tens of thousands, of privileged noblemen. Finally, the English peerage enjoyed considerable political power. Although the House of Commons was becoming increasingly important, the House of Lords shared legislative power with it. The highest offices in government, including the cabinet, remained in the hands of the peers and their relatives.

Yet the peerage was closely associated with the middle class. While some younger sons obtained valuable posts in the government, army, navy, and church, many others entered trade and the professions. Occasionally very rich men obtained titles, and the newest peer shared the privileges of the holders of the oldest titles. It is paradoxical but true that England was at once the most aristocratic and the most bourgeois country in Europe.

The representative institutions of Britain prevailed in her colonies on the American mainland. These colonies had been founded by royal charters and grants, some of which were constitutions in miniature. There was a very restricted suffrage, resting generally on the ownership of landed property, but since property was more widely distributed and inheritance laws were more egalitarian than at home, a greater proportion of the colonists was represented in their assemblies than of Englishmen in the House of Commons. Apart from this difference, the political system of the American colonies was similar to the system prevailing not only in the mother country but also in city-states of the Netherlands and Switzerland.

Dynasticism and Imperialism

The Atlantic world thus presented more varied and more flexible political methods than Eastern Europe. The states of both regions, however, were traditionally dynastic, imperial, and warlike. Their rulers belonged to a small and exclusive circle of families which derived originally from the nobility. They formed an international fraternity and usually had closer personal relations with one another than with the populations—even the native nobilities—they governed. Sovereignty was often determined by consanguinity, marriage, and inheritance, and domestic and international politics were to no inconsiderable extent influenced by such family affairs as the antagonism of aging fathers and impatient heirs, the rivalry of wives and mistresses, the intrigues of relatives and retainers, the accidents of heredity, and the effects of inbreeding.

The dynasts looked upon their countries as family estates. It was every monarch's ambition to add to his inheritance: dynasticism was hardly distinguishable from imperialism. Rule by foreign princes was common, and if England could be governed by a German family and Spain by a French, why could not Irishmen by Englishmen, and Americans by Europeans? When the noble Houyhnhnm asked why Europeans fought so much, Gulliver pointed to the drive for aggrandizement as one of the principal causes:

> Sometimes the ambition of princes, who never think they have land or people enough to govern.... Sometimes the Quarrel between two princes is to decide which of them shall dispossess a third of his dominions, when neither of them pretend to any right.... Sometimes our neighbors want the things which we have, or have the things which we want; and we both fight, till they take ours or give us theirs.... It is justifiable to enter into a war against our nearest ally, when one of his towns lies convenient for us, or a territory of land, that would render our dominions round and compact.

Universal competition created a kind of stability. Whenever any monarch acquired a considerable amount of territory, his neighbors demanded an equivalent profit. If any monarch threatened to achieve predominance or a monopoly of power, the others combined to frustrate him. Thus the principle of the balance of power kept the states tethered to each other. The traditional object of dynastic ambition was land, but the monarchs fell in easily with the competition for capitalist profits from commerce, shipping, and industry. Political and economic imperialism merged. War seemed to be an inevitable characteristic of Western civilization. The health of a state came to be measured by its military capacity. Confronting each other constantly on the battlefield, the states matched and tested alternative weapons and strategies, which thus tended to spread throughout the Western world, giving it a greater unity for martial than for peaceful purposes.

Eastern Europe provided unusual opportunities for an imperialist feast. Two of its largest states—Poland and the Ottoman Empire—were developing weaknesses so serious as to tempt their neighbors to intervene in their internal affairs and even to open the prospects of disintegration and partition. Austria, Russia, and Prussia were not slow to take advantage of these opportunities.

The countries of Western Europe found it more difficult to expand at each other's expense at home, but the world overseas presented them with dazzling opportunities. None of the Eastern powers, save Russia, had expanded in other continents, but all the principal Western countries had colonies overseas. They were all competing for the profits of oceanic trade and shipping and for control of sea routes and ports. The monopoly of empire and trade that Spain and Portugal had established following their geographic discoveries of the fifteenth century had in the course of time led to a more equitable distribution. In the seventeenth century, Holland, England, and France had become the leading colonial powers. By the mid-eighteenth century, Holland had lost her former eminence as a commercial empire, and a long struggle for colonial predominance between Great Britain and France was coming to a head.

While the prizes of ambition were as numerous and as great as ever, dynastic and imperialist policies were coming under critical scrutiny. There were persistent demands by enlightened men, particularly in the Atlantic countries,

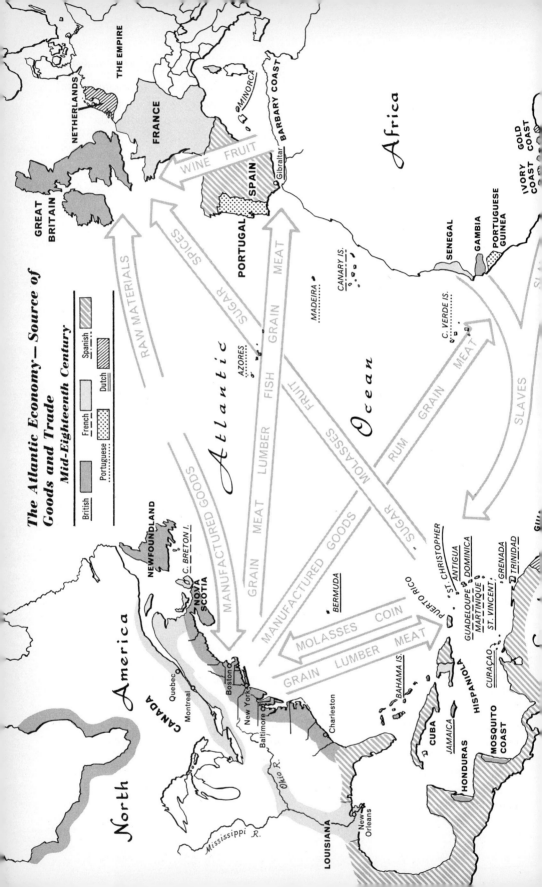

The Atlantic Economy— Source of Goods and Trade
Mid-Eighteenth Century

British
French
Portuguese
Spanish
Dutch

NORTH America

THE EMPIRE

NETHERLANDS

GREAT BRITAIN

FRANCE

SPAIN

PORTUGAL

MINORCA

BARBARY COAST

Gibraltar

Africa

IVORY COAST

GOLD COAST

SENEGAL

GAMBIA

PORTUGUESE GUINEA

Atlantic

Ocean

WINE   FRUIT

RAW MATERIALS

SPICES

SUGAR

MEAT

GRAIN

FISH

LUMBER

MEAT

GRAIN

FRUIT

MOLASSES

SUGAR

MANUFACTURED GOODS

MANUFACTURED GOODS

RUM   GRAIN   MEAT

MEAT

SLAVES

CANARY IS.

MADEIRA

AZORES

C. VERDE IS.

Canada

NEWFOUNDLAND

C. BRETON I.

NOVA SCOTIA

Quebec

Montreal

Boston

New York

Baltimore

Charleston

Ohio R.

Mississippi R.

New Orleans

LOUISIANA

HONDURAS

MOSQUITO COAST

BERMUDA

BAHAMA IS.

CUBA

JAMAICA

HISPANIOLA

PUERTO RICO

ST. CHRISTOPHER

ANTIGUA

GUADELOUPE   *DOMINICA*

MARTINIQUE

ST. VINCENT   *GRENADA*

CURAÇAO   *TRINIDAD*

MOLASSES   COIN

GRAIN   LUMBER   MEAT

that the interest of countries and peoples prevail over that of courts and privileged groups. "Patriotism" came to be opposed to dynasticism, and national autonomy to imperialism. There was a growing sentiment for "democracy," which connoted then not the rule of the masses but the participation of non-privileged groups in general, including the middle classes, in the formulation of policy and the framing of legislation. Public opinion was becoming a force to reckon with: the opinions that merchants, manufacturers, and investors held of the effectiveness of prevailing commercial, fiscal, and colonial policies; and the attitude of professional and educated persons toward government and society.

These tendencies were particularly apparent in countries ruled from a distance. Irish groups were growing restive under British domination. Spanish colonists were becoming more and more sensitive to the rigid controls of the mother country. The British colonies in America were developing a sense of common interests and of distinction from the Old World.

The largest part of the North American continent was held by Spain and France, and the British colonists nursed hopes of expanding in the interior. The proximity of the Catholic empires, in an age when religious antagonisms were still strong, was not the least of the bonds that tied the colonists to Britain. Yet there were signs of a growing feeling for autonomy and unity. This feeling was reflected in suggestions that the colonies establish a common legislature, that the imperial system develop into a partnership of autonomous countries, and particularly that the colonies rise toward equality with the mother country. It was reflected also in the criticism of mercantilist policies, which subordinated the interests of American merchants, shippers, and manufacturers to those of their counterparts in Great Britain. American nationality was taking shape.

Such was the variety, such the underlying homogeneity of Western civilization in the eighteenth century. In many aspects of life, in every region, the traditional was qualified by the modern. Nowhere were the two completely fused, nor could they be. There were signs, indeed, that such mutual accommodation as they had achieved in the past was diminishing. In Eastern Europe, the resources of aristocracy and absolutism were still impressive. In the Atlantic world strains accumulated apace in the second half of the century. Demands for the renovation of traditional practices and policies multiplied while the resistance of privileged classes stiffened. The peoples of absolutist rulers were impressed by the example of liberal institutions in neighboring countries, and these institutions were subjected to the criticism of reformers who proposed to strengthen and purify them. Enlightened thought and opinion acquired a sharp critical edge, and enlightened men proposed a resolution of the issues of despotism and liberty, power and intellect, tradition and reason. Finally, these issues were put to the test. Imperial rivalry and war abroad intensified controversy at home. In the seventies and eighties a series of revolutions broke out on both sides of the Atlantic. The prevailing order was challenged, and a modern society arose, first in the New World and then in the Old.

2. *The Enlightenment*

The eighteenth century has been called the Age of Reason, the age—to use a figure from the life of a man—when one arrives at reason and feels strong confidence in its promise. This is the light in which the German philosopher Immanuel Kant (1724-1804) saw his own time. To him the Enlightenment meant intellectual courage, a challenge to man to reject the tradition of accepting blindly the guidance of others. "Dare to know! Have the courage to use your own understanding; this is the motto of the Enlightenment."

This was the spirit of the Age of Reason, but it was the consequence rather than the source of its outlook. The men of that age felt that they must confront the world and come to grips with its problems more directly than their predecessors had done. They freed themselves from absorption with the old issues of metaphysics and theology: the ultimate nature of reality, the character of the afterworld, and the intricacies of infinity and divinity. Pure deduction and system-building did not appeal to them. They preferred to deal with other problems—those which yielded readily to reflection and experiment, and particularly those whose solution would improve human life.

In traditional thinking, political and moral questions often seemed to hinge on difficult metaphysical and spiritual issues. The men of the Enlightenment put first things first; they felt that it was possible to resolve issues affecting private and public behavior before settling ultimate questions. They conceived of philosophy and reason as the exercise of the energetic mind upon concrete questions of government, law, the physical world, economics, and morality. They had confidence in the basic harmony of nature and in the power of scientific procedures to reveal that harmony. Yet, combined with this confidence, they had an awareness of the vast realm of ignorance that surrounded mankind. The men of the Enlightenment considered themselves at the beginning of the quest for basic truths in every field of inquiry. Faith in science was balanced by an attitude of curiosity and tentativeness; ambitious ends were balanced by moderate means. Knowledge was shorn of dogmatism, and action of fanaticism.

The leading figures of the Enlightenment were sober and practical men. Their diagnosis of human problems was often sharp, but the remedies they proposed were seldom drastic. While they explored the most speculative suggestions, they submitted policies and institutions to the test of usefulness and effectiveness. They were content to mend rather than end old arrangements: not revolution but reform was their watchword.

The Scientific Spirit and Empiricism

Ever since the Renaissance there had been a growing tendency to inquire into questions that could be decided by observation and measurement. During the seventeenth century it became increasingly fashionable to devise theories to explain how things work in the practical world, to check these theories by experiment, to invent mechanical contrivances. Learned men began to classify observations of the operations of nature, to collect plants, to assemble and organize miscellaneous facts; they remodeled and improved tools, constructed precise instruments, and dissected corpses.

The spirit of experiment was akin to the spirit of questioning. On a memorable day in the history of the human mind (December 10, 1619), the French philosopher and mathematician René Descartes (1596-1650) hit upon the extraordinary suggestion that men ought to stop believing anything that could not pass the scrutiny of rigorous reason. They were to purge themselves of all accepted, habitual, and traditional ideas, even the most obvious, and even of sense impressions. They were to build their mental life from the bottom up, as it were, by entertaining only ideas which reason validated beyond any possibility of doubt. Logic, clarity, and certainty were the *liberté*, *égalité*, and *fraternité* of this first French revolutionist.

Reason and experiment changed man's view of the universe. Chemistry, geology, botany, and zoology all made germinal advances in the seventeenth and eighteenth centuries. It was astronomy and physics, however, that registered the most spectacular success. A long period of experimentation and speculation culminated in the formulation of the Law of Gravitation by Sir Isaac Newton (1642-1727): any two bodies are attracted to each other by a force corresponding to the product of their masses and inversely proportional to the square of the distance between them. The comprehensiveness, and yet the simplicity, of Newton's explanation of the coherence of the physical universe encouraged a belief in the harmony of the universe and in the power of man to penetrate its secret.

Modern science was born, and the search for laws became a passion among learned men. They were fascinated by the possibility that society and politics might also be governed by laws, laws as simple and general as those that governed the physical world, and that these laws might be discoverable by the same subtle mixture of induction and deduction. In his "Four Rules of Reasoning in Philosophy" (1687) Newton enjoined men to entertain only such

23

causes as are sufficient to explain the appearance of phenomena, to assign to the same natural effects the same causes, to infer that the truths they discover when observing phenomena are universal and apply to all similar phenomena, and to ignore contrary hypotheses that are not supported by observation. "Nature is pleased with simplicity, and affects not the pomp of superfluous causes." So it is with mathematics, the chief source of this fetching vision.

This vision was only one inspiration of the Enlightenment. Logic and observation had to be tempered with a sense of the limitations of our knowledge and the urgency of the problems of human life. It was John Locke (1632-1704), a great admirer of Newton, who achieved the synthesis of science, practicality, and social responsibility.

Teacher and physician, politician and publicist, Locke embodied his own view of life. In his *Essay Concerning Human Understanding* (1690), he shifted the attention of men from esoteric concerns to palpable aims, from speculative to empirical methods, by exposing the dangers of metaphysical, abstruse, and dogmatic thinking. It was generally accepted in Locke's day that man was born with certain ready-made ideas and principles which he must accept as a guide in life. Belief in an eternal God, the sense of the infinite, and the sense of beauty—all these were thought to be innate in man and above the need for demonstration. It was taken for granted that monarchs were appointed by God and that people were born to be ruled.

Locke cut the ground from under this kind of thinking by denying the existence of innate ideas. Everything we know, he contended, comes from experience. The senses report it and reflection interprets it. The most complex and abstruse ideas can be broken up into simple ideas, and simple ideas consist of experiences and sensations whose relations—their similarities and differences—are perceived by the mind. Ideas which cannot be so treated are mere imaginings or fond wishes. "Our business here is not to know all things, but those which concern our conduct."

Reason and the State

Experience and sober reflection, Locke believed, can yield an assurance of religious, moral, and mathematical truth. They can also give political guidance. In the Middle Ages, government was sanctioned by the Church, which claimed divine origin. Later, both Protestant and Catholic rulers and theorists argued that monarchy was also a divine institution, since the prophet Samuel had anointed Saul and David as kings by command of God. Monarchs had inherited the patriarchal authority of Adam, whom God had endowed with private property on the earth and control over his wife, children, and the remotest posterity. In his *First Treatise on Government* (1685) John Locke laid this argument out in shreds. Adam represents all men, said Locke, and God's grant to him established the common property of mankind in the land, its fruits, and its beasts.

Locke also repelled the argument that rulers ought to be absolute because men were contentious and selfish. In *Leviathan* (1651) Thomas Hobbes (1588-1679) had painted a desperate picture of man in the "natural" state, in which "every man [was] enemy to every man" and life was "solitary, poor, nasty, brutish and short." In order to escape the terrors of such an existence, Hobbes hypothesized, men agreed to establish an unlimited power over themselves. This power was not responsible to the people, who were bound to obey it. Hobbes was so obsessed with the ideal of order that he insisted on indivisible and unlimited sovereignty.

Locke thought neither so ill of man nor so well of authority. He agreed with Hobbes that the state of nature was dangerous and inconvenient and that society was as old as reason itself. (The state of nature was hardly more than a fiction: the controversy turned on the character of man and the proper functions of government.) Man in a natural state—so ran Locke's allegory—has the freedom of his own person, his occupations and activities, his thought and expression; the right to the product of his labor, enterprise, and skill, his inheritance, and his possessions; not to mention the freedom to enjoy "innocent delights." He also has the right to judge wrongs done to him, to punish an attacker and force him to repair the damage he has done. But so long as he acts alone, this right cannot give him stability and security. He therefore comes together with his fellows to form a society in which power, thus multiplied, will assure "peace, safety, and the public good of the people." To this society he gives up the right to dispense justice in order to preserve and strengthen all the other rights, which he retains in their fullness.

This was the "social contract" of Locke. Society appoints two trustees to fulfill its end: a legislature—preferably a representative parliament—to make the rules that hold between men, and an executive to enforce them. The function of government is limited to the natural rights surrendered by man to society. Government is an umpire—lawmaker, policeman, judge—but only when men clash with one another. Otherwise man is as free as if no government or society existed, although more secure. The trustees are responsible to society. The legislature is the supreme power so long as government fulfills its trust; when it does not, the authority reverts to society—that is, to the people—who may then transfer their trust to another government.

Rulers who usurp the legislative power and govern by capricious decrees instead of by fair, standing laws and who abuse the executive power by invading the rights and properties of their subjects convict themselves of breach of trust. They introduce "a state of war, which is that of force without authority." They are, in short, rebels. In such cases the people are absolved from obedience, resume their original liberty, and "are left to the common refuge which God has provided for all men against force and violence." What is generally called a revolution, therefore, is the self-defense of the people against arbitrary rulers. Not that the people are easily moved to take up the gage. On the contrary, they tend to be long-suffering, politically inert, and conservative. Rulers have only themselves to blame if "a long train of abuses, prevarications, and artifices, all tending the same way," finally drive their subjects to resistance. It is then too late to resort to argument:

> . . . cry up then governors, as much as you will, for sons of Jupiter: let them be sacred and divine, descended or authorized from heaven; give them out for whom or what you please, the same will happen. The people generally ill-treated, and contrary to right, will be ready upon any occasion to ease themselves of a burden that sits heavy upon them.

The Englishman Locke thus established the right of revolution and laid down the principles of policy in broad terms. A Frenchman, the Baron de Montesquieu (1689-1755), supplied the sophisticated analysis of law and government that was needed to implement Locke's purposes. Locke's writing was unadorned and conversational; Montesquieu's was brilliant and inspired. It crackled with a wry wit, pointed parables, and sudden indignation. *The Spirit of the Laws* (1748) is perhaps the most typical expression of the enlightened mind and manner. It is a treasury of legal commentaries, historical comparisons, sociological and philosophical insights, and political counsel.

Montesquieu observed that human society is governed by laws as invariable as those that govern the physical world. These "laws" consist of the application of reason to human affairs and the relations among men. But since man is fallible and has free will, he does not always obey even the rules he makes himself; hence society is not so well governed as the physical world.

Montesquieu reflected the thought of his time in ascribing to climate and the physical environment generally a significant effect upon government and society. The torpor of hot climates, it was thought, makes their inhabitants too lazy to withstand despotism; the energetic atmosphere of the temperate zone is more congenial to freedom. However, Montesquieu believed that the form of government is largely determined by the prevailing social ideals. Despotism, for example, is based on the principle of fear. If a society prefers the principle of ambition and "honor," or personal distinction, then monarchy is best suited to it. If it prefers moderation, it ought to choose aristocratic forms. If its ideal is virtue, or the disinterested love of the commonwealth, it ought to establish a democracy.

Montesquieu perceived, however, that there are practical limits to idealism. Democracy is the most desirable form of government, but it cannot function successfully amid inequalities of wealth. Wherever ultimate sovereignty may lie, liberty can be assured only if the legislative, executive, and judicial functions of government are performed by different bodies. Although it involves a certain amount of quarrelsomeness, freedom is a precious state. Montesquieu admired the free constitution of England, whose effectiveness he ascribed to the division of powers. He overlooked the tendency of the executive and legislative branches to grow together; the constitution was still in the process of development.

A discriminating relativism informed Montesquieu's conclusions. In free and democratic governments, he wrote, punishments must be gentler than in others, diplomacy more honest, and conquest more restrained. But taxes may be higher, since the citizens are more willing and able to pay them. "In moderate states there is a compensation for the burden of taxes: that is liberty; in despotic states there is an equivalent for liberty: low taxes."

Montesquieu did not propose a political form suited to all times, places, conditions, and cultures. "Men always accommodate themselves better to the mean than to the extreme." The statesman must strike a balance among the exigencies of environment and tradition, the attractions of ideals and values, the requirements of civilization, and the prejudices of men. For France and other Continental states which had fallen into a species of despotism, Montesquieu advised moderate and flexible reform. He counseled rulers to abandon the surveillance over the private financial affairs of men which provided the occasion for arbitrary and prejudiced laws; to avoid dealing with matters that were clearly not the business of the state, such as religion, opinion, intellectual activity, and commercial and industrial enterprise; and to restore the rights and liberties that the various groups in society had enjoyed before the rise of despotic monarchies. Thus, despite his attempt to preserve old institutions, Montesquieu is considered a founder of modern liberalism, for he contended that the reach of institutional and state authority should be limited in order to enlarge the opportunity for spontaneous individual or group activity, and that a legal framework should be established to guarantee the limitations of that authority.

Within the realm properly belonging to the state, no field stood in greater need of improvement than criminal law. In every country incoherence and cruelty characterized the penal system. Laws were antiquated, overlapping, and contradictory. Trivial offenses were punished by such savage sentences as torture, branding, transportation to distant and primitive penal colonies, and execution. Reason and humanity rebelled against procedures that were as impractical and ineffective as they were brutal.

The Marquis of Beccaria (1735-94) gave the classic expression to the views of enlightened men on penal legislation. In *On Crimes and Punishments* (1764) he started from the premise that the proper object of laws should be to advance "the greatest good of the greatest number." Crime must be judged by the extent of the actual injury to society, not arbitrarily by spite or abstract moral or theological considerations. Society must be concerned much more with preventing and diminishing offenses than with punishing them, except in so far and in such manner as to deter future criminals. Torture and capital punishment not only are barbarous but do not deter crime. Prevention is served much better by simple and mild laws, by swift and sure enforcement, and by procedures that protect the accused.

The Economics of Laissez Faire

Humanity and utility were sufficient guides for penal reform. Economic reform, however, was linked to scientific inquiry. Enlightened men tried to adjust policy to the conditions under which wealth was created. In order to find a method of increasing wealth, one must first find a way of measuring it. The physiocrats of France, a group of political economists, made the first attempt to estimate national income and identify its source. They found that source not in money but in goods, not in trade but in agriculture. The production of all goods, they believed, is the result of work on the land. The landlord, the farmer, the shepherd, and the miner all add to the stock of goods. The craftsman, the manufacturer, the merchant, and the shipper merely change the form or location of those goods.

The physiocrats concluded that government should encourage the development of the land. The yield of the land above cost and profit—the "net product"—was, they argued, the proper and sufficient object of taxation. Taxes should be levied on this surplus, not on business and industry, for these "parasitical" enterprises would only pass the tax burdens back to the ultimate producer.

For all their emphasis on land, the physiocrats were capitalist-minded. They wished to stimulate the investment of capital in land as well as in trade. They preferred large-scale cultivation to small. Only the individual competition of free workmen and free enterprisers, across regional and national boundaries, held the hope of a considerable accretion of goods. *Laissez faire, laissez aller!* There is, they contended, a "natural order," which, if allowed to proceed undisturbed, will weld all the rival individual interests into a common good. The physiocratic program implied the removal of all traditional restrictions, serfdom, guilds, and the policies of regulation, monopoly, and privilege.

The British economist Adam Smith (1723-90) and the philosopher David Hume (1711-76) agreed with the physiocrats that a scientific study of economics must start with production, but, unlike the physiocrats, they held that labor was productive whether it was employed in industry or in agriculture. They agreed that the system of regulation, monopoly, and privilege should give way to *laissez faire*—in foreign and colonial as well as domestic affairs. Whether at home or abroad, the spontaneous flow of capital and labor would make for greater production and lower prices than the artificial promptings of mercantilism. There is no need to establish tariffs in order to stimulate domestic industry or to impose restrictions in order to prevent the flow of capital abroad.

The industry and employment of a country, Smith observed in *The Wealth of Nations* (1776), depend upon the amount of capital available for enterprise. Enterprisers naturally prefer to keep their capital as close to home as possible. In a free economy an "invisible hand"—what the physiocrats called "natural order"—leads the enterpriser, by the road of private advantage, to the goal of social wealth:

> As every individual merchant . . . endeavors as much as he can both to employ his capital in support of domestic industry, and so to direct that industry that its produce may be of the greatest value; every individual necessarily labors to render the annual revenue of the society as great as he can. He generally, indeed, neither intends to promote the public interest nor knows how much he is promoting it. By preferring the support of do-

mestic to that of foreign industry, he intends only his own security; and by directing that industry in such a manner as its produce may be of the highest value, he intends only his own gain, and he is in this, as in many other cases, led by an invisible hand to promote an end which was no part of his intention.

The mercantilists assumed that the gain of one country was the loss of another. When David Hume demonstrated that the enrichment of France would be to the advantage of Britain, her great rival, he challenged the conception of trade as a jealous and individious game. By exchanging goods and services, Hume argued, the various countries could add to their wealth simultaneously. They would obtain from other countries the goods that could be produced more cheaply abroad and sell in a relatively free market what they could produce to best advantage at home. The result would be lower prices for consumers everywhere—itself a sign of enrichment—larger markets for the producers, and greater opportunities for the middlemen, as well as less bitter economic warfare.

If countries could become richer by trading freely with one another, there was no reason for colonialism. Colonies, Adam Smith contended, are a greater source of expense than of revenue; they contribute little to their own defense and drain the military strength of the mother country. The monopoly of their trade inhibits "the enjoyments and industry" of both empire and colonies. It is "a dead weight upon the action of one of the great springs which puts into motion a great part of the business of mankind." The control of colonial trade is less beneficial to the mother country than it is harmful to her rivals. Indeed, the benefits are largely illusory. For example, although England paid less than France for the tobacco of Virginia and Maryland, she paid more than she would if the trade were entirely free. Ever since the discovery of America, England had received much of the surplus produce of the colonies; she could receive a greater abundance if controls were removed. Thus mercantilism produced the satisfactions of spite rather than profit.

If the mother country benefits little from colonialism, Smith argued, the colonies benefit less. The American colonies, for example, were handicapped by regulations of Great Britain intended to secure "the monopoly of their commerce; to confine their market, and to enlarge her own at their expense; and, consequently, rather to damp and discourage than to quicken and forward the course of their prosperity." These strictures applied to other empires as well. The only thing that Europe had contributed to "the present grandeur of the colonies of America" was "the education and great views of their active and enterprising founders."

Smith objected particularly to the control of overseas governments by merchants, such as that exercised over Indian territories by the British East India Company and over Indonesian islands by the Dutch East India Company. "No two characters seem more inconsistent than those of trader and sovereign . . . The government of an exclusive company of merchants is, perhaps, the worst of all governments for any country whatever." The operations of business, Smith claimed, shorten the vision and lengthen the self-regard of the practitioner. They breed invidious rivalry, a sense of clique, and an easy adjustment to circumstances that offer opportunities of immediate enrichment—all dangerous qualities in a statesman and ruler.

Reason and Religion

Few issues seemed more important to enlightened men than that of religion. Wars of religion had ceased. Fire and sword were no longer used regularly to subdue or convert heretics, dissenters, and infidels. But occasional outbreaks of persecution showed that fanaticism and superstition simmered underneath. The world of thought and letters suffered under special difficulties, for religion stood at the center, as it were, of learning and inquiry. The clergy controlled most schools and universities. Taking holy orders was generally the condition for earning a higher degree or a teaching position. It was usually clergymen who exercised or inspired censorship. They kept a jealous surveillance over writings that touched on questions of morality and philosophy, not to speak of dogma or ecclesiastical institutions—and there was hardly a work of politics, science, or economics that did not touch on morality and philosophy.

In the seventeenth century a prolonged controversy developed over the validity of Revelation and the relation between dogma and morality and between theology and "natural religion." Enlightened men directed severe attacks against the belief in miracles, witches, and devils. The philosopher Benedict Spinoza (1632-77) had asserted boldly that belief in miracles was atheism. To claim that the Lord would interfere with the immutable order of the universe— the greatest work and evidence of His wisdom—was to reduce Him to a capricious being; in other words, to deny Him. Warier writers claimed that the Lord used to perform miracles but had apparently ceased to do so, since the evidence for latter-day wonders was inferior to that of the Apostles.

Moralists protested that Christianity had been reduced to external observance. An elaborate panoply of ritual, dogma, and clerical institutions rested on a narrowing base of inner feeling. The Jesuit order in particular was singled out for attack on the ground that it made religion subserve the material and political interests of the Roman Church. It was accused of condoning the moral offenses of men of power whom it wished to influence.

While the churches were losing the confidence of the public, they remained self-righteous. It was their intolerance and fanaticism that drew the heaviest fire of the Enlightenment. Awareness of the limits of human reason, uncertainty as to ultimate or metaphysical truths, and desire for harmony in human affairs combined to produce a widespread attitude of tolerance and reasonableness among cultivated men. In his *Letter on Toleration* (1689) John Locke questioned the good faith of persecutors.

If the gospel and the apostles may be credited, no man can be a Christian without charity, and without that faith which works, not by force, but by love. Now I appeal to the consciences of those that persecute, torment, destroy, and kill other men upon pretence of religion, whether they do it out of friendship and kindness toward them, or no: and I shall then indeed, and not till then, believe they do so when I shall see those fiery zealots correcting, in the same manner, their friends and familiar acquaintances, for the manifest sins they commit against the precepts of the gospel.

Locke insisted on a strict separation of the functions of the church from those of the state. The church is concerned with the direction of worship and the peaceable teaching of its tenets; it must not use the instruments of power to invade freedom or property; it should be "a free and voluntary society." The state, on the other hand, should not concern itself with beliefs and dogma. Diversity of religion does not disturb the social or civil order.

The limits of toleration were, to Locke, civil rather than religious. He would not tolerate churches which insisted on special privileges for their members, which did not "teach the duty of tolerating all men in matters of mere religion," and which were subservient to foreign governments. He would not tolerate atheists, because they did not acknowledge the existence of God and therefore, he and others of his day believed, could not take a proper oath and hence could not be trusted to keep faith. Yet Locke believed in man's right to his honest opinions. He wrote in his *Essay*:

> The conduct of our lives and the management of our great concerns will not bear delay: for those depend, for the most part, on the determination of our judgment in points wherein we are not capable of certain and demonstrative knowledge, and wherein it is necessary for us to embrace the one side or the other.
>
> Since, therefore, it is unavoidable to the greatest part of men, if not all, to have several *opinions* without certain and indubitable proofs of their truths; and it carries too great an imputation of ignorance, lightness, or folly for men to quit and renounce their former tenets presently upon the offer of an argument which they cannot immediately answer and show the insufficiency of: would, methinks, become all men to maintain *peace* and the common offices of humanity and *friendship in the diversity of opinions:* since we cannot reasonably expect that any one should readily and obsequiously quit his own opinion and embrace ours.
>
> . . . We should do well to commiserate our mutual ignorance and endeavor to remove it in all the gentle and fair ways of information; and not instantly treat others ill, as obstinate and perverse, because they will not renounce their own and receive our opinions . . . when 'tis more than probable that we are no less obstinate in not embracing some of theirs. For where is the man that has incontestable evidence of the truth of all that he holds, or of the falsehood of all he condemns; or can say that he has examined to the bottom all his own or other men's opinions? . . . There is reason to think that if men were better instructed themselves they would be less imposing on others.

31

If Locke was the strategist in the war against intolerance, Pierre Bayle and Voltaire (François Marie Arouet) were the generals in the field. Bayle (1647-1706) came from a family of Huguenot merchants and preachers who fled to Holland from the persecution of Louis XIV. His *Historical and Critical Dictionary* (1695-97) was an armory of arguments against Revelation, miracles, orthodoxy, and Biblical models. Bayle collected and catalogued the crimes, myths, and superstitions of crusaders and saints. He compared the behavior of believers and unbelievers with shocking results: free thinkers and atheists seemed to him more moral than Christians.

It was the great Voltaire (1694-1778) who mobilized the hosts against religious intolerance. In an endless stream of essays, poems, and histories, he mocked the self-assurance of the orthodox and satirized their follies.

Many a brutal hand was stayed by fear of his mordant pen. He compelled reversals of notorious judicial sentences and saved many men from the fires of fanaticism. "Écrasez l'infâme"—crush the infamous thing—was his war cry against fanaticism.

What could be done to reconcile religion with morality and reason? It must be possible to cut through dogma to the essence of religion and through external observance to the essence of morality. The men of the Enlightenment were much influenced by classical civilization, and they were impressed by the fact that many wise pagans, as well as the sages of the Mohammedan, Jewish, and Christian traditions, had been persuaded of the existence of a First Cause, or Creator, and of the probability of the survival of the soul. But what was the nature of the Deity? Newtonian physics had suggested that the universe was analogous to a watch, constructed and wound by a Great Watchmaker; the interference of the Creator was necessary only on the most extraordinary occasions, when the energy of the mechanism ran down and needed a stimulus from the outside. For normal operation His fixed and invariable laws sufficed. They might be expressed in the simplest language and sometimes in mathematical terms. It was the part of wisdom and virtue—the two were as one in this view—to decipher and to live by laws that were at once divine, natural, and rational. Sharply though the various religions differed on questions of theology, they agreed on the rules of conduct. There existed a "natural ethics" as there existed a "natural religion."

The consequence of these reflections was the evolution of deism. The "tenets" of deism were few: belief in a just God who governed the universe by unalterable and harmonious laws, adherence to a "natural morality," and often also a belief in a future life. Gone were original sin and the fall of man, the Trinity and the sacraments. The deists counted Jesus among the great moral teachers of mankind, perhaps the greatest, but they did not believe he was divine.

The practical consequence of deism was to make church and clergy superfluous. Since there were no dogmas to explain, no rituals to perform, and no sacraments to administer, priests and ministers lost their function. However, the deists conceded, a certain sophistication was needed before people were

Bust of Voltaire by J. A. Houdon (1741-1828.). In the Louvre.
ARCHIVES PHOTOGRAPHIQUES

ready for deistic views. The churches might continue to offer the familiar con-solations to humbler folk and to administer the familiar checks to misbehavior. For the mass of men, moral rules still needed the sanction of dogmatic author-ity; let the state continue to support official churches until all men should be-come enlightened. But persecution and invidious treatment of persons who stood outside official churches, censorship of reading and publishing, and surveillance of artistic consumption and production must cease.

The Influence of Asia and America

The Enlightenment was cosmopolitan. There was no place in it for sharp and invidious national distinctions. The enlightened man admired civic virtue and the love of one's community, but he did not magnify the peculiarities of his own nation or depreciate those of others. He had a wide-ranging curiosity about foreign countries and distant civilizations and a deep appreciation of their achievements. He was much impressed, for example, by Oriental civilizations. Buddhism and Confucianism, with their bent for secularism, practical morality, and intellectual achievement and their espousal of individual self-cultivation, seemed to confirm some of the tendencies of the Enlightenment. Neither Buddha nor Confucius stressed the belief in gods or devils. "Respect the spirits," the Chinese sage had said, "but keep them at a distance." He accepted the Golden Rule but not the principle of "turning the other cheek"; kindness he would reward with kindness, but enmity he would meet with "just treatment."

The enlightened man was struck by the extraordinary stability and continuity of Asian societies. He was not, however, an uncritical observer. Montesquieu described the Chinese as covetous, their emperors as despotic, and their customs as occasionally heartless, but he paid tribute to the sobriety of their laws, the equity of their taxes, the rationality of their administration, the secularism of their philosophy, the practicability of their religion, and the civility of their manners. He predicted that Christianity would never win over the Chinese and that their country could not be transformed by conquest. "Their customs, manners, laws, and religion being the same thing, they cannot change all these at once; and as it will happen that either the conqueror or the conquered must change, in China it has always been the conqueror."

The influence of the East was apparent in many fields. Its secularism and practical ethics strengthened deism. European artists introduced Oriental motifs and styles. In literature it became the fashion to cast the "wise man of the East" in the role of the objective and quizzical observer of the European scene.

While the Orient contributed the image of the noble sage, America supplied that of the "noble savage": the red Indian, virtuous and dignified, sober and kindly, and innocent of the prejudices and preconceptions of the European. Measured against this standard, the vanity, falsity, and vices of conventional European society seemed doubly ridiculous. Eventually the hardy and self-respecting settler and frontiersman—the American in general—slipped into the role, if not of the "noble savage," of the virtuous "natural man." There was great curiosity in Europe about the flora and fauna, as well as the communities, overseas. American travel books gradually became a part of the literary repertoire.

From the beginning America was a refuge for the persecuted people of the Old World. There was hardly a religious sect that did not find a home there. America was also the favorite seat of literary utopias. Sir Thomas More's original "nowhere" and many of the later utopias were located there. It was in America that speculative and even fantastic ideals might be realized, or at least experimented with.

The Enlightenment promoted an easy interchange of ideas. It made the European world, and particularly the countries bordering on the North Atlantic, a single cultural community. The leading men of France, Holland, Great Britain, and the American colonies maintained contact with one another by correspondence and visits. Locke and Newton were the patron saints of the French and American as well as the English Enlightenment. Montesquieu and Voltaire were widely read on both sides of the Channel, and on both sides of the ocean. In France, Anglomania and, later, enthusiasm for everything American were common. Businessmen crossed borders easily, and it was customary for investors and enterprisers to function with facility in several Atlantic countries. There were men who enjoyed citizenship and the privileges of natives in two or three countries simultaneously.

In each country the Enlightenment was naturally colored by local characteristics. In England the touch of empiricism was especially strong. France paid her traditional homage to logic, precision, and clarity. The American colonies were at once behind and ahead of England and France. They were both cultural and political dependencies, for they imported their reading matter and scientific knowledge, like their manufactured goods and luxuries, from Europe. Even their Bibles were European; it was not until 1777 that the first English version of the New Testament was published in the colonies. The Enlightenment crossed the ocean rather slowly, but the American had one advantage over the European: he was born more than half enlightened. In *Letters from an American Farmer* (1782), the fond eulogy of the French essayist and agronomist Hector St. John de Crèvecoeur (1735-1813), the American was a "new man." He had left behind

> . . . all his ancient prejudices and manners, receives new ones from the new mode of life he has embraced, the new government he obeys, and the new rank he holds. . . . From involuntary idleness, servile dependence, penury, and useless labor, he has passed to toils of a different nature, rewarded by ample subsistence. This is an American.

The transatlantic society was

> not composed, as in Europe, of great lords who possess everything, and a herd of people who have nothing. Here are no aristocratical families, no courts, no kings, no bishops, no ecclesiastical dominion, no invisible power giving to a few a very visible one; no great manufactures employing thousands, no great refinements of luxury. The rich and the poor are not so far removed from each other as they are in Europe.

Nor were the various nationalities. "I could point out to you," wrote Crèvecoeur, "a man whose grandfather was an Englishman, whose wife was Dutch, whose son married a French woman, and whose present four sons have now four wives of different nations." In America, "individuals of all nations are melted into a new race of men," deriving from that "strange mixture of blood, which you will find in no other country."

Crèvecoeur's picture was overdrawn. In many parts of America, particularly those that had been settled for a long time, national and religious groups preserved their distinctiveness. Yet more men of varied origins were brought together, placed on an equal level, and even assimilated than in the older countries. The image of the "new man" belonged as much to the future as to the present, but it was none the less potent for that.

There was, paradoxically, both greater religious earnestness and greater toleration in the New World than in the Old. Some of the colonies had been settled by religious sects, which found in America not only freedom to worship in their own way but an opportunity to organize homogeneous communities committed to their view of life. In such colonies as Massachusetts, which had been governed by theocracies in the early period, the relation between religion and society tended to be stronger than in Europe. Strict, somber, and rigid Protestant orthodoxies dominated much of colonial life, especially in New England. Powerful contrary forces, however, were making for toleration and rationalism. No single church was dominant in all the colonies. Four of the thirteen colonies—Rhode Island, Pennsylvania, New Jersey, and Delaware—had separated church and state to become the first secular polities in the Western world. The tendency of Protestant sects to divide, secede from the central body, and then further to subdivide drained the strength of ecclesiastical institutions. Finally, the advance of rational thought softened dogmatism. These circumstances, and the fact that there was greater literacy in the colonies than in most European countries, produced a growing though informal tolerance. Minority groups were on the whole treated better in America than in the Old World.

Apart from breeding an easier and more democratic atmosphere, America contributed to the Enlightenment a tart homeliness of expression. Benjamin Franklin (1706-90), the self-made printer and businessman of Philadelphia who was also a journalist, scientist, inventor, and politician, was the prototype of the enlightened American. His popular mouthpiece, Poor Richard of the *Almanac*, observed, "Kings and bears often worry their keepers," "Poverty, poetry, and new titles of honor make men ridiculous," and "Love and lordship hate companions." Franklin wrote,

> In old times it was no disrespect for men and women to be called by their own names. Adam was never called Master Adam; we never read of Noah Esquire, Lot Knight and Baronet, nor the Right Honorable Abraham, Viscount Mesopotamia, Baron of Canaan. No, no, they were plain men, honest country graziers, that took care of their families and their flocks.

Franklin's young compatriot Thomas Jefferson remarked with a rough directness, "It does me no injury for my neighbor to say that there are twenty gods, or no god. It neither picks my pocket nor breaks my leg."

There were two other ways in which American experience made a significant contribution to the Enlightenment. Some of the colonies had charters or "contracts" with the Crown which laid down procedures of government and lawmaking; thus the concept of written constitutions took root in the New World. Secondly, while representation in European parliaments or estates was often based on rank, class, office, or prescription, the need to grant representation to frontier settlers accustomed the American colonists to the idea of representation exclusively by township or territory. This idea became central in modern parliamentarianism.

The Edge of the Later Enlightenment

In the sixties and seventies, the European Enlightenment underwent a sea change. Its premises were pushed to extreme conclusions. The issue of socialism was raised, at least tentatively, and rationalism itself was challenged by both skeptics and romantics. The Enlightenment acquired an edge.

Amid the general acceptance of the property system, a few voices were raised against private ownership. Moralists inveighed against the ostentation, vanity, and luxury associated with unusual riches for the few and misery for the many. In a society primarily agricultural, justice suggested that land be divided equally among the cultivators. The Abbé Gabriel Bonnet de Mably (1709-85), reasoning from the doctrine of natural equality, reached the conclusion that equality ought to reign in the economic as well as the political field, in society as well as in law. The philosopher Morelly characterized the urge to possession as man's first vice. He described a utopia in which goods were distributed according to the need of the consumer and production was organized, to the minutest detail, by the community. The lawyer and journalist Simon Linguet (1736-94) stigmatized the state as an instrument for the legalization and preservation of private property, and property as the usurpation of social wealth. Only the establishment of economic equality, he claimed, could give substance to legal reforms.

Empiricism deepened into utilitarianism and materialism. For John Locke reflection was the agency which distilled sense experience into knowledge. Later philosophers, however, began to trace reflection itself to the senses. They made pleasure and pain the moving forces of action and the standard of ethics and politics. Happiness was a matter of multiplying pleasures and diminishing pains. The good state, the best laws, were those that promoted "the greatest happiness of the greatest number." At this point democracy became visible on the horizon, for everybody had sensations, and sensation, according to this philosophy, was the central fact of life. The objects of sensation, then, were the primary reality. Some philosophers, drawing the final conclusions of materialism, suggested that since the world, and man, were made up of material particles, the concatenation and movement of these particles accounted for thought as well as action, for ideas as well as events.

More important than the occasional expressions of materialism was the rise of skepticism. David Hume, "the great doubter," questioned whether we can ever know the real world outside ourselves. He denied man's ability to demonstrate that events had causes. Human reason, according to Hume, cannot penetrate the ultimate mysteries. The intellect is unable, by itself, to solve the problems of morality, beauty, and religion. Hume questioned the power of the mind to validate any general truth. Yet the world remained a fairly solid enterprise to the corrosive Scotsman. The inadequacies of the understanding, in his view, were fortunately supplied by the resources of feeling, imagination, belief, and habit. If we cannot be certain of cause-and-effect relations, we can be reassured by the probabilities of the case. The likelihood that these relations are real is endorsed by custom and by the results of human activity. This is sufficient for most purposes.

In narrowing the range of reason, Hume used the tools of reason itself. Other men appealed directly to feeling. The champion and symbol of romanticism was Jean Jacques Rousseau (1712-78), the son of a craftsman of the free Protestant city-state of Geneva, a vagabond, misfit, rebel, and writer of genius.

Rousseau drew a picture of civilization that chilled the heart. Primitive man was instinctive, solitary, and amoral, but he was free, and, unlike the beasts, he had the capacity for improvement. He learned to live in families and tribes and developed skills, crafts, and arts. These, however, bred invidious relations: "Iron and grain, which first civilized men, . . . ruined humanity." Private property completed the ruin. Rousseau wrote in his *Origin of Inequality* (1755),

> The first man, who, having enclosed a piece of ground, bethought himself of saying "This is mine," and found people simple enough to believe him, was the real founder of civil society. From how many crimes, wars, and murders, how many horrors and misfortunes, might not anyone have saved mankind, by pulling up the stakes, or filling up the ditch, and crying to his fellows: "Beware of listening to this impostor; you are undone if you once forget that the fruits of the earth belong to us all, and the earth itself to nobody."

The savior did not appear. The more wealthy, powerful, and refined society grew, the more vicious, artificial, corrupt, and mean men became.

Rousseau's answer, in *Émile* (1762) and *The Social Contract* (1762), was a new educational program and a new political system. He proposed education through experience to supplant education through precept, set tasks, and book learning. The child's body must be developed as well as his individual aptitudes. Conscience and the love of God were implanted in the heart of man and needed but to be awakened.

Rousseau endowed "society" with sentient being, distinct from and sovereign over what is usually called government. His politics begins with the determination of the "general will," the consensus of the citizenry as a whole arrived at directly, not through representatives. A society in which popular sovereignty reigns Rousseau considered a republic, regardless of the form of the government, for government is the subordinate agent of the sovereign in executive, legislative, and judicial matters. This agent may be a hereditary monarch, an aristocracy, or the citizenry itself, governing as well as reigning. By whomever exercised, the "general will" is unlimited in its reach. Rousseau identified the "general will" with public virtue and therefore saw no reason to restrict its power.

Rousseau's conditions for an effective democracy were forbidding: the state must be small so that its citizens can know one another and meet together readily; manners must be simple; rank and fortunes must be fairly equal, or rights cannot be equal; there must be no luxury, for luxury makes the rich possessive and the poor envious. "Were there a people of gods, their government would be democratic. So perfect a government is not for men." Rousseau settled for an elective aristocracy.

By Rousseau's test of popular sovereignty, virtually every state, feudal and modern, was condemned as illegitimate. However, his view that civilized society was corrupt justified every form of government, provided only that it gave expression to the "general will." For in a corrupt society there may be only a handful of selfless, authentic citizens who know what is the common weal and

Rousseau's attack on the "vices" of civilization, luxury, and formalism re-flected a powerful tendency toward natural simplicity and sensibility among French intellectuals. It became fashionable to affect rural simplicity. Even the Queen of France followed the fashion. This is Marie Antoinette's "mill" at the Petit Trianon *in the park of the palace of Versailles.* CULVER

are determined to achieve it. Perhaps there is but one such citizen: In that case, dictatorship is justified. Yet the sovereign, he wrote, cannot "exceed the limits of public expedience" or "general conventions," cannot impose "fetters that are useless to the community," and must allow the individual to do whatever "does not harm others."

Rousseau's ideal was the city-state of classical antiquity and Swiss democracy, but Europe could hardly be divided into small city-states. He promised that he would show, in a sequel to *The Social Contract*, "how the external strength of a great people may be combined with the convenient polity and good order of a small state." He never did so, but he intimated that he had in mind the principle of confederation.

Such were the contradictions of Rousseau's thinking. He loved freedom, yet insisted on moral discipline. What, then, was the source of his influence, which was considerable in his own day and grew greater afterwards? The charged flow of his style, the color of his images, the urgency of his sentiments set aglow every theme he touched. He indicted the rich and the fashionable, condemned arrogance and snobbishness, and vindicated the simple virtues and honest impulses of the lowly and unschooled with an eloquence that made his writings a trumpet call to sincerity and feeling. His declaration that "men will always be what women choose to make of them" bolstered the pride of half of the human race. His attacks on refinement pleased the middle classes. Finally, his exaltation of the purity and omnipotence of the "general will" gave confidence to democratic idealists. "Man is born free; and everywhere he is in chains"—the opening peal of *The Social Contract*—reverberated in the hearts of all men who felt the injustice and tragedy of human existence. Rousseau's fame is a triumph of art and imagination. He was a magician.

The Transmission of Ideas

The Enlightenment strayed onto radical paths indeed. Yet the philosophes, as leaders of the Enlightenment were called in France, did not propose to put all their ideas into practice. Hume was a Tory who supported the established order. He demolished the first cause in theory but was content to settle for deism in fact. Even Rousseau was no revolutionist. When he was asked to draft a constitution to arrest the internal anarchy of Poland, he produced a document that any of his moderate contemporaries might have written. In short, the Enlightenment was to the end temperate. It was the sobriety which accompanied its bent for improvement that made it an effective force. The principal carriers of the Enlightenment were men of letters, seconded by cultivated women. It worked its influence through the printing press, and through scientific and literary societies. A "fourth estate" was forming. Pamphleteers and journalists, satirists and playwrights—and a growing reading public—applied to public life the standards of reason and good taste. They scrutinized and discussed the defects, abuses, and incongruities of the prevailing order. They criticized the shifts and inequities resulting from the cross-fertilization of power, privilege, and capital. Enlightened writers addressed themselves to the ordinary literate man and the layman, avoiding esoteric ideas, pedantic allusions, pompous expressions, and technical terms. They appealed to everyday experience and relied on homely examples. To the weapon of simplicity and directness the philosophes added that of wit. The exigencies of censorship compelled them to resort to

40

Fig. 4.

Industrial illustration from Diderot's Encyclopedia. The glass blower twirls the glass in the flame, clips the rough edges, and puts the finishing touches on the goblet, which the boy lifts into the arch over the furnace.

understatement and indirect expression on sensitive subjects and to draw on their resources of irony, humor, and mock-seriousness. The result was a literature which was diverting as well as instructive. The age was rich in essays and satires and produced the most copious correspondence the world has ever known.

The master of the enlightened method and style was Voltaire, and its greatest product was the famous *Encyclopedia*. Voltaire was the most productive and entertaining of writers. The number and variety of his works—hundreds of plays, satires, stories, epics and histories, and thousands of letters— and the energy, consistency, wit, and persistence with which he attacked prejudice, arrogance, and bigotry made him a power to reckon with. With no less vigor, he popularized Newton and Locke and extolled science. His books and pamphlets circulated widely and were read with respect in royal courts and with admiration in *salons* and cafés. He treated great monarchs as his equals and lesser potentates accordingly. After two centuries his picture of human follies in *Candide* still makes the reader blush for his kind amid his tears of laughter. Of no modern writer can it be said with so much truth that the pen was mightier than the sword.

Encyclopedias in the eighteenth century were literary works, designed for reading and browsing as well as for reference. In Denis Diderot (1713-84), the age found the perfect editor. A writer of unusual energy, practical sense, and versatility, Diderot was the typical philosophe in action. He had moved from deism to atheism and materialism, but his modest and ebullient personality enabled him to temper his devotion to reason with an appreciation of sensibility.

Diderot assembled a brilliant group of philosophes, including Voltaire, Rousseau, Montesquieu, Robert Jacques Turgot (1727-81), a leading economist and administrator, and Jean d'Alembert (1717-83), an eminent mathematician, to collaborate on a vast survey of human knowledge. *The Encyclopedia, or rational systematic dictionary of the sciences, arts, and crafts, by a society of men of letters* appeared in seventeen folio volumes between 1750 and 1764. The governing aim of the Encyclopedists was to exhibit man's capacity and industry,

Fig. 5.

Fig. 6.

to expose the inadequacy of existing arrangements in society, notably the Church establishments, and to stimulate reforms that would promote the fulfillment of human potentialities. Industrial techniques and inventions were described and illustrated with minute care. Man the doer and contriver was the hero, and his setting was an orderly and potentially benign universe. The *Encyclopedia* found a powerful enemy in the Church, particularly in the Jesuit order. It was suppressed more than once, and Diderot was constantly harried. But the great editor finally triumphed, and the work was widely sold, read and imitated, translated, and pirated. It became the Bible of the Enlightenment.

The impact of the Enlightenment upon the various social classes was uneven. The tendency toward secular rationalism was qualified by a widespread craving for a warm and emotional religion. There were popular protests against doctrinal formalism in several parts of Europe. The German Pietists practiced a religion of the heart. The Moravian Brethren espoused a severe moral code and strove for "spiritual perfection." Driven out of Bohemia in the seventeenth century, the Brethren found refuge later in Saxony, England, and the southern American colonies. They were influential in converting to their views an intense Anglican minister, John Wesley (1703-91), who launched an evangelical campaign upon his return from a missionary voyage to Georgia. At large openair meetings, Wesley and a band of fellow preachers exhorted Christians to fervent prayer and spontaneous conversion. They painted in lurid colors the dangers of damnation and aroused emotional and even hysterical responses among their hearers, many of whom were untaught and poor people. They sought out the unfortunate and preached to miners, farmers, and prisoners. Their followers, the Methodists, eventually drifted out of the Church of England and, after the turn of the century, organized a church of their own.

In the mid-eighteenth century, a similar movement—the "Great Awakening"—swept the American colonies. Among its outstanding intellectual leaders were the brilliant Calvinist preacher Jonathan Edwards (1703-58) and the English evangelist George Whitefield (1714-70). Edwards' vivid descriptions of the eternal punishment awaiting sinners in hell deepened the sense of doom among New Englanders who had inherited a Puritan tradition. While Edwards attempted to reconcile reason and the Bible, science and Christianity, and emphasized the individual's responsibility for his actions, his final stress lay on deep faith. Whitefield and a succession of itinerant preachers, many of them followers of John Wesley, swayed greater numbers with more emotional appeals than those of Edwards. They established the first Methodist church in America in 1766. Eventually Methodism became one of the largest denominations in North America, with especial influence in the rural districts, the "back country," and the frontier. Most of the Protestant denominations were affected by revivalism, and some of the churches were divided by it. Revivalism, with its mass conversions, became endemic in America.

For all the conflict between emotionalism and rationalism, the religious movement incidentally reinforced some of the social influences of the Enlightenment. It weakened the prestige and the hold of established churches. The

Great Awakening increased the demand to separate church and state in America. On both sides of the Atlantic, revivalists advocated practical reform and social betterment. In the American colonies, where the people had unusual freedom to voice their sentiments and needs and to form new organizations and communities, the Great Awakening resulted in increased pressures for social equality, religious freedom, and political democracy.

In Western Europe and America the effect of the Enlightenment upon the classes that carried weight in society and government was much greater than its popular impact. In every age the practical consequence of a culture depends on the association between men of affairs and men of letters, and this association was particularly close in the eighteenth century. The fashion of the time commanded an interest in letters and the arts, and the classes that possessed wealth and controlled power followed the fashion. It was the middle and professional classes that were most deeply affected by rationalism, and these groups supplied most of the creative spirits of the Enlightenment. Voltaire's grandfather was a merchant, his father a lawyer; David Hume's father owned a small estate; and Diderot's father was a prosperous cutler. The humanistic education and training of professional men, in a day before narrow specialization, made them susceptible to new ideas. The ambitions of these men thrived on the recognition of the value of learning and intellectual discipline.

The businessman was susceptible to enlightened ideas for reasons of his own. He had prospered under the prevailing arrangements of society. For his more moderate ambitions—a stable income and a measure of social recognition—the atmosphere of aristocracy and absolute monarchy was congenial. But if business was to expand to its farthest limits, and if commercial ability and success were to entail social dignity, it was not enough to reduce annoying political controls over the economy or to abate the rigidities of tradition. It was necessary to reward all ability and to liberate all enterprise, for one could not claim recognition for mercantile talent alone. It was necessary to infuse society with new ideals and purposes.

This task the philosophes were performing. At the same time they showed an appreciation of the needs of business. Many of them combined the habits of enterprise and investment with literary and scientific pursuits; Voltaire, for example, engaged in financial speculation throughout his life. It was natural, therefore, that the man of letters and the man of business not only should be close but should even become the same person. Occasionally the two characters found such magnificent embodiments as Benjamin Franklin, the prototype of the businessman who takes a strong interest in learning and science, or of the man of science who succeeds in commerce and speculation. This merging did not diminish the distinction between the social functions of business and intellect, but it helps to explain the ease of their cooperation, the openness of the first to responsible reflection and the practical effectiveness of the second.

The effect of the Enlightenment upon the business classes had repercussions among the urban masses. That men of substance and learning should be critical of the dispositions of society was a matter of curiosity and interest to them. Evidently something was wrong, not only below—that they did not need to be told—but above.

From the town the Enlightenment moved to the palace, from the coffee house to the *salon* and the smoking room of the nobleman. As the printing press spread the ideas of the Enlightenment, cultivated women of social position or wealth opened their drawing rooms to men of learning, talent, and wit. Patrons of the arts and often mistresses of the great, they presided over *soirées* and receptions in which authors and scholars rubbed elbows with statesmen, aristocrats, and rich businessmen. The *salons* created an atmosphere of intellectual distinction, free controversy, and feminine grace. Able writers acquired political weight. Not since classical Greek times had women—a select few, to be sure—mingled so freely on a plane of equality with distinguished men.

Literary and scientific societies were the rage in Europe and America. In addition to debating and discussing, they encouraged literature and social criticism by offering prizes and running contests. Semisecret societies, notably the Masonic order, added a ritual touch to the new faith of deism and practical morality; their lodges multiplied and luxuriated from St. Petersburg to Philadelphia, and their membership included noblemen and squires as well as scholars, merchants, and professional men.

The Enlightenment reached into the highest monarchical and imperial quarters. The devout Empress Maria Theresa of Austria (1740-80) married a Freemason—Duke Francis of Tuscany—although Freemasonry had been condemned by the Papacy. Francis provided enlightened tutors for their two sons, Joseph and Leopold, as did the Empress Catherine II of Russia for her grandson, the future Czar Alexander I. Frederick II, King of Prussia, was a friend of Voltaire and an author in his own right. Many a lesser potentate took his cue from the greater, and the nobles followed suit. If the kings had not quite become philosophers, some of them listened to men who had.

Enlightened Absolutism

Enlightened men were not doctrinaire in matters of government, although they were not so indifferent as Alexander Pope's couplet implied:

> Of forms of government let fools contest,
> What's best administered is best.

In theoretical discussions, they preferred republics to monarchies, and parliamentary to absolute states. But they were not a political party, and they were willing to take half a loaf. They were intransigent only in their opposition to clerical intolerance, monastic idleness, and the more arrogant aristocratic pretensions. Since they laid most of the existing abuses at the door of the clergy and aristocracy, classes with which the monarchs and their bureaucrats were often at odds, a natural alliance between Enlightenment and absolutism suggested itself. Political institutions tended to be rigid, but policy might be flexible.

For their part, energetic rulers felt that some of the proposed reforms, apart from their intrinsic value, would strengthen the centralized state. Emancipation of the serfs, for example, would result in the transfer of much fiscal, judicial, and administrative authority from the local gentry and aristocracy to the monarchy. A serf was the lord's man, a freeman the king's subject. The definition of marriage as a civil contract would enable persons who did not belong to official churches to marry, inherit, and beget offspring legally—and it would incidentally shift the control of this important relation, its sanctions and its fees, from the church to the state. Simplification of the laws in the interests of fairness and humanity would also integrate the provinces of a country and make administration more efficient. Religious toleration, by attracting enterprising merchants and skilled craftsmen harried out of their homes by fanaticism, would enrich the country and increase the sources of taxation. The bargain was struck and enlightened despotism was born, the child of calculation and conviction.

The regional differences of the Western world stamped themselves upon the movement for reform. Empress Catherine II of Russia (1762-96) and King Frederick II of Prussia (1740-86), most of whose lands lay east of the Elbe River, were avid readers, who nursed literary ambitions of their own. They befriended fashionable authors, some of whom responded with eulogies of the "philosopher king" and the "Semiramis of the North." Both Frederick and Catherine looked upon the approval of liberal opinion in the light of a "good press."

Frederick II was all calculation. He inherited in 1740 a country poor in natural and human resources and a government which squeezed the last drop of fiscal and military blood out of it. For a long time Prussia had been forcing herself up to the rank of a great power; under the leadership of Frederick she achieved it. Frederick was so far in accord with the spirit of his time as to profess that "the monarch is only the first servant of the state." But he was a "servant" who had complete charge of the household and whose masters could not call him to account. Frederick preferred those reforms that filled the coffers of the state and strengthened its army. He drained swamps, built canals, subsidized new settlements, attempted to attract foreign craftsmen and manufacturers, abolished internal tolls, extended credit to landlords, and gave bounties to new enterprises. From all these "investments" he derived fiscal returns, and, although he helped to lay the foundation of future economic development, for his own time he did much more to improve the condition of his treasury than that of his people. He made his bureaucracy more efficient, though less enterprising, by exercising an iron control over it. Frederick was his own foreign minister, strategist, and army commander, watchdog of the accounts, and zealous overseer of his subjects' business, manners, and taste.

The tale of Catherine's reforms is soon told. She secularized church lands containing two million serfs and transferred them to the Crown; improved the administration and introduced a modicum of local and town government, without relaxing the power at the center; increased the freedom of commercial and industrial enterprise; and extended a measure of toleration to Christians who stood outside the Russian (Greek) Orthodox Church. She seized the initiative in promising projects, convoked a legislative assembly, suggested the liberalization and codification of the laws, and even broached the question of emancipating the serfs.

Next to nothing came of her projects. Catherine was no rebel. She remarked quite accurately: "I am an aristocrat—that is my business." Absorbed by the ambition to enlarge and strengthen the state and thus make her position secure, she showered the nobles with privileges in order to attach them to her cause. She released them from the traditional duty of service to the state, gave her favorites most of the secularized clerical lands, and tightened the control of the landlords over their peasants. The lord became not only master but judge and executioner. Serfdom, far from being abolished, approached the condition of slavery and was extended over the vast reaches of the southern "frontier." The frontiersmen—the Cossacks—lost much of their former freedom and became the auxiliary troops of the government to keep the other peasants in subjection. Wars for territorial expansion increased the fiscal and other burdens of the people. In 1775 Cossacks and peasants rebelled, under the leadership of a pretender to the throne, E. I. Pugachev (1741-75), and exacted a summary justice on the property and lives of landlords. They were suppressed with fury.

Catherine's reign consummated a long process of elevation for the nobility and degradation for the peasantry. At its end, of the thirty-six million people in Russia, some twenty million were private serfs; fourteen million were peasants on Crown lands, and only a shade less miserable. The Age of Enlightenment was really the "Golden Age of the Nobility" in Russia.

Enlightened reform was a greater reality in Western Europe. Tuscany, Spain, and Portugal led the van. The Hapsburg Archduke Leopold, who ruled in Tuscany from 1745 to 1790, before he ascended the throne of Austria as Leopold II (1790-92), found receptive soil for rational advance in Florence. He diminished the privileges of the clergy, particularly of the regular orders; sheared the Inquisition of its power of censorship; cleansed the criminal law of its barbarities, notably torture and capital punishment, in accordance with the proposals of Beccaria; granted a measure of self-government to the municipalities; fostered economic development and agrarian improvements; and spurred agricultural and industrial production. Leopold also encouraged artistic and literary activity. He reached out for support and sympathy by the publication of explanatory pamphlets. He even contemplated granting a modern constitution, in good time.

The Bourbon King Charles III began as a reforming monarch in Naples and Sicily (1734-59) and continued his activities when he fell heir to the more important throne of Spain, which he occupied until 1788. He simplified and humanized the laws, integrated the administration, encouraged higher education, and, above all, reduced the power and enormous riches of the Church by limiting the number of religious orders and levying heavy taxes upon religious foundations. The money thus raised was disbursed for new roads and bridges, secondary schools and colleges, and a better administration. Without challenging the functions and rights of the Church or tolerating attacks upon the Church or the Catholic religion as such, Charles tempered the sharpness of clerical censorship and checked the fanaticism of the Inquisition. It was regarded as a great advance that the dreaded institution dared to burn but few persons in Charles' reign.

In neighboring Portugal the daring minister Sebastian Pombal (1699-1782) struck at the most powerful representative of clerical dominion. The order of the Jesuits had long been under attack by enlightened men, and Pombal expelled it from the kingdom. France, Spain, and other Catholic countries followed suit. In 1773 Pope Clement XIV (1769-74), at their insistence, deprived the order of its functions and possessions and then finally "suppressed, extinguished, abolished, and abrogated it forever."

Among the numerous German states, Baden, Brunswick, and several others entered on the path of reform. Here and there, a ruler overreached himself. Denmark told a fantastic tale. An extraordinary German physician, John Frederick Struensee (1737-72), won the confidence of the Queen and of her incompetent husband, King Christian VII (1766-1808). In one feverish year, 1771-72, he issued more than a thousand reforming decrees. Few countries were so badly in need of them, but a strong group of courtiers and noblemen staged a palace revolution and "rescued" the King, forcing him to annul nearly all the decrees and to decapitate Struensee.

The fate of enlightened reform hinged, in great measure, on its introduction in France and England, for these countries exerted much influence throughout the Western world. They were the home of the Enlightenment, and criticism began at home. In both countries the question of reform involved imperial and colonial issues as well as domestic matters. Rational and economical policies at home entailed moderate aims abroad; Enlightenment therefore clashed with aggressive imperialism. French reformers proposed that the government concentrate its attention on improving internal conditions rather than on colonial rivalry and dynastic prestige. English reformers advocated a more liberal treatment of Ireland and the American colonies as well as the purification of the parliamentary system. The treatment of the colonies became a test of the application of enlightened views to relations between civilized communities. And this test became decisive for the conflict between the old order and the new.

3. *The First Atlantic Revolution*

The Revolution of 1775 was a European as well as an American event. It affected not only Great Britain and her colonies on the American mainland but most of the powers of Europe as well. It raised the question of freedom of the seas in which all the states with maritime interests had a stake. By changing the relation of the American colonies to their mother country, it influenced the relation of overseas colonies generally to the metropolis. To some extent it altered the distribution of power among the European empires. Not least, the Revolution tested the resources of various countries and the flexibility of their forms of government. It thus helped to decide the issue between traditionalism and Enlightenment.

The Rivalry of France and Great Britain

The occasion if not the cause of the American Revolution was the settlement, in 1763, of the old rivalry between France and Great Britain. For several generations France had been the leading state of Europe. Her luster was still bright, but her international position was deteriorating. She was being overtaken by her competitor across the Channel. In wealth, extent, and population England was still second to France, but she was assuming a leading role in commercial, maritime, and colonial affairs.

It is not easy to say which is more upsetting to domestic political equilibrium, a rise or a decline in international power. One thing was clear: the change in the relative position of England and France and the nearly continuous struggle between them complicated the domestic course of both countries. Each country felt an increasing pressure to set its house in order, even while it was challenged to maintain or assert predominance on the international scene.

The decline in the power of France was in a measure the result of forces and developments beyond her control. Nature, so generous to her otherwise—

no country in Europe had richer agricultural resources—had tipped the scales against her in naval fortune. The waters of the English Channel were the cross-roads of the maritime states, where sea predominance must first of all be decided. But there France suffered from severe disadvantages as compared with both Great Britain and Holland. Her Channel coasts contained no natural ports spacious enough to shelter large fleets, while the opposite shore contained several, and Holland was studded with ports and estuaries. The prevailing westward winds of the region favored the maneuvers of a fleet which issued from Channel ports into the Atlantic and blockaded Brest, the only considerable French port near the Channel; they discouraged the movements of a fleet moving northeastward from Brest.

Such being the dispositions of geography and the winds, there remained, for an ambitious France, only the possibility of gaining, by wars on land, a position in the delta of the Scheldt and Rhine rivers. In the sixteenth century the Protestant "sea beggars" of Holland had rebelled against the Catholic King Philip II of Spain, then ruler of the Netherlands, and had seized and "sealed" the mouth of the river Scheldt. The great Belgian port of Antwerp was ruined; its eminence passed to Amsterdam and then also to London. It had since been a cardinal point of the foreign policies of Holland and Great Britain that no important power with maritime potentialities should be permitted to establish itself in the delta. In alliance with the Hapsburgs, the two states had beat back the repeated attempts of Louis XIV to do so. In the Treaty of Utrecht of 1713, they had forced the transfer of the Spanish Netherlands (Belgium) to Austria, whose maritime interests were negligible. They secured Holland against another French irruption by setting up strong garrisons of Dutch troops in the (now) Austrian Netherlands.

This strategic condition had no little influence on the outcome of the struggle between France and Great Britain. The climacteric of that struggle was the Seven Years' War (1756-63), which was fought on many battlefields in Asia, America, and Europe, and on the high seas.

Since the sixteenth century the maritime powers of Europe had held scattered ports on the southern coasts of India, while the bulk of the subcontinent was ruled by the Mohammedan Mogul Empire. The Empire had deteriorated, however, and a multitude of confederacies and princes, whose allegiance to the ruler at Delhi was largely nominal, held sway. The divisions and quarrels of the princes offered a tempting opportunity for outside interference. European troops were better trained and armed than the Indian soldiers. By offering military assistance and supplies and by drilling native soldiers, trading companies and adventurers obtained economic and territorial concessions. The agents of the French East India Company were successful in imposing their leadership on a number of Indian states. When war between France and Great Britain broke out in Europe in 1756, Robert Clive (1725-74), an imaginative employee of the British East India Company, bested the French at their own game. Against heavy odds, he defeated the army of the native ruler of Bengal at Plassey in 1757 and made the English Company virtually sovereign in the rich district of northeastern India and in the Bengal capital, Calcutta. Clive filled the coffers of the Company with "gifts" from the native treasury while honoring the custom of European adventurers by stuffing his own pockets. The acquisition of Bengal was the beginning of large-scale European control of the interior of India.

In America the struggle between France and Great Britain was more direct. The French possessions in Canada, Florida, and Louisiana were larger, although far less populous, than the English colonies which lay between them. Working in close collaboration with Indian tribes, the French made ambitious efforts to secure the western hinterland and to merge their northern and southern holdings by gaining control of the routes of the Great Lakes and the Ohio and the Mississippi valleys. If these plans had succeeded, the English colonies would have been cut off from the land of the Mississippi and French domination of North America would have been established. Attempts were made to form a union of the English colonies to fend off this danger. In 1754, at a Congress in Albany attended by delegates of seven colonies, Benjamin Franklin proposed a plan for a federal organization. The colonies, fearing the loss of their autonomy, unanimously rejected it.

In America, where the "French and Indian War" between the British and French began two years before its European counterpart, the British conducted a daring campaign. The imperialist minister William Pitt (1708-78) energetically prosecuted naval warfare and increased the armed forces in the New World. In 1758 the British attacked and seized the strategic Fort Duquesne, on the Ohio River, and the stronghold of Louisburg, on Cape Breton Island, which controlled the entrance to the St. Lawrence River and therefore to the river ports of Quebec and Montreal. The following year they struck at the central stronghold of Quebec. Their troops scaled the Heights of Abraham in the dead of night, surprised the French garrison, and defeated it by superior numbers. They thus won control over Canada.

These victories and the advances in India were made possible by the energy of the British Navy. At the outset the government gave drastic indication that it expected the utmost in fighting. When the British Admiral George Byng showed hesitation in battle and lost the island of Minorca in the Mediterranean to a smaller French fleet, he was promptly court-martialed and executed—"in order to encourage the others," Voltaire observed. Subsequent naval actions left nothing to be desired. The British Navy transported troops to the distant continents, supported attacks on strategic ports, secured England against a French threat of invasion, won victories in the Caribbean, and isolated the French outposts in India from one another and from the homeland.

Yet the war was decided in Europe. Great Britain had a hired ally in Frederick II of Prussia. Because Frederick had seized Silesia from Austria in 1740, in an unprovoked and undeclared war, Austria supported France, and Russia joined her in the hope of participating in a partition of the Prussian holdings. Effectively surrounded, Frederick fought a brilliant but apparently foredoomed war. However, English subsidies kept him supplied, and in 1762, when his admirer Peter III ascended the Russian throne, Russia switched sides and came to his aid. France was strained by a war waged on three continents, and the financial resources and credit of her government proved inferior to those of the British. In 1763, Austria ceded Silesia to Prussia, which came of age as a first-rate power. In the Treaty of Paris, signed in the same year, France ceded Canada to Great Britain. In a secret treaty signed in 1762 she had ceded Louisiana to her ally, Spain, to compensate Spain for the loss of Florida to Great Britain. The dream of a French North American empire went a-glimmering, and the danger to the English colonies was removed. France was also forbidden to maintain troops in India and thus lost a military advantage—the chance for troublemaking—to the British. Great Britain emerged from the Seven Years' War as the leading imperial and naval power of Europe.

At the same time that France lost the colonial edge to Great Britain, a large displacement of states in Central and Eastern Europe weakened her Continental position. The eclipse and dismemberment, in whole or in part, of Sweden, Poland, and the Ottoman Empire disturbed the balance of power on which French diplomacy had rested for two centuries.

Considerations of political geography and strategy explain why France was affected so vitally by territorial changes on the other side of the Continent. So long as Europe is divided among a multiplicity of states, and so long as competition takes the form of wars between adjacent states, just so long will the fortunes of states depend on the number and strength of distant friends. For, in quarreling with its neighbor, a state will seek the aid of the neighbor's enemy; and since the neighbor is likely to quarrel with its neighbor, a state's neighbor's neighbor is its natural ally. Like the knight in chess, a state advances by jumping over its neighbors.

In his *L'Europe et la Révolution française* (1895-1904) the historian Albert Sorel observed that Sweden, Poland, and Ottoman Turkey were "like so many counterweights attached to the extremities of Europe, which made it possible to release the center. They supplied the "instruments and the theater of great diversions" and exercised "a decisive influence in the destinies of France." In previous centuries these countries had collaborated frequently with France against common enemies, notably the Holy Roman Empire and Austria. Commercial interest assisted this policy, notably in the case of Turkey, where the French held special trading privileges. The port of Marseilles had gradually taken the place previously held by Venice in the valuable exchanges of the Eastern Mediterranean.

Throughout the eighteenth century, however, the three northern and eastern "counterweights" were becoming dangerously light. Sweden lost most of the eastern and southern shores of the Baltic to Russia, in the larger measure, and to Prussia. The Ottoman Empire, internally demoralized and laboring under increasing foreign pressures, returned Hungary to the Hapsburgs. In a succession of wars the Romanovs seized the northern coast of the Black Sea and set out on the long and tortuous road to Constantinople. More serious, indeed critical, was the condition of Poland. Torn by inner factionalism, ruled by a monarchy which had to yield one after another of its powers to purchase votes at election, *51*

NORWAY

S W E D E N

Finland

Karelia

RUSSIA

Gulf of Finland

Ingria

Baltic Sea

Estonia

Livonia

DENMARK

Courland

Moscow

W. Pomerania
(to Sweden)

Lithuania

PRUSSIA

White
Russia

Pomerania

Bremen

Brandenburg

Berlin

POLAND

Duchy of
Bremen
(to Sweden)

Warsaw

Volhynia

Kiev

Dnieper R.

Elbe R.

Silesia

Podolia

Ukraine

Bohemia

Vistula R.

Dniester

Danube R.

AUSTRIA

K. OF HUNGARY

Yedisan

SWITZ.

Vienna

Styria

Budapest

Moldavia

C-r-i-m-e-a

Transylvania

O T T O M A N

Wallachia

Black Sea

Adriatic Sea

Bosnia

Danube R.

Serbia

Bulgaria

Albania

Rumelia

Constantinople

E M P I R E

Aegean Sea

Anatolia

Greece

1648

Sweden	
Poland	
Ottoman Empire	

0   *Scale of miles*   300

52   ***Receding and Advancing Empires, 1648-1795***

1795

Areas lost by Sweden

Areas lost by Poland

Areas lost by the Ottoman Empire

0   Scale of miles   300

misgoverned by an aggregation of petty and great nobles, her towns entirely excluded from political consideration—an imperial aristocracy masquerading as an elective monarchy—Poland underwent in 1772 the first of three partitions, the last of which, twenty-three years later, proved fatal. In 1772 Russia obtained the eastern areas, inhabited largely by Greek Orthodox serfs, and Prussia rounded out her territories by seizing western Prussia, Danzig, and, for a time, the capital of Warsaw. Austria, more behindhand, was contented with a slice of Galicia.

The strategic loss to France was great, for the prevalent conception of the balance of power required that when one ruler increased his holdings, the others must also do so in like proportion. Merely by standing still France seemed to have lost her rank at the head of the great powers. In 1756 she had concluded an alliance with Austria and sealed it by the marriage of the Dauphin—later Louis XVI—and Marie Antoinette, daughter of Empress Maria Theresa. In view of the designs of Austria upon Poland and Turkey, the marriage seemed to many ambitious Frenchmen symbolic of diplomatic defeat.

As the century grew older, the recession of France became apparent and painful. Her manufactures were advancing and her foreign trade was growing; it was not until the end of the century that British foreign trade overtook it. But France continued to hold her own rather in absolute than relative terms. The world was expanding: virgin areas and new markets were being opened by adventuring seamen, settlers, and merchants. The stride of France was not commensurate with opportunity. The dissatisfaction of imperialist elements reinforced the criticism of domestic reformers.

The Failure of Reform in France

The first reaction of French statesmen to the defeat of 1763 was to return to the fray. They strengthened the army and navy with a view to another challenge of Great Britain; they bought Corsica from the Republic of Genoa to advance their position in the Mediterranean; they sought to revive the bonds with old friends in the Near East; and they considered intervening in Egypt, where the Sultan's authority was tenuous, possibly as a strategic step toward the Indian Ocean. But soon, in other quarters, there were second thoughts: to set affairs in order at home, to improve the machinery of government, to meet the criticism of abuses and inefficiencies, meanwhile pursuing a less aggressive foreign policy.

The domestic condition of France was becoming as serious as her imperial and diplomatic position. The favors and sinecures of the court aristocrats aroused the jealousy of the lesser nobles, who languished in the provinces. There was increasing criticism of the system of privilege and of its evil effects upon the administration of the country. Enlightened officials and bureaucrats proposed to renovate and simplify the machinery of government. Their connections with the world of international exchange, shipping, and finance impressed them with the need for adjusting the state to new economic opportunities. In this aim they had the sympathy of business and professional men and men of letters.

The reformers' chance came with the accession of Louis XVI to the throne in 1774. A conservative but not averse to moderate reform, Louis appointed the able administrator Turgot as Comptroller General—in effect the principal minister—and supported Turgot's program with the royal power of decree. A learned physiocrat, Turgot was imbued with belief in the desirability of the unimpeded movement of wealth and labor and an economical administration. Expensive adventure abroad was as obnoxious to him as was wasteful meddlesomeness at home. The financial problem not only was most pressing, but it was crucial to other questions; for although the government was deeply in debt, powerful classes had a vested interest in the corruption and inefficiency that were chiefly responsible for the condition of the treasury. France was a rich country, and taxation could easily have reduced the large deficit. The total direct tax per head was some 32 *livres* a year, which was not high; nevertheless, as Adam Smith observed at the time, "the people of France, it is generally acknowledged, are much more oppressed by taxes than the people of Great Britain." The reasons were poor distribution of the load and expensive methods of collection. The indirect taxes fairly consumed themselves in the process of collection; of the worst, the *gabelle*, an impost on the compulsory purchase of salt, perhaps 80 percent was spent for enforcement. It was estimated that more than half the total revenue was drained off on the way to the treasury. The direct taxes were evaded by the powerful groups. Possibly 50 percent of the properties, those of the rich and the privileged, escaped their proportionate share. The more privileged provinces, again, were taxed lightly. On the whole, the poor paid too much, and the rich and noble far too little.

Turgot's answer was reform and thrift. There were to be no new taxes and no further borrowing. In a series of revolutionary decrees, he sought to reorganize the country into an integrated economic unit, undivided by provincial and municipal distinctions and taxes and undisturbed by the interference of privileged minorities. Notable among his decrees were those abolishing the *corvée*, or tax of forced labor, long imposed on the peasants, and the whole guild system of manufacture and business. The character of the state was being altered, without violence, from a system of estates, castes, corporations, and privileged to a system based on the free individual as the digit of administration and taxation. Turgot was on the path of a liberal revolution carried out by the fiat of the King.

He might have gone far had he not dared to reduce the size of the trough at which the King surfeited his favored nobles. In addition to effecting many savings and reducing the cost of tax collection, Turgot had attacked the country's financial difficulty by proposing to increase the *vingtième*, an income tax, the only charge that bore upon noble as well as commoner, and even to collect it. Thereupon, in 1776, the influential court aristocrats intimidated the King into dismissing the minister and abrogating most of his decrees. Turgot slammed the door hard as he left; he warned Louis, "It was weakness, Sire, that laid the head of Charles I [of England] on the block."

Queen Marie Antoinette of France, in the stately and sumptuous fashion of the great lady of the eighteenth century, a fashion that required not only wealth and leisure but the service of a whole regiment of craftsmen, tradesmen, and, above all, personal attendants. CULVER

The fall of Turgot was a dark day for the enlightened men of France. After stimulating the hopes of the reformers, Louis XVI had frustrated them. The dismissal of his able Comptroller General was the signal for an intensification of abuses. The King tightened the hold of the nobility on the higher offices in the army and the church and looked on while many a nobleman, flustered by rising prices, revived old and forgotten dues and services. Concentration on domestic reform gave way to adventure abroad. An opportunity to try imperial fortune again presented itself in the irresistible form of a British colonial revolution. The condition of France became involved with the fate of America.

Industrial Advance in Great Britain

The martial victories and colonial conquests of Great Britain were reinforced by economic advances. Since she had no provincial tariffs and relatively few guild controls, her domestic exchange thrived. Foreign and colonial trade was growing. A series of developments in commerce, agriculture, and transportation converged in striking technological improvements, especially in textile manufacture. While landlords assembled large estates and devoted themselves to scientific farming and production for the urban market, poorer farmers supple-

56

mented their reduced income by working in textiles for itinerant merchant-manufacturers. At first they worked in their own homes, with old spinning and weaving implements, and then in factories, usually located in the countryside, beyond the jurisdiction of town guilds. The improvements in transportation brought about by macadamizing roads and cutting canals facilitated contact between factory and town, mine and port.

This busy atmosphere stimulated enterprise and ingenuity. The expansion of the market for cheap cloth evoked sharp competition to supply it. Weaving wide cloth required the cooperation of two men standing at opposite sides of the frame and passing the weft thread over and under the alternate warp threads. In 1733 a watchmaker of Lancashire, John Kay, devised the fly-shuttle, a wooden box enclosing a spool of thread. By pulling strings attached to hammers, a single workman could throw the shuttle across the frame and bring it back, thus halving the labor requirement. When Kay's invention came into wide use, in the sixties, the demand for yarn increased, and other craftsmen and enter-prisers applied themselves to the production of more and finer thread. Invention in this case was the mother of necessity. In 1765 James Hargreaves, a carpenter and weaver, devised the spinning jenny, a hand machine which enabled a single worker to operate eight spindles—eventually as many as 100—at once, drawing fiber from a loose mass and twisting it into yarn. However, the yarn thus produced was rough and not strong enough to be used for warp, or longitudinal, threads on the weaving frame. In 1769 Richard Arkwright, an ingenious barber and wigmaker, invented the water frame, which produced a large number of threads of any required firmness and fineness. In 1779 Samuel Crompton, a weaver, constructed a "mule" which combined the advantages of the water frame and the spinning jenny. While Hargreaves' jenny and Kay's shuttle were worked by hand, the new frames required greater power. Before long the Lancashire countryside was dotted with mills operated by water power.

Textile manufacturers not only satisfied the existing demand but, by reduc-ing costs and prices, expanded it, making commercially produced cloth avail-able to additional layers of the population, at home and abroad. By the middle of the century England was importing three million pounds of raw cotton a year and exporting finished goods to the value of £45,000. By 1790 the imports had increased tenfold and the exports thirty-sixfold. The home market grew almost as rapidly as the foreign market. Prices of textiles dropped by as much as 50 to 70 percent, largely owing to the saving in labor costs. The quality of the cloth was superior to the product of the average spinner and weaver of the past. So fine were the new yarns that English muslins could compete with the imports from the Far East which had dominated European markets for centuries, and English manufacturers were eventually able to undersell the native producers of India. Mining, metallurgy, and pottery made similar, though less striking, advances. The machine was beginning to take the place of human skill.

The new industries became increasingly important in the national economy. Their masters emphasized their distinction from the older commercial and financial classes and drew together in influential organizations. They craved the protection of the prevailing mercantilist system. Industry secured legislation prohibiting the export of machines, miniature models and even sketches or descriptions of inventions, and discouraging skilled workers and mechanics from leaving the country. There was much spying and smuggling of "secrets" by other countries. No international law protected patents. France in particular sought to emulate and compete with Great Britain. By offering subsidies and prizes, she promoted the development, in her northeastern districts, of sizable industrial centers.

Although the new English manufacturers tried to monopolize industrial knowledge, they were critical of other aspects of the system of prohibition and protection. The expansion of foreign markets suggested to them the advantages of *laissez faire*. They could hardly expect other countries to admit British products if their country refused to admit foreign goods. They objected to the Navigation Acts, which, by restricting all imports to British ships, kept the cost of sea transport high. Enlightened writers had long advocated freer exchange between nations; they now had the support of a growing economic interest.

English Constitutional Questions

The old protective regime, however, was not to be dislodged easily. While industrial changes pointed to the extension of freedom, political developments strengthened traditional authority. The decisive Seven Years' War, which made the French monarchy momentarily cautious, made the British Crown willful. The attempt in France to revolutionize the administration of the country by absolutist means was matched in England by an attempt to strengthen the king's influence by parliamentary means.

The very extent of Britain's recent triumphs created serious problems. The Empire was heterogeneous: some colonies had a substantial degree of autonomy; others were administered by the government at London or by the British East India Company. The cost of defense rose, and new sources of funds were needed. A flexible imperial policy was called for.

Yet no time was less propitious for framing such a policy than the early sixties, for a domestic political struggle was brewing. In the preceding century two revolutions had advanced the power of Parliament, although they left the monarch with considerable strength. They had led to the entrenchment in ministerial office of a group of princely landlords, supported by mercantile interests and religious dissenters. This Whig oligarchy opposed the interference of the king in the conduct of affairs, which it came to regard as its monopoly. The first Hanoverian kings, George I (1714-27) and George II (1727-60), were much more interested in governing their native German state than England. By a kind of disuse and indifference, influence slipped from the Crown to Whig ministers.

On the whole, Whig rule was liberal and successful, although its political means were questionable. The ministers controlled Parliament, either through the purchase of seats—many were available on the market at about £2000—or through the dispensing of offices, pensions, sinecures, and outright gifts to members. The laws against religious dissent lost much of their severity in a loose enforcement. An easygoing rule preserved the traditional liberties of the country. Commercial and maritime interests were vigorously prosecuted.

At the moment of their greatest triumphs, the Whigs met their match in the young King George III (1760-1820). Unlike his two predecessors, George III was a native Briton. He had been brought up to resent the ascendancy of the Whig families. His mind was limited and intermittently unbalanced, but he had great earnestness and persistence. He ascended the throne in 1760 determined to emancipate the Crown and to rule as well as reign. Although the Whig ministers had governed under his predecessors, the cabinet system was not yet fully developed. Ministers could disagree on policy and vote on opposite sides in Parliament. It was recognized that the king had a right to choose the ministers, although his choices had to be approved by a majority in the House of Commons.

The methods of George III and "the King's friends," a group of noblemen and politicians who flocked to his support, were not revolutionary. They did not propose to revive the claim of a royal prerogative to act without parliamentary sanction, which had cost the Stuart dynasty two thrones and a royal head in the preceding century. Rather, they proposed that the King act like many another aristocratic politician—that is, that he control blocks of seats in the Commons by purchase or by influencing the electors to vote for his nominees. In such a game, however, the monarch had a great and, it seemed to his opponents, an unfair advantage, for he had at his disposal large funds from the state treasury.

The combination of royal and parliamentary influence would make the power of the King and his "friends" irresistible. It would diminish the distinction between legislative and executive power which was one of the principal guarantees of liberty. Although his methods were conventional, therefore, the success of George III as a political leader, with a party of his own, held distinct dangers for the constitutional development of Great Britain. The situation was worsened by the fact that the King and his supporters pursued their aims with an obstinacy that jarred political sensibilities and spilled over into the area of policy.

"The King's friends" abused their influence in Parliament to diminish its sense of independence and to encroach upon traditional liberties. In 1764, for example, John Wilkes (1727-97), a member of the House of Commons who had criticized the ministers and their policy, was arrested on a general warrant which, since it did not name a particular person, implied a power to seize anyone at will. The complaisant House of Commons withdrew the privileges which protected the speech of members and expelled Wilkes. When he was re-elected again and again by his constituency in London, the House expelled him, again and again. Freedom of the press and of speech, security of the person, and the independence of the voter—all were suddenly in danger. The Whig opposition seized the opportunity to refresh its role of liberal leadership. It found support and even stimulus in the popular meetings, demonstrations, and committees organized to support and cheer "Wilkes and Liberty." Political life, hitherto shut in the narrow circles of court and aristocracy, began to broaden out.

However, before the liberals could check "the King's friends" at home, colonial self-respect was roused to do them battle. The royal power was no less dangerous at home than in the colonies, where indeed it introduced fewer innovations; but these innovations confirmed exactions which had long been regarded as oppressive and therefore appeared in the unpleasant guise of imperialism.

The American Issue

The Whig oligarchy had treated the English colonies in North America with a salutary offhandedness. Until the middle of the eighteenth century the thirteen colonies had been neither rich enough nor populous enough to invite intensive exploitation; the West Indian islands, with their profitable sugar plantations and the ancillary slave trade, had attracted greater attention and interest. The king, as we have seen, usually appointed the governors of the American colonies, except for a few cases in which governors were elected or "proprietors" exercised executive powers on the basis of royal charters. The lower houses of the legislatures were everywhere elected by the colonists, while members of the upper houses were appointed by the governors. The colonists supplied the bulk of the administrators. The salaries of elected officials, and of most of the royal appointees, depended on the approval of the assemblies, a system which gave the colonists a measure of self-government and control over the executive. The corruption of politics in England was not matched in the overseas colonies. All in all, the colonies enjoyed a somewhat more liberal political system than the mother country.

However, the economic regulations imposed by the distant government in London were onerous. The American market was reserved for British manufactures, and local industries which competed with home enterprises were forbidden. The colonists were compelled to purchase most of their imports in England. When they were allowed to buy elsewhere, they had to transship through a British port, paying a substantial tribute to the British exchequer and a middleman's profit to British merchants, warehousemen, and factors. Many a colonial staple could be exported only to the mother country. Parliament sweetened the pill of these Navigation Acts by granting bounties on some important American staples which Britain needed, by giving the colonies a favored position in the British market as compared with foreign competitors, and by promoting and protecting colonial as well as British shipping. But the greatest "compensation" for these controls was their lax enforcement. Smuggling was common in that age everywhere, but it was practiced most widely in the New World, where it was hardest to check. The American colonists engaged tacitly in what amounted to an informal trade with non-British colonies and Continental countries, notably Holland.

European Empires in N. America, 1713-1763

British
French
Spanish

NEWFOUNDLAND

MIQUELON
& ST. PIERRE
(Fr.)

NOVA SCOTIA

BRITISH NORTH AMERICA

1763

NH
N.Y.   MASS.
OF   R.I.
PA.   CONN.
N.J.

Ohio R.   DEL.
PROCLAMATION LINE   MARYLAND
VIRGINIA

Mississippi R.   N. CAROLINA

S   Atlantic

P   GEORGIA   S. CAROLINA

A   Louisiana

N

I   FLORIDA   BERMUDA
(Br.)

S   Ocean

H   Gulf
of
Mexico

BAHAMA IS.
(Br.)

CUBA   SANTO
DOMINGO   PUERTO RICO   ST. CHRISTOPHER
(ST. KITTS)

W   BARBUDA
E   ANTIGUA

Belize   S   I N D I E S

JAMAICA   HAITI   GUADELOUPE   DOMINICA
(Br.)   (Fr.)   (Fr.)   MARTINIQUE
ST. LUCIA   BARBADOS

The Thirteen Colonies
and the Caribbean, 1763

British Territory

French Territory

Spanish Territory

Extent of settlement

Caribbean Sea   ST. VINCENT
GRENADA   TOBAGO

T   TRINIDAD

E

R

R

I

T

O

R   0   Scale of miles   500

Y

For these reasons, American opposition to mercantilism, although it was rising, was insufficient to produce a violent disaffection. Loyalty was further ensured by the colonists' fear that, unless they were defended by Great Britain, they might be conquered or hemmed in by the empires of France or Spain, which were more rigidly imperialistic, and Catholic in the bargain. Most of the colonists were Protestants, and in that day that meant decidedly anti-Catholic.

But the strength of an empire depends as much on the balance of forces among great powers as on the relation between a power and its colonies: sometimes, indeed, more so. The result of the Seven Years' War was, on the whole, a triumph for Great Britain, but one provision of the treaty which brought it to an end had the indirect effect of diminishing the colonists' sense of dependence upon the mother country. Since British statesmen were anxious to free their American colonies from the danger of future French attacks from the mainland, Great Britain demanded from France, and obtained, the cession of Canada instead of the West Indian islands she might have had. The choice was portentous. The colonists, freed from external danger, breathed easier, and developed ambitions of their own. Accompanied by a mild administrative policy, the acquisition of Canada might have become the starting point of a vast North American empire. Many colonists dreamed of such an empire, but they meant to share in its opportunities and its management. As it was, the acquisition turned out to be a mistake, for British statesmanship was blind. At the moment when it removed one of the reasons for the dependence of the colonists upon the mother country, it drew the reins of empire tighter. At a time when enlightened men of affairs had become persuaded that there was more economic profit in nurturing than in inhibiting commercial and industrial enterprise, the British government found it fitting to tighten mercantilist and financial controls.

Of the immediate issues that aroused the colonists, one was an irritation and the other a provocation. As a result of her defeat in the war, France had ceded to Great Britain the large area which lay between the Allegheny Mountains and the Mississippi River. By the Proclamation of 1763, Britain closed this region to American settlement, ostensibly to obviate conflict with the Indian tribes. By the Quebec Act of 1774, the British government transferred the land between the Ohio and the Mississippi Rivers to the Province of Canada, throwing into doubt the claims of several colonies to this valuable area. The colonists, moreover, feared that the government might assign huge estates in the territory to a few favorites and courtiers, a fear which, under the prevailing system of government, was only too likely to become a reality. Small folk became restless, although the government could not easily prevent them from settling on the frontier. Speculative companies were particularly disturbed, for they had hoped to buy large tracts and hold them for inflated sales to settlers. In a new and growing country, land represents the most important form of investment, and some of the leading capitalists and politicians held stock in such companies.

Of greater immediate consequence was the attempt to raise more money in the colonies. The British government was determined to compel Americans to contribute toward the support of imperial armed forces and to ensure their cooperation in time of crisis. It therefore attempted to strengthen the central authority. New laws and administrative orders issued in 1763-65 provided for the strict enforcement of trade regulations. New revenues to help defray the salaries of the royal governors and their appointees were raised—not, as formerly, by royal requisitions addressed to the colonial assemblies and approved by them, but by the action of the legislature at London. If both Parliament and the colonial assemblies could pass tax measures, the utmost circumspection was called for, in order to avoid a conflict. Yet the measures were approved by Parliament with hardly any discussion. The Americans protested immediately, and with a vehemence that astonished both the government and the opposition in England.

The colonists were even more deeply disturbed by Britain's evident intention to enforce and extend mercantilist controls and exploitation than by the fiscal program. But the right of the Parliament in London to regulate trade and impose external taxes—customs duties, for example—was securely established and recognized and could not be challenged. The colonists therefore selected the Stamp Act, among the many measures of 1763-65, as the main target of their attack. This law provided that no legal document was valid in a court unless it carried a stamp of a value proportionate to the financial transaction involved. The tax was not large, but such "internal" imposts had customarily been imposed only by the colonial assemblies. It was also a conspicuous tax, affecting poor men as well as rich, professional men and journalists—especially vocal groups—as well as landowners and businessmen: everyone who had to make a will, a contract, or a loan. In October 1765 a congress of delegates from nine colonies drew up a protest against internal taxes imposed from the outside: "...it is inseparably essential to the freedom of a people, and the undoubted right of Englishmen, that no taxes be imposed on them but with their own consent, given personally or by their representatives."

The Stamp Act Congress did not challenge the right of Parliament to impose the external taxes and duties which were the customary instruments for controlling shipping and commerce. This right was long recognized as valid. Yet the colonists had become increasingly critical of mercantilist regulations and exactions. They were able to express their protest by objecting to the internal taxes imposed by Parliament since such taxes were traditionally voted by their own assemblies. There was another aspect of this controversy. If the external revenue raised were sufficient to support royal officials and other imperial charges, then the British government would avoid the need to appeal for funds to the colonial assemblies, which would thus be deprived of the customary means of applying pressure on the executive. Englishmen, whether at home or in the colonies, were past masters at buying concessions with grants of money. The situation called for wary statesmanship, and this was conspicuously lacking in England.

The American Case

The substance of the American case, then, was rather different from its formalities. In essence, the colonists were insisting that they be treated on an equal basis with the Englishmen at home. They wished their assemblies to be able to bargain with and check royal power as the English Parliament could. They had come to think of America not as an inferior appendage of England, but as another England, or, better, a distinct commonwealth. Some of them believed that the British Empire must evolve toward a federal system.

The colonists arrived at this conception at least a century before any European government put it into practice. In the late eighteenth century, the government of England hardly shared their vision, although many enlightened men did. The controversy sharpened the constitutional issue in England. The King was at a great advantage, for, since many English groups profited from colonial control, he could defend his policy as patriotic. But his victory would be also a victory over the Whig theory of government as it had developed earlier in the century. Thus the issue of colonial freedom became one with that of enlightened reform and Parliamentary supremacy—and they were resolved together.

Even though the colonists were thus defending the cause of English as well as American liberty, the Parliamentary opposition to the King's policies could not help them much. The Whigs were in the minority. Besides, they were chary of diminishing the jurisdiction of Parliament, for whose independence they were striving. They therefore wished to retain the right, and continue the practice, though in attenuated form, of commercial controls. This was the position of the imperialist William Pitt, who applauded American resistance but added:

> Let the sovereign authority of this country over the colonies be asserted in as strong terms as can be assigned and be made to extend to every point of legislation whatsoever. That we may bind their trade, confine their manufactures, and exercise every power whatsoever, except that of taking their money out of their pockets without their own consent.

The Whig leader Edmund Burke (1729-97) pleaded, in a famous speech, for "conciliation" of America. The advanced reformers, notably John Wilkes and Richard Price (1723-91), Lord Mayor of London, defended the cause of the colonists as one with that of English reform. Wilkes protested the measures against America and petitioned the King to dismiss ministers who "carry them into execution by the same fatal corruption which has enabled them to wound the peace and violate the Constitution of this country."

Since the Americans had not challenged the right of the mother country to regulate their commerce, there was room for compromise. But George III and his compliant Prime Minister, Lord North (1732-92), who headed the government from 1770 to 1782, were resolved not to compromise. They treated the colonists with condescension. The Americans retaliated by ignoring the Stamp Act, intimidating the distributors of the stamps into inactivity, and agreeing to cease buying English goods. The Stamp Act was thereupon repealed, in 1766, but a Declaratory Act was simultaneously passed, asserting the right of Parliament to regulate the colonies in all matters. Since the Americans were contending for a real case, not a formal one, they enjoyed their practical victory. But in the following year Parliament passed the Townshend Acts, which provided for the collection of a variety of customs duties, partly in order to pay the salaries of royal officials in the colonies. The old argument was reopened, but this time the colonial assemblies clashed with the governors, and commercial intercourse with England was diminished by voluntary agreement among the colonies.

From this point, it was goad on one side and defiance on the other. The Americans resented particularly the revival of an old law under which they might be taken to England to be tried for treason. When the Townshend duties were repealed in 1770, a small tax on tea was retained in order to demonstrate the claim that Parliament could tax the colonies. Three years later the East India Company had an oversupply of tea on hand. The government remitted the duty collected upon imports into England and allowed the Company to reship its cargo to the colonies, where a somewhat smaller duty would be charged. Although the Americans would thus obtain unusually cheap tea, the incident illustrated some of the worst features of imperialism: favoritism to well-connected interests and discriminatory treatment of colonists. When the ships arrived in Boston Harbor, a group of disguised colonists boarded them and threw overboard the whole cargo of 340 chests. England's answer to the "Boston Tea Party" was coercion. The port was closed and the authority of the royal governor strengthened. The colonies promptly drew together in the First Continental Congress (1774), which denounced the enforcement of these measures and organized a commercial boycott of England. Organizations of patriots multiplied: Committees of Correspondence, to keep the colonies in close touch with one another and to coordinate their policies and activities; Committees of Safety, to take over the functions of government or to exert pressure upon the existing colonial parliaments or officials; and "Sons of Liberty," to press for direct resistance and to intimidate the "loyalist" partisans of the English government. The royal troops were bested by colonial volunteers in the first clash, which occurred at Lexington, near Boston, in April 1775. In August the King branded the colonists as rebels, and they besieged his army in Boston. The die was cast—yet many conservative Americans still struggled between loyalty and risk.

Into this inflammable situation a brilliant English pamphleteer, newly arrived in America, cast a lighted match. In *Common Sense* Thomas Paine (1737-1809) argued boldly for a rupture with the mother country. Hereditary monarchy, Paine asserted, has no basis either in natural or in divine right. The Lord was a republican, he reminded a generation which was familiar with the Old

Testament, for He had tried to argue the Hebrews out of their demand to be given a king: "Your wickedness is great, which ye have done in the sight of the Lord, in asking for a king." "One of the strongest *natural* proofs of the folly of the hereditary right in Kings is that nature disapproves it, otherwise she would not so frequently turn it into ridicule by giving mankind an *Ass for a Lion*." Royalty, wrote Paine, was born in conquest, usurpation, and robbery. Between such an institution and America there was no room for compromise. In independence only, and independence at once, lay the safety of the colonists and the best hope, not only of America, but of the whole Western world: "Freedom hath been hunted around the globe. Asia, and Africa, have long expelled her. Europe regards her like a stranger, and England hath given her warning to depart. O! receive the fugitive, and prepare in time an asylum for mankind." George Washington said that *Common Sense* "worked a powerful change in the minds of many men."

Waverers took sides. Most of the colonists split into supporters of independence and uncompromising loyalists. The former had the advantage of vigor and represented a broad cross section of the population. By the spring of 1776 royal authority had collapsed nearly everywhere, and the elected assemblies, seconded or rivaled by more spontaneous organizations, had informally taken over executive and even judicial functions. Separation was a fact, and in July 1776 the Second Continental Congress openly declared the independence of America and instructed the colonies to establish new governments and write constitutions.

66

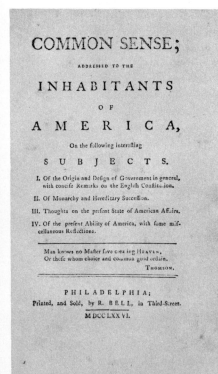

Title page of Common Sense, *the most influential pamphlet in the American Revolution. Its author, Thomas Paine, was active in the political life of Great Britain and of France during her revolution as well as in that of America.* LIBRARY OF CONGRESS

A Lockean Revolution

The Americans had made a Lockean revolution. To Locke revolution was the natural result of an abuse of power that is continued until it becomes insupportable by the community. The outbreak of revolution was prima-facie evidence that the rulers had exceeded their authority. In the Declaration of Independence, Thomas Jefferson (1743-1826) asserted that the King of England had committed tyrannical acts and infringed the rights of men as well as customary and traditional practices. The Declaration specified twenty-six "injuries and usurpations." However, it broadened the claims of the Americans of their rights as Englishmen into claims of their rights as men. By appealing on universal grounds for the support of enlightened opinion, it linked the fate of America with that of the whole Western world.

> ...We hold these truths to be self-evident, that all men are created equal, that they are endowed by their Creator with certain unalienable Rights, that among these are Life, Liberty and the pursuit of Happiness—That to secure these rights, Governments are instituted among Men, deriving their just powers from the consent of the governed,—That whenever any Form of Government becomes destructive of these ends, it is the Right of the People to alter or abolish it, and to institute new Government, laying its

67

Facsimile of Thomas Jefferson's original draft of the Declaration of Independence of 1776. In this first page of the American "manifesto," Jefferson gave eloquent voice to the principles of the natural rights of man as the basis of liberal government. The successful assertion of these principles by the former British colonies made them a revolutionary force in the Atlantic world.
LIBRARY OF CONGRESS

foundations on such principles and organizing its powers in such form, as to them shall seem most likely to effect their Safety and Happiness...

The fact that this high ground was taken was due to the participation of enlightened men in the revolutionary movement. Aggrieved merchants, planters, speculators, and elected officials had been the principal sources of opposition to the policy of Great Britain. These groups were soon supported by intellectuals, in both town and country. Many men belonging to the "capacities," as the French call them—college graduates, clergymen, lawyers, teachers, pamphleteers—wished to assert their natural interest in talent and ability, in free inquiry and expression, against the traditional claims of birth, favor, and social connection. They were prepared to pay to the principles of the Enlightenment the homage of a practical demonstration.

To this a social interest was added. Farmers resented the customary paramountcy of the owners of large estates in public office and in the shaping of public policy. A similar antagonism against the richer merchants inspired the shopkeepers, artisans, and workingmen of the towns. In an age when money meant specie and specie was in limited supply, and in a new country hungering for capital, the groups at the borrowing end of the credit system craved a more plentiful currency—that is to say, paper money. The imperial government, and many rich colonists, had frowned on this solution. Easy credit was the financial aspect of the popular passion for more equitable opportunities for property-owning, as it was the symbol of energetic native enterprise, for many a substantial merchant was also in favor of cheaper money.

The greatest rebel of them all was the infinitely receding and relatively empty American land. There was enough distance beyond the horizon to satisfy the deepest restlessness, and land enough to satisfy the greatest avidity, but too much to make it feasible for any government, whether transatlantic or domestic, to exercise more than a light surveillance over local affairs. The governments of colonies on the Atlantic seaboard were already unable to control effectively the mushrooming settlements in their western areas. A distinctive radicalism arose on the slowly peopling frontier. The ease of staking out a farm of one's own was matched by the glory of escaping the exclusiveness of the older society in the East. The ownership of property of moderate size became associated with democracy and liberty.

But if eventually the American frontier was too generous to be contained within a narrow dominion, foreign or domestic, its immediate future hinged upon the success of the Revolution; and it is not clear that the colonists could have prevailed without European assistance. The American army was small, uncertainly paid, and poorly supplied. Its staunch commander, George Washington (1732-99), made as great a contribution by holding it together year after year against discouraging odds as he did by winning battles. A major strategic difficulty the Americans faced was to budge British troops from the coast, where they were supplied by English ships. In 1775 the English suffered heavy losses at Bunker Hill, in Massachusetts. In 1776, the year of independence, they were forced out of Boston; farther south, however, they made good their hold on Long Island and the valuable port of New York. Washington retreated across the Hudson in November 1776.

The following year the honors were divided, the Americans doing better inland than on the coast. While a British force took Philadelphia, the seat of the Continental Congress, another army, 6,000 strong, was surrounded at Saratoga, in eastern New York, and forced to surrender. The winter was depressing: the harried American army encamped at Valley Forge, Pennsylvania, suffered from cold and want, the officers fell out with one another, and Washington was in danger of being forced out of his command. For the Americans it was the lowest point of the war. It was also, however, the turning point, for the international political weather was proving propitious. France had indirectly assisted the revolutionaries from the outset, but it was not until after the surrender at Saratoga that she entered into an alliance with them and declared war on England (1778). She hoped to restore the imperial balance in her favor by diminishing the British Empire and to obtain some of the American trade, from which British mercantile laws excluded her. The war became still wider. France's traditional ally, the other Bourbon power, Spain, followed suit in the same year, although disturbed over the effect the success of the rebels would have in the Spanish colonies. A combined Franco-Spanish fleet sailed up the Channel and threatened to invade England, and in 1779 Spain besieged Gibraltar by sea and land. Another French fleet assured aid to the American army and bottled up British troops in American ports. French money and men poured into the colonies—money which left the French treasury in worse straits than ever and men, soldiers and officers, who returned home inspired by the vision of a liberal society. Of these men the most eminent was the young Marquis de Lafayette (1757-1834), who combined an ancient lineage with liberal convictions.

Other European states assumed a belligerent or at least an unfavorable attitude toward Great Britain. In recent wars the British fleet had acquired the habit not only of attacking the commerce and seizing the goods of enemy countries but of interfering with the commercial traffic of neutrals as well. It would not permit a neutral to trade with a country at war with Great Britain or with the colonies of such a country. This policy amounted to an attempt to monopolize the sea trade of the world, since every state that had maritime interests was threatened or harmed by it. In 1780 Russia, Sweden, and Denmark joined in an Armed Neutrality: they threatened the British with hostilities unless their ships and those of other neutrals were permitted to carry any goods they pleased, even those belonging to enemy subjects, excepting only war materials. Prussia, Portugal, and Austria followed suit within the next three years. When in 1781 Holland recognized American independence and threatened to join the Armed Neutrality, Great Britain declared war on her.

The decisive blow in the Revolutionary War was struck in October 1781, when the principal British army, besieged by colonial and French troops in Yorktown, Virginia, and blockaded by a French fleet, surrendered. Lord North

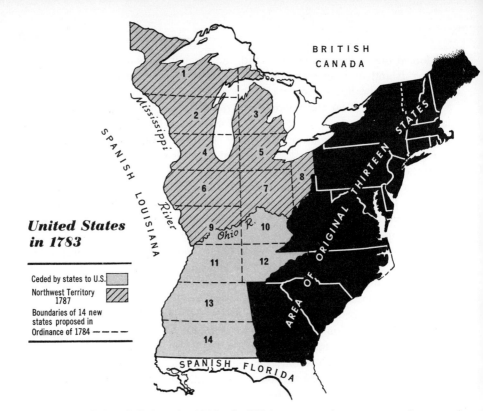

United States in 1783

BRITISH CANADA

SPANISH LOUISIANA

Mississippi River

Ohio R.

SPANISH FLORIDA

AREA OF ORIGINAL THIRTEEN STATES

Ceded by states to U.S.
Northwest Territory 1787
Boundaries of 14 new states proposed in Ordinance of 1784 — — —

resigned as Prime Minister in 1782; the Whigs returned to power and reversed British policy. In the Treaty of Paris of 1783 they recognized the independence of the American colonies and yielded to them all the territory lying between their borders at the Allegheny Mountains and the Mississippi River. This cession doubled the original area of the colonies. Britain's conflict with the other powers was less decisive. She had repelled Spanish attacks on Gibraltar and

The American horse topples its rider, King George III of Great Britain. Contemporary American cartoon. LIBRARY OF CONGRESS

re-established her domination of the Channel and her influence in West Indian waters. But she ceded to Spain Florida, which Spain had ceded to her in 1762, and added the island of Minorca. France obtained several small West Indian islands and gained fishing rights on the uninhabited coast of Newfoundland. However, Great Britain obtained from Holland, whose naval strength had proved unimpressive, the port of Negapatam in India and the right to trade in the Moluccas, or Spice Islands, in the Malay Archipelago. She ended the war without giving any promise to correct her maritime habits.

American independence had weighty commercial consequences. The former colonists were now able to trade with the world at large. Even before the colonies had repudiated the sovereignty of Great Britain, they had thrown their ports open to the ships of all countries; they now invited a reciprocal welcome elsewhere. Although trade with the colonies of other European powers was still subject to restrictions, American ships found their way increasingly to Continental ports.

The Liberal Experiment

The effect of the Revolution upon trade was eclipsed by a larger result: the establishment of a nation systematically organized to assure liberty. The United States was the first state of considerable size to assert explicitly the modern doctrine of natural rights and the social contract. After British authority was repudiated in 1776, and even while the war for independence was in progress, the Americans carried out, largely in the individual states, substantial changes in government and administration.

The federal union was most restricted and informal. The Continental Congress, which had coordinated the military efforts of the several states, was a temporary body. In 1777 it recommended the adoption by the states of the Articles of Confederation, "a firm league of friendship." Under this constitution, all states, regardless of size or population, had an equal voice in the new Congress, consisting of delegates appointed by the state legislatures. There was no executive body; executive functions were exercised by committees of Congress. The federal government conducted foreign relations but its powers of internal legislation were severely limited. It could deal only with the states, which were declared to be sovereign and independent, and not directly with individual citizens, whether for taxation or other purposes. The assent of all states was needed for a change in the Articles. Neither the federal government nor the states could issue titles of nobility. The opposition to the imperial authority which had inspired the Revolution was reflected in distrust of a strong central government.

The Articles of Confederation were not fully ratified until 1781 and did not go into effect until the war was virtually over. Meanwhile the colonists busied themselves to re-form the state governments, the real seats of authority. New state constitutions were written and laws enacted, the effect of which was

71

to weaken the hierarchical principle in government and society. Republicanism took the place of monarchical and aristocratic institutions; elections from below took the place of appointments from above; and there was a sharper division of powers. The executive authority, discredited by the colonial experience, was carefully hedged. The functions of administration, lawmaking, and judging were assigned to distinct groups of men, who were expected to be too jealous of one another to permit a new concentration of authority. Profiting by this preoccupation of the governing groups, the citizen would be able to live and work in undisturbed peace. This psychological principle was buttressed by legal safeguards. Emphatically and explicitly the new state constitutions asserted the right of the individual to think, write, publish, and worship as he pleased, to meet with his fellows, petition his rulers—which was as much as to say to warn them when they took a wrong course—and above all to be secure from sudden arrest without familiar legal cause and from imprisonment without prompt judicial action.

Before the Revolution, the colonies had had a limited suffrage based on the ownership of substantial landed property. Such ownership was far more common than in the Old World. The number of voters varied widely from colony to colony, ranging from 2 to 16 percent of the population, but on the average perhaps 10 percent of the population could vote. This was three times as many as the contemporary figure for England. Only in a few Dutch and Swiss city-states was suffrage as broad as, or broader than, in the American colonies, and in those Continental states its effect was considerably weakened by the power of the narrow oligarchies of the leading families which controlled public offices. During and after the Revolution, the American colonies, now states, drafted constitutions that somewhat enlarged the electorate by reducing the landed-property qualification or substituting for it proof of the ownership of other kinds of property; eventually tax qualifications supplanted the requirement of landed property. By such steps there was set in motion a continuing extension of the suffrage, which was accelerated by the fact that the new states admitted to the Union almost invariably omitted all qualifications and enfranchised all adult males. This process of gradual democratization, which culminated ultimately in the removal of tax qualifications, required more than a half century to complete. The American Revolution by no means introduced democratic suffrage, but it was a significant stage in the general evolution of the principle of universal enfranchisement.

It was as much to social as to political arrangements that Americans trusted their faith in the future. The old laws of entail and primogeniture encouraged permanent accumulations of property and a rigid social order. In the South there were many large estates which could not be alienated by their owners, neither sold nor given away, but had to be passed on to the first-born son or other heirs. These laws ensured that property would be kept, generation after generation, in the same group of families. Within ten years after the Declaration of Independence, entail was abolished in all thirteen states, and primogeniture was abolished within five more years. It was generally provided that, should a property owner die intestate, his children would inherit equal shares—the younger as well as the older, the daughters as well as the sons—and that all property would be subject to free sale.

During the war the estates of the British Crown and of leading loyalists were confiscated, broken up, and sold on fairly easy terms. Although it was generally propertied persons who thus increased their holdings, land concentration was sensibly diminished by this program. The abolition of quitrents eased the lot of many a poor farmer.

The demarcation line of 1763 became a memory. As soon as the war was over, thousands of Americans crossed the Alleghenies in search of homesteads. The thirteen states gave up to the Confederation government their claims to lands in the interior of the continent. These lands amounted to 430,000 square miles, or more than the combined territory of the states. How were they to be settled and governed? Were they to remain under the tutelage of the coast communities, or were they to become autonomous and equal to the existing states? Was the hinterland to enter into the subordinate relation to the states that the states themselves had had, until lately, to Great Britain?

The fact that the western territories were controlled by Congress and not by the states made a coherent program of settlement possible. At the suggestion of Thomas Jefferson, Congress in 1785 passed the Land Ordinance, which provided for a systematic survey and sale of the new lands. Parallel lines were drawn at regular intervals, producing townships consisting of thirty-six sections, each a mile square. Sections were to be sold to the highest bidder, at a minimum of a dollar per acre. The prices and the minimum lot were eventually reduced, but even the original procedure provided for a fairer distribution and a more orderly settlement than any other colonial country achieved.

For a country lacking the traditional supports of caste, privilege, aristocratic patronage, and continuity of family estates, a good education represented the principal avenue open to men of unusual talent and ability for the achievement of public recognition, influence, and office. In the circumstances of the American scene, public education therefore became, from the first, an essential complement of republicanism. "Religion, morality and knowledge being necessary to good government and the happiness of mankind," declared the Ordinance, "schools and the means of education shall forever be encouraged." It set aside one section in each new township, or about 3 percent of the land, as a bounty to public schools.

The European tradition strongly favored the claims of older over newer communities, of the metropolis over the colonies or frontiers. But the United States was fortunate in possessing a government so restricted in its functions that it could not be tempted by imperial designs. In 1784, eight years after he had written the Declaration of Independence, Thomas Jefferson drafted a document of equal importance. It was a plan to divide the Northwest Territory, as the cessions of the states were collectively called, into fourteen relatively small states—one more than the current membership of the Union. These new states were to enter the Union, as soon as they were settled, on terms of equality with their predecessors. Three years later Congress adopted Jefferson's proposal, modifying it somewhat by reducing the number of states to be carved out of the Territory and strengthening the control of the federal government during the interim period, which was somewhat prolonged. But the essentials of the proposal were retained. The Northwest Ordinance of 1787 provided that when a territory accumulated a population of 5,000 free males, it could establish its own legislature, although the laws must be approved by federal officials. When the population was 60,000, the territory could enter the Union on equal terms with the original members. The new states were to be cast in the liberal mold: their constitutions, which were in the nature of contracts with the Union, must be republican in form and must guarantee the familiar Anglo-Saxon freedoms. There was to be no slavery, but runaway slaves from the old states must be returned to their owners.

The Northwest Ordinance of 1787 was the most concrete expression of the basic ideals of America. It secured the essentials of fairness and self-respect for all future American communities. It excluded the possibility that the West would become a dependency of the East. More than that, by setting up the rules for the organization of the new communities, it fixed the goal toward which older communities, whether in America or in Europe, should tend. Perhaps more than any other act, the ordinance mirrored the vigor of American liberalism.

4. *The Revolution Crosses the Atlantic*

The American Revolution helped to precipitate a crisis in the Atlantic world. Unrest had been long gathering in Western Europe. In the 1780's a wave of protest and defiance swept a half dozen countries and city-states. Before the decade was over, civil war had broken out in Holland, the Austrian Netherlands (Belgium), Switzerland, and finally France, the leading Continental monarchy. The revolution had crossed the Atlantic Ocean.

The Constitutional Settlement in the United States

Yet the Americans had not yet finished their own task. They were still to determine the structure of the federal union and its relation to the member states. The thirteen states had an intense political life. Conservatives and liberals, aristocratic- and republican-minded men, creditors and debtors, merchants and artisans, bankers and farmers, all argued, contended, and competed for office and influence. The air was more democratic than in Great Britain; for the first time in a substantial community, popular groups voiced and pressed their demands along with the more powerful.

In the first years after the War of Independence, economic life became more stable. The Congress had issued paper money, which had fluctuated sharply in value. This money gradually disappeared from circulation, and the somewhat more reliable currencies of the individual states prevailed. Debtors agitated for further issues of paper money, but without much success. Domestic industry, freed from the mercantilist prohibitions of Great Britain and shielded by customs laws, grew slowly but encouragingly.

In the mid-eighties, however, a commercial depression developed and occasioned a political crisis. American merchants could trade with Great Britain but missed the freedom they had enjoyed as colonists to trade with the British West Indies. The government was finding it difficult to make commercial arrangements with other European countries and their colonies. The loose union under the Articles of Confederation was not presenting an impressive front to the suspicious Old World, where it must find friends and creditors. Its failure to pay European creditors hurt the standing of the country in foreign financial markets. Indeed, the government could not cover ordinary running expenses. The states had agreed to supply Congress with funds, in a settled ratio, but few of them met their obligations in time, and some of them failed to do so altogether. The Articles provided no means for bringing the recalcitrant states to book and no power to collect a federal tax.

Under the Articles of Confederation trade was regulated, not by the federal union, but by the several states. The states that possessed valuable advantages, such as convenient ports, did not disdain to exact tribute from their less well-placed neighbors. In several states the political pot boiled over. There were conflicts between the coastal and the frontier settlers—for example, between Virginians and Kentuckians—and between debtors and creditors. In 1786 farmers from the back country of Massachusetts, pressed by urban creditors and assisted by urban democrats, rose under the leadership of Captain Daniel Shays and were put down only after the state troops had been called out. Although the rebellion was suppressed, it alarmed men of order and stability.

Did these difficulties mean that the Union forged in the Revolutionary emergency could not be preserved, loose though that union was; that the states might quarrel and combine against each other, the large against the small, East against West, North against South, and even form agreements or alliances with foreign powers? Would the new states become the sport of rival empires? These problems were intensified by the conflict of political ideals. Many a substantial merchant and aristocratic-minded citizen still under the spell of the British system was disposed to favor a stronger central government, not only in order to ward off external danger but also to protect commerce from the interference of the states and to counteract the occasional democratic or agrarian tendencies of local legislatures. There were journalists and politicians who wished to release the energies of the nation, to give wings to extraordinary enterprise, to create in America an empire which might emulate the lustrous monarchies of the time.

The opponents of a drastic change in the Articles of Confederation comprised more modest, though not always poorer, merchants; local-minded landed gentry; and other citizens who were committed to the ideal of moderation. This party has been sometimes called democratic, not because of its program—for formal political democracy was unfamiliar to eighteenth-century politics—but because of the adherence to it of large groups in the population who were repelled by the proposal for a stronger government. These groups feared, not without reason, that a central government which was further removed from the citizen than the governments of state, county, or town was more likely to fall under the influence of powerful groups and should therefore be as limited in its functions and powers as was consistent with safety.

By providing for its financial needs, the friends of the Confederation government might have warded off the proposals to change it. But when a proposal was made to allow it to raise a tax of its own, they procrastinated. Most of them were absorbed in local affairs or did not appreciate sufficiently the importance of raising the credit and prestige of the Union in the eyes of the world. The advocates of a stronger government, seconded by citizens anxious over the condition of the Union, prevailed upon the state legislatures to send delegates to a Convention to revise the Articles. The Convention then took it upon itself to draft a new document altogether.

In the summer of 1787 fifty-five delegates, elected by the state legislatures, gathered in Philadelphia. Among them were some of the most eminent men in America: George Washington, James Madison, and George Mason of Virginia; Benjamin Franklin and James Wilson of Pennsylvania; and Alexander Hamilton of New York. The weight fell to men of relatively conservative views, partly because of the lack of readiness of the opposing group and the abstention of some of the more advanced republicans. The meetings were held in private and the members bound to secrecy. Insulated from outside pressure, the constitutional debate ranged freely for four months. In September 1787 the Convention presented to state conventions, specially elected for the purpose of examining it, a remarkable document which, with its subsequent amendments, is still the Constitution of the United States of America.

The new Constitution was the product of Anglo-Saxon political thought and experience, tinctured by the ideas of Montesquieu. In harmony with these ideas and the provisions of some of the state constitutions, the legislative, executive, and judicial branches of the federal government were sharply distinguished by function, term of office, and source of election and appointment. The new government was to be protected from the danger of excessive popular influence by the provisions that the members of the Senate would be appointed by the state legislatures and that the President would be elected indirectly by a complicated process intended to leave the choice to the leading men of the country. Members of the House of Representatives, on the other hand, were to be elected directly by the citizens of each state. The two-chamber Congress could alone declare war, make peace, sanction treaties, raise and supply armed forces or militias, regulate foreign and interstate commerce, and impose duties on imports. The power to coin money and fix its value was vested in Congress and denied to the states, so as to assure a more stable currency. The Constitution forbade the states to impair the obligations of contracts.

The framers of the Constitution were aware that provisions for a highly centralized government and a sweeping assertion of power over the states would preclude acceptance of the document. They reassured the small states by offering them an equal voice with the large in the Senate and the large states by providing for representation according to population in the House of Representatives. The democrats were conceded the rule that the voting qualification set up by each state for the more popular branch of its own legislature would prevail for the choice of federal Representatives and presidential electors. Congress could not suspend the writ of habeas corpus "unless when in cases of rebellion or invasion the public safety may require it." Neither Congress nor the states could impair the rights or possessions of individuals or issue titles of nobility. The American document was distinguished from the unwritten British Constitution by its systematic formulation of the rights of individuals and the duties of their governors and by its provision of fixed terms for all officials, which made it more difficult for cliques, parties, or families to perpetuate themselves in power. These features made the American system more attractive than the English to the liberals of other countries.

The Constitution confirmed the nonimperialistic policy of the Northwest Ordinance of 1787. A motion in the Philadelphia Convention that the representation of the Western states be limited in size to that of the Eastern states was voted down. James Wilson warned that jealousy of the colonies had wrecked the supremacy of Great Britain. "The fatal maxims espoused by her were that the colonies were growing too fast, and that their growth must be stinted in time. What were the consequences? first enmity on our part, then separation. Like consequences will result on the part of the interior settlements if like jealousy and policy be pursued on our part." George Mason opposed any discrimination against the West with a more profound observation on the decisive force of America, a force that distinguished it sharply from Europe—social mobility. "We are founding for our posterity, for our children and our grandchildren, who would be as likely to be citizens of the new Western States as of the old States."

When the new Constitution was submitted to the state conventions, the whole country became the stage of a stirring debate. The case for ratification was made most persuasively in a series of widely read newspaper articles, published under the signature "The Federalist," but written principally by Alexander Hamilton and James Madison. But the strongest argument was the fear of disunion and weakness. The Federalists agreed to append to the Constitution a "Bill of Rights" pledging that Congress would never establish an official religion; abridge freedom of speech, press, and peaceful assembly; forbid citizens to bear arms; quarter soldiers in private homes; issue orders of arrest without naming particular individuals; condemn anyone without a trial; or deny jury trials in civil or criminal cases. The last article of the Bill of Rights provided that "the powers not delegated to the United States by the Constitution, nor prohibited by it to the States, are reserved to the States respectively, or to the people."

Within less than a year, by June 1788, nine states accepted the Constitution, and the new American Union was launched. The first Congress was elected, and George Washington was chosen unanimously as President. The advocates of centralization, led by Hamilton, who became the first Secretary of the Treasury, transferred the war debt of the various states to the new government and paid off at face value the notes issued both by the states and by the Confederation, even though these notes had depreciated and had frequently fallen into the hands of speculators and financiers. The government won the support of the moneyed community, at home and abroad. It imposed tariffs and internal taxes and chartered a Bank of the United States with extensive functions.

These measures gave rise to new controversies. Nevertheless, the constitutional settlement was a triumph of reason and persuasion. By mutual concession, widely differing groups adhered in a political society.

Impact of American Independence on Europe

While Americans were solving their federal problem, Europeans were assimilating the lesson of their earlier successes. The Europeans paid little attention to the small gathering in Philadelphia, but they felt the impact of the Revolution in the easing of trade barriers and, above all, in the tensing of the movement of reform.

The former British colonies were not alone in enjoying a freer foreign trade as a result of their independence. Their victory was a blow to the mercantilist view that profitable trade depended upon conquest and political control. This was not because Great Britain had failed to keep the allegiance of the colonies but because, having lost it, she did not suffer commercially. British trade with the former colonies *increased*, to the surprise of the mercantilists and, incidentally, to the chagrin of French merchants, who had naturally hoped to derive commercial profit from the services of their country to America. The success of the North American colonists stimulated a movement for independence among the Spanish colonists in Central and South America; immediately it suggested the abandonment of the trade privileges of the mother country.

These events confirmed the views of such men as Adam Smith and Turgot and did much to persuade alert European statesmen that commercial freedom could be made to pay. This was particularly true of the ruling groups in Great Britain and France. In 1786 the two leading countries of Europe signed a commercial treaty which reduced custom duties between them. English manufacturers benefited from the reduction of French tariffs on cottons, hardware, and pottery. French wine growers profited from a corresponding reduction of British duties. Trade between the two countries rose in both amount and value. Abandoning customary practice, each country extended to the citizens of the other freedom to travel, to establish residence, to worship in their own faith, and to buy and use consumer goods.

The Americans had demonstrated the practical possibilities of vigorous organization and enlightened reform. Word had become deed. Their state constitutions, which limited the power of the executive and spelled out the inalienable rights of the individual, were translated and read widely in Western Europe. Intercourse with the Republic was lively. Apart from the constant stream of emigrants, many businessmen, investors, pamphleteers, and adventurers crossed and recrossed the ocean. For every American who traveled, lived, and did business in Western Europe there were several Englishmen, Frenchmen, Dutchmen, Belgians, Swiss, Italians, and Germans who explored the opportunities of the Republic.

The French philosophe Condorcet observed, in his *Influence of the American Revolution on Europe* (1786), that the United States had strengthened the idea of the rights of man by a practical example.

> The spectacle of a great people where rights of men are respected is useful to all others, despite the differences of climate, of customs, and of constitutions. . . . It becomes apparent what effect the enjoyment of these rights has on general well being. The man who has never feared an outrage on his person acquires a nobler and gentler soul; he whose property is always secure finds it easy to be honest; the citizen who is subject only to law has more patriotism and courage.

Americanism became a fashion, especially in France. Benjamin Franklin, who had negotiated the Franco-American Alliance during the War for Independence, was something more than a diplomatic agent: he became the ambassador plenipotentiary of the American idea. Everywhere he went he was lionized, and everything he said was quoted approvingly.

European governments had long been accustomed to discreet criticism. After the American Revolution criticism and satire became rougher. They overflowed from the aristocratic *salons* and playhouses into the streets and the market places. What had formerly been expressed cautiously in the learned treatise and the sophisticated essay, with their limited circulation, became the currency of the plain-spoken pamphlet, periodical, and popular play. All Europe rang with praise for a brilliant, and ominous, social comedy, *The Marriage of Figaro*. Its author, Pierre Augustin de Beaumarchais (1732-99), had been associated with the American struggle in the role of paymaster for the French king. His Figaro, the valet of a Spanish count, uttered a piercing cry against aristocracy:

> Because you are a great nobleman you think you are a great genius. . . . Nobility, riches, rank, appointments make people so proud! What have you done to deserve all these good things? You have taken the trouble to be born, and nothing more! Apart from that a quite ordinary sort of man! While I, lost in the obscure crowd's death, I have had to display more sagacity and ingenuity merely to exist than have been exercised in governing all the kingdoms of Spain during the last hundred years.

Fashionable audiences applauded Figaro's sentiments: the pretensions of the noblemen had become ridiculous to the noblemen themselves. Set to music by Mozart, the satire gained further currency. The fact that the Count of Almaviva, the great Corregidor of Andalusia, was rather an aristocratic mouse than a lion, that he treated his social inferiors with consideration, only added the sting of contempt to the satire. Beaumarchais' Count dropped twice to his knees, once before a chambermaid.

The reformers were emboldened by the atmosphere of criticism. Financial stringencies weakened the resistance of the governments to demands for improvement. This was especially true in countries which had taken part in the American war. In France, particularly, the burden of the treasury was greatly

Benjamin Franklin at the royal court at Versailles. Louis XVI and Marie Antoinette are seated. What a strange creature the "natural man" of America seems to the fashionable society of the Old World! BROWN

increased by the assistance France had given to the colonists. Reformers were disposed to adopt the methods used by the Americans—to defy the rulers with economic and, if necessary, military pressure and to mobilize the support of the citizens by setting up patriotic organizations, like the American "Committee of Public Safety."

The unrest of the 1780's was not confined to the propertied and influential classes of Europe. It also seized considerable segments of the popular masses, particularly in the larger cities and capitals.

The various layers of society were not always moved by the same conditions. If the religious orthodoxy of the upper and middle classes was weakened by rational criticism, that of the masses was weakened by evangelism. In times of scarcity, unemployment, and high prices, people rioted in the streets, attacking the stores and burning the houses of "grain monopolists" and wholesalers. In the seventies and eighties there were dozens of such riots in Paris and other large cities. With the growth of urban centers and slums the traditional methods of maintaining order, apprehending criminals, and enforcing the law became ineffective. The use of professional royal troops to put down riots was sanctioned by custom, but it more often provoked than allayed these new disturbances.

Now and then the rebels who had originally focused on economic abuses made political demands as well. Agitators learned to take advantage of this condition. In 1780, two years after the British Parliament had repealed the laws which debarred Catholics from inheriting land in England and Wales, an eccen-

81

tric nobleman, Lord George Gordon (1751-93), stirred up latent anti-Catholic passions and aroused a miniature rebellion in the capital. For three days London was in the hands of angry crowds, and looters and brawlers had a field day. Troops took a toll of several hundred dead and wounded persons before they restored the control of the authorities. The lax methods of maintaining order began to give concern to officials. There was no effective system of patrolling the streets, which were easily taken over by discontented groups. The complaint that crowded cities were foci of disorder and criminality became familiar. The urban revolution was on the horizon.

Popular Ferment and Radicalism in England

It was in the British Isles that urban unrest and the American example worked the most prompt effects. The Revolution was the period of gestation of English radicalism. Proposals for reform, which had been conceived in the sixties, assumed a bolder and more concrete shape. Royal favoritism, the unresponsiveness of the government to public opinion, and political corruption came under attack.

The irrationality of the system of parliamentary representation especially aroused reformers. Several dozen boroughs which had lost most of their inhabitants in the course of time nevertheless continued to elect members of the House of Commons. On the other hand, many populous cities, particularly those which had grown recently under the impact of industrial progress, sent no representatives. The cry against "rotten boroughs" became a constant refrain in English politics.

The radicals went still further, demanding a thorough renovation of politics. Influential societies were formed to work for the strengthening of individual liberties. They drafted comprehensive programs for the democratization of public life. In 1780 an organization of London democrats—the Westminster Committee of Association—proposed six fundamental reforms: the abolition of rotten boroughs and the establishment of equal electoral districts, universal manhood suffrage, vote by secret ballot, annual elections to ensure the responsiveness of Parliament to the electorate, payment of members of Parliament, and abolition of the property qualifications for election. The last two planks were intended to enable men of ability who did not possess independent incomes to serve in Parliament. Among the leading sponsors of these proposals were the Whig Duke of Richmond and the fiery Major John Cartwright, author of *American Independence the Glory and Interest of Great Britain* and organizer of the "Society for Constitutional Information." The radical programs became the fixed goal of English reformers.

The immediate consequence of the reform movement was to steel the Whig opposition in Parliament. The surrender of Yorktown in 1781 was not only a military disaster overseas but the end of a political system at home. The party of "the King's friends" had lost the colonies which, to the keener eye, had held

"Canvassing for Votes," one of a famous series of engravings by William Hogarth (1697-1764) exposing the abuses and corruption of English political life that aroused eighteenth-century reformers. Parliamentary candidates and their agents are scattering money among the voters, giving presents to their womenfolk, and bargaining for a citizen's support (center), while in the background a mob is attacking His Majesty's Excise Office. PRINT ROOM, NEW YORK PUBLIC LIBRARY

promise of becoming the chief jewel of the Crown. The pressure for legal and parliamentary reform increased apace; political societies redoubled their activities. In 1782 the conservative Lord North gave way to a new ministry of Whigs led by the Marquis of Rockingham and Charles James Fox, who received the support of Parliament and the consent, albeit reluctant, of the monarch. The new ministry compelled George III to relax his influence over the House of Commons and reduced the royal household and the favors at the disposal of the monarch. Revenue officers, who were royal appointees, lost the right to vote and, with it, the means of participating in politics. Government contractors were no longer to be permitted to sit in the House of Commons and influence voting in their favor. The resolution which had closed the doors of the Commons to John Wilkes despite his repeated election was dramatically torn from the Journals of the Commons. These measures did much to restore the dignity of Parliament and to vindicate the rights of the voters.

Electoral reform fared less well. Political leaders were agreed that the suffrage should be broadened and rotten boroughs abolished, but they did not press these issues. Some of the abuses of the slave trade in British territories overseas were removed, although the trade itself continued under the sanction of the law.

Although the government avoided radical political reform, it relieved the immediate pressures of financial stringency. The younger William Pitt (1759-1806), who became prime minister in 1783, invoked the traditional cooperation of the investing and banking community. The public debt was funded; that is, revenues were set aside to pay interest on new "consolidated" bonds—the so-called consols—which replaced many miscellaneous obligations of the Treasury. No provision was made for repaying the principal to individual subscribers, however, and thus government securities were confirmed as a permanent investment and the state became dependent upon financiers. By mortgaging future revenues and raising inequitable taxes, the state supplied its present needs, but in so doing it placed an unjust burden on future generations. The policy of "perpetual funding" was attacked by liberal economists as unwise and even ruinous. "To relieve the present exigency," Adam Smith wrote, "is always the object which principally interests those immediately concerned in the administration of public affairs. The future situation in the public revenue, they leave to the care of posterity."

America and Irish Autonomy

The revolutionary struggle overseas had strong repercussions in Ireland. Over the centuries, through several conquests, the English had established control over the smaller island, settled a substantial English town population there, and secured estates for English landlords. They had also established as official the Anglican Church, although the majority of the Irish population was Roman Catholic. The spirit of the age had attenuated religious prejudices, and Catholics and Protestants joined to imitate the American model. They had old grievances. The Catholic tenants in Ireland had been sacrificed to the profit of Protestant landlords, both native and absentee. Many farmers had been displaced to make room for grazing oxen and sheep, since the foreign trade in meat and wool had become very profitable to the great landowners, most of them British. The interests of the Protestant urban communities were equally sacrificed to their commercial and industrial rivals in Britain. Thriving industries were deliberately destroyed by prohibitions designed to benefit English exporters.

The parliament at Dublin, which represented only the Protestant minority, was doubly impotent to resist this selfish treatment: its acts were subject to the approval of the government at London, and its seats were purchased by supporters of that government with Irish money, offices, and sinecures.

In the seventies Catholic and Protestant groups in Ireland drew together in a movement for political autonomy. When British troops were withdrawn to fight Americans, the Irish grasped the opportunity to raise and equip large volunteer forces—theoretically to defend their island against a threatened French invasion but actually to assert their initiative and demonstrate their strength. Tens of thousands of Irishmen under arms could hardly fail to give point to the desires of their country. The government yielded a few concessions: it permitted Protestant Dissenters to hold office, nearly a half century before this was done in England; it lightened the disabilities of Catholics; and it relaxed the restrictions on trade, allowing Irishmen to trade freely with other British colonies. But so long as Ireland did not have the power to make its own laws, these concessions were as insecure as they were limited. In 1780, therefore, the first motion to secure legislative independence was introduced in the Dublin parliament.

In February 1782, while British and American agents were exploring peace terms, a convention of delegates representing some 80,000 armed volunteers met in Dublin. The soldiers' representatives, following the lead of the Americans, voted that "a claim by any body of men other than the King, Lords, and Commons of Ireland to make laws to bind this kingdom is unconstitutional, illegal, and a grievance." The Protestant Irish leader Henry Grattan (1746-1820) pressed the demand for legislative autonomy in the parliament at Dublin. Pointing to America, he pleaded with the English rulers:

> Do you see nothing in that America but the grave and prison of your armies? Do you not see in her range of territory, cheapness of living, variety of climate and simplicity of life, the drain of Europe? Whatever is bold and disconsolate . . . to that point will precipitate, and what you trample on in Europe will sting you in America.

Great Britain had already been stung. By the following month the government of "the King's friends" had fallen. The new Whig ministry hastened to make terms with the Irish as well as to negotiate with the Americans. It repealed Poyning's Act of 1494, which subjected all the laws of the Irish parliament to the veto of the English king and his council, and the Declaratory Act of 1719, which empowered the Parliament in London to legislate on Irish matters. The assembly in Dublin became autonomous, although it was still controlled by English settlers and landlords and its acts still needed the assent of the British sovereign.

These changes improved political relations between the two islands, but a domestic quarrel in England made it impossible to improve economic relations by easing trade between them. The government had proposed to lower tariffs on manufactured goods while continuing to protect merchants through the Navigation Acts. The manufacturers frustrated the proposal. Between a government which adopted laissez-faire principles incompletely and industrialists who insisted on being treated on equal terms with the favored trading classes, the cause of fairer commercial treatment of Ireland was lost.

Revolutions on the Continent

Neither in the British Isles nor in the American Republic was the crisis of the 1780's quite so deep or so portentous as in Continental countries. There were serious commotions in several Swiss cities and in the ecclesiastical principality of Liége, a territory which severed the Austrian Netherlands into two unequal parts. In the city-state of Geneva and in Holland there were civil uprisings that were put down by foreign intervention. But the severest troubles were experienced by two leading absolutist states: in the Austrian Netherlands, a rebellion against the Hapsburg ruler ended in repression; in France, the failure of the monarchy to reform itself led to a successful revolution.

Geneva, the wealthiest and greatest of Swiss cities (and the birthplace of Rousseau), was governed, like most independent burgher states, by a small group of leading families. In the early eighteenth century the body of the merchants and the people made several attempts to democratize the government; in 1738 they succeeded in compelling the aristocratic party to yield legislative and executive power to the assembly of citizens, to open the professions to all inhabitants, and to guarantee the right of petition. This was the first democratic revolution in Europe. In 1781-82, when the aristocrats intrigued to revoke these reforms and forestall further concessions, the citizens took arms and seized control of the city. The aristocrats appealed to outside help, and in 1782 an army consisting of French, Sardinian, and Bernese soldiers surrounded Geneva and forced it to capitulate. The aristocracy was restored and the citizens were stripped of all rights they had enjoyed since 1738. The leaders of the democrats were exiled, and some of them fled to France, where they soon had an opportunity to resume their activities.

The Dutch revolution suffered a similar fate. The government had joined the Americans in the war against Great Britain, but it exhibited much inefficiency and weakness and bought peace by making colonial concessions to the British. Although on the winning side, Holland had lost the war. This spectacle, and the example of the Americans, precipitated a rebellion against the narrow oligarchy that ruled most of the ports and cities and particularly against Prince **William V of Orange** (1766-95), the chief magistrate (*Stadholder*) of the United Provinces of the Netherlands. The power of the Prince, despite his apparently high position, depended on the pleasure of the constituent provinces. William aspired to establish a conventional hereditary monarchy. A "patriotic party" consisting of the majority of the burghers raised a volunteer army, organized demonstrations in the streets, and demanded the democratization of the government. In 1785-86 the "patriots" obtained control of several cities, including the great port of Amsterdam. Fighting broke out between them and the adherents of the Prince and the aristocrats.

France favored the democrats but had too many difficulties of her own to send help; Great Britain and Prussia assisted Prince William. King Frederick

William II of Prussia (1786-97), a brother of the Princess of Orange, marched an army into Holland and overwhelmed the rebels. The power of the Prince was strengthened, the aristocratic officials were restored to their places, and a campaign against the "patriots" was launched. About forty thousand of them, including their families, fled. Some of them found their way to the United States, but most of them took refuge in Belgium and France, countries which were on the eve of revolutions of their own.

Across the border, in the Austrian Netherlands, revolution was precipitated by the efforts of the most energetic of enlightened despots, Emperor Joseph II (1780-90).

The older enlightened rulers had proceeded cautiously. Frederick II of Prussia was bringing to an end a long reign in which imperialism and bureaucratic centralization rather than generous reform were the dominant notes. Catherine II of Russia continued to play at reform in a kittenish fashion, reserving her energies for the task of expanding Russia and solidifying the throne of the Czars. The more earnest reformer, King Charles III of Spain, persevered in the moderate and enlightened policy that he had initiated in the sixties.

It was left to the far-flung Hapsburg Empire to play out to the end the drama of enlightened despotism. Maria Theresa had been among the most moderate of reformers. She drafted projects for public schools and curbed arbitrary exactions on serfs. She was too devout to countenance a weakening of clerical privileges, despite the urgings of her son Joseph, who for fifteen years (1765-80) was her co-regent for the Austrian dominions of the Empire.

Joseph was an unusually potent blend of autocrat, imperialist, and reformer. He held strongly to his prerogative powers and had contempt for the classes whose special privileges reduced the jurisdiction of the state—particularly the aristocracy. He nursed strong ambitions to expand the boundaries of the Empire, and particularly to profit from the weakness of the Ottoman Empire by making territorial gains in the Balkan Peninsula. At the same time he had a professional conception of kingship. Kingship, to him, was the "trade" of administration with the view to assuring "the greatest good for the greatest number." If the will and power of traditional monarchy had sufficed for success, the administration of Austria and the other dominions of the Hapsburgs— Hungary, Bohemia, and Belgium among them—would have been modernized more thoroughly than that of any other Continental country.

Upon the death of Maria Theresa in 1780, Joseph, freed from her conservative inhibitions, launched a series of ambitious decrees. The Edict of Toleration granted freedom of worship and the right to marry legally to Protestants and Jews. Witchcraft and apostasy were no longer to be treated as crimes. How heavily the regime of intolerance had weighed upon the population was illustrated dramatically by the prompt increase in the number of Protestants. The Emperor disbanded the "contemplative" religious orders, preserving only those that devoted themselves to teaching, study, or nursing. He assigned their wealth to the support of hospitals and schools.

In 1782 the world was treated to an unusual spectacle. Pius VI traveled to Vienna—the first time a pope had visited Germany since the fifteenth century—in an attempt to turn Joseph from his attack upon the functions and wealth of the clergy. The attempt proved futile: there was no moving the Emperor. Four years later the Holy Roman Emperor looked on with approval as a group of leading German Catholic archbishops, in a meeting at Ems, declared their virtual independence of the papacy, particularly in respect to fiscal contributions and local clerical appointments. They asserted that the powers exercised by the papacy since the early centuries of the Christian era "can no longer be considered valid; they belong among the usurpations of the Roman curia, and the bishops are entitled, since peaceful protests are of no avail, themselves to maintain their lawful rights under the protection of the Roman-German Emperor...." In the Tuscan dominions of Joseph's brother, the Archduke Leopold, a group of bishops made a similar pronouncement.

Turning from the field of religion, the Emperor decreed the equality of all subjects before the law, especially for the purpose of taxation; gave the press a wide range of expression; and permitted a greater freedom of bequest by will. Finally, he granted the peasants the right to marry freely, to leave their villages, to choose their own occupation, and to own property in their own name. He encouraged the activities of the middle classes and gave hope to talent and ambition. The Emperor felt that a modern administration must be uniform in all the areas and provinces of a country. He therefore strove to render more compact the scattered inheritance of his dynasty. He tried to break down the tariff wall that enclosed Hungary and to exchange distant Belgium for Bavaria, which was adjacent to his dominions in Austria and Bohemia. The first attempt

Emperor Joseph II, ruler of the Hapsburg dominions and head of the Holy Roman Empire, tries his hand at plowing. This picture is an amusing example of the popular, and accurate, belief that enlightened monarchs were as concerned to improve the economic condition of their peoples as they were to reform law and administration. BETTMANN

was resisted by the magnates of Hungary; the second was frustrated by an alliance of German states formed for the purpose by Frederick II of Prussia. But Joseph had nevertheless defined more clearly than any other enlightened monarch the geographic as well as the administrative conditions of the modern state.

The revolutionary Austrian Emperor, however, overstepped the customary bounds of enlightened absolutism. Other reforming princes had attempted to introduce a more rational administration, but without altering the institutions of society or changing the traditional "constitution." They had introduced changes sparingly and had concentrated on the abuses of the clergy, which of all groups was the most subject to criticism and therefore the most vulnerable. The policy of Joseph was more far-reaching. In the mid-eighties he prosecuted an administrative and judicial renovation that involved the transfer to the central government of functions and jurisdictions traditionally exercised by influential groups and provincial assemblies, generally controlled by local noblemen, town councilors, and privileged corporations of magistrates. All these groups were stirred to remonstrance. In 1787 the Emperor turned down a proposal to take counsel on these matters with the leaders of the aristocracy. Bargaining with the privileged estates was of the essence of the old "constitution," which Joseph was eager to put to an end.

The opposition prepared to take a stand. In 1787 the local Estates of Brabant (representative bodies of clergy, nobles, and privileged burghers) in Belgium protested that Joseph's administrative changes contravened the *Joyeuse Entrée*, the fourteenth-century charter of the province. They voted to suspend the payment of taxes. In several provinces the Estates began quietly to raise an army to resist the Emperor's officials and even sounded out foreign powers on the possibility of intervention. Determined up to that point, Joseph decided to retreat. It was, however, late in the day. When he withdrew the administrative decrees, in 1788, fighting had already broken out. Belgian liberals who feared the strengthening of the centralized authority joined forces with clergymen who opposed the Emperor's religious policy. Enlightened absolutism was caught between two fires: its reform program aroused the defenders of traditional institutions, and its arbitrary methods of rule antagonized the defenders of local autonomy. The imperial troops failed to subdue the rebels. In December 1788, the Estates General—the feudal parliament—of the Austrian Netherlands deposed the Hapsburgs and proclaimed the United States of Belgium. The new republic was destined to be short-lived, however. Shortly after Joseph's death in 1790, his successor, Leopold II, dispatched a powerful army that destroyed it.

At the other end of his far-flung realm, Joseph II had made a more timely retreat. His centralizing measures had aroused the powerful and arrogant nobility of Hungary. On the other hand, the brutality with which the landlords put down a *Jacquerie* revolted the humanitarian Emperor. Joseph's hands were tied by the rebellion in Belgium and by his absorption, and expenses, in a war with Turkey as a result of his efforts to expand the Empire southeastward. As Turgot had said, Enlightenment and empire did not mix well. Joseph decided to conciliate the aristocratic Hungarian opposition. Before his death he rescinded a good many of his reforms; most of the rest were later withdrawn by the equally enlightened but more cautious Leopold. The defeated ruler wrote his own epitaph: "Here lies Joseph II, who was unfortunate in everything he undertook."

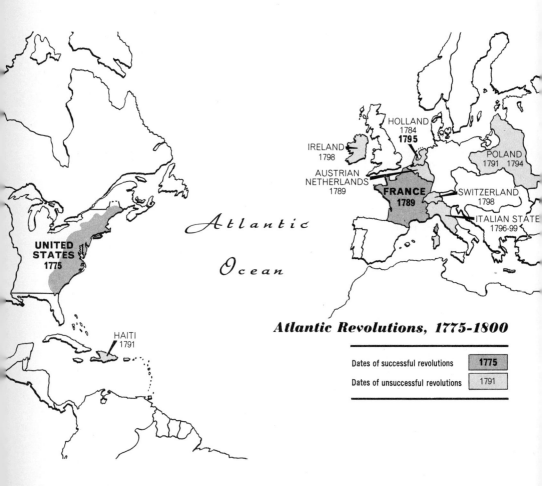

HOLLAND
1784
1795

IRELAND
1798

POLAND
1791 1794

AUSTRIAN
NETHERLANDS
1789

FRANCE
1789

SWITZERLAND
1798

ITALIAN STATE
1796-99

UNITED
STATES
1775

Atlantic

Ocean

HAITI
1791

Atlantic Revolutions, 1775–1800

| Dates of successful revolutions | **1775** |
| Dates of unsuccessful revolutions | 1791 |

Joseph was less unfortunate than he thought. His program, known as "Josephism," became the magnet against whose attraction Austrian conservatism fought for nearly a century. The Austrian rulers had learned that the privileged classes were neither wise enough to reform themselves nor weak enough to allow their sovereigns to do it. The brother-in-law of the two emperors, Louis XVI of France, gave a more spectacular demonstration of the same truth in a more advanced country.

The Deepening Crisis in France

Paradoxically, it was during the reign of the mildest of the Bourbon line that French absolutism appeared most capricious. Louis XVI was by no means a rigid conservative, yet he came to be distrusted by the reformers; he was not an insistent reformer, yet he came to be condemned by the party of privilege. In the end he was isolated, just as the more energetic and intelligent Joseph of Austria had been.

At the beginning of his reign, in 1774, Louis had played the part of the enlightened ruler, with Turgot as his Finance Minister, but he soon yielded to the opposition—the queen and the court aristocrats—and dismissed Turgot. He then tried solutions of a different sort, with Jacques Necker (1732-1804) as Comptroller-General. The policy of the economist Turgot, as we have noted, was to reduce expenses and avoid further borrowing. But Necker, a banker, was naturally at home in the atmosphere of credit and not at all adverse to admitting financiers and investors into official confidence. In Great Britain, in Holland, and latterly even in the United States, the investors and speculators exerted no little political influence. Like William Pitt and Alexander Hamilton, Necker favored cooperation with these elements, in the belief that funds would be forthcoming if a future income were set aside to service interest and capital, and if the affairs of the government were so run as to give assurance of its reliability and solvency. The first condition implied new taxes, and new taxes pointed to a contest with the privileged orders.

Necker tried to build up the confidence of the financial community, by demonstrating that the government was improving its budgetary procedures. In 1781 he made public for the first time the *Compte Rendu au Roi*, an estimate of income and expenditure submitted annually to the King by the comptroller of France. Although the surplus he indicated was largely imaginary, his recognition of the obligation of the government to submit to public accountability pleased financiers and reformers. But the Old Regime was accustomed to secrecy. Publicity would disclose fiscal habits that could not stand the light of day. The king might have to take financiers into his confidence in framing policies that involved expenditures, and there were few policies that did not. Necker was dismissed. He had succeeded in borrowing heavily and left the treasury in a worse state than he found it. But since he had displeased the King, he became a popular hero. Indeed, his fall was the signal for a reactionary offensive.

The nobility had for some years been reviving and exacting of the peasants old services and dues which had long fallen into disuse. The *parlements* (or courts of high instance) now increased the number of titled ancestors in the direct line of inheritance that a candidate needed in order to qualify for a commission in the judiciary, and the King raised the number of such ancestors required for a commission in the army. He had already excluded commoners from the higher positions in the church. The judiciary, the army, and the church were thus closed to recently ennobled bourgeois. The clergy applied the rule of the tithe to the new crops which were then being introduced—to potatoes, for example. When in 1781 the Parlement of Paris objected to a badly needed new tax, the government was driven to establish additional useless offices and then put them up for sale. The only alternative to reform seemed to be an aggravation of abuses! In 1780 the King forbade the use of torture to obtain confessions from persons accused of crime. But torture was retained for the purpose of forcing the accused to reveal his accomplices—even though the justification for one was no better than for the other. Matters were not improved when an abuse was abolished and then restored. Such was the case of the onerous road service called the *corvée*.

Louis disappointed the reformers without winning over the privileged orders. He then proceeded, as if by deliberation, to weaken the bonds that tied the magistracy and nobility to the Crown. The royal judges were generally bourgeois in more or less distant origin but rigidly aristocratic in privilege and pretension. The more important of them sat in the parlements, which often criticized royal legislation, especially reform measures. The principal parlement, at Paris, had long enjoyed the privilege of registering royal decrees and thus investing them with the indispensable sanction of a public record. It began in time to claim the right also of refusing to register decrees—in effect exercising a veto. Louis XV (1715-74) had abolished the parlements in 1771, but his successor revived them in the bright morning of his reign. The judges returned to the fight and threw out many a measure of Louis' reforming ministers. He thereupon exiled them to the provinces and reduced their functions and powers. They retaliated by protesting that only the Estates General—the old feudal parliament, which had not been convened since 1614—had the right to approve fundamental changes in taxation and government. Since they stood on old privileges, the judges are now justly regarded as reactionary, but their defiance was loudly applauded and they became the heroes of the day. Their action was highly significant, for it meant that considerations of reform were being subordinated to the wider issue of royal power, and that a fiscal matter was taking the dangerous form of a constitutional issue.

After the magistracy, the nobility. Juggle finances as he might, one minister after another concluded that the privileged must accept a fair share of the burden. If the prevailing system of society was not to be disturbed, they must do so voluntarily. The issue hung on the moderation and responsibility of the privileged orders. They were found wanting, more so than the Crown. In Austria and Spain, the wealth of the monastic orders was being tapped for secular purposes. The French clergy, which held perhaps one fifth of the real property of the country, refused to increase its contribution to the treasury. Since all the bishops and most of the wealthy abbots were scions of noble families, the refusal was that of the nobility as well as the clergy. In 1786 the

Finance Minister, Charles Alexandre de Calonne (1734-1802), told his master that a crisis had been reached:

> Piecemeal measures are of no use for the salvation of the State; if ruin is to be staved off, it is indispensable to start reconstructing the whole edifice.... It is impossible to increase taxation and ruinous to be always borrowing; it is not enough to confine ourselves to economic reforms. The only thing to be done, the sole means by which the finances may at least be reduced to order, must consist in infusing life into the whole State by recasting all the vicious elements in its constitution.

In one of his rare exhibitions of firmness, Louis decided to bring the mighty to terms. Calonne proposed an "Assembly of Notables," and early in 1787, when Joseph II was turning down a similar suggestion, the French king summoned this gathering, composed largely of nobles and titled officials. In accordance with what was becoming an established practice, the royal minister delivered an indictment of the royal administration. He came to the prosaic conclusion that the nobles should accept equal liability to taxation. The oration of Calonne was the funeral oration of the Old Regime. The Notables were not satisfied merely to reject his advice; they declared that the authority to create new taxes belonged not to them but to the Estates General. The Notables were dismissed.

The suggestion to convene the Estates General was interesting indeed. It was upon the grave of such institutions, and chiefly on that of the Estates General, that Cardinals Richelieu and Mazarin and King Louis XIV had erected the royal monopoly of political power. Since the last convention of the Estates, in 1614, the monarchy had grown fat with functions and jurisdictions. The resurrection of the Estates was therefore unwelcome to the court. At first the aim of the privileged orders in proposing that the Estates be called was to escape responsibility and adjourn the issue of taxation. But then they began to see the prospect of extracting valuable concessions from the monarchy and reversing the trend of their diminishing political importance.

The Estates General consisted of three chambers. The First Estate represented the clergy, the Second the nobility, and the Third the rest of the nation: merchants, craftsmen, professional men, and peasants. The old rule was that no legislation touching the rights or the pockets of an Estate could be enacted without its consent. This rule gave each Estate bargaining power with the Crown. The Estates might be summoned individually, but even when all three were called, they met and voted separately. Since the high clergymen were noblemen, the nobility in effect controlled two houses out of three.

So far the privileged orders were safe. But they were playing with fire— 1787 was not 1614. In the interim the middle and professional classes had become a power in the land. With a twist here and there, the Estates General might be transformed from a feudal parliament dominated by noblemen into a modern parliament. Suppose that the representation of the Third Estate were   *93* increased and that the Estates met and voted as one body. The result would be a legislature dominated by the nonaristocratic groups. This was precisely what the reformers now proposed. In either case—whether the aristocrats or the reformers prevailed—the royal power must recede, especially if the two factions should combine against it.

In 1788 such a combination came to pass. In the southern province of Dauphiné, the nobility, clergy, magistrates, and middle-class and professional groups agreed to revive the local Estates without asking the King for approval. The three Estates were to meet in one chamber, and the Third was to have as many representatives as the other two put together. Faced with this revolution, the government forbade the meeting, which was to take place at Grenoble, the old capital of Dauphiné. The Estates defiantly met at near-by Vizille. It claimed the right to refuse payment of taxes it did not approve and petitioned the King to call the Estates General.

Pressed from all sides, Louis recalled Necker, who had acquired the reputation of a reformer, and convened the dreaded legislature on January 27, 1789, fixing the meeting for May 1 of that year. He split the difference between the traditional and the modern conceptions of a parliament. The Third Estate was to have six hundred members while the other two were to have about three hundred each. But the Three Estates were to meet and vote separately, as before. This concession to the nobles canceled out the concession to the Third Estate. Despite its double size, it was to count for no more than the other two. The summons of the King was like the unfurling of a flag in the wind. Louis appealed to the electors to voice their grievances and demands. He promised, in effect, to grant the country a new constitution. His letter of convocation was to be read to the people in all the parish churches:

> We need the cooperation of our faithful subjects to help us to overcome all the difficulties in which we find ourselves concerning the condition of our finances, and to establish, according to our wishes, a constant and invariable order in all the parts of the government which affect our subjects and the prosperity of our kingdom. These great purposes have determined us to convoke the assembly of the Estates of all the provinces of our obedience, as much to counsel and help us in all the things that shall be submitted to us as to make known the wishes and grievances of our peoples; so that, in a mutual confidence and reciprocal affection between the sovereign and his subjects, there may be reached, as promptly as possible, an effective remedy for the evils of the State, and that all the various abuses, the abuses of all sorts, be reformed and avoided by good and practical, strong, solid means that assure public happiness, and that restore to us particularly the calm and tranquillity of which we have been deprived for a long time.

Alas, the King of France was never again to know "calm and tranquillity." Nor was many another Continental ruler. In the preceding decade, several parts of Western Europe had experienced civil war. The reformers in every case had been beaten back. Would this also happen in France? Contemplating the scene of the eighties, Thomas Jefferson, the American Minister to France, drew the contrast between Europe and America, with a touch of satisfaction:

> Happily for us that when we find our constitution defective and insufficient, to secure the happiness of our people, we can assemble with all the coolness of philosophers and set it to rights, while every other nation on earth must have recourse to arms to amend or restore their constitutions.

The French Revolution

War and Democracy

Imperial and Intellectual Adventure

Bonapartism and Republicanism

The Duel for World Empire

"*La Liberté guidant le peuple,*" *by the Romantic painter Eugène Delacroix (1798-1863), was occasioned by the July Revolution of 1830 in Paris. Its style of dress belongs to that period, but its spirit is that of all the many revolutions in the Atlantic world since the eighteenth century. The fighters on the barricades represent a cross section of the urban revolutionary groups—rough-hewn workers and middle-class intellectuals. The tricolor carried by La Liberté is the flag the Revolution of 1789 substituted for the white flag of the Bourbons. In the right background is the great city; in the foreground are the bodies of a royal soldier and a fighter for the people lying on the debris of wood and cobble stones, the typical material of the improvised barricade.*

The Revolutionary Alternatives

5. *The French Revolution*

The French Revolution began with a stupendous misunderstanding. The revival of the old feudal parliament in 1789 held out contradictory promises to the various classes of France. The King looked upon the convocation of the Estates General as a tactical maneuver in his campaign to compel his subjects, particularly the aristocracy, to replenish his treasury and so refresh his financial credit and ability to borrow. The aristocrats hoped that, by controlling the Estates General, they would regain a political influence that they had not had for centuries and would cause the pendulum of power, which had swung to the monarchy, to swing back in their direction.

In these calculations, the Court and the aristocrats were at odds with the people of France. The professional and middle classes, and enlightened men of all classes, intended to transform what had been a feudal assembly guided by aristocrats and clerics into a modern parliament responsive to public opinion. They proposed comprehensive reforms in the administration and policy of the country. The hopes of the lower classes soared still higher. The convocation was an extraordinary event and suggested to them an extraordinary effort on the part of the King to listen to the woes of the poor and to relieve them. Why else, humble folk in town and country asked each other, did the King invite them in paternal tones to tell him their "wishes and grievances" and hold out the prospect of remedying "the evils of the state" and "all the various abuses"? Was not the poverty of the masses the greatest evil and abuse of the state?

The King opened the mouth of France, and a flood of words poured out. He virtually ended censorship. It was still necessary to obtain official licenses to publish periodicals, but pamphleteering was free, and it flourished luxuriantly. Thousands of essays, appeals, addresses, letters, debates, replies, rebuttals, and surrebuttals inundated the country. In the six months following the convocation of the Estates General, perhaps a hundred thousand pamphlets were circulated.

Parisians storm a printing establishment in their eagerness to get news of the progress of the Revolution. The press was becoming an increasingly important factor in political life. Contemporary drawing. BETTMANN

The Voice of the Nation

In his letter of convocation, Louis XVI had asked the voters to provide their deputies with "instructions and large powers sufficient to propose, remonstrate, advise, and agree regarding whatever may be the need of the state, the reform of abuses, the establishment of a fixed and durable order in all the parts of the administration, the general prosperity of our kingdom, and the welfare of all and each one of our subjects." If words meant anything, the King was inviting the country to help him to write a constitution. The French rose to the challenge. Every town, every district, every last hamlet in the country, every organized craft and trade, and every local and provincial estate drew up its own *cahier de doléances*. Twenty thousand of these "bills of complaint" are in print, and they still keep turning up in local archives, old chests, and attics.

The peasants of France—the "dumb beasts of burden" of the Old Regime —found their voice at long last. They bethought themselves of their many heavy troubles. Model *cahiers* were circulated and copied. Not infrequently an educated priest or lawyer guided the pen of an ignorant townsman or countryman. Their *cahiers* ranged from reports of the most homely and local grievances —"The village bridge is badly in need of repair; last week the leg of Pierre's horse was caught between the planks," or "The principal street should have

99

lights at night"—to comments on the most general issues of concern to the country—liberty of opinion, equality of taxation, and a better form of government.

The more articulate urban groups produced an impressive series of statesmanlike *cahiers*. Paris fulfilled its responsibility as the leading city of France. Boxes were set up to gather the suggestions of the citizens. The city forwarded to the Estates General a complete draft of a new constitution of the state, the church, and the administration.

Taken together, the *cahiers* of the Third Estate spelled out the will and the hope of France. From myriad proposals there emerged a consensus which transcended the barriers of class, tradition, and geography. This was the consensus:

The monarchy should be preserved in a dignified, strong, and yet limited form. The king was inviolable, but his ministers should be indictable for any abuse of their office. (The implication was that the rulers of France had been lawbreakers but were above judgment.) The king should share his powers, particularly the function of legislation, with an elected and independent legislature, which was to hold the purse strings of the country.

The arbitrariness and secrecy of Court government should be brought to an end. There should be an unvarying and uninvidious rule of law—a simple law known to all beforehand—sober and economical budgeting, a fair and economical administration of justice. Local government should have substantial autonomy. The individual citizens should be trusted with a few precious freedoms, notably the right to make up their own minds on controversial subjects without the coaching of their betters, to discuss their opinions with their neighbors, and to argue orally or in print.

There should be greater opportunity for members of all classes to advance in life, economically, politically, and culturally. Manorial dues and guilds should be abolished. The government should show some concern for the needy sections of the people. The aristocracy might preserve its honors, but it should assume its proper share of the tax burden and surrender its onerous exactions on the countryman. The Roman Catholic Church should remain the official church, but it should become more modest in its pretensions and expenditures, and less censorious of other faiths. Its fashionable bishops would do well to reside in their dioceses and pay more serious attention to their duties than had been their custom of late. Finally, the Church should pay the parish priest a greater respect and, particularly, a larger salary.

Such was the mandate which the voters of France entrusted to a broad anti-aristocratic party.

The elections of 1789 were free even by later standards. The privileged elements were divided. There had never been much love lost between the greater and lesser nobility or between the upper and lower clergy. In the Second Estate the provincial nobles outnumbered their superiors, the Court aristocrats. In the First Estate, the higher clergy were outnumbered two to one by the humble *curés*, who belonged socially to the peasantry.

The Third Estate was more closely knit. The liberal suffrage qualifications made the election the first popular canvass in any large country in modern times. Most male heads of a family who were over twenty-five years of age and were inscribed on the tax rolls could vote. Since direct taxes were common under the Old Regime, some 90 percent of the adult male population was eligible. In laying down these democratic suffrage rules, the Court hoped to profit from the old mistrust between country and town, between the poor and the capitalists, and between the unlettered people and the educated classes. It was the second group in each case that the Court feared more. But the monarchy's calculation that it could set the various classes against each other proved as wrong as its conception of the function of the Estates General. It turned out that both the peasants and the townspeople accepted the leadership of the enlightened bourgeoisie and liberal young noblemen. The result was a Third Estate which was representative of the whole nation, although it consisted largely of lawyers, journalists, merchants, and men of independent means. This Estate supported by liberal nobles and lower clergy commanded a large majority of the members of the Estates General.

For the first time in modern history, and as happened but rarely thereafter, a large nation spoke as with a single voice. Much of the best ability, earnestness, and good will of France was embodied in the Estates General.

The people of France had done their work. It remained for their ruler to do his. But when the Estates General met in Versailles, in May 1789, Louis, addressing the three orders together, told them that they had better find money for the treasury and leave reform to him! He failed to present a program and thus missed a precious opportunity for leadership, for the Estates General, and the nation, were disposed to follow him. The initiative passed by default to the Third Estate, which seized it promptly.

If the three Estates were to meet separately, as they had done in the past, the reformers would be divided and so weakened. The Third Estate therefore refused to organize itself as a distinct body, with its own chairman and secretary. Instead, it invited the other two Estates to join it and to agree to a common verification of the certificates of election of the members of all the Estates. The aristocracy and clergy turned down the invitation, over the objection of sizable minorities of their bodies. The Third Estate thereupon proceeded to verify the certificates not only of its own members but also of a number of individual members of the other two Estates (notably a few parish priests) who came over to join it. This was a revolutionary act, for no one of the three bodies had authority over the members of the others. When this verification was completed, on June 17, the Third Estate assumed the name of the "National Assembly," in which capacity, it declared, it would write a constitution for France. It threatened that, if the Assembly were dissolved, taxes would cease to be paid.

Two days later, the majority of the clergy voted to verify mandates together with the Third Estate, but not necessarily to merge the two bodies. This was a significant step: the priest had joined the Revolution. The issue between the aristocracy and the bourgeoisie thus became sharper. The King stood by the aristocracy, for a time. On the same day, he summoned a joint session of the Estates for June 23. Meanwhile, in order to prepare a meeting place for the joint session, he closed the largest available hall in Versailles—a hall which had previously been assigned to the Third Estate, as the most numerous of the three. But the Third Estate was not informed in time, and, when its deputies appeared on June 20 at the hour set for their deliberations, they found the door closed and assumed that they had been deliberately locked out. The National Assembly of France was forced to meet in the street. It adjourned to an indoor tennis court nearby and there took a wrathful oath: the Assembly would not disband until it had given the country a new constitution. Two days later, on June 22, about 150 clergymen, including two archbishops, joined the Assembly, which thus came to represent two of the three Estates as well as a majority of the membership of the combined body.

At the royal session on June 23, Louis announced that he was willing to concede a moderate program of reform, However, he was adamant on the constitutional issue. The Third Estate was not the "National Assembly." The three Estates must preserve their identities, meeting separately except to discuss matters which did not touch the privileges of the upper orders and, in any case, voting separately. The King answered defiance with a threat: "If by any chance (as I should be sorry to think) you fail to support Me in this high endeavor, I shall by Myself do what is best for My people."

After delivering his ultimatum and advising the deputies to separate for their future meetings, the King left the hall. However, the members of the Third Estate, a majority of the clergy, and a sprinkling of the aristocracy remained in their places. Commanded a second time to disband, this time by a messenger of the King, they retorted that they would not leave except by force. Force Louis was not prepared—at the moment—to use. "Very well," he is said to have remarked, "let the bastards stay."

A few days later, Louis yielded; he commanded the aristocrats to become members of the National Assembly. The aristocrats protested angrily but obeyed. France now had a parliament, recognized by the King and pledged to write a moderate constitution. The broad outlines of this constitution had been limned for a century by liberal writers, spelled out in practice by English and American lawyers and politicians, and endorsed by the thousands of *cahiers de doléances*.

Townsmen and Peasants Defend the Revolution

It soon became apparent that the King's concessions had not been genuine. On July 11, Louis dismissed for the second time the timid but popular Necker and began to move troops from the provinces to Versailles and Paris. Since Versailles was inhabited chiefly by courtiers and their retinues, the position of the deputies there became awkward. If the King should use his growing force, what counterforce could they oppose to it? Only their votes and their voices— or the energy of the French people.

Sporadic disorder had already broken out in the cities of France. Like most of Western Europe, France had suffered from the poor harvest of 1788. Food had been short throughout the winter, and the price of bread and other staples was higher than it had been in generations. Thousands of unemployed men and women flocked into Paris. Economic distress was now added to anger at the King's threatening behavior. Journalists, lawyers, and liberal deputies from Versailles appealed for support to the disaffected populace of Paris. In frenzied speeches, pamphlets, and posters, they pleaded with the Parisians to save the National Assembly, and with it the hope of improvement and reform. There were bankers who distributed money strategically and hardware merchants who left the doors of their munition stores suggestively unlocked. Some of the royal soldiers fraternized with the orators and the people.

The stage was set and the little folk of Paris stepped upon it to inaugurate, quite simply, a new era in history. The principal actors were the inhabitants of the district of St. Antoine—craftsmen, journeymen, shopkeepers, and their customers. These people lived in the shadow of the royal stronghold of the capital, the notorious prison of the Bastille. On July 14, seconded by other Parisians, they broke open arsenal after arsenal, increasing their means of resistance while diminishing the King's means of attack. Finally they came to the fortress itself, whose guns were pointed ominously at St. Antoine. Guided by the professional skill of rebellious soldiers, and generously laying down sixteen lives to one, they stormed the grim Bastille—the symbol of tyranny—and destroyed the garrison.

The effect was disproportionate to the event, for the Bastille actually contained very few prisoners at the time. It was, however, the principal fortress of

The storming of the Bastille, July 14, 1789. This contemporary drawing stresses the cooperation of the King's troops with the citizens of Paris. From Armand Dayot, La Révolution Française. COURTESY OF THE METROPOLITAN MUSEUM OF ART, ROGERS FUND, 1952

the King, and now it had fallen to the people. The uprising was contagious. It was repeated in so many other cities of France that it appeared that the whole urban population had repudiated royal authority. In Paris and elsewhere new communal governments were set up.

The fall of the Bastille saved the Assembly. The King removed his troops from Versailles and Paris and confirmed the authority of the new Paris Commune. He thus advertised to the world that he had lost control, both military and administrative, over the capital of his realm.

The success of the Parisians was not lost on the peasantry. They had drafted piteous *cahiers* asking for relief from their burdens, but what chance was there that the powerful and learned men of the Assembly—much less the King—would trouble their heads about them? Most of the countrymen had elected men of the richer and enlightened classes as their representatives. There was a good deal of sympathy in the National Assembly for the condition of the peasantry, but no daring programs to deal with it were framed. The villagers were looked on as primitive and inert, and it was not suspected that they could act as a unit. There had been rural uprisings before, but none had assumed the sweep of a national movement.

But now that the townsmen had risen and asserted themselves, the peasants followed suit. The revolution which the noblemen had unwittingly begun by forcing the convocation of the Estates had finally percolated to the bottom of the social heap. After the fall of the Bastille, royal power seemed no more, and primeval fear returned. From village to village the rumor sped that "the brigands"—the terror of the countryside at that time—were coming. At first "The Great Fear" was merely a reflection of the general disorder and uncertainty, but it promptly pointed out to the peasants the source of their age-long misery. If "brigands" were coming to despoil and destroy them, who could have incited and dispatched the plunderers but the aristocrats, for who else hated the peasants so much? Arming themselves with anything that came to hand, the peasants descended upon manor houses and castles, where they shrewdly took care to set aflame the records and rolls of servitude and obligation, the "feudal contracts." For the sanctity of the written and signed deed was formidable. No proof, no obligation!

The movements of July, although they were neither organized nor universal, were sufficiently broad and simultaneous to take on the proportions of a general uprising. Not since the fourteenth century, the classic age of agrarian revolt, had any Western country witnessed a *jacquerie* of such scope and violence.

The urban revolutions had saved the National Assembly, but the peasant revolutions spurred it to reject the Old Regime with a unique thoroughness. Up to that moment the Assembly had contemplated moderate fiscal and political reforms. Now France, in one high leap, surpassed the liberal achievements of the more evolutionary Anglo-Saxon models. Two years of discussion and repeated mass movements in city and country were required before this immense renovation was spelled out in law and code, but in essence it was the work of a single day. On the morning of August 4, 1789, the Assembly decided to follow the example of the American revolutionists in drafting a formal statement of the aims and principles of their new government. On the night of the same day, it announced, with a daring simplicity, "The feudal system is entirely abolished."

This was not the first reaction to the peasant disturbances. The new town governments and guards had been preparing to put them down. And at the opening of the night session of the Assembly, some bourgeois had suggested that troops be sent against the rural rioters. The aristocrats were bound to suffer more than the bourgeois from the wrath of the peasants: they were caught between fear of making concessions to the peasants and fear of reprisal for repressing them. At this juncture, a minority of advanced liberals, among them a few aristocrats, took history by the forelock. A liberal nobleman, the Vicomte de Noailles, proposed that all personal privileges in the village be surrendered; that the corresponding servitudes and servile obligations be abolished without compensation; that other obligations, notably those connected with property, be declared subject to redemption; and, finally, that all groups be taxed equally. The assembly responded with instant and enthusiastic approval. The dam was down; surrender followed surrender and sacrifice, sacrifice. When the sun dawned on August 5 the slate had been wiped clear not only of a myriad of abuses, injustices, and inequalities but of the whole old system of government, administration, and law. The Declaration of August 4-5 pledged that manorial courts, territorial and urban privileges, tithes, hunting privileges, perpetual rents or dues, and the sale of judicial or municipal offices would be abolished.

The Assembly then began to draw up a statement of principles for the new order of things. The more famous Declaration of the Rights of Man and of the Citizen, adopted on August 27, was to be the preamble of the Constitution. It proclaimed the equality of all men before the law, provided for a government of separated powers responsible to the citizens, and carefully spelled out the freedoms of the individual.

The Declaration of August 4-5 proclaimed Louis XVI as the restorer of French liberty, a gracious compliment the King neither appreciated nor deserved. He procrastinated, prevaricated, provoked. The large changes proposed by the two Declarations must have his consent—there was no thought of doing without him; the French were not republicans. He claimed a power of veto over both the constitution that was being written and the laws of the assembly to be established under it. The Marquis de Lafayette, Commander of the National Guard, mediated between the supporters and the opponents of the royal veto, with the advice of Jefferson, then Minister of the United States to France. A compromise was worked out. The King would grant his consent to the fundamental constitutional laws—the two Declarations—and, in exchange, he would obtain a veto which could be overcome only by the action of three successive sessions of the legislature. While the Assembly carried out its part of this bargain by submitting the Declarations to the King, the monarch broke faith again. Yielding once more to the advice of the intransigent Court nobles, he began to assemble troops at Versailles for a show of strength.

"Monsieur Veto" and especially "Madame Veto," as Louis and his queen, Marie Antoinette, came to be known, became extremely unpopular. Paris was suffering from high prices as well as political frustration. The dismissal of servants and the depression of the luxury trades caused by the flight of thousands of aristocrats from the seething country increased the ranks of the unemployed. On October 5, a group of Parisians, many of them women, marched on Versailles, asking quite simply for bread.

In the afternoon, a deputation of the marchers appeared before the National Assembly, which sent its chairman, Mounier, with the Parisians to the palace to ask the King not only to provision the capital but to sanction the Declarations. Louis granted the first request at once but, with his advisers divided, struggled to decide between surrendering to the new principles and fleeing from Versailles to set up a rival capital and authority in some provincial town. Finally, in the evening, Louis accepted bitterly the Declarations and the suspensive veto.

At midnight, there was another invasion of Versailles. Lafayette had been reluctant to exercise his powers as Commander of the National Guard either to stop the marchers from leaving Paris or to coerce the King to grant their requests. But, pressed by his soldiers and instructed by the Paris Commune to bring the Court to the capital, he led his troops to Versailles. Two armies confronted each other in the very palace and palace yard. The night watch was divided: within the palace, sentries of the King's Guard took their posts; outside, in the palace yard, was the National Guard of Paris; between, evidently overlooked, was an unobtrusive side door. At dawn, a crowd of Parisians opened it and penetrated to the apartments of the Queen, who fled to the King. Lafayette arrived and, to prevent an outbreak, persuaded the King and Queen to appear with him on the balcony. The people then made the demand that the Commander had delayed: the King to Paris! Louis acquiesced at once; the game was over. The people had appropriated the King—this was never forgotten by either side.

Later in the morning of October 6, the women and the National Guard returned to Paris, bringing with them "the baker, the baker's wife, and the baker's errandboy"—*i.e.*, the royal pair and the Dauphin. "Now," they exulted, "we shall have bread!" The Assembly followed—but the royal regiment did not.

Individualism and the Fluid Society

Internal deterioration over a long period of time had prepared the ground for the Revolution, and the determined action of the principal nonaristocratic classes at the strategic moments had sealed its victory over the old state and society. But it was one thing to destroy the Old Regime and another to create a new and better order. Only a fertile idea, honestly pursued and applied, could give shape to a new state and society, in harmony with each other and with the hopes and ambitions of men. The natural rights of man was such an idea. The Declaration of the Rights of Man and of the Citizen spelled it out clearly:

> All men are born and remain free and equal in rights. . . . The purpose of all political association is to conserve the natural and imprescriptible rights of man. These rights are liberty, property, security, and resistance to oppression. The principle of sovereignty resides essentially in the nation. . . . Liberty consists in doing everything that injures no one else; hence the exercise of the natural rights of each man has no limits except those that assure to the other members of society the enjoyment of the same rights. These limits can be determined only by law. . . . Law is the expression of the general will. All the citizens have the right to participate personally, or through their representatives, in its formation. It should be the same for all, whether it protects or it punishes.

From these principles flowed the new polity, and from their implicit assertion of the rule of equality and fairness, the new society.

For two years, from August 1789 to September 1791, the National Assembly drew the outlines of the new order and proceeded to fill them in. In some matters this task was continued and completed by its successors, the Legislative Assembly of 1791-92 and the Convention of 1792-95. The National (Constituent) Assembly wrote a new Constitution, codified criminal law, recast the local and national administration of the country, rearranged the relations between church and state, and passed a multitude of laws regulating economic, family, and personal affairs.

France became a vast public forum. The actor in it was neither the caste nor the class but the independent and articulate citizen, in motion among his fellows. The new citizen was assumed to be mobile, responsible, and concerned with public affairs. He could "go anywhere, remain anywhere, or leave, without being arrested, accused or detained." He could practice any religion he wished or express any religious views. He was free to meet and assemble with his fellow citizens, provided that he was unarmed. He might petition the government, but only as an individual, not as a member of a group. He could not be arrested without cause, tortured, or tried for a crime except by a jury of his peers. Unless and until an accuser could prove him guilty, he was presumed to be innocent. He might "speak, write, print, and publish his thoughts, and his writings cannot be submitted to any censorship or inspection before their publication." The "free communication of ideas" was acknowledged as "one of the most precious of the rights of man."

France rose to this challenge. A constant stream of pamphlets, newspapers, and addresses flowed from the emancipated press; the walls were covered with posters, appeals, and the text of speeches and laws; the uncensored theaters multiplied rapidly; discussion clubs and debating societies proliferated by the thousands.

France found a common tongue. In 1789, classic French was not the everyday speech of most Frenchmen, though it was being used increasingly by literate men and by townspeople. Latin was associated with "aristocracy." The dozens of *patois* of the countryside, dialects of Basque, Provençal, and German as well as of French, were associated with the parochialism and ignorance bred by "feudalism." "With thirty different *patois*, we are still a Tower of Babel," observed Abbé Henri Grégoire (1750-1831), the energetic leader of the movement to promote a single language.

> One can at least give a great nation a uniform language so that all the citizens who compose it might communicate their ideas without hindrance. . . . So many jargons are so many barriers that impede the movements of commerce and weaken social relations. Through the influence of custom upon language, of language upon custom, they prevent political amalgamation and make of a single people thirty. . . . In order to extirpate all prejudices, to develop truths, talents and virtues, to melt all the citizens into the national mass, to simplify the mechanism and ease the play of the political machine, we must have one language. . . . The unity of idiom is an integrating part of the Revolution. . . .

Variety yielded to unity. The exclusive use of French was encouraged officially. It became a badge of devotion to the country and to the Revolution. Every child was to be taught French. The principle of free public schools was asserted, for education and discussion were essential to the open forum.

Man was to be equally free in all the corners of the country. "Must the same man be right in Brittany and wrong in Languedoc?" Voltaire had asked. Under the Old Regime, a chaotic variety of conditions had prevailed within the boundaries of France—and France was not unique in this respect. In the southern part of the country, the courts generally dispensed Roman law based on the code formulated by the Emperor Justinian in the sixth century. In the north, the tradition and oral custom, often primitive and barbarous, of each particular locality or district held sway. The result was that in civil law, for example, some 360 different "codes" were identifiable. In some provinces, the amount of taxes to be raised was apportioned among the towns and villages by appointed royal officials; in others, by local assemblies representing the various estates and corporations. Most provinces, indeed, had no such assemblies, whether for this or any other purpose. In some provinces, the indirect taxes, notably the notorious *gabelle*, or salt tax, were set at exorbitant levels; in other, perhaps adjacent, areas, taxes were moderate or even nominal, owing to old feudal or contractual arrangements. In some areas, the principal direct tax, the *taille*, was assessed on the valuation of land and other real property; in others, it was based on the valuation of all the property of the taxpayer. Here the provinces were large and compact; there they were microscopic or sprawling. Boundaries were always traditional, never convenient or rational. This town had bought from the Crown the right to elect its own mayor and aldermen from among its principal guildsmen, but in the next town quite other electoral or appointive rules prevailed. For a century, goods could move within a large

France Before the Revolution

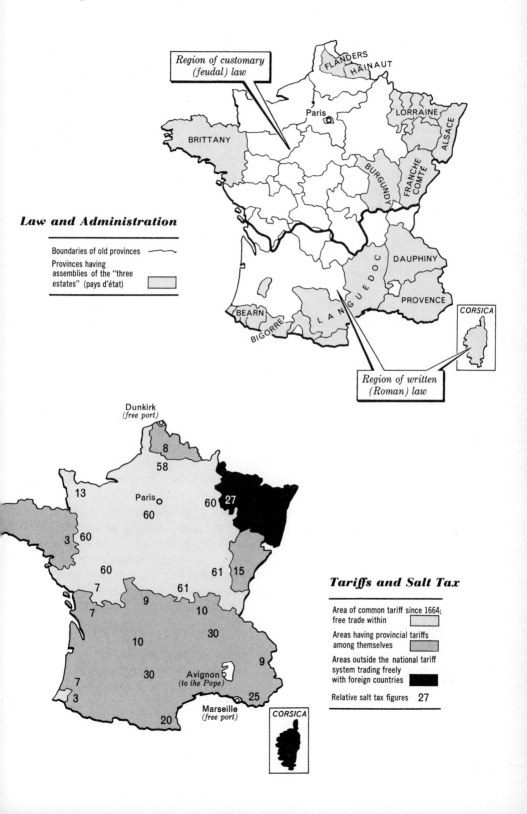

Region of customary (feudal) law

FLANDERS
HAINAUT
Paris
LORRAINE
ALSACE
BRITTANY
BURGUNDY
FRANCHE COMTÉ
DAUPHINY
LANGUEDOC
PROVENCE
BEARN
BIGORRE
CORSICA

Law and Administration

Boundaries of old provinces ——
Provinces having assemblies of the "three estates" (pays d'état)

Region of written (Roman) law

Dunkirk (free port)

8
58
13
Paris
60
27
60
3 60
60
61 15
7
61
9
10
7
10
30
9
30
Avignon (to the Pope)
7
3
25
20
Marseille (free port)
CORSICA

Tariffs and Salt Tax

Area of common tariff since 1664; free trade within

Areas having provincial tariffs among themselves

Areas outside the national tariff system trading freely with foreign countries

Relative salt tax figures 27

part of north-central France without the payment of internal customs duties, but a duty had to be paid in order to penetrate into the rest of France, and more duties to move from one point in southern France to another. Finally, the boundaries of these fiscal, commercial, legal, judicial, and administrative jurisdictions never coincided, unless by accident.

A rational geometry now disciplined this jungle. With a greater thoroughness, and against heavier odds, the French outdid the simplicity of American administration. Sweeping away the accretions of tradition, prescription, habit, and chance, they divided the country into eighty-three *départements* of about equal size, subdivided the *départements* into uniform districts, and further divided the districts into communes. These three became the units of a homogeneous political, administrative, and even ecclesiastical system. The law, much simplified and made more coherent and humane, applied to all corners of the realm without distinction. Places were now "free and equal in rights," for otherwise men could not be free and equal.

As there was no room for privileged provinces, there was no room for guilds, private associations, secret organizations or orders, and, above all, secret government. The individual had rights, the government duties. According to the Declaration of the Rights of Man and of the Citizen, "society has a right to demand of any public official an accounting of his administration." This was a novel idea for the eighteenth-century monarchy. "Those who solicit, expedite, execute, or cause to be executed, arbitrary orders must be punished." The debates of the Constituent Assembly and of the Legislative Assembly were held in public, unlike those of the English Parliament of the day. The army was not to serve "the private convenience of those to whom it is entrusted," notably the king. It is significant that this needed to be spelled out. Sovereignty was declared to reside in the nation, and "no body, no individual, can exercise any authority that does not issue from it." The "king does not rule, save by the law."

In order to prevent the various parts of the government from combining to limit the rights of the individual, the executive, legislature, and judiciary were separated from one another, almost as sharply as in the Constitution of the United States. The king lost the power to declare war or to sign treaties, although he could negotiate international agreements and conduct foreign relations. He remained the chief central administrator and enforcer of the laws. As the head of the army and navy, he could appoint the higher officers, leaving most of the lower posts to be filled by promotion or election by fellow officers. His veto on legislation was suspensive, but stronger than that of the American president, since only the vote of three successive legislatures could prevail over it; this might mean a delay of anywhere from two to six years.

The power to make war, to sign treaties, and to initiate and frame laws was given to a unicameral Legislative Assembly. (After a sharp debate, a second chamber was rejected as "aristocratic," since in European states the upper house usually consisted of noblemen or appointees of the Crown.) This body had a broader base than the American federal and state legislatures and the

British House of Commons of that day; yet it was not elected democratically. In the "primary" assemblies, from which the poorest third of the population was excluded (and hence called "passive citizens"), adult males who had paid a small direct tax ("active citizens") elected both local officials and delegates to a "secondary" assembly. This secondary assembly, composed of the richer men, elected both the departmental officials and the deputies to the Legislative Assembly. But the property requirement for the deputies was lower than that for their electors—a bow to ability. Thus, supported by a broad base of the population, the men of wealth controlled power but shared leadership with the men of brains and cultivation. Among the careers opened to talent there was, notably, the political career.

The Rule of Equality and Fairness

Under the aristocratic Old Regime, social relations were tainted by cruelty and discrimination. The new society would be governed by the rule of fairness, even a fairness occasionally tinged with sentiment. The Revolutionary legislation attenuated the old distinctions between aristocrats and the nonprivileged, free men and serfs, Catholics and non-Catholics, natives and aliens, landlords and tenants, creditors and debtors, prosecutors and accused, and respectable professional men and those who earned their livelihood in "derogatory" pursuits. The Revolutionary broom also swept through the pre-eminences of family life, so seldom reviewed by a society—the superiority of men over women, of fathers over children, of old over young, and of legitimate over "natural" children and foundlings.

The new Constitution freed the citizen from all the old strait jackets:

> There is no aristocracy any more, nor peerage, nor hereditary distinction, nor distinction of orders, nor feudal system, nor patrimonial rule, nor any title, denomination or prerogative that derives from it, nor any knightly order, nor any corporation or decoration for which proofs of nobility used to be required, or which presumed distinctions of birth, nor any other superiority except that of public officials in the exercise of their duties.

Hereditary titles and privileges at one end, slavery and serfdom at the other, were abolished. Colonial slavery survived, but only until 1793. One of the greatest of privileges, that of avoiding or evading taxes, was ended; every person was now taxable in proportion to his means.

The native could henceforth emigrate if he wished to do so. The right of the king to inherit the property of aliens, which had fallen into disuse, was now formally abolished. The dishonesty of creditors and the vengeance of prosecutors were curbed. It had been customary to take the word of the creditor in preference to that of the debtor. Both were now equal before the law: the former had to present written evidence of the debt; the latter could not be   *111* imprisoned for failure or inability to pay. The burden of proof was placed upon the accuser and the prosecutor. Torture was abolished in all its various forms and for any purpose.

The Revolution dared the act which had tempted all the enlightened rulers. The Catholic Church continued to be the official church, but its vast holdings—estimated at 20 percent of the land of the country—as well as its buildings and tenements were "nationalized" by the Assembly in November 1789. In exchange, the state undertook to pay the salaries of the clergy. The Bishop of Autun, Charles Talleyrand (1754-1838), who had proposed "nationalization," estimated that after paying clerical salaries the state would have a surplus of some two million pounds sterling a year. The Assembly also abolished the tithe and fees for religious services. Under the Civil Constitution of the Clergy of 1791, the clergy was made elective, as in the early days of Christianity. In the future the state was to defray the cost of educating the young, caring for the sick, and relieving the poor. The revolutionaries established the principle of universal education, in schools supported by the community, although the financial stringency and disorder of the time prevented the immediate realization of this goal.

The church was bereft of its control over thought and printing. No longer were non-Catholics, whether Protestants, Jews, or nonbelievers, subject to civil and legal disabilities. The registry of births, marriages, and deaths was transferred in 1792 from the priests to clerks of the state. As people were born equal, so they were to die: the distinction between different types of funerals, at graduated fees, was ended. The status of the clergyman was changed by the assertion of equality: he could now own and inherit property and, if he wished, could leave the Church and marry. The monk and nun could quit their orders at will and re-enter society: they were rather encouraged to do so. No vow, no contract, no obligation was any longer to be regarded as "eternal."

With a noble impatience, the Constituent Assembly gave a new law to the family and tried to recall it to love. Marriage became a simple civil contract between two equal and independent parties. Like any contract, it could be terminated. Divorce was at last possible, and on seven different grounds. The father's power, especially the power that he exercised from beyond the grave, was much diminished: no children could be wholly disinherited. If a man died intestate, all his heirs would share equally, women as well as men. The position of the illegitimate child was improved somewhat. Even the young aristocrat shared in the gains of the Revolution. The rebellious son was no longer at the mercy of the rich and influential father, who, under the Old Regime, might even imprison him, virtually at will, with the aid of the infamous *lettres de cachet*.

The emancipation of women was begun, although it could not, in the circumstances and habits of the time, be carried very far. A woman could henceforth become a party to a contract. A wife could own property in her own right. Her children by a former husband preserved their rights in her inheritance. The authority to consent to the marriage of minors passed from the father to a council of the nearest relatives, female as well as male. Like the state, the family became parliamentary.

There were no more "derogatory" professions; the actor, for example, could now marry legally. The Jew no longer paid the same toll as a pig wherever he went. It had been considered a privilege to be executed by decapitation, a disgrace—reserved to the lower orders—to be hanged; the distinction was erased. The Revolution, in abolishing torture, insisting on kind and rational treatment of the insane, and trying to lessen pain and suffering in general, showed a high charity.

The Emancipation of Property and Ability

The emancipation of ideas and men was complemented by the emancipation of property and ability, goods and services. To the free forum was added the free market.

Under the Old Regime, ownership had been overlaid by a medley of overlapping rights and claims. Land property, for example, whether in the hands of tenants, sharecroppers, or owners, was subject to the "superownership" of the seigneur, who had heavy claims when property changed hands through death, marriage, or sale. The seigneur and the family had the right to retrieve property sold to an "outsider" at the price he had paid. Gifts of property were suspect, and mortgaging was not altogether free.

Henceforth property was to be mobile. It was tied exclusively to one individual. No one else, no institutional group or rule, could influence its use or disposition. The owner could dispose of it at will. Purchase, sale, and gifts were now final. Tenancy, sale, transfer, mortgaging, gifts, and inheritance were freed of all exterior conditions, fees, reversions, and claims; they were subject to the simple conditions of sale, rent, payment, and public record. The emancipation of the mortgage was especially noteworthy, for it meant that the owner of land or buildings could now "liquefy" them, obtaining credit and beginning to share in the advantages of investment and speculation. The fixed property of France took wing in the brisk air of enterprise.

The farmer could now fence in his fields, extinguishing the traditional right of the other villagers to graze their cattle on them after harvest or in fallow seasons. If his land abutted on a river, the shore line was his and not, as of old, the seigneur's or the king's. The owner could keep out the aristocratic hunter, even after the crops were gathered. In short, he owned the land fully and everything on it—even the fruit of his neighbor, if it happened to fall on his land.

Neither guild nor government could any longer inhibit the production, supervise the quality, or control the price of goods. Commodities were no longer bowed down by a burdensome variety of local imposts, held up at the gate of towns for the old *octroi*, or impeded in their movements from region to region by internal customs duties. Profit from loans—the "usury" of old—became as legal as rent from land, under the less repulsive name of "interest." The National Assembly provided for uniform weights and measures, but it was left to the National Convention to implement this decision by adopting the metric system in 1793. Eventually this system was introduced by most countries of the Western world, with the significant exception of England. The United States adopted it only for money measures.

Professions, offices, crafts, and occupations were thrown open to all men "without distinction of birth." Advancement was to depend only on individual "virtue and talent." The creations of the mind and imagination, the stake of the writer, composer, or inventor in his product, were protected by new copyrights and patents, made temporary in character so as to preserve the interests of society. The entrepreneur in business and industry was protected equally against monopoly and against the combination of his employees.

Economic emancipation was to serve the aim of a more fertile exploitation of material resources and human energies, a greater production of goods and services, and greater consumption of goods and enjoyment of exertion. The French Revolutionaries, in common with liberals and democrats on both sides of the Atlantic, believed unshakably in the principle of private property. In that age no responsible or influential group seriously advocated communism or socialism. What was then called the "agrarian law"—that is, the proposal of a general redistribution of the land among all the people—did not receive much support even among radicals.

But this does not exhaust the social view of the Revolutionaries. It was felt rather generally, and not only by advanced reformers, that more men, as many men as possible, perhaps most men, should have an opportunity to acquire at least a modest competence and property. The importance of this conviction may be appreciated if it is recalled that the men of that time regarded educational, political, professional, and other opportunities in life as dependent upon the possession of such a competence. In short, the "natural right" to property was interpreted by many leaders to mean not only the security and preservation of private property but also a broadened opportunity for acquisition. It was hoped that a number of laws in various fields, such as inheritance, would operate in the direction of diminishing the distance between the extremes of riches and poverty and would thus tend to produce a relative and flexible equality.

Much was done to make property more mobile, to place it in more hands, and in hands that could not hold on to it forever and under all circumstances—in short, to release it from the grasp of permanent corporations and foundations and to turn it over to mortal individuals. The greatest single corporation was the Church; its greatest beneficiaries, the small group of leading and aristocratic ecclesiasts. These economic and social as well as political considerations led to the "nationalization" of the property of the Church. In the spring of 1790 the properties of the Crown were also nationalized. King, bishop, and abbot had been great landlords; they now became salaried employees of the state. Two years later, the properties of the more defiant among the emigré aristocrats were seized, without any compensation.

The new laws were designed to prevent indefinite accumulations and the growth of idle and frozen properties. It was provided, for example, that owners must actually put their land to use; that leases were to be limited to three lives, or ninety-nine years, at the most; that there were to be no clerical or other "eternal" foundations; that no charge or obligation was to be created which could not be reversed or ended by reimbursement or purchase.

The immediate occasion of the confiscations, as of the Revolution itself, was the condition of the treasury. The state issued notes (*assignats*) which the buyers could present as payment for Church and Crown lands and buildings. The hope was that the state debts would be paid with the money received for *assignats* and the notes thereupon destroyed. At first the larger holdings were broken up into moderate-sized units and the terms of payment were easy—12 percent down and twelve years in which to pay the rest. Smaller farmers and tenants were able, sometimes by pooling their funds, to get a foothold on the land or to increase their holdings, while richer men also gathered in property; only the cash-poor tenants and laborers could not make hay while this brilliant sun shone. With so much property thrown on the market, land values in general dropped sharply. It was a buyers' holiday. By 1791, however, the *assignats* had been overissued and their value had dropped—but the treasury was still ravenous. The easy policy of the preceding few years was sacrificed; estates were sold in larger units, the terms of payment tightened, the down payments increased, and the number of years of settlement extended. The middle group of the population—landlords and burghers—and the rich, of course, were placed in a better position for extending their properties. Altogether, during this period perhaps one third of the fixed property of the country passed into private hands.

Land Reform

There was another, more direct, way in which the farmers were benefited, and this time the farmers as a whole. Under the Old Regime, the privileged groups had not only avoided their duty to contribute to the support of the state but had levied what was in effect a huge tax upon the bulk of the population, a tax so enormous that it made or kept them extraordinarily rich while forcing millions of others to live in the direst poverty. This was composed of a varied complex of dues, rents, services, payments in kind, and gifts on holidays or other special occasions that the occupier traditionally owed to the seigneur, regardless of whether the occupier was a serf or a freeman, a tenant, a sharecropper, or an "owner." Relatively few Frenchmen were still serfs—their number in the eighteenth century has been estimated at about one million—and they were generally concentrated in the northeast areas, recently acquired from German princes. But most of the land had been classified as "servile," on the clever rule which the barons of old had imposed: *nulle terre sans seigneur* (no land without a lord). This was the core of what was called the "feudal system" in the village, and sometimes "real serfdom" to distinguish it from personal servitude. The Declaration of August 4 abolished personal serfdom without compensation and declared real serfdom redeemable at a rate to be fixed later. But the opening statement of the Declaration read: "the feudal system is entirely abolished." This pledge; the difficulty of distinguishing fair contractual rents from traditional and arbitrary payments; the difficulty of producing written documents to validate a just obligation and prove a mutual agreement; the conviction of the peasants, despite all enactments, that the land ought to belong to them without conditions; their realization that the collapse of effective authority provided a golden opportunity to assert that conviction; and, finally, their sporadic uprisings whenever the Assembly debated the terms of redemption—all these combined to turn the Declaration into an effective, if not a formal, act of abolition of all traditional payments whatever.

The position of the small farmers, who accounted for a third of the agricultural population, and of the tenants and sharecroppers, who accounted for another third (the rest were laborers), was improved and consolidated. At a time when most Continental farmers remained in thralldom and the enclosure movement was gradually divorcing the English farmer from landownership and from the land itself, the French farmer, like the American, struck root in the moderate holding. The American had an enormous advantage, of course, in the availability of unoccupied land on the frontier. During the American struggle for independence, the rules of entail and primogeniture were either weakened or abolished in the several states, with the result that in the settled areas many a large estate was pulverized or thrown upon the market. In France, the confiscations and *assignat* sales and the laws guaranteeing every child a share in his father's estate had similar effects. The Revolution "Americanized" the French farmer.

In another respect, also, the American and French Revolutions are similar in their implications. With extraordinary luck, extraordinary ability, a small family, and great shrewdness, sagacity, and calculation, a Frenchman, like an American, might still attain sizable and even considerable wealth. Whether large or small, private possession was to be secure; the state, American and French alike, promised never to confiscate it. Nevertheless, the tendency of much of the legislation was to narrow the gap between the very rich and the very poor, or at least to create a considerable class of middling men, principally on the land.

Such was the work of the National Assembly in the relatively brief span between June 1789 and September 1791, when its Constitution went into effect and a new legislature was elected. By establishing the free market, the Assembly benefited the consumer and enriched the enterpriser. It left political leadership in the hands of the rich, the trained, and the able. But by multiplying the opportunities of craft, calling, and profession, by stimulating the extension of educational opportunities, by bringing the possession of property within the reach of a considerable part of the population, and, above all, by abolishing invidious distinctions in the family and society as well as in the political forum and the state, the Assembly benefited all Frenchmen—indeed, all men everywhere. It raised man to a new stature and dignity. That is the reason for the enthusiasm with which the Revolution was carried out at home and was received at first, abroad, and for the admiration, almost the veneration, in which it has been held since by disinterested men. The contemporary philosophe Condorcet summed up, in somewhat exaggerated terms, the difference between the two revolutions of the eighteenth century:

> The Revolution in France was more far-reaching than that in America... for the Americans, who were content with the civil and criminal code that they had received from England; who had no vicious system of taxation to reform; and no feudal tyrannies, no hereditary distinctions, no rich, powerful, and privileged corporations, no system of religious intolerance to destroy, limited themselves to establishing a new authority in place of that which had been exercised up till then by the British. None of these innovations affected the ordinary people or changed the relations between individuals. In France, on the contrary, the Revolution was to embrace the entire economy of society, change every social relation, and find its way down to the furthest links of the political chain, even down to those individuals who, living in peace on their private fortune or on the fruits of their labor, had no reason to participate in public affairs.

It was the sweep and thoroughness of the French Revolution that distinguished it from the American and accounts for its singular fame.

6. *War and Democracy*

The first steps of France toward freedom were received everywhere with a pleased astonishment. The fall of the Bastille in particular became the symbol of the death of the Old Regime. The English Whig leader Charles James Fox pronounced it "the greatest and best event that had ever happened." Englishmen and Americans were flattered that France had paid their own revolutions the compliment of imitation. Enlightened men, and particularly the young, were enthusiastic. At nineteen, the Romantic poet William Wordsworth (1770-1850) felt that it was

> Bliss. . . in that dawn to be alive
> But to be young was very heaven!—O times,. . .
> When Reason seemed the most to assert her rights. . . .
> When most intent on making of herself
> A prime enchantress. . .
> Not favored spots alone, but the whole earth
> The beauty wore of promise. . . .

Before long, however, public opinion became divided. The removal of the French King and Queen from Versailles to Paris, the nationalization of the property of the Church, the democratic tendency of some of the new laws and codes, the emigration of aristocrats and priests—such developments provoked a sharp and prolonged controversy over the Revolution.

The Great Debate

Edmund Burke, who had defended the American revolutionists, initiated the controversy in 1790 with a slashing attack on all efforts to refashion society and polity according to a rational plan. His *Reflections on the Revolution in France* pictured society and polity, not as mechanisms or instruments, subject to change by human will, but as living organisms of which institutions, customs, religion, and hierarchy of classes are integral parts. Society, Burke contended, cannot be improved by being dissected into parts and dealt with piecemeal or by being treated as a logical scheme. The social contract is not an agreement between people and rulers about methods of government.

> . . . It is a partnership in all science, a partnership in all art, a partnership in every virtue and in all perfection. As the ends of such a partnership cannot be obtained in many generations, it becomes a partnership not only between those who are living, but between those who are living, those who are dead, and those who are to be born. Each contract of each particular state is but a clause in the great primeval contract of eternal society, linking the lower with the higher natures, connecting the visible and invisible world, according to a fixed compact sanctioned by the inviolable oath which holds all moral natures each in their appointed place. . . .

To Burke, a revolution was a fatal rending of the relations that hold the social organism together and the vital links that bind the present to the past and to the future. Every country ought to continue its old institutions, which embody its collective and accumulated wisdom. Only small and peripheral reforms should be made, and not even these when the political atmosphere is unquiet and puts a premium upon change.

The *Reflections* became the "manifesto of the counterrevolution." It ran through many editions and was praised by monarchs and princes. It provoked a war of ideas: dozens of writers rushed to the defense of revolutions in general, and of the French Revolution in particular.

Perhaps the most cogent reply to Burke was the *Vindiciae Gallicae* (1791) of Sir James Mackintosh (1765-1832), a Scottish philosopher and historian. History, Mackintosh pointed out, belied Burke's theory that tranquil and gradual methods were responsible for true reform:

> Whatever excellence, whatever freedom is discoverable in governments, has been infused in them by the shock of a revolution, and their subsequent progress has been only the accumulation of abuse. . . . Whatever is good ought to be pursued at the moment it is attainable. . . . No hope of great political improvement. . . is to be entertained from tranquility, for its natural operation is to strengthen all those who are interested in perpetuating abuse.

"Where would be the atrocious guilt of a great experiment," asked Sir James, "to ascertain the portion of freedom and happiness that can be created by political institutions?"

More popular was the reply of the pamphleteer whose *Common Sense* had been the bugle call of the American revolutionists. Thomas Paine dedicated *The Rights of Man* (1791) to George Washington, who had assumed the presidency of the United States at about the time the French Revolution broke out. In it he expressed the hope that the "principles of freedom" asserted in America

might become universal and that the New World might "regenerate [the] Old."
If monarchies and aristocracies are essential to the well-being of nations, he
asked, why are Americans happier and more prosperous than Europeans? He
proposed a "triple republican alliance" of the United States, France, and Great
Britain.

Paine mocked a lachrymose passage in the *Reflections* in which Burke be-
wailed the humiliation of the Queen of France: "he pitied the plumage and
forgot the dying bird." He attacked Burke's argument from tradition:

> There never did, there never will, and there never can exist a parliament,
> or any description of men in any country, possessed of the right or the power
> of binding and controlling posterity to the "end of time," or of commanding
> forever how the world shall be governed, or who shall govern it. . . . Every
> age and generation must be free to act for itself, in all cases. . . .

Paine argued that "the error of those who reason by precedents. . . respecting
the rights of man, is that they do not go far enough into antiquity. . . ." If they
did they would come to the act of creation and discover that it was God who
had bestowed on man his "natural rights."

To Thomas Jefferson, Secretary of State in Washington's first administration, the French Revolution was "the most sacred cause that man was ever
engaged in." The American poet and pamphleteer Joel Barlow (1754-1812)
issued some practical *Advice to the Privileged Orders* (1792). The system of freedom,
he argued, would serve their future material interests as well as those of the
people at large. He assured them "that the establishment of liberty will be less
injurious to those who now live by abuses than is commonly imagined; that protected industry will produce effects far more astonishing than have ever been
calculated; that the increase of enjoyments will be such as to ameliorate the
condition of every human creature."

The debate over the French Revolution stimulated the activity of reformers
much more than the American war for independence had done. To Europeans,
France was a more apposite example than the United States. Western Europe
was astir with hopes for renovations similar to those which followed from the
events of 1789. The veterans and exiles of the recent Dutch, Belgian, and Swiss
revolutions became active again. In the United States, the bourgeoning distinction between conservatives and liberals—or Federalists and Republicans, as they
were called—was sharpened by the controversy. The reform societies that had
arisen in England during the struggle with America multiplied in number and
renewed their efforts for parliamentary reform. In England as elsewhere in the
Atlantic world, a pattern of popular agitation and pressure developed: pamphlets, leaflets, handbills, political cartoons, and petitions were printed and
distributed; posters were displayed; networks of political clubs and "corresponding societies" multiplied and exchanged ideas; open-air meetings and "national
conventions" were held and popular demonstrations took place in important
squares and before palaces and parliamentary buildings.

Response of the Powers to the Revolution

At first the war over the French Revolution was one of ideas alone. For the powers, although concerned over the growth of reform movements and active in repressing them, were pleased with the course of events in France herself. So long as France was disturbed within, her international influence might be discounted. Reckoning by past experience, the powers assumed that the Revolution could only weaken France. They proceeded to make hay. In 1790, for example, a controversy arose between Spain and Great Britain over Nootka Sound in Vancouver Island, off the Pacific coast of North America. Spain appealed for assistance to the French King, who was bound to her by alliance. The National Assembly took the opportunity to discuss the procedure of treaty-making and concluded that no treaty was valid without parliamentary sanction. In the circumstances, the British Prime Minister, William Pitt, was able to intimidate Spain into yielding her claims to the Sound, with its large possibilities for trade with the Far East. Nor was it unwelcome to the powers that, during this controversy, the French Assembly asserted that "the French Nation will refuse to undertake any war of conquest and will never employ its forces against the liberties of any people." Free from the prospect of French interference, Pitt toyed with the idea of a war to check the progress of Russia toward the Mediterranean Sea. Russia, Prussia, and Austria conspired, more effectively, to carve up the remainder of the Polish republic. The four did not exclude the possibility that, should France continue to be disturbed internally, she might also undergo an amputation.

Even though the powers did not intervene directly in France, they drifted, largely because of their depreciation of the Revolutionary government, into a concert with one of the most irresponsible parties in modern history. The French aristocrats had become so accustomed to social primacy and had been for so long removed from actual leadership that they had lost all sense of political reality. They could not command the Revolution, compromise with it, or deflect it. Their first instinct was to flee and return with an invading army. Upon each outburst of the Revolution—after the fall of the Bastille, after the march on Versailles—a wave of emigration spilled abroad. Finally it became a continuous flood. Conservative clerics, army officers, and politicians joined the aristocrats. It was estimated that by 1792 the emigration counted 50,000 of the leading men of the Right. The *émigrés* fell under the influence of the most reckless of their number. They plotted, raised troops, pressed foreign monarchs for aid, and offered territorial concessions in exchange. In the spring of 1791 they drew the French King into a plot to flee Paris, place himself at the head of a loyal army in the north, establish a rival government, and march on his refractory capital.

Louis had accepted the Revolution in form but not in spirit. After his forcible removal to Paris he regarded himself as a prisoner and, therefore, though   *121* an honest man, he did not feel bound by his word. It must be said that he gave plenty of evidence of his reluctance to become a constitutional ruler: he balked, equivocated, and intrigued. In June 1791, he and his family fled Paris in disguise and headed for the North, where troops and noblemen were waiting for them. The citizens of the village of Varennes, however, recognized Louis and escorted him back to Paris. For the first time, it was proposed to abolish the monarchy. The majority of the Assembly, however, preferred to revise the constitutional draft in a conservative direction, in order to make it palatable to the monarch. If the King could be brought to accept his position as a limited ruler, the new order would be preserved, on the one hand against the aristocratic party and on the other against the democratic forces that the Revolution was arousing. Few aspects of this fascinating story are more fascinating than the game between a simple-minded king who was coy and a revolutionary assembly which was legalistic.

On September 30, 1791, the King affixed his signature to the Constitution. The National Assembly dissolved itself, pronouncing the Revolution at an end, and the new regime was launched with the election of the Legislative Assembly as provided for in the Constitution.

Two months later Louis sent the following letter to the King of Prussia:

I have just written to the Emperor [Leopold II of Austria] and the kings of Spain and Sweden, to lay before them the idea of a congress of the chief European powers, supported by an armed force, as the best means of re-

THE NATIONAL ASSEMBLY PETRIFIED, AND THE NATIONAL ASSEMBLY REVIVIFIED.

1. BARBER—" De King is escape! de King is escape!"
2. COOK—"Aha! be gar, de King is retaken!! Aha! Monsieur Lewis is retaken, aha!!"

This lampoon by the English caricaturist James Gillray (1757-1815) sug-
gests the emotion that the French Revolution aroused in some of its British
opponents. Gillray is commenting on the flight of Louis XVI to Varennes in
June 1791 and his forced return to Paris.

establishing a more desirable order of things and preventing an evil which is harassing us from spreading to other European states.

The appeal fell on unwilling ears. The rulers would not intervene directly in French affairs, which, they thought, could not go too badly to suit their interests. Leopold II, who was connected with the French Bourbons by blood as well as alliance, was determined not to press matters to the point of war. He had little respect for the judgment of his sister, Queen Marie Antoinette, or his brother-in-law, or for the intrigues of the *émigrés*. He had already gone as far as he wished. After Louis' frustrated flight to Varennes, Leopold and the King of Prussia issued the Declaration of Pillnitz (August 27, 1791), expressing concern over the fate of the French king and his family and threatening to send an army into France, but only if other powers joined them, which was highly unlikely. This qualification did not diminish the outraged reaction in France.

The French Court then proposed to provoke foreign intervention by the simple means of declaring war on the powers whose aid it craved. It was to be a "little" war which would frighten France into supporting her King. If Louis lost it, he would be in the gentle hands of his royal colleagues. Louis wrote to his prospective "enemies":

> . . . The physical and moral state of France is such that it is impossible for her to carry on [this war] for half a campaign, but it is necessary that I should appear to enter upon it wholeheartedly, as I should have done in former times. . . . It is necessary that my course of action should be such that the nation may find its only resource in its troubles in throwing itself into my arms.

There never was a more naïve project. The prospect of war tempted revolutionary leaders for precisely the opposite reasons. Competing pressures were rising to pull the Revolution back and to push it forward. The Pope's refusal to sanction the Civil Constitution of the Clergy raised the threat of heresy and aligned many a priest and devout layman with the aristocratic party. Louis showed where his heart lay by vetoing a law to punish priests who refused to take the oath to the Constitution and another to confiscate the estates of *émigrés* who rejected a summons to return to France. Suspicious of the Court, popular groups in Paris voiced republican demands and redoubled their efforts to extend the Revolution in a democratic direction. There were again disorders in the countryside and demands for the abolition of the last remaining rents and charges of feudal landlordism.

A majority of the deputies of the newly elected Legislative Assembly believed that a war could unite the country and consolidate the Revolution. Prices were rising, and many moneyed men felt that economic instability could be ended only if the Revolution were recognized by the states of Europe—as would be the case if France were victorious in a war. A powerful group headed by the lawyer Brissot de Warville (1754-93) hoped to secure their own middle-ground position against the pressures of aristocrats and extreme democrats alike. A war which they directed, they believed, would align both King and country behind them and brand counterrevolutionaries as traitors. "A people which, after a thousand years of slavery, has achieved liberty needs war," Brissot declared. "It needs war to purge away the vices of despotism. It needs war to consolidate its freedom. It needs war to banish from its bosom the men who might corrupt its liberty." There were those who were eager to spread the blessings of liberty to "less happier lands," and many a foreign revolutionary who urged them on. In vain a sober minority protested. Maximilien Robespierre (1758-94), of Artois, warned that "armed missionaries are loved by nobody." Let France complete her revolution; other countries may make their own. "To whom," he asked, "would you entrust the conduct of this war? To the agents of the executive power? If so, you will be abandoning the safety of the empire to those who want to ruin you. . . . War is the very thing which we ought most to fear." Worst of all, if the war were successful, a victorious general would be likely to seize power and put an end to the Revolution.

The Brissot group, backed by the Assembly, brought matters to a head: it demanded of the Emperor of Austria that he repudiate the Declaration of Pillnitz. Meanwhile, on March 1, 1792, the cautious Leopold II died. His son and successor, Francis II (1792-1835), listened to bellicose ministers and returned a defiant refusal. On April 15 the Assembly thereupon declared war upon Austria and Prussia. Queen Marie Antoinette promptly betrayed the French plan of campaign to her nephew, the Emperor.

The Outbreak of the War and the Fall of the Monarchy

The war lasted, with few interruptions, for nearly a quarter century, shook all the monarchies of Europe, and destroyed many of the accomplishments of the Revolution. It disappointed the expectations of everybody concerned.

For France, the war began badly. Her army crossed the frontier into the Austrian Netherlands but melted away at the smallest resistance. Whole regiments disbanded or passed to the enemy; royalist officers deserted. The commanders wished to call off the campaign. Meanwhile, the King challenged the Assembly by vetoing a measure to establish an armed camp in order to defend the capital. On June 29, he tried to steal out of Paris in order to hear mass from a "nonjuring" priest—that is, one who had refused to take an oath to the Civil Constitution of the Clergy. When several thousand citizens burst into the palace to detain him, Louis toasted the health of the nation; but he persisted in his refusal to sanction the military measure. This "humiliation" of the monarch moved the commander of the Austro-Prussian army, the Duke of Brunswick, to issue a contemptuous threat that if any harm came to Louis he would level Paris to the ground.

Brunswick's declaration was the last straw. From many parts of France came the demand to depose a king beloved of the enemy. The Assembly failed to act with the speed and vigor that the compounded danger of invasion and treason called for, and what might have been a semilegal coup became the first planned revolution of modern times. The previous uprisings had been characterized by a certain spontaneity. Now insurrection was organized by a committee of five men unknown to fame, truly leaders of and from the populace, who were advised by such radical politicians as Robespierre and Georges Danton (1759-94). The ranks of the Parisians were swelled by several thousand provincial volunteers who were on their way to the front; notable among them was the contingent from Provence, which arrived singing the most famous of marching songs, the "Marseillaise."

During the night of August 9-10, 1792, the masses swept into the streets of Paris. The legal Commune yielded its position, without a struggle, to a new body representing the insurrectionists. While the Mayor of Paris assured the King that he had nothing to fear, the National Guard of the capital went over to the insurrection. In the morning, several thousand volunteers marched on the palace. Leaving its defense to the professional Swiss Guard, Louis sought refuge in the Legislative Assembly, which was meeting nearby. A fierce engagement broke out in the palace yard, in which most of the Swiss Guard and a much larger number of citizens laid down their lives. Nevertheless, the citizens prevailed. While the issue hung fire, the Assembly respected the royal office, but when the victorious populace streamed into the hall, the Assembly, still refusing to depose Louis, "suspended" him from office. It abrogated the Constitution of 1791, under which he had reigned, and called for the election, early in September, of a new Constitutional Convention.

The disillusionment of the politicians who had hoped that the war would unite the country in support of the settlement of 1791 (and, incidentally, in support of their leadership) was only slightly less profound than that of the Court. For, having given up the Constitution of 1791, the moderate majority of the Assembly was helpless to resist the wave of democracy. For the first time in any modern state, not excepting the young American republic, the masses were invested with effective sovereignty: the new Convention was to be elected by universal male suffrage. Only the aristocrats were disfranchised, together with their servants, on the ground that the lackey outsnobs the master.

The agrarian reform was now completed, and the peasants were attached to the Revolution. The last remaining feudal rents and charges, which in 1789 had been declared redeemable against compensation to the landowners, were abolished without payment. They were to be honored only if the owners produced written evidence of liability—a feat that few of them could perform. The "common lands" of the village were divided among the inhabitants. The confiscated lands of the *émigrés* were to be parceled out in moderate lots and sold on easy terms.

The established church lost no less than the aristocracy and the monarchy. The nonjuring priests were ordered out of the country: some 25,000 clergymen left. The remaining religious orders were dissolved.

Austria and Prussia were still to be disillusioned, but they did not have to wait long. Since their eyes were turned to the East, where a second partition of

Poland was impending, they had been slow to begin their campaign against the French and used a small army. Although the war broke out in April 1792, it was nearly mid-August before they crossed the border. They advanced rapidly against a disintegrating royal army. By the end of the month, the Austro-Prussian army had taken the strategic fortresses of Longwy and Verdun, and the road to Paris lay open.

The crisis of the Revolution was at hand. On September 2 the news of the fall of Verdun threw Paris into panic. Enraged and frightened citizens, unrestrained by the government, broke open the prisons and put to death more than a thousand prisoners, with the barest appearance of justice, in the so-called September Massacres. The Commune closed the gates of the city and organized battalions of volunteers for the front. For the next few weeks volunteers left the city at the rate of 1800 men a day. The Assembly decreed the death penalty for citizens who refused to serve or to contribute arms.

At the front, loyal officers experimented with novel tactics. Professional troops were scarce, and the raw recruits were not experienced enough to stand firm at the cannonade with which the attacker in the eighteenth century opened battle. A simple stratagem became the germ of the modern cadre army. The ranks of the volunteers were stiffened with seasoned professionals. This alternation of the two kinds of soldier combined discipline with revolutionary fervor. The test came on September 21. At Valmy, thirty miles north of Paris, the military amalgam stood its ground in the face of a cannonade of the Prussian army. Surprised—and, incidentally, suffering from scurvy—the invaders turned and took the road back.

The French Republic and the First Coalition

On the same day, and before the news of the victory of Valmy had reached Paris, the new Convention met and proclaimed a republic. Conceived in defeat, the First French Republic was born with victory perching on her banners.

One of the staunchest assemblies in history, the Convention combined legislative and executive with constituent functions. It consisted of 750 deputies, principally lawyers, journalists, teachers, and other professional men, and some businessmen and landowners. Liberal nobles at one end and workers and peasants at the other counted but a handful of deputies. Gone were the large ranks of aristocrats and clergy of the National Assembly.

One can hardly speak of anything so coherent in organization and program as parties. The two leading groups were the Girondins and the Jacobins, each of which could count on the support of a fluctuating minority of some 200 deputies. The Girondins stood for freedom of political expression and action, for the inviolability of property rights, and for freedom of trade, of enterprise, and even of financial speculation. Since these policies found support among commercial elements, the Girondins drew close to them. Most of the Girondins hailed from the provinces and therefore preferred a federalistic to a centralized government.

Their rivals were members of the Society of Friends of the Constitution, formed in 1789. Their popular name derived from an old Jacobin monastery which the Society used for its meetings. Jacobin clubs had multiplied and spread to every corner of the country; their membership, originally quite select, had become larger. The Jacobin deputies and leaders had cooperated with popular groups in the rising of August 10 and, without developing a systematic doctrine, had become accustomed to making concessions in the direction of democracy and egalitarianism. They were willing to improvise novel measures. They used the network of Jacobin clubs to integrate the efforts of the country and place it under the leadership of Paris.

Between the Jacobins and the Girondins lay the more or less inchoate "Plain" of the Convention. About as large as, and sometimes larger than, the other two groups combined, the Plain was ill defined politically and less capable of leadership. It was opposed to a return to an unreconstructed Old Regime but was otherwise conservative in tendency. It favored a moderate regime equally removed from aristocracy and equalitarian democracy. The decisions of the Convention, especially when the Girondins and the Jacobins disagreed, rested with the Plain. Domestic policies, however, waited upon the outcome of the war.

Valmy was the prelude to a victorious military campaign. By October France was cleared of invaders. The government was then faced with the decision whether the revolutionary armies were to go on to the Netherlands— or beyond—and whether the French should assist the liberals of adjoining countries to imitate their reforms. For a time the Convention hesitated. Robespierre, the leader of the Jacobins, had opposed the war to begin with and now opposed the advancement of reform through conquest or the justification of conquest by reform. "To give laws is to conquer," and conquest had been abjured. He warned against "the danger of starting all over again with the Belgians the painful and bloody struggle which we had to carry on with our own priests."

But there were leaders—notably the Girondin Brissot—and military men who were tempted by imperial stakes. Besides, who was to pay for the war if the armies could not lay their hands on the riches of the nobility and the Church in occupied countries, particularly those lying close at hand in the Austrian Netherlands? Foreign sympathizers were eager to welcome the French as liberators, fearing that their peoples could not or would not imitate the French of their own will. Some of them came to Paris, where they urged the Convention to spread the revolution by the sword. Dutch, Belgian, and Swiss rebels were particularly impatient.

Fired by the victory of Jemappes on November 6, 1792, which secured the Austrian Netherlands, the Convention declared on November 19 that it would "grant fraternity and assistance to all peoples desirous of recovering their liberty" and charged "the executive power to give the generals the necessary orders to bear aid to these peoples and defend their citizens who have been or may be molested in the cause of liberty." On December 15 the Convention instructed its generals abroad to abolish tithes, serfdom, and feudal dues; to hold elections for new administrative bodies; and to set aside the property of rulers and of religious corporations and orders as backing for *assignats*, which must be accepted as legal tender.

Thus the Revolution became European. French armies occupied the Austrian Netherlands and the principal cities of the Rhineland, where they encouraged and enforced liberal revolutions. Confiscations of clerical properties yielded much-needed treasure. Revolutions broke out spontaneously in Savoy and Nice, and France was invited by native liberals to incorporate those territories, then subject to the King of Sardinia, into her own realm. Avignon, the Pope's enclave in France, had been thus absorbed in the preceding year.

This forward policy stimulated the demands of reformers elsewhere in Europe, and the activities of the governments against them. But neither the danger of domestic discontent nor the propaganda war declared by the Convention aroused the powers so much as the exhibition of armed strength. The French victories of the autumn posed an unexpected threat.

No power was more sensitive to this threat than Great Britain. Ever since 1789, the government of William Pitt the Younger had pursued a calculated policy of nonintervention. As late as October 1792, after the French King had been "suspended," the Republic proclaimed, and many aristocrats massacred, Pitt still predicted a long period of peace. But in the next month, when the

James Gillray's satire on the methods by which the French revolutionaries brought liberty to foreign lands. It ignores the fact that French reforms were usually welcomed by the population of conquered countries. The man feeding John Bull from the right is Charles James Fox (1749-1806), British Whig leader and friend of the French Revolution. PRINT ROOM, NEW YORK PUBLIC LIBRARY

French armies swept into the Austrian Netherlands, he became alarmed. Holland might fall next, and with it the strategic estuary of the Rhine, Meuse, and Scheldt rivers. The sealing of the Scheldt to navigation had become a symbolic condition of the commercial prosperity and imperial security of Great Britain and Holland. These countries had provided for the closing of the river mouth in various international treaties to which France was a party. The French revolutionaries now gave an old controversy a new turn: they proposed to reopen the Scheldt, contending that sailing down a river to the sea was one of those "natural rights" in whose name they had recast so many institutions. (The issue was essentially the same as the one the Americans were contending for in seeking from Spain a guarantee that their ships and goods could move freely out from the Mississippi past New Orleans into the open waters.) A few years earlier, Great Britain, then at loggerheads with Holland, had encouraged Emperor Joseph II in his efforts to force open the mouth of the Scheldt. But the maritime potentialities of the Austrian Empire were not impressive. France was a different case, and Pitt now invoked against her the sanctity of the treaties to which she was a party. Only an occasion for war was needed. This was provided by the trial of Louis XVI.

The disposal of a dethroned ruler is a delicate problem. A monarch cannot retire into obscure privacy. If he is permitted to go abroad he might become the center of conspiracy and return with foreign help. He cannot properly be tried, for in monarchical states the law itself speaks in his name. Since loyalty is defined as loyalty to the king, how can a king be a traitor?

However, the Constitution of 1791, which followed custom in declaring the king inviolable and his ministers responsible for his official acts, also contained this suggestive provision:

> If the King place himself at the head of an army and turn its forces against the nation, or if he does not explicitly manifest his opposition to any such enterprise carried out in his name, he shall be considered to have abdicated his royal office,

On November 2, 1792, a secret iron chest was discovered in the palace, containing correspondence of the King with foreign Courts in which he asked for assistance to punish his own subjects. The correspondence revealed deeper intrigues and conspiracies than Louis had been considered capable of; it convicted him of a mixture of ingenuousness and cunning. In January 1793, Louis was tried for treason by the Convention sitting as a court. He denied the jurisdiction of the court, as Charles I of England had done a century and a half earlier: subjects could not try sovereigns. "A subject and a sovereign," Charles had said on the scaffold, "are clean different things." But even if Louis were convicted of leading an army against his own country, the constitutional penalty was only abdication.

The Jacobins insisted that Louis and the Revolution could not both survive. One of them must die. "Cruel necessity," Cromwell is said to have muttered at the bier of his King. Robespierre also appealed from law to political necessity: *129*

> A dethroned king in a Republic can only serve one of two purposes: to disturb the tranquility of the state and upset liberty, or else to establish both of them firmly at the same time. ... Now, what course of action does a sane policy dictate with a view to consolidating the infant Republic? It is to stamp indelibly upon our hearts a contempt for royalty and to paralyze all the partisans of the King. ...

Brissot, speaking for the Girondins, proposed in vain the compromise of submitting the verdict to a popular plebiscite; he warned that the Convention was not keeping "Europe sufficiently in view." But the Jacobins did not appreciate the fact that Louis' death might weaken the Republic abroad as much as it would strengthen it at home. Robespierre retorted that the Girondins, only a few months earlier, had "provoked the war and hailed the progress of revolutionary ideas." The vote, on January 17, was 361 for execution, 72 for a death sentence accompanied by a reprieve, and 288 scattered votes for imprisonment, exile, or death in case of invasion. This gave a clear majority of *one* in favor of execution. A second vote of 380 to 310 rejected a reprieve.

On January 21, 1793, the King of France was guillotined in the Place de la Révolution in the presence of thousands of his subjects. (His queen was executed nine months later.) "We will throw down the head of a King as a gage of battle," Danton exclaimed. The gage was picked up with a fury that was to outlast Danton's generation. Great Britain, already resolved upon a rupture, dismissed the French envoy; the Convention replied to this action with a declaration of war. Spain and Sardinia then declared war on France. With Great Britain, these states joined Austria and Prussia to form the First Coalition, thus surrounding France with enemies. Nearly all the other states of Europe severed

The executioner showing the head of King Louis XVI in the Place de la Révolution, later named Place de la Concorde. Some of the soldiers and civilians are cheering. From Les Principales Journées de la Révolution, *engravings by Helman after the drawings of Monnet, Paris, 1838.* SPENCER COLLECTION, NEW YORK PUBLIC LIBRARY

Queen Marie Antoinette of France, hands bound, in the tumbrel on the way to the guillotine. Jacques Louis David (1748-1825), the official painter of the revolutionary government and later of Napoleon, was a witness to the scene and caught in this sketch the unbending pride of the Queen. LOUVRE

diplomatic relations with France. The United States had been allied to France since the struggle for independence. George Washington's conservative Secretary of the Treasury, Alexander Hamilton, argued that the alliance was no longer valid; the liberal Secretary of State, Thomas Jefferson, insisted that it was. It was agreed, however, that for the moment neutrality was the only practical course. The isolation of France was complete. The duel between conservative Europe and the Revolution had begun.

The Jacobin Commonwealth

The struggle was joined both within and without France. In the spring of 1793, the armies of the First Coalition expelled the French from the Netherlands and the Rhineland. They pierced the French border at a half dozen points and penetrated deeply into France: English, Prussian, and Austrian troops in the northeast, Sardinian in the southeast, Spanish in the southwest. Simultaneously domestic tensions snapped. Opposition to the religious legislation and to the military draft burst into flames in the districts of the Vendée, in the west. The opposition of upper-middle-class groups and moderate liberals to the radical proceedings of the Convention broke out into open rebellion in some of the largest cities of the country—Lyons, Marseilles, Bordeaux, and Toulon, the principal naval base in the Mediterranean. Foreign war and civil

131

strife became one. The Vendée rebels received aid from the British, and Toulon was turned over to a British fleet by the insurrectionary leaders. In March and April, three armies of rebels set out for Paris, determined to make an end of the government of the Convention.

The greatest crisis of the Revolution was at hand. The authority of the Convention had been repudiated in important areas, the administration had been decentralized by the first Constitution, the machinery of government had been shaken by the almost constant changes of personnel. It was imperative to enlarge and inspirit the army, to tighten the grip of the government upon the country, and to repress the enemy within. Extraordinary measures were needed, but they were likely to play havoc with liberty and normal politics and trade.

Many Girondins shrank from these measures. Their supporters in the provinces had added to their difficulties. Bordeaux, capital of the Gironde, whence some of their principal leaders came, had rebelled against the radical actions of the Convention and against the dominating influence of the people of Paris. The Jacobins were less inhibited. They were ready to meet the crisis on its own terms. Only they were in a position, because of their past record, to make the ultimate appeal to the people at large to save the state. This was acknowledged by the support they received from the Plain in the Convention.

First the Jacobins obtained control of the Commune of Paris. Then, on June 2, 1793, Commune troops beleaguered the Convention hall. In the presence of a large number of citizens who had swept into the hall to watch the proceedings, the Convention suspended thirty-two Girondin deputies. It set up executive committees endowed with unusual powers and elected the same small group of Jacobins to serve on them. The broadest discretion and decree powers for punishing the enemies of the Republic were vested in the Committee of General Security and, for administration and the conduct of the war, to the all-important Committee of Public Safety. Special tribunals were established for the rapid trial of suspects. It is estimated that some 20,000 persons were executed during this "Reign of Terror," which lasted for more than a year.

The Committee of Public Safety, led at first by Danton and then by Robespierre, galvanized the energies of the country. It remained responsible to the Convention, which invested it with the duty of accelerating and supervising the action of ministers and officials and of taking, "under urgent circumstances, measures of external and internal defense." The Committee stirred the local authorities into action, coordinated their activities with the decisions of the Convention, and punished laggards and traitors. The urgency of the moment precluded considered and gentle pressure, and individual agents committed hysterical and even barbarous acts. The principal task was military. The famous decree of August 23, 1793, the *levée en masse*, ordered a draft of the whole population: "Young men will go to the front; married men will forge arms and transport foodstuffs; women will make tents and clothes and will serve in the hospitals; children will tear rags into lint; old men will get themselves carried to public places, there to stir up the courage of the warriors, hatred of the kings, and unity in the Republic." Unmarried men between the ages of 18 and 25 streamed into the army. The new recruits were "amalgamated," as before, with professional and experienced soldiers. Able subaltern officers who could not hope to rise to high rank in the old army faced golden professional opportunities.

These drastic measures were seconded by an elaborate apparatus of extra-official action. Thousands of Jacobin clubs throughout the country acted both directly and by exerting pressure upon local officials. They coordinated their action, taking their cue from the Jacobin Club of Paris. Jacobin leaders in the Convention kept in close touch with popular groups, particularly in Paris. On occasion, they encouraged massed demonstrations to apply pressure on the moderates of the Convention.

The partnership between the Jacobins in the government and the people was reflected not only in military and administrative measures but also in the social legislation of this year of emergency—in the regulation of the market, the promotion of agrarian democracy, and the passage of a host of measures designed to give reality to the "natural equality" of men. In order to protect the consumer in a period of scarcity and inflated prices, the Jacobin government passed the "Law of Maximum" (September 17, 1793), limiting prices for necessaries. The fall of the currency was momentarily checked, and the profits of speculators and monopolists were curbed. Terroristic measures were directed against economic speculators as well as political enemies. The last vestiges of claims for the compensation of feudal charges were abolished. Local governments provided employment to needy persons.

Children and women, whose position had been improved by earlier legislation, were now raised to a plane of equality with that of their former superiors. Inheritance was to be divided equally among all heirs, not excluding illegitimate children. At the age of 25, an heir could claim his share and start on an independent course in life. A young woman could marry against the wishes of her parents. In specifying grounds for divorce, the law no longer discriminated against women.

The Convention abandoned the old Gregorian calendar, with its saints' days and religious holidays. It decreed a new calendar, in which the year was divided into twelve months of equal length, with three ten-day "weeks" in each. There was one day of rest in ten, instead of seven, days, but the five or six days left over at the end of the twelve equal months were a prolonged holiday. The months had "natural" names: Vendémiaire, month of vintage; Brumaire, month of fog; etc. The Christian era was replaced by the new revolutionary era: the numbering of the years began with the autumnal equinox (September 22) of 1792—incidentally, the day after the proclamation of the Republic. The Convention severed the relations of the state with the Catholic Church. It asserted simply that the French people acknowledged the existence of a Supreme Being and the immortality of the soul.

The first thoroughly democratic constitution of a large country—if we except the constitutions of several American states—was adopted by the Convention on June 22, 1793, and was sent to the primary assemblies for ratification, but its application was adjourned until the end of the military emergency. The

Constitution stresed local autonomy and entrusted the executive power to a committee of twenty-three men chosen by the departments, an interesting innovation.

Victory and the Retreat from Democracy

The measures of the Jacobins preserved the territorial integrity of France. By the autumn of 1793 the invaders were held; in the following spring, the French armies gained the offensive, recaptured the Austrian Netherlands, and occupied Nice and Savoy. For the middle classes the emergency was now over; for egalitarian democracy it was about to begin.

Although the democratic program had been largely improvised, some of the more radical Jacobin leaders proposed to carry it out to the end. This was notably true of Robespierre, who, during the critical period, had become the spokesman of the democratic forces. Robespierre was not a socialist, perhaps not even an advanced political democrat. Like other radicals of his time, he took for granted a society of private property and even social distinctions. But he did not like a government that catered to the special interests of the rich and the powerful. He wished to make it possible for the little man of country and town to obtain a moderate property. Since a general confiscation and repartition was not considered either feasible or fair, this leveling or egalitarian program could be carried out only indirectly, by curbing large-scale privileges and monopolies, whether in land, credit, capital, or power. It presupposed enlightened leadership close to the masses, but not necessarily of them.

A beginning had been made. But great temptations still beckoned to the shrewd and unscrupulous. One year under the emergency government of the Committee of Public Safety had hardly sufficed to extinguish the advantages of the upper classes of society and give secure foundations to the "Republic of Virtue." The strongest of measures had been invoked against the foreign enemies of the Republic; Robespierre believed that equally strong measures were needed to humble the enemies of social fairness and civic virtue.

For most members of the Convention, on the other hand, the end of the military emergency was the end of the need for concessions to democracy. Three events brought this difference of opinion to a head: the Ventôse decrees of March 3, 1794, providing for the distribution of the estates of *émigrés* to landless peasants; the passage of the Law of Suspects on June 10, which empowered the revolutionary tribunal to convict without hearing evidence; and the victory at Fleurus, in the Netherlands, on June 26, which disposed definitively of the threat of invasion. Members of the Convention who feared for their lives should the Law of Suspects continue in effect plotted with Jacobins who were jealous of Robespierre's ascendancy. On July 26 Robespierre made a speech demanding strong measures against corrupt politicians, including deputies, and refused to name names, thus sowing fear broadside. The next day—9 Thermidor by the revolutionary calendar—these groups stampeded the Convention into ordering his arrest. He hesitated too long in appealing to the poorer sections, and their little army eventually made a sad showing against the determined leadership and troops of the Convention. Robespierre was lost; on July 28 he and his closest collaborators were guillotined.

Robespierre has become the prototype of the fanatical dictator who sacrifices humanity on the altar of an *idée fixe*. If is difficult to do him justice. Robespierre was intelligent, able, and thoroughly honest, but he was also pedantic and doctrinaire. Above all, he shared with Rousseau a dangerous blend of stoicism, sentimentality, and doctrinal rigidity. If Rousseau was the man who thought he had discovered the magic formula for combining democracy with discipline and authority, Robespierre was the sorcerer's apprentice who tried to apply the formula. Neither man had Voltaire's gift of contemplating his own ideas with skepticism and humor. Hence the solemnity and literalness with which Robespierre adhered to doctrines, some of which, when carried to extremes, were contradictory and delusive. He despised militarism, yet prosecuted the war with the utmost determination. He loved the people, but allowed no consideration of humanity to deflect him from what he considered his civic duty. He was opposed in principle to the death penalty (before the Revolution he had resigned a judgeship rather than apply it), yet engaged in mass executions. He loved liberty, yet practiced intimidation and terror. Like Rousseau, he would force men to be free.

When Robespierre fell, the Convention faced the problem of dismantling the apparatus of emergency political and economic control and restoring a constitutional regime. Curiously enough, there were those who perceived no such problem, among them the Jacobins who had led the struggle against Robespierre. A "tyrant" had been removed—that was all; the emergency government could continue, with only this difference, that men could engage in politics with greater profit and safety to themselves.

The Thermidoreans, as the deputies who had brought about Robespierre's fall were known, were astonished to discover that the death of Robespierre was as significant to France as his life had been. His Jacobin opponents found that they could spare him less than they had thought: he had acquired a symbolic significance. His name had become so closely associated with the principles of the Revolution that his fall disheartened its adherents and inspirited the conservatives and even the royalists, who had brooded in helplessness for several years. It became difficult for the Jacobins to defend the emergency regime without seeming to vindicate its principal champion. The bourgeois Plain found its long-lost voice and pressed the advantage. Within a few months after the execution of Robespierre, radical judges were removed from the revolutionary tribunals, which were shorn of their power. The jurisdiction of the Committees of General Security and Public Safety was shrunk, and most of their functions were distributed among a dozen commissions, answerable to committees of the Convention. Then, through the introduction of a speedier rotation of members, the

135

Committees were purged of their radical members. Jacobins who had long sat on the Committee of Public Safety with Robespierre were shortly replaced by moderates. The stability and the continuity of the executive were much weakened.

Would the populace accept this assault upon its friends in the government? For the Thermidoreans in the Convention had yielded economic as well as political ground to the demand of the Plain. The Ventôse decrees, which had given the poor an opportunity to acquire land, were soon annulled; payment for attendance at district meetings, which had given them an opportunity to exert political influence, was discontinued. The most important concession wrung from the Thermidoreans was the repeal of the Law of Maximum in December 1794. Prices were once more allowed to find their competitive level, which meant, in that unsteady time, that they were allowed to increase rapidly. To meet the rising costs, the government printed *assignats* at an astronomical rate, and this caused further increases in the price of commodities. By the end of 1794 the *assignats* had lost two thirds of their purchasing power. Inflation was a runaway horse and the cost of living the helpless rider.

Into the bargain, the crops of 1794 had suffered from drought. The winter of 1794-95 proved most trying for the lower classes in towns, especially in the capital. People were literally dying of famine. Popular uprisings broke out in Paris in April 1795. The Convention could now count on fresh resources, however: with the support of the richer sections of Paris, it introduced regular troops into the city for the first time since 1789. The rebels of the radical district of St. Antoine were forced to capitulate.

The results of this popular defeat were decisive. The *assignats* were allowed to drop still further, and more freedom was granted to individual trade. A guerrilla campaign against the die-hard Jacobins broke out and was tolerated if not encouraged by the Convention. Some of its members, who were experienced in street warfare, organized and turned loose "gilded youth" of the old and *nouveaux riches* and like-minded bank and shop employees. In the provinces, such political gangs as the notorious "Companies of Jesus" were murdering Jacobins. The Reign of Terror had not ended; it had merely changed color. The "White Terror" of 1795 probably exacted as many victims as the "Red Terror" of 1793-94, without, however, the excuse of civil war and foreign invasion.

But the most lasting results of the defeat of the Jacobins were the dispersal of the cadres of the democrats and the dismantling of their mechanisms. The radical ranks were decimated, and renewed collaboration between politicians and the populace was made difficult and dangerous. Several leading Jacobins were deported to Oléron Island, off the Breton coast, despite the fact that none of them was involved directly in the risings; many a lesser Jacobin was treated more harshly.

The Jacobin clubs were forbidden to engage in concerted action, to correspond with one another, or to send delegations or collective petitions to the Convention. The autonomy of the Commune of Paris and those of other cities was abolished or reduced; the administration of the country was subordinated to the central government. The Paris Commune was forced to surrender its supply of cannon. Not until 1830 were the people of Paris to move again into the "forum" of the streets with political effect.

The Turn to Conservatism and Empire

Democracy was arrested, but the government was now menaced by the forces it had released. After Thermidor, the Convention had softened its attitude toward royalists and priests. Nobles returned surreptitiously, and royalist agents and journalists became active. Plot after plot was hatched to put an end to the Republic.

The Convention became increasingly conservative; a sizable group of its members was not disinclined to restore the monarchy, provided that the changes of the first years of the Revolution were retained. But the royalist leaders would make no concessions. On June 8, 1795, Louis XVII, the son of the executed king, died at the age of ten in a Paris prison. His uncle, the reactionary Count of Artois, assumed the succession with an intransigent declaration: upon being restored to the throne, he proposed to punish the regicide deputies, to re-establish a system of Estates, and to restore the position of the Church. That he would conclude a peace favorable to the enemies of France went without saying. The Convention, a majority of whose members had sent Louis XVI to the guillotine, could hardly hope for an agreement with such a Bourbon. For the Convention, then, and particularly for those members who had voted for Louis' execution, preserving the Republic and strengthening the position of France in Europe became matters of life or death.

The struggle against the royalist danger confirmed a turn toward an ambitious foreign policy which had been some time in preparation. In the spring of 1795, defeated in the field and weakened financially, Prussia, acting independently of her Coalition allies, proposed superficially tempting terms. She would withdraw from the war in order to assure herself a large share in the third and final division of Poland. She would assent to French control over the German states lying on the left bank of the Rhine, provided that she obtained compensation on the right bank for the small losses this concession would involve for her. She promised to prevent any North German state from attacking France, which implied French acquiescence in the hegemony of Prussia in North Germany. The effect of these terms would be to increase the enmity of Austria toward France, and thus to adjourn the prospects of a general peace; to commit France to a policy of meddling in and reorganizing Germany; and to compel her to abandon her interest in the affairs of Eastern Europe.

The Republic hesitated before these dangerous possibilities. Although there were many who counseled moderation, their pleas were weakened by the activities of the royalists, who agitated in favor of a humiliating retreat before the powers. Finally, on March 5, 1795, France accepted Prussia's terms and concluded the Treaty of Basel.

137

The First Coalition crumbled with the defection of Prussia and that of several smaller German states. In the autumn, in another treaty concluded at Basel, Spain ceded San Domingo to France. Her failure in the war against France advertised her weakness to her Latin American colonies and whetted the ambitions of England and the United States in the Western Hemisphere. England and Austria remained in arms against France.

At the same time that the Convention concluded peace in a manner which committed France to imperialistic policies, it resolved the constitutional question in a conservative spirit. It scrapped the democratic Constitution of 1793, which had never been in effect, and substituted a new document. The object of the Constitution of 1795 was to prevent the concentration of political power and to lay the ghost of democracy. In order to achieve the first aim, the balance of powers was carried almost to the dead point. Limited executive functions, notably excepting the initiative and veto of legislation, were vested in a committee of five "Directors" (hence the term "The Directory"), to be chosen by the upper chamber of the legislature—the council of 250 *Anciens*, or "Elders"—upon nomination by the lower chamber—the Council of Five Hundred. The members of the smaller council had to be at least forty years old and either married men or widowers. The judiciary was elective and independent of the executive. Every year one third of the legislature was to be renewed by the voters, and one new Director chosen.

Universal suffrage, which was used to elect the Convention and was provided for in the Constitution of 1793, was abandoned. Any direct taxpayer over twenty-one years of age—that is, a majority of the males—could join the primary assemblies, which chose the local officials and members of the secondary assemblies; but to be a member of the secondary assemblies, which chose the national deputies and departmental officials, a voter had to be the owner of substantial property and at least twenty-five years old. Only some 30,000 of the total population of about 25 million Frenchmen could qualify. Yet, to become a deputy there was only an age qualification—thirty years. This electoral system placed effective power in the hands of the rich but still kept political careers open to less wealthy men of ability and talent.

The new Constitution stifled all hints of social improvements by state action. "They'll come again to ask for bread," a deputy cried, and the pledge of the Constitution of 1793 that "the aim of society is the general welfare" was omitted. The principle that "all men are born and remain free and equal in rights," expressed in the Declaration of the Rights of Man of 1789 and the Constitution of 1793, was excised. The new statement that "the law is the same for all" did not have the same suggestive ring. A catalogue of duties counterbalanced the statement of rights, and the right to revolt against oppression was omitted.

The country was secured against a revival of egalitarian democracy.

But the leaders of the Convention did not feel secure against the wrath of aristocratic electors. It was expected that the first elections, in September, would return a strong antirepublican or proroyalist group. To protect the old membership, therefore, the Convention decreed that two thirds, or 500 members, of the new legislature must be recruited from among the members of the Convention. Both Constitution and decree were submitted together and accepted by a plebiscite held late in September 1795.

The action of the so-called "Perpetuals" in the Convention was anticonstitutional in spirit and was generally resented, especially by conservative and royalist groups, since it threatened to entrench the regicide heirs of the Convention. In October 1795—Vendémiaire by the revolutionary calendar—the richer sections of Paris rose in armed insurrection. The Convention tacked, appealing now to republican sections for sympathy and help, but relying largely upon the army. General Paul Barras (1755-1829) was entrusted with the defense of the Convention, and Barras placed command of the troops with a young artillery lieutenant, Napoleon Bonaparte.

Bonaparte was a native of Corsica—born in the very year, 1769, when the Republic of Genoa sold the island to France. As a means of conciliating the population of Corsica, the French government admitted a few young Corsicans to the military schools that were open only to aristocratic Frenchmen. Bonaparte had been one of these. In his youth he was a follower of the Corsican patriot Pasquale Paoli (1725-1807), who worked, with the assistance of the British, for the independence of the island from both Genoa and France. But Bonaparte now had a commission in the French army and had distinguished himself in 1793 in the siege which ousted the British and their French royalist friends from the port of Toulon. In those years Bonaparte professed Jacobin sentiments, but he was, at bottom, a soldier who had contempt for the failure of governments to seize control of the streets from the people.

Barras' assignment was made to Bonaparte's hand. Artillery had previously been confined to field and siege operations, but Bonaparte believed that it could also dispose of the power of citizens in the streets. Although his troops were outnumbered by the rebels of Paris, he outmaneuvered his opponents and quickly suppressed the revolt by a "whiff of grapeshot." The reprisals were on the whole mild—rich people must be treated more gently than poor—but the results were decisive. In October the elections returned 374 "Perpetuals" to seats in the new legislature. The Convention annulled 126 of the other mandates in order to fill the quota of 500 seats with its own members. The Constitution of the Directory was born with the taint of original sin.

7. *Imperial and Intellectual Adventure*

The repercussions of the French Revolution reached the utmost bounds of the Western world. The collapse of the Old Regime and the swift alternation of absolutism, limited monarchy, democracy, and conservative republicanism suggested the possibility of new political forms and social philosophies. Turmoil in economic life—due to the confiscations, inflation, and unusual transfers of property—stimulated speculative enterprise. The victories of France exposed the brittleness of old empires and opened the prospect of a vast redistribution of territories and colonies. Extraordinary opportunity beckoned to the thinker and the politician, the trader and the soldier. The world seemed plastic to the hand of man.

The Intellectual Ferment

The Revolution experimented with policies and institutions which had been discussed only in theoretical works, in private *salons*, or in the *tabula rasa* of the New World, and some which had not been proposed before at all. Reality had outsped theory. Academic issues became practical politics. Enlightened men had leaned toward republicanism but had regarded it as unsuited to large and ambitious countries; yet America and France were now republics. They had discounted the force of democracy; and a democratic government had successfully defied the monarchs of Europe. The consequence was that hesitancy was banished from political thinking. Ideas became programs.

The innovations of the Revolution inspired some thinkers to sketch the outlines of a perfect society and others to resort to drastic devices to shore up the walls of the old order. Modern utopianism—both radical and conservative—was born. System-building became the fashion.

The Revolution opened an epoch of projects: to organize world peace, to establish social equality, to emancipate women, to assure the progress of civilization, and so on, truly *ad infinitum.* Many of the utopian schemes that won a following in the next century germinated in the 1790's. Robert Owen and Charles Fourier (see pp. 262-64) conceived their visions in the wake of the Revolution. The young Count Claude Henri de Saint-Simon (see pp. 223-24) responded to the feverish atmosphere by speculating boldly on the stock market, planning vast roads and canals to connect various parts of the Continent, gambling in depreciated *assignats,* and evolving schemes for a new elite of ability and learning to govern the world.

The most significant intellectual event of the nineties was the debate on "the great question," as the Reverend Thomas Robert Malthus (1766-1834), one of the principal participants, put it: ". . . whether men shall henceforth start with accelerated velocity toward illimitable, and hitherto unconceived, improvement; or be condemned to a perpetual oscillation between happiness and misery, and after every effort remain still at an immeasurable distance from the wished for goal."

The opening gun of the controversy was fired by William Godwin (1756-1836), an English philosopher and novelist, with the publication of *Enquiry concerning Political Justice and Its Influence on Morals and Happiness* (1793). Godwin characterized his book as "a child of the French Revolution," the product of "the concussion that the minds of men suffered" in their political thinking and of "the materials that have been furnished by the recent experiments of America and France."

The *Enquiry* was a defense of individual freedom. Godwin contended that the greatest obstacles to human progress are coercive laws and institutions, aristocracies, churches, monopolies, and wide inequalities of wealth. Government, he said, is the embodiment of that inhibition of reason and morality which

David's famous painting of Mme Récamier (1777-1849), the presiding beauty of Parisian intellectual and political salons in the period of the Directory. CULVER

is responsible for poverty and ignorance, crime and war. The decrease of the power and functions of government is the beginning of reform. Empires and nations should be broken up into smaller and more manageable units, each with complete autonomy. Gradually advice and remonstrance by respected leaders would take the place of coercion. The individual would at last be free. Reason would persuade him to use his property to help those whose need is greater than his own. Equality—or, rather, the absence of sharp and invidious inequalities —would thus be the result of growing morality.

Man, Godwin believed, cannot become perfect, but he is "perfectible, or in other words, susceptible of perpetual improvement." For the moment, Godwin was content with moderate advances. The French and American Revolutions had hardly established a regime of equality. But the abolition of social ranks, political privileges, and monarchical and aristocratic institutions seemed to him to point to that goal.

A more discriminating vision of the future possibilities of man was born in France. The Marquis de Condorcet was the only member of the galaxy of philosophes who survived to participate in the Revolution. An advanced liberal, Condorcet was active in promoting projects for public education and constitutional reform. In 1793, having criticized the Jacobin Constitution, he was ordered arrested, along with the Girondin leaders. He hid successfully for ten months. While living in fear of imminent arrest and execution, he wrote the first history of civilization, in a style which revealed only hope and magnanimity. His faith in the Revolution remained undimmed. Finally captured, Condorcet died during his first night in prison. After the fall of the Jacobins, a contrite Convention published and distributed his *Sketch for a Historical Picture of the Progress of the Human Mind* (1795).

Condorcet's view of history was based on a theory advanced by Turgot before him. By "the alternation of calm and agitation, of good conditions and of bad," mankind "marches always, although slowly, towards still higher perfection." Condorcet divided history into nine epochs, distinguished by the condition of the economy and society, by the attitude of the state and society toward intellectual enterprise, and, above all, by the state of learning, science, and inquiry. The Enlightenment, the ninth epoch, carried forward the accumulated thought of the past and aroused in men a sense of their powers. It would be followed by a tenth and crowning epoch.

Condorcet felt that a certain amount of inequality was rooted in natural distinctions. But inequalities due to circumstances of birth, wealth, sex, and education would shrink constantly through the abolition of privileges of status and heredity, the repeal of laws that encouraged the accumulation and combination of fortunes, the establishment of freedom of trade and occupations, the elimination of ostentatious spending on the one hand and hoarding on the other, and the institution of public schooling, adult education, simplified methods of teaching—the use of graphs and other visual aids, for example— and the education of women.

Condorcet foresaw wide application of scientific, mathematical, and statistical skills to the problems of government and society. He envisaged, for example, the application of the principle of mutual savings and insurance to the relief of orphans and the aged, to the launching of young men in careers and family life, and to the provision of credit for economic enterprises, thereby making great capitalists superfluous. Political democracy would be improved by devising scientific means to determine the will of the majority, the weight of public opinion, the degree of social utility, and the probable success of proposed policies. Condorcet proposed the invention of a universal language to facilitate the exchange of information and ideas among all men. He foresaw the substitution of brotherhood for imperialism in the relations of Europe with Asia and Africa. International organization would assure amity among the nations, and wars would come to "rank with assassinations as freakish atrocities, humiliating and vile in the eyes of nature and staining with indelible opprobrium the country or age whose annals record them."

With Godwin, Condorcet believed that disease would be eradicated and that the span of life would grow longer and longer. The success with which domestic animals had been bred and his observations of human change suggested to Condorcet the possibility that new skills and capacities might be transmitted by heredity. He believed that even the biological frame might be improved.

One great difficulty remained. Progress might encourage the growth of population. Would not a time come when the limit of Nature's capacity to feed man is reached? Would not society then start on the downward path? Godwin contended that no immutable law prescribed the constant growth of population. "In a certain stage of the social progress, population seems rapidly to increase; this appears to be the case in the United States of America. In a subsequent stage, it undergoes little change, either in the way of increase or of diminution; this is the case of the more civilized countries of Europe." Should population press upon the means of subsistence, men might marry later in life and raise smaller families.

As the "perfectibilists" appealed to scientific "laws" to accelerate progress, conservatives mocked them with other "laws" that seemed to condemn mankind to permanent misery. In 1798 there was published one of the gloomiest productions of the human mind, Malthus' *An Essay on the Principle of Population; As It Affects the Future Improvement of Society, with Remarks on the Speculations of Mr. Godwin, M. Condorcet, and Other Writers*. Malthus had at first been "warmed and delighted with the enchanting pictures" of future improvements drawn by idealists. But one consideration convinced him that perfectibility was "little better than a dream": the disproportion, in the world of men as well as in that of animals and plants, between population and food. Benjamin Franklin had observed that only lack of space and the competition for food keeps the numbers of animals and plants down. In the hands of Malthus this view became a mathematical formula: the instinct of sex presses population forward in a geometric ratio: 1, 2, 4, 8, 16, 32 . . .; food can increase only in an arithmetical ratio:

1, 2, 3, 4, 5, 6. . . . No matter how sparse the population of a country or how plentiful its land resources, the increase of people will outrace that of food before long. The example of new countries is not to the point, except to show how fast population grows when not checked by the shortage of food. "In the United States of America, where the means of subsistence have been more ample, the manners of the people more pure, and consequently the checks to early marriages fewer, the population has been found to double itself in twenty-five years." This rate of increase was "probably without parallel in history." It was due not to the superiority of civilization but to "the great plenty of fertile uncultivated land" characteristic of new colonies. In older countries, the rate is kept down by "the vices of mankind," which are "active and able ministers of depopulation," and by misery—*i. e.*, poverty, unhealthy cities, debilitating luxury, "vicious practices with respect to women," unwholesome industrial occupations, pestilence, and war. The chief killer of people is famine, "the last, the most dreadful resource of Nature."

By a somber decree, Nature had vetoed the perfectibility of man. The view of Malthus made every effort at amelioration appear only as an aggravation of the evil, for every measure that improves the lot of men without adding to the food supply merely increases the number of future victims of vice and misery. The Poor Laws of England, for example, might relieve an individual here and there, but they merely "spread the general evil over a much larger surface," for, by proportioning benefits according to the number of the recipient's children, they encouraged reproduction. The laws should be abolished in favor of county workhouses for extreme cases of distress. "The fare should be hard, and those that were able obliged to work."

Malthus felt that man's "original sin" was laziness and inertia—that Providence had arranged the disproportion between population and food in order to awaken man from savagery, to develop his mind, "to elicit an ethereal spark from the clod of clay." From such a point of vantage human suffering fell into perspective: for "there is no more evil in the world than is absolutely necessary as one of the ingredients in the mighty process." This was reassuring, but Malthus's *Essay on Population* raised a nightmare that has haunted mankind ever since.

Perfectibility was only one of many issues of the nineties. The German philosopher Immanuel Kant drafted a "treaty of perpetual peace." If all states became free and republican, he argued, if they entered into a federation that reduced standing armies, forbade debts for foreign adventure, and put an end to the acquisition and transfer of states by inheritance or bargaining, war would be banished from the earth.

The domination of woman by man is possibly as old a phenomenon as war. In 1792, Mary Wollstonecraft (1759-97), an English writer and the wife of Godwin, delivered a philippic against female slavery from which the male sex has not yet recovered. Her *Vindication of the Rights of Women* excoriated the despotism which made women "immoral dolls" and creatures of vanity and whim, repudiated female submissiveness, and demanded equal educational opportunities for the sexes and a chance for women to earn their own livelihood. She believed in female suffrage but was afraid that her English contemporaries would find the suggestion laughable. She hoped that the French would give women the vote as a deed of "justice for one half of the human race."

On the conservative side, Joseph de Maistre (1754-1821), a nobleman exiled from his native Savoy, began, with the *Considérations sur la Révolution*, to lay the foundation of an extreme antirational doctrine. To write constitutions, in his view, was to presume upon the privilege of God. It was He who created nations and cities, gave them names, and wrote their constitutions. The oldest societies are those which bear most clearly His imprint. Hence the example of the United States did not count. The Republic was still an "infant." To De Maistre, there was something devilish and unreal in any deliberate human project of a grandiose kind. The plan, drafted by his compatriot Pierre Charles l'Enfant (1755-1825), to construct a new American capital was going the rounds in Europe. De Maistre wagered "a thousand to one that the city will not be built, that it will not be called Washington, and that the Congress will not meet there."

In one case the word became deed. François Noël Babeuf (1760-97)—better known as Gracchus Babeuf, after the agrarian rebel of the Roman Republic—had been employed, as a domestic servant of noblemen, in the invidious task of reviving old exactions upon the peasants. During the Revolution, he developed a rather simple platform of communism, or equality, as it was then called. Pointing to the fact that the agrarian reforms had not provided *all* the peasants with land, he proposed that the government possess itself of all property, particularly the land, by abolishing inheritance and similar measures. It should then allow all the citizens equal access to property by assigning uniform lots to everyone.

Babeuf formed the Society of Equals to advance his program. In 1796, when the masses of Paris were suffering from food shortages and inflated prices and radical Jacobins were eager to revenge themselves on the Thermidoreans, the leaders of the Society entered into a plot to overthrow the Directory, shrewdly aiming their appeals at soldiers as well as at proletarians. In the *Manifesto of the Equals* they called for another, "far greater revolution which will be the last." This first attempt at a communist revolution was nipped in the bud by agile police work. Secret agents insinuated themselves into the councils of the conspirators and cooperated with them, the better to prepare them for defeat. When the Equals had compromised themselves enough, they were arrested and tried. Most of them were exiled, but Babeuf died on the guillotine in April 1797.

Economic Speculation

The intellectual controversies of the nineties were part of a larger ferment—financial, military, and political—which particularly affected the Atlantic world. Adventurous enterprise was the order of the day in Great Britain and America as well as in France and neighboring countries. The alarums and turns of war, state loans, and contracts for military and naval supplies stimulated stock-exchange operations. Government secrets, advance knowledge of official action, and first reports of victories or defeats were grist to the mill of speculation.

Britain's economy was stimulated by the war with France. War loans benefited investors and financiers. The seizure of belligerent and neutral ships, which the British maritime code encouraged, added to the wealth of the country. Profits from familiar enterprises were supplemented by the less spectacular but eventually more significant progress of industry, particularly in cheaper textiles. Britain profited from the application of the advances in technology which had begun in the sixties.

Toward the end of the century, the age of steam came into its own. The steam engine was devised by a Frenchman, Denis Papin (1647-1714), and improved in 1702 by the Englishman Thomas Newcomen (1663-1729). It was used at first to pump water out of open-cut coal or metal mines. The Newcomen engine was a clumsy machine, consisting of a cylinder containing a piston. Steam introduced at one end of the cylinder pushed the piston to the other end. The cylinder was then cooled by the application of cold water; the steam condensed and shrank in volume; a vacuum was created, and the atmospheric pressure in the other chamber pushed the piston back. The alternate heating and cooling of the cylinder wasted energy and time. In the 1760's another Englishman, James Watt (1736-1819), added a second cylinder in which the

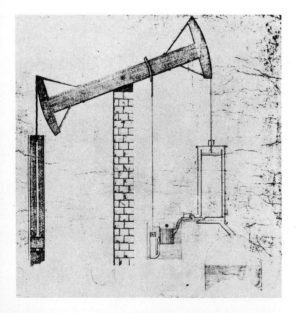

Drawing of an early steam engine by James Watt. This drawing was made in 1765, but steam power was not used in factories on a large scale until the turn of the century. The steam engine was the most important invention of the Industrial Revolution and was based on French as well as English experiments. WERNER WOLFF, BLACK STAR

steam, after pushing the piston to one end, escaped and was condensed. The original cylinder remained hot. In 1782 Watt improved the engine by using steam to push the piston back. The piston was thus kept moving constantly back and forth by steam power alone, instead of by the alternation of steam and atmospheric pressure. In the nineties an increasing number of textile and other mills installed steam engines. Freed from dependence upon water-power sites, factories rose in towns. The modern industrial city began to take shape.

Next, iron was added to steam. In the eighteenth century the production of iron and iron goods had declined in Great Britain owing to the scarcity of forest land, which supplied the charcoal traditionally used for smelting. The country became increasingly dependent upon foreign iron, particularly from Sweden. The discovery that coal, in the form of coke, could be used for smelting laid the foundations of a new iron industry.

The result of these developments was that in the nineties, while domestic turmoil disrupted the industry of France, British industry took a decisive lead. It was during the revolutionary years that Britain's foreign trade for the first time surpassed that af France.

The United States also felt the surge of economic expansion. The American Republic was, for the moment, the only important commercial state which was not at war. Following the treaty between France and Spain in 1795, the British fleet withdrew from the Mediterranean and Great Britain relaxed her pressure on trade in the Atlantic. French and neutral ships, and most of all American ships, increased their activities.

Land had been, and continued to be, the principal object of investment within the United States. Several states disposed of tens of millions of acres, sometimes at ridiculously low prices and as a result of questionable bargains between politicians and traders. The friendly legislators of Georgia, for example, sold to the four so-called Yazoo companies the title to twenty million acres of Indian land, which today comprise two large states—Alabama and Mississippi —for a half million dollars. The following year, however, the sale was rescinded and the lands were ceded to the federal government. Eventually the previous buyers were reimbursed.

It was France, however, that offered the greatest opportunities for personal enrichment. Her whole property system was in flux. Old established groups were scattered by exile or imprisonment and their estates were lost or diminished by confiscation, forced sales, and emergency disposals for ready cash. An enormous amount of real estate—rural and urban, clerical, aristocratic, and even bourgeois—was thrown upon the market. Townsmen and landlords with cash in hand assembled large estates overnight.

Inflation completed the ruin of the dispossessed classes in France, as it effected that of less wealthy men who depended upon fixed money incomes. In 1797 the state canceled two thirds of its debt. Many a creditor was wiped out; many others were close enough to the government to save themselves by advance knowledge of these measures. Feverish sales and purchases, whether of property or government notes (*assignats*), frequent turnovers, and brokerage fees provided splendid opportunities for the class of men who bought, not to keep and improve, but to sell quickly at a profit, and who gambled on the fluctuating market in land and stocks.

The Dilemma of the Directory

In France, the opportunities in politics and empire were even greater than those in business and finance. The course of events hinged on the question of whether the Directory could stabilize conditions at home and make peace with the enemies of France abroad.

The new regime retained most of the legal and administrative achievements of the Revolution. Its religious policy was more radical than that of the Convention. It completed the breach with Christianity. Religious pilgrimage, street processions, and the public exhibition of crosses and other symbols were forbidden, although enforcement was not always severe and the nonjuring clergy were pursued less energetically than before. The influence of Freemasonry spread in official circles. A new official religion was proclaimed—Theophilanthropy ("the love of God and man")—with a whole set of festivals, holidays, observances, and ceremonies.

The Directory pursued the vision of a bourgeois society. It made it easier to carve large estates from the clerical domain. These lands were not, as previously, broken up and sold in small plots; public sale to the highest bidder was permitted for the first time. The war industries were denationalized: one by one, the factories, the shoe and clothing enterprises, the cannon foundries, and the transport system were turned over to private hands. The Directory replaced the new method of direct requisition of goods for the armies, adopted in the earlier years of the Revolution, with the older method of private contracting. It permitted private import and export trade, which had been forbidden by the Convention government. It threw open sea enterprise, then the most fertile source of large fortunes.

Inflation was checked by stringent measures. When the *assignats* were demonetized in 1797, many holders were impoverished, but dealers with political connections were able to unload in good time. The government budget, whose imbalance had been the occasion of the Revolution, was steadied at last. The national income was enhanced by the large "contributions" received from conquered countries.

Society became "respectable." Divorce was made more difficult; illegitimate offspring lost their recently acquired right to an equal share in inheritance, and the head of the family regained his power through the abolition of the parliamentary *tribunal de famille*. Public educational opportunities were extended to the secondary level, but principally for the children of the propertied. It seemed like old times, with the difference that the middle classes had taken the place of the aristocracy.

148 The loyal support of these classes was essential to the stability of the Re-

Paper money of the French Revolution, secured by the nationalized property of the Church. Issued in extravagant amounts, the assignats *deteriorated in value rapidly. In 1797, the government "demonetized" them in the process of balancing the budget, thus impoverishing citizens who held large quantities of them.*

THE CHASE MANHATTAN BANK MUSEUM OF MONEYS OF THE WORLD

public and the achievement of peace. Yet—and this is the paradox of the heart of the failure of the Directory—this support never fully materialized. For in these very years, in the mid- and late nineties, the revolution in property and the adventures of speculation altered the composition and the character of the class of property owners. The old property system was gone, along with the old aristocracy; the new bourgeoisie was already born, but not yet grown up. Hence the spectacle of moneyed men who had profited from the Revolution but became royalists; hence the resurrection of aristocratic vanities. The *nouveaux riches*, who set the tone of the time, were savagely competitive. They could not infuse the newly emerging bougeoisie with responsibility—only with bumptiousness. They could not commit their loyalty to the government; they could only seek to penetrate it for the sake of profit. The Directory had to endure assaults from the conservative side no less, indeed more, than from the Left.

Every domestic crisis was exploited for *coups* on the stock exchange. Every military conquest enhanced the lust for profit and the power of contractors as well as of generals. The abolition of nationalized industries threw open a wide range of businesses for supplying the needs of the army and provisioning the hungry cities. Official favors and contracts were tempting to the watchful enterpriser—and to the politician. Most of the Directors and many of the legislators were moderate men and tried to keep their heads in this whirl. But there were others. In the "high society" of the time, which became notable for its impudence, men "on the make" rubbed elbows with high officials. Alliances were struck between contractors and generals, speculators and legislators, bankers and politicians, to their mutual advantage and corruption. At the center of affairs were General Paul Barras, who was one of the five Directors; Talleyrand, former Bishop of Autun and for two crucial years—1796-97—Foreign Minister; Jean Tallien (1767-1820), the leader of the Convention and later of the Council of Elders; and the adventurer Joseph Fouché (1759-1820). These men and their fellows were eager for sudden wealth and exalted position.

Thus nurtured, the spirit of speculation confronted the spirit of the Revolution in the inner citadel of the Republic.

149

Military and Imperial Adventure

In the early months of the Directory—in 1795-96—peace still seemed attainable. France had not only defended herself successfully but had much enlarged her boundaries. Although the Treaty of Basel, by implicitly recognizing Prussian hegemony in north Germany, had made peace with Austria more difficult, a moderate strategy was likely to reconcile Austria and isolate Great Britain.

More aggressive counsel prevailed, however. On the ground that Austria might be offered compensation for her losses on the left bank of the Rhine by cessions nearer Austria, a daring campaign was launched, in 1796, in northern Italy, where the Hapsburgs already controlled Tuscany and smaller principalities. The campaign proved all too successful. The speed of movement made possible by requisitioning local supplies instead of relying on supply trains; the concentration of forces at vital points; the increased use of artillery in battle; the use of cavalry detached from the main body of the troops to pin down slower moving enemy troops in terrain favorable to attack—these elements of the new strategy, developed by revolutionary statesmen and generals, were brought to their highest effectiveness by a military genius. The "hero" of Vendémiaire had

General Bonaparte at Arcola. A highly romantic treatment by a contemporary artist of a famous episode in the Italian campaign of 1796-97 when Bonaparte seized the flag and led his soldiers across a bridge. VERSAILLES MUSEUM

been rewarded by the Directors with the command of the campaign in Italy. In a few weeks, Bonaparte won a series of brilliant and decisive victories. North-central Italy was at his feet. By the Treaty of Campo Formio, signed in October 1797, Austria ceded the Belgian provinces and the left bank of the Rhine to France but received Istria and Dalmatia. France retained the Ionian Islands, which she had just seized.

In an age of speculators, the young Corsican was a master. He was all the greater gambler for being also a precise craftsman in military and administrative affairs. He had a superstitious belief in his star, whether for glory or for doom. A revolution in Venice had overthrown the ancient oligarchy and established a constitutional state. Bonaparte seized it by trickery and gave it to Austria. With the assistance of local liberals, he reorganized Genoa, Piedmont, and Lombardy on the French administrative model. In defiance of the advice of civilian agents assigned to his command by the Directors, he kept control of the new states through subordinate generals and army contractors associated with them. He carried the war south into Tuscany and the Papal States. His imagination took flame: a connecting military road must be cut through Switzerland; to the Ionian Islands Malta must be added, in order to master the Mediterranean; beyond, Egypt beckoned, and then the Near East, perhaps India. . . .

This was romantic imperialism with a vengeance. If Bonaparte had his way, France would stand committed to the defense of distant lands and the other powers would be driven to fight for their existence. Some of the Directors favored moderate policies in order to preserve the spirit of republicanism, but there were others who were not principled. And Bonaparte came bearing gifts: he had a draft of a treaty with Austria; cash contributions and art treasures streamed in from the subdued Italian states; Bonaparte supported his own army; and the Italian victories brought prestige not only to him but to the Directory. It would have taken a strong government to repudiate the triumphant general. Such a government might have preferred a real peace with Great Britain to his seeming peace with Austria. But, in the summer of 1797, the Directory's efforts for a peace with Britain were negated by its own divisions and indecision, and by the meddling of speculators, royalists, and unscrupulous politicians. Its domestic position was weakened by unfavorable elections, and it had to appeal to the army for protection.

A financial crisis had broken out across the Channel, forcing the Bank of England to suspend specie payments; the price of consols fell sharply. Had leading merchants not accepted bank notes at par, the public credit would have collapsed; even so, it was severely shaken. The "corresponding societies," organized to press for domestic reform, agitated for peace with France as well, and petitions to end the war poured in to Parliament from many parts of the country. And then the power of Great Britain was touched at the root. A series of mutinies incapacitated the home fleet in the Thames and the North Sea fleet. By May 1797, twenty-six ships were in the hands of rebels, and the infection seemed about to spread to the army.

In July, the British and French met for negotiations at Lille. The British were willing to agree to French annexation of Belgium, but they hoped to retain their own conquests from Holland and Spain, countries now allied to France. The Directory insisted on the return of the Cape Colony, in Africa, to Holland and of Spain's West Indian islands. But the position of the government was undermined from within; Talleyrand, Minister of Foreign Affairs, was opposed to war with England. He and Barras, or their agents, asked the British for a bribe in exchange for using their influence to secure favorable peace terms. The British held out, hoping that dissensions within France would bring about the same result. Everything hung in the balance until the showdown between the conservative Councils and the republican Directors.

The Councils had been spoiling for a fight for some time. In the spring of 1797, the elections held annually to replace a third of the legislature syphoned another conservative stream into it. Few "Perpetuals" were returned. The surviving leadership of the Revolution was in danger—and the danger was more than personal. A majority of the members of both new Councils favored a revision of the revolutionary legislation; the extreme wing called boldly for its total repeal. In the summer, the Councils weakened the provisions against *émigrés* and returned many churches to Catholic worship.

Unwilling and unable to appeal to popular Jacobin groups to stem the rising conservatism. the Directors relied on the army. Bonaparte, still in Italy, was ready with his support—all too ready. On July 14, 1797, the eighth anniversary of the fall of the Bastille, he proclaimed to his troops: "Mountains separate us from France; you will cross them with the speed of the eagle if it becomes necessary . . . to protect the government and the republicans." The Directors preferred the more moderate and sincere republican General Lazare Hoche (1768-97), but an arrangement to shift his army, destined for an invasion of England, nearer to Paris miscarried. A bargain was struck with the Corsican. The government approved his Italian policy, and he sent his adjutant, General Pierre Augereau (1757-1816), to take command of the troops in the French capital. On the night of September 3-4, 1797 (17-18 Fructidor), Augereau seized the Tuileries, the official meeting place of the Councils. The conservative leaders fled, and a legal majority of the legislators assembled at the Odéon, on the other side of the Seine, and annulled the mandates of 154 seats. Fifty-odd politicians, including two conservative Directors, were transported to penal islands. The laws against *émigrés* and priests were again tightened, and anti-republican newspapers were subjected to police approval.

The consequences were far-reaching. The basic revolutionary settlement was preserved, at the price of constitutionalism. The influence of the military chiefs, and of the irresponsible politicians acting with them, was increased. Several generals became candidates for ministerial and even for directorial posts. Bonaparte's reward was the leadership of the French delegation to the Congress of Rastatt, where the territories of Germany were to be unscrambled. The victory of the Directory convinced the English negotiators at Lille that they could not hope for a relaxation of French terms. Negotiations were broken off.

The strategy of France took another aggressive turn. General Hoche had urged a descent upon Ireland in order to weaken England and to initiate the revolutionary land program in still another country of Western Europe. But Bonaparte's Roman heart was drawn to the Mediterranean, where the imperial possibilities were more enticing and revolutionary reform less relevant. "On the one side were all the opportunities for the country, and all the risks for the general. ... On the other were all the opportunities for the future of a despot and all the risks for France." Bonaparte chose the road to Egypt, and Hoche, whose armament was diminished by Napoleon's requisitions, made an unsuccessful attempt to invade Ireland in the winter of 1796-97. His ships were scattered by a storm. He landed a small army but was unable to help the Irish rebels, who had dovetailed their plans with those of the French. The following year, while Bonaparte fought his campaign in Egypt, two more unsuccessful attempts were made in Ireland.

Reaction in England and Federalism in the United States

Great Britain responded to the prolongation of the war by tightening her imperial system and intensifying the repression of political activity at home. The repression had begun in 1793-94, when the Tory government of Pitt interdicted meetings of more than fifty persons and judges punished active political reformers by exiling them to penal colonies overseas. "Corresponding societies" now became illegal. Debating halls and reading rooms were subject to the same penalties as prostitution houses. It became virtually impossible to advocate even moderate reforms energetically. The Habeas Corpus Act was suspended, and the government was now free to hold "agitators" in prison for years without trial. The leaders of the Whigs were so disheartened that they ceased to attend Parliament. The government subsidized the *Anti-Jacobin*, a periodical which satirized the foibles of the reformers. An attack was launched on the incipient trade unions, as much for political as for economic reasons: the Combination Acts of 1799 forbade the organization of either employers or workmen, but omitted any penalties for the former. The shortage of food during the war years provided the occasion for the passage of a general Enclosure Act, under which millions of acres of land were removed from common use and were put under cultivation by better-off farmers and landlords. This increased the dislocation and distress of poorer farmers and laborers.

Ireland lost her parliamentary autonomy. Despite the failures of the French interventions, insurrection became endemic and flared up into civil war. Great Britain quelled it with ferocity and determined to bind Ireland closer to herself. Prime Minister Pitt proposed to abolish the Irish Parliament and admit one hundred Irish members to the Parliament at London. He bought enough members of the Irish Parliament, with offices, sinecures, and the promise of a measure allowing Catholics to sit in the English Parliament, to ensure approval of the "union," which in 1800 was voted by both bodies. However, King George insisted that Catholic emancipation would violate his coronation oath, which pledged him to protect the established Anglican Church. Pitt yielded to the King and broke his own promise to the Catholics. The influence of the King was strong enough to postpone, in effect, religious emancipation for a generation.

As Great Britain and France descended into the maelstrom of war, they threatened to drag the United States after them. The debate in America over the French Revolution deepened a political division that had appeared at the foundation of the Republic. The Republicans, led by Thomas Jefferson, would limit the functions of the federal government, thereby increasing those of state and local bodies. They were supported by the agricultural population and by democrats who suspected the Federalists of harboring aristocratic prejudices. The Federalists, led by Alexander Hamilton, advocated a strong federal government and policies designed to advance the interests of business and investment. The more extreme among them hoped eventually to give the Republic a conservative European cast. Hamilton favored changing the presidency into a lifelong office and the Senate into an aristocratic body of very rich men elected by rich men. He wished to divide the states into smaller units amenable to management by the central authority and to strengthen that authority by establishing a large standing army. When, in 1794, the farmers of Pennsylvania resisted a tax on whiskey, Hamilton demonstrated the ability of the government to enforce obedience by marching troops into that state.

President Washington tried to keep aloof from these incipient political parties; in his first cabinet, of 1789, he included both Hamilton and Jefferson as Secretary of the Treasury and Secretary of State, respectively. Yet he leaned strongly toward the Federalists.

In 1794 Washington negotiated a commercial treaty strikingly favorable to Great Britain. Although it was confirmed by the Senate, the treaty aroused general disapproval. The President denounced the "democratic societies" that had sprung up to support the French cause.

The divergent views of the two groups were naturally reflected in their attitudes toward events in France. The Federalists ranged themselves against the Revolution, especially after the turn toward democracy in 1792, and sympathized with Great Britain in her war with France. The Republicans, on the other hand, sympathized with the effort to establish a republican regime on the Continent. The controversy was sharpened by a dispute with France. The French navy pursued the strategy of striking at merchantmen dealing with the enemy rather than at the British navy. It harried American ships, among others, and seized many cargoes. For several years, American merchantmen engaged in informal hostilities with French warships.

In October 1797, shortly after the purge of the Councils, an American commission arrived in Paris to settle the dispute. The commissioners were treated by Talleyrand with little dignity. The agents of the Foreign Minister—

known to history as Messrs. X, Y, and Z—suggested to them that a bribe of a quarter of a million dollars would facilitate terms. When this suggestion became known, Congress denounced the Treaty of Alliance of 1778 and appropriated funds for the construction of a larger navy. The more extreme Federalists whipped up the dogs of war and Congress passed the Alien and Sedition Acts, ostensibly directed against the activities of aliens in domestic politics and of native seditionists but really intended to weaken the Republican opposition. Aliens—that is to say, French refugees—who "defamed" the government were to be deported; citizens who did so were to be given substantial prison terms. Shiploads of Frenchmen fled in fear of arrest, and peace-minded editors were prosecuted and jailed. The period of naturalization was extended from five to fourteen years, and aliens were placed under official supervision.

The Republican leaders, driven by this hue and cry, retired from the federal scene to the more congenial atmosphere of the state legislatures, where their influence, particularly in the South, was not easy to destroy. Jefferson rallied them for a stand. The legislatures of Virginia and Kentucky passed bold resolutions asserting that the Alien and Sedition Acts contravened the guarantee of rights in the federal Constitution and that the two states would refuse to recognize the validity of such legislation within their borders.

The recent alliance of Spain with France suggested the possibility of an attack on Spanish possessions in America, particularly on the Floridas and Louisiana. Subject to Washington's nominal command, Hamilton became the chief of the army. He officered it with his partisans and, during 1798-99, engaged in a far-flung intrigue for concerted action with Great Britain and Spanish rebels. War with France was averted by President John Adams (1735-1826), who succeeded Washington in 1797. Adams was a more moderate Federalist than Hamilton. The Directory having indicated its agreement with his belief that a war was unnecessary, Adams dispatched a new commission to negotiate the dispute. The Federalist party was split down the middle. In 1800, it lost the presidency to the Republicans. Jefferson assumed the office in March 1801 and promptly reversed the conservative policies of the Federalists.

Bonaparte and the Destruction of the Republic

At the same time that republicanism was reaffirmed in America, it was undermined in France. Bonaparte's Egyptian enterprise was an attempt to take the growing Asian empire of Great Britain in the flank and, incidentally, to acquire for France an empire in the Near East. The western Mediterranean was still regarded by France and Spain as their province, but for more than a century Britain had been sending fleets into those waters. She had held Gibraltar since 1702 and for a few years occupied the Balearic Islands. British penetration now proceeded apace. Britain had recently given naval support to the independence party of Corsica, to which Bonaparte and his family had once adhered. The usual route to the East from Europe lay around the Cape of Good Hope, but there was an old project to find a short cut through the Mediterranean and the Red Sea. The question of conquering Egypt as a path to the East had been explored by Louis XIV in the late seventeenth century, when the sovereignty of the Ottoman Empire over the whole coast of North Africa was beginning to weaken.

The Directors hesitated before sanctioning an attack on Egypt. Although that country was ruled by the Mamelukes, a body of feudal cavalry, it was still formally subject to the Ottoman Empire, with which France had long had friendly relations. The venture was a gamble. But Bonaparte found support within the government. Talleyrand had always been disinclined to attack England directly, and he had good reasons of his own for wishing to leave Paris: the "X-Y-Z affair" had just become known through the publication of the correspondence of the American commissioners and the Foreign Minister's agents. With the annual elections in the offing again, the Directory wished to get these dangerous confederates out of the way. Talleyrand was dispatched to Constantinople to explain to the Sultan that an attack upon his Egyptian lands was meant as a friendly gesture—a job for a clever man. And Bonaparte was placed at the head of a large naval and military expedition, which was assembled secretly at the port of Toulon.

In May 1798, the expedition sailed from Toulon. Bonaparte's fleet eluded the British patrol under Admiral Horatio Nelson (1758-1805) and stopped to seize the island of Malta, strategically situated at the center of the Mediterranean, from the Knights of Saint John, the order of financier-monks. Again avoiding, by the merest chance, the cruising British fleet, Bonaparte landed at Alexandria at the end of June. In a few swift battles he overran Egypt and pushed on toward Syria. While his armies scored one victory after another, a grievous blow befell the naval power of France.

Nelson had crossed and recrossed the Mediterranean in search of the French ships. On August 1, 1798, he came upon them as they rode at anchor in the well-protected Aboukir Bay, near the mouth of the Nile. Throwing aside conventional tactics, Nelson shoved his fleet through the narrow and reef-ridden entrance to the bay, matched ship against ship, and shot it out. Tethered to heavy anchors, with most of its sailors on shore leave, the French fleet was at a disadvantage. It was virtually destroyed. Nelson was showered with kingly honors and gifts; he became a millionaire overnight. Bonaparte had opened wide the Mediterranean to his enemies, who made it a British lake for more than a century.

It remained now for sea power and land power to meet. They could do so only at a port. In the winter and early spring of 1798-99, Bonaparte had conquered Palestine and pierced Syria. In March he took Jaffa, where plague exacted a heavy toll of his men. He pressed on and besieged the fortified port of Acre, famous in the period of the Crusades. The Turkish garrison was assisted by a British naval officer, Sir Sidney Smith; it was provisioned from the sea, now safely in British hands; and, the coast being flat at that point, the artillery fire of the fortress was supplemented by the guns of the British warships.

Portrait of Lord Nelson in 1798. The great admiral had already lost an arm and the sight of one eye and later was to lose life itself fighting the French. In the National Portrait Gallery, London. BETTMANN

Bonaparte failed to carry the walls. In May he raised the siege, adjourned his dreams of a march to Constantinople and India, and dragged his army back to Egypt at an appalling cost. A few months later he administered another defeat to the Turkish army at Aboukir. But, having heard news of interesting events in Europe, he abandoned his soldiers and left for France, to which he had sent reports of his victories in the East, but not of his defeats.

A series of military defeats on the Continent in the winter and spring of 1798-99 had plunged the Directory into another crisis. Austria had repudiated the Treaty of Campo Formio; Russia, risen sated from the feast of Poland, had entered the lists against France for the first time since the war broke out in 1792. Both powers received heavy British subsidies—about a pound a day for every soldier put into the field. The Second Coalition came into being. In the spring of 1799 a combined Austro-Russian army had driven the French out of northern Italy and followed them into Switzerland. In the north, French-held Holland was threatened with invasion from the sea by a combined force of British and Russians. In the south Nelson had assisted the incompetent Bourbons to regain Naples, where they were conducting a terror against liberals. By summer the revolutionary armies had been pushed back to the borders of France.

But the crisis was not only external. The renewed wars had made trade with neutrals more difficult. The richer farmers and landlords blamed the government for the low prices induced by deflation. Political *coups* had become normal and habitual; the new military defeats resulted in a strengthening of the Jacobins in the May elections; in June, the Councils, thus nerved, intimidated three Directors into resigning and replaced them with men who, it was hoped, would prove determined republicans. Meanwhile, by unfortunate chance—for the Directors drew lots on who was to retire each year—Jean François Reubell (1747-1807), the strongest man in the executive, retired. The "Perpetual" Emmanuel Sieyès (1748-1836), who had always been critical of the existing Constitution, took the vacant seat.

The climax of the crisis came after the tide of war had turned in favor of France. In September an Austro-Russian army was repulsed; in a resounding victory, the French regained their position in Switzerland; and the Russians, after quarreling with the Austrians, withdrew from the campaign. When Bonaparte returned to Paris in October, plots were brewing. The stirrings of Jacobinism helped to unite Sieyès, Talleyrand, and their colleagues, who were conspiring to impose on France a more conservative constitution. They needed the help—so conventional had the combination of political and military maneuvering become by then—of a successful general. As in 1797, the politicians tried to avoid Bonaparte and find a more moderate soldier. But Barthelemy Joubert, who might otherwise have been their choice, had died in a battle in Italy, and Jean Moreau (1763-1813), the victor in Switzerland, refused to betray the Republic. Bonaparte's conscience was light as a feather, and the failure of his Egyptian campaign was not yet known. Unless he forged ahead now, his position might become difficult: he had returned without orders; he had no command in Europe; if victory came it would not be his. He had just turned thirty, which was too young by a decade for membership in the Directory, and it would take nine years to change the Constitution legally. Bonaparte and Sieyès were too shrewd not to distrust each other, but Talleyrand brought them together. An army contractor advanced a large sum to further their plans against the promise of future financial favors.

Money, plot, politicians, general—everything was ready. On November 8, a deputy who was involved in the plot arose in the Council of Elders and denounced a conspiracy—how true!—which he ascribed, however, to the Jacobins. He secured a vote convening a session the next day at Saint-Cloud, outside of Paris and hence removed from the direct influence of the people. Bonaparte was given command of the troops by the Council, although this was a prerogative of the Directors. On November 9 (18th Brumaire), the conspirators tried to intimidate the legislature into entrusting them with a revision of the Constitution. Bonaparte appeared before the Councils, but he behaved so tactlessly that he strengthened the suspicion of many deputies that the country stood in greater danger from him and his friends than from the "conspiracy" they pretended to combat. Shouted down as disloyal, Bonaparte withdrew. The day was saved by his brother Lucien, who had recently been elected President of the Council of Five Hundred. Lucien declined to put a motion to outlaw his brother, abandoned the tribune, and, clad in the Roman toga then affected by French lawmakers, rushed out into the courtyard and harangued the soldiers: their general had been assaulted by assassins who were terrorizing the Council within; Bonaparte was loyal to the Republic; if he ever betrayed it, Lucien himself would kill him. The troops marched into the hall, with drums beating, to defend their commander. The legislators fled through the doors and windows. A few hours later, a small minority reassembled and appointed commissions to rewrite the Constitution and three "Consuls" to form a provisional executive: Sieyès, Bonaparte, and Pierre Roger Ducos (1754-1816), a former President of the Council of Five Hundred. "Citizens," Bonaparte declared, "the Revolution has remained faithful to the principles from which it sprang. It is now at an end."

He was half right.

After the *coup*, Sieyès pulled out his old draft of a constitution. He announced the new dispensation in aphoristic style: "Confidence should come from below, authority from above." Manhood suffrage, abandoned after the fall of Robespierre, was now revived. The new Constitution was submitted to a popular vote and received a huge majority, although, since the opposition had been silenced, the vote was meaningless. Moreover, the legislature provided under the Constitution was organized, and its personnel selected, by the leaders of the *coup*—*before* the first elections were held. Thus chicanery as well as force attended the birth of dictatorship.

The Constitution disposed of liberty: the conventional declaration of the rights of man was conspicuous by its absence. Sieyès contrived a maze in which power was concentrated and responsibility obscured. There were to be three Consuls, or executives, and four legislative bodies. The Senate, to be appointed by the First Consul, was to select the members of the Tribunate, which could discuss legislation but not vote, and those of the Legislative Corps, which could vote but not discuss. The Council of State, whose appointment was left indefinite, alone could prepare and introduce bills. The Senate was to pass on the constitutionality of laws, thus closing the cycle. The First Consul would stand for re-election every ten years.

Sieyès suggested that among the three Consuls there be "but one head and but one sword, to execute what that head proposed." Since Bonaparte was the sword, Sieyès must be the head. To the surprise of Sieyès, the young general cast himself for the head as well. Sieyès was shocked by his impudence, but it was too soon for the conspirators to fall out. He yielded, after accepting a rich estate, and Napoleon became First Consul.

8. *Bonapartism and Republicanism*

On the morrow of the coup of Brumaire, France was still at war with Austria and Great Britain. In the spring of 1800, General Moreau engaged Austria in southern Germany, and Bonaparte, now First Consul, led an army to attack her in northern Italy. Instead of taking the narrow road between the Ligurian Alps and the Mediterranean, he repeated the feat which the great Carthaginian commander Hannibal had accomplished 2000 years before. Unencumbered by the African's elephants, Bonaparte pierced the Swiss Alps in only nine days. In nine days more he descended upon Milan, the richest city of Lombardy. Eleven days later he faced the Austrian army on the plain of Marengo, farther to the south. He had, to all appearances, lost the battle when General Louis Desaix unexpectedly appeared on the field with fresh regiments. That reversed the decision; the Austrians fled; Desaix, the real victor, died on the battlefield. A few months later, General Moreau won a brilliant battle at Hohenlinden, in Bavaria. The dazed Austrians agreed to surrender their holdings both in central Italy and in western Germany. To all intents and purposes, the Holy Roman Empire was dead.

The Restoration of Peace

Of the host of enemies that had hung on the flanks of France in the midnineties, only Great Britain remained to be dealt with. But no army could get at her easily, and the seas were still dangerous to her rivals. The neutrals, like France herself, denounced Britain's practices of seizing and searching ships and confiscating cargoes. In 1800 they banded together, as they had done during the American struggle for independence, in an attempt to force Britain to change her ways. Russia, Denmark, Prussia, and Sweden—all the Baltic powers —closed their doors to British goods and demanded respect for their commerce and shipping. The United States, whose trade had gained remarkably at the expense of the warring powers, was naturally sympathetic to this Second Armed Neutrality of the North.

It was a critical moment for Great Britain. Bonaparte had prevailed on the Continent and was building a flotilla to take an army across the Channel. The Baltic powers projected a combined naval force to assert their rights. Britain struck with desperate speed and questionable morality. Denmark held the key to the Baltic: she guarded the narrows of Skagerrak and Kattegat, and she possessed the largest single navy in that sea. Without troubling to issue a declaration of war, Nelson sailed into the shallow port of Copenhagen, the Danish capital, and bombarded the peaceful city and the navy lying unsuspectingly at anchor before it. The Danes capitulated. A few days later came the news that Czar Paul I, who had held the throne since 1796, had been strangled by palace conspirators, with the apparent acquiescence of his son Alexander. The late Czar had been a member of the Second Coalition but had changed his policy in admiration of Bonaparte's campaign in Egypt. He had embargoed the valuable trade that Russian aristocrats and noblemen carried on with British merchants, sending wheat and naval stores and receiving textile goods and a very favorable balance in specie. And he had been the heart of the alliance of maritime neutrals. His successor, Alexander I (1801-25), purchased popularity in aristocratic circles by raising the embargo. The Second Armed Neutrality was no more.

The victories of Bonaparte established French influence in Germany and Italy. But Britain proved invulnerable on the sea. France was unable to strike down British commerce, and the British were unable to reopen French and French-controlled ports. In 1802, the protagonists negotiated the Treaty of Amiens, which restored the colonial losses of France and her Dutch ally and provided for the return of Malta, which Nelson had seized in 1799, to its military order. The French held out the hope that they might open their ports to British goods, sometime in the future.

The Western world was again at peace. But it was no longer the world of 1789. The old order survived, but in an amputated form. It had lost France and the adjacent countries to the east. The hereditary rulers had been humbled by mass armies and forced to come to terms with a military upstart. Experience, however, is a clumsy teacher. Only a few of the traditional governments used the respite to take stock of domestic deficiencies. In Great Britain William Pitt resigned as Prime Minister in 1801 and was succeeded by his friend Henry Addington (1757-1844). Charles Fox (1749-1806) reorganized the liberal ranks, which had been scattered by the panic of the Revolution. The repression of the nineties slackened. There were fewer prosecutions for political pamphleteering, and the critics who had been imprisoned without trial were released. The government made the first grudging admission that it bore some responsibility for the inhuman conditions prevailing in the new factories. The first Factory Act, passed in 1802, provided that pauper children who were "let out"— virtually sold, that is—by Poor Law commissioners to mill owners should be   *161* given proper quarters and religious instruction. Unfortunately, however, no provision was made to enforce the law.

Without abandoning its maritime principles, the British government abated some of their more extreme applications. It agreed to permit neutrals to trade between European countries and their colonies overseas, provided that they "broke" the voyage by calling at ports in their own countries. They must pretend that they were engaged in their own trade and pay the cost in time and profits that this pretense entailed. This relatively mild rule benefited particularly American shippers, who took over much of the colonial trade of Spain, France, and Holland.

At the eastern end of Europe, Czar Alexander I of Russia inaugurated his reign in 1801 with a program of reform. He abolished torture, opened the doors to exchange with the West through emigration and the import of books, eased censorship, and established many secondary schools and universities. He increased the efficiency of the executive machinery by introducing a modicum of regularity in its operations; ministries were for the first time entrusted with the various functions of administration. An imperial decree allowed the middle classes to purchase landed property, hitherto the monopoly of the landowning class. (It should be said that the membership and rights of the various classes were strictly defined in Russian law.) However, the fundamental questions of constitutionalism and serfdom were treated with the utmost caution. A bill of rights was drafted on the model of the French Declaration of the Rights of Man and of the Citizen of 1789, but it was never promulgated. The Emperor officially invited the landowners to allow their peasants to purchase land and freedom. A small minority of the peasants, about 50,000, eventually attained freedom through the benevolence of some of the landowners and the calculation of others, who hoped to manage their estates more profitably by hiring free labor.

Prussia took a few halting steps toward reform: guild restrictions were removed, private industrial enterprise was encouraged, internal tariffs were ended, and the Crown serfs were freed. However, the enlightened minister, Baron Heinrich vom und zum Stein (1757-1831), was frustrated in his attempt to put through a comprehensive program of renovation despite his warning that without reform "the Prussian state will either be dissolved or lose its independence, and ... the love and respect of the subjects will entirely disappear."

Reform fared worse elsewhere. In Austria the only changes introduced were designed to strengthen the armed forces, and in Spain, which had a distinguished record of improvement, the monarchy became steadily less enlightened.

Jefferson and Napoleon

On the whole, the experience of the French Revolution made the traditional ruling classes more conservative rather than less. Yet the danger in which they stood was growing. In the first years of the nineteenth century there developed two alternatives to the old order. Napoleon Bonaparte established a modern Caesarism, and republicanism, destroyed in France, assumed a bolder and more finished form in the United States.

Less than two years after he became First Consul, Bonaparte became virtually a monarch. Following a plebiscite in 1802 he became Consul for life with the right to appoint his successor. In 1804 another plebiscite sanctioned a proclamation by the Senate and Tribunate naming him Napoleon I, hereditary Emperor of the French. Napoleon was then thirty-five years old.

In America, the election as President of the leader of the Republican party, Thomas Jefferson, in 1800 was as significant an event as the *coup* of Brumaire in France the year before. In 1809 Jefferson was succeeded as President by the Republican James Madison. After two terms Madison was succeeded by another Jeffersonian, James Monroe, who was also elected to a second term. This quarter century of Jeffersonian rule set the United States firmly on a democratic course.

Thomas Jefferson sensed more clearly than any American leader the possibility of creating a distinctive and fair society in the New World and did more

A bust of Thomas Jefferson by the French sculptor Houdon. AMERICAN PHILOSOPHICAL SOCIETY

to bring it about. A blend of civilization and the frontier, he was descended from one of the "first families" of Virginia but grew up on an "up-country" estate, where he imbibed the attitudes and ideals of the newly settled neighborhood. Jefferson also had strong cultural bonds with Western Europe. He was the typical philosophe. His ideal was to realize in the New World the fondest dreams of the Old.

By contrast, Bonaparte brought to the Old World the spirit of a turbulent land. In his native Corsica, blood feuds were common and family was the only tie of loyalty. The clan of the Bonapartes was poor, but it nurtured aristocratic pretensions. It supplied rebels equally against the original master of Corsica, the Republic of Genoa, and its successors, monarchical and republican France.

The inspiration of both leaders was classic. But while the Corsican evoked Alexander the Great, Caesar, and Italian *condottieri*, the Virginian evoked Greek and Roman stoics, Hebrew visionaries, and Anglo-Saxon jurists. Jefferson struck the note of political consent, maturity, and responsibility; Bonaparte, that of authority, tutelage, and caprice. The talents and temperaments of the two men were appropriate to their principles. Jefferson was moderate and prudent. A wily political manager, he insinuated his influence rather than imposed his will. Bonaparte, a brilliant soldier—indeed, a military genius—was self-willed, dramatic, and opinionated. While Jefferson emphasized republican simplicity, Bonaparte outdid the traditional monarchies in splendor, ostentation, and expense.

For all his extraordinary effect, Bonaparte was conventional in his thinking, and Jefferson, for all his reserved quality of mind, was a daring and flexible idealist. Jefferson was firmly rooted in the traditions and texts of Anglo-Saxon liberalism. Bonaparte was unruly. He reveled in the opportunity for extraordinary action that difficult challenges presented. From domestic dictatorship, his road led to empire, then to European hegemony, and finally to world dominion. His horizon was constantly receding. The dictator was, of course, the more glamorous figure. As the "Spirit Sinister" of Thomas Hardy's historical drama *The Dynasts* observed,

> . . . My argument is that
> War makes rattling good history; but
> Peace is poor reading. So I back
> Bonaparte for the reason that he will give
> Pleasure to posterity.

Jeffersonianism in Practice

Jeffersonianism may be described as aristocratic democracy. Jefferson believed in the rule of the best with the consent of the people. The best, in his view, were able and talented persons, of whatever social class, trained and educated at the public expense. Not everyone is fit to rule, he believed, any more than everyone is able to assert leadership in the sciences and arts, but every-one—assuming an educated and independent electorate—is capable of under-standing the problems of government, of choosing among candidates, and of judging rulers and officeholders. Thus he made democratic citizenship and leadership by a "natural aristocracy" compatible.

No electorate can be self-reliant, however, which is economically dependent or servile. Only easy access to and widespread ownership of land could supply the basis for a virtuous democracy in an age when the majority of the popula-tion was engaged in agriculture and when property was essential to security of life, personal independence, and disinterested public activity. It was, indeed, the availability of land on the North American continent that made it possible for the Americans to attain what seemed difficult, if not impossible, in Europe—a large propertied electorate. Hence the interest of Jefferson and his followers in acquiring, settling, and developing the Western frontier.

But Jeffersonianism was not simply agrarianism. The Republicans were aware that the graces of life, the advance of technology and crafts, the spread of ideas and learning, the intercourse between nations and continents—in short, culture and cosmopolitanism—presupposed town life and the activities of com-merce, shipping, and industry. In the eighteenth century, however, it appeared that some of the worst vices of society were most conspicuous in great cities: sharp inequalities of wealth, wasteful luxury, decadent oligarchies, mob fren-zies, the poverty and oppression of the new factories. The Jeffersonians therefore deemed it desirable to maintain a proper balance between town and country life.

In his first inaugural address in 1801, Jefferson described his goal as "a wise and frugal government, which shall restrain men from injuring one another, shall leave them otherwise free to regulate their own pursuits of industry and improvement, and shall not take from the mouth of labor the bread it has earned." In his first term as President (1801-05), Jefferson and his Republican followers gave a practical demonstration of these principles. They curbed the temptation for excessive activity at the center of government by reducing the military, naval, administrative, and diplomatic establishments. They made provision for the extinction of the national debt in order to eliminate the temp-tation to run the government by excessive taxation and borrowing. They abolished taxes on whiskey and paper and postage for newspapers, and they reduced the appropriations for the army and navy. By keeping down the number of collectors and officials, they hoped to lighten the political as well as the fiscal burden of society. Although the Republicans leaned strongly toward free trade, they relied for revenue on customs duties, which were easier and less costly to collect than excise taxes and were paid by people who could afford expensive imports. It was expected that the national debt would be paid off shortly; the resulting surplus from the customs they hoped to use in building roads and canals to bring the states closer to one another.

Jefferson regarded education as a public function, "not that it would be proposed to take its ordinary branches out of the hands of private enterprise, *165*

Thomas Jefferson unhitching his horse at a boardinghouse in Washington to ride to his inauguration as the third President of the United States on March 4, 1801. Washington had just become the capital of the Republic, but it was still "a backwoods settlement in the wilderness." The French architect P. C. L'Enfant (1754-1825) had prepared an elaborate and beautiful plan for its future development.

which manages so much better all the concerns to which it is equal; but a public institution can alone supply those sciences which, though rarely called for, are yet necessary to complete the circle, all the parts of which contribute to the improvement of the country, and some of them to its preservation." In his own state, Jefferson later used his influence to found the University of Virginia.

The principle of individual freedom was strikingly confirmed. Jefferson freed from jail the victims of the nefarious Alien and Sedition Acts. The laws themselves were allowed to lapse. The House of Representatives impeached Justice Samuel Chase (1741-1811) of the Supreme Court, who had handed out harsh sentences under these laws and had used the bench to make vindictive attacks on republicanism and Republicans. The impeachment failed, but the judiciary was somewhat chastened. Jefferson urged Congress to extend a warmer welcome to immigrants: ". . . shall we refuse the unhappy fugitives from distress that hospitality which the savages of the wilderness extended to our fathers arriving in this land? Shall oppressed humanity find no asylum on this globe?" Congress responded by reducing the period of waiting for naturalization from fourteen to five years. The control and registration of aliens, initiated during the war hysteria of 1798, were abandoned.

A humane policy toward the Indian tribes was a deep concern of the Jeffersonians. The government obtained from Georgia the rights to the huge Yazoo lands, which had been ceded by Indian tribes. It attempted to compromise the long-drawn-out struggle between the avidity of the frontiersmen and the attachment of the Indians to their ancient soil.

Although they were anti-imperialistic, the Jeffersonians were expansionists. Since their political ideal was based on an electorate of small farmers, more land was needed as the population grew. Alert to the danger presented by adjacent European empires in America, they had additional reasons for securing the hinterland of the Republic. Their idealism as well as their interests led to the ambition to control as much as possible of the North American continent. One of Jefferson's most farsighted measures was to dispatch the Lewis and Clark expedition, which ascended the Missouri River to its source, crossed the continental divide, explored the Columbia River, and finally reached the Pacific Ocean. The expedition laid the basis of future claims to the Pacific Northwest, even though much of the West was then thought to be too arid for settlement.

Expansion was to subserve the aim of democracy. The new communities of the West were to be master in their own house. This attitude won for the Republicans the support of the frontiersmen. Western land policy was liberalized. The minimum lot was reduced to 160 acres. Eighty dollars down and a promise to pay the balance in four years secured a farm. These conditions favored quick settlement, and the Jeffersonians encouraged the formation of new states. Since these states generally had broader suffrage provisions than the older states, their entry into the Union made for its democratization. Ohio's admission in 1802 as the first state carved out of the Northwest Territory was a symbol of the times. By promulgating a democratic constitution, Ohio carried out the promise of the great Northwest Ordinance of 1787.

These were the policies of the federal realm; but that realm itself was meant to be as restricted as possible. The Jeffersonians were more active on their favorite ground—state, county, and town governments. There they secured passage of a multitude of acts adjusted to the needs of the several communities and tending generally in the direction of greater religious toleration, a gradual broadening of the suffrage, a preference for elective over appointive offices, and a preference for fixed instead of life tenure for judges.

The Pattern of Modern Caesarism

While Jefferson carried forward principles inherent in the American Revolution, Bonaparte bore an equivocal relation to the French Revolution. He rejected its liberal policies and procedures and its sympathy with the abused elements of society, although he preserved its administrative and legal contributions. Napoleon was neither an enlightened despot nor a revolutionary; he was, rather, the first modern Caesar. In a time of social stress, Julius Caesar had been the leader of the popular party of Rome, which included many impoverished and dispossessed farmers. He had gathered the military power in his hands and subverted the traditional institutions of the landlords and aristocrats, particularly the Senate. The pattern of militarism and empire, democratic claims and aristocratic subversion, came to be known by his name.

Caesarism adapted to modern conditions was Bonapartism. French society was not composed, as ancient Roman society had been, of patricians, plebeians, slaves, and mercenaries; the country was not made up of varied provinces

167

paying homage to different gods and tribute to the same treasury; nor did the Empire comprise a net of commercial centers encircling the Mediterranean Sea, themselves encircled by a hinterland of agrarian and barbarous provinces. Capitalists and free farmers were now as influential as landlords; the country was a homogeneous legal and administrative unit; and commerce ranged the seven seas of the globe. But the emphasis on the power of the central government, on military eminence, on imperial conquest and expansion, on revolutionary and democratic claims, and on the extraordinary attributes of the ruler characterized Bonapartist France as it had Caesarist Rome. Napoleon revived the titles and slogans of the dictatorship that supplanted the Roman Republic. He filled the political stage with consuls, senators, tribunes, and legionnaires.

After the coup of Brumaire Bonaparte reshaped the Constitution along dictatorial lines with a few strokes. He preserved, for a time, the intricate façade of four legislative bodies, but he himself appointed the Council of State. Within a few years, he abolished the articulate Tribunate, whose Roman counterpart had been the special guardian of democratic interests. He preserved universal suffrage as a sign that his power rested on popular sovereignty. But the voters did not choose the legislators. They merely established lists of "notabilities," from which the First Consul selected legislators and local officials at his discretion. Within a few years, it was provided that these "notabilities" must be eminent and rich men.

Napoleon used "democracy" for propagandistic purposes. Questions were placed before the voters and yes-or-no answers stipulated. The dictator had the advantage of phrasing the questions. Voting proceeded in the enforced silence of the press and the platform, and in the absence of political organization and activity. Bonapartist "democracy" was not representative but "plebiscitary" and tutelary. It was used not to choose or to punish lawmakers and executives or to decide policy but to lend a popular glow to decisions made in advance by the ruler.

Napoleon applied the second half of Sieyès formula—"authority from above"—with greater honesty. While Jefferson was bolstering liberty in America by releasing from prison the victims of the Sedition Acts and Great Britain was easing the pressure on political pamphleteers and organizers, Napoleon was abolishing the freedoms of the forum. Journalists, orators, playwrights, actors, callers of meetings, and organizers of political clubs and parties had no place under his regime. Napoleon patronized art and science, but only those branches that had no moral or political connotations. He distrusted writers above all, sensing correctly that literature has a bearing upon social conditions and ideals. Books were censored, plays discouraged, and newspapers virtually abolished. Literary output and quality declined. "People complain that we have no literature," Napoleon remarked. "That is the fault of the Minister of the Interior." The contrast with the Anglo-Saxon countries was sharp. Jefferson said that if he had to choose between "government without newspapers, or newspapers without a government," he would prefer the latter. "But I should mean," he added, "that every man should receive these papers, and be capable of reading them." When Charles James Fox remarked to Napoleon that in England the politicians did not mind too much the criticism of the press, the Consul strode out of the room shouting: "It is not so here!"

Local autonomy went the way of the independent legislature and the independent voter. The French revolutionaries had created uniform departments and communes, but they had also assigned them considerable powers and made their officials elective and responsible to the local citizenry. Simplicity and uniformity thus promoted decentralization. But they could as easily promote its opposite. Under Napoleon, the equality of autonomy became the equality of obedience. A simple stroke sufficed: the hundred-odd prefects who ruled the *départements* were not to be elected by local citizens but appointed by the First Consul; and the officials of the thousands of communes and towns were to be appointed either by the Consul or by his prefects. A hierarchical bureaucracy covered France, and authority was guaranteed by a large and successful army. Napoleon expanded the system of conscription introduced by the Directory. "I can use up 25,000 men a month," he boasted, and he was sometimes better than his word. Thanks to the Revolution, the state was more efficient and rational than the Old Regime. Thanks to his military power, it was also more coercive. Under the Old Regime, the citizen was often lost in a bewildering maze of antiquated and overlapping jurisdictions; he now marched in the straight corridors of a systematic despotism.

The functions of the executive were gathered into a single pair of hands. All discretionary power—the choice of peace or war, the initiation and approval of new laws, and constitutional changes—was held, in effect, by Bonaparte: no group, no class, no official body dared to oppose him. Step by quick step, the executive became more and more monarchical and Napoleon more exalted, always with the approval of the popular plebiscite but without public discussion. In 1802, when he became Consul for life, he dropped his family name. Two years later, he made himself hereditary Emperor of France. The title of Emperor still carried the old connotation of ruler of the whole Christian world. There were many kings, but there could be only one emperor. After Napoleon's assumption of the title, the Hapsburg ruler dropped his own title of Holy Roman Emperor. In the ceremony at Notre Dame Cathedral, Napoleon seized the iron crown of Lombardy—which had sat on the brow of Charlemagne— from the startled Pope Pius VII, who had been invited to crown him, and placed it on his head himself. He remembered that a thousand years before, on Christmas Day 800, Charlemagne had allowed the Pope to crown him, and that his successors were never allowed to forget that their authority was invalid without papal sanction. None of this for Napoleon, who was fond of reading history.

Abroad, the Emperor's brothers and sisters, his uncles and his cousins and his aunts, became kings and queens, duchesses, cardinals, princes, highnesses, and consorts, and enjoyed emoluments appropriate to their dignities. Napoleon bowed to fashion, but he had little respect for bearers of titles. He considered the rulers of Europe to be, almost without exception, fools and madmen, and the members of his own family incompetent. He made no friends; the

169

only person he respected was his mother, whose comment upon her son's fantastic success was "Provided it lasts!" The fanfare and tinsel was meant to impress and dazzle people and to throw the other monarchies into the shade. At odd moments Napoleon also regarded it as a travesty, a practical joke on a continental scale. There was much of the actor in him, and while he half-believed in the role he was playing, he enjoyed the joke as well as the power. For a long time, following the Roman tradition to the letter, he refused to abjure republicanism. Until 1807 his coins carried the device: "République Française —Napoléon I, Empereur," while the sonorous "Liberté, Égalité, Fraternité" was discarded.

Although men remained, as the Revolution had decreed, equal before the law, imperial pomp required aristocratic and clerical circumstance. Noblemen were tempted back from exile to adorn the new court with the old gold of tradition and to lend it an air of authenticity. One can manufacture anything, except tradition. The overwhelming majority of the nearly 150,000 *émigrés* returned to France. Napoleon added a nobility of his own by creating, in 1802, the Legion of Honor, membership in which was a reward for civil or military merit. Never fanatical, Napoleon preserved religious toleration, but he re-established as official the Roman Catholic Church. He exercised a greater control over clerical appointments than had the Bourbon kings and exacted more onerous political services from the clergy. This applied not only to the Catholic but also to the Protestant and Jewish churches, which he also recognized as official, in an effort to broaden as much as possible the religious sanctions of his authority and of

The coronation of the Empress Josephine by Napoleon in the Cathedral of Notre Dame. A few minutes before, Napoleon had snatched the crown from Pope Pius VII (1800-23), sitting behind him, and placed it upon his own head. Napoleon's mother is watching the scene from the circle above. An engraving after the painting by David. CULVER

his system of conscription. Only the Catholic priests, however, were paid by the state. The recognition of three churches was a *reductio ad absurdum* of the idea of an established religion, but Napoleon's mind was at home in strange arrangements. His aims were thoroughly practical. He used religion deliberately to instill loyalty in the young. The catechism approved by the Catholic Church left nothing to the imagination in spelling out the duties of French children:

> Christians owe to the princes who rule them, and we in particular owe to Napoleon I, our Emperor, love, respect, obedience, loyalty, military service, the dues laid down for the conservation and the defense of the empire and of his throne; we also owe him fervent prayers for his safety and for the temporal and spiritual prosperity of the State.
>
> —Why do we owe all these duties towards our Emperor?
>
> Firstly, because God . . . plentifully bestowing gifts upon our Emperor, whether for peace or for war, has made him the minister of His power and His image upon earth. Secondly, because our Lord Jesus Christ, both by His teaching and His example, has taught us Himself what we owe to our Sovereign. . . .
>
> —Are there not particular reasons which should attach us more closely to Napoleon I, our Emperor?
>
> Yes, because it is he whom God has sustained, in difficult circumstances, so that he might re-establish public worship and the holy faith of our fathers, and that he might be their protector. He has restored and maintained public order by his profound and active wisdom; he defends the State with his powerful arm; he has become the anointed of the Lord by the consecration he has received from the sovereign Pontiff, head of the universal church.
>
> —What must one think of those who should fail in their duty toward our Emperor?
>
> According to the Apostle Paul, they would resist the established order of God Himself, and would render themselves worthy of eternal damnation.

When Napoleon turned from imperial to legal and social concerns he revealed the mentality of an ordinary burgher. He revised revolutionary legislation and assembled it in the Code Napoléon, which brought order and security to property and propriety to the family. It extended protection to the buyers of the liberated and confiscated lands thrown upon the market by the Revolution. It confirmed the superiority of the employer over the employee. Workers were forbidden to form unions, to call strikes, or even to move about the country without a "passport" issued by the police. It was made difficult for a worker to get a job unless his former master gave him a good character. In wage disputes, the word of the employer was always credited. The Code stiffened the penalties for offenses against persons and property. It revived some, though not all, of the barbarities of the Old Regime—branding, for example.

Napoleon believed in social inequality. As security went with property, property went with honor. The officials and dignitaries of the state were showered with gold and lands. Senators and marshals received large salaries and estates. Dignities were open to men of unusual talent and ability, but once attained they must be shored up by wealth. The egalitarian and leveling features of the revolutionary legislation were absent from the Code Napoléon. Men regained their superiority over women, the old over the young, legitimate children over illegitimate. The husband controlled the wife's property, and also her conduct. His power over the children was restored. Most important of all, equality of inheritance was weakened. The revolutionary code had provided that only one tenth of a property might be distributed at will; the rest was to be divided equally among the heirs. The Code Napoléon raised the discretionary portion to one quarter, and to one half if the testator had only one child. Bastards were again disinherited. Entail was revived, but it was valid for only one generation.

With the Code and the sword, Napoleon restored public security. He snuffed out the brigandage and the disorder of the countryside, which had become endemic during the revolutionary years. The peasants regarded the successful general as the guardian of their recent gains. Free political life interested them less than it did the urban population. The state was better organized to deal with town radicals, street marchers and demonstrators, and organizers of clubs. The police and spy system directed by the notorious Joseph Fouché—a former Jacobin, like Napoleon himself—was efficient, and the military could be used for domestic repression as well as foreign conquest. What, above all, kept the towns orderly was the acquiescence of the bulk of the middle classes. They preferred, at least for the moment, the comforts of order to the dangers of freedom. They were relieved to see an end to democratic and radical experiments. Only consistent liberals, Jacobins, and a few intellectuals and men of letters remained unreconciled, and Napoleon pursued them with the same persistence with which he fought William Pitt and Horatio Nelson.

It was in the highly qualified form of the Code Napoléon that the revolutionary settlement of France spread to other countries, by conquest and later

172

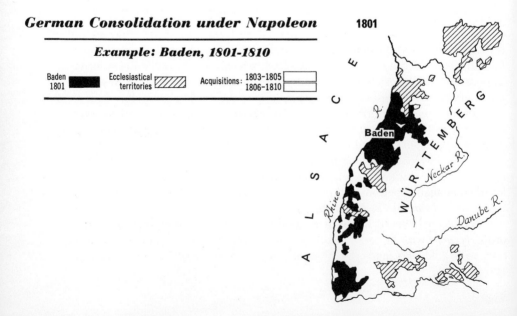

German Consolidation under Napoleon   1801

Example: Baden, 1801-1810

Baden 1801   Ecclesiastical territories   Acquisitions: 1803-1805 1806-1810

also by imitation. The regions subject to France or obedient to her influence had more reason than France to be grateful to Napoleon. He completed the process of reorganization that the revolutionary armies had begun in the Netherlands and the Rhineland. In Germany, Napoleon destroyed the system of petty states and ecclesiastical sovereignties. The dozens of small states were assembled into fewer and larger units for the sake of uniformity of administration. The ecclesiastical states were merged with secular units, as were the small independent baronies and most of the city-states. In all, 112 sovereignties were wiped out. In Italy, similarly, the half dozen principalities of Lombardy became a single state, and several principalities farther to the south another one.

The compact state and uniform administration spread from the Atlantic countries eastward. In western Germany and Italy, semifeudal obligations, provincial distinctions in law and taxes, ecclesiastical monopolies and exemptions, aristocratic privileges, restrictions on the movement of men or goods, restrictions on the choice of occupation and professions—these and their numerous and colorful kind were suppressed. In their place came simpler laws, fewer imposts, equal taxation for all areas and classes, religious toleration, and a greater centralization of administration. New elements were drawn into public service, chiefly landed proprietors, merchants, and professional men.

Napoleon "sold" reform at a high price. He levied money and goods to support the liberating armies, some of which were stationed permanently in the conquered areas. He allowed his generals and bureaucrats to line their pockets at the expense of the local population. Yet, taken all in all, the German and Italian states were paying a smaller price for reform than France had paid, whether measured in gold or in blood. But they imported a truncated "French Revolution." Large-scale proprietorship was not diminished as in France; no serious attempts were made to institute constitutional government and republicanism. Napoleon did not propose to establish abroad the free political life that he had destroyed at home.

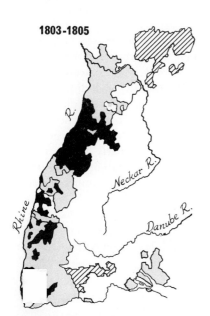

1803-1805

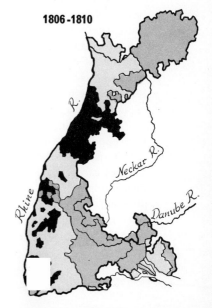

1806-1810

The Louisiana Purchase

Both Bonapartism and republicanism were daring and, for their time, novel creations. For the moment, Bonapartism was much the stronger of the two. Its wealth, population, and military resources were imperial. But what of the future? Bonapartism depended on the constant exhibition of force and on artifice. In the constricted Old World, a new government could get elbow room only by pushing and attacking. In his inaugural address of 1801, President Jefferson exulted that America had "room enough for our descendants to the hundredth and thousandth generation." Republicanism could afford to trust its fate to the operation of the natural forces of the environment and of human ability. The Republic must improve the advantage that derived from its distance from the rivalries and threats of Europe and its possession of a freedom-loving, agrarian population scattered over generous areas. "I know," Jefferson said in his address,

> that some honest men fear that a republican government cannot be strong; that this [American] government is not strong enough. But would the honest patriot, in the full tide of successful experiment, abandon a government which has so far kept us free and firm, on the theoretic and visionary fear that this government, the world's best hope, may by possibility want energy to preserve itself? I trust not. I believe this, on the contrary, the strongest government on earth. I believe it is the only one where every man, at the call of the laws, would fly to the standard of the law, and would meet invasions of the public order as his own personal concern. Sometimes it is said that man cannot be trusted with the government of himself. Can he, then, be trusted with the government of others? Or have we found angels in the form of kings to govern him? Let history answer this question.

There was one qualification to the accessibility of the hinterland to Americans: half the continent, beyond the Mississippi River, was held or claimed by European empires. Some elements in the United States were disposed to appeal to force and intrigue in order to supplant the European powers, but there was danger that in doing so they would turn the United States into a militaristic state and exalt the authority of a few leaders. In expanding the body of the Republic by force, they could, Jefferson felt, destroy its soul. He preferred to exploit natural circumstances cautiously, but with perseverance.

For a while, fortune smiled on his policy. Without his raising a finger, his chief opponents within and without the Republican party destroyed one another. As late as 1798, the Federalist leader Alexander Hamilton had dreamed of a military career that would enable him to reopen the possibility of a conservative development of the American system. In a quarrel with Aaron Burr, the Republican Vice President, in 1804, Hamilton accepted the challenge to fight a duel rather than forfeit the "honor" essential to a military mind. He was mortally wounded. Sometime before his end, Hamilton had written the epitaph of his strivings: "Every day proves to me more and more that this American world was not made for me."

The climax of Burr's own career was unenviable. In 1806 he assembled an informal and secret maritime expedition on the Mississippi in order to invade Louisiana, or to descend upon New Orleans, or to invade Mexico—nobody knows which and very likely Burr had not decided. This adventure threatened to involve the United States in war with Spain, and Burr was arrested and tried for treason. Although he was acquitted for lack of adequate information, his position in the Republican party was irretrievably compromised. The tide of adventurism was ebbing.

Jefferson succeeded beyond the dreams of Burr and Hamilton in the very realm they had aspired to win, but by his own moderate methods. In 1800 Napoleon, hoping to revive the French Empire in North America, constrained Spain to yield Louisiana, the large basin of the Mississippi on its western bank. This territory included the port of New Orleans, which, situated near the mouth of the Mississippi, controlled the trade moving up and down the river. By a treaty with Spain the United States had obtained the right to navigate the Mississippi and to establish a place near its mouth in which to deposit and reload goods for further shipment. But France was a greater and more aggressive force than Spain, and her renewed interest in the area made the future uncertain. The right of deposit was suspended in 1802. The Western areas of the United States depended on the Mississippi as an outlet for their produce. Might they not be drawn toward the power that controlled the river?

"There is on the globe one single spot, the possessor of which is our natural . . . enemy," President Jefferson wrote to his Minister in France, Robert R. Livingston. "It is New Orleans, through which the produce of three eighths of our territory must pass to market, and from its fertility it will erelong yield more than half of our whole produce and contain more than half of our inhabitants." As a solution to the problem, Jefferson proposed that France sell New Orleans to the United States.

Napoleon was at the moment in no position to prosecute his ambitions in America. Under the brilliant Negro leader Toussaint L'Ouverture (1743-1803), rebels had seized control in San Domingo. A French army was having difficulty in suppressing the rebellion; indeed, the army was eventually defeated. Without a secure foothold in the West Indies, an empire on the mainland seemed untenable. War had broken out again between France and Great Britain, and there was a possibility that the British navy would wrest from Napoleon his newly acquired territory in America. All these circumstances, however, are inadequate to explain the step Napoleon took. Suddenly, and against all counsel, he offered to sell not only New Orleans but the whole of Louisiana—a veritable empire—for fifteen million dollars. He probably hoped to recapture it somehow: he delighted in transferring and retaking lands and in scrambling the map.

It was an extraordinary opportunity. Yet the United States did not find it so easy to buy as he to sell. There were sections of the country—New England was one—which were apprehensive lest their influence diminish with the indefinite expansion westward. The Constitution made no provision for buying land or expanding the boundaries of the Union, and the Republicans were committed to its strict interpretation. Jefferson would have preferred to wait until a constitutional amendment authorized him to act. But there was no time and no alternative. In 1803 Jefferson accepted Napoleon's offer. "The Executive," he said openly, "has done an act beyond the Constitution. The legislature must ratify it and throw themselves upon the country for an act of indemnity." The Senate approved the purchase by twenty-four votes to seven. Louisiana was organized as a federal territory with an autonomous government and a governor appointed by the President. When the population increased and became accustomed to Anglo-Saxon law and institutions, it would be divided into individual states and members of the Union.

The acquisition of Louisiana, more than any other act, assured the material greatness of the United States. It nearly doubled the territory of the Union and contributed, eventually, twelve states of unusual size. The American Republic became the largest country in the Western world, save Russia. It now measured almost two million square miles and was more extensive than the Roman Empire in the golden age of the Antonine Emperors. In a few years, the basin of the Mississippi was made more productive, and its distant corners more accessible, by the application of the steam engine to river transportation. Settlers in large numbers and freight in bulk began to move up and down the tributaries of the great river.

The faith of the Constitutional Convention of 1787 that republicanism and federalism were suitable to extensive states was reaffirmed by Jefferson:

> I know that the acquisition of Louisiana has been disapproved by some, from a candid apprehension that the enlargement of our territory would endanger its Union. But who can limit the extent to which the federative principle may operate effectively? The larger our association, the less it will be shaken by local passions; and in any view, is it not better that the opposite bank of the Mississippi should be settled by our own brethren and children, than by strangers of another family? With which shall we be most likely to live in harmony and friendly intercourse?

The final condition of American security, after land and republicanism, was peace. Jefferson and his followers associated the habits of aggression with the old order. They hoped that economic pressure might prove an adequate substitute for war. European statesmen, however, often resorted to war precisely in order to apply economic pressure. Jefferson soon had plenty of opportunity to put his hope to the test. For in 1805 a gigantic struggle opened which involved all Europe and ultimately the United States as well.

9. *The Duel for World Empire*

The conflict initiated by the wars of the French Revolution lasted nearly a quarter century and had two phases. In the 1790's France defended her political and territorial integrity against the assaults of conservative Europe and built a wall of dependent states, re-formed on the republican model, around her eastern borders. The second phase was less ideological. Napoleon fought to make the Continent a French empire, and that empire dominant in the world. The European powers strove to maintain their international position as well as their old institutions.

For France and Great Britain, these struggles were the culmination of a contest that had lasted for more than a century, since the wars between Louis XIV and the Dutch and British empires. Napoleon made an extraordinary effort to destroy the commercial and colonial power of his competitor. Great Britain fought to preserve her trade with the Continent and to enlarge her share in the colonial, shipping, and commercial wealth of the world.

Napoleon vs. Nelson

The occasion of the war symbolized its aims: Napoleon refused to open French ports to British ships. He baited the British with a threat to sail to the Near East, as he had done in 1798, and proceed to India, as he had failed to do earlier. The British refused to return the island of Malta to the ancient order of the Knights of St. John, although they had promised to do so in the Treaty of Amiens. They were determined to maintain their newly acquired position in the Mediterranean Sea.

Napoleon severed diplomatic relations in 1803 and prepared to invade England. Nobody to this day knows whether he intended to do so or merely wanted to keep the British under the threat of invasion; probably Napoleon himself was undecided. He assembled an army at Boulogne, on the Channel, and

177

built a flotilla of small boats, the harbor being too shallow for large ones. The plan was to row the boats across the Channel in foggy and still weather when the British fleet was blinded and becalmed. As additional security, a French fleet was to take off for the West Indies, incidentally destroying merchant shipping on the way, to entice the British to give chase and so leave the Channel unguarded. The French fleet would slip back to cover the invasion while the British were looking for it in American waters. It was not a bad strategy. The British had the choice of defending the West Indian islands and abandoning the Channel, thus exposing their country to invasion, or lingering in the Channel and losing the American islands.

The choice did not seem so narrow to the British, however. The government roused the patriotic fervor of the people and improvised a home-defense army while the fleet maintained a continuous watch over the naval shelters of the enemy. Nevertheless, the French fleet escaped and drew the British vessels in pursuit across the Atlantic Ocean. It returned quickly, following the plan, but hesitation and bad weather kept it out of the Channel.

Early in 1805, William Pitt, an advocate of war *à outrance* and of aggressive imperialism, returned to power in Britain. He proffered a treasure of subsidies to the Continental enemies of France. Napoleon's assumption of the imperial title implied claims to European rule. His unprovoked seizure of the Republic of Genoa in 1805 led the powers to fear that if he did not invade England, Napoleon would attack them instead. In August 1805, therefore, Russia and Austria joined Great Britain in a new coalition—the third. Their fears came true at once.

Napoleon immediately abandoned Boulogne and, pitting leg power against geography, forced his army to march five hundred miles southeastward in ten days. He suddenly appeared before the fortress of Ulm, on the Danube, where the Austrian troops were gathered. Another French army cut off their retreat. In October the Austrians capitulated. Napoleon sped on to Vienna and captured it without a fight. A combined Austro-Russian force retreated to Bohemia, and he followed. On December 2, at the village of Austerlitz, he tempted his enemies to stretch out their armies in a thin arc in order to attack the flanks of the French army. When they did so, he speared the center of the arc and threw the enemy force into confusion. The Austrians made peace while the Russians withdrew eastward. This was the moment that Prussia, avid for British subsidies, chose to break her ten years' peace with France. Napoleon not only bested Prussia at Jena, in October 1806, but dismantled her military system. No state and army defeated by the French collapsed so completely and ignominiously; Napoleon toyed with the idea of wiping Prussia off the map of Europe.

Russia held out for a few more months. In July 1807, following a moderate French victory at Friedland, Napoleon met Czar Alexander on a raft in the Niemen River, near Tilsit in Poland, and concluded an agreement. Russia joined the French attack on Great Britain and pulled in Denmark, whose dynasty was allied to the Russian. By closing the entrance of the Baltic to British ships, Denmark indirectly involved Sweden, which formally remained neutral. Napoleon and Alexander projected farther flung but vaguer plans. The Czar hoped to obtain Constantinople, which Napoleon appeared to promise but meant to withhold. There was talk of an overland attack, across the Caucasus mountains and through Persia, upon the great prize of India.

While he won on the Continent, Napoleon lost on the ocean. On October 21, 1805, four days after the French had captured an Austrian army in Ulm, Admiral Lord Nelson won a decisive naval victory. Commanding twenty-seven ships, he met the combined French and Spanish fleets, counting together thirty-three ships, near Cape Trafalgar off the coast of Spain. The allied fleet was arrayed in the conventional single file, expecting to pair off ship for ship for a broadside engagement. Nelson avoided this familiar strategy in a maneuver resembling that of Napoleon at Austerlitz. The Emperor had aimed his stroke at the center of the opposing army. Nelson divided his fleet into two forces which advanced perpendicularly on the long line of the enemy and severed it into three parts. One of Nelson's squadrons isolated the enemy ships in the rear

The Attack at Trafalgar, October 21, 1805

➡ **British, 27 ships**
▷ **French, 18** ⎰ **33 ships**
▷ **Spanish, 15** ⎱
   V—*Victory*, the flagship of Admiral Lord Nelson
   B—*Bucentaure*, the flagship of the French Admiral Pierre
   de Villeneuve
   The French and Spanish ships marked + were taken or destroyed.

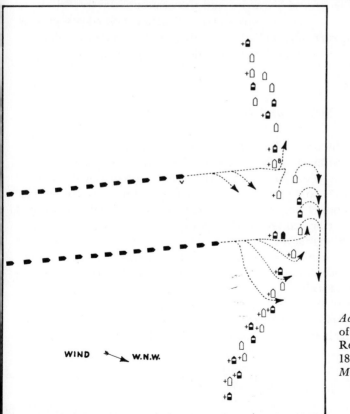

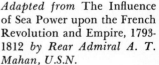

Adapted from The Influence of Sea Power upon the French Revolution and Empire, 1793-1812 *by Rear Admiral A. T. Mahan, U.S.N.*

to prevent them from coming to the assistance of their sister ships. The other tackled the center group ship for ship. The French-Spanish fleet forfeited the advantage of superior numbers and lost twenty-two ships. Nelson virtually annihilated the naval power of France and Spain and inaugurated a century of British control of the oceans. The price Britain paid for this victory was the great admiral himself—Nelson was killed in the last moments of battle.

There remained one threat to Britain's new-won supremacy: France might make up her losses by obtaining the aid of the fleets of Denmark, Sweden, and Portugal. Great Britain secured her position by a piratical act. George Canning (1770-1827), the Foreign Secretary, ordered the most important surviving navy, that of Denmark, seized. In August 1807, a British fleet appeared suddenly before Copenhagen and bombarded the city, as it had done in 1801, without a declaration of war. Its shells killed nearly two thousand civilians. The Danes surrendered eighteen ships of the line and forty frigates.

Napoleon thereupon tried to seize the Portuguese navy. A French army under Marshal Andoche Junot struck out across Spain for Lisbon, marching twenty uphill miles a day. The British raced them by sea. On November 30, 1807, the Portuguese capital surrendered to the fifteen hundred famished French soldiers who had survived the brutal march. On the day before, the British navy had forcefully persuaded the Prince Regent of the country to come aboard and sail to his colony of Brazil, his naval and merchant fleet in tow. A Russian fleet which arrived to help secure the Portuguese ships for the newly concluded Franco-Russian alliance was blockaded and then captured by the British. In the Baltic Sea, a tacit agreement between Great Britain and Sweden kept their fleets from engaging each other in battle. The Russian ships in that sea also were blockaded. Thus were all the fleets of Europe destroyed, immobilized, captured, or blockaded.

The Continental System and the British Empire

Mars divided the prizes of war evenly. While Britannia ruled the waves, the French controlled much of the Continent. The stage was set for a decisive test between the two imperial systems. The British system rested on naval control, overseas trade, and industrial production. The French rested on military and territorial power, the extension of moderate reform, and a centralized administration. Great Britain used her sea power to advance a profitable mixture of mercantilism and *laissez faire*. She monopolized trade and shipping in the areas and routes under her control and claimed the benefits of free trade elsewhere. France used her military predominance to enforce mercantilist policies on a Continental scale.

Napoleon enlarged the French Empire and organized most of the Continent around it. At its greatest extent, the Empire included not only Belgium, Holland, and the Rhineland, but Catalonia, most of the Italian peninsula, and the North Sea coast of Germany. It stretched to the Baltic and Balkan coasts. Russia, Austria, Prussia, and all the smaller states were bound to the Empire by alliance. Sweden and the Ottoman Empire were lonely exceptions.

In Germany and Italy, the influence of Prussia, Austria, and the papacy gave way to that of France. Napoleon reduced the Kingdom of Prussia to less than half its former size and pushed its western boundary back across the Elbe. The Hohenzollerns were confined to their old holdings in Pomerania and Prussia proper. In 1807 Napoleon combined the Prussian and Austrian gains from the partitions of Poland to form the Grand Duchy of Warsaw, which joined his allies. In July 1806 fourteen German states west of the Elbe were grouped into a Confederation of the Rhine, with Napoleon as "protector." The members of the Confederation abolished aristocratic and clerical privileges and local distinctions of law and taxation. Completing a process begun in 1803, they assimilated some two hundred intervening and neighboring statelets. The internal state lines of Germany were settled until the advent of Hitler.

The central and some of the northern areas of Italy became part of the French Empire. The other northern states of the peninsula were grouped together as the Kingdom of Italy, with Napoleon as king. When his son François (1811-32) was born, Napoleon incorporated the Kingdom into the French Empire and named the infant King of Rome. As Rome and Constantinople had once been the twin capitals of the Roman Empire, Rome and Paris were now the capitals of the French Empire. The Kingdom of Naples, in the south, was turned over by Napoleon first to his brother Joseph Bonaparte and then, when the Bourbon ruler of Spain was dethroned and Joseph promoted to his place (in 1808), to Marshal Joachim Murat (1767-1815), his favorite cavalry leader. Murat had married Napoleon's sister Caroline.

Hoops of iron and gold held together Napoleon's empire and alliance system. Military predominance was assured by limiting the armies of Austria and Prussia to 150,000 and 42,000 men, respectively. The Italian and German states pledged financial tribute and, in time of war, military assistance to France. This enabled Napoleon to avoid borrowing from financiers and investors and to lighten the burden of the French taxpayer. He subsidized home manufactures, particularly those that suffered from the struggle with Great Britain. A rigorous tariff excluded the goods of other Continental states from France, or raised their price, while the satellite states were forced to accept French goods free of duty. Russia and Austria, by agreeing to shut out British goods, favored imports from France. French commerce and manufactures prospered to an unusual degree.

Napoleon locked the doors of the Continent against British trade. He multiplied prohibitions of imports. Whole classes of goods—for example, cotton, woolen, and muslin stuffs—were defined as British, regardless of the port of immediate origin or place of manufacture, and banned from the French market. Foreign goods on the prohibited list were confiscated and burned publicly.

In November 1806, Napoleon issued the Berlin Decree, in which he announced that, since Great Britain made war unfairly by attacking all commerce on the high seas, all commerce with her was to cease. He declared the British Isles blockaded, although he could not patrol their coasts. Henceforth any vessels sailing to or from them would be seized, wherever they were found. British subjects in French-held lands were liable to imprisonment and confiscation of their goods. These rules were stiffened in the Milan Decree of 1807.

Napoleon compelled virtually all the states of Europe in effect to blockade themselves against British products. The satellites fell into line by command; Prussia, Austria, Russia, and Denmark by agreement. The Continental System was complete.

To this system Great Britain opposed one that transcended the boundaries of Europe. She spread a network of strategic posts around the seven seas, penetrated the maritime empires of France and her dependents, and intensified industrial production. After the naval victories of 1805 Great Britain struck in every direction. She lunged at Turkey, forcing the entrance to the Dardanelles, but was unable to capture Constantinople. She landed an army in Egypt, although it was soon ousted. Elsewhere, Britain prevailed. She added the Ionian Islands, off the coast of Greece, to her Mediterranean possessions. By supporting the Bourbon dynasty, which had been forced to quit the mainland, Great Britain dominated the policy of Sicily. She attempted in vain to seize the port of Stralsund in the Baltic.

In the East, Britain's success was noteworthy. The conquest of the interior of India, which had begun in the mid-eighteenth century, continued apace. The Dutch colonies of Java, Ceylon, and Amboyna and the French outposts in India were captured. So were the valuable calling places for ships in the Indian Ocean, the French islands of Bourbon (later named Réunion) and Mauritius, and the Cape Colony itself, the Dutch tip of Africa. The route to India and the opportunities for Eastern trade and riches became a virtual British monopoly.

In the Western Hemisphere Great Britain prosecuted "the policy of filching sugar islands." One after another, she took over the Dutch, the French, and the Spanish possessions in the West Indies. By 1810 all the islands were under the British flag. Following Trafalgar, the British navy seized the ports of Montevideo and Buenos Aires on the east coast of South America and dispatched an expedition to occupy Chile on the west coast. The fact that these attacks were repelled or withdrawn suggested that there were limits to the territorial expansion of an essentially maritime power.

Napoleon's replacement of the Bourbon ruler of Spain by his brother Joseph in 1808 provided Spain's American colonists with a long-awaited opportunity to win their autonomy. Proclaiming their allegiance to Ferdinand VII, who had never reigned and was in French captivity, the Latin Americans proceeded to elect their own officials and set up their own provincial governments. Since England had allied herself with the deposed Bourbons, she claimed a right to trade with South and Central America. In the absence of French vessels, even merchants in French possessions in the Western Hemisphere traded

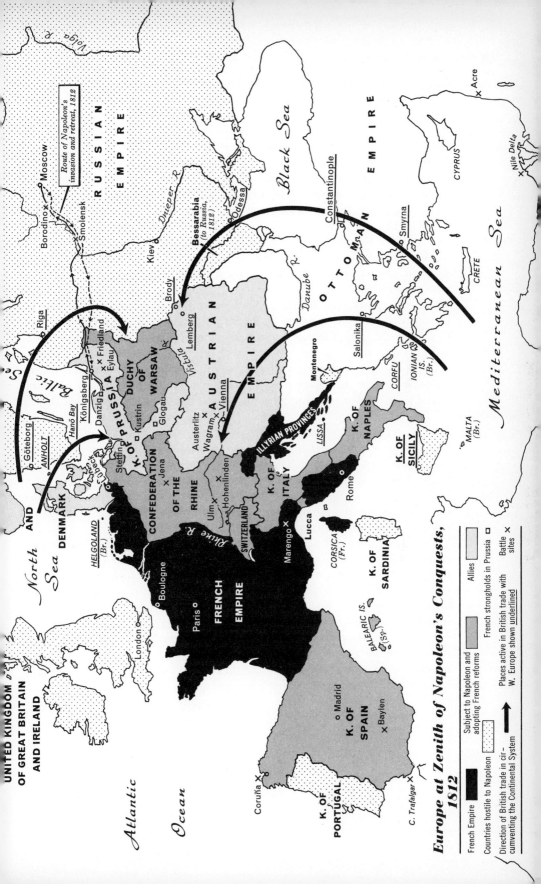

Europe at Zenith of Napoleon's Conquests, 1812

Legend:
- French Empire
- Countries hostile to Napoleon
- Subject to Napoleon and adopting French reforms
- Allies
- French strongholds in Prussia
- Battle sites ×
- Direction of British trade in cir-cumventing the Continental System
- Places active in British trade with W. Europe shown underlined

UNITED KINGDOM OF GREAT BRITAIN AND IRELAND
- London o

RUSSIAN EMPIRE
- Moscow ×
- Borodino ×
- Smolensk ×
- Kiev o
- Odessa o
- Riga
- Route of Napoleon's invasion and retreat, 1812

OTTOMAN EMPIRE
- Constantinople
- Smyrna o
- Salonika o
- Montenegro
- CYPRUS
- CRETE
- Acre ×
- Nile Delta ×

DUCHY OF WARSAW
- Lemberg o
- Brody o
- Danzig
- Königsberg ×
- Friedland ×
- Eylau ×
- Küstrin o
- Glogau o
- Bessarabia (to Russia, 1812)

K. OF PRUSSIA
- Stettin
- Lübeck

AUSTRIAN EMPIRE
- Vienna ×
- Austerlitz ×
- Wagram ×
- Hohenlinden ×

CONFEDERATION OF THE RHINE
- Jena ×
- Ulm ×

FRENCH EMPIRE
- Paris o
- Boulogne o
- Marengo ×
- Lucca ×
- Rome o

K. OF ITALY
- ILLYRIAN PROVINCES

K. OF NAPLES

K. OF SICILY

K. OF SARDINIA

K. OF SPAIN
- Madrid o
- Baylen ×
- Coruña ×
- C. Trafalgar ×

K. OF PORTUGAL

DENMARK
- Anholt
- Hanö Bay
- Göteborg o
- HELGOLAND (Br.)
- MALTA (Br.)
- CORSICA (Fr.)
- BALEARIC IS. (Sp.)
- IONIAN IS. (Br.)
- CORFU
- LISSA
- SWITZERLAND

Seas and waters:
- North Sea
- Baltic Sea
- Black Sea
- Mediterranean Sea
- Atlantic Ocean

Rivers:
- Volga R.
- Dnieper R.
- Vistula R.
- Danube R.
- Rhine R.

with the British. The opening of these new markets at a time when Napoleon was closing more and more European ports was a godsend to British commerce, shipping, and industry.

On the seas, British warships and merchantmen seized ships flying the flags of the "enemies," who numbered as many as the allies and dependents of Napoleon. While manufacturers reaped the advantages of reduced foreign competition, the owners of privateers and the naval crews pocketed more direct profits: the courts awarded them the goods they captured. The interests of traders, shippers, and naval officers were thus conjoined.

The British did not propose to abandon the European continent to their rivals. When Napoleon declared a blockade of England, England declared a blockade of the Continent. "As France had said she would have no trade with England, she was to have no trade except with (or through) England." Both were "paper blockades" since they were not enforced by a naval patrol of the interdicted coasts. The British allowed neutral ships to sail to the Continent provided that they first called at British ports and paid the usual duties and fees. They thus levied tribute on all trade with Europe. Napoleon retorted with a decree that any ship which called at British ports or whose captain allowed it to be searched for enemy or contraband goods would be fair French prey. In order to save such ships from the wrath of the French, British firms sold forged ships' papers, showing that the owners had not called in Great Britain.

Behind the appearance of retaliation there was a difference between the French and British policies. Napoleon was engaged in an effort to destroy the trade of the enemy. The British strove to frustrate that attempt; but their design was more ambitious. They used war measures as an excuse to seize the trade of neutrals and of countries nominally subject to Napoleon or allied to him, which meant the trade of virtually all commercial European countries; such trade as they did not seize or supplant they taxed heavily when the neutrals called at their ports.

The militancy of Britain's statesmen and sailors was matched by the ingenuity of her manufacturers and merchants. The war and the sharpened competition for markets intensified advances in industry. Napoleon made strong efforts to revive French manufactures, but Great Britain had a head start. The application of steam power led to an increase in the number and variety of manufactured products and a reduction in their price, at a time when the commerce of Great Britain had need of every resource. The textile industry continued to be the principal contributor and index of economic advance. At the opening of the nineteenth century, England imported about 60 million bales of raw cotton per year and exported finished goods valued at 8 million pounds sterling. By 1810, at the height of the struggle with Napoleon, both imports and exports had more than doubled.

The Economic Stalemate

The long conflict strained the energies of France and Great Britain. Napoleon waged endless war with smugglers and traders, and indirectly with the European consumer. When Napoleon closed French and Belgian ports to the British, their ships siphoned goods through the ports of northern Italy and Holland. Napoleon's allies in those countries could not enforce his regulations. His own brother, King Louis of Holland, had not the heart to ruin the business of his subjects. Napoleon thereupon annexed Holland and Genoa and incorporated them into his own administration.

The British sailed further east. They occupied the island of Helgoland, off the northern coast of Germany, and dealt with smugglers operating through the busy estuaries of Bremen and Hamburg. In the south their ships pressed into the Adriatic docks and beaches. Napoleon followed them along the coast, wrested Venetia and Dalmatia from Austria, and occupied the northern coast of Germany. British fleets then appeared in the Baltic and in the many bays of the Aegean Sea, looking for opportunities to push goods into the Continent. Gothenburg in the Baltic and Salonika in the Aegean became flourishing entrepôts. Land routes shifted from west to east, and the commercial importance of Central and Eastern Europe, which had been dormant for centuries, was revived. From beaches and small landings, from obsolete and abandoned docks, through undeveloped and pastoral regions, over the roughest mountain trails, up the Danube and the rivers of the north, a wealth of tropical, colonial, and industrial goods moved into the heart of the Continent.

Napoleon paced the coast and pursued. He extended his empire across the base of Denmark and occupied the old Hanseatic emporium of Lübeck in the Baltic Sea. But he could not be sure that Russia would continue to keep the rear door to Europe locked. Was he to make war on the Ottoman Empire in order to repair the breached wall of the Balkans? He had already twisted his empire out of shape; two long and thin arms protruded from its western mass and stretched to Lübeck in the north and Dalmatia in the south. Moreover, military occupation was not completely effective. Napoleon found no new means to deal with smuggling, the twin brother of restriction. Even in times of peace, the eighteenth-century monarchs had had to employ agents by the thousands to prevent smuggling. The agents often supplemented their income by cooperating with their quarries. There are naturally no official figures for smuggling trade, but students of the subject suspect that it amounted to as much as the legal trade throughout the eighteenth century. In some cases it is known to have amounted to much more. The Continental System sharpened the ingenuity of the smugglers. Camouflaged carriages, even hearses, moved forbidden goods. Napoleon confiscated and burned more and more goods and jailed more and more violators and complaisant officials. This made business more risky and pushed up prices, but the market seemed insatiable. Napoleon

185

finally decided that, since he could not destroy illegal trade, he might as well share in its proceeds. His tariffs of Trianon and Fontainebleau in 1810 permitted the entry of goods at a duty which was slightly lower than the estimated charges of the smugglers. He became his own smuggler.

Napoleon was at war not so much with smuggling as with the widespread craving for sugar, cheap cloth, and modern credit. How was he to assuage the taste for tropical luxuries which the upper and middle classes had developed? Sugar, spices, tea, and coffee could be supplied only through British or British-controlled shipping. The same was true of the all-important quinine, which was used as a specific for most ailments. How was Napoleon to stop a trade which profited everybody? A pound of sugar, for example, which brought eight cents in the West Indies, sold for $1.20 to $1.45 in France and Germany. How were Continental manufacturers to meet the low prices resulting from a series of improvements in the English textile industry or to obtain raw materials, such as cotton, from overseas? Napoleon made brave but futile efforts to find substitutes. He encouraged experiments with beet sugar, which was not manufactured on a substantial scale until long after his death.

Napoleon's economic ideas were conventionally mercantilist, with a touch of physiocracy. He tried to undermine the British financial structure by hoarding precious metals and drawing them out of Britain. The British threw a bridge over every financial chasm. Lacking specie, the Bank of England had stopped redeeming paper notes in coin in 1798 and did not resume for twenty years. But the faith and discipline of the business community made up for the shortage of specie. Leading merchants continued to accept payment in paper notes at face value. Although the charges on the national debt grew rapidly, financiers continued to advance loans to the government. By shipping goods through devious channels, the merchants established credits on the Continent which they sold to the government in exchange for paper notes. The government then sent instructions to transfer the money from Continental consumers and middlemen to military contractors. Thus the British raised troops against Napoleon by using the Continent's own supply of specie.

But in 1810-11, when Napoleon's position was still strong, the island empire experienced an economic crisis. Although the French navy could not challenge British supremacy on the high seas, divided into hunting packs, it was able to sink and seize much shipping. In 1809 it seized 571 British ships, and in 1810, the extraordinary number of 619. Insurance rates in Britain went up sharply. Trade diminished and factories were shut down. Unemployment rose, and in the winter of 1811-12 workers rioted in the streets. Sometimes men destroyed the machines that were the symbol, if not the cause, of their misery. A series of bad harvests reduced the supply and increased the price of food. In 1812 Great Britain was close to famine. Napoleon acted on mercantilist principles: you fed your enemy and took his money. If you sold your rival as much as possible and bought from him as little as possible, you would drain off his specie and destroy his credit. The Emperor dispatched ship after ship of grain, with instructions to buy nothing in return and bring back specie. The national debt of Great Britain was snowballing to a degree that seemed fantastic to Englishmen as well as to Frenchmen. The Chancellor of Austria, Prince von Metternich, concluded that the British Empire was about to founder. Yet the year 1812 proved to be the turning point of the long conflict.

Religious and Nationalist Opposition to Napoleon

The fact was that economic forces did not alone decide the war. France could not seal off the Continent, but Great Britain could not carry on normal trade with it. There was one striking difference in the positions of the two countries: the difficulties of the British were chiefly commercial and financial, but those of Napoleon were political and cultural as well.

In France, a substantial group of Jacobins and influential men of letters remained unreconciled to Bonapartism. They protested that constant warfare drained the manhood of the country and the inflated foreign policy defied common sense. Like Napoleon's own mother, many politicians and military men suspected that the Emperor's grandiose structure was brittle. They were alert to the first signs of cracking. The most disquieting rumbling came from abroad. From various sources—religious, national, and military—and from different points of the compass—Prussia, Spain, and Austria—movements and ideologies arose to challenge Napoleon.

A religious opposition had been forming since the earliest days of the Revolution. Burke had pointed to religious sentiment, and De Maistre to religious organization, as necessary to public order. The established churches and devout Christians throughout Europe were scandalized by the confiscation of clerical property and the toleration of dissenters in France and French-held states. The national catastrophes and the personal tragedies of the long succession of wars bred psychological tensions and superstitious fears. Mystics, seers, demagogues, and charlatans drew crowds with threats of doom and promises of salvation. They searched the apocalyptic portions of the Bible for hidden and prophetic meanings. How appropriate to the time were the images of *The Revelation of St. John the Divine*: the Beast with ten crowns, the Four Horsemen, the Avenging Angel. Who was the Satan, the beast that toppled thrones and enchained nations, if not Napoleon? Was not the season of the Avenging Angel at hand? It was with the shout of Antichrist that Andreas Hofer (1767-1810), an innkeeper of Tirol, in 1809 aroused a rebellion against Napoleon. Thousands of peasants joined him to smite the Beast. They were smitten instead, but it was not to be the last rebellion.

Another development was more portentous. Subjection to Napoleon aroused patriotic resentment in many countries. An assortment of grievances brought various classes together in common opposition to the foreign invader. Many merchants and manufacturers envied the special favors enjoyed by French trade. Peasants resented the requisitions of food and cattle by Napoleon's armies. Some of the rulers tried to find a way to the hearts of their subjects.

They appealed, in words strange to their lips, to "the interest of the people" and the "love of the nation." The vogue of romanticism reinforced these tendencies. Poets sang of the beauties of the soil, the glories of the past, and the virtues of the countryman. The medieval, the provincial, and the peculiar—so repellent to the enlightened mind—came into their own. Attempts were made to fuse all interests in one national aim.

In Germany these attempts were prosecuted with a special energy. Much of Germany had become virtually a French colony. The abolition of many tiny states stimulated the desire for a united Germany. German thinkers, who enjoyed a reputation for abstract theorizing, isolated a factor that seemed to them to justify the consolidation of their country. This factor was the national tongue. Although the German language had many dialects, it was the possession that most conspicuously set Germans apart from other Europeans and gave them a claim to territory imperial in extent.

Two men gave direction to the quest for a national philosophy: Johann Gottfried von Herder (1744-1803) and Johann Gottlieb Fichte (1762-1814). Both men were critical of the patrimonial rule of the princes. The fact that Austria had been associated with the now defunct Holy Roman Empire while Prussia had produced, in Frederick II, an aggressive ruler inclined them to look to Prussia for leadership. Herder gave "the nation" a special meaning. To men of the Enlightenment, a "nation" or a "people" had been a representative sample—a smaller edition, as it were—of the human species. Herder's "nation," however, was incomparable. Each nation had its own mysterious and inexpressible "genius." That "genius" was "nowhere more displayed than in the physiognomy of [the nation's] speech." It was reflected in folk poetry and popular idiom. The loyalty of the individual belonged not to humanity but to the nation.

Herder disliked the French but admired Rousseau. He exalted the Germans, yet also prized the Slavs. Fichte was made of sterner stuff. His doctrine raised the Germans high above other peoples. "To possess character and to be German are the same thing." Like Herder, Fichte defined the nation largely by language. "Man," he wrote, "is far more shaped by language than language is by man. . . . Language . . . breaks out as a direct, natural force from intelligent life [and] . . . has directly the power to lay hold of life and to arouse it."

It could hardly be argued that language generally has this power. German, Fichte claimed, was one of the few languages in human history that did. This gift made the Germans not only the greatest but also the only true nation in Europe. "The distinction of the Germans is the fact that they have an original language, while the other [neo-Latin] peoples have an unoriginal, a borrowed, a mixed language. . . ." The ancient Greeks also had an original language, but they were dead. Germany, Fichte claimed, was uniquely great from the beginning. European civilization had been saved by the "heroic" struggle of the early Germans against Rome. The world was again in need of salvation, and it was up to the Germans to repeat the feat of their fathers. In his *Addresses to the German Nation*, delivered at the newly founded University of Berlin in 1810, Fichte called upon the young to abandon the quest for individual freedom and rights, to lose themselves in the nation, to dedicate themselves to the aggressive spirit of their primitive ancestors and smite the latter-day "Romans."

"Turnvater" Friedrich Jahn (1778-1852) gave a more primitive expression to the new nationalism. Jahn brewed a heady mixture of xenophobia, anti-Semitism, and chauvinistic boastfulness. For the classical ideal of "a healthy mind in a healthy body," he substituted a program of patriotic *Turnen*, or gymnastics. He drilled masses of young Germans in the open air and taught them to reject refinement and sophistication as "foreign." He filled them with an admiration of national prejudice and aggression.

While some Germans were exalting their national virtues, others proceeded to imitate French reform. After the defeat by Napoleon at Jena, the Prussian king, Frederick William III (1797-1840), recalled to ministerial office Baron vom Stein, an intransigent enemy of Napoleon and an earnest reformer. Vom Stein worked to modernize the administration, release economic enterprise, and attach the middle and professional classes to the state. He did away with professional castes and opened the occupations to all. Noblemen might henceforth go into trade, and townspeople might buy and sell rural property. He introduced a measure of local administrative autonomy but stopped short of a thorough land reform, freeing the serfs without giving them land. There was talk—which turned out to be only talk—of drafting a constitution. Meanwhile, a council of ministers was established, which made the power of the monarch somewhat less arbitrary.

A group of able younger officers made efforts to infuse brains into the leadership of the army, to diminish the ignorance and brutality of the aristocratic officers, and to break down the wall of mutual contempt that separated them from their soldiers. They persuaded the reluctant King to establish a General Staff of able strategists and schools to train them. Members of the Staff were appointed to guide the commanders in the field. By gradual steps, the King introduced the principle of universal liability to service. He told his officers to stop beating their men and treating them like cattle. He decreed that promotion would henceforth rest

> . . . only on knowledge and education in times of peace, and exceptional bravery, initiative, and perception in times of war. Those individuals, deriving from any part of the nation, who possess these qualities can lay claim therefore to the highest military positions of honor. Because heretofore only one estate had these privileges, all the talent and knowledge of the rest of the nation were lost to the Army, and this estate did not feel at all the necessity to develop their military ability, since birth and long life carried it to the highest military posts of honor. That is the reason why the officers remained behind all the other estates in education. For this reason the Army was regarded as a state within a state, and earned the hatred and to some extent the contempt of the other estates, when instead the Army should represent the union of all the moral and material energies of all the citizens of the state.

The King's words were bolder than his deeds: the officer corps remained aristocratic. But the reformers did achieve three results: young officers were forced to compromise with the "bourgeois" virtues of industry, enterprise, and education; incompetent generals were removed; and positions on the General Staff were reserved to men of ability. Within a few years, the army was invigorated and strengthened. The regular troops, limited by Napoleon to 42,000 men, were supplemented by auxiliary levies of men to perform police and guard service behind the lines.

While Prussia imitated the military organization of France, other countries developed counterstrategies. From 1808 to 1811, when Napoleon stood at the zenith of his political power, Spanish guerrillas and British commanders blunted his sword in a series of campaigns in the Iberian Peninsula.

Speed of movement and reliance on local food supplies were essential to Napoleonic strategy. Now it appeared that the British could march as fast as the French. A British expeditionary force had landed in Portugal in 1808 under the command of Lieutenant General Sir Arthur Wellesley (later the Duke of Wellington, 1769-1852) and besieged the army which Napoleon had dispatched in a vain attempt to seize the Portuguese fleet (see p. 180). The French were compelled to capitulate. A small part of the British force, led by General Sir John Moore (1761-1809), then penetrated northern Spain to assist the rebels against French rule and to divert Napoleon from Portugal. The Emperor himself rushed through mountain passes in bitter December weather to engage Moore's troops, throwing away in the effort three thousand men and horses. But the British general outsped him. Moore forced his troops to march by night as well as by day, losing six thousand men to weariness and the weather. He himself was killed in a final engagement, but the bulk of the British force managed to embark for home at the port of La Coruña.

In Portugal Wellington built three heavy lines of fortification across the peninsula on which the capital of the country stood. Outside Lisbon, the Portuguese militia were ordered to harass the French invaders. The rest was achieved by hunger. At Wellington's insistence, the Portuguese government ordered the rich to the capital with their movable wealth. The peasants were ordered to destroy roads, bridges, and river boats, to burn their provisions, and to abandon their homes for the mountains. When the French army arrived in the autumn of 1810 it found the land a desert. Marshal Masséna stood for months before the fortifications of Torres Vedras; his troops starved or fell at the hands of peasants and guerrillas while foraging for food. He finally withdrew after losing some 25,000 Frenchmen. Wellington's losses were mostly Portuguese soldiers and peasants.

Napoleon's brother Joseph ruled in Madrid, but the provinces and the hinterland were alive with guerrillas. In strategy as in politics, Napoleon presupposed a state of order. To defeat an army in the field and to bend a regime to his will, he had to discover an army that could fall apart, a regime coherent enough to fight or to surrender. But the Spanish Junta, the rebel government, could not control its own territories nor coordinate its campaigns. Local districts raised their own troops and improvised their own campaigns. Again and again, Napoleon defeated large armies only to find that marauding and guerrilla warfare continued. The country was too disorganized to be defeated definitively. The French armies were large enough to win battles, but not large enough to patrol every town and village.

While national movements were arising in Spain, Prussia, and elsewhere, Napoleon was diminishing France's reputation as the leader of reform. In the revolutionary years, wherever French armies arrived they brought administrative and fiscal improvement. As general and First Consul, Napoleon had balanced innovation with expansion. But as Emperor, he tipped the balance against reform. The farther he marched from France, the more he left the Revolution behind. When he organized the Grand Duchy of Warsaw, his outpost in Eastern Europe, he bestowed upon it his Code but withheld the agrarian reform of the Revolution save for the abolition of legal serfdom. Prussia was reorganizing herself by her own efforts. In Spain, King Joseph found a host of competitors. Where his control was effective, Joseph confiscated clerical lands, abolished the rebellious Córtes (parliament) in southern Spain. In 1812, Spanish reformers adopted a constitution modeled principally on the draft of the French National Assembly of 1791, although it profited from English and American examples as well. The term "liberal" was first used to designate the reform party in the Córtes.

Lo Mismo (The Same—With or Without Reason). *This etching, from "Disasters of War" by Francisco de Goya (1746-1828), illustrates the fierceness and desperation of the struggle of Spanish guerrillas against French regulars and the primitive weapons the guerrillas used.*
THE METROPOLITAN MUSEUM OF ART, ROGERS FUND, 1922

America Fights for Freedom of the Seas

The international tension induced by the French-British conflict finally broke at the periphery of the Western world. Russia, at the eastern extremity, and the United States, at the western, rebelled against the efforts of France and Great Britain to force them into their economic systems.

Although Russia was an ally of Napoleon and the United States was neutral, both countries chafed under the restrictions and impositions of economic and maritime warfare. Both wished to secure the freedom of the seas and the rights of neutral shippers. Like France, Russia had looked upon the transatlantic republic as a welcome counterpoise to the maritime ambitions of Great Britain. During the American War of Independence and again during the French revolutionary wars, she strove, in common with other commercial states, to curb British practices on the seas. In 1808, when Russia and the United States were at odds with Great Britain over sea rights, each, acting independently, appointed its first diplomatic representatives to the other.

Geographic and political circumstances led the United States to challenge one of the protagonists and Russia to challenge the other.

The United States was being caught between the devil and the deep blue sea. Great Britain seized any ship that proceeded to Europe without calling at a British port or accepting the visit of a patrol and paying for the privilege in both cases. France seized any ship that did these things. American trade dropped to one third of its former value. As if this were not enough, the British continued an old practice of impressing, or kidnaping, sailors. The American merchant fleet employed many Englishmen who preferred its higher pay and better treatment. Some of them became American citizens, but Great Britain, like many European countries, did not recognize transfers of citizenship. The British fleet was in need of trained sailors, and its traditional method of recruitment was to send gangs to raid port towns and drinking places. This method was extended to the decks of American ships.

The American government protested against impressment and tried to persuade Great Britain and France to relax their claim to control all commerce. The Republicans were inclined to greater antagonism toward Great Britain than toward France, not only because Britain was in a position to do American trade greater harm but also because war with France would strengthen the groups in America—particularly the Federalists—that admired British aristocratic institutions. To avoid choosing between two enemies, President Jefferson resorted to economic pressure. In 1807, at his request, Congress passed the Embargo Act, prohibiting trade with foreign countries.

Although the embargo hurt them, both France and Great Britain refused to modify their restrictions. Jefferson's assumption that nations follow their economic interests was correct, but the European empires did not share his view that the goal of these interests ought to be moderate. Moreover, economic pressure worked both ways. The embargo infuriated the commercial classes of New England, which suffered from the suspension of shipping. American freight found its way promptly to British vessels.

Jefferson wrote later,

> My hope was that, by giving time for reflection and retraction of injury, a sound calculation of their own interests would induce the aggressing nations to redeem their own character by a return to the practice of right. But our lot happens to be cast in an age when two nations to whom circumstances have given a temporary superiority over others, the one by land, the other by sea, throwing off all restrains of morality, all pride of national character, forgetting the mutability of fortune and the inevitable doom which the laws of nature pronounce against departure from justice, individual or national, have dared to treat her reclamations with derision and to set up force instead of reason as the umpire of nations. Degrading themselves thus from the character of lawful societies into lawless bands of robbers and pirates, they are abusing their brief ascendency by desolating the world with blood and rapine.

The embargo was lifted when Jefferson left office, in March 1809. Under James Madison, his successor, Congress passed the Non-Intercourse Law, which barred trade with France and Great Britain but permitted it with all other countries. Then, in May 1809, it passed Macon's Bill No. 2, which provided that trade would be restored with whichever of the two embargoed countries first withdrew her restrictions on American trade. The Non-Intercourse Act would remain in effect against the recalcitrant power. Napoleon took immediate advantage of these terms. He declared—untruthfully, it turned out later—that he was revoking the Berlin and Milan decrees, which had proscribed all commerce, including that of neutrals, with Great Britain. President Madison thereupon proclaimed nonintercourse with Great Britain and dispatched an agent, the poet and merchant Joel Barlow, to seek a broad commercial agreement with France. Napoleon did not keep his word and, after long hesitations and delays, Great Britain, pressed for food and supplies, decided herself to yield to American pressure. On June 23, 1812, she suspended the restrictions of the Orders in Council which applied to American shipping. But it was too late. Five days earlier, Congress had declared war on Great Britain. A group of young representatives from Western states, some of them hoping for territorial conquests in Florida and Canada, had insisted on more drastic action than an embargo. Faster international communication than sailing vessels would have alerted the American government to the imminent suspension of the Orders in Council and thus might have prevented the declaration of war. So close to success had the Jeffersonian policy of economic pressure come.

Napoleon's Campaign in Russia and His First Abdication

War between France and Russia broke out at the same time—in 1812. The Continental System affected Russia's whole foreign trade, overland as well as overseas, and was more onerous for her than the restrictions imposed by the British. Russian noblemen and merchants yearned for the lost profits of trade with Great Britain. Napoleon's hegemony over the Continent threatened Russia's future as a great power. Czar Alexander chafed under Napoleon's refusal to concede him Constantinople, the Holy Grail of Russian imperialism. In 1810 the Czar began to withdraw from the Continental System. The following year he opened Russia's doors to tropical produce and shut them against some of the products of French luxury industries. In June 1812 he made his peace with Britain and concentrated his troops on Russia's western borders. Although they were aligned on opposite sides, Russia and the United States continued their friendly relations.

Napoleon had anticipated Russia's reversal and was considering the possibility of war. His advisers counseled him against a campaign in Russia as too risky. But Napoleon felt that not only his economic system but his European dominion was at stake. If Russia made good her defection, other states were sure to follow suit. By embroiling Great Britain with the United States Napoleon had secured his rear. He recalled troops from Spain and raised new levies in France; he commanded his satellites to march and Austria and Prussia to assist him with troops; he assembled an army of nearly 600,000 men, the largest that the Western world had seen up to that time. In June 1812 he pitted the Grand Army against the vastness of Russia.

The Russian army, which had been split into two groups, counted 300,000 men. Its commanders declined to grant Napoleon an engagement and retreated constantly, calling on the peasants to destroy crops and so starve the French. Russia had even less coherence than Spain and much vaster escapes. Napoleon sliced into the country easily, yet each part continued to live, like the segments of a gargantuan amoeba. The Russian commander, Mikhail Kutuzov (1745-1813), finally turned up on the strategic Borodino River, thinking that it would make a sorry impression if Moscow, nearby, were given up without a show of a fight. Five thousand French soldiers and more Russians died to dispel the rumor that the Czar could not fight because he had no army. Kutuzov succeeded in drawing back with most of his army, and Napoleon entered Moscow on September 14.

Her ancient capital in enemy hands, Russia had now to sue for terms: such was the rule of the game. The Prussian king had sued for peace when Napoleon approached Berlin; the Austrians, when he entered Vienna. For five weeks the conqueror waited for the Czar to surrender. But Alexander could wait longer than Napoleon, who soon discovered that no vital artery led from the heart of Russia to St. Petersburg or anywhere else. Lacking provisions and quarters for his troops—much of Moscow had been burned by the retreating Russians—and with the first snow of the bitter Russian winter falling, Napoleon was finally compelled to make a retreat. He had failed to subdue Russia; and the worst was to come.

The strategy of Kutuzov was to chase the French army out of the country but not to destroy it, for that would benefit Napoleon's Western enemies, particularly Great Britain, more than Russia. A thorough victory, moreover, would tempt the Czar to lunge westward, and Russia would be forced to reorganize herself in order to deal at close quarters with more advanced countries. The guarantee of Russian isolation and conservatism was a modest victory.

The winter of 1812-13 frustrated both Kutuzov and Napoleon. Hardly a tenth part of the Grand Army returned to Poland in disciplined ranks. For every man who fell in pitched battles, many fell to guerrillas, starved, or froze to death. The American reaction to European militarism was epitomized by Joel Barlow, who had followed Napoleon on the Emperor's promise—never

A detachment carrying the Emperor Napoleon's proud "eagles" on his disastrous retreat from Moscow in 1812.
CULVER

fulfilled—to discuss a commercial treaty with the United States. Barlow, who died in Cracow after having witnessed Napoleon's ruinous retreat, spoke, in his "Advice to a Raven in Russia," as the peaceful messenger of the New World to the martial scourge of the Old: The bird of prey had no better friend than "the

195

Great Napoleon." To John Quincy Adams, then American Minister at St. Petersburg, the rout of Napoleon's army was a vindication of the military tactics employed by the American revolutionists against the British: delaying tactics, harassment, and avoidance of direct, full-scale engagements. This so-called Fabian system of warfare was used successfully against Napoleon's generals in Portugal and then against the Emperor himself, the greatest exemplar of professional military "science." A weapon had been found against invaders.

The disintegration of the Grand Army dispelled the myth of Napoleon's invincibility. His enemies came out of hiding. In Paris, as soon as the news of the Russian debacle was known, a plan was hatched to unseat the Emperor. A small group of royalists and republicans announced that he was dead, seized several imperial offices, and was about to proclaim a new government. Apprised of the affair, Napoleon abandoned his retreating army in Russia and sped back to his capital to exact vengeance and reassure his subordinates. It did not escape his notice that nobody had proposed the accession of his son to the throne in the event of the Emperor's death. Caesarism had failed to become hereditary monarchy.

Napoleon found it less easy to put out the fire abroad. The forces of nationalism and religion, joined to those of aristocracy and monarchy, prepared the first broad uprising against French power. Patriotic burghers and professional men who dreamed of a constitutional state and aristocrats to whom such a dream was a nightmare marched together under the indiscriminate banner of nationalism.

The old order found a new voice. In March 1813, King Frederick William III of Prussia issued an appeal "to my people" to rise up for "freedom of conscience, honor, independence, [free] trade, industry, and science." Villagers and townsmen, professors and students rushed to the colors. It is true that the appeal of the King had been in effect forced by the resurgent movement of the patriotic officers and professional classes. It was all the more significant on that account. A traditional monarchy was being propelled by the energies of the middle and professional classes.

The aims of Czar Alexander were bolder than those of Frederick William. The desecration of the "Holy City" of Moscow by the "Dragon" and the "miraculous" salvation of Russia gave his ambition for European leadership an apocalyptic confirmation. A mystic, Baroness Barbara von Krüdener (1764-1824), persuaded Alexander that he was the destined savior of Europe, citing as her authority *The Revelation of St. John the Divine.* The Czar found no difficulty in blending his imperial ambitions, his liberal leanings, and his mystical inclinations. He appeared in Prussia at the head of the soldiers who had harassed the Grand Army and proclaimed his determination to bring freedom, "brotherhood," and political independence to all peoples.

In the spring of 1813 Napoleon faced larger hosts than the French had ever met before. The Prussian army which had formerly protected his right flank became his enemy. Sweden, whose crown prince, Bernadotte, was a former

196

French marshal and had commanded regiments in the Grand Army, also changed sides. Another ally, Austria, insisted that the Czar and Napoleon must accept her mediation, at a suitable middleman's fee. From 1813 to 1815, Great Britain lavished thirty-two million pounds to subsidize Continental armies. Napoleon confronted his greatest enemy: arithmetic. Russia and Prussia, joined later by Austria, had collected an army of nearly 900,000 men; all Napoleon could put into the field was 700,000. Thus outnumbered, he was worsted at the battle of Leipzig in October 1813. At the end of the year, as Napoleon withdrew into northeastern France, Wellington crossed the Pyrenees into southwestern France.

It was the end, but Napoleon declined the boundary of the Rhine proffered by the allies as a condition of peace. Early the following year he fought one of his most brilliant campaigns against engulfing odds. He won one local engagement after another only to find fresh armies advancing against him. "Why then," a general asked him, "does not Your Majesty think of something to stir up the people?" "Chimeras!" Napoleon exclaimed. "How can I hope to stir up the people in a land where the Revolution has destroyed the nobility and the priesthood, and where I myself have destroyed the Revolution?"

In March 1814 the allies entered Paris, and in April Napoleon was forced to abdicate unconditionally. Louis XVIII, brother of the executed Louis XVI, ascended the throne of France. The victors, respectful of the miseries of the great, allotted the deposed Bonaparte an annual income of two million francs from the treasury of France and made him the ruler of the small island of Elba in the Mediterranean. Napoleon remained an Emperor—the Emperor of Elba!

Peace in America

The honors of the American war were divided. The Americans had staged a few spectacular naval exploits and inflicted some commercial damage on the enemy, but they could not shake the mastery of the British navy in the Atlantic. They made several abortive attempts to invade Canada. In 1814, the British and Canadians staged their own invasion of northern New England and New York. Another British force landed in Washington, set fire to the city, including the unfinished Capitol and the White House, and were finally repulsed at Baltimore. A third British force landed at the mouth of the Mississippi in an attempt to seize the port of New Orleans. The American defenders, under the command of General Andrew Jackson (1767-1845), decisively defeated the invaders on January 8, 1815. Again, as at the start of the war, delayed communications played a part at its finish, for the battle of New Orleans was fought two weeks after Britain and the United States had signed a treaty of peace.

In the final months of war, however, neither side was disposed to continue the struggle. The opponents of the war in New England, chafing under the embargo, called a convention at Hartford, Connecticut, in December 1814. The delegates threatened that their states would withdraw from the Union unless the power of the federal government to declare war was abolished and the influence of the Southern states reduced. Although the threat of secession was not serious, it dramatized the unpopularity of the war in an important part of the country.

Great Britain sent fresh troops overseas after the fall of Napoleon, but her military leaders at home, notably the Duke of Wellington, were not confident of the results of a large-scale compaign in America. They did not find Napoleon's recent experiences in Spain and Russia reassuring as to the risks of a war waged against a patriotic population. There were, moreover, considerations of international relations that made a speedy peace desirable. It was well known that Great Britain's ally Russia, which had offered to mediate between her and the United States, shared the American views on sea rights. Britain was also disturbed by the Russian suggestion to bring American issues before the European powers, then meeting at Vienna for a general European settlement. She wished to prevent the interference of Continental powers in overseas questions.

The consequence was that Britain rejected Russia's offer to mediate but undertook direct negotiations with the United States at Ghent, in Belgium. The treaty, signed in December 1814, left all the outstanding issues unsettled and restored the *status quo ante bellum*. Disputed boundary questions were left to be determined by joint commissions of the two countries.

The Hundred Days and Waterloo

In the spring of 1815 there was peace in America as well as in Europe. In Europe, however, it was a quarrelsome peace. The victorious allies, assembled at Vienna, could not agree on how to divide the spoils. Czar Alexander demanded the Grand Duchy of Warsaw, then occupied by his army. Prussia agreed, on condition that she be permitted to swallow Saxony, whose ruler had been consistently loyal to Napoleon. Austria and Great Britain, fearing an unusual accretion of power to these states, were prepared to go to war to stop them. War indeed came—not from Vienna but from Paris, via Elba.

Louis XVIII (1814-15, 1815-24) had been installed on the throne of France and had been instructed by Czar Alexander to grant a constitution. Returning *émigrés*, however, clamored for the abrogation of all changes made since 1789. There was much discontent in the country. These difficulties were promptly exploited by the Emperor of Elba. On March 1, Napoleon suddenly landed in the south of France. He outfaced the troops and officers sent to seize him, took them in tow, and, on March 20, entered Paris in triumph. Louis XVIII fled without being able to resist.

Back in power, Napoleon outbid the Bourbons by making concessions to public sentiment. He invited the liberal writer and politician Benjamin Constant (1767-1830) to supply him with a constitution. He acknowledged that constitutionalism and imperialism did not mix well: "I endeavored to set up a world

The Powers are busy carving up the map of Europe at the Congress of Vienna, when Napoleon returns from Elba, wielding thunderbolts. Contemporary American cartoon. PRINT ROOM, NEW YORK PUBLIC LIBRARY

monarchy, and for this I needed unfettered power. . . . But if France is to be the whole of my dominions, then a constitution is better." Actually, he hoped to use the constitution as a steppingstone to empire. "I foresee," he said, "a terrible war. In order to win through I must have the support of the people. The people will ask for freedom in exchange for its support. Very well, the people shall have freedom." Napoleon accepted a parliament and a modicum of ministerial responsibility, granted liberty of the press, and abolished feudal titles. He insisted on retaining hereditary titles and the right of confiscating property. He swore allegiance to the constitution, but how lightly his word was regarded was indicated by the fact that only one and a half million Frenchmen bothered to vote in the plebiscite held in May to sanction the document. The old plebiscites had run to four and five million.

Napoleon had no chance to test his constitutional experiment or France his capacity to work in harness with parliamentary leaders. The allies adjourned their quarrels, closed ranks, and quickly raised an army of 600,000 soldiers. Great Britain alone spent 5 million pounds sterling to mobilize troops and prepare them for the field. With the addition of the soldiers of other nations, the hosts against Napoleon numbered nearly a million men. Even by drastic measures, which somehow avoided the dread word "conscription," Napoleon was able to gather only 400,000 men. Many of his soldiers were raw recruits. He had already sacrificed his best-trained officers and men.

Napoleon attempted to compensate for this imbalance in numbers by being more speedy and catching the allies one by one. In June, Wellington waited for him at Waterloo, near Brussels, with 67,000 British, German, and Dutch troops stretched thinly on a line of thirty miles. The Prussian leader Blücher was farther south with an army scattered even more thinly. Some nine days would be needed to assemble these and the other allied hosts for striking. On June 13, Wellington judged from reports of a deceptive speech made by Napoleon at Paris that the Emperor was not likely to leave the capital soon. He had in fact left that very evening and slept only ten miles from the Belgian border, where his army had already been massed quietly.

Napoleon caught the Prussians near Ligny and overwhelmed them with superior forces. Blücher retreated northeastward, pursued by a French army. Napoleon himself, with 74,000 men (the main body of his troops), turned north to confront the isolated Wellington. The allied commander deployed his troops in squares, facing outward, so that they were able to shoot in every direction and thus defend themselves against an infantry or cavalry charge from any side. They formed a kind of human fortress nerved for a siege. This delayed Napoleon for a few precious hours, which Blücher employed in eluding his pursuers and turning westward to join his allies with 30,000 of his men. Arithmetic quickly changed sides. The Prussians and British attacked. Napoleon fled the field, leaving over 40,000 dead and wounded. This was nearly twice as great a loss as that of his enemies. Wellington's casualties were 15,000 and Blücher's 7,000.

On June 22, Napoleon abdicated again. Making his way to the coast, he made an attempt to escape to the United States but was compelled to surrender instead to a British admiral. Taking no chances, Great Britain, with the approval of the other powers, put him away under heavy guard on the desolate island of Saint Helena in the South Atlantic. There he died in 1821, at the age of fifty-two.

The Emperor of Europe—for Napoleon was hardly less than that at the peak of his career—spent the last few years at Saint Helena pouring out his memoirs. He pictured himself, for posterity, as the builder of a new Europe, free and disciplined, humane and orderly, progressive and practical. There was much of the gambler in Napoleon; he pointed out the chances he had missed and how, with a little management, he could have improved his luck.

The fact was that he had made his contributions as a representative of the great Revolution that he had betrayed; it was his failures that were original. Napoleon was a great organizer; in the republican days of his Consulate he completed the administrative changes of the Revolution. He brought the basic French reforms to western Germany and northern Italy, his first conquests. His domination gave them a sense of political unity. But his insatiable militarism cost millions of lives and eventually undid him and his country. He led one million Frenchmen and two or three million other Europeans to a violent death.

Although Napoleon ended his days as a prisoner of his enemies, it was France that drained the Napoleonic tragedy to the dregs. For centuries past, every French ruler—king or republican, "glorious" or dull—had left the country greater in size, if not always in spirit. Napoleon alone left it smaller than he received it, in both respects. The most spectacular military genius since Alexander the Great, if not in all history, was the only modern ruler of France who could not defend her against invaders. Not in four centuries had Paris been occupied by an enemy, as she was in 1814. Abroad, Napoleon made the name of France more feared but less admired. His career demonstrated the sterility of militarism, the difficulty of uniting the Continent, and the importance of sea power in a world of which Europe was the center but which stretched beyond the oceans to the four points of the compass.

For the most dramatic event in modern history, the great warrior prepared a commonplace denouement. He reduced issues which went to the root of Western civilization—reason versus prescription, equality versus privilege, freedom versus tutelage—to a confrontation of armies on a strip of Belgian soil. He reduced the French Revolution to an ordeal by fire.

Swift, elegant, and efficient, the American clipper ship was the Queen of the North Atlantic in the mid-nineteenth century. She had the tallest masts, slimmest "waist," and broadest spread of canvas of any sailing vessel in history. Carrying freight, immigrants, and mails, she was a potent force in an age of enterprise and of busy intercourse between Europe and America. The clipper shown here is the Dreadnought—*a name later appropriated by England for more deadly ships—on her "celebrated passage" in 1854 from New York to Liverpool, which she made in 13 days and 11 hours, dock to dock. The clipper was shortly supplanted by the more economical and mechanical, but less attractive, steamship.*

III   *The European*

European Conservatism and the Debut of America

European Liberalism and American Democracy

Atlantic Enterprise

Slavery and the Social Question

Conservative Europe and Nationalism

1848—The Great Watershed

and American Solutions

10. *European Conservatism and the Debut of America*

The Congress of Vienna

The Congress of Vienna of 1814-15 functioned in the spirit of the aristocratic society that it was determined to restore. All the great and the small powers of Europe were represented in the Austrian capital. But there was no true Congress. The full group was never convened, no general deliberations were ever held, and no final treaty covering all the conclusions reached was ever signed. The important decisions were made in tête-à-têtes of sovereigns and ambassadors, between the courses of state banquets or in the interludes of festivities. In the antechambers, the agents of smaller states intrigued with the entourages of the leading monarchs. The unending round of splendid dinners, soirées, and receptions strained the purse of the host, the Emperor of Austria. The masked balls at which emperors and kings rubbed elbows with humble counts and daring courtesans became the very symbol of the Congress. A contemporary observed, "The Congress dances but does not move."

"The Adonis of the salons," Prince Klemens von Metternich (1773-1859) presided over this diplomatic waltz. Metternich was the scion of a lesser noble house of the Rhineland who had begun his diplomatic career by marrying the granddaughter of Prince von Kaunitz, the chancellor of Empress Maria Theresa and of her sons, the Emperors Joseph II and Leopold II. In 1809 Metternich became the unquestioned master of the foreign policy (although not of the domestic administration) of the Austrian Empire, a role he played without interruption until 1848.

Metternich was sinuous in both figure and character. As acting president of the Congress, he struck the official keynote of the age the Congress introduced: immobility. Metternich was too intelligent to justify the irrationalities and deficiencies of the old order. His own Austria was a museum of historical antiques. Nor did he fail to see that some of the consequences of the Revolution and Bonapartism were irreversible. The trouble was that the Revolution was contagious and the "disease" of progress and innovation incurable. Metternich did not believe that the old order had the energy both to improve and to preserve itself; it had to do either one thing or the other. He concluded that safety lay only in avoiding all change. He treated the old order as if it were a precious Dresden doll. The porcelain was already chipped and cracked; to touch it, much less to attempt a complete restoration, would prove disastrous. Only the most careful management could assure the continuity of the old system, and perhaps only for a time. In his own eyes, and eventually in the eyes of many conservatives, Metternich became indispensable to that delicate task.

Metternich was outranked by Alexander I of Russia, whose views were more liberal but also more enigmatic. The Czar, indeed, cast himself in the role of the leader of the forces of improvement. He wished to extend westward not only Russia's boundaries but her prestige. His insistence that Louis XVIII grant France a constitution, and the presence of Russian troops in Paris in 1814, testified to the influence of the easternmost empire of Europe. Napoleon had predicted that in a century Europe would be "republican or Cossack." Alexander seemed to dream of its being republican *and* Cossack.

The spokesman of Great Britain was Viscount Castlereagh (1769-1822). Although he represented a parliamentary country, Castlereagh vied with the Continental aristocrats in hauteur and rigidity. He had no interest in reform, either in Britain or on the Continent. The representative of Prussia was Karl

The Congress of Vienna, 1814-15. Metternich stands at the left, in front of a chair. The figure at the right with his arm resting on the table is Talleyrand. At the extreme left stands the Duke of Wellington. Seated in center is Castlereagh. Engraving by Godefroy after Isabey. THE METRO-POLITAN MUSEUM OF ART, *Gift of Miss Georgiana W. Sargent, in memory of John Osborne Sargent*

Augustus von Hardenberg (1750-1822), who had formerly been an enlightened bureaucrat but now practiced conservative diplomacy, without striking success. France, in her defeat, was represented by a spiritual emptiness. Talleyrand, a high clergyman of the Old Regime and Prince by the grace of Napoleon, had served every government since Louis XVI—except the Jacobin—with equal fidelity to its principles. Through his genius for intrigue and maneuver, he insinuated the influence of France into the council of the victors. He supplied the Congress with a needed principle: the legitimate rulers were to resume their inherited places. The powers accepted the principle of legitimacy, although they honored it as much in the breach as in the observance. They restored the dynasties of the Bourbons in France and in Spain, the Oranges in Holland, the Braganzas in Portugal, and the Hapsburgs in Italian duchies. Legitimacy was often sacrificed, however, to the overriding aims of the members of the Congress —to secure the maximum territorial profit for themselves, to see to it that France behaved herself in the future, and to guarantee themselves against one another's cupidity by maintaining the balance of power.

The territorial distribution began with a vast "deal." The Polish-Saxon issue was compromised. Russia acquired the Grand Duchy of Warsaw, which comprised the gains of Prussia and Austria in the last two partitions of Poland. Prussia received half of Saxony, the other half being left to its legitimate monarch. In "compensation" Prussia also received the valuable Rhineland. The Hohenzollern state now protruded deep into Western Europe. Austria realized one of the dreams of Emperor Joseph II: she gave up to Holland the Austrian Netherlands for territory nearer home. Not only did she regain the lands yielded after a succession of disastrous wars with Napoleon but she acquired also, with Lombardy and Venetia, the bulk of northern Italy, notably excepting Genoa, which went to Sardinia. The dynastic connection of the Hapsburgs with the rulers of several Italian states and their influence with the rest made Italy virtually an Austrian dependency. The Austrian Empire did not have a uniform or centralized administration, but its territories were at last contiguous. In the north, Russia retained Finland, but as "compensation" Sweden obtained Norway from Denmark, and Denmark received the Duchy of Lauenburg. It was a game of musical chairs.

Great Britain obtained the restoration of the British monarch as ruler of Hanover. Otherwise she left the Continent to her allies, on condition that they leave the rest of the world to her. Already possessed of the greatest navy afloat, she extended her maritime empire, secured it with strategically situated harbors and islands, and did everything in her power to restrict to the Continent the activities of the other powers. The very suggestion that the United States might be represented at Vienna and that Russia and other powers might participate in decisions affecting the New World caused Britain to hasten the conclusion of the Treaty of Ghent in 1814, terminating the war with America. For its part, the American government was reluctant to participate in the Congress lest it become "entangled" in European disputes.

During twenty years of warfare, Great Britain had acquired the bulk of the overseas colonies not only of France but of the other Continental empires as

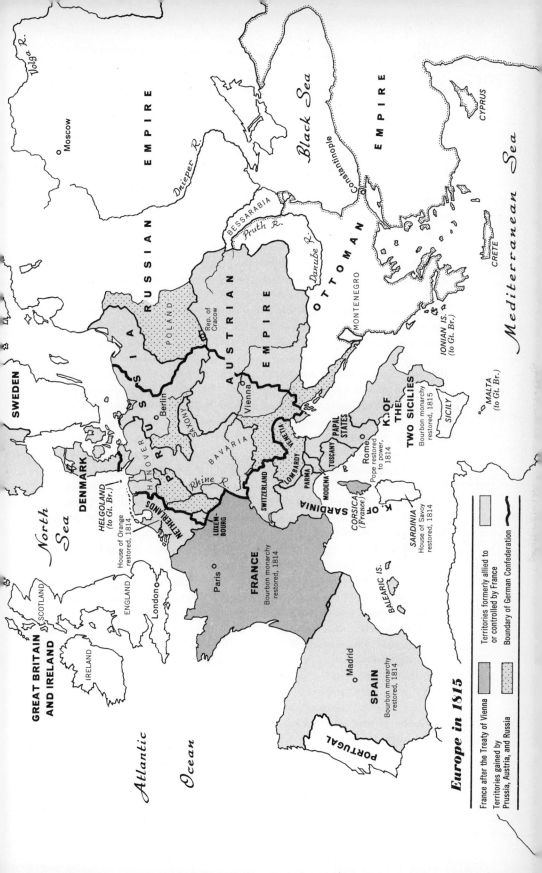

Europe in 1815

France after the Treaty of Vienna

Territories formerly allied to or controlled by France

Territories gained by Prussia, Austria, and Russia

Boundary of German Confederation

GREAT BRITAIN AND IRELAND

SCOTLAND

IRELAND

ENGLAND

London

North Sea

Atlantic Ocean

SWEDEN

DENMARK

HELGOLAND (to Gt. Br.)

House of Orange restored, 1814

NETHERLANDS

LUXEMBOURG

HANOVER

P R U S S I A

Berlin

SAXONY

BAVARIA

Rhine R.

FRANCE
Bourbon monarchy restored, 1814

Paris

SPAIN
Bourbon monarchy restored, 1814

Madrid

PORTUGAL

BALEARIC IS.

CORSICA (France)

K. OF SARDINIA

SARDINIA
House of Savoy restored, 1814

SWITZERLAND

PIEDMONT

LOMBARDY

VENETIA

PARMA

MODENA

TUSCANY

PAPAL STATES

Rome
Pope restored to power, 1814

TWO SICILIES
Bourbon monarchy restored, 1815

K. OF THE

SICILY

MALTA (to Gt. Br.)

A U S T R I A N

E M P I R E

Vienna

POLAND

Rep. of Cracow

R U S S I A N   E M P I R E

Moscow

Volga R.

Dnieper R.

Danube R.

Pruth R.

BESSARABIA

MONTENEGRO

O T T O M A N

E M P I R E

Constantinople

Black Sea

IONIAN IS. (to Gt. Br.)

CRETE

CYPRUS

Mediterranean Sea

well. Of these she returned only a few—for example, Java and Dutch Guiana to Holland. Her haul was impressive. Malta and the Ionian Islands, added to Gibraltar, helped her to maintain naval predominance in the Mediterranean Sea. She kept the French islands in the West Indies but returned Guiana. The former Dutch colony of the Cape of Good Hope and Ceylon and the former French islands in the South Atlantic and Indian Oceans—Ascension, Seychelles, and Mauritius—gave Great Britain control of the all-important route to the Far East. During the long war in Europe she had extended her holdings in India, so that by 1815 she had become the dominant power in the subcontinent. The East India Company was engaged in a profitable trade with China. Ports and coast areas had been seized in Malaya. In Australia, Britain had occupied New South Wales and had launched a colonization program. The Portuguese and Spanish colonies in America were restive, and Great Britain was doing a thriving trade with them.

In short, in the years when her European rivals were embattled on the Continent, Great Britain assembled her modern empire. She destroyed or diminished the holdings of her old rivals—notably France and Holland. Of the great powers on the Continent, only Russia, whose navy was no match for Britain's, had overseas ambitions. Neither Austria nor Prussia had colonies. Britain's network of strategic islands and shelters gave her naval supremacy. Whereas in Europe the post-Napoleonic period was characterized by balance among several great powers, overseas it was characterized by the virtual monopoly of the British Empire.

There remained for the Congress the question of security. First France was shorn of much of her strategic and military power. She was reduced to the boundaries she had had in 1792, when the Revolutionary wars broke out, and she lost many of her colonies. The cession of the Rhineland to Prussia brought the might of a great power to her doorstep. The incorporation of the Austrian Netherlands into Holland bolstered the ability of the Dutch to prevent another irruption by France in that strategic region. The acquisition of Genoa strengthened France's neighbor to the southeast, the Kingdom of Sardinia. The restored Bourbon returned to the system of a limited professional army. As indemnity for the expense to which she had put the powers when she welcomed Napoleon back in 1815, France was to pay the sum of 700 million francs.

Finally, the powers protected themselves against one another. Austria, Great Britain, Prussia, and Russia signed the Quadruple Alliance, guaranteeing the possession of the newly acquired territories. They provided for future diplomatic meetings to enforce or alter the provisions of the treaty. This was the basis of the "Concert of Europe." In 1818, when France had demonstrated her good behavior, she was admitted to the partnership. The Quintuple Alliance proved successful. It was nearly forty years before any great power went to war with another great power.

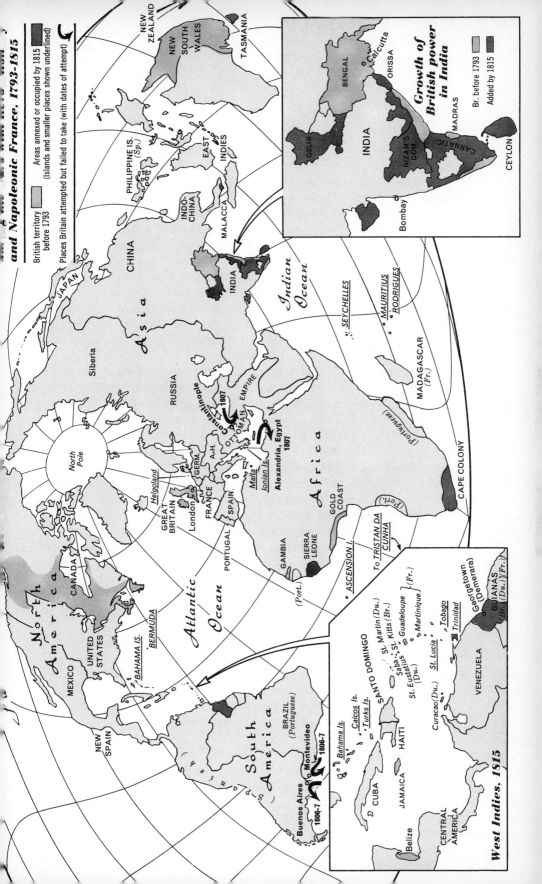

and Napoleonic France, 1793-1815

British territory before 1793

Areas annexed or occupied by 1815 (Islands and smaller places shown underlined)

Places Britain attempted but failed to take (with dates of attempt)

Growth of British power in India

Br. before 1793

Added by 1815

DELHI • Cawnpore • Calcutta
BENGAL
ORISSA
INDIA
NIZAM'S DOM.
MADRAS
CARNATIC
CEYLON
Bombay

NEW ZEALAND
NEW SOUTH WALES
TASMANIA

PHILIPPINE IS. (Sp.)
EAST INDIES
INDO-CHINA
MALACCA
CHINA
JAPAN
Asia
Siberia
RUSSIA
INDIA
Indian Ocean
SEYCHELLES
MAURITIUS
RODRIGUES
MADAGASCAR (Fr.)

North Pole

North America
CANADA
UNITED STATES
MEXICO
NEW SPAIN

Constantinople 1807
OTTOMAN EMPIRE
Alexandria, Egypt 1807
Malta
Ionian Is.
GERM.
A.-H.
London
GREAT BRITAIN
FRANCE
SPAIN
PORTUGAL
Helgoland

Africa
GOLD COAST
GAMBIA (Port.)
SIERRA LEONE
CAPE COLONY
(Portuguese)

Atlantic Ocean
BERMUDA
BAHAMA IS.
ASCENSION I.
To TRISTAN DA CUNHA

South America
BRAZIL (Portuguese)
Buenos Aires 1806-7
Montevideo 1806-7

West Indies, 1815

CENTRAL AMERICA
Belize
CUBA
JAMAICA
HAITI
SANTO DOMINGO
Bahama Is.
Caicos Is.
Turks Is.
St. Martin (Du.)
Saba • St. Kitts (Br.)
St. Eustatius (Du.)
Guadeloupe (Fr.)
Martinique (Fr.)
Curaçao (Du.)
St. Lucia
Tobago
Trinidad
Georgetown (Demerara)
GUIANAS (Br.) (Du.) (Fr.)
VENEZUELA

The New Conservatism

By making this territorial and colonial settlement, the Congress of Vienna met only half—the easier half—of the problem that faced the European world. This was the question of the Revolution. It seemed reasonable to expect that the fall of the military dictator would benefit liberty. In the hour of his need, many a ruler had appealed to his people for support. Reformers were led to believe that their patriotism would be rewarded by constitutional concessions. Although Czar Alexander encouraged them, Prince Metternich used all his influence to quash these aspirations. The Czar ruled as an autocrat at St. Petersburg but behaved as a limited ruler in Warsaw, where he appointed a ministry and had a parliament elected. He induced the Continental rulers to subscribe to a Holy Alliance in 1815, binding themselves to treat one another and their subjects according to "the precepts of Justice, Christian Charity, and Peace"—an unheard-of innovation. Most rulers thought the idea silly though harmless but signed in order to please the "mystical" Czar.

In France, Louis XVIII, a practical man, made no attempt to disturb the land settlement of the Revolution, the centralized administration, or the rule of equality before the law. He restored to the ancient aristocracy its dignities but not its confiscated estates. He increased the influence of the Church. In place of a constitution based on popular sovereignty he promulgated a charter, "by the grace of God." The Charter promised to respect the freedom of the individual. It established a bicameral parliament consisting of a powerful House of Peers and a lower house, the Chamber of Deputies, elected by the 200,000 wealthiest landowners of the country. Louis XVIII was prepared to rule in the spirit of compromise, remarking that he did not propose "to go on his travels again."

The German princes assembled at Vienna signed a treaty agreeing to fulfill the pledges of constitutional government made to the people in the "war of liberation" from Napoleon. The legal and administrative system introduced by the French in western Germany and northern Italy and the consolidation of provinces were preserved. Prussia retained the Code Napoleon in the newly acquired Rhineland. The restored rulers of Sardinia and the Two Sicilies and of Spain promised to grant constitutions.

German liberalism meant unity as much as constitutionalism, and Metternich was equally opposed to both. Under another name, the Holy Roman Empire was reconstituted. The new German Confederation contained only thirty-eight states as opposed to the three-hundred-odd states of the Germany of 1789. But the union was loose, and the Austrian ruler was still its head. In Austria herself, there was no concession to constitutional demands.

King George III resisted pressure to grant a constitution in Hanover as firmly as he resisted attempts to improve the English parliamentary system. The Tory groups, which had held power almost without interruption since the 1780's, refused to consider issues which had long been settled in the minds of liberal men—the emancipation of Catholics, the political equality of Protestant dissenters, and the removal of political and legal abuses. The Foreign Secretary, George Canning (1770-1827), one of the ablest and most cynical of British statesmen, felt that it was not "a British interest to have free states established on the Continent."

> The principle which for centuries has given ascendancy to Great Britain is that she was the single free state in Europe. The spread of the representative system destroys that singularity, and must (however little we may like it) proportionally enfeeble our preponderating influence—unless we measure our steps cautiously and accommodate our conduct to the times.

With this nationalistic conservatism was associated a highly protectionist economic policy. In 1815, fearing the competition of foreign grain, the Tories had passed the first of the Corn Laws, which increased the duty that protected the price of grain, and the profits of the large landlords, at the expense of the consumers of food. A wing of the Tory party, as also of the Whig party, supported by the mercantile interest, had become persuaded of the desirability of removing certain old commercial prohibitions. In 1814 Great Britain had agreed to allow American ships to bring goods from any country to Great Britain and most English colonies. In 1825 foreign countries were allowed to trade with English colonies, although only in products of their own. The intercolonial trade, the trade between Britain and her colonies, and the coastal trade in Britain were still reserved to imperial shipping.

On the Continent, as in Britain, the policy of political "immobility" gained ground, in the years following the Congress of Vienna, through the evolution of conservative doctrines, the demands of restored *émigrés*, and the reaction to the resurgence of revolutionary activity. Distilled through romantic literature, conservatism emerged as a sentimental worship of tradition, an exaltation of monarchical, aristocratic, and clerical principles, a contempt for rationality, and a revival of the values and images of the Middle Ages. Perhaps the most prominent figure in the vogue of medievalism was Sir Walter Scott (1771-1832). In his "Waverly" novels, Scott painted a world in which chivalry reigned and religious and social harmony prevailed. The success of these novels was enormous, both in England and on the Continent. It mattered little that the images of Sir Walter and other romantic novelists bore scant resemblance to the actualities of medieval times.

The French politician and writer François René de Chateaubriand (1768-1848) developed a romantic argument in defense of Christianity. Christianity was good, not because it was true, but because it was beautiful. In the eighteenth century, he felt, the churches had fallen into a trap as a result of their own strategy. By using rational arguments to defend religion, they had enchanced the prestige of reason, which must ultimately corrode faith. Religion, he asserted, must be revered precisely because it is mysterious.

More significant than the evocation of romantic images and the discrediting of reason was the elaboration of dogmatic philosophies of tradition, stability, and authority. De Maistre in France and G. W. F. Hegel in Germany developed novel premises for a bold conservatism.

Since the nineties, when he had entered the lists in the debate on the French Revolution (see p. 145), De Maistre had filled in the outlines of a pessimistic and obsessive doctrine. His books, particularly the gloomy *Nights of St. Petersburg* (where De Maistre spent years as an ambassador of the King of Sardinia), became a staple of romantic literature in Roman Catholic countries. De Maistre was haunted by the prevalence of bloodshed and guilt in history. The fact that states rested on brute strength proved to him that it is God's way to appeal to force in managing men. The fact that war confounds the innocent with the guilty merely confirmed the ancient doctrine, held by pagans as well as Christians, that innocent blood is essential to spiritual purification: it is always the lamb that is sacrificed. God, according to De Maistre, makes kings in a quite literal sense; how else can we explain how the most unlikely people, hailing from the most obscure origins (for example, Napoleon) become sovereigns? In short, De Maistre turned around the liberal argument against war and tyranny. He was not a man to shrink from the conclusions of his position. Secular and religious authority must be one, and they must be absolute. De Maistre announced that human society rested on two pillars: the Pope and the Executioner. The Pope should be declared infallible, and the Protestant and Eastern Orthodox nations must return to his allegiance. Otherwise there would be no divine sanction for the coercive authority that government needs.

The philosophy of Hegel (1770-1831) has played an extraordinary role in the history of Europe, and of the world at large. In the lifetime of its creator it was accepted as a defense of conservatism because of its exaltation of the state. Later, in Marxist adaptation, it exercised a wider influence.

Hegel deduced from the events of history not only the meaning of human existence but its correct and future course. Unlike De Maistre, he exalted freedom above all other values. But he gave freedom a definition that negated its familiar characteristics. To the liberal, freedom consisted of the release of the individual from external authority and, in particular, of the restriction of the jurisdiction of the state. Hegel followed Rousseau in making political authority absolute. Like Rousseau he reconciled the love of freedom and authority by a deceptively simple device—he melted the individual into the state. But whereas Rousseau's ideal state was a democratic republic, Hegel's was an improved version of the familiar Prussian apparatus of his own day. In Hegel's language, which was a creation as strange as his philosophy was bold, freedom was reason; since the state embodied reason, dissent was madness. When a man was arrested, it was his own reason that slipped the manacles on his wrists. The state was "a great architectonic edifice, a hieroglyph of reason," "the realization of the ethical idea." It was "the march of God through the world." The idea that every man should have the right to say or write whatever he pleases seemed a piece of "uneducated crudity" to Hegel. The press represented "what is most transient, particular, and accidental in human opinion. . . ." Hegel would rather trust the great man. "The great man of his time is he who expresses the will and the meaning of that time, and then brings it to completion; he acts according to the inner spirit and essence of his time, which he realizes. And he who does not understand how to despise public opinion as it makes itself heard here and there, will never accomplish anything great."

Different though they were, the views of Hegel and De Maistre converged on a single political result: they lent weight to the defense of existing institutions against the assertion of natural rights. They appealed to those members of the middle classes who had been repelled by the radical aspects of the Revolution. They took hold particularly among the ruling groups, who used them to justify the most extreme measures. Many rulers and aristocrats had spent years in exile and had lost touch with the sentiments of the populace. They persuaded themselves that in destroying Napoleon they had also destroyed the Revolution and, with the Revolution, the enlightened ideas that had flourished for generations before its outbreak. They wished to give European society a fixedness that it had not possessed in centuries, if ever.

While their policy was ostensibly based on the values of tradition and continuity, it was actually novel. Tradition was not, to them, the salting down of experience over a long period. It was the evocation of medieval images, many of them false, that gave a glow to institutions whose shape was of more recent origin. Their link with the past was poetic rather than genealogical. In consequence, the monarchy, aristocracy, and clergy of the restoration bore little resemblance to their counterparts of the preceding century. Before the Revolution, some of the monarchs, seconded by the middle and professional classes, had countenanced reforms at the expense of the aristocracy and clergy. They were now blamed for adopting the persuasive counsel of reason. It became unfashionable even to seem to be enlightened. The aristocracy and clergy became equal partners with the monarchy at the expense of the middle and professional classes. They reclaimed functions which they had lost long before the Revolution. For their part, the monarchs were determined to rule without consulting the interests and wishes of their people. Emperor Francis II of Austria is said to have observed of a prominent subject: "I know that he is a patriot for Austria, but the question is whether he is a patriot for me."

In many countries the restoration spelled brutality and obscurantism. In Spain, for example, the constitution of 1812, which had been drafted by the liberal opponents of Napoleonic rule, was abrogated, and a dishonest fool ruled "by the grace of God." King Ferdinand VII (1814-33) prosecuted his reactionary policy to extreme lengths: he revoked the abolition of serfdom—this was done nowhere else—and restored to the Church its confiscated estates. Another Bourbon, on the throne of Naples, governed by violent and corrupt means. Even in more advanced countries, the rulers carefully avoided any measure that might disturb the aristocratic and clerical groups. Secret police, spies, and *agents provocateurs* swarmed like flies. Liberal professors were dismissed and critical journalists silenced. The governing classes everywhere, including those of Great Britain, refused to consider even the most moderate proposals for improving existing institutions.

On the Continent, the military apparatus of the state was again based on   *213* reliable professional troops. Conscription was abolished; it might make a citizen a soldier without wiping out the citizen in him. Prussia alone retained conscription, but in a characteristic form: a professional cadre of officers drawn from the aristocracy was combined with a short-term soldiery.

Official churches were strengthened everywhere. So much was religion now considered the essential cement of society that Great Britain increased her support not only of the Anglican Church but of the Roman Catholic Church in Ireland as well. The papacy revived the militant Jesuit order, which the Catholic countries had banished from their dominions in the period of the Enlightenment. A new deference to papal authority appeared in Ultramontanism—literally, "beyond the mountains"—a movement to close ranks around Rome. The papacy became more influential than it had been for more than a century. In the schools and universities, the clergy ruled without challenge. Protestant as well as Catholic churches worked in close association with repressive governments.

Finally, conservatism descended to the ridiculous and the petulant. In honor of liberty, trees had been planted in avenues, squares, and parks wherever French influence had spread. Many of the "liberty" trees were now uprooted angrily. Street lighting had been much promoted during the revolutionary years; the lights were now turned out in many cities. It was said of the typical restoration ruler that, had he been present at the Creation, he would have cried: "*Bon Dieu, conservons le chaos!*"

The "Era of Good Feelings" in America

The triumph of conservatism in Europe coincided with the confirmation of Jeffersonian democracy in America. There were European reformers who still regarded the United States as a model for the Old World. Jeremy Bentham (1748-1832), the great English legal and constitutional reformer, pronounced the American government "the best that is or ever has been." The Reverend Sydney Smith (1771-1845), an essayist and wit, commended American simplicity. "The Americans, we believe, are the first persons who have discarded the tailor in the administration of justice, and his auxiliary the barber—two persons of endless importance in the codes and pandects of Europe. A judge administers justice without a calorific wig and particolored gown, in a coat and pantaloons." Like many other friendly observers, however, Smith was critical of the state of culture, science, and crafts in America. "In the four quarters of the globe who reads an American book? . . . What new constellations have been discovered by the telescopes of Americans? . . . Who wears American coats or gowns? . . . Finally, under which of the old tyrannical governments of Europe is every sixth man a slave . . . ?"

But while liberals mixed praise of the Republic with criticism, conservatives and aristocrats were contemptuous of the United States. "Nothing makes me more impatient," wrote De Maistre, "than the praises heaped upon this child in arms. Let it first grow up." Thomas Jefferson observed that the monarchs looked upon the Republic as a "splendid libel on their [own] governments." Gone were the days when transatlantic rebels, like Benjamin Franklin, were lionized in royal courts and aristocratic salons. The separation between the two worlds was accented when the political leadership of the Continent shifted to the Eastern powers, whose connections with America were slender.

Conservative antagonism was increased rather than diminished by the circumstance that the Republic was maturing and expanding. No longer a fledgling state, she had emerged unscathed from the ordeal of fire and internal dissension. By the purchase of Louisiana she had nearly doubled in territory. In 1819 she rounded out her southern coast by purchasing Florida from Spain, after a show of force.

In the early twenties, two Founding Fathers and former presidents, in an exchange of letters, cast up the accounts of aristocracy and republicanism in America. The old Federalist John Adams persevered in his political pessimism. He felt that mankind could not avoid rule by the few, whether the few were distinguished by superior birth, wealth, talent, or learning. Jefferson rejected the rule of birth and wealth as "a mischievous ingredient in government" and proposed that "provision should be made to prevent its ascendency." A true aristocracy of virtue and talents, however, is "the most precious gift of nature . . . That form of government is the best which provides the most effectually for a pure selection of. . .natural *aristoi* into the offices of government."

America, wrote Jefferson, was discovering a new way which the Old World would eventually follow:

> Before the establishment of the American States, nothing was known to history but the man of the old world, crowded within limits either small or overcharged, and steeped in vices which that situation generates. A government adapted to such men would be one thing; but a very different one, for the man of these States. Here everyone may labor for himself, if he chooses; or, preferring the exercise of any other industry, may exact for it such compensation as not only to afford a comfortable subsistence, but wherewith to provide for a cessation from labor in old age. Everyone, by his property, or by his satisfactory situation, is interested in the support of law and order. And such men may safely and advantageously reserve to themselves a wholesome control over their public affairs, and a degree of freedom which, in the hands of the *canaille* of the cities of Europe, would be instantly perverted to the demolition and destruction of everything public and private.

Despite recent setbacks, Europe will eventually move in a republican direction, for

> science has liberated the ideas of those who read and reflect, and the American example has kindled feelings of right in the people. An insurrection has consequently begun, of science, talents, and courage against rank and birth, which have fallen into contempt.

Jefferson's confidence reflected the political and material progress of the Republic. The Federalist party that Adams had led was in ruins, discredited by its pro-British sympathies and the efforts of some of its leaders in New England to disrupt the Union during the War of 1812. The rival Republican party controlled most national and state offices. In the election of 1816 the Federalist candidate, Rufus King (1755-1827), carried only three states and James Monroe (1758-1831), a Virginia planter of the school of Jefferson, was elected by a large vote. Adams' own son, John Quincy Adams (1767-1848), served as Secretary of State under Monroe, who was re-elected in 1820 virtually unanimously. The disappearance of the Federalist party and the assimilation of its members into the Republican party resulted in a high degree of political agreement, which a contemporary commentator dubbed the "era of good feelings."

The American Republic and the earlier colonies had depended for manufactured goods upon European imports. During the long wars normal trade channels were disrupted, and Americans began to supply themselves. Native industry bourgeoned. Paper mills, iron foundries, and particularly textile mills multiplied. An industrial proletariat, as well as industrial capitalism, began to develop, largely in the Northern states. In 1816 Congress enacted a protective tariff to safeguard the interest of "infant industries."

Resurgent Revolution and Intervention

The political contrast between the United States and Europe seemed sharp. On the morrow of the Congress of Vienna, the victory of European conservatism seemed complete. Underneath, however, Europe simmered with criticism and protest. Many secret societies sprang up; their membership embraced liberal army officers and professional groups, particularly teachers and students. In Germany the press and university groups insistently reminded the rulers of their promise to establish constitutional regimes. In Italy the secret society of the *Carbonari* (literally, "charcoal burners") engaged in political plotting for republican government. Still hoping that the Czar would some day honor his promises of reform, Russian army officers engaged in heated discussions of methods that might urge him on. In Great Britain, a quiet agitation for political reform was reinforced by the unrest of industrial workers. Peace had brought on economic depression and unemployment, and the Corn Laws brought widespread hunger. The scenes of 1811 and 1812, when the workers had vented their fury on the new machines, were repeated on a larger scale beginning in 1816.

In 1819-20, violence broke out. A young German student assassinated an agent of the Czar. The heir to the French throne was shot dead. In Great Britain, a plot was uncovered (the so-called Cato Street conspiracy) to blow up the whole Tory cabinet while it was dining. A peaceful meeting at Manchester in August 1819, called to discuss demands for broadening the suffrage laws, was invaded by troops. Many participants were killed and more wounded in what became known as the "Peterloo massacre." The government obtained Parliamentary

" Portentous, unexampled, unexplain'd !
————— ————— What man seeing this,
And having human feelings, does not blush,
And hang his head, to think himself a man ?
————————— I cannot rest
A silent witness of the headlong rage,
Or heedless folly, by which thousands die——
Bleed gold for Ministers to sport away."

THESE ARE

THE PEOPLE

all tatter'd and torn,

Who curse the day

wherein they were born,

On account of Taxation

too great to be borne,

And pray for relief,

from night to morn ;

Who, in vain, Petition

in every form,

From " The Political House That Jack Built," a leaflet on the Peterloo massacre in England in 1819, when troops attacked a meeting for parliamentary reform. PRINT ROOM, NEW YORK PUBLIC LIBRARY

approval for a series of laws—the notorious Six Acts—which abridged the right of Englishmen to assemble peacefully and imposed a heavy tax on pamphlets, thus making popular expression more expensive and hence more difficult. Repression was intensified elsewhere as well. Metternich prevailed upon the German Confederation to issue the Carlsbad decrees, which imposed a stricter watch over the press, over meetings, and over university life and teaching. Louis XVIII yielded to reactionary nobles and diluted the pledges of the Constitutional Charter: he imposed a strict censorship of the press and a virtual prohibition of political gatherings. His brother, Charles X, who succeeded him in 1824, introduced an extreme conservative regime. He revived the medieval

217

trappings of the monarchy. Like the rulers of the Middle Ages, he had himself anointed at the Cathedral at Rheims.

The excesses of Ferdinand III of Spain had provoked frequent popular outbreaks ever since his restoration in 1814. Finally, in January 1820, rebellion broke out among the officers of an expeditionary force about to sail across the Atlantic to suppress rebellious Spanish colonists. Ferdinand restored the 1812 constitution and installed a liberal ministry. The liberals of other countries followed the Spaniards' lead. In July there was a successful revolution in Naples. In August the liberals of Portugal rose and summoned a constitutional assembly. Since the Portuguese royal dynasty was divided into liberal and conservative branches, the conflict took the form of a family quarrel; rival candidates for the throne began a struggle that lasted for a generation. In March 1821, Piedmont had a revolution. Farther east, Greek liberals and merchants rose against the rule of Ottoman Turkey.

The powers met these defiances by organizing an international system of repression. The Czar had considered giving assistance to the Greek rebels, in pursuance of the old Russian policy of weakening Turkey. But at a meeting of the powers held at Troppau in October 1820, Metternich persuaded Alexander to stop flirting with liberalism. The Austrian Chancellor obtained the assent of Prussia and Russia to an agreement to take concerted military measures. It was accepted as an international policy that revolutions must be suppressed by the interested power, wherever they occurred.

Austria promptly dispatched an army to Naples. The liberal government was overthrown, and the Two Sicilies were delivered to Bourbon "legitimacy" and terrorism. In the north, Austrian troops helped the King of Sardinia to put down his critics. In 1823, after a congress of powers in Verona (1822) had decided to intervene in Spain, a French army was commissioned to dispose of the Spanish revolution. It accomplished its purpose in a few battles and restored one of the worst of European regimes, which reveled in an orgiastic punishment of the rebels.

There was one country in which it proved impossible to arrest revolution. The spectacle of a Christian people rising against Mohammedan rulers aligned even many conservatives with the Greeks, and the Western governments hesitated to apply the rule of intervention in this case. For a while, Metternich had induced the Czar to repudiate the rebels, but in 1822, when the Greeks declared their independence (see pp. 227-28), Alexander found it difficult to restrain his sympathy. Great Britain, which had extensive interests in the Mediterranean, was making efforts to reduce Russia's influence over the Greeks.

The United States was the first government to express official sympathy with the Greek patriots. It was "natural," declared President Monroe in his message to Congress in 1822, that the reappearance of a "classical" people "in their original character, contending in favor of their liberties, should produce that great excitement and sympathy in their favor which have been so signally displayed throughout the United States."

The International Debut of the Republic:
The Monroe Doctrine

Between 1809 and 1812, the Spanish colonists in Latin America had rebelled against the authority of the mother country, often ostensibly in support
of the legitimate Bourbon dynasty against the Napoleonic usurper. By 1816 the
rebellions had been suppressed almost everywhere except in Argentina. Yet, in
the several years following, the movement surged up again and, despite the
dispatch of expedition after expedition from Spain, the colonists established new
states. They were assisted by American and British soldiers and sailors of fortune.

It became clear that Spain alone could not enforce obedience, and some
of the more extreme conservatives in Europe proposed to extend the policy of
intervention overseas. If Russia and France came to Spain's assistance, as was
suggested, it was likely that they would be rewarded with American territory.
European imperialism in the Western Hemisphere, which had waned during
the revolutionary and Napoleonic conflicts, would be revived on a large scale.
It would be, moreover, an old-fashioned mercantilist imperialism. The colonies
would be recalled, not to the values of religion and tradition, but to their duty
to serve as the milch cows of the favored classes of the mother country. Monopolies, prohibitions of trade, and political privileges would be imposed again.

These plans had hardly jelled before they aroused the opposition of the
United States and Great Britain. The United States, which was the first country
to recognize the new South and Central American states, was naturally alarmed
at the prospect of European intervention in the Western Hemisphere. Great
Britain was almost equally disturbed, but for commercial and naval rather than
political reasons.

The former Spanish colonies had thrown their ports open to all countries,
and no country was in a better position to take advantage of this concession than
Great Britain. Now there seemed to be a possibility that the colonies might again
be brought into the exclusive system of Spain or perhaps of France. The supremacy of the British navy might be threatened by expeditions in the Atlantic. When
the powers at the Congress at Verona decided to intervene in Spain to suppress
the liberal rebellion, Foreign Secretary Canning warned that Britain would not
give up the economic relations she had established with the old Spanish colonies.
If France conquered Spain, it must be Spain without the West Indies or any
other part of America. Great Britain in effect withdrew from the Concert of
Europe.

Canning then proposed that the United States join Great Britain in issuing
a declaration that they would resist intervention in Latin America. President
Monroe insisted that Great Britain first recognize the new republics. The Americans regarded Canning as an enemy, and with good reason. He wished to prevent any close understanding between the United States and Latin America,
fearing that such an understanding would give the United States leadership of

the Western Hemisphere. In confidential memoranda written during the dispute over neutral rights which led to the War of 1812, the Minister had expressed his "apprehension of the ambition and ascendency of the United States." "I need not say," he wrote, "how inconvenient such an ascendency may be in time of peace, and how formidable in time of war." With the recent war experiences in mind, he reflected that "sooner or later we shall probably have to contend with the combined maritime power of France and the United States." Canning hoped to edge out the United States by inducing the Latin-American colonies to import the British mixture of monarchy, aristocracy, clergy, and representative institutions instead of the more republican institutions of the United States or of revolutionary France.

For their part, the Americans considered that joint action of two unevenly matched powers would place them in an inferior position, especially since the greater power was the former mother country. They were aware, however, that the naval power of Great Britain was the greatest obstacle to European intervention and was, therefore, their own shield. Certain of British support, the Americans acted independently. On December 2, 1823, President Monroe issued the famous declaration which set the limits of European imperialism in the New World. The declaration was directed not only against intervention in Latin America but also against recent efforts by Russia to extend her claims to the northwest coast of America to include a part of the Oregon country. It was in reference to these efforts that Monroe announced as "a principle in which the rights and interests of the United States are involved, that the American continents, by the free and independent condition which they have assumed and maintain, are henceforth not to be considered as subjects for future colonization by any European powers."

After deploring the failure of the recent liberal revolutions in Spain and Portugal, the President declared:

> The political system of all the allied powers is essentially different . . . from that of America. . . . We owe it, therefore, to candor, and to the amicable relations existing between the United States and those powers, to declare that we should consider any attempt on their part to extend their system to any portion of this hemisphere as dangerous to our peace and safety. . . . We could not view any interposition for the purpose of oppressing them [the new independent governments], or controlling in any manner their destiny, by any European power, in any other light than as the manifestation of an unfriendly disposition toward the United States.
>
> . . . It is impossible that the allied powers should extend their political system to any portion of either continent without endangering our peace and happiness; nor can anyone believe that our southern brethren, if left to themselves, would adopt it of their own accord.

Monroe's message was received with enthusiasm by liberals in Europe and with contempt by conservatives. Canning approved of the stand of the United States against intervention, but he was displeased with Monroe's attack on conservative principles. The Continental allies abandoned whatever thought they might have had of sending an expedition overseas and passed over in silence the large claims asserted by Monroe. Great Britain extended recognition to the South American states in 1825.

The independence of South America was now secure. But the consequences of the dispute were even more far-reaching. Not only old-fashioned imperialism but the whole conservative system suffered a grievous blow. For one thing, Great Britain could no longer be counted upon to cooperate in her foreign policies with the conservative Continental powers. The Concert of Europe had been riven. This division could hardly fail to benefit the liberal critics of that system. And Monroe's message clearly stated what many of these critics in Europe felt. No one sensed this more strongly than the leader of conservatism, Chancellor Metternich of Austria, who wrote:

> These United States in America, which we have seen arise and grow. . . have suddenly left a sphere too narrow for their ambition and have astonished Europe by a new act of revolt, more unprovoked, fully as audacious, and no less dangerous than the former [the American Revolution]. . . . In their indecent declarations they have cast blame and scorn on the institutions of Europe most worthy of respect, on the principles of its greatest sovereigns, on the whole of those measures which a sacred duty no less than an evident necessity has forced our governments to adopt to frustrate plans most criminal. . . . If this flood of evil doctrines and pernicious examples should extend over the whole of America, what would become of our religious and political institutions, of the moral force of our governments, and of that conservative system which has saved Europe from complete dissolution?

Although the Chancellor exaggerated the immediate impact of American policy, his fears of discontent nearer home were realistic enough. For in the mid-twenties a revival of the European liberal movement was preparing.

11. *European Liberalism and American Democracy*

The defection of Great Britain from the Concert of Europe and the assertion of the Monroe Doctrine struck severe blows at the policy of intervention to suppress revolutions. But if the arm of European conservatism was not long enough to reach across the Atlantic, it was strong at home. The revolutions of the early twenties had been crushed everywhere, in some cases by the troops of the great powers. By the mid-twenties only Ottoman Turkey was still wrestling inconclusively with the Greek rebels.

Yet even at home the victory of conservatism was not definitive. Despite all the efforts of the governments, an opposition was gathering, particularly in Western Europe—an opposition more comprehensive and more determined than that which had challenged the old order in the late eighteenth century. At the same time, America presented Europeans—liberals as well as conservatives—with the striking image of a democratic society in a large country.

The most noteworthy aspect of the opposition to conservatism was the character of its adherents—the bulk of the middle and professional classes—and their participation, or at least acquiescence, in the political activities of the lower classes. Recent advances in industry and commerce had increased the numbers, wealth, and confidence of the middle classes. The repressions and excesses of the restoration seemed to them to demonstrate the incapacity of the titled classes, whose leadership they were no longer content to accept without question. Absolutism and despotism—enlightened and unenlightened—had been tried and found wanting. Constitutional government was the only remaining alternative. But men of property felt that it must be a less sweeping constitutionalism than that which had inspired the French revolutionists; unless liberal principles were applied with moderation they might lead again to the democratic measures of French Jacobinism. These men rejected the doctrine of natural rights and popular sovereignty as radical; they insisted on less inflammable philosophies of government and on the influence of the wealthy classes in the framing of policy and legislation. They were encouraged by the rise of doctrines which recognized

222

the role of superior talents, emphasized the importance of practical ability, and exalted commercial and industrial enterprise. The most influential of these doctrines were Saint-Simonianism, utilitarianism, and classical economics.

Saint-Simonianism and Utilitarianism

Saint-Simon, a fantast of genius, whom we met in the revolutionary nineties, threw off enough ideas to feed a half dozen movements. He proposed that governments base their policies upon "positive knowledge"—fact finding and scientific planning—that an international parliamentary system be formed to keep the peace; that Great Britain and France join forces as a nucleus for a European and then a global government; that a world parliament undertake gigantic public works—great canals, improvement of communications, the eradication of disease—that the Pacific and Atlantic Oceans be connected by a canal cut in Nicaragua.

Saint-Simon searched for a principle of society that would restore the stability which the Revolution had shattered. He found this "cement" in the idea of a modern elite to take the place of noblemen and warriors of the past. At the turn of the century Saint-Simon had sketched a plan for the government of the world by an aristocracy of scientists, writers, and artists. The advance of science, he believed, would elevate more and more people into the propertied class, and society would eventually approximate a democracy led by an intellectual elite.

After the fall of Napoleon, Saint-Simon was struck by the contrast between the incompetence of the restored monarchs and noblemen and the energy and ability of businessmen. Encouraged by the financial as well as the moral support of wealthy bankers and merchants in France, he merged his thinking with the interests and aspirations of the business world.

The keynote of Saint-Simon's new idea was production, and he traced its source to his service during the American Revolution as a young officer in the French army. "It was in America, while fighting for the cause of economic freedom [*la liberté industrielle*], that I first conceived the desire to watch this plant of another world blossom in my own country." Saint-Simon summed up the essential character of America as "peace, production, and economy." In the New World, he said, a great statesman is one who reduces taxes without doing harm to the public service; in the Old World, he is one who finds a way to increase revenue without too much complaint from the taxpayer.

Saint-Simon proposed to put the "producers" in charge of the country. By "producers" he meant all the creators of "pacific works of public utility"—farmers, manufacturers, merchants, scientists, professional men, artists, civil servants. But Saint-Simon assigned leadership increasingly to great financiers, businessmen, factory owners, and engineers. These groups composed the new elite to which he would turn over the world for benevolent management. The banking community in particular, which provided capital for great undertakings, came the closest to embodying Saint-Simon's vision of an "industrial" elite. He was convinced that such an elite would act in a disinterested fashion for the benefit of mankind and that it would raise the material level of the masses. Political government, or the "administration of men," would give way to an "administration of things," a government devoted to a rational and scientific organization of the productive forces.

The impact of Saint-Simonianism was felt largely in France and adjacent Continental countries, where it evoked a response among able and enlightened men of affairs. Elsewhere, particularly in England and the United States, a greater influence flowed from the doctrines of utilitarianism and classical economics.

Utilitarianism was an old idea. Many eighteenth-century writers had said that human actions and institutions should be judged by their practical results. They had noticed the tendency of men to seek pleasure and avoid pain and suggested that government should aim at "the greatest happiness of the greatest number." But it was the English jurist Jeremy Bentham (1748-1832) who made utility the criterion of morality and taste as well as of law and politics.

To Bentham, society was a "fictitious body"; it was merely "the sum of the interest of the several members who compose it." Laws therefore must be framed with a view to enlarging and multiplying the pleasures and diminishing the pains of the greatest possible number of individuals. Bentham's pleasures and pains were available to ordinary men. There were fourteen simple pleasures— the pleasures of sense, wealth, skill, amity, a good name, power, piety, benevolence, malevolence, memory, imagination, expectation, association, and relief. There were twelve simple pains—the pains of privation, awkwardness, enmity, and ill name, and eight others which, under happier circumstances, might become pleasures: the pains of sense, piety, benevolence, malevolence, memory, imagination, expectation, and association. If the view of human nature that this list reveals seems commonplace, it made the list all the more effective with large numbers of busy men. Bentham was directing the attention of lawmakers to those interests that touch the lives of the generality of men. "Everybody is to count for one and nobody is to count for more than one." Bentham prepared a "calculus of felicity" for computing the intensity, duration, certainty, propinquity, fecundity, and purity of pleasures and pains. Lawmakers could use this calculus to determine which of two laws was more likely to promote the "greatest happiness of the greatest number."

The older philosophy of liberalism had recognized the role of society and culture in checking the selfish impulses of individuals. Bentham assigned that role to the state. The legislator must leave the individual free to act on his own judgment, but he must contrive ways of enlightening him and influencing him to choose those actions that would benefit others as well as himself. While Bentham rejected "natural rights" as decisively as the most conservative writers, his conclusions often coincided with those of French liberals. He advocated free public schooling for the children of the poor, savings banks for workers, health

legislation, and new and economical administrative methods. Not even the

English language escaped his attention. It owes "international," "maximize," "minimize," and "codification" to him.

Bentham was a severe critic of the customary laws of England, their technical complexity, their verbal confusion, and their "feudal" accretions and over-lappings. Laws should be so simple and consistent as to make contending lawyers and interpreting judges superfluous. Punishment should provide an example that will prevent repetition, inflict as little pain as possible, compensate the victim, reform the offender, and avoid shocking the sentiments of the population. Prisoners should be taught trades, put to work, and compensated for it. Bentham would have the state provide employment for able-bodied paupers.

In politics, Bentham was for a long time a Tory. Like Saint-Simon and other contemporary reformers, he tried at first to enlist the support of noblemen and monarchs for his projects. When he failed, he turned republican, even democrat. In urging the establishment of a broad suffrage, Bentham was in advance of most middle-class liberals. For fifty years he was busy drafting codes, constitutions, and administrative rules for the world at large. He helped to write the constitutions and statutes of the newly founded republics of Latin America.

In the hands of his followers, who were known as the "philosophical radicals," Bentham's "principle of utility" became the raw material of a veritable industry of legal reforms and administrative and political devices. The philosophical radicals were technicians of government and engineers of social efficiency as well as reformers. They were the English counterpart of the French revolutionists. To mention but a few of the brilliant band, there were James Mill (1773-1836), Bentham's closest collaborator, who developed the political instruments of utilitarianism, notably broader suffrage rules; John Austin (1790-1859), who prepared the ground for scientific jurisprudence and rational codification; Sir Samuel Romilly (1757-1813), who fought in Parliament to put an end to the barbarities of criminal law; and David Ricardo (1772-1823), who worked out the implications of utilitarianism for political economy.

Ricardo was probably the most influential of these men. His doctrines of prices and rent influenced both liberals and socialists. The price of agricultural produce, Ricardo contended, is set by the effort and cost of cultivating the poorest soil in use. Were the price lower, such land would be withdrawn from cultivation, for the cost of using it would not be met. It follows that the owners of fertile soil receive an increment over and above the return on their cost of cultivation. This unearned increment is rent. When the return on land covers only the cost of the labor and capital spent on it, it is not rent but wages and interest. All rent is, therefore, properly speaking, unearned. As industry develops and population increases and poorer lands are put under the plough to supply the growing demand, the price of produce naturally rises. The owners of previously cultivated land receive a higher profit, without having lifted a finger. Thus industrial progress enriches landlords.

The siphoning off of wealth to the unproductive class, Ricardo claimed, has a depressing effect upon the accumulation and employment of capital. He defined capital as everything that makes human labor productive: tools, materials, storehouses, food, clothing, skills. It is clear that the progress of society rests on the increase of capital, so defined. The welfare of workers as well as of capitalists depends on it. Labor is the ultimate source of wealth, and capital itself is merely the embodiment of the labor of the past. The market value of labor, like that of other things, is determined by supply and demand. It tends to oscillate around the "natural wage"—that is, around the amount required to maintain and reproduce the labor force. Ricardo accepted the implications of Malthus' "law of population": when wages rise, the supply of workers also rises. Wages tend to the level of subsistence, but that level is not a fixed physical factor but a resultant of the customs and traditions of the country; it is higher in countries which possess more capital. In order to raise it, capital must be increased while population is kept in check.

The sacrifices that the growth of capital and industry entail are, in Ricardo's view, necessary though tragic incidents in man's effort to wrest from nature a richer and more congenial environment. Society and the state can do nothing to diminish the pain inevitably associated with progress. They can, however, do much to speed the prospects of improvement; by removing the hindrances to the operation of this process—tariffs, monopolies, privileges, and favoritism to one class or another—and by promoting individual enterprise and competition. The outstanding obstacle to such a policy is the provincial and national exclusivism of the conservative system, particularly as it is embodied in the raising of food prices, to the advantage of the powerful class of landlords, by protective and prohibitive laws. In England the abolition of the Corn Laws became the chief economic demand of the philosophical radicals. England was becoming more and more dependent on imported grain. If the corn laws fell, the whole protective system would fall with them. The abolition of tariffs would reduce the income of the state, and the weight of new taxation could be shifted to the shoulders of the landlords.

Ricardo built his theory on the foundation laid by the physiocrats and Adam Smith. But his view of the value of the activities of landlords and capitalists differed from theirs. The physiocrats had singled out the landed classes as the only productive element in society. Adam Smith had identified the interests of the landlords with those of the community. He had strong reservations about the civic responsibility of the mercantile classes; it was only "the invisible hand" of a harmonious Nature that transmuted self-interest into social gain. Malthus had endorsed the influence of landlords as beneficial. Ricardo shifted the accent of social utility from landlords to capitalists and workers. His law of rent made parasites of the most influential class of traditional European society.

The Greek Revolution and the Revival of Liberalism

The doctrines of Saint-Simonianism, utilitarianism and classical economics provided the middle and professional classes with an armory of weapons and emboldened them to seek not only influence but a place in the halls of legislation and the bureaus of administration. In this ambition, the liberals were not slow to enlist the support of the lower classes.

A striking sign of the resurgence of liberalism in the mid-twenties was the wave of sympathy for the Greek revolution. That rebellion was calculated to arouse all the sentiments of the critics of Western governing classes—economic, cultural, and political. The Greeks were commercially the most highly developed of the peoples subjugated by the Turks. The deterioration of the Ottoman Empire encouraged Greek shippers, merchants, and sailors to avoid customs regulations and duties and to engage in informal wars with the Sultan's naval patrols. On the mainland of Greece, Christian shepherds and farmers formed the habit of assaulting Mohammedan officials, particularly tax-gatherers. There were mountaineers and sailors who found it profitable to combine rebellion with robbery and to enact the role of patriotic Robin Hoods. To hold up tax-gatherers and customs patrols was just as patriotic as to attack imperial forces, and more rewarding.

The Greek rebels were not only merchants, sailors, and mountaineers; they were also educated youths and professional men of the towns and ports, who were influenced by Western ideas. The chief intermediary with the West was Adamantios Koraïs (1748-1833), a merchant's son who had been living in Paris since the early years of the French Revolution. In pamphlets, manifestoes, and letters, he appealed to his compatriots with a program of constitutionalism and national independence. He reminded them of their nearly forgotten classical glories, so cherished by the French revolutionaries. In order to revive the ancient tradition, Koraïs worked to purify the popular Greek language and bring it closer to its classic origins. Some years before, the patriotic poet Constantine Rhigas (1760-98), also an expatriate, had written a Greek version of the *Marseillaise* and organized a powerful "society of friends"—the Hetairia—for the liberation of his country. Rhigas established the first modern Greek press, published translations of foreign works in the popular dialect, and collected and published Greek songs.

In 1820 cultural, political, and economic unrest had flared up in armed conflict on the Greek mainland. The resulting disorders on land affected largely the native population, but the disorders in the Aegean Sea concerned foreign shippers and traders and their governments, notably Great Britain, whose commerce in that area had grown appreciably since the collapse of Napoleon's Continental System. When a ship was held up for duty by Greek rebels and then forced to pay the customary charges to the Turkish officials as well, the calculations essential to the strategy of commerce became impossible. The first instinct of the foreign trader was conservative: let the government restore security by suppressing the rebellion. But when the Turks proved unable to do so and rebel merchants obtained loans from English investors, Great Britain became sympathetic to Greek independence. In 1823, at the same time that George Canning and James Monroe were throwing a shield before South America, the British Foreign Secretary recognized the Greeks as belligerents. It was impossible, he said, to treat "as pirates a population of a million souls."

227

The story of South America was repeated: Great Britain was again supporting revolution. Russia now betrayed an irresistible eagerness to help the Greeks. For more than a half century the czars had nursed the hope of seizing Constantinople or at least of assuring Russian shipping a free outlet from the Black Sea into the Mediterranean and thence to the oceans of the world. It was a Greek general serving in the Czar's army, Alexander Ypsilanti (1792-1828), who had raised the banner of Greek revolt in 1821, not in Greece herself, but in the Danubian principalities—now Rumania—where Russia had exercised a protectorate since 1812. Years of ferocious but indecisive warfare followed.

In 1825, on the appeal of the Sultan, an Egyptian army landed in the Morea and seemed to be about to carry the day for the Turks. The European powers sought to force the Sultan to agree to a truce. In 1827 an Anglo-French-Russian fleet, commanded by a British admiral, blockaded the Egyptian fleet of Mohammed Ali at Navarino, presumably to prevent the Sultan from moving supplies up to his fighting forces. An accidental altercation brought about an engagement, and the allies destroyed the Egyptian fleet. In 1828 a Russian army marched through Bulgaria and in 1829 took Adrianople, just north of the Turkish capital. Another Russian army seized Turkish territory at the other end of the Black Sea, in eastern Asia Minor. In the negotiations that followed Russia demanded autonomy for the Greeks. In order to outbid her for influence in the new state, Great Britain insisted on full Greek independence—that is, independence from Russia as well as from Turkey. Pressed from all sides, the Sultan yielded. In the Treaty of Adrianople he not only recognized Greek independence but loosened his grip on the Danubian Principalities. He promised to raze his fortresses there, but Russia was to occupy the Principalities until the Sultan paid a war indemnity. Greece finally became a constitutional monarchy in 1832 under King Otto I, a Bavarian prince imported from the dynastic hothouses of Germany.

Philhellenism was, after the outburst of enthusiasm for the French rising in 1789, the greatest expression of liberal sentiment on an international scale. The governments found it difficult to discourage or repress it. Educated men were more familiar with the history of Greece than with that of their own countries. Philhellenists subscribed money, held demonstrations of sympathy, and delivered orations in praise of liberty in the best classical style. French, English, American, and Russian liberals volunteered to fight against the modern "Persians." The most renowned poet of the day, Lord Byron, sang the cause of Greece and died in Missolonghi in 1824.

Liberal discontent went deeper, of course, than opposition to Turkish absolutism. There were percipient conservatives who were prepared to make timely concessions. In Great Britain, for example, the rigidity of the Corn Laws was somewhat eased in 1825. Grain might henceforth be imported at any time, on a sliding scale of duties which rose when the price of grain fell and fell when it rose, with the double result that the country would not want for food and the landlords' profits would be protected from close foreign competition. The movement to emancipate the Catholics, which Tory statesmen had promised to do for nearly fifty years, was proving irresistible. Daniel O'Connell, the eloquent organizer of Irish resistance to British rule, was elected to Parliament by huge majorities again and again, although the Test Act of 1673 had made it illegal for any non-Anglican to hold public office. The Act was repealed in 1828. The following year, Parliament repealed other laws that effectively excluded Roman Catholics from public life. Non-Anglicans now became the political equals of the members of the Established Church. The reform of the brutal penal laws was also begun.

In France a liberal majority was elected to the Chamber of Deputies in 1827 and a moderate ministry was installed. Censorship was attenuated, liberal professors were restored to the chairs from which they had been driven, and the suffrage was somewhat extended for the election of local officials. In common with contemporary English officials, the French ministers tried to develop methods of maintaining order without calling out the troops, which often had a provocative effect. In 1828 new police systems were launched experimentally in both Paris and London. The policemen would wear simple, unostentatious uniforms, carry no arms, and seek to win the favor of the populace. They were to repress political outbreaks and criminal activities, but by preventing them from occurring rather than by acting after the fact.

The liberal opposition, however, was not to be won over so easily. An imaginative priest, Felicité de Lamennais (1782-1854), who began his career as a defender of absolute monarchy and unquestioning faith, raised a storm by proposing that the Roman Catholic Church, to preserve its independence, sever its alliance with the Bourbon rulers. In 1828 he launched a periodical, *l'Avenir*, with the startling motto "God and Liberty." He urged the papacy to separate the Church from the state and to lend its support to freedom of the press and of speech, which, he argued were as necessary for the activities of an independent pulpit as for those of an independent press. *L'Avenir* was eventually (1832) condemned by Pope Gregory XVI (1831-46), but meanwhile it influenced younger priests, not only in France but also in Belgium and Poland, where a Catholic population chafed under foreign rule.

The Revolution of 1830

Alarmed by the resurgence of liberalism in France, the arch-conservative group of royalists—called the "Ultras"—abandoned caution and put pressure on King Charles to arrest the trend. In 1829 he dismissed the moderate ministers and appointed as chief of government the "Ultra of the Ultras," the Prince of Polignac. The Prince announced his intention "to reorganize society, to give back to the clergy their weight in state affairs, to create a powerful aristocracy, and to surround it with privileges." Since his ministry did not have the support of the Chamber, his appointment defied the principle of ministerial responsibility. Tension rose. In March 1830 a large group of deputies presented an address to the King protesting his appointment of an unconstitutional ministry. The

King replied by dissolving the Chamber and ordering new elections. Hoping to distract the country and tap strength abroad, the government decided to conquer Algiers, where for some years insults and blows had been exchanged between the local ruler and French officials. The expedition sent in June 1830 was successful—in a short campaign the French army occupied the coast and the capital—but meanwhile domestic critics had formed societies to defend the Charter by refusing to pay taxes. For some years a republican movement had been growing in Paris; it now became threatening. When the new elections resulted in another liberal Chamber, the King abandoned all constitutional pretense. On July 26 he issued ordinances which dissolved the Chamber before it had met, changed the electoral system so as to ensure a subservient majority in the future, and muzzled the opposition press.

This was too much. Deputies, writers, printers—even moderate conservatives—called upon the republicans and the people of Paris to rise. On July 28 thousands of Parisians poured into the streets and raised barricades. In a few days of fighting they overcame the royal troops and took possession of important public buildings. On August 2 the King abdicated and fled to England.

The triumphant people of Paris were persuaded by General Lafayette to accept as king Louis Philippe, head of the younger (Orléans) branch of the royal family. The new king, on his part, agreed to accept a constitution, not to "grant" one, as a condition of his rule. The House of Peers was purged of intransigent conservatives, and the electorate of the lower house was expanded to include not only the 200,000 richer landowners of the country but an additional 100,000 persons who had a large income from any sort of property. Thus the money principle supplemented the land principle, and business property became as influential as agrarian property. The disillusioned democrats and republicans soon renewed their demands for universal suffrage, with greater persistence.

The crash of Bourbon obstinacy in France had repercussions throughout Western Europe. Under pressure, several German rulers promised to grant liberal constitutions. Sympathetic risings against the Pope and Hapsburg princes occurred in several cities of central Italy, but they were put down by Austrian soldiery.

The most successful imitation of the July revolution in Paris occurred a month later in nearby Belgium. The Treaties of Vienna of 1815 had attached Catholic Belgium to Protestant Holland, and the vogue of the time had imposed an absolutist rule upon both. In Belgium, however, the rule of the Orange dynasty appeared foreign and heretical as well as illiberal. Belgian liberals had the same grievances as Dutch liberals, but they also had the support of the Catholic Church, which objected to being "tolerated," along with various heresies, by the official Protestant Church. Catholic Belgians accounted for one third of the population of the united Kingdom of the Netherlands and for much of its wealth, but they were far outnumbered by Dutch in the appointive bureaucracy and judiciary. In these circumstances, the Catholic elements in Belgium drew close to the liberals, making the movement "national," and accepted the program of constitutionalism. In August 1830 the people of Brussels came

Atlantic Revolutions, 1800–1830

Countries where revolutions succeeded

Countries where revolutions failed

(Dates of successful revolutions in darker type)

out into the streets, fought off royal troops, and proclaimed the separation of Belgium from Holland and its independence as a constitutional state.

Louis Philippe hoped to place one of his sons on the new throne. Great Britain, bristling at the possibility that her naval position on the Channel might be weakened by the accretion of French influence, secured the selection of King

Leopold, a prince of the German house of Coburg and an uncle of the British heiress presumptive, Victoria. Belgium modeled its constitution largely upon that of the British. In August 1831, when Holland dispatched a large army and defeated the Belgians, the French crossed the border and defeated the Dutch in turn. Later, with the aid of a British fleet, they expelled the Dutch from Belgium. In 1839 France and Britain secured their own interests as well as those of Belgium by inducing Prussia and other European powers to sign a treaty guaranteeing the neutrality of the new state. They also declared the River Scheldt (on which Antwerp stood) open to navigation and free from Dutch control and duties, although its mouth was in Dutch territory. They thus assured the Belgians of a valuable outlet to the sea and promoted easier trade generally.

Intervention by the powers in favor of a revolution was a novel spectacle. In 1830, when the French and the Belgians rose, Russia was determined to march across the Continent in order to re-establish legitimate rule. Czar Nicholas I, who succeeded his brother Alexander in 1825, was an uncompromising conservative. For once, however, Austria held back. Chancellor Metternich had long been critical of the obduracy of the French royalists, and the far-flung military operations of Russia alarmed him: they threatened to make the Czar as powerful in the West as he was in the East. Quite opportunely, Polish patriots foiled the plans of the Czar. Encouraged by the French example, they staged a rising in Warsaw, on the eve of the projected departure of the Russian troops to the West, in November 1830. Again, as in 1793-95, Poland's loss was France's gain. The Polish civil war lasted a whole year before it was put down, and Nicholas was forced to abandon his intention of intervening in France. The Czar employed more than military means to best the rebellious Poles: he wooed the peasantry by giving them the land of patriotic noblemen. The failure of the rebellion enabled Nicholas to extend absolutism to Poland by abrogating the constitution Alexander had granted in 1815.

The English Reform Bill and Its Significance

The French success in July 1830 supplied the spark for an attack on conservatism that had been gathering in Great Britain for some years. In an election held in August, the opposition to the Tory government much increased its strength in the House of Commons. Until the revolution in France the opposition candidates had stressed demands for the abolition of slavery and for lower taxes; after the revolution they concentrated on the constitutional question. The movement for parliamentary reform, which had been dormant during the wars with France and the long ascendancy of the Tories, came alive again in the twenties. The working classes, hoping that political changes would lead to social legislation in their behalf, were the first to espouse reform, followed later by the middle classes. Events in France had shown that the combination of these two classes was irresistible. The majority of the Whigs had opposed extensive constitutional change almost as strongly as the Tories had, although they were willing to sponsor other reforms. But the Whigs had been out of office almost continuously for forty years, and they were now ready to make concessions.

In November 1830, when the new Parliament was assembled, the Prime Minister, the Duke of Wellington, asserted that "the system of representation possessed the full and entire confidence of the country." Such was the outcry against this statement that Wellington resigned and the King, William IV (1830-37), called on the Whig leader, Earl Grey (1764-1845), to form a government.

In March the Whigs introduced a bill to redistribute Parliamentary seats, in order to give representation to populous towns, and to extend the suffrage moderately. The bill was narrowly defeated by the House. Parliament was thereupon dissolved and a new election called. The results of the election—a Whig triumph—showed that the country was strongly in favor of reform. The Second Reform Bill was passed in the new House of Commons, but the House of Lords rejected it by a majority of forty-six votes on October 2. Seldom had English public opinion been more aroused. It seemed clear that a handful of lords and bishops were defying the express will of the nation. In October and November there was an outburst of popular demonstrations and riots. The agricultural districts of the south were swept by disorders. In industrial districts, where trade was depressed and unemployment common, workers drilled and gathered arms for a war on the Lords. Bristol was seized by insurrectionists and the palace of the Bishop, an opponent of the bill, was burned. The troops quickly recaptured the city, but only after killing twelve and wounding ninety-four persons, according to an official count.

The fear of a full-dress revolution helped to turn the tide. In March 1832 the Commons passed the Third, and final, Reform Bill. The House of Lords obstinately insisted on watering it down. The riots of the previous fall were not repeated, but the working and middle classes were more determined to win, and they were better organized. Impressed by the strength and unity of the reformers, King William promised Earl Grey to create enough peers to secure a majority for the bill if the House of Lords persevered in its opposition. The prospect of a dilution of their order persuaded enough peers to change their vote or abstain from voting. The bill became law in June 1832.

The Reform Bill was a veritable political revolution. It altered a representation system that had continued unchanged for centuries. It abolished "rotten boroughs" and boroughs controlled by aristocratic families and reduced the representation of others. The seats thus gained were assigned to the more populous counties, chiefly industrial centers in the Midlands which had been totally or largely unrepresented. The Bill simplified the qualifications for voting. It wiped out the traditional mélange of charters, privileges, personal grants, guild membership, and town corporation rights which gave the electorate a motley and uneven character. Here and there some poor citizens had been entitled to vote, but the weight of the electorate lay with landlords and propertied townsmen. Henceforth tenants and leaseholders of substantial real estate, as well as the owners, could vote. As in France, the money principle was honored alongside the land-tenure principle, the mobile wealth of the capitalist alongside the property of the landowner.

The change in the size of the electorate was not striking. Slightly more than 100,000 persons became voters, making a total of about 300,000. It was the composition of the new electorate that was significant: it included the urban classes recently enriched by industrial development. The indirect effect of the Reform Bill was to weaken further the influence of the nobility and monarchy. The humbling of the House of Lords added to the prestige of the House of Commons. The king had occasionally exercised the privilege of selecting the personnel of the ministry, although he had to choose among leaders who could obtain a majority in the House of Commons. After the thirties, the Crown never rejected a favorite of the Commons for its own favorite. The "Civil List"—the salary of the king—was reduced, and with it the largess at his command. Ever since the "panic" of the French Revolution the government had often interfered with and abridged the rights of assembly, association, habeas corpus, and publication. The defeat of a rigid conservatism bolstered the practices of freedom.

The passage of the Reform Bill advanced the eventual prospects of democracy, although its voting provisions bitterly disappointed the advocates of universal suffrage. Within a few years there arose the great Chartist agitation for the thorough democratization of the parliamentary system. Yet the Whig leaders agreed with the Tories in regarding the concessions in the Reform Bill as final. They proposed to restrict political power to the middle and upper classes. The fact remained, however, that the Bill had been carried by the pressure of public opinion and popular agitation. This meant that if the people were determined on a change, and a considerable portion of the leading groups and politicians endorsed it, the government would find it difficult to resist.

Finally, after the Reform Bill, Parliament proved amenable to a gradual easing of imperial controls in colonies settled by Englishmen, notably in Canada. Eastern Canada consisted of two provinces—Lower and Upper Canada—ruled by royal governors and appointed councils which represented aristocratic and bureaucratic cliques. For many years the popularly elected lower houses of the legislatures had demanded control of the purse and the power to appoint judges and protested the privileges and land grants bestowed on the established churches. The unrest of Lower Canada was particularly intense, since the majority of the population was French and the oligarchical government English. In 1837 both provinces rose in arms. The rebellion was a successful failure, for, although it was easily put down by royal troops, the new Governor General, Lord Durham, in a famous *Report on the Affairs of British North America* (1839), endorsed the principle of self-government. Influenced by the philosophical radicals, Durham recommended that the two provinces be combined and that they be granted a government responsible to the voters. The first recommendation was carried out in 1840 when the British Parliament passed the Union Act, and shortly thereafter the principle of executive responsibility to the legislature was also conceded. The Canadian government was to control all matters except foreign relations, trade regulations with other countries, and the disposal of public lands.

Democracy and the American West

The political overturns of 1830-32 changed the relations among the principal regions of the Western world. In the countries of Western Europe, they put an end to the rigid conservatism induced by the "panic" of the French Revolution. The very nomenclature of politics changed. In England Tories became Conservatives and Whigs Liberals. There, as everywhere in Europe, "liberal" became the fashionable term of the nineteenth century, as "democrat" was to be that of the twentieth century. It was the certificate of modernity. The label was appropriated by every group, and especially every political movement, that wished to keep abreast of the times. Eventually there were Liberal Protestants, Liberal Catholics, Liberal Socialists, and even Liberal Conservatives.

After the "defection" of France and Great Britain, the governments of Austria, Prussia, and Russia became more, rather than less, repressive. As Western Europe moved farther away from the absolutist powers, it moved closer to the United States. The acceptance of a flexible constitutionalism vindicated the American example. Transatlantic contacts multiplied rapidly. Free trade, individual enterprise, legal and humanitarian reform and social experiments swept both sides of the Ocean. Economic advances or crises in any country of the North Atlantic region affected all the others. Yet the more Western Europe and America confronted each other, the more glaring appeared their differences. While Western Europe accepted constitutionalism, America proceeded beyond it to democracy. A European ideal became an American reality. In the Old World, individualism and democracy did not cohabit comfortably. In the New, they entered into an enduring union which became one of the distinctive features of its character. Finally, the Republic endured a tragedy that Europe was spared—the tragedy of Negro slavery.

American democracy had been germinating for a long time. Its spirit had been evident in the Revolution and was strengthened by the victory of Jeffersonianism. After the War of 1812, most of the older states rewrote their constitutions and broadened the base of the suffrage by reducing or removing property qualifications. Many appointive offices became elective. The principle of the separation of church and state was widely accepted.

In this evolution the growth of the American West played a large role. After peace with Great Britain was restored in 1814, the settlement of the interior became greatly accelerated. While farmers, land companies, and landlords staked out the nearer lands, the more adventurous and footloose frontiersmen followed the sun and pierced the Rocky Mountains beyond Louisiana. Some of them even reached the Pacific Coast, where they added the claims of the United States to the older claims of Russia, Great Britain, and Spain. From Louisiana, and from the older Northwest Territory, eleven additional states had been carved out and admitted to the Union by 1821. In these states most of the citizens owned land, and the traditional qualifications for suffrage were therefore meaningless. The constitutions of the new states provided for simple manhood suffrage.

But Western society was not simply politically democratic. It was a mixture of individualism and egalitarianism, social flexibility and cultural conservatism. Origin and inheritance counted for little, enterprise and ability for much more. An exaggerated emphasis on personal independence led to exhibitions of pride that were almost aristocratic. It was as much as a man's life was worth to insult another man. Yet the spirit of equality and cooperation was strong. Most men owned land and helped one another in the exigencies of life in new communities and the emergencies of the frontier. There was an easygoing relationship among the various religions and nationalities of the region. Yet the breezy environment acted also as a preservative of tradition and culture. Migration and resettlement revolutionized a man's way of living and working, but it did not change the content of his mind or supply him with new spiritual alternatives. The Westerners and the frontiersmen clung to their national and religious memories. They were drawn to their own kind. Religious sects and social practices that could not survive in older communities found a home among them.

The old distinction between the New World and the Old was reflected in the differences between the West and the East in America. Finance, industry, higher education, and fashion were concentrated largely in the older states. To a lesser degree, political leadership of the Republic also rested with the older states. As conservative Europeans were condescending toward Americans, conservatives in the East set Westerners down as "wild men," without breeding and discipline. But just as the older colonists had asserted their rights and their dignity against European claims of superiority, so now the Westerners claimed equality with the Easterners.

For some years, the Western areas had tried to break into the magic circle of national leadership. In 1824 General Andrew Jackson of Tennessee (then considered a Western state) stood for the presidency. Jackson had distinguished himself in wars with the Indians and was the hero of the defense of New Orleans in 1815 against the British. Although he obtained the largest number of electoral votes, he lacked a majority, and the election was thrown to the House of Representatives. Henry Clay (1777-1852), a defeated candidate from Kentucky, persuaded the representatives of his state to vote for John Quincy Adams of Massachusetts, son of the second chief of the Republic. Their votes, combined with those of Eastern representatives, gave Adams the presidency. Clay became Secretary of State. Four years later, however, Jackson was elected by the votes of Western farmers, and urban artisans and middle-class groups in the East. He also received the votes of supporters of state banks and those of financial elements, notably in New York, which chafed increasingly under the ascendancy of Philadelphia, headquarters of the powerful Bank of the United States. By the mid-twenties, manhood suffrage had become the rule in most of the states; Jackson was therefore the first popularly elected President of the United States.

Andrew Jackson inaugurated a new era in the American presidency. He had ended his education early, and his gruffness and frontier manners tempted his enemies to mock him as boorish and vulgar. These taunts only endeared him the more to the people. Yet Jackson was hardly a "common man." He had ample means and lived as a plantation gentleman. He had the pride and touchiness of a hidalgo, and high political sophistication. He did much to raise the prestige of the presidency. Federal judges were appointed, and the members of Congress were chosen by individual districts and states. Only the President was chosen by the American people as a whole; therefore, Jackson felt, the President represented the people in a unique way. When he asserted the power of his office, he was giving effect to the popular will. Jackson urged legislation upon Congress, appealed to popular opinion in support of his policies, and vetoed more measures than had his six predecessors combined. The voters endorsed his conception of the President as a strong leader in close touch with popular sentiment by re-electing him in 1832 by a larger majority than he had obtained in 1828. The Whig candidate, Henry Clay, received 49 votes in the electoral college to 219 for Jackson. The American presidency has been a more influential office since Jackson's day, although not all its holders have asserted its prerogatives and prestige as vigorously as he did.

In the Jacksonian era, parties and electoral methods assumed a shape which henceforth became characteristically American. Candidates for federal office had traditionally been nominated by caucuses of members of Congress and state legislatures; they were now nominated by conventions of delegates representing the rank and file of the party supporters. The new system was first used on the state level, and in 1832 the presidential candidates were selected by national conventions. The ordinary voter began to have a voice in the nomination of candidates for the highest offices in the Republic. Popular appeal became an essential of political success. An aspirant for public office must have the "common touch" or at least affect it.

Party alignments and nomenclature were suited to the new mood. In the "era of good feelings" of the early twenties, most factions—including many former Federalists—were merged in the comprehensive ranks of the Republican party. (The four candidates for the presidency in 1824—Jackson, Adams, Clay, and William H. Crawford—all called themselves "Republicans.") The bulk of the old Republicans accepted the leadership of Jackson and assumed the name of "Democrats." The conservative groups drew together, first under the name of "National Republicans" and finally under the liberal-sounding name of "Whigs." In England this name connoted opposition to royal authority. To complete the image, the Whigs charged "King Andrew" with dictatorial ambitions as well as demagogic leanings. The Whigs were actually a loose aggregation of financial groups, a faction of Southern planters and slaveholders, and a scattering of mercantile and industrial leaders, held together by a common opposition to Jacksonian policies. Eventually, however, they took a leaf from Jackson's book in an attempt to appeal to the mass of the voters. In 1840 they won the presidential election by promoting their candidate, General William

Henry Harrison (1773-1841), a well-to-do Ohioan of Virginian antecedents, as a man of humble origin and tastes. The Whigs set up log cabins and served hard cider to the voters in order to demonstrate Harrison's "folksiness."

The American liberal distinguished himself from the Western European liberal by his view of the state as well as of suffrage. In the Old World, the tradition of political authority was strong. Just as the aristocrats had used legislative and executive power to maintain their privileges, the philosophical radicals of England and the Saint-Simonians of France proposed to use it to establish the new order. Economists who believed in the automatic action of "natural laws" used man-made laws to provide the setting for their operation. While the European liberals emancipated the individual from the authority of various institutions, they gave the state itself a more rational and imposing structure and promoted an improved civil service.

The American liberal rejected this emphasis on management. The Jacksonians not only reduced the functions of government but made the operation of government informal and loose. The theory that government was so intricate and mysterious as to require a political "priesthood" of long training and breeding seemed to them a cloak for hereditary oligarchical rule. At the lower levels, they advocated and practiced rotation in office. The result was that the weight and sometimes the efficiency of administration were inferior to those of Western European states. At the higher levels, the new leadership included men of ability and substance. Jackson himself was one of the ablest men who attained to the presidency.

In his Farewell Address of 1837, Jackson described the moderate, self-reliant, and liberal character of American democracy:

> The planter, the farmer, the mechanic and the laborer all know that their success depends upon their own industry and economy, and that they must not expect to become suddenly rich by the fruits of their toil. Yet those classes of society form the great body of the people of the United States; they are the bone and sinew of the country—men who love liberty and desire nothing but equal rights and equal laws, and who, moreover, hold the great mass of our national wealth, although it is distributed in moderate amounts among the millions of freemen who possess it.

Europe Looks at America

The growth of American democracy at a time when democratic movements were making their appearance in Western Europe turned the attention of Europeans across the Atlantic. The opinion of the lower classes and of those members of the middle classes who found the European atmosphere constricting was eloquently expressed in the increasing emigration to America.

A host of travelers descended upon the United States. Their opinions were often divided along party lines. John Stuart Mill (1806-73), son of the philosophical radical James Mill, observed that "the progress of political dissatisfaction, and the comparisons made between the fruits of a popular constitution on one side of the Atlantic and of a mixed government with a preponderating aristocratic element on this side in England, have made the working of American institutions a party question. For many years, every book of travels in America has been a party pamphlet."

The literature on America was therefore also a literature on Europe. The English utilitarian Harriet Martineau (1802-76), who visited America in 1834-36, commended the Americans for having "established for ever . . . two things before held impossible: the finding a true theory of government, by reasoning from the principles of human nature, as well as from the experience of government; and the capacity of mankind for self-government." In his *Lettres sur l'Amerique du Nord* (1836), Michel Chevalier (1806-79), a leading French Saint-Simonian, described the Americans as "the most enterprising of men and most ambitious of nations." The United States was "Europe turned upside down." In America public opinion was formed by the general population; in Europe, by the rich and noble. The "plague of pauperism" which was undermining European societies had been all but banished from America, at least in the Northern and Western states where there was no slavery. America seemed to Chevalier the last projection of civilization; she was destined, he believed, to surpass Western Europe, as Western Europe had surpassed earlier civilizations. The Republic still lacked traditions, but time would eventually produce them.

Many European travelers were considerably more critical. *Domestic Manners of the Americans* (1832) delighted Tories and snobs. Its author, Mrs. Frances Trollope (1780-1863), described the men of America as selfish, the women as petty and provincial, the servants as impudent, religious camp meetings as orgiastic, and the people generally as vulgar, materialistic, and contemptuous of eminence, quality, and talent. Americans behaved as if the government could not go on "without their bawling and squalling, scratching and scrambling to help it."

The novelist Charles Dickens (1812-70), a democrat and a reformer, went to America prepared to like it but was disillusioned. His *American Notes* (1843) depicts the Americans as sharp traders and disrespectful voters, with familiar manners, unsanitary habits, and a licentious press. As an author, Dickens resented the failure of the United States to punish publishers who pirated books originally issued abroad—a practice that continued until the enactment of a copyright law in 1891. Dickens was piqued by the attitude of Americans toward England. The English hero of his novel *Martin Chuzzlewit* (1844) was accosted by an American: "Well, how's the unnat'ral old parent by this time? Progressing back'ards, I expect, as usual." Dickens' humor deserted him when he pronounced Americans "dull and gloomy."

From a French aristocrat, the prospect of democracy tore an anguished cry. Count Alexis de Tocqueville (1805-59) came from a family that supported the Bourbon monarchy. His *Democracy in America* (1834, 1840) is a critical analysis of democracy and a nostalgic evocation of aristocracy. De Tocqueville acknowledged that the American Republic possessed "the most perfect federal

constitution that ever existed." He commended the prevalence of local autonomy, the dispersion of property, the public spirit and common sense of the citizens, their ability to come together spontaneously and form associations for a
rich variety of purposes, their free press, their practical versatility, their respect
for women, family, and all natural bonds and affections, and, finally, the wide
dissemination of information and of the elements of a common education which
made the masses "the most enlightened in the world." But he found the political
leadership of Americans undistinguished, their literature and art imitative, their
journalism irresponsible, their taste vulgar, and their science backward. The
"despotism" of mass opinion, he contended, weakened individualism, freedom
of thought, and freedom of discussion. Democracy satisfied large numbers of
men, but it promoted only minor virtues: moderate intelligence, kindliness,
sincerity, comfort, and tranquility. It ignored the great passions and the loftier
attributes associated with aristocracy. Aristocracy, however, was doomed—this
was God's will. "What appears to me to be man's decline is, to His eye, advancement; what afflicts me is acceptable to Him. A state of equality is perhaps
less elevated, but it is more just." The Lord apparently had lower cultural
standards than De Tocqueville.

It had been easy in the past for conservatives to dismiss small democracies,
such as the Swiss, but America, De Tocqueville perceived, was potentially a
world power. And was not the portent of America redoubled when one considered that another power was arising which was also dangerous to the traditional civilization of Europe? Like the United States, Russia had a youthful
energy that contrasted with the lethargy of the Continental countries which
had reached maturity. "The principal instrument of the former [the United
States] is freedom; of the latter [Russia], servitude. Their starting point is
different and their courses are not the same; yet each of them seems marked out
by the will of Heaven to sway the destinies of half the globe."

If, at best, democracy portended cultural death, at worst it threatened to
become Caesarism or despotism all the more crushing because it spoke in the
name of the people. This danger, in De Tocqueville's view, was less serious in
America than in Europe, with its tradition of centralized administration, militarism, and one-man rule. To diminish this danger, and to mitigate the evils
of democracy, De Tocqueville counseled Europeans to secure the rights of the
individual, to nurture religious feeling, to encourage free association, to establish local government and a free press, to moderate the effect of the ignorance of
the majority by providing for indirect election of officials, and to limit legislative
power while increasing the power of an independent judiciary.

Democracy in America fixed the image of America in the minds of many
cultivated Europeans. It was especially welcomed by conservatives. Sir Robert
Peel, the Tory Prime Minister, recommended it in an important political address. But De Tocqueville's book did not go without challenge. In a critical
review, John Stuart Mill praised it as a brilliant analysis but took issue with
some of its conclusions. Political leadership in America compared well, he
thought, with contemporary British statesmanship. It was a mistake to think

that aristocracies are more prudent than democracies. "The opinion of a ruling class is as fluctuating, as liable to be wholly given up to immediate impulses, as the opinion of the people. Witness the whole course of English history." Lacking the extremes of aristocracy and peasantry, the United States was pre-eminently a middle-class country, and the defects singled out for attack by De Tocqueville were defects of the commercial spirit everywhere. The English middle class exhibited the tendencies criticized as American. The danger, both in America and in Europe, lay in the predominance of that class, and in general of any one interest or class. The remedy lay in balancing the commercial class with an agricultural and a learned leisure class. "One of the great advantages of this country over America" was that Britain possessed a learned class. Mill counseled the British middle class to tolerate a balance of interests and America, which boasted the greatest diffusion of general intelligence and education, to develop its facilities of higher education.

De Tocqueville's book understandably was received less favorably in the United States than in Europe. Many Americans found his generalizations too broad and arbitrary. They looked upon him as an aristocrat whose social prejudices were confirmed by his anti-Jackson hosts in America. Yet they acknowledged the justice of some of the observations of De Tocqueville and other critics. They found their own De Tocqueville in the romantic novelist James Fenimore Cooper (1789-1851). In *The American Democrat* (1835) Cooper charged his country with cultural provincialism, which he blamed on the sparseness of settlement, the competition and fanaticism of religious sects, and the oppressive authority of public opinion. Democracy replaced "one tyrant by many" and bred demagogy and mediocrity.

Cooper's was a minority voice. A more representative and influential spokesman was the poet and essayist Ralph Waldo Emerson (1803-82). Emerson ascribed American provincialism to business drives and practices and to a tendency to think in terms of groups, masses, and geographic sections instead of in terms of individuals. He placed much of the blame for cultural deficiencies on American dependence upon European values. In an address on "The American Scholar," delivered at Harvard University in 1837, he called on his compatriots to free themselves from cultural colonialism. "We have listened too long to the courtly muses of Europe," Emerson said. "The spirit of the American freeman is already suspected to be timid, imitative, tame." He foresaw a day

> . . . when the sluggard intellect of this continent will look from under its iron lids and fill the postponed expectation of the world with something better than the exertions of mechanical skill. Our day of dependence, our long apprenticeship to the learning of other lands, draws to a close. . . . Events, actions arise, that must be sung, that will sing themselves. Who can doubt that poetry will revive and lead in a new age? . . . We will walk on our own feet; we will work with our own hands; we will speak our own minds. The study of letters will no longer be a name for pity, for doubt, and for sensual indulgence.

*The debilitated situation of a monarchal Government when puffed up
by pride and self-importance whose resources must be wrung from the people's
hands. The difficulties to which such a State must ever be exposed.*

*The flourishing condition of a well-formed industrious Repu-
willingness displayed by the citizen of a free State to serve his co
his blood and fortune.*

*An American cartoon on the difference between America and Europe. Presi-
dent Andrew Jackson is demanding that King Louis Philippe fulfill a
treaty granting compensation for American ships seized by Napoleon. The
French Parliament had refused to vote the necessary moneys. On the left:
"The debilitated situation of a monarchal Government when puffed up by
pride and self-importance, whose resources must be wrung from the people's
hands. The difficulties to which such a State must ever be exposed." On
the right: "The flourishing condition of a well-formed industrious Republic.
The willingness displayed by the citizen of a free State to serve his country
with his blood and fortune." Between the two captions is a stanza from
Byron's* Childe Harold's Pilgrimage. PRINT ROOM, NEW YORK PUBLIC
LIBRARY

As Emerson spoke, three American writers were on the threshold of careers that
brought them lasting international fame. They were Edgar Allan Poe (1809-49),
Herman Melville (1819-91), and Walt Whitman (1819-92). Emerson's declaration of independence was not premature.

Jacksonian democracy and the European reactions to it set a pattern of
contrast between the New World and the Old. Yet, when the pattern emerged,
the countries of the Atlantic were not so dissimilar. Their mutual influences
were many and strong. They pursued similar economic policies and responded
to similar ideas and movements. Different though they were, American democracy and European liberalism stimulated and reinforced each other. They introduced a generation of adventure in material, moral, and intellectual life.

242

12. *Atlantic Enterprise*

The revolutions of 1828-32 released the energies of the Atlantic world. Opportunities for economic expansion and individual enterprise multiplied. The settlement of new lands was accelerated. The revolutions stimulated the rise of a profusion of practical reforms, idealistic projects, and utopian experiments. Liberalism regained the momentum it had lost during the long wars against republican France and the subsequent denouement of Bonapartism. It laid the foundation for nearly a century of unprecedented advances in industry, transportation, and communication.

Laissez Faire in Western Europe: The Repeal of the Corn Laws

The liberals of Western Europe rationalized the machinery of the state, abolished monopolies and privileges, and provided for free economic exchange. They swept out a multitude of superfluous offices, sinecures, and jurisdictions that had grown around monarchical and aristocratic institutions. They streamlined the duties and expenses of local administration, justice, poor relief, and official churches. They abolished old imposts which were annoying to the taxpayer and costly to collect. Their keynote was simplicity, uniformity, and economy. The sphere of the state was highly restricted, but within that sphere its administration was strengthened and, both in England and on the Continent, the civil service became more efficient and honest.

Liberals put an end to the combination of political and economic power that had made the fortune of privileged classes. In England, for example, the trading monopoly of the East India Company was abolished in 1833. Henceforth the Company was restricted to the administration of the Empire in India. Independent merchants and shippers legally penetrated that old preserve of mercantilism, although the Company retained the monopoly of the trade between India and China.

The classical economists and the utilitarians had long contended that free trade among countries would enlarge markets, stimulate production, and promote prosperity. It would increase the riches of society and the profits of merchants and manufacturers while benefiting the consumer by bringing down the cost of living. If countries could exchange goods freely, they would not go to war for trade or colonies. Expensive naval and military establishments would become superfluous. Free trade would introduce the reign of political freedom and universal peace.

Free trade naturally appealed to exporters and importers. English industry was so far in advance of that of other countries that it did not fear the competition of foreign imports. The adoption of free trade by England would encourage its extension elsewhere, for if England agreed to accept the agricultural products and raw materials of other countries, they in turn would admit her industrial goods. Both sides would benefit through the lowering of prices of agrarian as well as industrial goods. Lower prices meant lower costs of production, and cheaper goods meant more customers.

English free-traders found strong support for their argument in the distress of the lower classes. The main item in the workers' budget was food, and the price of grain was kept high by tariff duties. Repeal of the Corn Laws would mean cheaper bread and—many employers hoped—lower wages. This in turn would mean lower prices of manufactured goods and hence potentially greater markets. The free-traders singled out the Corn Laws for attack as the vulnerable heart of the protective system. These laws were dear to the landed interests and to the Conservative party.

In 1836, after a business depression, the Anti-Corn Law League was founded, with the financial help of factory owners. Richard Cobden (1804-65) and John Bright (1811-89), who had been engaged in textile manufacturing, became the leaders of the movement. They launched an agitation remarkable for that time, using methods familiar to today's pressure groups. They distributed popular propaganda and mass advertising, held mass meetings, and, appealing to both self-interest and humanitarianism, formed alliances with politicians of both parties. They struck out against stodgy conservatism and aristocratic selfishness, on the one hand, and socialistic proposals, on the other. To the urban masses, they held out the promise of cheap food.

Hunger came to the assistance of the Anti-Corn Law League. Half the population of Ireland lived on potatoes, and in 1845 blight struck the potato crop. The following year the English wheat crop failed and the Irish potato crop was again ruined by blight, as it was again in 1847—the worst year of all. The Irish starved to death by the thousands and hungered by the hundreds of thousands. It became necessary for the government to import food, and even to distribute much of it free. The Corn Laws became synonymous with famine. Within the next few years one million of a population of eight million fled to the United States, under miserable conditions of travel, in an anger which still glows in their descendants.

Instead of a revolution in the state, a revolution occurred in the structure

Anti-Corn Law cartoon of 1839 by W. M. Thackeray (1811-63), the English novelist who was also an illustrator. A policeman, a soldier, and a beadle are preventing a Russian and a Pole from landing grain for the starving people of England.

of parties. The Conservative party had come into power in 1841, under the leadership of Sir Robert Peel (1788-1850), on a platform of protection. Under pressure of events, Peel, who was the heir of a millionaire textile manufacturer, embraced free trade and carried with him his cabinet and a hundred Conservatives in the House of Commons. These, combined with two hundred Liberals and philosophical radicals, voted to repeal the Corn Laws in June 1846.

The landed interest suffered a resounding defeat, and the Conservative party was divided. The followers of Peel formed an informal third party, which often cooperated with the Liberals. Eventually many leading Peelites joined the Liberal party. Profiting from the division, the Liberals returned to power for a decade and a half. They proceeded to draw the obvious conclusion from the victory of free trade: they repealed the old Navigation Acts, which had reserved to English ships the trade between England and her colonies as well as England's coastwise trade, and Parliament began a long-range overhauling of the protective, fiscal, and imperial system.

Laissez Faire in America: The Bank and the Tariff

In Great Britain *laissez faire* was an issue between agrarian and industrial interests. In the United States, however, it was an issue between conservative-minded men and democrats, and between sections of the country.

Jacksonianism, like Jeffersonianism, had a strong tendency toward *laissez faire*. The tradition of states' rights and the fear of a strong federal government

245

and bureaucracy reinforced the influence of the classical school of economics. The result was that the principles of *laissez faire* were applied more literally in America than in Europe. The European tendency toward reliance on the mechanisms of authority was represented in the United States by the advocates of the "American System" of mutual economic interests. Although the Whig party did not present a clear-cut program, a good many of its members, notably its leader, Henry Clay, subscribed to the System. They proposed that the federal government levy high tariffs in order to encourage the rapid development of industry and provide funds for an ambitious program of internal improvements. The building of roads and canals, they contended, would foster the integration and mutual intercourse of the various parts of the large country. It was suggested that additional revenue might be obtained by setting higher prices on the sale of public lands. The effect of this System would be to concentrate capital and finance through an officially sponsored exploitation of men and resources.

Under the leadership of Jackson, the Democratic party opposed the System, arguing that federal appropriations for internal improvements were in effect grants to large private corporations. In 1830, in a resounding message vetoing a bill authorizing the use of federal moneys to help construct the Maysville Road in Kentucky, Jackson asserted that such a law would be unconstitutional. It was more important, he claimed, to reduce taxes and the national debt in order to "rivet the attachment of our citizens to the government of their choice by the comparative lightness of their public burdens" and to spread the influence of "liberal principles and free government throughout the world."

The principal struggle between Democrats and Whigs, however, was engaged not over the American System as a whole but over the Second Bank of the United States. The Bank had been chartered in 1816 by the federal government and endowed with valuable privileges. Like the Bank of England, on which it was modeled, the Bank of the United States held the deposits of the government, made loans to it, and had the power to issue notes. One fifth of the capital was subscribed by the government. The rest was held by private capitalists, who controlled the operations of the Bank. Its prestige, size, and official connections gave the Bank the leadership of the financial community.

The Democrats were not in principle opposed to the regulation of financial practices. The regulation of currency issue and credit conditions, to ensure fairness to all parts of the business community and to prevent the use of financial power for political purposes, was an integral part of the creed of the liberal economists. There were, however, two difficulties involved. Neither the United States nor the European countries had established a uniform system of money. The notes of various private banks, both domestic and foreign, circulated and competed with one another, with the result that there was much uncertainty and confusion in all transactions based on money. Unscrupulous financiers manipulated these various currencies to their profit. The second difficulty was that the Bank of the United States, like the Bank of England, was both an official institution and a commercial bank. There was always the possibility that the directors would use their privilege of receiving deposits from and lending money to the government to contract or expand credit or to reduce or raise prevailing interest rates so as to increase their profit and gain an advantage in competition with other, less favorably placed bankers and financiers. England met this difficulty by passing Peel's Bank Charter Act of 1844, which separated the banking operations of the Bank of England from the department that issued paper money. Beyond a fixed amount which was determined by the debt of the government to the Bank, every paper pound had to be backed by gold. The issue of money was gradually restricted almost entirely to the Bank of England.

This solution was not as yet open to the United States. The individual states as well as the federal government chartered banks. The Jackson administration felt that the Bank of the United States had not stabilized the issue of money. In a new country which was short of capital and had to borrow heavily from abroad, control over the flow of credit was a powerful tool in the hands of financiers. Democrats, particularly in the West, had a great distrust of the "money power." It was feared that the leaders of the Bank, many of whom were allied with conservative Whig politicians, might become a power in the government. This fear gained substance from the contemptuous attitude exhibited by select circles in the East toward the presence of new and "untaught" men in the government. In short, the technical problem of regulating currency and banking became a conflict between adherents of oligarchical and democratic views.

When, in the summer of 1832, Congress passed a measure renewing the charter of the Bank, President Jackson vetoed it. He acknowledged that "a Bank of the United States is in many respects convenient for the government and useful to the people." The existing bank, however, had excessive and unconstitutional powers and was "dangerous to the liberties of the people." The proposed law seemed to him to be "predicated on the erroneous idea that the present stockholders have a prescriptive right not only to the favor but to the bounty of Government. It appears that more than a fourth part of the stock is held by a few hundred of our own citizens, chiefly of the richest class." There were not enough votes to supply the two-thirds majority needed to override the veto. The President, interpreting his re-election later in the year as a "popular mandate" to destroy the Bank, withdrew the government deposits and distributed them among a number of state banks.

The defeat of an institution that tended to dominate credit accented the tendency to extend the principle of competition to the financial field. In the past, the privilege of organizing a company of limited liability required a special legislative act and was granted only to favored groups engaged in unusually large enterprises, such as the building of railroads or canals. It was often accompanied by monopolistic privileges. In the thirties and forties, a number of American states extended the right of limited liability to any combination of enterprisers operating in any field of activity. "General incorporation" acts made the formation of companies a simple formality which did not require action by the legislature. They enabled investors to pool their capital and to engage in varied enterprises by buying stock in a number of companies.

The advance of enterprise was reflected also in tariff policy. The proposal

"*The Downfall of Mother Bank.*" *Contemporary cartoon shows President Andrew Jackson as the American Samson destroying the Bank of the United States, a financial power he regards as an "aristocratic" threat to the Republic. "Old Nick"—with horns and tail—is Nicholas Biddle (1786-1844), president of the Bank and leader of a pack of venal politicians and editors.* NEW YORK HISTORICAL SOCIETY, NEW YORK CITY

of classical economists to ease restrictions on foreign trade found a hearing in most of the Atlantic countries. In the United States the question of the tariff had constitutional as well as economic aspects, regional as well as national implications. Industrial development was concentrated in the Eastern states, and the manufacturing interests of those states, as well as some Western agricultural groups, favored protectionism. Northern shipping firms supported freer trading practices, but it was, above all, the Southern states, whose principal activity in foreign trade was the export of cotton to England, that demanded lower tariff duties.

In 1828, when a high tariff called the "Tariff of Abominations," was passed, Vice President John C. Calhoun (1782-1850) of South Carolina, the spokesman of the South, elaborated a novel version of an old doctrine in his *South Carolina Exposition and Protest.* The American people, Calhoun argued, had established the individual states, and the federal government was but a voluntary contract of these states. True sovereignty resided in the states. Each state might judge for itself when that contract had been infringed by law of the federal government. When it felt that such an infringement had occurred, it might declare a law unconstitutional and of no effect—at any rate, within its own borders. The explicit approval of three quarters of the states would make a law constitutional but the aggrieved state would have the choice of seceding from the Union or accepting the judgment of its partners.

The implications of this "nullification" doctrine were ominous. The federal government could legislate only on matters which the most literal reading of the Constitution indicated were within its province. Once it concerned itself with controversial issues, particularly issues which divided regions, it risked the break-up of the Republic. Under such conditions effective government would become impossible.

The Whig Senator Daniel Webster (1782-1852) of Massachusetts, in a historic debate with Senator Robert Hayne (1791-1839) of South Carolina, defended the principle of a Union invested with flexible and dignified powers. The federal government, he contended, was not "the servant of twenty-four masters [states], of different wills and different purposes, and yet bound to obey them all." The old Confederation of 1781 was indeed a mere compact among sovereign states, but it was precisely in order to repair the inadequacies of that system that the Constitution had been written. That Constitution was an instrument of government "made for the people, made by the people, and answerable to the people," not the individual states. Webster concluded that, if matters were pressed to a showdown, the antinullificationists would "call the *People* to come to the rescue."

In 1832, South Carolina declared the Tariff of Abominations and the somewhat lower federal tariff of 1832 unconstitutional and void within that state. It threatened to secede if the federal government insisted on enforcing the law. President Jackson promptly issued a proclamation which asserted that the claim that a state might annul a federal law was

> incompatible with the existence of the Union, contradicted expressly by the letter of the Constitution, unauthorized by its spirit, inconsistent with every principle on which it was founded, and destructive of the great object for which it was formed. . . . Secession, like any other revolutionary act, may be morally justified by the extremity of oppression; but to call it a constitutional right is confounding the meaning of terms, and can only be done through gross error or to deceive those who are willing to assert a right, but would pause before they made a revolution or incur the penalties consequent on a failure.

There was recourse under the Constitution for fundamental complaint: three quarters of the states could ask Congress to call a convention to amend it. This South Carolina had not done. The federal government was ready to execute its laws. Congress passed the Force Bill in March 1833 authorizing the President to use troops to enforce the tariff law.

Neither side, however, meant to carry things to extremes. On the same day that it passed the Force Bill, Congress enacted the Compromise Tariff of 1833, which provided for a gradual reduction of duties to a moderate rate of 20 percent ad valorem. South Carolina, which stood alone in its act of nullification, accepted the new tariff and revoked its Ordinance of Nullification.

In the forties and fifties the tariff duties dropped lower and lower, in line with the tendency of the time. The South was satisfied, but the constitutional issue of states' rights and of the limits to which a state could go in resisting federal authority remained unresolved, with eventually tragic results.

Industrialization and Overseas Settlement

Laissez-faire policies in Europe and America emancipated and assisted the activities of business. Savings in taxes increased the capital available for investment. Commerce, industry, shipping, and banking made large strides.

The economic advance was not continuous or steady. Investment was often venturous, particularly in railway construction. In the thirties and forties, there was much speculation in shares of companies engaged in building canals and turnpikes. Hope sometimes outran common sense. The first railways, for example, were not always built where they were most needed, and competing companies frequently built duplicate lines covering the same areas. Canals eventually proved to be much less useful and profitable than they had seemed, principally because of the advent of the much cheaper and faster railways. Demand did not always catch up with supply, and overproduction resulted. High peaks of feverish activity alternated with sudden and moody crashes. The Western world experienced its first general financial crises. In 1817, 1825, and again in 1836 and 1847, waves of bankruptcies swept over the various countries. Capital and credit became scarce, and many debtors were driven to the wall. The epidemic of depressions was the sign of a new and tragic unity that capitalist expansion was impressing upon the Western world.

In France the production and export of wine and grain increased apace, and industrial development benefited sensibly from the more reliable credit policies of the new regime of Louis Philippe. Private banks multiplied, and the use of machinery in industry was promoted. The number of mechanical looms rose from 5000 in the early thirties to more than 30,000 in the late forties. Steam engines, which had once been counted in the hundreds, came to be counted in the thousands. The first railways were built. Both tracks and cars were at first light in construction and therefore unsuitable for high speeds or heavy freights. But they facilitated the movement of passengers, mails, and light goods in peacetime, and promised to do the same for soldiers and supplies in time of war.

Belgium, like England, was fortunate in possessing supplies of iron and coal located conveniently near each other, and she made greater proportionate advances than France. She imported much English machinery, and her new outlet to the sea, the reopened Scheldt River, reanimated her foreign commerce. The western and eastern extremities of Germany, notably the districts of the Ruhr and of Silesia, experienced a similar though slower and spottier initiation into modern industrial technology.

The expansion of the United States was chiefly agricultural, but industry nevertheless struck hardier roots, especially in the Northern states. A large textile industry was developing in New England, where first water power and then steam power was used to propel machines. By 1840 woolen factories alone employed 21,000 workers, and in another decade 35,000. The number of cotton spindles in 1840 was two and a quarter million; twenty years later three million more were in use. The amount of cotton consumed and the value of the final product increased fourfold. It was nearly the same story in metals, transportation, and other enterprises.

Nowhere was progress so rapid as in Britain, the original model of the industrialized country. By our present standards, no country was highly industrialized in the mid-nineteenth century. Even in Britain, many industries were still unmechanized; most of the wealth was still derived from agriculture, and most of the population was engaged in that pursuit. But Britain was so far in advance of other countries, her wealth was increasing so much more rapidly, and industrial production already played such a considerable role in her economy, public policy, and the daily life of a substantial sector of her population that she may be called. without exaggeration, the only great industrial country in the world at that time. A few indications of her outstanding eminence will suffice. British production of coal tripled in the first half of the century. By the 1840's it was perhaps ten times as great as that of the rest of Europe combined. Railroads had not yet become the essential carrier of a complex economy, but the English trackage of nearly two thousand miles was by far the largest in the world. Steam shipping was growing more rapidly than anywhere else. The first large stock and trades exchanges appeared in Great Britain. And that country had already become the chief investing, as well as industrial, center of the globe.

Business ventured overseas. It pried open old empires long closed to commerce with the West and opened new territories to settlement and trade. It scored a spectacular success in China. The "Celestial Empire" forbade the entry or residence of foreign merchants. Venal Chinese officials and privileged foreign merchants, however, carried on a restricted informal trade at the port of Canton. The British East India Company had established a quasi-legal export of opium produced in India for Chinese addicts. When the Company's trade monopoly with China was broken in 1833, independent British merchants, eager to cash in on newly opened markets, greatly increased the pressure for establishing a regular and legal trade. Meanwhile, the Emperor, disturbed over the spread of the opium habit, decreed that the traffic must stop. Local officials exploited the decree by raising their demands for bribes to allow the trade to continue. It was a three-cornered contest among the imperial administration, whose controls were inefficient; local officials, who exercised a virtual autonomy; and the foreign merchants at Canton, where the traffic was concentrated. In 1839 a high imperial emissary confiscated and burned the stocks of opium in the port. The

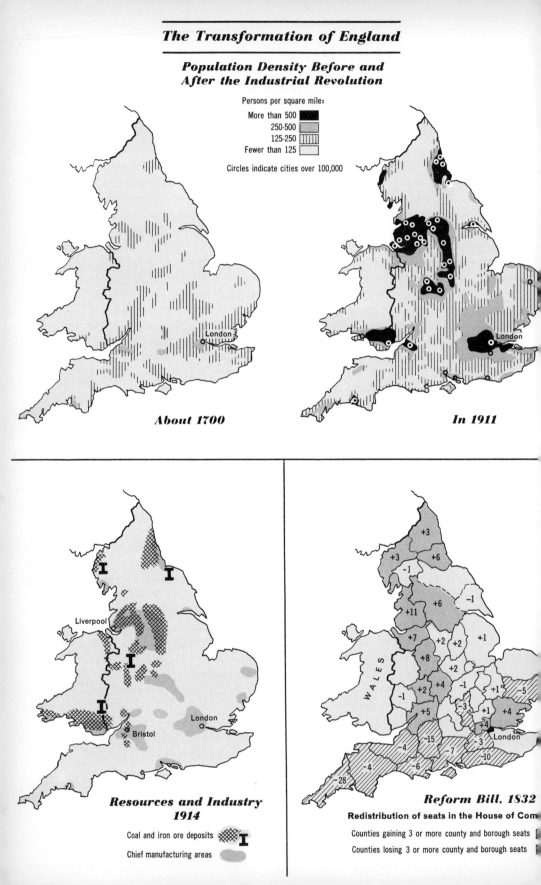

The Transformation of England

Population Density Before and After the Industrial Revolution

Persons per square mile:

More than 500
250-500
125-250
Fewer than 125

Circles indicate cities over 100,000

London

About 1700

London

In 1911

Liverpool

London

Bristol

Resources and Industry 1914

Coal and iron ore deposits

Chief manufacturing areas

+3
+3   +6
-1
-1
+6
+11
+7   +2 +2   +1
+8   +2
+2
-1   +2   +4   -1   +1 -5
+5   -3   +1   +4
-1   +4
-4   -15   -7   -3   London
-28   -4   -6   -10

W A L E S

Reform Bill, 1832

Redistribution of seats in the House of Com

Counties gaining 3 or more county and borough seats

Counties losing 3 or more county and borough seats

British opened war and dispatched a fleet which blockaded Chinese ports, bombarded coastal cities, and occupied the island of Hong Kong. China could interpose only a weak defense, and it became apparent that the grandiose and ancient Empire was largely façade. In 1842 the Emperor signed a treaty with Great Britain opening five ports to regular trade, providing that imports would be taxed at the low duty of 5 percent ad valorem, agreeing to pay a war indemnity, and ceding Hong Kong, which commanded the Bay of Canton. In order to prevent Great Britain from reaping the advantages of a monopoly, the Emperor soon extended the same terms of trade to the United States, France, and other Western countries. For the first time in centuries, the Chinese market lay open to the shippers and traders of the world.

Since colonial days, American seamen, notably those of New England, had conducted trade in the Far East and a large whaling industry in the North Pacific Ocean. American whalers and Dutch and French shippers, in need of shelter and revictualing places, began to knock at the doors of the empire of Japan, which had been closed for centuries against foreign intercourse.

Agriculture as well as commerce felt the impulse of *laissez faire*. In Great Britain, the philosophical radical E. G. Wakefield (1796-1862) applied the theory of economic liberalism to land settlement. England had surplus capital and surplus labor, but she lacked enough land to satisfy her needs. On the other hand, the colonies overseas had much virgin land but lacked capital and labor. The problem was how to combine the interests of England with the promotion of emigration and settlement. Wakefield's answer was "systematic colonization" to create an environment in which the "natural laws" of individual enterprise and competition could operate without hindrance.

Chinese painting of about 1800, showing the compound of warehouses and offices of foreign traders in the port of Canton. BETTMANN

The first principle of his scheme was that the government had to prevent land from falling into the hands of poor people. It should forbid "squatting" and set the price of land too high for the ordinary man. It then should proceed to sell the land to settlers of means and to capitalists, on condition that they lay out the money to "import" English poor, clear the forests, build roads and houses, and initiate the cultivation of the land. The immigrants had to be young people of both sexes. The government would use the receipts from land sales to promote migration. By keeping the price of land high, it would force immigrants to work for wages, at least for a number of years. By the time that some of these workers, by dint of saving, had established themselves as farm owners, other immigrants would take their places as wage earners.

The settlement of several points in eastern Australia had begun in the late eighteenth century. That of western Australia was begun in the 1820's, but the first settlers did not prosper, and the British government shipped convicts in order to supply the necessary labor force. The trials of the new colony spurred Wakefield to try his own scheme in southern Australia. In 1834 he formed the South Australia Association, which bought land from the government at 12 shillings an acre and sold it to the settlers at 20 shillings, or four times the price of American land. For some years the colony was in bad straits, owing to insufficient planning, but in the forties its condition improved and the population grew to 50,000 persons.

Wakefield and his followers were responsible for the British acquisition of New Zealand. In 1837 they formed a company similar to the South Australia Association for the settlement of that territory. Their initiative in sending out an expedition, and the fear that France, whose agents were active in the region, might forestall her, led Great Britain to proclaim annexation in 1840. Although the British government assured the native Maori chiefs that the tribes would not be disturbed in their possessions, the company acquired large tracts of land at nominal prices. Bitterness and warfare ensued. But the company was successful in settling 15,000 Englishmen within a half dozen years.

The conception of "systematic colonization," combined with the liberal program of political autonomy, produced a new conception of empire. Wakefield and other philosophical radicals envisaged colonies whose bonds with the mother country would rest on common institutions and culture and on mutual economic benefits. They dreamed of an empire without imperialism—a free association of like-minded commonwealths. In this respect, they were in the tradition of the Americans who had proposed a free imperial association before their Revolution. The philosophical radicals, however, differed from the Americans in projecting colonies that were replicas of the mother country. They wished to reproduce overseas the social structure of the Old World, with its capitalists and laborers, its rich and poor.

The Movement for Free Land in America

The expansion of American settlement was greater, and more democratic in character, than that of the British colonies. This was one of the most important indirect results of American independence. The Western farmers and Eastern workingmen who supported Jackson and the Democratic party demanded a liberalization of land policy. The policy that had been inaugurated in the Northwest Ordinance of 1787 was to survey the unoccupied areas in lots of 36 square miles, the future townships. The townships were divided into 36 sections, each a mile square (640 acres). One section in each township was set aside for educational purposes. A proposal to reserve another section to support religion had been defeated. The land was sold at auction, either in whole townships or in one or more sections. In 1820 the sections were broken up into lots of 80 acres and the price, which originally was a minimum of $2 an acre, was reduced to $1.25. A sizable farm thus might cost only $100. There was no limit to the number of sections anyone could buy.

This was only half the story. The Western states, as well as the federal government, had originally made large grants of land both to companies and to individuals, especially to war veterans. Much of the land passed into the hands of speculators and financiers. The small man who wanted a farm often had to have substantial savings or to borrow money. Since the frontier (officially defined as the area where two to six persons lived in a square mile) moved faster than the government was able to survey it, farmers often staked out and occupied new land at will, without bothering to pay or to get official title to their homesteads.

The increase of the population of the West and industrial developments in the East combined to increase the pressure for free settlement. The availability of free land, industrial workers believed, would slow down the movement of workers from country districts to factory towns, and so improve the bargaining position of urban employees.

The federal government responded slowly to the rising pressure. In 1832 President Jackson declared in his annual message to Congress that the public lands should cease as soon as possible to be a source of revenue, that the price set on them should cover merely the cost of surveying and the sums paid to Indian tribes for some of the lands. "The government should afford to every American citizen of enterprise the opportunity of securing an independent freehold." In 1841 Congress made a significant concession. A settler who had occupied land, whether surveyed or not, cleared the forest, and laid out a farm without the formality of a purchase could obtain full title by paying the minimum price of $1.25 an acre without submitting to competitive bidding. But he might have to borrow to meet the payment, or else buy on credit from speculators. In 1854 it was provided that the price of land which remained unsold after being on the market for thirty years be reduced to only 12½ cents an acre.

The gradually liberalizing land policy placed the seal on an irresistible   *255* movement of migration and settlement. Although the United States extended to the Rocky Mountains, only its eastern half was occupied in 1830. The line of the frontier stood in Iowa, Missouri, and Arkansas, on the western bank of the Mississippi River. The prairie lands beyond the Mississippi Valley were long regarded as uninhabitable. In the twenties and thirties, explorers brought back reports of fertile valleys in the Oregon country beyond the Rocky Mountains. Opportunities beckoned in the vast territories of Mexico. Adventurers, government agents, and traders penetrated into Texas and New Mexico. Frontiersmen had developed the habit of pulling up stakes whenever greener fields beckoned. Unpopular religious sects longed for a new Zion beyond the hostile environment of the settled communities. Secular idealists plotted the perfect society in the security of distance and isolation. Frequent business crises, notably the "panic" of 1837, turned the eyes of Americans westward. By the thirties, the tide of migration, which had wavered between 10,000 and 25,000 newcomers annually, rose to between 50,000 and 100,000 a year. It passed the 100,000 mark in the late forties, when economic conditions worsened and crops failed in Europe.

In the forties, large parties began to set out on the great adventure. They generally started from Kansas or Missouri in covered wagons and journeyed 2000 miles across prairie, mountains, and desert. The trip, which took about six months, was not for the poorest, since the equipment, oxen, and food for a family cost about a thousand dollars. Communities and sects pooled their resources for migration. Every year the parties grew larger. The Western adventure was replete with hope and fantasy. It was not infrequently punctuated with tragedy and failure and, at least in one disastrous case, when in 1846 the Donner party was trapped for a winter in the mountains, with the horrors of starvation, freezing, and cannibalism.

The migration described a great arc from Puget Sound on the Pacific to the

Frontiersman's progress. Two stages of occupation, clearing, and settlement. Engravings fr
Pioneer History of the Holland Purchase of Western New York, *by Orsamus Turner, 18.*

Gulf of Mexico. The settlers were first attracted by the Oregon country. The area was, however, under dispute with Great Britain, or rather with the powerful Hudson's Bay Company, whose trappers and Indian agents collected the furs of the primeval forests and uncharted waters. American settlers first staked out farms, built homes, and established small communities in the fertile Willamette Valley in the thirties.

The original settlers consisted of a group of Methodist missionaries who went out to convert the Indians of the Northwest and remained to till the land and raise cattle. By 1845 there were six thousand settlers in Oregon. The following year Great Britain yielded her claims to the territory south of the 49th parallel and migration on a large scale started. In 1846 a band of Mormons who had been hounded and persecuted in Illinois set out for the West and freedom. When in 1847 they reached the desert wastes surrounding the Great Salt Lake, their leader, Brigham Young, announced that the Lord had revealed to him that this was the Promised Land. By the end of the year, four thousand "Saints" had arrived and proceeded to turn a treeless and waterless plain into excellent farmland, fulfilling Young's revelation.

Most tempting to the pioneers were California and the Southwest, then under the formal, but loose, rule of the Republic of Mexico. Mexico at first encouraged migration from the United States into Texas and permitted the American settlers to manage themselves. But the settlers, many of them immigrants from the Mississippi Valley, could not reconcile themselves to indefinite allegiance to distant rulers in Mexico City. Mexico emancipated the slaves in 1829, but many of the Americans owned slaves and opposed the application of the law. Mexican rule, moreover, was uncertain; across the stage of politics, generals, dictators, and constitutional presidents followed one another in quick and bewildering succession. Restiveness and ambition on one side and incoherent rule on the other could have only one result. In 1836 the Texans declared themselves independent; after a short war with Mexican troops, they made good their claim and began to bargain for admission into the United States. There was

controversy and uncertainty in the United States regarding the legality and practicability of such an annexation, since Mexico did not recognize Texan independence and Great Britain and France showed an interest in the area. Critics of slavery opposed annexation, and advocates of peace opposed the war that might result from it. In order to force the hand of the government in Washington, the Texans threatened to seek the protection of Great Britain, but meanwhile caution prevailed both in London and in Washington.

By the mid-forties, however, the pressure had become irresistible. Expansionist groups proclaimed that it was the "manifest destiny" of the United States to take over the whole of North America (and why only *North* America?). The dispute over Oregon with Great Britain, the temptation to annex Texas, and the fear that Great Britain and France might intervene as long as the situation remained unsettled brought matters to a head. The election of 1844 was fought on the issue of expansion, and the annexationist Democrat James K. Polk became President. Events now moved with startling speed. After brief negotiations, Great Britain agreed to extend the boundary line between Canada and the United States—the 49th parallel—to the Pacific. This gave the Oregon country to the Republic but secured to the European power unchallenged control over the area to the north—now British Columbia. Texas was admitted as a single state in 1845, although Southerners had wished to carve it into several commonwealths. Mexico had not recognized the independence of Texas and now refused to recognize its admission into the Union. Moreover, the Texans claimed an area far beyond Texas as their own. Mexico owed compensation to American citizens for damages during its many revolutions and disorders. But the overriding issue was Mexico's fear that, if she made any concessions, the United States would go on swallowing her up piece by piece; the Texans and their supporters in the United States would not abate their ambitions or contemplate a future of control by a power which did not inspire them with respect. Attempts to negotiate the various disputes and even to buy California failed, and in 1846 war broke out. Mexican troops were defeated several times, and an American army landed in Veracruz and marched into the capital of Mexico City. Thereupon Mexico ceded not only Texas and its claims to the Southwest but also the whole province and coast of California.

In a matter of four years, the American Republic had swelled its territory by a million square miles—nearly a third of its former size. Except for a small area bought from Mexico in 1853 (the Gadsden Purchase), the continental boundaries of the Republic were complete.

Spurred by the discovery of gold in 1848, an avalanche of migrants descended upon California. When it was acquired from Mexico, California had a handful of American settlers; in 1848, about six thousand persons arrived; the next year, when news of the gold discoveries had spread, nearly 80,000 persons migrated. Although the California experience was hardly typical, the expansion of the forties transformed the pattern of settlement. Settlers began to move inland from the Pacific coast, while the migration from the East continued. Settlers moved into the mining region of Nevada (then called Western Utah) and

Growth of the United States, 1783-1867

Alaska, 1867
(by purchase from Russia)

Oregon Country 1846 (by treaty with Gt. Britain)

Louisiana Purchase 1803 (from France)

United States in 1783

Mexican Cession 1848

Texas Annexation 1845

Gadsden Purchase 1853 (from Mexico)

Florida 1819 (by treaty with Spain)

scattered over the areas east of the Rocky Mountains. As a result, the old frontier —the line between settled and unoccupied land—became gradually blurred. Within a generation, nearly a million people had migrated to the area between the Mississippi Valley and the Pacific Ocean. They eventually added a dozen new states to the Union. They accomplished the most remarkable settlement in the history of the Western world.

Adventures in Reform and Utopia

It was not only agricultural, commercial, and industrial life that felt a forward impulse after the revolutions of 1828-32. The atmosphere was favorable also to educational, religious, and spiritual enterprise.

France and England adopted the principle of state responsibility for primary education. They were more effective, however, in advancing secondary and higher education. In the United States popular education made striking progress. Elementary schooling was an essential part of the Western settlements. Free schools, provided for on the frontier by the land grants of the federal government, were launched in the older communities of the East as well. Large American cities experimented, as did English cities, with free adult education in the evening, both for training in the crafts and for general cultivation. In 1847 the first free college in the Western world was founded—the College of the City of New York.

After the long hibernation of Toryism, induced by the "panic" of the French Revolution, Great Britain followed the earlier examples of France and the United States and abolished, in the twenties and thirties, the myriad infamies of her penal code: capital punishment for hundreds of trivial offenses, inflicted even on children; branding, mutilation, and the public stocks; and transportation for life to the distant wilderness of penal islands and the antipodes of Australia. The United States became a pioneer in the humane treatment of convicted criminals. As the death penalty and corporal punishment were invoked in fewer cases, fines and imprisonment took their place, and the number of people locked up increased. Reformers who believed that imprisonment might be used to reform the convict made efforts to improve the prisons, which were in effect graduate schools of crime, with inmates living in large, promiscuous groups under highly unhealthy conditions. Reformers prevailed upon the legislatures of New York and Pennsylvania to provide separate cells for prisoners at night. Discipline and punishment for infractions of rules were made less harsh. European countries sent investigators—France dispatched Alexis de Tocqueville—to study American penal innovations.

Official churches lost many of their privileges. In France the Catholic Church continued to control primary education, but secular scholars directed the secondary schools and universities. The Church no longer influenced the training of the sons of the middle and professional classes, the new rulers of society. The state voted salaries to Jewish and Protestant as well as Catholic clergymen. England made long strides toward equality among the various religions. Marriages performed by Dissenting ministers received legal sanction. The government ended the scandalous discrepancies of income in the established Anglican Church by reducing the salaries of the bishops and raising those of the curates. An Ecclesiastical Commission was set up to supervise the financial affairs of the church. The unpopular tithe, levied in kind upon the farmer, became a money payment by the landowner. In Scotland, the liberal elements among the Presbyterians, with many of the poor, founded a Free Church, in protest against the authority of the old church officials.

Rebelliousness swept various parts of the American religious scene. Liberal Presbyterians in America, like their coreligionists in Scotland, broke away from the Calvinistic orthodox church and formed a church of their own. Congregationalist ministers in New England turned increasingly toward unitarian views. Universalists denied the existence of Hell and emphasized moral values rather than theological dogmas. Liberal clergymen and men of letters in New England reacted against old-fashioned theologies and rigid morality by appealing to a mixture of romanticism, idealism, and deism called "Transcendentalism." The Transcendentalists, whose leading figure was the essayist and poet Ralph Waldo Emerson, rested man's future on his capacity to cultivate himself, to grow by asserting and fulfilling his individuality, and to translate his ideals into action. In rural areas, especially on the frontier, religious heterodoxy luxuriated. Revivalism became more popular and frenetic. The public confessions and emotional conversions of the "camp meetings," accompanied by groaning, dancing, trembling, screaming, and fainting, scandalized orthodox and conventional Christians. The feverishness of revivalism bespoke the dourness and loneliness of frontier life.

There were insistent demands to abolish slavery. In England the first Parliament elected after the Reform Bill became law put an end, in 1833, to slavery in the British colonies. The owners were conciliated by a payment of twenty million pounds, which covered the market value of their "property." The West Indies, with their sugar plantations worked by chattels, and South Africa were the areas principally affected. France weakened the legal privileges of the masters.

In the United States, an impetuous reformer, William Lloyd Garrison (1805-79), began an antislavery crusade in 1831 with the publication of *The Liberator*. He apologized for once having assented to "the popular but pernicious doctrine of gradual abolition." He insisted that "every chain be broken, and every bondman set free!"—immediately.

> I will be as harsh as truth and as uncompromising as justice. On this subject, I do not wish to think, or speak, or write, with moderation. No! No! Tell a man whose house is on fire to give a moderate alarm; tell him to moderately rescue his wife from the hands of the ravisher; tell the mother to gradually extricate her babe from the fire into which it has fallen;—but urge me not to use moderation in a cause like the present. I am in earnest—I will not equivocate—I will not excuse—I will not retreat a single inch— AND I WILL BE HEARD.

Garrison's intransigence seemed intemperate to many Northerners as well as Southerners. But the ranks of the abolitionists grew.

Demands also multiplied for birth control, for a reformation of the traditional organization of family life, and for the equality of the sexes. Even in the United States, women were still the wards of their nearest male relatives. In many matters they had no independent legal existence. They did not, for example, control their own earnings. A husband could discipline or silence his wife by beating her "with a reasonable instrument." Masculine domination evoked stronger opposition in the New World than in the Old. Women knocked at the doors of colleges, medical schools, and even religious seminaries, and occasionally broke them down. (Oberlin College, for example, founded in 1833, admitted women and Negroes.) An extreme group of feminists gave up corsets, petticoats, and corkscrew curls and adopted loose dresses, Turkish bloomers, and short hair. American women showed up as delegates to the World Anti-Slavery Convention in London in 1840. (The scandalized males of Europe refused to seat them and placed them in a special enclosure behind curtains.) The energetic Scottish reformer "Fanny" Wright (1795-1852) emigrated to the United States, where she campaigned for equal rights, free education, and state care of children. In 1848 a Women's Rights Convention held in Seneca, New York, issued a "Declaration of Independence" modeled on the Declaration of 1776. It charged that man had "endeavored, in every way that he could, to destroy [woman's] confidence in her own powers, to lessen her self-respect, and to make her willing to lead a dependent and abject life." The Declaration demanded the extension of full civil rights and privileges, including suffrage, to women.

While some reformers attempted to remake existing institutions and rules, others experimented with new societies. At the turn of the century, Robert Owen (1770-1857), a humanitarian textile manufacturer, had established a model industrial village at New Lanark in Scotland. His enterprise was successful, from both the social and the financial point of view. Its fame spread, but it found few imitators. The mincing progress of factory reform persuaded Owen that society would not be regenerated by the generosity of legislators and statesmen; mankind must help itself. He asserted, in *A New View of Society* (1816), that the environment was responsible for the fact that men were on the whole mean and selfish. Men must gather in voluntary associations to provide decent working conditions and educational opportunities. By changing the environment they would improve the character of future generations. Owen later suggested cooperative villages of about a thousand persons, who would be employed in both industry and agriculture. He worked out elaborate plans for the layout, equipment, system of distribution, and educational and social activities of the proposed community. After disappointing experiences with two such communities in the twenties, the untiring reformer proposed the formation of cooperative societies whose members would deposit their product and receive "labor notes" equivalent to the time each had spent in production; with these notes they could purchase articles of an equivalent labor value. Under this exchange system, profit would be abolished and a "just price" established.

A group of French Saint-Simonians, pursuing a suggestion by the master, organized in the thirties a hierarchical society, headed by a chief "father" and chief "mother," and characterized by the rituals of a new religion. They were particularly concerned to reward unusual ability, to discourage idleness and inherited wealth, and to place the sexes on an equal plane.

The most suggestive of the socialist schemes was that of the French utopian Charles Fourier (1772-1837). It seemed to Fourier that man had organized his work as if deliberately to frustrate natural instincts. The result was inefficiency and boredom, which led not only to poverty and waste but also to psychological misery. One must start, Fourier believed, with human nature and build around it. In addition to the familiar drives and instincts, Fourier stressed man's passion to distinguish himself from his fellows, his tendency to become bored with any prolonged activity, and his desire to form small groups to compete with other groups. He proposed the establishment of communities, or "phalansteries," of about two thousand persons, so organized as to fulfill these "passions." Occupations would be changed often and regularly; small groups would emulate and rival one another in the same tasks; and labor would cease to be a curse and become a pleasure. People would be paid in accordance with the labor, talent, and capital they contributed to the community. Each member would be at once a worker and a shareholder. To ensure economy and comfort, cooking, heating, and lighting would be organized hotel-style. The scheme was rigid and artificial,

A BIRD'S EYE VIEW OF ONE OF THE NEW COMMUNITIES AT HARMONY,
IN THE STATE OF INDIANA NORTH AMERICA.
AN ASSOCIATION OF TWO THOUSAND PERSONS FORMED UPON THE PRINCIPLES ADVOCATED BY
ROBERT OWEN
STEDMAN WHITWELL, ARCHITECT.

ABOVE *Proposed sketch of a Utopian community. The caption reads: "A bird's eye view of one of the new communities at Harmony, in the state of Indiana, North America. An association of two thousand persons formed upon the principles advocated by Robert Owen. . . . The centres and extremities are occupied by the public buildings, the parts between are the dwellings of the members. In the interior of the square are the botanical & other gardens, the exercise grounds, &c. . . . The disposition of every . . . part is so regulated by a careful attention to the most important discoveries & facts in Science, as to form a new combination of circumstances, capable of producing permanently, greater physical, moral, and intellectual advantages to every individual, than have ever yet been realized in any age or country."* LIBRARY OF CONGRESS

BELOW *New Harmony as it appeared in 1831, shortly after its establishment. At the right is the community hall.* AMERICAN PHILOSOPHICAL SOCIETY LIBRARY

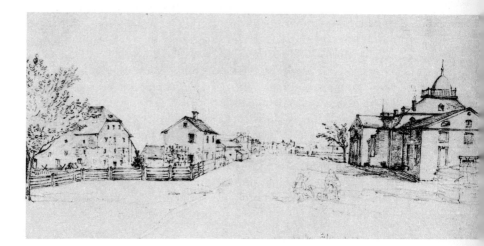

but it reflected many a psychological insight. The idea of combining individual reward, social cooperation, and team competition was shrewd. Fourier threw much light on the relation between fatigue, boredom, and inefficiency. A few phalansterian communities were organized in France and England but many more found a home overseas. Fourierism attracted an influential following

263

among American men of letters, idealistic politicians, and journalists. For a while Horace Greeley (1811-72), editor of the New York *Tribune*, made the newspaper a Fourierist publication. Between forty and fifty "phalansteries" were launched in the United States.

Utopianism was religious as well as secular. Although many of the utopian communities originated in Europe, it was in the United States that they found their most congenial home. The Mormons, who practiced polygamy, established populous communities successively in New York, Missouri, Illinois, and, finally, in 1847, in distant Utah. Organized hierarchically as a theocracy, the Mormon church-state controlled commerce and industry and distributed land to its members according to the size of their families and the nature of their occupation; with those qualifications, land ownership was equal. In 1848 another Christian sect, the Perfectionists, led by John Humphrey Noyes, founded in Oneida, New York, a community based on communion with God, communism in property, and eugenic mating. A small sect of German Zoarites, who believed in brotherliness in property arrangements, were helped by English Quakers to settle in Ohio. In Pennsylvania a community of German Harmonites combined celibacy and a strict schedule of prayer with communism in property. Other German sects and Swedish sects as well were scattered from New York to Iowa.

The religious and utopian societies attempted to realize one of the oldest and fondest dreams of men—the unstrained and orderly community of equal brothers. They appealed to the idealistic and devout of all classes, not to farmers or proletarians alone, or even particularly. They were a reaction to the increasingly competitive spirit of modern society and a protest against age-old inequalities. Membership in these communities, and resignation from them, was a matter of personal choice, conviction, or conversion. And so, although their ideal was communal, they thrived, if only for a while, in an atmosphere of freedom. Most of the communities were short-lived. The availability of land and work for fair wages in the world outside, the rigid character of many of the communities, and their heterogeneous composition operated against them. The astringent air of individualism dispelled the dream of Utopia.

Utopia, the equality of the sexes, and servile emancipation did not exhaust the aims of the reformers. International congresses were held to protest against military aggression, demand disposal of the weapons of war, and propose a world parliament, a world court, arbitration clauses in international treaties, and a United States of Europe. Other congresses proposed the abolition of tariffs and the emancipation of colonies. Technocracy, anarchism—even new diets and forms of dress—there has hardly been a proposal, idea, or fad in the past century that did not find a voice, a hearing, and a following determined to put it into effect. Freedom, which in the economic atmosphere of the time meant individualism, stimulated social and moral enterprise. Seldom were the social imagination and sensibility more alive than in the stirring decades of the thirties and forties.

13. *Slavery and the Social Question*

The advance of enterprise had its victims as well as its heroes. In America Negro slavery became deeply entrenched in the very decades that brought democracy to white men. For the native tribes of America, New Zealand, and Australia, every advance of the frontier and of settlement spelled retreat and dislocation, and in some cases even virtual extinction. A still greater problem, in the number of its victims, was the inhuman conditions under which the growing proletariat was living and working, particularly in the factory towns and slums of Western Europe.

Negro Slaves and Native Tribes

At the time of the establishment of the American Republic, Negro slaves numbered 700,000, or one fifth of the population. In his draft of the Declaration of Independence, Thomas Jefferson had delivered a fierce attack on slavery as a "cruel war against human nature itself" and on the slave trade as "execrable," an "assemblage of horrors." These passages were deleted to conciliate the slave-holding colonies. For the same reason, the Constitution of 1787 provided that the government would not interfere with the slave trade for twenty years. In 1808 the provision lapsed, and the trade was forbidden by federal law. The Founding Fathers had hoped that slavery would disappear gradually, by private manumission and action by individual states. Within a generation after the Revolution, half the states of the Union, all in the North, abolished the institution. The Ordinance of 1787 forbade it in the Northwest Territory. Free states—Ohio, Michigan, Indiana, Wisconsin, and Illinois—were carved out of this territory.

However, in the South economic fate decreed another development. In 1793 a Northerner, Eli Whitney (1765-1825), had produced an invention that had momentous consequences. Previously the United States had grown a little cotton of the long-staple variety, the fiber of which could easily be separated from the seeds by hand. Such cotton could be raised only near the sea. Short-staple cotton could grow almost anywhere in the South, but the separation of the seeds was prohibitively costly if done by hand. With Whitney's invention, the cotton gin, a worker could clean out the seeds speedily merely by turning a hand crank. As a result, cotton culture spread to the interior, arresting the development of diversified agriculture and creating a demand for slave labor. The continuous advances of the textile industry, particularly in Great Britain, offered a ready and avid market.

Southern plantation owners rushed into the new business. By 1820 they were producing 180 million pounds of cotton a year, a figure that was doubled in each of the four succeeding decades. Cotton soon accounted for more than half the value of the exports of the whole country. These developments increased the value of slaves and stimulated the illegal slave trade. In 1820 there were about 1,500,000 Negro slaves, or more than twice as many as there had been in 1790. And the number was increasing rapidly.

In the circumstances, the old hope of emancipation waned, to the dismay of many Americans. Jefferson did not speak for himself alone when he exclaimed "I tremble for my country when I reflect that God is just; that his justice cannot sleep forever." Already conflicts were arising between plantation owners and free-soilers over the question of the Western lands: were they to be slave or free? With them arose sectional conflicts. In the Missouri Compromise of 1820 it was agreed to divide the Louisiana Territory into a large area in the north in which slavery was forbidden and a smaller area in the south in which it was permitted. The numbers of free and of slave states were then equal. Thereafter it became the custom to admit one free state for every new slave state.

This balance lasted for a generation. But neither the slave system nor the world at large stood still meanwhile. The number of slaves rose to nearly four million in 1850 through natural and occasionally forced increase (slaves were actually "bred" in some cases) and illegal importation from Africa. The average price of a slave rose from $200 in 1800 to $500 a half century later. The settlement of Southwestern regions and the annexations from Mexico swelled the areas of slaveholding. The treatment of the slaves varied considerably from region to region, and even from master to master, but it varied within a narrow range. At worst the slaves were treated brutally; at best they were treated like expensive chattels. No Southern state recognized the marriage of slaves as legal, and some states made it illegal to educate slaves, on the theory that education might give them a taste for freedom. The masters formed a small though powerful minority of the white population. The census of 1860—the last one that counted slaves—showed that only 384,000 of a population of about eight million Southerners owned slaves, and that only 107,957 of these owned more than ten slaves. The great plantation masters formed a tiny oligarchy: 10,781 owned fifty slaves or more, and only 1,733 owned one hundred or more.

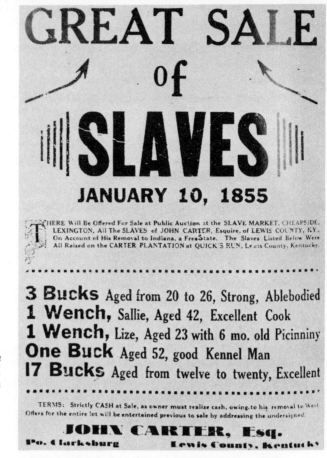

Poster announcing a slave auction in Kentucky, 1855. From J. W. Coleman, Slavery Times in Kentucky.

Even as slavery was spreading and creating a strong vested interest in the American South, the world was abandoning it. The neighbors of the United States—Canada and Mexico—had ended it, as had most of the South and Central American states: only Cuba and Brazil still permitted slavery. Colonial slavery was on the way out: Britain, as we have seen, abolished it in 1833, and France diminished the privileges of the masters. Even serfdom, long since wiped out in Western Europe, survived on the Continent only in the absolutist regimes of Austria, Russia, and Ottoman Turkey.

In the circumstances, the position of the Southern slaveholders became morally untenable. Although most Americans in the North were opposed to slavery, they hesitated to agitate the matter for fear of offending Southern sentiments and endangering the Union. But in the thirties public opinion grew restive. It was proposed to free the Negro slaves and colonize them in Africa, although little progress was made in that direction. In 1831 an ill-planned uprising of Negroes was put down by Virginia, but it inspired fear throughout the South.

In that same year, William Lloyd Garrison started his abolitionist agitation. Abolitionist societies and petitions to Congress multiplied. In 1838-39, 267

Southern politicians prevailed upon Congress to pass the "gag rule"—that is, to refuse to receive and consider antislavery petitions. Representative John Quincy Adams, a former president and son of a president, fought a long and ultimately victorious battle to reverse the gag rule and preserve the right of petition.

In the controversy over the tariff (see pp. 248-49), Southern leaders had made it clear that they would take drastic action—perhaps even seceding—if the slave interests were attacked, and Northern leaders had replied that the North would fight to preserve the Union. Between these extreme positions the political parties were unable to find a compromise. Both Democrats and Whigs depended upon Southern as well as Northern support. Southern influence was strong enough to prevent the government from cooperating with European countries to suppress the African slave trade, which, because of the rising demand, rose to its largest dimensions after 1830. As the opposition to slavery grew in the North, its defenders in the South resorted to novel arguments. They asserted that slavery, far from being a necessary evil, as had been argued formerly, was a beneficent institution, and that a society that had no slaves was backward. This set them in opposition not only to the North and to European countries but also to the whole trend of Western civilization. The rapid growth of Western settlement and the expansion of the boundaries of the United States as a result of the Mexican War made the debate still sharper, for they raised the question of the spread of slavery and its competition with the system of free settlement in the vast regions beyond the Mississippi. Indeed, many Northern liberals opposed both the annexation of Texas and the Mexican War because the slaveholding interests stood to gain from territorial acquisitions in the Southwest. Slavery, already an issue that divided the states, threatened to become a power that overshadowed and dominated the whole Republic. In this new form, the question became a good deal more serious than it had been before.

Territorial expansion aggravated the problem of the native Indian population as well as that of the Negroes. The policy of the Republic since its foundation was to respect the perpetual right of the Indian tribes over the land they occupied. It had even been proposed to admit an Indian state to the Union. But as the line of settlement moved westward, frontiersmen came into close contact, and almost constant conflict, with native tribes. A long-drawn-out struggle for Indian lands was carried on in the hinterlands. The federal government was not prepared to withstand the pressure of would-be settlers and protect the rights of the Indians. When the Supreme Court ruled, in 1832, that Georgia's attempt to break up tribal organization was illegal since the states had no jurisdiction over the Indians within their borders, Georgia defied the court, and President Jackson made no effort to enforce the decision. He was engaged upon a drastic plan to put an end to the conflict. In 1825, John C. Calhoun, who was Secretary of War at that time, had proposed that the Indians be removed west of the Mississippi, a region then regarded as unsuitable to agricultural settlement but ideal for Indian life because of the abundance of game. Jackson negotiated ninety-four treaties providing for the removal of the tribes to distant reservations beyond the western borders of Missouri and Arkansas. Many of these reservations, like the utopian societies of an earlier generation, succumbed to the irresistible example of the dominant society around them and became individualistic: they divided the communal or tribal lands and Indians became private owners, some of them rich and many more of them poor. Many Indians, however, resisted resettlement, and several wars were waged before the transfer was finally effected.

The removal was the most dramatic event in a long and tragic history. The last military stand of the Indians—to pursue the story beyond the mid-century—was made in the sixties and seventies, when many bloody battles were fought. By the early eighties they were all driven to enclosed and remote "reservations." Dislocation and fighting greatly reduced the Indian population. Some tribes, notably the Seminoles, were virtually exterminated. It has been estimated that when America was discovered there were more than 800,000 Indians in the region that eventually became the United States. By the end of the century their number had been reduced by almost 70 percent. It has been only recently that the government has made serious attempts to repair the injustice done to the original Americans.

The story of the Indians was repeated in its essentials in other parts of the globe where weak native peoples confronted white settlers. In Australia a fierce three-cornered struggle developed among the bushrangers (the most unscrupulous of the frontiersmen and squatters), the aborigines, and the more respectable settlers. It led to the reduction of the Australian natives and the complete extermination of the Tasmanians, the last of whom died in 1876. The Maoris of New Zealand survived but lost much of their land. Despite a treaty guaranteeing the possessions of the Maori chiefs, encroachment was constant. By the end of the century, most of the better land had passed into the hands of English immigrants.

The Evils of the Factory System

The tragedies of native tribes and slave labor affected the agricultural areas of the American South and the peripheral regions of the Western world. The plight of the industrial proletariat, however, was a cancerous growth in the very heart of that world. It was worst precisely in those countries and areas that were registering the greatest advances in industry and commerce, wealth and population.

From its beginnings in the eighteenth century in England, the factory system brought in its train low wages and inhuman working conditions for a considerable segment of the population. For others, it meant technological unemployment—supplantation by machines. It is true that some of the early factories paid rather better wages than the depressed agrarian and craft occupations from which they drew their workers. But after a while the labor force lost all contact with the village and craftsmanship, became urbanized, and rapidly increased in numbers and density. In these circumstances, the position of the workers worsened and became all but uniformly bad. Wherever the factory system spread, the customary labor market was disturbed and the traditional craft organization disrupted. This was notably true in the textile field, the outstanding example of industrial transformation. Hand-weaving and spinning were replaced by machine production. The product was more abundant and cheaper, though less fine, than the product of the skilled craftsmen. The factory owner profited from the increase in sales, and the foreign consumer from the decrease in price. Only labor lost. Skilled and experienced craftsmen were thrown out of work. In the new factories, their places were often taken by their wives and children. Training and skill were not required for tending the new textile machines. Women and children had the necessary aptitude for the work and, as the weakest of classes, could be underpaid and exploited with impunity. Wages hovered around the level of bare subsistence and often sank even lower.

Working conditions were primitive. In the new factories, little or no provision was made for ventilation, light, heat, and adequate meal periods, not to mention occasional spells of rest. Hours were unconscionably long. A six-day working week of twelve to fourteen hours a day was regarded as normal, and a longer working day was not uncommon, even for young women and children. Five- and six-year-olds worked in crowded and windowless mills alongside their mothers, while the heads of the family, as likely as not unemployed craftsmen, turned housekeepers, cooks, and alarm clocks. The natural order of family life was reversed. Many of the children who were employed—it is not too much to say used up—in these early mills were recruited from orphanages and poorhouses. Public officials often virtually sold or rented them, to save themselves expense and trouble. The special horrors of child labor in coal and iron mines deserve the pen of a Dante or a Swift.

The industrial proletariat resembled a standing army. It was herded and disciplined in factories by day and packed away in slums at night. In the absence of sanitary facilities and clean water supplies, epidemics of disease were frequent, particularly of cholera. However, population grew as never before. The more miserable the conditions of the urban masses, the more they multiplied. Thousands upon thousands were crowded into the noisome districts that festered around the factories. Decency, morality, and restraint all but disappeared.

To these "normal" miseries of the factory system were added the ups and downs of unemployment and depression, speculation and panic. The economic crises which broke out with increasing frequency in the thirties and forties had one effect upon the business community and another on the armies of labor. Many businessmen went under in times of slack, but there were some who not only survived but profited from the bankruptcies of others. Few if any employees, however, escaped the harsh effects of general financial disasters. Enduring quietly in prosperous times, they suffered spectacularly in depressions. Wages dropped sharply or disappeared altogether in the darkness of unem-

Engraving of an urban slum, by Paul Gustave Doré (1832-83). The scene is London. BETTMANN

ployment. On occasion these conditions were aggravated by grain shortages or crop failures, which raised the prices of necessities. The forties witnessed a series of especially disastrous crop failures in several countries, notably England and Ireland.

The classic description of industrial conditions, particularly of child labor, is contained in the testimony given in 1831-32 before an English parliamentary committee headed by the reformer and economist Michael Sadler (1780-1835), and the subsequent reports of factory inspectors appointed as a result of its revelations. The testimony of William Henden, aged nineteen, is typical:

What time did you begin to work at a mill? When I was six years old. *What were the hours of work?* We used to start at five and work till nine at night. *What time had you for your dinner?* Half an hour. *What time for breakfast and drinking?* A quarter of an hour at each end of the day. *What wages had you?* Two shillings and sixpence. . . .

How were you kept up to your work during the latter part of the day? The over-looker used to come with a strap and give us a rap or two, or if they caught us asleep they would give us a pinch of snuff till we sneezed; they would give us a slap with a strap if we did not mind our work. *Was the strap an instrument capable of hurting you badly?* It was a heavy strap with a small handle to it. *Where did they strike you with it?* Generally in the small of the back and over the head. *Did they strike the young children as well as the older ones?* Yes. *And the females as well as the males?* Yes. . . .

State the effect upon your health of those long hours of labor. . . . It produced a

271

weakness in my knees; I was made crooked with standing the long hours. *Just show the gentlemen your limbs.* (The witness exhibited to the committee his limbs, which appeared exceedingly crooked.) *Are you quite sure you were, as a child, perfectly straight and well formed?* Yes. *How old were you before your limbs began to fail you?* About eight years and a half old. *Had you any brother or sister working at the mill?* Yes, I had two sisters and a brother. *Have those long hours of labor had any effect upon the rest of your family?* Yes, upon one of my sisters. *Is she crippled?* She is nearly as bad as I am. *Was she originally perfectly straight and well formed?* Yes. *To what age did she continue to be perfectly well formed?* Till she was about nine years old. *How tall are you?* About four feet nine inches. *Are you quite certain that the deformity of your limbs was not consequent upon the accident you had?* No, it was not owing to that. *You were deformed, as you are now, before that?* Yes. *Were the children unhappy at the state in which they were?* Yes, they were. *Have you seen them crying at their work?* Yes. *Had you time to go to a day school or a night school during this labor?* No. *Can you write?* No, not at all. *Had you to work by gaslight?* Yes. *What effect do you think that has upon the eyes?* It nearly made me blind; I was forced to go into the infirmary; I was seven weeks there, and the doctors said, towards the latter end of the seven weeks, they did not expect they could cure me. *What do you do now?* I sell potatoes.

The Modern Social Question

Whether the evils of the factory system exceeded in depth or extent the miseries of the poor under the old order may be an open question. Women and children had always been exploited on the farm and in the cottage, journeymen and apprentices in craftsmen's shops, clerks and salesmen in stores and offices, and workers in warehouses and wharves. But the old society did not know the telescoped misery and the enforced unemployment of large masses of people. The distresses of the factory town and slum were also more uniform and obtrusive than those of the old shop and village. Since the industrial units were relatively large and workers were more concentrated, the social by-products of the factory system were, on the one hand, a greater threat to health—that of others as well as of the slum population—and, on the other hand, more susceptible to public control and correction. Whereas the great landowners were wont to profess, although not always to practice, the ideal of *noblesse oblige*, the "captains of industry" were apt to be devoted adherents of the colder policy of *laissez faire*. They were therefore magnetic targets of criticism.

Finally, the modern industrial problem was distinguished from its earlier counterpart by the faith of reformers that it could be solved. Poverty had always been taken for granted. It had seemed to be unavoidable, particularly in large, complex, and, paradoxically, rich societies. Few observers had suggested that poverty could be ended or even considerably alleviated by public action, and those who did were not taken seriously. The availability of free land and the relative scarcity of labor made extreme poverty unnecessary for the majority of Americans, but the United States was regarded as an exception.

Now, for the first time in the history of old societies, it appeared possible to exorcise this secular evil. The advances in production, the opening of new fields to enterprise, and the development of new markets were multiplying consumer goods to an extraordinary degree. As the factory system attained large proportions in England and began to spread to other countries in Western Europe and to the United States, its power to reduce the price of staple products and thus make them available to wider segments of the population became apparent to all. The more optimistic utilitarians and free-traders were convinced that the application of their principles would eventually take the sting out of poverty. Meanwhile, the contrast between the riches of the captains of industry and commerce and the misery and insecurity of their workmen struck sensitive observers with dramatic force.

The social problem became acute at a time when laissez-faire doctrines gained general acceptance. The classical economists had not been averse to legislative action to remove blatant social evils. But many of their followers, particularly manufacturers, often took a literal and narrow view of *laissez faire*

THE CONDITION

OF

THE WEST INDIA SLAVE

CONTRASTED WITH THAT OF

THE INFANT SLAVE

𝔍n our 𝔈nglish 𝔣actories.

WITH FIFTEEN ILLUSTRATIONS FROM THE GRAVER OF

ROBERT CRUIKSHANK.

" Truth is strange,—stranger than Fiction."

NEGRO SLAVERY.   ENGLISH LIBERTY.

It was a common argument of English reformers that American slaves were better off than child laborers in England. This argument was sometimes based on a romantic view of the life of slaves in the New World. PRINT ROOM, NEW YORK PUBLIC LIBRARY

LONDON:
W. KIDD, CHANDOS STREET, WEST-STRAND;
AND SIMPKIN AND MARSHALL,
STATIONERS'-HALL-COURT.

and denied the responsibility of the state and the community for the humanization of the industrial process. To these men, *laissez faire* meant state inactivity, even though the establishment and maintenance of *laissez faire* itself required the intervention of lawmakers. They proposed to ensure a hands-off policy by keeping the state weak and poor. This could be done simply by lowering taxes.

There were also economists who thought that the industrial system was a delicate mechanism that would get out of order if it was modified in any important respect. The English economist Nassau Senior (1790-1864) argued that any reduction in hours of work was bound to raise prices, diminish consumption, and destroy the foreign market for English textiles. If prices remained the same while hours were reduced, the profit of the manufacturers would be lost and business destroyed. This was because "the whole net profit is derived *from the last hour.*" Andrew Ure (1778-1857), a Scottish writer, eulogized the factory and the machine as a means for disciplining and civilizing human labor by eliminating man's congenital laziness, inattention, and willfulness. He praised Richard Arkwright, the "father of the factory system," as "a man of a Napoleon nerve and ambition" who had subdued "the refractory tempers of work-people accustomed to irregular paroxysms of diligence. . . . The more skillful the workman, the more self-willed and intractable he is apt to become. . . . The grand object therefore of the modern manufacturer is . . . to reduce the task of his work-people to the exercise of vigilance and dexterity—faculties . . . speedily brought to perfection in the young."

The result of such attitudes and ideas was to weaken the modicum of special responsibility that the community had traditionally accepted. The change in the British Poor Laws in 1834 was a case in point. Under legislation dating back to the sixteenth century, each parish was responsible for relieving its indigent out of the proceeds of a local tax levied for the purpose. At the end of the eighteenth century, when unemployment and low wages became a problem in industrial areas, this law was supplemented by the Speenhamland Plan, which provided that wherever wages were insufficient for subsistence the parish would make up the difference. The intent was praiseworthy, but the effect was to shift part of the burden from the wagepayer to the taxpayer and thus to enable unscrupulous employers to pay low wages with impunity. The corruption and wastefulness of the traditional local administration added to the cost of poor relief.

The utilitarians and economic reformers were as much concerned to put an end to waste and inefficiency in administration as they were to promote individual enterprise and self-reliance. In 1834 they replaced the old Poor Laws and the Speenhamland system by a cheaper, more efficient, and crueler law. "Outdoor" relief—that is, relief in the homes of the indigent—was ended. Persons who applied for relief were herded into prisonlike "workhouses." Families were separated. A law passed in the following year reformed local administration and created a better and more uniform parish government. These two laws did away with much of the old corruption and reduced taxes, but they also aggravated the plight and offended the dignity of the lower classes. The same emphasis on individual rather than state action was reflected in the reluctance to protect the workers while on the job.

Reformers and Socialists

The wound that industrialism inflicted on society had festered in England for a long time without attracting public attention. But now that industry employed hundreds of thousands of people, of both sexes and all ages, now that its masters had acquired great wealth and an influence in national policy, now that factory chimneys darkened the skies not only in the English Midlands but also in northern France, Belgium, the Rhineland, and Silesia, a moral rebellion broke out. The rebels were a motley crowd: men of tender consciences from all classes, noblemen and rich men with a sense of *noblesse oblige*, Christian clergymen and laymen who took their religion seriously, esthetically inclined persons who were repelled by the ugliness of the factory town and the tasteless-ness of its products, idealists who beheld a vision of the perfect society, and system-builders and inventors of mechanisms for the more efficient organization of the economy and society. Their proposals fell into three categories. Some of the critics wished to ameliorate industrial conditions without altering the tra-ditional order of society and government; others proposed to recast the eco-nomic and political structure; still others worked to broaden suffrage as a means of influencing policy in the interest of the mass of the population. They proposed reform, socialism, or democracy.

Conservative reformers looked upon the proletariat as the ward of the ruling class. This was the point of view expressed in the social novels of the Tory Benjamin Disraeli (1804-81), who later became Prime Minister. Disraeli warned that the policy of neglect was dividing the English into "two nations" glowering at each other. The masters of industry, he charged, were lacking in *noblesse oblige;* a reinvigorated aristocracy and monarchy would treat the work-ing class with decency and dignity. The people must once more come to regard their "betters" with submission and deference, but the upper classes must de-serve their esteem. A flexible conservatism, not laissez-faire capitalism, was the hope of the future. The Scottish essayist and historian Thomas Carlyle (1795-1881) agreed with Disraeli that mankind must be ruled by aristocrats but contended that the "captains of industry," having possessed themselves of the principal sources of wealth, must rise to the obligation of leadership. Strength and wealth imply moral responsibility and the duty to protect the weak of society. In *Past and Present* (1843), Carlyle criticized the dissociation of the upper classes from the destiny of the lower. The fact that the rich contract cholera from the poor, he claimed, is a macabre illustration of the natural "sisterhood" of the social classes. Lord Ashley (1801-85), a persistent and ef-fective social reformer, was a Tory of strong antidemocratic and evangelical convictions who later became the Earl of Shaftesbury. He observed that "in proportion as a man is a deep, sincere, and consistent lover of social, civil, and religious liberty, he will be a deep, sincere, and consistent hater of pure democracy, as averse to all three." His interest in relieving the conditions of the poor apparently stemmed largely from a concern with their spiritual and moral welfare: he was as vigorous a champion of religious education and Sabbatarianism as of factory legislation. In France, Bonapartism became associated with advanced social ideas. Louis Napoleon (1808-73), the exiled head of the Bonaparte family, promised in a pamphlet entitled *The Extinction of Pauperism* (1844) that a revived Empire under his rule would be less militaristic and more paternal than the regime of his famous uncle.

Many of the reformers were "free lances." They did not combine forces or engage the support of organized movements or political parties, either on the Continent or in England. Although they secured acceptance of the principle of reform, their practical effectiveness was meager and limited. In England, Robert Owen prepared a generous bill to reduce the evils of factory work only to find that the measure finally enacted in 1819 was a mere shadow of his original proposal. Its provisions were rendered useless by the strategic failure to supply funds and appoint factory inspectors to enforce them. The passage of legislation without financial appropriations or administrative implementation became the standard evasion of reluctant lawmakers. Owen became disillusioned and turned his efforts to organizing trade unions.

In 1833, following the revelations of the Sadler committee, Lord Ashley secured the passage of a law forbidding the employment in textile mills of children under nine years of age. Children under thirteen were to work no more than forty-eight hours a week; those between thirteen and eighteen, no more than sixty-nine hours a week. Inspectors were empowered to enter factories, inquire into working conditions, summon witnesses, and draft rules for the enforcement of the law. In 1842 mine owners were forbidden to employ women, girls, and boys under ten. A law passed in 1847 further reduced the hours of work of women and children in textile factories to a maximum of ten a day. These concessions were not extended to adult males: they were applied, on grounds of morality, to persons who were not regarded as full and self-reliant members of the system of voluntary contracts and free enterprise.

France adopted similar measures. A law passed in 1841 regulated child labor, not only in textile mills and mines, but in all industrial establishments that used motive power or machinery and employed twenty persons or more. The minimum working age was set at eight years, one year lower than in England. The law was inadequately enforced, and early in 1848 another law was passed providing for the appointment of factory inspectors.

While reformers were trying to remove the worst abuses of the factory system and utopian socialists were experimenting with "perfect" small communities, other socialists proposed to recast the industrial society as a whole. An English group drew radical conclusions from some of the premises of *laissez faire*. David Ricardo's "iron law"—that wages tend to the level of subsistence—

had condemned labor to a permanent inferiority, although his view that the level was relative to the wealth of a country qualified its harshness. On the other hand, Ricardo had followed earlier economists, including Adam Smith, in assigning to human labor the principal role in the creation of economic wealth and value, apart from Nature herself, which supplied the materials of work. "Ricardian socialists" defended labor's claim to a larger share in its own product. They proposed, variously, that the income of capitalists be paid only for the managerial and other contributions they made to the process of production; that the price of goods be fixed by society in accordance with the amount of labor they represented; that workers associate themselves to produce and be paid in accordance with their contribution to the common effort; and that producers, working independently, combine to market their goods. Ricardo had contended that land rents, when they represented no effort or outlay by the landlord, were "unearned," in contrast to wages and interest on capital. Would not the collection of unearned income be the fairest of taxes? Ricardian socialists drew the more drastic conclusion that land ought to be confiscated from its owners and distributed among the poorer farmers and unemployed proletarians.

In France, the home of utopian socialism and of the modern revolution, radicalism was both more idealistic and more activist than in England. Saint-Simon was essentially a conservative in search of a new elite that would hold society together as effectively as the old nobility had done. But his view of history as a struggle between propertied and unpropertied classes, his proposal for a scientific organization of production, and his confidence that poverty could be ended earned him the reputation of a socialist. The Saint-Simonian writer Pierre Leroux (1798-1871), who was among the first to use the term "socialism," denounced the manifestations of despotic controls in the family as well as in the economy and the state. He assigned to society the duty "to give all its members, to each according to his needs, his capacity, and his work, the enjoyment of common labor, whether such labor be an idea, a work of art, or material property." The Catholic writer Lamennais, who had defied both the Bourbon state in asserting the rights of religious thought and the Pope in defending constitutionalism, became one of the earliest proponents of "social Catholicism." The "permanent revolutionist" Louis Auguste Blanqui (1805-81) advocated a "proletarian dictatorship" modeled on the Committee of Public Safety of 1793-94 but adapted to latter-day economic ends. Under his plan the government would confiscate large estates and distribute them to poor peasants, gain control over the factories, and impose heavy taxes on the rich.

The most influential of the new doctrines in France were those of Pierre Joseph Proudhon and Louis Blanc. Proudhon (1809-65) was one of the pioneers of anarchism. He regarded existing society as the embodiment of injustice since it was based on property, which, Proudhon observed simply, "is theft." "Liberty is the sum total of my system—liberty of conscience, freedom of the press, freedom of labor, of commerce, and of teaching, the free disposal of the products of labor and industry—liberty, infinite, absolute, everywhere, and forever." In order to ensure justice and equality among men, the individual must be given the opportunity to work for himself. Proudhon proposed that capitalism be abolished through the establishment of mutual credit companies. These companies would provide craftsmen and small producers with free credit to enable them to establish their own shops. Having eliminated the capitalist entrepreneur, the self-employed workers would go on to eliminate the middleman and competition itself by organizing to sell their products cooperatively and sharing in the profits.

The proposals of Louis Blanc (1811-82) were better adapted to the factory system than were those of Proudhon. Blanc, too, would abolish capitalist enterprise and competition; *laissez faire*, he averred, was *laissez mourir*. But unlike Proudhon, who had a predilection for crafts and small-scale production, Blanc proposed that the state supply credit to enable groups of workers to establish factories of their own. These "social workshops" would compete in the free market with capitalist enterprises. In the course of time, they would drive the capitalists out of business by superior efficiency and lower prices. Painlessly, capitalism would yield to a new system of ownership and production.

Finally, in the mid-forties, a German form of socialism was developed, the last in the crowding field. To Karl Marx (1818-83), socialism was the last stage of a hierarchical series of class societies and economic systems which composed Western civilization. In each stage, the dominant class adapted government, policy, and morality to its own interests. Currently, the bourgeoisie was that class. Its function was to introduce the system of production that, fully developed, was the answer to the recurrent problems of poverty and class division itself. This task the bourgeoisie was meeting successfully, although only in England was it meeting it fully. "The bourgeoisie was the first to show us what human activity is capable of achieving. It has executed works more marvelous than the building of Egyptian pyramids, Roman aqueducts, and Gothic cathedrals; it has carried out expeditions surpassing by far the tribal migrations [of the early Germans] and the Crusades."

However, in the process the bourgeoisie, according to Marx, was turning all the other classes into wage slaves. In prosperous times, the industrial proletariat earns a bare subsistence. Since unrestricted competition leads to crises, which are bound to become more frequent, regular, and prolonged, unemployment, insecurity, and even starvation result. The remedy Marx proposed was that the proletarians combine in unions and political parties, overthrow capitalism, and supplant it with a planned economy that would exploit to the full the modern techniques of production and introduce an age of plenty. The proletarians were to re-enact the role of the bourgeoisie in the French Revolution, that of leading society toward a higher form of organization. Early in 1848, Marx, in collaboration with Friedrich Engels (1820-95), published *The Communist Manifesto*, a rough first installment of his doctrine. The peroration of the *Manifesto* was dramatic: "Let the ruling classes tremble at the prospect of a communist revolution. Proletarians have nothing to lose by it but their chains. They have a world to win. *Proletarians of all countries, unite!*"

Marx did something that few social thinkers had ever done before. Reformers had appealed chiefly to the generosity and public spirit of the governing groups, and socialist writers had addressed themselves to radical intellectuals and enlightened members of the middle and upper classes. Marx not only made the industrial proletariat the agent of its own salvation but called upon it to lead mankind toward a happier future for all classes.

Trade Unionism and Democracy

Although socialists and reformers were concerned about the condition of the lower classes, their contact and relation with these classes were tenuous and indirect. It was only in France that the new doctrines, notably those of Proudhon and Blanc, obtained a popular audience. Elsewhere the proletarians trusted their fate to labor organizations. The industrial proletariat was better placed for combining its forces than the older proletariat of town and country. Peasants worked on scattered holdings and lived in isolated villages. Craftsmen worked in small groups, typically in the homes of the masters and under their eye, and journeymen met only at crossroads, when shifting from one temporary employer to another. It was difficult for them to communicate, to plan concerted action, or to exert pressure on their employers. Industrial workers, on the other hand, were pressed together in large numbers. City life was busy and gossipy. The increase of literacy and the appearance of cheap pamphlets and newspapers disseminated information and ideas. The spread of constitutional freedoms in Western Europe opened the mouths of the advocates of the poor as well as those of the rich.

If the opportunities for organization had improved, legal and political conditions were unfavorable to unionism. Most activities of labor organizations were still illegal. In 1833 Robert Owen, who had made varied attempts to solve the social question, attempted to combine all the workers and their existing organizations into a Grand National Consolidated Trades Union. Within a year, after a series of disastrous strikes, the ambitious project collapsed. Similar misfortunes beset French efforts. Many unions were organized half-secretly, notably among the weavers of Lyons and the printers of Paris. But strikes were repressed with brutality, especially the great strike of silk weavers in Lyons in 1831.

From such disillusionments, the workers and their sympathizers drew the conclusion that political reform must precede social reform. The establishment of middle-class suffrage in 1830-32 had strengthened the advocates of *laissez faire;* democratic suffrage would redress the balance in favor of the lower classes. In France a broad movement for a democratic republic arose in the thirties. Lamennais, Louis Blanc, and Leroux led the demand for universal suffrage. Similar demands were made in Belgium.

The most spectacular agitation took place in England. There proletarian and lower-middle-class groups joined in the powerful movement of Chartism.   *279*

Their immediate aim was the democratization of the parliamentary system. The famous Charter drawn up in 1836 contained six points: universal manhood suffrage, secret ballots, annual Parliaments, abolition of the property qualification for election to Parliament, provision of salaries for members of Parliament, and equal electoral districts. Behind political reform, however, lay broader social purposes. Some of the Chartists wished to resettle urban proletarians on the land, others proposed the use of a general strike to enforce labor's demands, and still others suggested the formation of producers' and consumers' cooperatives. In any case, social amelioration was to follow political emancipation.

Chartism gathered momentum in the late thirties but foundered against the resolute understanding between Liberals and Conservatives to regard the Reform Bill of 1832 as final and to refuse further additions to the electorate. Huge popular demonstrations, processions, and petitions to Parliament did not avail. The "physical force" wing of the movement won support in a convention held in Birmingham in 1839, and riots promptly broke in that industrial center. When Parliament rejected a Chartist petition by the decisive vote of 235 to 46, an armed rising in full style broke out in Newport, in South Wales. The constabulary was called out, ten Chartists were killed, and the leaders tried and condemned to long prison terms. The following year, the agitation was renewed with violence. It was again sternly repressed. Soon the pressure of the Chartists was deflected; another movement promised more immediate, though less drastic, relief. The Anti-Corn Law League was appealing for support among the urban poor as well as the middle classes. Its proposal to eliminate the duties on grain promised to reduce the food bill of the worker as well as the wage bill of the manufacturer. "Cheap bread" was a popular cry, and supporters of Chartism became supporters of free trade. The success of the League in bringing about the repeal of the Corn Laws in 1846 did much to assuage proletarian unrest.

While many workers strove for democracy and cheap bread at home, others found them overseas. Upwards of 330,000 persons emigrated from England between 1840 and 1842, more than 220,000 in the three years following, and 130,000 in 1846 alone. Then the stream rose higher and became more regular. For some years after 1846, a quarter of a million persons left England every year. On a much smaller scale, a similar emigration occurred in Western and Central European countries.

The United States attracted the majority of these emigrants. It was also an inspiration for those who stayed at home. For in the very years when a considerable movement for universal suffrage arose in Western Europe, democracy was becoming a reality in America. A sizable urban industrial class was developing in the Eastern states. The lot of the working man and woman was not good; hours were long and wages low. Yet working conditions were better than in Europe, and the special horrors brought to light by the Sadler Committee in England were unknown in America. As in Europe, the workers organized unions, largely in the skilled and better-paid trades. The first considerable strikes occurred, but after the depression of 1837 unionism was weakened.

HERE AND THERE;
Or, Emigration a Remedy.

*English view of the misery and repression that drives people to emigration
and the prosperous conditions prevailing in Australia and other overseas
countries. Cartoon from* Punch *of 1848.* © PUNCH, LONDON

The American workingman possessed considerable advantages over the
European. He was not competing in quite so crowded a labor market, he could
vote, and he could hope that the availability of free land might improve his
position by keeping the labor force relatively small. Here and there workingmen's parties arose and exercised local political influence. Their program not
only called for the improvement of working conditions and wages but included
broader demands: free trade, an end to monopolies of any sort, freely chartered
banks, easy credit, and the extension of limited liability to any enterprise.
They endorsed the farmers' demands for free land in the belief that Eastern
landlords, in order to retain a working force, might reduce their rents. Eventually, they reasoned, rent would cover merely the cost of improvements on the
land, and thus the lower and middle classes in the towns would be benefited
as well as those in the country. This expectation fell in with the thinking of the
Ricardian school.

In America, as in Western Europe, the movement to improve the condition
of the industrial proletariat was often directed against landlords—both rural
and urban—as well as against manufacturers. In Central and Eastern Europe
industry was poorly developed, and the landed classes were deeply entrenched
in absolutist and aristocratic regimes. There the old antagonism between urban
liberals and rural conservatives held the center of the stage. The opposition to
the established order took the form of liberal and agrarian nationalism.

281

14. *Conservative Europe and Nationalism*

Every step that the Atlantic world took toward liberalism increased its distance from the countries of Eastern Europe. For these countries not only persevered in their policy of repression but intensified it. Even in Prussia, which, as the westernmost state of Eastern Europe, felt the contagion of Western thought most directly, the monarchy abandoned all thought of redeeming its past promises of constitutional reform. There was a widespread opinion that Frederick William IV (1840-61), who ascended the throne in 1840, would react against the political inertia of his predecessor, Frederick William III, but he proved to be, if anything, even more conservative.

Austria stagnated. She did not lack statesmen who recognized the need to remake the administration and the laws on a rational and economical plan. Prince von Metternich was one of these. But he was in control of foreign affairs, and domestic matters were the preserve of traditionalist bureaucrats. Metternich was driven to conclude that the security of the regime depended on his ability to outmaneuver the hosts of liberalism advancing from the West. He came to think of himself as the "indispensable" man. And Metternich was mortal.

The Russian autocracy acted with greater vigor to shore up conservatism. It had special reasons to do so. In December 1825, when Alexander I died, a small group of liberal army officers led their troops in a revolt in an effort to wrest a constitution from the new czar, Nicholas I (1825-55). Decisive artillery action prevailed against the rebels, who were sentenced to savage punishment. Five years after the so-called Decembrist uprising, as we have seen, Czar Nicholas put down another rebellion, this time in Poland. Nicholas did not share the occasional liberal tendencies of his brother Alexander. A changeless social order and a military government were more congenial to him. He proceeded to develop a regime of comprehensive and unsleeping repression. He established a powerful secret-police and spy organization to keep watch over "unorthodox" opinions and to restrain the least sign of active opposition. He forbade travel abroad, particularly for the purpose of study in Western universities, instituted a rigid control over the importation of scientific and liberal books, regimented the press and the educational system, and kept a suspicious watch over domestic critics and Western sympathizers. Banishment to the cold wastes of northern Siberia became the capstone of the "Nicholas system," under which Russia was governed in the spirit of the barracks.

The Ottoman Empire was not only unreformed but was becoming progressively less able to withstand any challenge to its authority, from within or without. It could no longer effectively control its holdings, which were still considerable: the Balkan Peninsula, Asia Minor and the northern coast of Africa. The local governors and military leaders often ruled as independent despots. The professional standing army obstinately refused to permit the Sultans to reform the administration, which some of these rulers were minded to do. Every effort to bring the military potentates to book or to protect the population against their depredations led to convulsions, mutinies, and massacres.

Nationalism and Its Varieties

The opponents of conservatism in Eastern Europe shared many of the aims of Western liberals: parliamentary government, legal and fiscal equality, personal freedom, administrative uniformity, easier economic exchange, and occupational mobility. But they lacked some of the supports available to liberals in England and France. Town life was restricted, the professional classes were relatively weak, industry was but little developed, and the large mass of the population consisted of oppressed and ignorant serfs. Above all, the nationalist movements did as much to confuse and divide the liberal ranks as to reinforce them.

Nationalism is one of the most controversial ideologies of modern times. It is not merely patriotism, which means devotion to one's native country or district. The object of nationalism is the "nation," a term which has variously been applied to groups that share a territory, a political or religious tradition, historical experience and customs, ideas, or even a "destiny." There has been an inclination to reduce nationality, wherever possible, to the palpable test of common language. Yet people shed and acquire languages more readily than they can change traditions, religions, or customs. Indeed, there have been many instances of groups creating new or reviving old languages in order to qualify as nations. Under the circumstances, the appeal of nationalism has been wide, but its connotations have often varied from region to region.

In Western Europe, "nation" connoted a compact territory of considerable size, a centralized state of some weight and importance, and a fairly homogeneous population. The national was the obverse of the local, provincial, or partial interest. "When portions of mankind, living under the same government . . . feel towards each other either as enemies, or as strangers, and [are] indifferent to each other," wrote John Stuart Mill, "they are scarcely capable of merging into one and the same free people. They have not the fellow feeling   *283* which would enable them to unite in maintaining their liberties, or in forming a paramount public opinion." "Free institutions are next to impossible in a country made up of different nationalities."

This conception was the result of a long historical process. The frequent interchange of goods and skills among the various regions gathered by the monarchs under their control: the extension of royal power, taxes, and the administration of justice; the work of literary men and scholars who fashioned the languages that supplanted the many dialects in common use in the Middle Ages; and occasionally a deliberate policy to promote the use of a common language—such influences stretched a uniform web of language and culture to fit political boundaries. In Great Britain the language of the people became that of the royal Court, which had spoken French as late as the sixteenth century. The dialect of London eventually became the language of the country. In France the rulers imposed the dialect of the capital as a symbol of authority and a means of centralization. They encouraged scholars and men of letters to discipline and refine the speech of Paris. During the Revolution the abandonment of local dialects became a sign of patriotism: a uniform national language corresponded to the uniformity of law and administration, and to the principles of equality and fraternity, that the Revolution was seeking to establish.

In the nineteenth century, national terminology gained a wide currency, used by widely differing groups. To Western liberals, the assertion of the public interest against that of privileged classes or traditional institutions was a "national" obligation. Englishmen noted ironically that institutions of prestige —the navy and the army, for example—were royal but that the burdensome debt was "national." Conservative groups defended as "national" the policy of asserting the dignity and functions of the monarchy and aristocracy and of maintaining the British Empire. The opposition to the regime of Louis Philippe in France was "national" as well as social. Manufacturing interests demanded the reservation of the home market to native industries as a patriotic duty. Bellicose politicians condemned the desire of the government to avoid friction with Great Britain as injurious to the "national" dignity. The restiveness of peasants, who were falling in debt to financiers, took the form of Bonapartist nationalism. In the thirties, romantic writers, disillusioned by the humdrum regime of Louis Philippe, created the Napoleonic myth, of a hero who had introduced social harmony and made France glorious. There were peasants who had never believed the reports of Napoleon's death and looked forward to the day when he might reappear, rescue them from their creditors, and restore the martial glory of France. Napoleon's son had died in 1832, but his nephew Louis Napoleon was waiting in the wings to step on the stage as his heir.

In the United States national phraseology was used to describe the emphasis on federal as opposed to state action and the movement to extend the boundaries of the Republic. Expansionists, as we have seen, argued that it was the "manifest destiny" of the nation to extend its domains to the Pacific Ocean, and leaders of the conservative Whig party proposed the American System to nurture native industry and bring distant regions into intimate contact with

284

each other. Since their program contemplated a large working force, the proponents of the American System did not view with favor the rapid development of the Western states and the acquisition of new territories, which would tempt workers away from the industrial centers of the East. Thus one nationalist tendency canceled another.

Italian and German Nationalism

If one traveled southward or eastward, across the Alps or the Rhine, another face of nationalism came into view. Increasing numbers of Italians and Germans were attempting to emulate, in telescoped time, the long evolution of France and England and to assemble the numerous independent provinces into large, compact states, homogeneous within and influential without.

Nationalists argued that Italy and Germany were already nations which needed only political consolidation in order to attain to full stature. This was only partly true. Italy possessed geographic and religious unity, but southern and northern Italians could hardly understand each other's dialects. Nationalists were inspired by the history of the empire which had dominated the ancient world and that of the Renaissance, when Italy had been the cultural and artistic leader of Europe. Germany had no clear physical boundaries; its linguistic diversity was less pronounced than that of Italy, but religious contrasts made up the difference. Protestantism was strong in the north, Catholicism in the south and west. Germany and Italy both had long commercial histories, but the northern states of these regions—Prussia and Sardinia, respectively— were more developed economically than the states in the south. Nationalists hoped that political and economic consolidation would supply some of the existing gaps in homogeneity. They intensified the efforts initiated in the preceding century to develop uniform vocabularies and literary styles and to discourage local dialects.

Two classes in particular were eager to consolidate Italy and Germany. Merchants and manufacturers perceived the advantages of combining the various provinces into a single large market. Lettered and professional men craved free expression and communication, and they associated freedom with the supersession of the multitude of conservative states by a single, liberal state. The demands for constitutionalism and for unity became one. Civic rights were essential to any element that aspired to public activity and influence, whether it was democrats who wanted a parliamentary regime based on a broad suffrage or the handful of radicals who wished to regenerate society. All these groups envisaged a large state with uniform laws. Their methods as well as their aims were necessarily national. The policy of the Continental powers in intervening, by diplomatic and military pressure, to prevent the introduction of constitutions made piecemeal and gradual reform impossible. The inhabitants of the various states must strike at once and together or they would fail.

There were substantial differences between Italy and Germany, however.

The central regions of Italy were controlled by the head of the Roman Catholic Church, who was traditionally an Italian. The Kingdom of Sardinia, which included Piedmont in the northwest as well as the island of Sardinia, was governed by the native House of Savoy. Otherwise Italy was ruled by foreign princes. The Spanish branch of the French dynasty of Bourbon had controlled southern Italy and Sicily since the early years of the eighteenth century. Tuscany and several smaller states had Hapsburg rulers. The valuable provinces of Lombardy and Venetia, with their capitals of Milan and Venice, were part of the Hapsburg Empire. In effect, Italy had been a protectorate of Austria since 1815. For Austria not only supplied several rulers but claimed the right to intervene anywhere in Italy to put down revolution—a right which she exercised more than once. Italian conservatism rested on Austrian arms.

In the circumstances, liberalism and nationalism became one in the *Risorgimento* (literally, "renewal"), the movement for political unity in Italy. Proposals for a new form of government ran the gamut from federal clericalism to democratic republicanism, but Italian patriots were agreed in opposing foreign domination. The Piedmontese priest Vincenzo Gioberti (1801-52) contended that the supremacy of a reformed and liberal papacy, freed from the influence of the Jesuit order, not only would bring unity to the peninsula but would strengthen the moral tone of European civilization. The pope, responsive to public opinion, would become the head of a confederation of states. Another leading Piedmontese, Count Camillo Cavour (1810-61), was an admirer of English liberalism and constitutionalism. He was active in promoting economic enterprises, particularly railway construction, believed in free trade, and advocated a unitary state on parliamentary lines. But the most influential propagandist for nationalism was Giuseppe Mazzini of Genoa (1805-72). Mazzini regarded mankind as a harmonious family of nations, each with a special function to perform and a special virtue to exemplify. A resurrected Italy, he believed, had the mission of restoring to European civilization the sense of unity it had had in the best days of the Roman Empire and the medieval papacy.

The revolutions of 1830-32 stimulated political activity and the multiplication of political societies everywhere, but particularly in Italy, where the tradition of conspiracy and movement across provincial boundaries was strong. In 1832, Mazzini founded the society of Young Italy, and tens of thousands of his compatriots joined it. He proposed that the provincial diversities associated with absolutism, clericalism, and Hapsburg influence yield to the unity of a democratic and republican Italy. On the flag of the new society the slogans of unity and independence appeared alongside the old French revolutionary slogans of liberty, equality, and fraternity. The substance was liberal and fraternal, the form was national. Several years later, Mazzini organized a Young Europe movement, composed of Young Italy, Young Germany, Young Poland, and various other national groups, with the eventual aim of forming a federation of republics.

North of the Alps, nationalism struck a less liberal note. The three-hundred-odd states and statelets of Germany had been pressed into thirty-eight units of the German Confederation with the help of Napoleon and the armies of the French Revolution. The score of states in the Rhineland were welded into a consolidated area during their annexation by France. A few German states were substantial in size: Hanover, Saxony, Bavaria, Württemberg, and Baden. Two—Austria and Prussia—were great powers. But Austria and Prussia, though the leading members of the Confederation, were, in large measure, non-German states. Much of their territory, including Prussia proper, lay outside the boundaries of the old Holy Roman Empire and the Confederation. In Austria, the Slav, Hungarian, Italian, and Rumanian subjects far outnumbered the Germans. Prussia contained a large number of Poles. A "united" Germany must therefore include non-German populations. In this sense, Germany differed from Italy, which was populated almost exclusively by Italians. The result was that German nationalists exalted the claims of the Germans above those of other peoples. In his famous "Song of the Germans," Hoffman von Fallersleben extolled

> *Deutschland, Deutschland, über alles,*
> *Über alles in der Welt.*

The middle classes of Germany, like those of Italy, were eager to establish internal free trade over a large area. But free trade between nations implied cosmopolitan attitudes that Italian nationalists accepted but many German nationalists abhorred. In the Napoleonic period the nationalist philosopher J. G. Fichte had advocated a "closed commercial state" with quasi-socialist policies. Now the economist Friedrich List (1789-1846) revived Fichte's theory— with a difference: he also advocated a protective policy but in order to stimulate the growth of *capitalistic* industry. List envied English success and conceived of a united Germany as a rival of the British Empire for world influence, industrial production, and colonial power. A promoter and publicist, List spent several years in the United States, where he put his pen at the service of the protectionist interests. Returning to Germany in 1832, List imported the American System, but he gave it a more aggressive cast than it had in the United States. In *The National System of Political Economy* (1841), List placed the nation above the individual. He attacked the cosmopolitanism of the classical economists: "Only England . . . could afford the luxury of free trade, since she could defy industrial competition. Other countries must build up industry by the protective system. To do this, they must cherish the ideal of national power above that of individual welfare and international harmony."

List felt that the German states alone did not form a sufficiently large and coherent "natural" market. "A nation without extensive territory and with otherwise limited resources, which does not control the mouths of its rivers [the mouths of the Rhine and of the Moselle were in Holland], or which does not have suitable boundaries, cannot resort to the protective system, or at least cannot employ it with full success. It must be first enlarged by way of conquest or negotiation." Although List agreed with the adherents of the American System in opposing the rapid expansion of the American West, he proposed that Germany should take into her economic system not only Holland and Denmark but also the Danubian basin—Austria, Hungary, and several other countries. He urged Germans to emigrate—not to the United States, where they would become assimilated to the English ways, but to Latin America and Pacific areas and islands, where they might pave the way for German trade and influence. Translated into German, the American System had become an imperial program.

For the moment List's ideas were influential mainly in stimulating railroad building and the growth of free trade among the German states. Since 1819 Prussia had concluded treaties with seven small northern states providing for the abolition of tariff duties among them. In 1828 Bavaria, Württemberg, and two tiny neighbors organized a similar but separate Southern *Zollverein* (customs union). A third customs union was organized by Saxony for the intermediate states. The Prussian and Saxon unions for a time suspended the customs duties at their common borders. For trading with the world beyond, the duties became moderate as the years passed. By 1834, the various Zollvereins had merged and expanded to include nearly the whole Confederation except the Austrian dominions, Hanover, and a few small states. Yet Austria was the controlling power in the Confederation. The economic system, of which Prussia was the leader, thus came into conflict with the political system.

National, Economic, and Religious Differences in Eastern Europe

In Germany and Italy, nationalism represented an effort to emulate the coherence of France and Britain. Farther east, however, it often made for division rather than unity. There, the relation of language, territory, and politics was so different as to suggest another world. Townsmen and villagers, landlords and peasants, rulers and subjects, were often divided by language, religion, and sentiment.

In Bohemia the bulk of the peasantry spoke Czech, while many landed noblemen were Germans or Germanized Czechs, although Czechs and Germans were both Roman Catholic, the sense of separation was sharp. In Galicia the peasants were mostly Ruthenians, who were Uniat in religious affiliation, while their masters were Roman Catholic Poles. In Slovakia the peasants were Slavs and many landlords Hungarians. In Transylvania the peasantry spoke Rumanian and adhered to Eastern Orthodox Christianity, and most of the landlords were Hungarians who worshiped variously as Roman Catholics, Calvinists, or Unitarians. Many a town in these and adjacent countries was populated by Germans, Germanized Slavs, or Jews, while the enveloping countryside was Czech, Hungarian, Rumanian, Polish, or Ruthenian.

In the Balkan Peninsula an additional distinction crossed the others. The

Prussian Tariff Union (Zollverein)

Prussia in 1818 (common tariff union)

Accessions to Tariff Union: 1818-1834 · 1836-1854 · 1867

Boundary of the German Confederation

army and central administration were Mohammedan, while the subjects were Christian, largely of the Eastern Orthodox persuasion. The Sultans governed from a distance and concentrated their interest on the collection of tribute. They "subcontracted" much of the local administration to ambitious members of the wealthy Greek community of Constantinople. Greeks obtained high posts in the Eastern Orthodox Church as well as political posts throughout the Empire, as Italians obtained the leading positions in the papacy. Turkish rule assumed the form of Greek supremacy. A Bulgarian or Rumanian peasant was likely to prefer the distant Turkish master to the Greek cleric or taxgatherer close at hand.

The only country of Western Europe in which economic, religious, and political differences reinforced one another on a large scale was Ireland. The bulk of the population consisted of poor tenants adhering to the Roman Catholic faith; the landed proprietors, many of them Protestant, ruled through their influence in London. In Ireland, therefore, nationalism assumed the character it had in Eastern Europe.

Eastern nationalism was protean. It gave expression to the most varied and contradictory interests and sentiments. It transmuted issues that in the Atlantic world were discussed or fought out in terms of class interests, political ideals, or economic policy into questions of national pride and national character. Here it was a movement of peasants—Czech, Ruthenian, Rumanian, or Ukrainian, as the case might be—confronting landlords—German, Polish, Hungarian, or Russian; there it was the nationalism of the urban group recently recruited from the countryside confronting older town-dwellers of another tongue or religion. Here it was the nationalism of nations seeking to regain the vast boundaries of a glorious past which enclosed other nationalities in a condition of subordination. There it was the nationalism of the smaller groups who were content with local autonomy on a modest scale and with equality. Finally, there was the nationalism of the dominant elements of the existing kingdoms and empires—Prussians, Austrians, Great Russians—which sought to shore up their position by impressing the stamp of their "superior" language and culture on heterogeneous and "inferior" populations. Liberals evoked the Western image of a parliamentary nation, and aristocrats evoked the patriarchal relations of a feudal nation.

The transmutation of economic and political issues into national questions was in full swing in the first half of the nineteenth century. Since the French Revolution, the Eastern peasant had begun to stir and to awaken. There was pressure to relax servile bonds and rural dues. Town life was undergoing change. Napoleon's measures to close the Continental economy to Great Britain revived the activity of many old towns, markets, and trade routes. Looking for economic opportunity, peasant youths migrated to the towns in increasing numbers. There they competed in trades and professions with older townsmen. The social and religious composition of many a city changed substantially. In several German cities, for example, large Slav minorities arose. In 1815 Prague had 50,000 Germans and 15,000 Czechs. Forty years later it had 73,000 Germans and 50,000 Czechs, and this was but the beginning of a trend. In 1880 Prague had 80,000 Germans and 126,000 Czechs.

The Rise of National Movements

These social changes were occurring at a time when cultural developments accented national tendencies. The romantic movement turned the attention of writers and scholars to the study of folklore, tradition, and custom. It stimulated the study of the mysterious past—the glories and the tragedies—of peoples. Poets and novelists were absorbed by the "soul" and destiny of nations and races as well as by the feelings of individuals.

The study of philology suggested a relation between language and national character. The German romantic philosopher Herder (see p. 188) had popularized the idea of national "genius." He had exalted the "genius" not only of the Germans but also of the Slavs, and he had located this "genius" in their respective languages. The conservative French philosopher Louis de Bonald

(1754-1840) regarded language as having a divine origin. His argument was fetching: man is a thinking animal; thought is impossible without speech; speech could not have been invented by man for he could not think without it; ergo, speech comes from God. This was as much as to say that each linguistic group was the mysterious and permanent creation of God.

While conservative publicists pointed to the importance of historical tradition, liberal revolutionists awarded all human groups an equal right to just laws and governments. Romantic poets, above all Lord Byron, exalted the heroism of national rebels against foreign oppressors. Responding to both tendencies, nationalists developed elaborate justifications for the claims of their peoples to a place of honor as well as equality among the great nations of the world.

Gradually cultural and social tendencies came together. The growth of towns and the decreasing costs of printing and paper encouraged the spread of literacy. The conflict between the traditional and modern forms of government suggested new opportunities for the educated and professional classes. The royal and imperial bureaucracies, developed in the seventeenth and eighteenth centuries by traditional states, had dealt generally with the larger fiscal, military, and diplomatic policies, leaving rural administration to the devices and mercies of the local squires and aristocrats, The modern state advocated by European liberals and democrats could not be run so informally. It required a large body of clerks, officials, judges, lawyers, and teachers. This placed a premium upon literacy and education and upon the ability to use the official language. Since the uniformity of the modern state requires the use of a single language for law, administration, and education, the adoption of a language would confer great advantages upon the group that spoke it.

Politics and culture became one. The typical nationalist of Eastern Europe was the literate son of a prosperous farmer or of a tradesman or craftsman settled in a town dominated by a "foreign" people or state. He was, or would be, a lawyer, teacher, bureaucrat, or journalist. But his prospects were limited. He might be a Czech in German Prague, a Hungarian in German Vienna, a Slovak, Croatian, or Rumanian in Hungarian Budapest, a Rumanian in a Bucharest controlled by Greek officials, a Pole in centers subject to Russian, Austrian, or Prussian rule, a Ukrainian or Lithuanian in a city whose population was largely Polish. The young man was willing enough to assimilate. His schooling and his customary language were often those of the dominant people or official state. But cultural assimilation did not spell equality of opportunity. He was often treated condescendingly as an "inferior" newcomer by members of the dominant nation or representatives of the official state. Instead of attempting to climb toward his "betters," he reacted by identifying himself with his own people. (Naturally, a good many of his kind continued on their course of assimilation, with the consequence that some of the leading nationalists stemmed from the "wrong" nations. Many a German and Hungarian nationalist, for example, was a Slav by origin.) In order to assert his claims to equality, the young nationalist strove to match the cultural and literary achievements of his rivals. He had seldom written the language he had learned at his mother's knee and perhaps had forgotten it. He now refreshed his memory. He discovered the rough beauties of popular speech and the simple virtues of the peasant masses.

On the model of developed literary languages, nationalists produced grammars in order to standardize speech and eliminate local dialects. They collected folklore and transcribed oral traditions and popular legends. With this raw material, they improvised popular poetry, romantic epics, and short stories—the staples of new literatures. Archivists and historians ransacked the records of churches, monasteries, and manors to disclose the glories, the achievements, and the tragedies of the past.

Nationalism—nationalisms—were born. In seeking to raise the level of their own people, the nationalists appealed to the universal values of equality and often of democracy. In magnifying the distinctive values and attributes of their people, they deepened national divisions. As the movement spread, its ruder followers confused attachment to one's own with a dislike of others. There was a tendency to look upon use of the native language as a value in itself and to make it the seat of national and political virtue. Nationalism ran the risk of becoming xenophobia.

What the Germans called the "historical nationalities" had been the first in the field. These were peoples which were dominant in established kingdoms or empires—the Germans in Austria and Prussia, the Great Russians in the czarist Empire—or which possessed powerful landed aristocracies and had had success and power. German and Great Russian nationalists were determined to extend the influence of their language, culture, and religion and to pre-empt the best administrative, military, educational, and professional opportunities. The subject nationalities had to defer and adapt to their "superior" culture and claims.

Hungary boasted a famous history, although she had to reach back centuries for it. Her gentry and aristocracy were descended from the Mongol invaders of the ninth century and looked down upon neighboring peoples as conquered natives. In the fifteenth century Hungary was one of the principal powers of Eastern Europe, and her fame spread into Asia. The Hungarian magnates were among the richest and proudest landlords in Europe. They perceived in nationalism a means of increasing their political authority. A minority among them took more exalted views. A public-spirited aristocrat, Count Stephen Széchenyi (1791-1860), led a movement to advance the economic growth of Hungary by building bridges, improving cattle stock, and breaking down the tariff wall along the border of Austria, which discriminated in favor of Austrian goods. The journalist and orator Louis Kossuth (1802-94), a half-Slav, demanded complete autonomy for Hungary, a modern constitution, the breach of aristocratic privileges, and political rights for the middle and professional classes. The chief popularizer of nationalism was Alexander Petőfi (1823-49), the "Robert Burns of Hungary," also a Slav by descent. In his poem "The Hungarian Nation," Petőfi cried:

> Shame on thee, outraged nation! Shame on thee
> Who once didst fill, in the heroic age
> Of history's pages, a transcendent page,
> And now thou kneelest in thine infamy,
> A poor slave victim on the vulgar stage.

The magnates insisted that the Austrian emperor frequently consult the Hungarian Diet. They were supported in this demand by the liberals, who hoped to transform the aristocratic legislature into a modern parliament. Both groups demanded that Magyar be made the official legal language of Hungary, and in 1840 they won their point. They forced the Rumanians and Croatians within the borders of Hungary to accept the new usage and thus submit to the hegemony of the Hungarians.

Polish nationalism was a movement of resurrection. Two centuries earlier, Poland had been one of the largest kingdoms in Europe. At her greatest extent, her boundaries extended from the Baltic to the Black Sea, and from the Oder River through much of what is today western Russia. Prussia proper, Lithuania, Courland, and the Ukraine were once under Polish suzerainty. Poland, however, had never had an integrated administration, her local and central affairs being controlled by an anarchic gentry and a proud aristocracy. By three strokes of the sword—in 1772, 1793, and 1795—Russia, Austria, and Prussia had carved up Poland and divided it, the lion's share going to Russia. This division was confirmed in 1815, when Russia's share was increased.

After the unsuccessful revolution of 1830, thousands of liberal Poles, stemming from the gentry and the middle and professional classes, emigrated voluntarily or were exiled. The exiles became active in the revolutionary circles of every European center, particularly in Paris. Two parties were distinguished among them: the aristocratic nationalists, who hoped for a revival of the social structure of the old Poland, and a liberal group, which agitated for the abolition of aristocratic privileges, the emancipation of the peasantry and its endowment with land, and a modern administration and legal system. Both groups were determined to reassemble Russian, Austrian, and Prussian Poland.

The spiritual and intellectual leader of the nationalists was the classic poet of the Polish Renaissance, Adam Mickiewicz (1798-1855). In *The Book of the Polish Nation and of the Polish Pilgrimage* (1832), Mickiewicz celebrated national ambition, individual virtue, liberal ideals, and international brotherhood. He called for "a universal war for the freedom of the nations" and hailed Poland as the "Christ of the nations," whose resurrection was the condition of universal emancipation.

Whenever the ambitions of Germans or Great Russians, of Poles or Hungarians, prevailed, other peoples were condemned to inferiority and dependence. These were peoples which had not in centuries, if ever, played an important role on the stage of politics or culture. They consisted largely of peasants and had few landed aristocrats, townsmen, craftsmen, or capitalists. The southern and western Slavs, for example, had lost their upper and middle classes through military defeats stretching over several centuries. In mixed districts, these peoples—Czechs, Moravians, Croatians, Serbs, Ruthenians, Rumanians, and Ukrainians—supplied the bulk of the rural proletariat. In order to strengthen their claims to equality and autonomy, they developed a nationalism of their own. For no people was so poor as to lack the raw materials of nationalism. Any native tongue or dialect might become a literary language. Every people had a folklore and an oral tradition. History was a game everyone thought he could play at. When the Hungarians claimed Transylvania by right of conquest in the ninth century, the Rumanians discovered an older claim in the colonization of Transylvania by the Roman Emperor Trajan (53-117 A.D.) long before the invasion of the Mongolian Magyars. They went still further and claimed the boundaries of Dacia, the ancient kingdom which, when subdued by Trajan, included not only Transylvania but the Danubian provinces, now held by the Ottoman Empire and Bessarabia, held by Russia. Similarly, the Czechs and Poles countered claims of the Germans, derived from the eastward migration of traders and knights, by claims based on prior occupancy and political hegemony in the Middle Ages.

While some nations invoked the glories of their past, others drew inspiration from the tragedies. Romantic writers were as apt to extol death and defiant failure as life and success. While Hungarian and Polish nationalists dwelt on their medieval fame, the Czechs sang the dirge of the Battle of the White Mountain, in 1620, when the army of the Hapsburgs had crushed an attempt to establish the independence of Bohemia. The Serbs celebrated as their national holiday the anniversary of their worst defeat in history. At the Battle of Kossovo in 1389 their ancestors had fallen before the Turks as defenders of the largest empire that any Balkan nation had ever assembled. All the nationalities could claim to have been, at one time or another, the guardians and saviors of Christianity and European civilization—against the Mohammedan Turks, against the pagan Huns, or against other "barbarians."

Among the earliest national movements were those of the Greeks (see pp. 226-27) and the Czechs. As the Greeks evoked the ancient glory of Hellas, Czech patriots recalled that Bohemia had once been the political and cultural center of the Holy Roman Empire and Prague had one of the oldest universities in Europe. Modern Czech history, Czech literature, Czech culture were born. And since the language of the new culture, which was developed by urban lettered and professional men, was that of the peasant majority, the road was open for an alliance between the two elements. Czech nationalism was liberal and democratic.

The journalist Charles Havlíček (1821-56) published the first Czech newspaper. Forbidden by the Austrian authorities to report and discuss domestic events, he filled his journal with "Letters on Ireland." It turned out that Irish and Czech problems were strikingly similar. Havlíček went to prison for this transparent joke.

Francis Palácky (1798-1876), the "father" of Czech history, published an elaborate *History of Bohemia* in which he traced the long struggle of the Czechs against German dynasts and aristocrats. He hailed his ancestors as the earliest liberals and "protestants" of Europe and ascribed their defeat to the fact that they were premature pioneers. His political demands were moderate: he worked for Czech equality and autonomy within the borders of a reformed Hapsburg regime. Other Czech nationalists demanded equality with the German element, the official use of their own language, relief of the conditions of the peasantry, political autonomy, and civic liberties.

While the Czechs, in the northern areas of the Hapsburg Empire, strove for equality with Germans, the Croatians, in the south, defended their rights against Hungarian encroachment. When Magyar took the place of Latin as the official language, nationalists demanded the substitution of Croatian. Both in Croatia and in Serbia, linguists and grammarians prepared a common orthography and literary language that could assimilate the many dialects of the South Slavs. A new Serbo-Croat language, with alternative Latin or Cyrillic letters, became the basis of the South Slav literature. Only religion and politics remained a divisive element, for the Croatians were Roman Catholics under the rule of the Hapsburgs, and the Serbs were Eastern Orthodox and all but independent of the Turks.

In Transylvania, subject to the Hapsburgs, and in the Danubian principalities ruled by the Sultan, there was a growing movement to advance the claims of the Rumanian population. Literary men explored the Rumanian "soul" and Rumanian history and asserted the special virtues of Rumanian peasants. A Transylvanian romantic poet, Andrei Mureşeanu (1816-63), wrote a call to arms that became the hymn of Rumanian nationalism:

> Wake up, Rumanian, from the sleep of death
> To which your barbarous enemies have condemned you—
> Now or never fashion yourself a better fate.

The "King of Rumanian Poets," Vasile Alexandri (1821-90), in his "The Awaking of Rumania" (1848), cried:

> Enough has the foreigner lorded in our land
> . . .
> To arms, brave ones, let the world see
>   on Rumanian fields
>   Proud legions of Rumanians

The "foreigners" in the Danubian principalities were Turkish pashas and Greek bishops; in Bessarabia, the Russian rulers; and in Transylvania, Hungarian landlords. A common protest against all of them was found in linking Rumanian nationalism with the ancient Kingdom of Dacia. Rumanian was a highly mixed language but, since it had many Latin words and forms, nationalists came to look upon their people as the heirs of Roman glory and the re-   *295* presentatives of Latin civilization. They "purified" the Rumanian tongue by emphasizing Latin roots and borrowing words from the "sister" Latin nations—above all, from the French. Francophilia became one of the chief characteristics of Rumanian nationalism, as Francophobia was typical of German nationalism.

"The Sick Man of Europe"

Nationalism threatened to recast the political map. The ambition of Italian and German nationalists endangered the position of the Hapsburg emperor, not to speak of the multitude of lesser dynasts who would lose their thrones if their lands were melted into national states. The claim of the Magyars to the historical boundaries of Hungary included more than half the Austrian Empire. A common interest in the continued division of Poland had long been the strongest bond of Russia, Austria, and Prussia. The revival of a unified Poland would strike simultaneously at all of them. Since these powers were the mainstays of conservatism, the cause of Poland became the cause of liberals everywhere. The demands of the smaller nationalities were more moderate. They craved a modicum of equality and opportunity rather than political power. Yet even this modest aspiration implied a reform of the centralized bureaucracies and an attenuation of national and religious favoritism and monopolies.

Empires which suffered from inner political weakness were especially sensitive to national strains. Spain's American empire had fallen apart into a dozen pieces, even though the colonists had a common religion and language. How much greater was the prospect of disintegration in regions of mixed populations! The danger was compounded by the temptation offered to other empires to intervene to exploit domestic unrest. How serious the case might become was demonstrated by the experience of the Ottoman Empire with the Greek rebellion—the first successful nationalist movement in modern times. The Treaty of Adrianople in 1829, which recognized Greek independence, also guaranteed the autonomy of Serbia and compelled the Sultan to withdraw all Moslems from Moldavia and Wallachia and to raze all his fortresses in these principalities. Russia was to occupy them until the Sultan paid a large war indemnity. North Africa presented even more serious challenges to the Turks than the Balkan Peninsula. The year after losing Greece, the Sultan lost Algiers, whose allegiance to him, it is true, had been only nominal. France had seized it in order to destroy its nests of pirates.

Egypt offered a different case of nationalism. Since the beginning of the century it had been ruled by a Mohammedan despot of Christian origin. Mohammed Ali (1769-1849) was appointed leader of an army of Albanian soldiers sent by the Sultan to wrest control of Egypt from another professional army, the Mamelukes. Ali massacred the Mameluke chiefs, made himself absolute ruler, turned the Egyptian masses into state serfs, and established state monopolies of the most important trades, manufactures, and exports. With the assistance of French experts, he built a navy and an army along Western lines. Then he threatened to take over the whole Ottoman Empire. Making war upon his sovereign, in 1832 he occupied Syria—from time immemorial the ambition of Egyptian rulers—penetrated into Asia Minor, approached the strategic Straits (the Dardenelles and the Bosporus), and finally stood before Constantinople.

The Sultan appealed for help to the powers. Russia sent a strong fleet into the Straits and landed an army on the shores of Asia Minor. Mohammed Ali was stopped, but he retained possession of Syria. Although Russian soldiers held the heart of the Ottoman Empire, Nicholas I preferred to dominate rather than to conquer or partition it. It sufficed that the Sultan promised, in the Treaty of Unkiar Skelessi (1833), to close the Straits virtually at the pleasure of Russia. Russian warships might issue from the Black Sea into the Mediterranean and come back at will, closing the "door" behind them; other warships would find the Straits closed.

Russia's success aroused the other powers, particularly Great Britain, who feared that Russia proposed to swallow her client. If Russia occupied Asia Minor and penetrated into Persia, she might secure an entry into India by the northwest route, the favorite path of the conquerors of the wealthy subcontinent. Recent technological advances, moreover, enhanced the strategic importance of the Eastern Mediterranean. In the thirties a chain of steamers connected English ports with Egypt, notably with Port Said on the Mediterranean. By a short portage, passengers and light freight arrived at the Red Sea port of Suez and then embarked on other steamers for India. The whole trip took one month and at once supplanted, except for heavy freight, the old route around the Cape of Good Hope, which was longer by five thousand miles. The Ottoman Empire now stood, as the Byzantine Empire had once stood, athwart an important route between Europe and Asia.

The fate of the Ottoman Empire became an international concern. France at first sympathized with Mohammed Ali, who had been much influenced by Napoleon. But she preferred to befriend Great Britain and so joined Britain in competing with Russia for the privilege of defending the Sultan against his ambitious vassal. British and French forces helped to defeat Mohammed Ali and to compel him to withdraw from Syria and content himself with the governorship of Egypt. In 1841 the Treaty of Unkiar Skelessi was virtually annulled by the Straits Convention, in which the powers agreed that the Straits should be closed in peacetime to all foreign warships. Thus balked, Russia proposed to Great Britain that since "the sick man of Europe" might expire momentarily, the two countries should agree to divide the Ottoman inheritance. Great Britain might take Egypt and Crete, Russia most of the Balkan Peninsula. Only Constantinople—the coveted prize—would remain Turkish. Britain refused: the prospect of a Russian empire on the Aegean or the Adriatic Sea was unpleasant to contemplate. She preferred nursing the sick man along to speeding his demise.

The example of Egypt and Greece was not lost on Europe. Even in strong

Punch *cartoon, 1853: the concern of France (Napoleon III) and Great Britain over the condition of "the sick man of Europe"—the Ottoman Empire—threatened by the Russian angel of death, knout in hand.*
© PUNCH, LONDON

A CONSULTATION ABOUT THE STATE OF TURKEY.

states, the unrest of subject peoples was portentous. Nationalism, observed Prince Metternich, "means everything and nothing, but today it sweeps the world." Concerned above all with preserving the *status quo*, he had tried unsuccessfully to restrain conservative powers from assailing the old-fashioned Ottoman Empire and thus abetting the Greeks. Metternich's diagnosis was perceptive, but his prescription was an ineffective mixture of sedation and coercion. National unrest could be allayed by local autonomy, toleration of religious minorities, and the admission of members of the various nationalities to government employment and to economic and professional opportunities. It was partly by pursuing such policies that the United States, which was even more varied ethnically than any of the European empires, had avoided national friction. But the Austrian government, like other conservative powers, exploited linguistic and religious differences to frustrate demands for equality. National reform required energetic and flexible government, and the conservatives made a fetish of inertia and rigidity. By keeping their territories isolated from one another and by preserving traditional customs, they prevented their peoples from coming together and combining their efforts. They used troops of one area and nationality to police other areas. In Austria, Czech troops kept Hungary in order. Hungarians and Croatians patrolled Italy; and Germans and Italians disciplined Poland. Russia relied on the Cossacks of the southeast to restrain dissatisfied nationalities and peasants in all parts of the country. The rulers learned the advantages of recruiting infantry in one region, cavalry in another, and artillerymen in a third. It was government by mutual distrust.

The smaller or weaker nationalities were often inclined to come to terms with the "foreigners" at distant royal and imperial courts in order to concentrate their attacks on opponents nearer home. Thus the Croats and Rumanians sought the support of the Hapsburg ruler at Vienna against the Hungarian nationalists. The emperor encouraged these peoples to resist the introduction of Hungarian as an official language, regarding with favor their efforts to develop a common orthography with Latin characters to diminish the difference between the various dialects of the South Slavs. He approved the administrative separation of Transylvania from Hungary. "Divide and conquer" was his motto.

In the circumstances, many nationalists came to feel that a change in the system of government was a prerequisite to their emancipation. They demanded constitutional rights. To conservatives, therefore, nationalism appeared as but a new form of an old enemy, a patriotic-seeming incarnation of the dreaded Revolution.

15. *1848 — The Great Watershed*

The Revolution of 1848 was the most spectacular and comprehensive revolution the Western world has ever experienced. It struck with the speed and force of an electric storm, zigzagging across Europe from one end of the continent to the other. Large empires and small countries, capital cities and provincial towns, rich burghers and depressed proletarians, all rose in unison. Dozens of thrones were shaken, kings fled from their capitals, and governments lost their grip and scattered to the four winds. The stunned rulers made extraordinary concessions to the opposition.

The Revolution seemed to be strikingly successful. Yet the anticlimax came promptly and was equally electric. The Revolution, although widespread, was not the result of a concerted and organized movement. The rulers, on the other hand, had long been accustomed to uniting for purposes of repression. After their initial shock, they gathered their energies, divided the opposition, and came to one another's aid. They succeeded in canceling most of the concessions they had made to the revolutionaries.

The storm was over. Within a year and a half Europe had run the gamut from democracy and fraternity to conservatism and reaction. It was never to be quite the same again. Before long, the issues of 1848 were posed again. They were met, however, in a manner quite different from that proposed by the revolutionaries. Someone has said that 1848 was a turning point in history—at which history refused to turn. This is quite wrong. History *did* turn, but in a direction that surprised contemporaries and puzzled later generations.

Revolution Becomes Endemic

Although the rapid spread and wide ramifications of the Revolution were astonishing, few of the individual rebellions were unexpected. The elements that produced them had been present and visible for a long time. Throughout

300

Europe there was a rising demand to bring traditional society into alignment with the needs of modern commerce, urban life, and liberal culture.

The reforms proposed were on the whole moderate. But through long neglect, they had become urgent. Some of them had been adjourned since the eighteenth century. And although the proposals varied from region to region, and even from country to country, they all found vent in the common cry for constitutionalism and democracy. Liberal democracy was broad enough to encompass the needs of the most disparate classes and countries. To the unity of the opposition, the established order opposed rigidity. Its policy was nearly everywhere inflexibly negative. Since the French Revolution of 1789, a bitter and prolonged struggle against the spirit of change and innovation had frozen conservatism into immobility. Even mild reform, even improvements that were admitted to be inherently desirable, were rejected as threatening to the very foundations of society. The absolute monarchies of the Continent met every demand of liberals or nationalists with the naked blade. In Western Europe the ruling groups set their face stonily against the proposals of social reformers. Their doctrinaire adherence to the "laws" of *laissez faire* placed a heavy burden on the industrial masses.

It was the confrontation of the immobility of the rulers with the pervasive insistence on bringing Europe up to date that produced the Revolution of 1848.

Every region of Europe had its tensions. In Eastern Europe the chronic discontent of serfs and peasants and the rising claims of submerged nationalities reinforced one another. Italian and German liberals and democrats, free-traders and republicans, were swept up in an overriding movement to combine the fragmented provinces of their countries and to establish a constitutional order. In countries which were already consolidated and constitutional, democracy and republicanism commanded a large following. Industrial centers, notably in Western Europe, suffered from fluctuating employment, low wages, and barbarous working and living conditions. Finally, most of the countries of the Western world were affected by the commercial crises that punctuated the thirties and forties. Crop failures compounded the distress in Europe, and in the late forties the social scene became dismal.

At the same time, however, the influence and energy of urban society were advancing apace. The cities and industrial centers had grown remarkably in size and wealth since the beginning of the nineteenth century. They formed a brotherhood, exchanging ideas, opinions, and reading matter. The speeding up of communications through the introduction of the railway and the telegraph, and the increase of newspapers, promoted this exchange.

Government had not kept pace with the growth of urban civilization in administrative or military techniques. Only in England and France had any attempt been made to develop a police system adequate to the needs and the character of the modern city, and France had soon abandoned her attempt of 1828. The weapons of the military were not superior to those that civilians could obtain or improvise—flintlocks, gunpowder, pikes, knives—except in artillery and cavalry. But artillery and cavalry were not always effective in the   *301* narrow and twisting streets of the old cities. Yet the rulers relied largely on the armies to repress rebellion, even though the arrival of the troops nearly always made matters worse, politically and psychologically.

Under the circumstances, uprising and street fighting became normal instruments of politics and pressure. Revolution became not only respectable but fashionable. Substantial burghers, professional men, and persons of standing in society often cheered the barricade fighters on. It was in capital cities that barricades were usually thrown up. There urban civilization faced the traditional order at close range. In the centers of capitals shone the palaces of the kings and princes, the offices of the ministers, and the winter residences of the aristocrats. Around them ranged the counters and the workshops, the markets and the stores, the cafés and the homes of the commercial, industrial, and professional classes, rich and poor, lettered and unlettered. The capital cities became the principal stage of the Revolution.

The overthrow of the Bourbon monarchy of France in 1830 had convinced the opposition that the old order was not unshakable. On the morrow of that overturn the French romantic poet Victor Hugo thought he "heard on all sides . . . the dull sound of revolution, still deep down in the earth, pushing out under every kingdom in Europe its subterranean galleries from the central shaft of the mine which is Paris." Indeed, uprisings broke out in a crescendo series. In 1832 the Bourbon party of France rose against the regime of Louis Philippe, and two years later the republicans followed suit. Both risings were unsuccessful, as was an attempt by Louis Napoleon, nephew of the Emperor, to seize the garrison of Strasbourg in 1836. Louis Napoleon was exiled from France, but four years later he returned and plotted to incite a regiment in Boulogne to rise. He was captured and imprisoned in the fortress of Ham but escaped to England in 1846 to wait for a better opportunity. The most irrepressible revolutionist was the communist Louis Auguste Blanqui (see p. 277). Assisted by a small band of followers, Blanqui struck in 1830, in 1839, and several times later. He spent about half of his eighty-four years in prison, directing further *coups* from his cell.

In Italy uprisings were equally numerous. The organization Young Italy, directed by Mazzini, incited mutinies in the Sardinian army and staged rebellions in Genoa, Naples, and Sicily. A small army of Germans, Poles, and Italians invaded Sardinia from Switzerland, to help the rebels. The German Confederation experienced fewer political but many industrial disturbances. In Prussian Silesia the protests of skilled weavers against the introduction of machinery and the harsh conditions of labor more than once led to local wars with the royal troops.

Methods of agitation were as radical in England as on the Continent. Huge demonstrations and petitions to Parliament were among the more peaceful, although a large demonstration always carried the threat of violence. One wing of the movement of Chartism, as we have seen, advocated "physical force."

The disposition to drastic action infected some areas of the United States.

An anticipation of the doom of the traditional order. The spirit of revolution is blowing down a series of cards—the monarchs of Europe—resting against each other on a table supported by the backs of the people. Caricature by Honoré Daumier (1808-79) published in 1834 in the comic journal Charivari *of Paris.*

Rhode Island was the only state without a written constitution and one of the few that had not adopted virtually universal male suffrage. In 1842, the democrats of Rhode Island called an extralegal convention to rewrite the royal charter of 1663, which had continued to define the state government even after the Revolution, and elected new officials. A group of democrats, the Dorrites, so named after their leader, T. W. Dorr (1805-54), armed themselves and were put down by state troops. Shortly thereafter, however, the charter was superseded by a democratic constitution.

In Continental Europe tensions increased in the late forties. A number of agrarian and industrial riots broke out as a result of crop failures and unemployment. In 1846 there was a rebellion in the last remnant of free Poland. As a minute concession to the proprieties, the Congress of Vienna had set up the city of Cracow as an independent republic. Cracow became the natural center of conspiracy for exiles from the Polish areas of Russia, Prussia, and Austria. These states cooperated to suppress the rebellion and abolished the Republic of Cracow, assigning it to Austria. Since many of the rebels were landlords, the Austrian government promised the peasants relief from servile labor and set them to attack their masters. The extinction of the Republic shocked public opinion in both Europe and the United States into vigorous though ineffective protest. A new wave of Polish emigration rolled westward. Exiles moved clandestinely from country to country and cooperated with, and even led, the disaffected. There was hardly a conspiracy in which these "traveling salesmen of revolution" did not have a hand.

While the Republic of Cracow was foundering, Switzerland was riven by civil war. The Protestant and Catholic cantons had long been at odds over the efforts of the former to enforce, through a strengthened federal government, a policy of religious toleration, secular schools, and other liberal measures. In 1846 the Catholic cantons formed a separate league (*Sonderbund*), virtually seceding from the ancient confederation. The Protestant cantons equipped a large army, and the *Sonderbund* was defeated in 1847. The confederation was preserved intact, and its path was to be liberal. Prussia and Austria threatened the victors with military punishment, but events in Italy and France soon made the threat empty.

In 1846 Pius IX began the longest (1846-78) and one of the most remarkable pontificates in history with a series of liberal concessions. He initiated constitutional and educational reforms, granted freedom of the press, and amnestied political prisoners. Conservative leaders were shocked; Metternich exclaimed that he was prepared for anything except a "liberal Pope." "God does not grant amnesties," the Chancellor fumed; "God pardons!" Gregory XVI, Pius' predecessor, had opposed railroads on principle, as the material symbols of modernity. Pius IX, who had a refreshing curiosity, laid out several lines to connect Rome with provincial cities.

Public opinion in Western Europe and the United States greeted with delight the actions of the new pontiff. A mass meeting attended by thousands of Protestants and Catholics in New York praised the "noble attitude of Pius IX" as "the grandest spectacle of our day, full of encouragement and promise for Europe, more grateful to us and more glorious to himself than triumphs on a hundred fields of battle." In 1847 President James K. Polk (1795-1849) recommended to Congress that official relations be opened with the Holy See, and the following year he appointed the first American diplomatic representative to the Vatican.

In January 1848, riots in Florence and Turin persuaded Leopold II, Grand Duke of Tuscany (1824-59), and Charles Albert, King of Sardinia (1831-49), to imitate the Pope's example of liberal reform. In the same month, revolution broke out in Sicily and Naples. In February, the Bourbon king, Ferdinand II (1830-59), who was an old hand at making concessions (and repudiating them at the first opportunity), accepted a constitution, his fourth.

The Springtime of Revolution

At last, in February 1848, the "Gallican cock" crowed. For some years, middle-class liberals and republicans in France had been engaged in a campaign against the government of Louis Philippe and his favorite minister, François Guizot (1787-1874). That government had become increasingly corrupt. By dispensing large sums of money and offices to deputies, it kept the legislature under control. In some districts a few hundred voters were sufficient to swing elections, and voters were wooed by shameless appeals to their cupidity. Alexis de Tocqueville protested that the regime encouraged the view that "the man who possesses political rights owes it to himself, owes it to his children, to his wife, and to his relations, to make a personal use of those rights for their benefit."

At the beginning of 1848, the public weather turned ugly. Since political meetings were forbidden, the campaign against the government had lately been conducted by means of banquets, at which politicians and writers delivered increasingly defiant toasts and orations. They made contact with restive popular groups and in February arranged for a demonstration in the streets to coincide with a banquet attended by propertied and professional men. Alarmed, the government intervened. On February 21, the day before the scheduled banquet, the republican leaders agreed to call off the demonstration. But their liaison with the poorer districts was slack. On the following morning, large groups of workers and students poured into the center of Paris. Both regular troops and bourgeois guards looked on sympathetically. King Louis Philippe took the hint and dismissed Guizot. He did not, however, promise to change his policy and reform the government. On February 23, a small group of soldiers commanded by an overzealous officer fired on a crowd and killed more than twenty persons, including some women and children. At once Parisians armed themselves, raised barricades, and attacked the troops. Abandoned by respectable burghers, Louis Philippe fled to London. In his wake, the Republic of 1792 came back to life. A provisional government, consisting chiefly of liberal republicans, was established.

From the heart of the Revolution, on the banks of the Seine, the news traveled, over the new telegraph and railway lines, to the heart of reaction, on the banks of the Danube. Chancellor Metternich and Czar Nicholas were considering measures to intervene against the French republicans when revolution broke out in Vienna. On March 13, liberal students and proletarian groups clashed with imperial troops. As in the French capital, the burghers stood by in stolid sympathy with the revolutionaries. The bourgeois Civil Guard remained neutral, which, under the circumstances, signified that it also was on their side. Metternich was dismissed, and his "reign" of nearly forty years came to an inglorious end. Like the former French king, he fled to London, where he found refuge in the very atmosphere of personal and political freedom that he had striven to dispel. The Austrian emperor, Ferdinand I (1835-48), installed a liberal ministry, abolished censorship of the press, promised a constitution, and established a new National Guard.

The *coup* in Vienna resounded throughout the Empire. There were revolutions in Hungary, Bohemia, Lombardy, Venetia, and later also Croatia. In Budapest a liberal regime with a separate parliament was installed, with the approval of the Emperor. German and Czech liberals rose in Prague and forced Ferdinand to grant an autonomous regime for Bohemia. In Lombardy and Venetia the Revolution took the form of a war between Italian patriots and Austrian troops. After five days of fighting in the streets of Milan, the imperial garrison withdrew from the capital of Lombardy. The Venetians revived the

305

old republic that Napoleon had wiped out, but in a liberal instead of the traditional oligarchical form. The Hapsburg Empire appeared to have disintegrated into its constituent parts.

In rapid succession, a host of cities in the German Confederation, Italy, Holland, and Denmark rose against their masters. A mass demonstration in the capital of Prussia led to a clash with the troops in which twenty citizens were killed. With the news of Vienna still in his ears, King Frederick William IV apologized to his "beloved Berliners," bowed his head before the bodies of the slain, and ordered his troops out of the capital. He cried out that he would "merge Prussia in Germany" and pledged a constitution. A dozen smaller German potentates echoed his pledge.

To the east, in the Ottoman Empire, the Danubian principalities rose and obtained the promise of autonomy, constitutionalism, and the emancipation of the serfs. Of all the large countries of Europe, Russia alone did not experience an uprising. But even she was not entirely unaffected. Rebellions of serfs, endemic for a generation, greatly increased in 1848 and were repressed with the customary brutality. Polish and Russian exiles and refugees participated actively in many a rising elsewhere on the Continent. This was not without meaning for the future of czarism.

The fire also singed the British Isles. Famine-stricken Ireland flared up promptly with several risings, which were as promptly repressed. Rioting broke out in industrial districts on the larger island. Chartism, which had become quiescent in the early forties, came to life again. Its leaders organized a march of citizens to carry a petition for manhood suffrage to Parliament. The petition was said to contain several million signatures and it was rumored that half a million petitioners would be present in person at the demonstration. In one vital respect, however, political conditions in Britain differed from those on the Continent. Across the Channel the middle classes and the national guards generally sided with the populace. In Britain they ranged themselves behind the government. The Chartist demands for a redistribution of political power seemed to threaten their position as well as that of the aristocratic and landed classes. The government appealed to the citizens of London to volunteer for a special constabulary force, and 170,000 men (including, incidentally, the French *émigré* Louis Napoleon) responded to the call. This force was placed under the command of the aged Duke of Wellington, who had conquered the first Napoleon at Waterloo in 1815.

But the heart had gone out of Chartism. Only one tenth of the expected half million persons gathered for the march on April 10. There was no disorder. The marchers were virtually surrounded by policemen and special constables. They were not allowed to proceed to the Houses of Parliament but sent a delegation to present their petition, which was contemptuously rejected.

The United States presented a strong contrast both to England and to the Continent. Not only was she apparently immune to the European commotion of 1848 but she was experiencing unusual prosperity. The news that Europe was introducing liberal democratic institutions pleased American public opin-ion—the Old World was paying the New the compliment of imitation. Ameri-cans attended countless meetings and banquets and marched in large demon-strations and torchlight parades to celebrate the Revolution.

It was the uprising in Paris that aroused the greatest enthusiasm in the United States. James Russell Lowell (1819-91) caught the spirit of the time in his *Ode to France*:

> The brute despair of trampled centuries
>> Leaped up with one hoarse yell and snapped its bands. . . .
> And down the happy future runs a flood
>> Of prophesying light;
> It shows an Earth no longer stained with blood,
> Blossom and fruit where now we see the bud
>> Of Brotherhood and Right.

The United States hastened to be the first to recognize the new republic. President Polk, in a message to Congress, described the rising as a "sublime spectacle" and praised the French people for introducing institutions "similar to our own." Congress followed suit in a resolution congratulating France. In the debate over the resolution, Senator John C. Calhoun struck a discordant note: He objected to an amendment commending the abolition of slavery in the French colonies. The amendment was defeated but the resolution won by a large majority, which included Representative Abraham Lincoln of Illinois.

Calhoun linked the cause of democracy in Europe with that of antislavery in the United States. He regarded both American abolitionism and European socialism as products of the doctrine of natural rights and equality. In a letter written in the summer of 1848, he criticized the conception that political liberty and social equality might be combined:

> It is this false conception that is upheaving Europe, and which, if not corrected, will upset all her efforts to reform her social and political condi-tion. It is at the same time threatening our institutions. Abolitionism origi-nates in it, which every day becomes more formidable, and if not speedily arrested, must terminate in the dissolution of our Union, or in universal confusion, and overthrow of our system of government.

Advances of Liberal Democracy

The defeat of European conservatism was, for the moment, complete. It had lost control of the centers of political, commercial, and intellectual life. For the Revolution was originally, and essentially, an urban movement. The peasants followed rather than initiated political action. There were, indeed, no peasant risings on a large scale, although agrarian reforms—above all the abolition of serfdom in Eastern Europe—were among the demands of the day. The conservative regimes had never fully appreciated the strength and the promise of the modern city. It became clear that they could not hold it against a united population.

On the Continent the propertied classes in the cities and many young liberal aristocrats had seconded the rising of the ordinary citizens and often spurred them on. The citizens, for their part, had accepted without question the leadership of middle-class politicians and men of letters. The massed citizens and the bourgeois national guards were more than a match for the small professional armies, whose tactics were better adapted to the field and the fortress than to the street and the square. The imbalance was so evident that in most cases there had been no serious struggle and the regular troops were promptly withdrawn or immobilized. In but few cities had the fighting been prolonged or bitter. Nowhere save in France was a throne overturned. Nowhere was a crowned or titled head harmed. Nowhere was a constitution refused. The ease with which the cities prevailed produced an atmosphere of apparent social harmony.

On the very day of the Revolution, February 23, the provisional government of France had established universal manhood suffrage. Elections for a constituent assembly were set for the end of April. To see to the needs of the workers in a period of economic depression, two socialists were appointed to the ministry. The government abolished "sweated labor" and piecework and established free labor exchanges. It reduced the hours of labor to ten per day in Paris and to eleven in the provinces. It granted workers the right to set up cooperative producing enterprises, extended them credit, and gave them orders for military equipment. Foreign workers were allowed to take jobs in industry.

A large massing of the populace of Paris on March 17 constrained the government to proclaim a new right—"the right to work." An official decree announced that the Republic "undertakes to guarantee the existence of every worker by means of his labor. It further undertakes to give work to all its citizens." A commission, headed by the socialist Louis Blanc, was set up to inquire into means of implementing the decree. The government established "national workshops" for unemployed citizens, reminiscent of the "social workshops" that Blanc had proposed earlier as a solution to the industrial problem. But these workshops, subsidized by the government, were designed to provide temporary relief to the unemployed rather than to initiate a new kind of industrial organization.

In the German confederation, the Diet was persuaded to assent to a call by leading liberals for the meeting of an informal "pre-parliament" to discuss a closer union. At the end of March, the pre-parliament ordered the holding of elections by universal manhood suffrage for a constituent body, the National Assembly. In May the Assembly met at Frankfurt. It included a large body of professional men and government officials elected in their individual capacity, as well as landlords and merchants and a sprinkling of aristocrats. The Assembly improvised a central government and appointed the Archduke John of Austria, who had attained some popularity by his liberal leanings, as imperial regent. The new executive was recognized by several German states, and the Diet relinquished to the Archduke its federal jurisdictions and functions.

In the Hapsburg Empire, national differences forced the revolutionaries onto a double path. The revolutionaries of Vienna insisted on the liberalization of the Empire as a whole, while those in the provinces demanded liberal regimes of their own. Emperor Ferdinand responded in both directions. First he promulgated a constitution, in April. But, after a new rising in Vienna the Austria Assembly (*Reichstag*) rejected the imperial constitution as too conservative and proceeded to write one of its own.

The most important act of the *Reichstag* upon its meeting in July was the abolition of the notorious *robot*, the labor services to lords which sometimes consumed as much as a third of the peasant's time. The *Reichstag*, however, stipulated that the provinces must raise special funds to compensate the lords for the abolished services. The peasants remained unsatisfied, but a secular grievance was removed.

The work of writing a new constitution and of dovetailing it with concessions to the individual areas was then begun. For a polyglot empire, the obvious solution was federalism. The Czech leader Palácky proposed to divide the country into national states and set up a central government with limited functions, on the model of the United States and Switzerland. His proposal was watered down by the *Reichstag*. The "historical" boundaries of the old kingdoms and provinces were preserved. However, they were to be divided into ethnic districts wherever necessary for the performance of local functions. In districts of highly mixed populations, special tribunals representing the various groups were to be organized to arbitrate national disputes. In addition to a central parliament, there were to be local representative bodies and governors responsible to them. The constitution struck a fair balance between central and local governments and placed the nationalities on a plane of equality. It was the most successful attempt made in Austria to solve both the problem of nationalities and that of self-government.

Meanwhile the Emperor had agreed to the autonomy of Hungary, Bohemia, and Croatia. Hungary promptly organized a separate government, for the new constitution was not to extend to her territory. In Bohemia, Czech liberals issued a call for a Pan-Slav Congress to ensure equality of treatment for the Slavic peoples under the new institutions. The Congress, held at Prague in June, was attended by representatives of Slovak, Yugoslav, and Polish groups, but most of the delegates were Czechs, who were primarily concerned to ensure their equality with Germans and Hungarians. Members of the Congress drafted a petition to the Emperor, a call to the Slav peoples to establish a permanent organization for common action, and a manifesto to the peoples of Europe. The manifesto protested against national oppression and asserted that the Slav claimed "liberty for himself and for all." It urged that European nations call a congress to discuss their problems in the spirit of friendship. The tone of the Pan-Slav Congress was moderate, but there were members who propounded ambitious plans to unite all the Slavs into a single state. The Russian firebrand Michael Bakunin (1814-76) envisioned a Slav empire stretching from Prague eastward to the Pacific Ocean—incidentally, the limits of the Soviet empire of the mid-twentieth century.

The Italian problem was simplified by the fact that the alien Hapsburg dynasty, which controlled the northern provinces and had long protected the conservative system throughout the peninsula, was a magnetic target for the revolutionaries. The Savoy dynasty of Sardinia had shown liberal tendencies and was eager to extend its dominions. To many revolutionaries, except convinced republicans, King Charles Albert of Sardinia was the logical candidate for the leader of a united Italy. When Milan and Venice rose in rebellion in March 1848, an Austrian army under General Radetsky retired into the "quadrilateral" formed by the fortresses of Verona, Legnano, Mantua, and Peschiera, the key to the control of northern Italy. Charles Albert declared war on Austria on March 22. The revolutionaries, disregarding existing boundaries, raised volunteers everywhere to assist the Sardinian army. They constrained the Grand Duke of Tuscany, the Pope, and the King of the Two Sicilies to send detachments to the north. These rulers found themselves in the extraordinary position of fighting the power which had defended them against past uprisings. The Sardinian army won victories over the Austrians in May and June. Venetia and Lombardy merged with Sardinia: northern Italy was one. Several smaller states to the south also adhered voluntarily to the enlarged kingdom. The old dream of a united Italy seemed to be coming true.

The Crisis of the Revolution

All was hope in the spring of 1848. The Revolution had been successful beyond the dreams of the most sanguine men. In fact, it had been too successful. It was hardly possible that the whole old order, heavy with riches and tradition, would vanish without resistance. It soon appeared that there was something unreal about the great achievements of the spring.

The European Revolution, it turned out, was not one but many. The general currency of liberal and democratic ideas gave it an intellectual and spiritual unity. Journalists, orators, and conspirators moved from country to country. But there was little organized political and military cooperation across borders. There was, indeed, no disciplined revolutionary party that could have arranged such cooperation. Within each country, also, the Revolution had stopped halfway. The rulers, on the other hand, had long experience in moving armies from country to country to put down rebels. They were prepared to do so again at the first opportunity.

The revolutionaries accepted the concessions of the rulers at face value. They entered many ministries and influenced policy. But they neither laid hands on the apparatus of power nor dismantled it to make room for an apparatus of their own. They were not minded or prepared to take over the administrative offices, the bureaucracy, the judiciary, and—most important of all, in the circumstances—the army and its weapons. The old officials and generals retained their places. The new leaders exploited the facilities of the press and the platform and trusted for their continuance in power to the same more or less spontaneous action of the popular masses that had put them at the head of affairs. Only in Italy, where the Kingdom of Sardinia was on their side, and in Hungary did the revolutionaries possess the instruments of force, and there they were dislodged only by prolonged fighting.

While the revolutionaries took the rulers at their word, the old officials and generals discounted their concessions as made under duress. The promised constitutions were still to be drafted, promulgated, and applied. Meanwhile, the bureaucracies and the armies continued to function. The very lack of integration of the traditional administrations stood them in good stead. In the moment of need it appeared that the old governments rested much more on aristocratic bureaucracies and armies than on the principles of monarchical absolutism.

The outcome of the Revolution hinged on two questions: Would the cooperation of the urban classes continue, and would the rural areas continue to acquiesce to the leadership of the cities? Could the governments reconquer the streets from the people or transfer the struggle from the streets to the fields to give effect to their military power?

The answers to both questions were discouraging. Nearly everywhere the middle classes took alarm at the democratic political and social measures, even though these were highly tentative, and at the effectiveness of popular pressures. They began to cooperate with governments and standing armies to recapture control of the streets from the populace—they changed sides. In many areas, after the first concessions to them, the peasants stood aside and in effect supported conservative leaders or monarchs. In Eastern Europe, national questions divided liberals and democrats. And, as the struggle grew fierce, the opportunity for field and siege operations, in which the standing armies excelled, grew greater.

The shift of power occurred first in France. There democracy provided its own antidote. The urban democrats and socialists had insisted on universal suffrage, only to discover that the peasants, the bulk of the population, gave their votes to many a monarchist, Bonapartist, clerical, and conservative. The National Assembly which met in Paris in May turned out to be a moderate, if not a conservative, body. A majority of its members was opposed to the influence of the urban democrats and liberals who had called it into being. The issue was joined over the "national workshops." Since business was still depressed, many idle workmen flocked into the capital from the provinces, and the rolls of the "workshops" rose to more than 100,000 men. Although these enterprises were in the nature of improvised relief rather than rivals of private industry, they aroused a furious opposition. They were regarded as concessions to socialism and therefore as threats to private property. In any case, the propertied classes would have to foot the bill. The anxiety of these classes was intensified by the memory of the fierce Jacobin democracy of 1793-94, although leftist leaders like Louis Blanc were as unlike Robespierre as it was possible to be. "I do not believe," observed Alexis de Tocqueville, "that people were ever so frightened at any stage of the great Revolution, and I think their terror can only be compared with that of the civilised communities of the Roman Empire when they saw themselves in the hands of the Goths and the Vandals."

On June 21 the Assembly abolished the "national workshops." Two days later the workmen protested by staging a militant demonstration. Tens of thousands marched through the streets. Barricades were raised in the poorer quarters. The Assembly, the propertied classes, and the National Guard closed ranks. For three days the battle raged. Professional troops led by General Louis Cavaignac (1802-57), who was voted dictatorial powers by the Assembly, carried the fight, but it was a dearly bought victory. About 1600 soldiers were killed or wounded and, though accurate figures for civilian casualties are lacking, probably many more citizens. The aftermath was equally bitter. There were more than 11,000 arrests, and 4300 rebels were sentenced to transportation to colonial prisons. The repression deeply embittered the working classes of France.

The "June Days" were the chief turning point of the Revolution of 1848. Conservatives everywhere took heart from the defeat of the workingmen of Paris. In the ensuing weeks, the French government suppressed critical newspapers, harried political societies, and stamped out radical activity. The Assembly repealed the law limiting the hours of work. It drafted a constitution which accepted the principles of liberal democracy but erected a strong executive power. The "right to work" was not mentioned. The chief of government was to be, as in the United States, a president elected by universal suffrage. But the French president's term of office was to be not four but seven years, and he was to manage a centralized administration and a large army. In December the electorate chose as president a politician whose inheritance and ambitions predisposed him to dictatorship and empire. He was Louis Napoleon, whose uncle had invented the modern formula for combining popular phraseology with imperial power. Only the low opinion in which the new president was held explains his election; many liberals and republicans who voted for him felt that he would neither dare nor know how to repeat the fabulous career of his uncle. In politics as in life, it is unwise to underestimate the other man.

Hesitation and Nationalism in Germany

The Frankfurt Assembly proved the least energetic and independent of the constituent bodies established in the turbulent year. The middle and professional classes of Germany, like those of France and England, were determined to arrest the rise of urban democracy. But, unlike the French and the English, the Germans still had to curb monarchical and aristocratic power and to establish a unified state. The French Revolution of 1789 had shown that a struggle with the Old Regime could not succeed without the support of humble townsfolk and peasants and the good will of neighboring peoples. The Frankfurt Assembly ignored the interests of these groups and offended their dignity. From the beginning it opposed the activities of the urban democracy that had given it being. It rode roughshod over the claims of the Slavs. Yet the rulers could hardly be coerced into accepting a liberal solution to the German question while they were encouraged to deny a similar solution to the Polish or Czech questions. The Frankfurt Assembly chose the course that delivered it into the arms of the conservatives.

Liberal principle implied the unqualified extension of equal rights to Slavic minorities of Prussia and Austria. Since language had become the symbol of nationality, it implied the use of Slavic languages in the courts, schools, and administrative offices. Above all, it implied the assurance of fair opportunities in government employment, the professions, and trade. If, on the other hand, German nationalists insisted on a more unitary and homogeneous state, the alternative was to show modesty in territorial demands and not claim areas which, like Bohemia, contained a majority of Czechs and a minority of Germans. However, German nationalists were generous in their territorial claims and sparing in their concessions to other peoples.

Even radicals who had no national prejudices, such as Karl Marx and Friedrich Engels, drew a sharp distinction between the "historical" nations and all the "benighted" Slavic peoples except the Great Russians and the Poles. They had a reason of their own for rescuing the Poles from the general condemnation of the Slav world: a restoration of Poland would spell the defeat of the three conservative powers which had divided her. Engels pronounced the other Slav nationalities "inert" and "unprogressive," dependent for economic leadership and cultural nourishment upon Germans and Hungarians and doomed to succumb to "the action of historical causes that inevitably absorbs people into a more energetic stock."

The Slav nationalities could hardly be expected to accept such judgments. They did not concede that their lack of haughty aristocracies and affluent middle classes and their oppression by others in the past should condemn them to permanent inferiority or extinction. To a young, romantic Czech, the fact that in recent centuries the Germans had made a greater splash in the world did not justify their airs of cultural superiority and their pre-emption of the best economic, professional, and political opportunities. Since the Hungarians treated the Croatians with similar arrogance, the Slavs preferred the reform of the Austrian Empire to its partition between new German and Hungarian states. The Czech leader Palácky felt that the continual expansion of Russia held the threat of the establishment of "a universal monarchy," a gigantic absolutist state which would be an unmitigated evil for all men. The Austrian Empire united the various peoples of the Danubian region against this danger. If the Empire did not exist, Palácky observed, it would be in the interest of Europe to create it. The Czechs therefore refused to be represented in the Frankfurt Assembly, whose attempt to include Bohemia and Austria proper in a German state would have disrupted the Danubian organization. The Germans, in their turn, withdrew from the revolutionary body at Prague. Thus the German and Bohemian movements were sundered, as were the Hungarian and Croatian, to the profit of the Hapsburgs.

Developments in Prussian Poland were equally damaging to the cause of the Revolution. In the first flush of the Revolution, under the pressure of the democrats of Berlin, Frederick William had approved the establishment of an autonomous government in Posen. It proved difficult to draw a line of demarcation between German and Polish territory, since the population in border areas was mixed. Royal officials and generals took advantage of this circumstance. Defying the liberal ministry at Berlin, the local commander attacked the newly formed Polish army and dispersed it. The Duchy of Posen was split by the sword, and the lion's share was assigned to German rule. The German area contained more than a million people (a majority of them Poles) and the Polish area a little more than 300,000 persons. The Prussian parliament refused to sanction this arbitrary decision, but the Frankfurt Assembly approved it, so eager was it to extend the boundaries of German power and so contemptuous of the rights of the Slavs.

By autumn, when the Frankfurt Assembly launched its constitutional debate, it had already compromised its political independence and liberal principles. While the peoples of Italy, Hungary, and Austria were in arms against the Hapsburg monarchy and the conservatives were gaining confidence that they could crush them, the Frankfurt deputies spent valuable months drafting "the fundamental rights of the German people." They produced a more elaborate statement than any English, French, or American declaration of rights: one which guaranteed, in addition to the customary freedoms, the right to teach, the freedom of "knowledge," and the freedom to migrate. The proposed Constitution would preserve existing states and thrones for local functions but provided for a central federal government with wide powers. There was to be an upper chamber representing the states and the rulers and a lower chamber elected by universal suffrage.

The advocates of a "Great Germany" proposed to include in it the German lands of the Hapsburgs— that is, lands that were "historically" German, since the "German" province of Bohemia contained a majority of Slavs. The partisans of Prussian leadership preferred a "Small Germany" which excluded all Hapsburg areas but included all of Prussia, with Polish territories that had never been part of the old Confederation or of the Holy Roman Empire. The "Great Germans" were in the ascendant, and the Assembly resolved the issue in their favor. The Austrian ruler, however, would not accept a federation that excluded Hungary, Croatia, and Galicia and severed his Empire in half. In April he promulgated an Austrian constitution which provided for the unity of all his lands. In one stroke, he nullified the attempt of the Frankfurt Assembly to create a "Great Germany" and that of the Austrian *Reichstag* to write a liberal and federal constitution for the Empire. The Emperor boldly proposed that the old Confederation be revived, under the leadership of Austria and Prussia, in that order. The Frankfurt Assembly thereupon voted to exclude all the Hapsburg territories from the new federation. Its most distinguished members journeyed to Berlin, amid the plaudits of their fellow citizens, to lay the crown of "Little Germany" at the feet of Frederick William IV.

Like the Austrian Emperor, the Prussian king had recovered his freedom of action. In November 1848 he had marched troops into Berlin, encountering no resistance from the population. He suspended the Prussian parliament and decreed a conservative constitution. The deputies called upon the citizens to refuse to pay taxes; the Frankfurt Assembly, however, encouraged them to pay. Elections for a new parliament were held in January 1849, but when the new chamber protested the continued imposition of martial law, the King sent it packing and changed the rules of the game in order to secure a more manageable successor. His constitution followed the letter of democracy by permitting all male citizens to vote, but in May 1849 the King frustrated its spirit by instituting a combination of indirect voting and the three-class system. The richest taxpayers, a tiny minority, voted separately to elect one third of the members of a local assembly, which selected the deputy. Another third of the local assembly was elected by a second class of moderately well-to-do citizens. The bulk of the population, more than 80 percent of the taxpayers, elected the rest of the assembly and therefore carried little weight. Such "universal manhood suffrage" was equivalent to a heavy property qualification for voting.

Having thus secured a conservative system in Prussia, Frederick William was ready to deal with the more democratic constitution drawn up by the Frankfurt Assembly for a federal state. He disapproved of many things in it, but particularly of the provision that accorded the ruler a merely suspensive veto over legislation: his veto in Prussia was absolute. Above all, he refused to honor the principle of popular sovereignty by accepting a dignity from an elected assembly. The King declined the offer to rule as Emperor of the Germans with the remark that he would not pick up a crown "from the gutter."

Civil War in the Hapsburg Empire

The restoration of monarchical authority in Austria was a longer process. The first contest between the military and the revolutionaries occurred in Bohemia in the summer of 1848. In Prague tension mounted as the speakers at the Pan-Slav Congress in June protested the traditional domination of Germans. The Czech democrats were emboldened to demand of the imperial commander, Prince Alfred von Windischgrätz (1787-1862), supplies of cannon and ammunition. When the general refused to comply, the Czechs raised barricades and engaged the troops. Windischgrätz first tried to fight it out in the streets. Thinking better of this plan, he contrived, by the ruse of an armistice and exchange of prisoners, to withdraw his soldiers and his artillery to the heights which commanded Prague. After a heavy bombardment of a day and night, he compelled the revolutionaries to surrender. The Pan-Slav Congress was dissolved, and its members were dispersed. One of the three principal cities of the realm of the Hapsburgs was safely in the hands of the imperial army.

In the early spring of 1848 the campaign of Sardinia and her allies had all but welded northern Italy into a single state. In April, however, Pope Pius IX recalled his troops from the war against Austria. In Naples the soldiers of King Ferdinand II of the Two Sicilies had fallen upon and massacred hundreds of liberals and democrats. The King ignored the constitution he had conceded in February and, following the example of the Pope, withdrew his troops from northern Italy. Considerably weakened, the Sardinian army suffered a severe defeat at Custozza at the hands of General Radetzky. King Charles Albert signed an armistice which canceled his recent gains. Although the Republic of Venice continued to hold out, northern Italy returned to the sway of the Hapsburg emperor. The Italian republicans braced themselves for another effort farther south. The German assembly at Frankfurt congratulated General Radetzky upon his victory over the Italian liberals.

The victory of the Hungarians had been more prompt and complete than that of any other people of the Empire. Having obtained, in April 1848, the Emperor's consent to set up a separate government and constitution, the revolutionaries fancied the possibility of accomplishing their aims by legal means. They were careful to preserve the niceties of loyalty: they did not recall the Hungarian regiments which General Radetzky was using to suppress the Italian Revolution.

As the Germans of Bohemia were chary of accepting Czechs and Ruthenes as equals, the Hungarians assigned an inferior position to the Croatians, Serbs, and Rumanians in the territory they claimed as their own. Yet the five million Magyars were outnumbered by non-Magyars: there were in Hungary five million Croatians and Serbs and two and a half million Rumanians, not to mention more than a million Germans in Transylvania. The Magyar leaders assumed a haughty air. In April a delegation of Serbs asked the Diet to recognize the official use of the Serb language in their own districts. The delegation argued that any group which had a common language, culture, and tradition was entitled to the rights of a distinct nation. Louis Kossuth, the principal leader of the Hungarian revolutionists, retorted that no group was a true "nation" unless it had a government of its own, as the Hungarians did. He had no objection to the use of other languages for private purposes, but Hungarian was to be the sole official language of the state. Non-Magyars would be allowed to hold minor offices only. In short, Kossuth would not grant a "second nation" a full share in leadership and full equality of rights and opportunities. When the Serbs demurred, he replied that the sword would decide the issue. He thus enriched the conception of the nation with the connotation that it was a government that could win wars.

In these circumstances, the Croatians, Serbs, and Rumanians drew away from the revolutionaries of Hungary and tried to get better terms from the Emperor. Baron Jellachich, governor of Croatia, was empowered by the Court to attack Hungary, which was still formally loyal, with a Slavic army and was promised the support of German soldiers from the garrison of Vienna.

While German and Slav soldiers were preparing to march against Hungarian revolutionaries, the democrats of Vienna took up the Hungarian cause; they had scores of their own to settle with the Emperor. The government of Vienna, like the French provisional government, had proclaimed "the right to work" and initiated public works to give the proclamation effect. But it did not have the cooperation of the imperial ministers. Encouraged by the repression of the Paris proletariat in June, the treasury officials had reduced relief to the unemployed. A popular demonstration of protest was repelled by soldiers, with many casualties. When it was proposed to send a part of the garrison to join Jellachich against the Hungarians, the Viennese democrats rose en masse. On October 6, students and workers looted ammunition depots to arm themselves and hanged the Minister of War. A Hungarian army in chase of Jellachich came close to Vienna. It hesitated for a brief and vital moment: some of the generals were chary of crossing the line lest they lose their standing as loyal subjects of the emperor. When they finally did so, at the insistence of Kossuth, it was too late. General Jellachich had had time to prepare, and he defeated the Hungarians within sight of Vienna. Meanwhile General Windischgrätz bombarded the city. After a gallant fight (led, incidentally, by a Polish general, Joseph Bem), the Viennese surrendered to imperial troops on October 31. A score of revolutionary leaders were executed.

The Empire then strengthened its dynastic position. In December Ferdinand I, incompetent and epileptic, abdicated in favor of a youth of eighteen, his nephew Francis Joseph. The new emperor repudiated the varied and contradictory promises made by his uncle. The liberal ministry was dismissed and conservatives were installed in office. The counterrevolution had triumphed in Austria, the center of the Hapsburg Empire.

Intervention in Italy and Hungary

By the end of 1848 the monarchs and conservative groups had turned back the revolutionary movement in Austria, Bohemia, France, and Prussia. In northern Italy only Venice still held out. Yet the struggle was by no means over. Italian and Hungarian revolutionaries were still in arms in the spring of 1849.

In the preceding fall Italian liberals and democrats had launched a second series of uprisings. Left in the lurch by the Pope and the King of the Two Sicilies, disillusioned by the weakness of the Sardinian monarchy, they abandoned the north for the center and south of the peninsula, and monarchy for republicanism. In Tuscany, in Rome, and in Naples, the more extreme partisans, reinforced by republicans from other parts of Italy, came to the fore. The climax came in November, when a popular insurrection in Rome forced the Pope to flee to Gaeta, under Neapolitan protection, and ousted his government. A new Roman Republic, the fourth in the annals of the "Eternal City," was proclaimed on February 9, 1849, and a democratic electorate chose a constituent assembly. A similar assembly was convened in Florence. Since the Grand Duke had fled, Tuscany became in effect republican.

King Charles Albert of Sardinia, perceiving another opportunity to challenge Austria, renewed the war in northern Italy in March 1849. His army, led by the Polish General Albert Chrzanowsky (1788-1861), attacked the imperial forces in Lombardy. It was once more severely defeated by General Radetzky. The hapless King abdicated in favor of his son Victor Emmanuel II (1849-78) and died soon afterward in lonely exile. The Austrian armies marched into Tuscany, took rebellious town after town, and restored the Grand Duke. They occupied the Venetian mainland, although Venice itself held out until the end of August. Everywhere the Austrians exacted a savage vengeance; General Julius von Haynau so distinguished himself by the indiscriminate murder of democrats and liberals that he became known as "General Hyena." Nevertheless, the success of the reactionaries was not complete. The Republic of Rome still stood as the summer of 1849 drew near.

The war in Hungary was long indecisive. Twice imperial troops took Budapest—in January and in April—but the Hungarian armies still held the field. In March, indeed, the Revolution took a more dangerous turn. Hungary declared herself independent, disowned the Hapsburg ruler, proclaimed a republic, and made Kossuth her "Governor-President." The leaders tried to repair their earlier errors by broadening the suffrage and proclaiming the complete equality of nationalities. While the official language was to be Magyar, the language of local administration was to be that of the majority of the local population. Public offices were to be open to all regardless of nationality or religion. These concessions were a year late, for many Rumanians and Croatians were already fighting in the armies of the Emperor, who had made larger

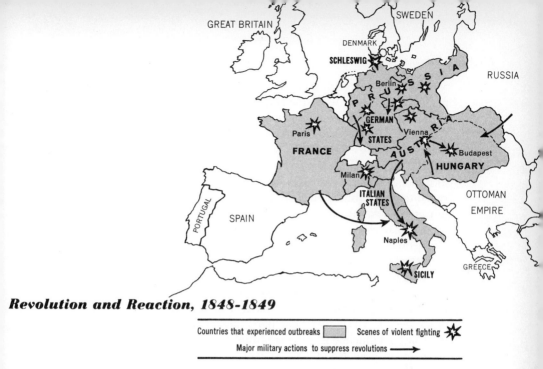

GREAT BRITAIN

SWEDEN

DENMARK

SCHLESWIG

Berlin

RUSSIA

GERMAN
STATES

Paris

Vienna

FRANCE

Budapest

HUNGARY

Milan

ITALIAN
STATES

OTTOMAN
EMPIRE

PORTUGAL

SPAIN

Naples

GREECE

SICILY

Revolution and Reaction, 1848-1849

Countries that experienced outbreaks ▢   Scenes of violent fighting ✴

Major military actions to suppress revolutions ⟶

promises to them. Even so, the Hapsburgs were unable to prevail against the new republic; they did not dare to withdraw their troops from Italy, and in June the Hungarians recaptured their capital.

In the summer of 1849 one thing had become clear: conservative rulers could not always deal with their own revolutionaries. Only outside intervention could repress the Hungarian and the Roman Revolutions. This was also true of the revolution that broke out in Baden and Saxony in May of that year. But intervention was more possible than it had been in the preceding year. The conservative paralysis of 1848 had been overcome. There were now fewer centers of defiance, and the economic depression which had stimulated much of the urban unrest of 1847-48 was being overcome. The only government that had shown a consistent sympathy for the democrats was three thousand miles away; nor was it the policy of the United States to interfere in European affairs. The Holy Alliance sprang to life again. Prussia intervened in Baden and Saxony, France rushed troops to suppress the Roman Republic, and Russia sent a large army to destroy the Hungarian Republic and complete the restoration of the Hapsburg Empire.

Prussia's task was the easiest. In May Prussian troops were marched in to suppress the Saxons; they dispersed the leading rebels, captured the Russian anarchist Michael Bakunin, who had led the rebellion, and turned him over to Austria. (Austria turned him over to the Czar, who put him away in prison.) The following month, large bodies of Prussian troops fought and finally defeated the insurrectionary armies of Baden, led by a Pole, Ludwig von Mieroslavsky (1814-78), and a German, Franz Sigel (1824-1902). Thousands of the rebel soldiers and officers, including young Friedrich Engels, crossed the border to

319

Switzerland. The Prussian government then attempted to improve its influence in Germany while the Hapsburgs were still heavily engaged in Hungary. It organized a monarchical union of the smaller German states under its own control. Whether this maneuver could prevail depended largely on the strength of the Hapsburgs; but the German revolution was over.

The deepening reaction in France had found expression in foreign as well as domestic policy. The advanced democrats had clamored to support foreign revolutionaries, but their star was in the descendant. Their antagonists were just as eager to intervene abroad, but on the other side. As early as the summer of 1848, General Cavaignac, who had so efficiently put down the workers of Paris, offered his assistance to the hard-pressed Pius IX. The Pope, however, preferred at the moment to secure the assistance of the more reliable traditional monarchies. But when in March 1849 he was forced to flee from Rome, he became less particular. The new president of France, Louis Napoleon, was allied to the powerful Catholic party and was eager to intervene in Italy, in order both to strengthen that party and to derive prestige from challenging Austria for influence in the peninsula. In the spring, therefore, he dispatched an army to seize Rome for the Pope. But since the new constitution, under which he had just been elected president, forbade intervention in conflicts between rulers and people, he pretended that the expedition was intended to bring the Pope and the people together peaceably.

The Roman Republic was supported by democrats from all over Italy. Mazzini of Genoa was its head and Giuseppe Garibaldi (1807-82) of Nice was its military commander. The French landed in April at Cività Vecchia and marched on Rome; to their surprise they were promptly repulsed by Garibaldi, who then turned south and repelled a Neapolitan army also marching against Rome. France signed an armistice with Garibaldi, but as soon as the French had been quietly reinforced from home, the army fell upon Rome. After a long and brave defense, Rome was taken on June 30 and returned to the Pope. A large part of the French army remained to protect him against his own people. Papal power thenceforth rested upon French bayonets. In the north, the Austrians besieged and bombarded Venice; ravaged by cholera and threatened with starvation, the city surrendered in August. The Italian revolution had been destroyed.

So had the Hungarian revolution, but not before demonstrating that the Hapsburg Emperor was no more able than the Pope to rely on his own strength. Despite considerable victories after the collapse of the Viennese rebellion of 1848, by March 1849 the new emperor, Franz Joseph, had to appeal for foreign support. Prussia's aid could be obtained only at the price of acknowledging her hegemony over Germany. The Czar had all along been willing, even eager, to intervene to restore the conservative order, fearing that the success of the Hungarians would encourage the Poles of Russia as well as those of Austria and Prussia to imitate them. In March the Austrian Emperor applied to Russia for help. In June the Czar dispatched an army of 80,000 men, larger than any single Austrian army in the field. The Hungarians were finally defeated in August but no one would mistake the true victor in the war: the rebels insisted on surrendering to the Czar instead of to their own ruler.

The Death of an Age

The restoration of conservative governments in Hungary and Italy rang down the curtain on a concentrated drama of eighteen months. It brought to an end a whole epoch in Western life, the epoch that began with the Atlantic revolutions of the eighteenth century. These revolutions enlarged the vision of liberty to include the material betterment and spiritual dignity of the poor and untaught, as well as propertied and lettered men. The dream of liberty of the religious dissenter, the enterprising merchant, and the writer and artist became also the dream of the worker and the farmer. For three generations, these men had often stood together against absolutism, privilege, intolerance, and inertia. Liberalism blended into democracy, and democracy blended into social reform.

In the spring of 1848 this vision had illumined and startled all Europe. But climax turned swiftly into anticlimax. Europe did not repeat the French adventure or the American experiment. It was too variegated, its peoples were too isolated, and, above all, the Western countries were too different from the Eastern. The middle classes and many intellectual leaders took fright at the social movements that had arisen since the French Revolution, and particularly since the introduction of modern industry in Western Europe.

The eventual result—which took a generation to jell—was a change in the character and the relations of liberalism, democracy, and conservatism. The political bonds between the two great regions of Europe grew slacker, and nations were set against each other. Immediately, there was great disillusionment among democrats and intellectuals and a narrowing of the views of liberals. Popular groups turned away from militant political action. Chartism in England and proletarian radicalism in France petered out. The practical form of socialism proposed by Louis Blanc was discredited after its unfair trial in the spring of 1848. The energy of urban workers flowed into the more modest channels of trade unionism. Peasant movements in Central and Eastern Europe suffered a similar attenuation. Even undismayed young radicals like Karl Marx were immobilized momentarily. Tried on a political charge by a jury in his native Rhineland, Marx was acquitted but deported by the Prussian government to France, which deported him again. He settled in England, where he launched the studies which provided the most acid critique of the origin and ways of capitalism. "Another revolution," he wrote with glum determination, "is only possible as a result of another [economic] crisis. But one is as sure as the other."

A sizable number of liberals, democrats, and trade unionists found the air too stifling in Europe and turned their back on it. English Chartists, German liberals and socialists, Hungarian, Italian, and Polish revolutionists crossed the Atlantic Ocean. In the measure that the political life of the Old World was impoverished, that of the New was enriched. Many of the political exiles found in the abolitionist movement an outlet for the idealism and energy that Europe had rejected.

The American people welcomed the defeated soldiers of the Revolution of 1848 with open arms. Giuseppe Garibaldi fled to the United States, where he lived until 1854. Louis Kossuth came over to receive an extraordinary reception. He was invited to address Congress, although the government discountenanced his effort to obtain help to renew the struggle. To Americans, poorly informed on conditions in Eastern Europe, he seemed the hero of the Revolution.

American enthusiasm for Hungarian independence led to a dramatic quarrel with the Hapsburg Empire. President Zachary Taylor in 1849 had instructed a diplomatic agent to recognize Hungary as soon as possible. The Hungarian Republic was destroyed before this could be done, but the Austrian government protested that the United States was interfering in its domestic affairs and threatened retaliation. The Secretary of State, Daniel Webster of

No figure of the Revolution of 1848 aroused so much admiration in America as Louis Kossuth, president of the Hungarian republic which was crushed by Czar Nicholas I. Below is a contemporary drawing showing the reception of Kossuth in New York in 1851. The Hungarian leader went on to Washington, where he addressed the Congress. CULVER

Massachusetts, rejected the protest in a thundering reply. He observed contemptuously that, compared with the American Republic, the Austrian Empire was "but a patch on the earth's surface." He reminded the rulers of Europe how often they had spoken disparagingly of the American system of government and exulted that "the prevalence of sentiments favorable to liberty is the result of the reaction of America upon Europe; and the source and center of this reaction has doubtless been, and now is, in these United States."

The fact was, however, that revolution was going out of fashion in Europe. For three quarters of a century, it had been the customary method of political opposition. There were few European countries that did not experience it, and quite a number of them did so more than once. Although the fear, or hope, of political overturns lived on for a time, there were few outbreaks on a large scale until 1917-18. Of the principal risings after 1848—those of the Paris Commune of 1871 and the Russian Revolution of 1905—the first was completely unsuccessful and the second largely so.

Thus 1848 appears in retrospect as the culmination of a long series of revolutions and as the dividing line between a period of deep unrest and one of growing stability. After 1848, liberals became wary of political conspiracy, secret organizations, and the adventures of the barricade. Many lettered and professional men who had flirted with democracy and social reform did penance. The middle classes of town and country drew away from movements that appealed to workers and peasants and from leaders who consorted with the lower classes. They became obsessed with the importance of "order." Although they deplored the savagery with which the popular movements were repressed, the propertied classes of Western Europe reconciled themselves to dictatorial and clerical measures to restore and safeguard stability. In Eastern Europe, aware of their weakness, they moved toward an accommodation with traditional authority. Everywhere they embraced mores and moralities that made for cautious and correct behavior. The age of idealism and democratic liberalism gave way to the age of respectability and propriety—in England, of Victorianism.

IV   *The Liberal World*

*Abraham Lincoln, leader of the successful war to preserve the Federal Union and
emancipator of the Negro slaves. His judgment, in the famous Gettysburg Address, was that
the American Civil War was fought to determine whether a "nation, conceived in liberty
and dedicated to the proposition that all men are created equal . . . can long endure."
Lincoln's statesmanship was an essentially cautious mixture of traditional Anglo-Saxon
principle with practical politics at its best. He lived in a time when Russia also faced the
problem of personal servitude and Italy, Prussia, and Austria-Hungary that of national
unification or consolidation. These problems Lincoln, Czar Alexander II, Camillo Cavour,
Otto von Bismarck, and Emperor Francis Joseph resolved variously, each according to his
particular character and the character of the regimes and principles he represented.*

16. *Prosperity and National Consolidation*

Although the Revolution of 1848 failed, it had a profound effect upon conservatism as well as liberalism. This effect did not become fully apparent at once. On the heels of the Revolution, most of the Continental regimes resumed their accustomed practices—above all, that of political repression. They treated the experience of 1848-49 not as a challenge to modify their policies but as a military engagement which they had won after much trouble. The German poet Heinrich Heine (1797-1856) caught the official mood in a satirical poem on the advice of the fathers of a small German town to its citizens:

> Have faith in your own magistrate,
> Who lovingly protects the state
> Through laws benevolent and clever.
> *Your* duty: Shut your traps forever.

Reaction in Austria and Prussia

Yet the restoration was not unqualified, even in Eastern Europe. There had been no political commotion in Russia, and Czar Nicholas, who had destroyed the Revolution at his doorstep in Hungary, was confirmed in his reactionary course. But the regimes that had been shaken betrayed the signs of incipient and reluctant change. They felt the need to rationalize and tighten their administrations, if only in order to forestall future demands for reform and avert future outbreaks.

In Austria, the youthful Emperor Francis Joseph governed with the advice of a council nominated by himself. He disbanded the provincial and autonomous diets, which had proved rebellious. By decree, he transferred police and judicial functions from the local magnates and their assemblies to the central administration at Vienna. Gathering his dominions into one customs system, he reduced the tariff to a moderate scale. Taxes were simplified and made more uniform. Serfdom, which had been abolished in 1848, was not revived, but the Emperor gave the owners financial compensation for their loss. A concordat with the Roman Catholic Church in 1855 gave the bishops and priests control over education and marriage and promised to restore the monastic estates confiscated seventy-five years earlier by Joseph II.

The German language was imposed on all occasions which brought the subject face to face with the state. Hungary and Bohemia lost their former linguistic privileges. A hierarchical German bureaucracy ruled. The pledges made to the Croatians and Rumanians, who had assisted the Empire, were disregarded as thoroughly as those made to the rebellious Czechs and Hungarians. "What we get as punishment," Hungarians twitted Croatians, "you get as reward." When Francis Joseph visited Transylvania after the Revolution, Avram Iancu, who had led a Rumanian army against the Hungarian rebels, refused to see him. "What could a madman like me," he exclaimed, "say to a liar like him?"

The policy of integration was daring, but not consistent. While the Hapsburgs imposed a central control over the many provinces of the Austrian Empire, they insisted on the preservation of the traditional political division of Italy and Germany.

In the north of the Italian peninsula Austria restored her control and the old conservative policies. She supported similar action by the Papal States and the Kingdom of the Two Sicilies in the south. Hundreds of liberals and republicans were hanged, and thousands languished in the medieval dungeons of Palermo, Naples, and Rome. Austria exercised a veto upon the plans to unify Italy and barred the road to the expansion of the Kingdom of Sardinia, which alone of all the Italian states preserved her constitution and thus threatened to become the rallying point of liberals and patriots throughout the peninsula. The Sardinian *Statuto* of 1848 provided a restricted suffrage. In 1850 a series of laws made marriage a civil contract, abolished the special jurisdictions of old ecclesiastical courts, and forbade the acquisition of property by religious orders without the permission of the government. In the atmosphere of legal and civil equality, the middle classes thrived and their progress was promoted by the government.

Austria cooperated with other German states, notably Prussia, in diluting the recent concessions to liberalism. Prussia emasculated her own constitution of 1848 by transferring, in 1850, important functions from the elected chamber to the executive and the aristocratic bureaucracy. The judicial power of the aristocracy in their local bailiwicks and of the provincial aristocratic diets was revived. Moreover, high state offices came to be increasingly and almost exclusively filled by noblemen. As though that were not enough, stringent control of the press was instituted. Many liberals and democrats abstained from voting under these frustrating conditions. By 1855 the chamber consisted entirely of conservatives—many of them officials of the royal administration.

Although Hohenzollerns and Hapsburgs were equally conservative, they did not see eye to eye on the project to integrate the German states economically or politically. The Hapsburg Empire first tried to put an end to the *Zollverein*, of which Prussia was the strongest member. When this effort failed, the Emperor made the interesting proposal that the union be joined, not only by Austria, but also by the rest of Central Europe, even the Balkans and Italy. The suggestion was grandiose, but the relatively backward industry of the Empire needed higher tariff protection than that of the other German states. Prussia stood her ground and, by lowering tariffs, prevented Austria from entering the customs union.

Austria prevailed in the political field, however. In 1849 Prussia had launched at Erfurt a project to combine the German states under her leadership. Fearing her power, the smaller states entered the union. The following year, Austria reconstituted the looser Confederation of 1815 and challenged Prussia to give up the Erfurt Union. War seemed imminent, and Russia threw her influence on the Austrian side. Prussia capitulated at a conference at Olmütz, in Moravia. Austria became once more the mainstay of the status quo in Germany. The issue between Austria and Prussia, like the dispute between Austria and Sardinia in Italy, could be settled definitively only by force. Thus reaction set the scene for war.

The Second French Empire and the Papacy

In France and the Papal States, conservatism struck out on more novel paths than in Austria and Prussia.

Like his uncle, Louis Napoleon posed as the shield of the people. The French National Assembly proposed to qualify manhood suffrage by stipulating a condition of permanent residence that many industrial and rural wage earners could not fulfill. For the ears of the people, the President cried out against this invasion of democracy; for the ears of the still-shivering propertied classes, he announced the existence of a dreadful (and imaginary) "communist conspiracy." Napoleon I had come to power in 1799 by raising the cry of a "conspiracy" against the Republic. In order to lend his projected coup the aura of his uncle's fame, Louis Napoleon scheduled it for the anniversary of the victory at Austerlitz. On December 2, 1851, he declared a state of siege and marched out his mercenaries, whose loyalty had been stiffened by the distribution of liquor in the barracks. He forcibly dissolved the National Assembly and arrested with impartiality the leaders of the various parties. Having "saved" democracy by destroying responsible and parliamentary government, he instituted a severe censorship and then managed, with a mixture of cunning, corruption, and terror, a plebiscite which—lo and behold—approved a new constitution. This first constitution, modeled on the consular document of 1799, abased the legislative power and exalted the executive.

The following year, another constitution, approved in due order by another plebiscite, made the President hereditary emperor, Louis Napoleon III. (The "second" Napoleon was the only son of Napoleon I, who had never sat on the imperial throne and died in 1832.) The new constitution virtually nullified the integrity and independence of the legislative body and removed all restraint upon the executive. Universal suffrage was preserved, but the freedom of opinion and of political action that were needed to give it reality were denied. Only officially approved candidates could present themselves to the voters. The lower chamber could not debate publicly or initiate legislation.

Europe rubbed its eyes in astonishment. "The old Napoleon has come back in person, though ridiculously transfigured," exclaimed Karl Marx. "Hegel says somewhere that, upon the stage of universal history, all great events and personalities reappear in one fashion or another. He forgot to add that, on the first occasion, they appear as tragedy; on the second, as farce." Yet, while the political forms were similar, the substance of policy was different. Napoleon III poured new wine into old bottles. The repression of political, personal, and public freedoms, the bloating of executive power, the diminution of legislative functions, the abolition of ministerial responsibility, the abuse of democratic suffrage for plebiscitary homage—all these followed the pattern of modern Caesarism. But Napoleon I had been a military genius and an administrative despot sensitive to the demands of an agrarian society. His nephew was a shrewd and demagogic politician, sensitive to the pressures of an industrial society and to urban public opinion.

Napoleon III erected his power on a series of compromises with clerical, middle-class, and even proletarian groups. He pursued a traditional religious policy. The Falloux Law of 1850—passed during his presidency—placed secondary schools under the control of the clergy. In the universities, the chairs of history and philosophy were abolished as too modern. The Emperor retained in Rome the army that had won the city for Pius IX.

At the same time, Napoleon posed as the patron of the workingman. Had he not coquetted with socialism and written *The Extinction of Pauperism?* If his uncle had sometimes regarded himself as "the peasants' emperor," Napoleon III would be more up-to-date as "the social emperor." He initiated elaborate public works, which provided much employment. In the art of electioneering he rivaled the greatest practitioner of the craft—the American politician. The Emperor enriched the ritual of vote-getting by kissing the babies of the voters, and he invariably shook the grimy hands of the engineers of the trains on which he traveled.

Napoleon III had less to offer to the peasantry. The first Napoleon had protected the land settlement of the Revolution by humbling the *émigrés* and their foreign confederates. But the latter-day problems of the peasant were financial: he was heavily mortgaged. Napoleon III was too committed to the interests of the financial classes to reduce interest rates. Fortunately for him, the Napoleonic myth was nowhere so alive as in the countryside.

Finally, the Emperor played upon the prejudices of the middle classes, their fear of "socialism," and their cupidity. He encouraged profit-making, fortune-hunting, and commercial and industrial enterprise. His public works stimulated investment and increased the issue of government bonds. The construction of canals and railroads and the modernization of cities attracted the imaginative and wealthy followers of Saint-Simon, the father of industrial and financial planning. Speculative ventures and stock-exchange gambling were hallowed by the blessing of the Emperor, whose relatives, ministers, and minions were not above profiting from stock-market manipulation. While republicans and liberals suffered imprisonment, transportation to miasmic prison islands, or exile, many members of the middle classes sacrificed their political principles to material interest.

While making concessions to various classes, Napoleon grasped the reins of domestic legislation and foreign policy. But the preservation of his discretionary power was not easy. Middle-class secularists disapproved of the extreme clerical reaction; financial speculation displeased the more sober property owners and the proletarians; liberals and democrats remained unreconciled. To maintain the delicate domestic balance, the dictatorship must preserve the appearance of effective power. For this the prestige of a successful foreign policy was essential.

Napoleon III had neither the talent nor the ambition to revive his uncle's policy of Continental conquest. France feared another holocaust, another Trafalgar and another Waterloo, while the great powers, particularly Great Britain, had too lively a recollection of the many defeats that preceded their victory at Waterloo to tolerate a new challenge by France. Soon after his *coup d'état*, Napoleon III had allayed these fears by proclaiming *"L'Empire est la paix."* The problem was how to maintain a stance of victory without incurring the risks of great wars. The Emperor's solution was to cooperate with Great Britain and to exploit the difficulties of the more traditional conservative empires. In France, as in the German states, reaction entailed war.

By his clerical policy, Napoleon III was committed to the support of the temporal power of the papacy. But while the Emperor had a tendency to accommodate himself to strong opposing forces, Pope Pius IX was unbending. Two years before the Revolution of 1848, he had inaugurated his pontificate by reforms that delighted European and American liberals and attenuated anti-Catholic feeling in Protestant countries. But the experiences of 1848—the assassination of his minister Rossi, his own flight from the Vatican, the proclamation of a Roman Republic led by laymen—shocked the Pope into a reversal of his political course. Pius had a rough directness and obstinacy; he was as thorough and sincere in his new policy as he had been in his old.

The eagerness of conservative governments to strengthen the official religions enhanced the Pope's position abroad. Not only Austria but Baden, Württemberg, Hesse, and Spain concluded concordats favorable to the Catholic clergy. In his own dominions, Pius IX restored arbitrary rule by clerics, a rigorous police and spy system, brutal methods of imprisonment and torture, and a fiscal system which had become a byword of corruption and unfairness. His secretary of state, Cardinal Giacomo Antonelli (1806-76), amassed a huge fortune by his proximity to the treasury. Rome vied with Naples for the distinction of being the worst governed state in Europe.

Yet the papacy had virtually lost its independence. The French army stationed in Rome was its sole remaining guarantee of temporal power. To this circumstance was added the fact that Roman Catholicism, along with other orthodoxies, was feeling the pressure of scientific and national movements. Pius responded by strengthening religious dogma and counteracting liberal tendencies. In 1854 he made the Immaculate Conception of the Virgin Mary a binding article of Catholic faith. He also appointed a commission to collect and classify the "errors" of liberalism with a view to anathematizing them.

The Modern Police System

Perhaps the most novel antirevolutionary measure of the time—and the one that had the most permanent effect—was the tightening of state control over urban life. The lively and spontaneous movement of the people on the streets and thoroughfares, in the squares, parks, and sidewalk cafés, facilitated political discussion, the rapid dissemination of news and rumors, and the circulation of criticism and satire of rulers and officials. Ever since 1789 the cities had been the chosen battleground of the revolutionaries and the scene of their triumphs. The governments were not unaware that, while they had won all their engagements in 1848-49 in the field, they had lost many within city walls. They were struck by the contrast presented by Great Britain, whose government retained its grip on the urban centers and had turned back the Chartists. The repeal of the Corn Laws accounted in large part for the relative peace in England during the period of turmoil on the Continent, but contemporary observers ascribed London's apparent immunity to revolution to its new police system. French officials, some of whom, like Napoleon III himself, had had firsthand experience with British methods, were particularly impressed.

For nearly a generation Great Britain had been slowly developing a form of authority and a police system adapted to the peculiar conditions and needs of the modern city in a liberal state. The informal local watchman and volunteer constable had been found too inefficient and the armed mercenary and soldier too provocative and tardy to satisfy the demands for public order, whether these demands required repression of crime and enforcement of the laws or repression of the urban challenge to political authority. From the fifties on, more and more cities in Europe and the United States introduced modifications of the British police system. Paris was one of the first to do so.

But on the Continent the imitation of the British system was compromised to some extent by a characteristic military turn. The British constables were not armed, and their uniforms were modest, designed to distinguish the police from the civilians rather than to impress or abash citizens. On the Continent police were always armed, even if only with side arms or blunt swords or daggers. They were dressed in the military tradition—that is, gaudily, color-fully, imposingly. A representative of authority who did not look glossy and a trifle ominous was inconceivable to the conservative Continental mind. The policemen were recruited generally from among the noncommissioned officers and volunteers of the regular army, which groups were principally of peasant stock. In effect, the village was mobilized to discipline the city.

There was another movement which, beginning in the fifties, incidentally strengthened the influence of authority. This was the movement to improve public health and to rebuild and beautify old cities. In Paris an official of the Empire, Baron Georges Haussmann (1809-91), laid out parks, cut wide avenues through crowded districts, installed a system of water supply and sewage, and constructed bridges and public buildings. Modern Paris is largely his creation. On a smaller scale, similar plans were carried out in Vienna and other capitals.

These improvements served the interests of order as well as of aesthetics and health. The narrow and crooked streets, so advantageous to the barricade fighter, were cut through and replaced by straight and extremely broad ave-nues. The fortified walls which surrounded many of the inner parts of the old cities were taken down and replaced by circles of boulevards. (The word "boulevard" originally meant the top of fortified "bulwarks.") The circles, in turn, were connected by broad radii with the important squares and political structures and royal palaces. Broad avenues led straight to the outskirts of the overgrown cities. It became possible to dispatch troops promptly into the heart of the city, to deploy them in the huge squares which were cleared in front of the important and strategic public buildings, and to concert effective artillery and cavalry action in all directions. Railroad lines were laid partly with the view of rushing troops to the capitals from a distance in case of trouble.

Such changes, augmented and improved later in the century, notably by the growth of standing armies, altered the ratio of strength between govern-ment and people on the Continent. The year 1848 divided the era between the French Revolution and the first Russian Revolution of 1905 into two approximately equal periods: in the first fifty-odd years, few European capitals were spared the experience of urban revolutions, and many capitals had re-peated experiences; in the second period, with one exception (during the Paris Commune of 1871), no government lost control of its capital.

Gold and the Iron Horse

It appeared in the early fifties that Continental conservatism had re-estab-lished itself. The middle and lower classes were uncommonly quiescent. Yet Europe—indeed, the world at large—was astir as seldom before. The economy revived from the depressions of the forties. The increasing application of steam power to industry and, above all, to transportation and the opening of fresh avenues of trade spurred production and exchange.

In 1848, thousands of miles away from the cities where conservatives and liberals stood embattled, a spectacular event had helped to lift capitalism from its trough. Gold in abundance was discovered in California, which was then a virtually empty territory just taken from Mexico. Thousands of farmers, sailors, tradesmen, and soldiers of nearby states and towns abandoned their occupations and rushed to the gold-fields. The rush attracted thousands more from the Eastern states and then from Europe. Within two years the population of California rose from 5000 to 50,000. A decade later it was 100,000. Then the shower of Danaë fell in the Antipodes. In 1851 gold deposits were discovered in Australia. Again, tens of thousands of gold-hunters streamed in, largely from England and other European countries. In the first half of the century, the world had produced gold worth about 800 million dollars. In the first three years after the discoveries in California and Australia, it produced 4242 million.

Sailing vessels consumed valuable weeks turning Cape Horn on the way to the Australian and American El Dorados. The gold rush revived and intensified the old interest in a passage between the Atlantic and Pacific Oceans, by canal or rail, across the narrower parts of Central America. More significant was its effect upon the world economy. Business transactions were limited by the amount of precious metals available and in circulation. Paper money was backed by gold or silver, and international payments were made by transferring metals from country to country. The increase of metal facilitated and multiplied purchases and sales and pushed up prices, which were essentially a ratio between the total amount of goods and the total amount of specie. The new treasure helped the Western world to pay for its adverse balance of trade with India and China: Eastern exports were larger than imports. The growth of California and Australia themselves benefited the older areas, for example, for the gold-hunters became heavy importers of various commodities.

The early industrial progress and the flexible commercial policy of England placed her in an advantageous position to profit from the economic upswing. When the first World Exposition was held, in London in 1851, English goods stood out in both high quality and low price. England demonstrated her strength by discarding the shield of tariffs; year after year she abolished more and more customs duties and direct taxes. By 1860 her fiscal system rested only on duties on tea, taxes on alcohol and playing cards, and a low income tax.

On the Continent, the most energetic economies were those of France, Belgium, Prussia, and Sardinia. The French and Belgian governments laid out, built, and operated national railway lines. Count Cavour, the Sardinian Prime Minister, initiated new enterprises and gave state support to those of other investors. He simplified the fiscal system, effected economies in the budget, negotiated treaties that broadened commercial opportunities, and accelerated railroad building.

In Germany, Prussia was assuming industrial leadership as she had assumed leadership of the movement for freer trade. Railroad construction provided an outlet for the energy and the capital of her middle classes. In order to connect important centers, it was often necessary to cross state boundaries, obtain land grants and franchises from various governments, and conclude elaborate treaties. The cupidity and ambition of petty rulers came into play. Now and then political considerations frustrated the needs of economics. Hanover, for example, for a long time obstructed the rail connection between Hamburg and the free city of Bremen, situated only a hundred miles apart. The German states were to some extent shaped by the parallel and north-flowing rivers and, as in the United States, the new railroads created an east-west axis. Prussia derived great advantage from this circumstance, for she was the only state that extended all the way from the eastern to the western extremes of Germany. The growth of railways thus reinforced the stimulus that commerce had given to the integration of northern Germany. The network of customs treaties which Prussia had concluded by 1844 with most of the states of the German Confederation (significantly excluding the Hapsburg territories) was continued and strengthened in the fifties.

Overseas, the only region which paralleled Western European countries in economic and technological development was the northeastern area of the United States. The greatest American industry—cotton goods—doubled its production and labor force in the forties and fifties. American iron mills began to manufacture rails, although they could not as yet compete with the English on equal terms. Railroad mileage rose rapidly, from 2818 in 1840 to 9021 in 1850 and 30,626 in 1860. The victory of the "iron horse" over steamboat and canal coach and rubble or macadam road, was decisive. By 1860 perhaps two thirds of all internal freight was being shipped by rail. Rates tumbled. The Middle West, already linked to the Southern states and the port of New Orleans by the Mississippi River, now was linked by several rail lines to the Northeast. The new connection ultimately became more important than the old.

The economic advances which began in the fifties promoted free intercourse and trade. Western Europe was in a better position than Eastern Europe to take advantage of economic opportunities, and the Northern states of America were similarly favored over the Southern; the ensuing disproportion of wealth and strength aggravated old frictions. Beginning in the mid-fifties, a series of conflicts swept the Western world. In 1853-56, Turkey, Britain, France, and Sardinia went to war against Russia; in 1859, France and Sardinia fought Austria; two years later civil war broke out in America; in 1864 Austria and Prussia fought Denmark and two years later each other; and, finally, Prussia fought France in 1870. Every confrontation demonstrated the ineffectiveness of traditional conservatism, and many concessions refused to revolutionaries on the barricades were yielded to soldiers on the battlefield. In every confrontation the protagonists that commanded greater industrial power prevailed. The same railroads and steamships that sped the movement of samples and salesmen, mails and goods, facilitated the deployment of troops and sped the transport of army supplies.

War and Reform in Russia

In the first of these contests, Russia went to war over the "Eastern question": what to do about the progressive inner rot of the Turkish Empire, and how to profit from it? Russia suggested to Britain that the two might divide up the Empire, but Britain would not anticipate the demise of the "sick man"; the possibilities were too incalculable and the threat of Russian domination of the Aegean or Adriatic Sea too real.

The Czar resorted to direct pressure. In 1853 he demanded the right to "protect" the Greek Orthodox subjects of the Sultan and to control the Holy Places of Jerusalem. But Napoleon III, as an ally of the clerical party, could not fail to enforce the traditional claim of France to protect Roman Catholic interests there. He therefore joined England in declaring war on Russia. While a Russian army occupied the Danubian principalities of Turkey—Moldavia and Wallachia—the two Western powers sent their fleets to assist the Sultan. The Western powers carried the war into Russia herself. British and French steamers bore troops to the Crimean peninsula, where they effected a landing in September 1854. The objective was to take Sevastopol, the principal Russian fortress and naval base on the Black Sea. Sardinia formally entered the war in January 1855 and sent a small army to join the British and French in Crimea. The Russians were handicapped by the fact that, lacking adequate railway facilities, they could not bring troops from the interior of the country with sufficient speed. After a long siege, Sevastopol fell to the allied army in September 1855.

During the fighting in Crimea Austria had exploited Russia's difficulties by checking Russian ambitions to expand in the Balkan peninsula. She had mobilized her troops and, with Turkish approval, replaced the Russians in the occupation of the Danubian principalities. After the fall of Sevastopol she threatened to enter the war against Russia. The Czar promptly came to terms with all his enemies. In view of the fact that a Russian army had helped the Hapsburgs to defeat the Hungarian Republic in 1849, Russia had reason to resent, and to remember, Hapsburg "ingratitude."

The Crimean War affected the domestic affairs as well as the international position of the participants. In England it led eventually to a reform in army organization, for British troops had perished by the thousands as a result of disease, malnutrition, cold, and, not least, incompetent leadership. The purchase of commissions was ended, the period of service shortened and a reserve system organized. Nevertheless Britain's military prestige suffered, and the powers henceforth largely discounted her ability to intervene successfully by arms in Continental affairs. The heroic work of the nurse Florence Nightingale (1820-1910) in succoring the wounded and sick led directly to the improvement of medical care for British soldiers everywhere.

The Turkish Empire was preserved and the interests of the Western   *335* powers in the Mediterranean were safeguarded. Under pressure of the powers, Turkey agreed to a broad program of reform, which brought more liberty to the Christians under her control. At the Congress of Paris in 1856, Russia agreed to dismantle her naval installations and forts in the Black Sea, which was neutralized. The weapon of sea power was struck from her hands in the southern waters.

The Congress made a significant contribution to international law on the sea. In the Declaration of Paris it abolished privateering, or the practice of arming private vessels in order to carry on war, and asserted unequivocally that the neutral flag protected from capture the goods of an enemy, except for contraband of war. It further provided that neutral goods could not be captured even when carried in a ship under the flag of an enemy—again, unless they were war contraband—and that a blockade was not legal unless it was effective —that is, unless the blockading state maintained a naval force sufficient actually to prevent access to the enemy coast.

Russia had lost a war on her own soil. The humiliation convinced her rulers that the modern world could be fought only with its own weapons. Nicholas I, who had constructed a system of extreme repression and obscurantism, died a few months before the collapse of Sevastopol. His successor, Alexander II (1855-81), launched a program of reform calculated to improve the economy and administration of the country without hurting the dominant landed classes or diminishing the absolute power of the Czar. In 1861 he issued the Emancipation Edict, abolishing serfdom without compensation to the owners. He decreed that the land belonged to the nobles, although many of the original titles were communal rather than individual or manorial. The government then bought, at good prices, one third to one half of the land, for resale to the peasants. The government alone bore the charges on the loans it raised to pay the landlords, and the peasants were given forty-nine years in which to reimburse it for the principal. But the prices paid by the government for the land were sufficiently high to make even these gentle credit terms a heavy burden for the peasants. The former serfs of the lords were now debtors of the government. The economic difference was not always apparent to the naked eye.

Nor did emancipation bring complete liberty for the serfs. The government sold land not to individuals but to the old village communes, now revitalized for this fiscal purpose. The communes (led by the elders) assigned land to the large "tribal" families, which were headed by the oldest male. These families consisted of several ordinary families and might therefore include as many as twenty or thirty persons. Individual members of a "tribal" family could not leave their village or acquire land in another one.

This agrarian reform was accompanied by administrative improvements. The Czar organized limited local self-government and local councils were charged with the superintendence of schools, roads, bridges, and hospitals and empowered to raise the necessary taxes. He instituted a system of courts and decreed jury trial for criminal charges. However, he kept the central government in his own hands.

For a short time, a milder wind blew over the Russian domain of Poland. The Czar reinstituted the parliament and guaranteed limited civil freedoms. This was much more than the Russians themselves obtained, but much less than true constitutionalism. It could hardly satisfy either the liberals or the radicals of Poland. The Czar's attempt to quell religious dissent by drafting the dissenters into the Russian army—which was regarded as severe punishment, since service lasted twenty years—was the signal for an insurrection in 1863. England, France, and Austria interceded jointly for the liberties of Poland, but Prussia assisted the Russian armies by catching fleeing rebels. In order to divide the Polish opposition, the Czar confiscated the estates of aristocratic rebels and turned them over to the peasants, on terms far more advantageous than those granted to the Russian peasants. The rebellion was drowned in blood and a severer repression organized. All autonomy disappeared in Poland, and the Russian language—the symbol of external constraint—was made obligatory in all schools.

Italian Unity and the Liberal French Empire

In the Crimean War Russia had been disappointed by the neutrality of Austria, whose regime she had saved in 1849 by crushing the Hungarian Republic. Imperial rivalry in the Balkans had prevented the cooperation of the conservative powers. Three years after the war, Austria faced alone, as Russia had, a war with Western states. The Italian question simmered once again.

By assisting Great Britain and France in Crimea, Sardinia had earned a seat at the Congress of Paris and sympathy for her aim to unite Italy. To this claim Napoleon III was especially sensitive. In his youth he had taken the oath of the *Carbonari*, a secret society whose aim was to free Italy from foreign domination and unify the peninsula. (In 1858 Felice Orsini, a *Carbonaro*, nearly succeeded in an attempt to assassinate the Emperor for his procrastination.) Napoleon had another reason for supporting the claims of the Italians, and those of other nationalities: he perceived an opportunity to shore up his dictatorship at home by exploiting the national difficulties of older empires. His intervention in the Crimean War had enabled him to use his influence to secure autonomy for the Danubian principalities from Turkey and had earned France the gratitude of their leaders. Intervention in support of Italian claims against Austria had the additional advantage of offering the prospect of territorial profit.

Count Cavour, Prime Minister of Piedmont (Sardinia), tempted Napoleon with an offer to cede Nice and Savoy to France in exchange for French assistance in wresting Lombardy and Venetia from Austria and uniting them to Sardinia. This action would please French liberals; however, it was not desirable from the imperial point of view for France to nurture a strong and completely united Italy. Further, Napoleon's clerical policy prescribed the preservation of the Papal States. Beset by contradictory impulses, Napoleon accepted Cavour's terms, and Sardinia assumed a provocative attitude toward Austria. The Austrian finance minister advised Francis Joseph against a war, for the condition of the treasury was poor, but the Hapsburg Emperor was more concerned with the political traditions of his dynasty than with economic considerations. In April 1859 he declared war on Sardinia. A French army, seconded by Sardinian troops, invaded Lombardy and within two months forced the Austrian army to retreat, first at Magenta and then at Solferino. Napoleon III, without consulting his ally, made peace with Austria in July, obtaining Lombardy but not Venetia for Sardinia. He had already taken Nice and Savoy and hoped that, if the growth of Sardinia remained thus restricted, the integrity of the papal dominions might be maintained. Cavour resigned in protest.

But there was another force in the peninsula. Immediately after the collapse of the Austrians, liberal and democratic groups rose in many parts of Italy and called for plebiscites. Nine months later, large majorities voted for annexation by Sardinia. In May 1860 Cavour, returned to office, encouraged a filibustering expedition, led by the republican general Garibaldi, to win the Bourbon south. The attempt was successful, but then Garibaldi's army turned north and occupied the papal territories (avoiding Rome, still defended by a French army). Would the republican turn over his conquests to monarchical Sardinia? The rest of the country had been united, and civil war was not

Giuseppe Garibaldi (1807-82), popular leader of the Italian unification movement. BROWN

The Unification of Italy, 1859–1870

Dates show when states joined with
K. of Sardinia to form K. of Italy (proclaimed 1861)

Venetia ceded by Austria, 1866;
Rome annexed, 1870

an attractive prospect. Garibaldi reluctantly accepted the monarchy, and Victor Emmanuel was proclaimed king of all Italy in March 1861. The dream of a democratic republic, realized for a moment in 1848, was dispelled. But, save for the province of Venetia and the city of Rome, Italy was one.

The Pope would not recognize the new state. Premier Cavour (who died three months after the Kingdom of Italy was born) had advocated "a free Church in a free State," which meant that the two institutions would not impinge on each other's jurisdictions. But Pius IX characterized Victor Emmanuel as "a Catholic King" who, "forgetful of every religious principle, despising every right, trampling upon every law," had "despoiled the august head of the Catholic Church of the greatest and most flourishing portion of his legitimate possessions."

The clerical party in France blamed Napoleon III for the seizure of the papal territories and the weakening of the temporal power of the papacy. It was not conciliated by the fact that French troops were still protecting the Pope's position in Rome itself. In an attempt to compensate for the loss of Catholic support, Napoleon made a few concessions to the liberals. In 1860 he sanctioned negotiations by the Saint-Simonian economist Michel Chevalier with Richard Cobden, the English free-trade leader, for a commercial treaty between France and England. The treaty abolished old prohibitions against the importation of certain English products, established moderate tariff rates, and provided that French goods were to be admitted to England free of duty. Each country was to grant to the other whatever concessions it made in the future to "the most favored country." The Cobden-Chevalier treaty aroused the opposition of French manufacturing interests, traditionally protectionist, but it pleased laissez-faire liberals and earned the friendship of England.

Napoleon shored up his position politically as well as economically. He granted amnesty to political offenders and permitted republican leaders to return from exile, lifted the prohibition on the publication of parliamentary debates, and permitted the chambers to criticize the government and to amend the budget. He curried favor with proletarians by legalizing labor organizations and strikes.

In Austria also there were attempts to liberalize the Empire. As the Crimean defeat had undermined the "Nicholas System" in Russia, so the Italian defeat weakened the centralist regime established by the Hapsburgs in the wake of the Revolution of 1848. Emperor Francis Joseph declared himself ready to put an end to arbitrary government. In October 1860 he decreed a constitution and restored the historical distinctions of Hungary, Bohemia, and the German provinces of the Empire. Local parliaments and administrations reappeared, and bureaucratic influence at the center was supplanted by aristocratic influence in the provinces. But the settlement was not solid. Fearing that the Hungarian nobility would gain strength from these arrangements, Francis Joseph in 1861 promulgated a second constitution more centralistic in tendency. Thereupon Hungary refused to elect delegates to the central diet and insisted on a separate administration. Whether the Hapsburg government could maintain its position and avert another constitutional experiment depended on the outcome of the continuing competition with Prussia over influence in the Germanies. The Hungarian and the German questions thus became one. And the German question was taken in hand by a more daring politician than Francis Joseph.

The Triumph of Bismarck's Prussia

Otto von Bismarck (1815-98) was a Prussian landlord employed in the royal diplomatic service. He was characterized by shrewdness, complete freedom from preconceptions—including conservative preconceptions—thorough opportunism, and an overriding will to power. The Revolution of 1848 convinced him that the day of Metternichian immobility was over and the success of Napoleon III in exploiting liberal doctrines and demagogic democracy for absolutist ends impressed him. He concluded that an apparent adaptation to the demands of liberalism and democracy could preserve the substance of conservatism and fulfill the old Prussian dream of dominating Germany. "There is no room," he wrote, "for both Austria and Prussia in Germany; one of us must yield; until one does we must be enemies."

Prussian noblemen, true to the conservative tradition, were loath to contest

*Portrait of Prince Otto von Bismarck made
in 1888, toward the end of his career.*
BETTMANN

Austrian power for fear of strengthening the liberal elements, which were the principal advocates of the integration of the German states. But Bismarck had no such inhibitions. He was prepared to strike a bargain with the liberals, even though he had only contempt for representative government and for personal freedom. His conception of an acceptable parliamentary regime was one in which "our humble cousins the tailors and shoemakers become the lords of the state until they have once more opened their purses," so that the true lords of the state—the monarch and aristocrats—once more run it in their own way. The reward of the Prussian liberals must lie in the humbling of Austria, the principal upholder of a conservative German system; in the economic consolidation of the country; and in the introduction of constitutional formalities. Parliamentarianism would be negated in practice by enlarging Prussia and establishing her control over other German states and by extending the Prussian system, under which the monarchy and the aristocratic bureaucracy controlled the executive, the administration, the army, and foreign affairs.

Such a solution to the German problem was unlikely to appeal to the king, the aristocrats, the middle class, or the populace. But if their active cooperation could not be enlisted their weaknesses might still be exploited. Bismarck regarded the middle classes as selfish and opportunistic, the masses as sentimental and gullible, and the ruling groups as simple-minded. The conservatives might be kept in place by concessions to the middle classes, the middle classes by concessions to the masses; and, of course, vice versa. If any group became obstreperous, a neutralizing pressure from another group would restore the balance. So complex and delicate a balance could hardly remain steady long, and expert manipulation would be required to shift the weights and restore it. Bismarck had a candidate for the job—himself.

Bismarck's opportunity came in 1862, when he was recalled from his post as ambassador to France in circumstances that were extraordinary. After the Franco-Sardinian-Austrian War of 1859, which had revealed the military weakness of Austria, King William I, who succeeded his brother Frederick William IV in 1861, had determined to enlarge the Prussian army. This required an increase in taxes, for which, under the constitution, the consent of the lower chamber (the *Landtag*) was necessary. The liberal groups, unwilling to strengthen the armed forces at the command of the monarch, mustered a majority against the proposal. The *Landtag's* refusal set a precedent for the indirect control of the military by the elected representatives. True to the Hohenzollern tradition, however, William insisted on unquestioned and exclusive control of the army. Rather than yield, he was prepared to abdicate. As a last resort, his alarmed ministers persuaded him to summon Bismarck, who had already earned a reputation for iron tenacity.

Bismarck, appointed president of the Prussian cabinet and foreign minister, promptly decided to collect the new taxes—without the approval of the parliament, if necessary. He was quite ready to meet the defiance of the liberals by abrogating the constitution and appealing to force. It was a crucial moment for Prussian liberalism. In the seventeenth century, a proud and well-to-do English citizen had started King Charles I on the way to the scaffold by refusing to pay a tax unsanctioned by Parliament. There were no John Hampdens in Prussia; the taxpayers paid obediently. Henceforth the grateful King regarded Bismarck as indispensable, and the threat of resignation, which Bismarck used freely, always bent him to the minister's will.

Bismarck hoped to reconcile Prussian liberals to an emasculated constitutionalism by his advocacy of a German union. Since Austria had in 1861 adopted a more advanced constitution than that of Prussia and so became a rival for the support of German liberals, Bismarck outbid her with the proposal that a new German parliament should be elected by universal manhood suffrage. While he was cajoling democratic opinion in the German states and frustrating representative institutions in Prussia, Bismarck prosecuted his program for the aggrandizement of Prussia. This program contemplated war. Prussia, however, did not possess the resources for a war against two great powers, and if the conflict with Austria were not decided quickly there was the possibility that other powers would intervene to check Prussian gains. It was therefore necessary to isolate Austria and to prepare a military campaign that would be so quickly successful as to forestall intervention. Russia was in the best position to frustrate Bismarck's plans by inclining toward Austria. The conciliation of Czar Alexander became, therefore, the cornerstone of Bismarck's policy. He was assisted by Russia's resentment at Austria's antagonism in the Crimean War. Bismarck's antiliberal measures in Prussia pleased the Russian ruler. In 1863, during the Polish rising, Bismarck confirmed his good will by sending four Prussian army corps to the

Polish frontier in order to prevent assistance from reaching the rebels and by seizing and handing over to the Czar fleeing rebels who sought refuge in Prussia.

Bismarck was now free to deal with Austria. In 1863, Denmark had tried to assimilate the duchies of Schleswig and Holstein into her own administration, although the union between Denmark and the duchies was merely a personal and dynastic one. The majority of the people of Holstein were Germans; most of the population of Schleswig was Danish. In 1864, Prussia joined Austria in a brief war which wrested both duchies from Denmark. Bismarck then made their joint administration by the conquerors the occasion of a quarrel with his erstwhile partner. Since speed of attack would be of the essence in a war with Austria lest the other powers be tempted to interfere, the General Staff, headed by Helmuth von Moltke (1800-91), made careful preparations. The first railroads had been laid in Prussia with military ends in view. Moltke added a few short lines which would make it possible to mass troops at vital points on the border of Bohemia; the movement of troops would be coordinated by telegraph from a desk in Berlin.

The General now waited for a signal from Bismarck that Austria was without allies. Great Britain had dynastic ties with Prussia: the eldest daughter of Queen Victoria—the Princess Royal—had married the heir to the throne of the Hohenzollerns. British free-traders approved of the Prussian *Zollverein* and the prospective consolidation of Germany. To Napoleon III, in October 1865, Bismarck hinted that Prussia might acquiesce if the French were later to detach a western slice of the German Confederation, or even seize Belgium. (Napoleon, however, wagered on Austria's strength and on the hope that he might collect his compensation when the two powers were locked in combat.) Bismarck arranged a trade treaty between Italy and the *Zollverein* and then an alliance, in April 1866, which bound Italy to join Prussia if she went to war with Austria within three months. Bismarck promptly marched troops into Austrian-administered Holstein and provoked Francis Joseph into declaring war in June 1866. The Diet of the German confederation protested Bismarck's actions, and Prussia withdrew from the confederation. Saxony, Hanover, and several south German states came to the assistance of Austria, but their military movements were sluggish.

Prussia was ready to seize the initiative. Three convergent railways sped her troops to Bohemia. Austrian troops had the use of only one railway, and most of them marched on foot. The use of the new breech-loading gun made Prussian fire swifter. At Königgrätz in Bohemia, the Prussians outnumbered and defeated the enemy. The whole campaign—known as the "Seven Weeks' War"—was over by the end of July. The speed of the Prussian victory astounded Europe. Italy obtained Venetia, but Bismarck exacted no Hapsburg territory, hoping to earn the future friendship of Austria.

In the Hapsburg Empire, the Austrian defeat at Königgrätz was a victory for the Hungarian upper classes. In 1867, one year after the battle, Francis Joseph agreed that Hungary was to be governed and administered independently of the Austrian, or western, half of the monarchy. The connection between the two halves was to be largely dynastic. Francis Joseph was to be emperor in Austria and king in Hungary, and there were to be only three common ministries: those of foreign affairs, finance, and the army. There was to be complete freedom of the market in each half. Within a constitutional framework, the old institutions were to be preserved. Suffrage was highly restricted. In each parliament the power of the landed gentry was to be superior to that of the middle classes. This predominance of noblemen and landholders implied a national predominance also, particularly in Hungary, for the upper classes were largely Hungarian whereas the bulk of the peasantry was Slav or Rumanian. In Austria, German noblemen shared their power, though on unequal terms, with the German upper middle classes and with the Polish magnates in Galicia. The German language became symbolic of their superior status in political and administrative affairs. In Hungary the magnates maintained a more exclusive control over the state, public education, and the bureaucracy. Croatians, Slovaks, and Rumanians were jauntily disregarded and dominated, and the use of their language was discouraged.

While defeat compelled the Hapsburgs to loosen their grip on Hungary, victory enabled the Hohenzollerns to tighten theirs on Germany. For Bismarck's consolidation of Germany was Prussian rather than national. The Polish regions in the east and the Danish areas in the north were included as part of Prussia, but the German provinces of the Hapsburgs were excluded, in order to ensure Prussia's hegemony in the rest of Germany. The southern kingdoms of Baden, Württemberg, and Bavaria, which leaned toward Austria, were left independent for the moment. In 1867 Bismarck organized the North German Confederation, which included all the states that had sided with Austria—Hanover, Electoral Hesse, Nassau, and Frankfurt—and incorporated them into the Prussian administration. Prussia now comprised three fourths of northern Germany. She pressed the remaining northern states—twenty-one minuscule principalities—into the Confederation.

The constitution of the North German Confederation was ostensibly federal, liberal, and democratic. The functions of local administration, justice, and education were left to the individual states. The lower house of the federal legislature, the *Reichstag*, was elected by universal manhood suffrage and apportioned by population. No law or budget was valid without its approval. (Theoretically, the *Reichstag* could have used its control of the purse to increase its power at the expense of the monarchy. But the experience of the Prussian *Landtag* was hardly reassuring; as a reward for his successful war, it had just agreed to "forgive and forget" Bismarck's illegal collection of taxes.) Laws could be initiated only by the *Bundesrat*, the federal council, whose discussions were secret and whose members were appointed by monarchs of the member states. Of the forty-three delegates to the *Bundesrat*, Prussia had seventeen while all the other members together had twenty-six. With the help of several small partners, which was always available, Prussia controlled the *Bundesrat*. The Confederation thus contravened the essential principle of federalism—equality among the members—which is assured in the American Constitution by the equal representation of the states in the Senate.

**Political Consolidation
of Austria-Hungary, 1867-68**

Showing principal nationalities
G = Germans

The Prussian king, as permanent president of the federation, appointed the federal chancellor and could remove him at will. Control of the army and of foreign affairs was in the hands, not of the federal legislature, but of the king-president. The executive was responsible neither to the *Reichstag* nor to the *Bundesrat,* and his actions could not be controlled by them. The constitution was drafted by Bismarck—who was, of course, named chancellor—and approved by the King of Prussia and the other monarchs before it was submitted, as a *fait accompli,* to the various state legislatures and the *Reichstag.* There was no thought of submitting it to a popular vote.

As chancellor, Bismarck held an extraordinary position. It was not the king-president but the chancellor who appointed the federal ministers. Since all seventeen of Prussia's votes in the *Bundesrat* were cast as a unit, on instruction from the Prussian government, and since Bismarck was also Prime Minister of Prussia, the Chancellor controlled the council. The king-president could remove the chancellor, but he could not alter the character of the office. In the hands of an insistent and strong man, its power could become virtually absolute. In the hands of a moderate minister, it would tempt the king-president to participate actively in government. By tailoring the chancellorship to his capacity for manipulating the various elements in the state and to his ambition to hold the lead rein, Bismarck satisfied his own drive for power, but he also exposed the constitution to the perils of divided authority.

The Bismarckian system was, in its essentials, complete. Only the adherence of the south German states was needed to confirm its strength and security.

The Franco-Prussian War and the Paris Commune

The speedy triumph of Prussia without a countervailing gain for France was a blow to the prestige of Napoleon III. The opposition to his regime at home became militant. In 1868 and 1869, the Emperor responded to the pressure of strikes, demonstrations, and popular criticism by enlarging the freedom of the press and the power of parliament in framing the budget. But these measures only whetted the appetites of liberals and democrats. Napoleon could not, without a virtual abdication, grant the full freedom and parliamentary control that alone would satisfy them. The conventional remedy for domestic tension was a foreign success. Napoleon tried to secure a railway concession that would tie Belgium closer to France: in vain. He tried to obtain Luxembourg: in vain. In May 1870 he sought to refresh his domestic power by holding a plebiscite to endorse his concessions since 1860. The plebiscite yielded the usual results: seven and a half million voters expressed approval and only one and a half million disapproval. But the significance of plebiscites under dictatorial rule was heavily discounted. The fact was that the regime was growing weaker daily.

This was a situation made to Bismarck's hand. He needed a "national" war in order to persuade the south German states to merge in a German union that seemed to them indistinguishable from a Prussian empire, and he needed it soon. There had been negotiations for Austrian assistance to France in case of war, but there was as yet no formal alliance. Bismarck decided to pick a quarrel with Napoleon's government quickly. In Spain, a revolution in 1868 had deposed Queen Isabella II (1833-68), and the new government was trying to find a new monarch. In early 1870 Bismarck gave his support to the candidacy of a Hohenzollern Prince, fully aware that France could not tolerate a dynastic connection between her western and eastern neighbors. When the French government protested, King William agreed to withdraw the candidacy and nearly spoiled the game for Bismarck. But the French, eager for a diplomatic victory, demanded of the King, who was vacationing at the watering place of Ems, a promise that the candidacy would not be renewed in the future. William returned a curt but not provocative refusal. Bismarck, however, would not give Napoleon a diplomatic triumph or his King a pacific solution. He then published an altered version of a dispatch from Ems describing the King's exchange with the French ambassador to make it appear that France had made insolent demands and had been insulted in turn. This was calculated to enrage both German and French "patriots."

Thereupon, in July 1870, Napoleon declared war. The world believed that he had made imperialistic demands and that France was the more aggressive power. To the south German states Bismarck divulged an indiscreet memorandum in which Napoleon betrayed his covetousness for German territory. Bismarck appeared in the role of the patriotic defender of national territory, and the states offered military cooperation. Russia's neutrality was bought with an

EUROPE

CARTE DE L'EUROPE EN 1870

"*Angleterre, isolée, peste de rage et en oublie presque l'Irlande qu'elle tient en laisse. L'Espagne fume, appuyée sur le Portugal. — La France repousse les envahissements de la Prusse, qui avance une main sur la Hollande l'autre sur l'Autriche. L'Italie, aussi, dit à Bismarck: Ôte donc les pieds de là. La Corse et la Sardaigne... un vrai Gavroche qui rit de tout. Le Danemark, qui a perdu ses jambes dans le Holstein, espère les reprendre. La Turquie d'Europe bâille et s'éveille. La Turquie d'Asie aspire la fumée de son narguilé. La Suède fait des bonds de panthère; et la Russie ressemble à un croquemitaine qui voudrait remplir sa hotte.*"

An animated French map of the international troubles of Europe in 1870. The "degrees of longitude" are measured on a rifle. The caption explains the state of affairs: "Isolated, England fumes with rage and almost forgets Ireland, whom she holds on a leash. Spain smokes, while leaning heavily on Portugal. France repulses the invasions of Prussia, who stretches one hand toward Holland and the other toward Austria. Italy also says to Bismarck: Take your feet away from there. Corsica and Sardinia . . . a regular urchin who laughs at everything that is going on. Denmark which has lost her legs in Holstein, hopes to get them back. European Turkey yawns and awakens. Asiatic Turkey puffs on her Oriental pipe. Sweden leaps like a panther, and Russia looks like a bogie-man who wishes to fill up his basket [usually, according to legend, with bad little boys]."

agreement to support her denunciation of the clauses of the Treaty of Paris of 1856 which forbade her to build naval power in the Black Sea. Great Britain was reassured by Bismarck's promise to respect the neutrality of Belgium. Austria moved slowly, counting on the strength of the French army as France had

The Prussian Consolidation of Germany 1864-1871

Boundary of the German Confederation, 1815 ━━━━ Kingdom of Prussia, 1864

Annexations and conquests from Den- Joined Prussia to form
mark, Austria, and other German states N. German Confederation, 1867

Annexations from France, 1870-71 United with N. German Confederation,
                                         1871, to form German Empire

Boundary of the German Empire, 1871 ∙∙∙∙∙∙∙∙∙∙∙

counted on hers four years earlier. Prussia's enemy had once more been isolated. While the half-prepared French army entered the Rhineland, three Prussian armies, which outnumbered the French by 100,000 men, sped on strategic railways to converge at Sedan, in northern France. Their superiority of numbers and staff work brought rapid victories. Surrounded, the Emperor himself surrendered with 80,000 men on September 2. Bonapartism never recovered from this anticlimax; appropriately, it fell on the battlefield, where it had first risen.

A revolution promptly broke out in Paris, and the successful mob obliged the reluctant Assembly to proclaim a republic—the third. While two German armies besieged Paris, Bismarck negotiated with the south German states for their entry into the Confederation of 1867. On January 18, 1871, while Paris was starving and struggling desperately to hold out, a mass of gilded uniforms met in the Hall of Mirrors in the palace of Louis XIV at Versailles. The Kings of Bavaria, Württemberg, and Baden hailed William I of Prussia as German Emperor. Ten days later, the French capital capitulated.

The conquerors allowed the French to hold an election in order to provide a government that would be empowered to sign a peace. Conservative French groups, fearing a renewal of revolutionary activity, pressed for a quick peace, at almost any price. Republicans and democrats urged resistance both to the invader and to the conservative groups. The majority of peasants voted for the peace-minded conservatives—royalists, Orleanists, and Bonapartists.

The National Assembly met in Bordeaux on February 13. It declared the Emperor "responsible for the ruin, invasion, and dismemberment of France" and formally deposed him. (After being kept a prisoner by the Germans, Napoleon settled in England, where he died in 1873.) The Orleanist Adolphe Thiers was elected as head of the executive power. On March 1 the Assembly accepted Bismarck's harsh terms. They provided for a huge indemnity—two hundred million francs—the support of an occupation army that would stay in France until the sum was paid, and the cession of Alsace and part of Lorraine. Lorraine had been French for a century and Alsace, although its inhabitants were bilingual, had been French for more than two centuries. The populations of these provinces did not consider themselves German, but they were not consulted. Even after Waterloo, the powers had not touched the territory of France, seizing only lands that the revolutionists and Napoleon had recently conquered. Bismarck gave military reasons for the seizure, and they seemed to him adequate.

The terms of peace deepened the cleavage within France. The radicals suspected the conservatives of treachery, feeling that the war had been conducted with one eye on the Prussian army and another on the French republicans. Paris had been poorly defended although its garrison was large. General Bazaine had surrendered at the decisive battle of Metz under suspicious circumstances, with 173,000 men. The National Assembly indefinitely postponed discussion of the form the government was to take but was obviously unfriendly to the idea of a republic. Social distress increased the political unrest. In the spring of 1871 unemployment increased, and the Assembly refused to prolong the moratorium on debts and rents that had been proclaimed during the war.

On March 18 the people of Paris rose, supported by the National Guard, which the Germans had failed to disarm. Thiers's government fled to Versailles. A week later, by universal manhood suffrage, the capital elected a general council, or Commune, consisting of moderates and liberals with a sprinkling of socialists. Alongside the Commune, a committee of the National Guard exerted a partial authority. The Commune repudiated the Thiers regime, abolished conscription, and revived the militia. It established secular education, remitted the rents of the last critical months, and extended the moratorium on commercial debts. Its policy was radical but not socialist, as was also true of the revolutionary communes set up at Lyons, Marseilles, and other cities in the south.

349

This did not prevent Thiers from raising the cry of "red." Prussia rushed to the assistance of the deposed conservative government. While Bismarck's troops held Paris in a vise, Thiers attacked the suburbs. Barricades were erected and savage fighting developed. After two months of struggle, the Commune expired in "Bloody Week" (May 21-28). During the period of fighting, the Communards had executed many hostages, including the Archbishop of Paris; the victors retaliated by killing, deporting, or imprisoning an estimated twenty thousand Parisians, among them the most active radicals and socialists.

On the Continent liberalism and conservatism had reached a compromise of their differences. The sword had decided the character and the extent of the compromise. Across the Atlantic Ocean there had also been an appeal to the sword, to settle the question of Negro slavery and national unity.

17. *The American Civil War*

The roots of the Civil War lay deep in the American past. The introduction of Negro slavery by the colonial empires of Europe, the rise of cotton culture in response to the demands of the modern textile industry, the avid expansion of the United States in the forties, the uncertain line between the jurisdiction of the federal government and that of the states, the divergent development of the various sections—such was the tangle of events and circumstances that led to the greatest crisis of the Republic. In this tangle were strands of movements that coursed through the whole Western world. The conflict between the federal principle and the centralized state, the differences between industrial and agrarian areas, the advance of steam power, and the drive for domestic free trade within large markets precipitated wars in Italy and Germany—not to mention events farther afield—as well as in the United States.

The movement to emancipate slaves and serfs had been gathering momentum throughout the Western world. Great Britain had abolished the African slave trade in 1807 and the United States followed suit in the next year. At the Congress of Vienna in 1815 the European powers agreed to cooperate to stop the African trade. The French Revolution put an end to serfdom in Western Europe, and Napoleon ended it in Poland. Prussia abolished serfdom in 1807, and in 1833 Great Britain ended slavery in her colonies. The Revolution of 1848 achieved the abolition of slavery in the French colonies and of serfdom in the Austrian Empire and parts of the Ottoman Empire. Late in the fifties, the Czar prepared to free the peasants of Russia. This was done in 1861. The last bastion of bondage in the Western world was crumbling. Except for Brazil, the United States remained the only large Western country where slavery existed.

Slavery and Conservatism

In the early fifties, when reactionary policies prevailed in Continental Europe, restrictive and antiforeign movements came to the fore in American politics. A group of "patriots" launched the American party, which came to be called the "Know Nothing" party because its members were instructed to maintain secrecy about the organization. The party proposed to restrict the rights of immigrants, to prolong the period of naturalization from five to fourteen years, and to work for the continued monopoly of Protestants of English origin in elected offices. This movement was directed against all immigrants but particularly Irish Catholics, who, fleeing from the famines of the forties, were arriving at the extraordinary rate of almost a hundred thousand a year.

In 1854 the Know Nothing party elected a large number of members to Congress and state legislatures in the Northeast, where most of the immigrants were settling. It won control of Massachusetts, where it undertook a grotesque investigation into the morals of the monastic orders. But two years later its presidential candidate, Millard Fillmore, won only the small state of Delaware, although he gathered 875,000 votes throughout the country out of a total of 4,050,000 votes cast. The party had been split by the slavery issue: Know Nothing leaders in the Northeast gave their support to the newly formed Republican party. Antiforeignism, along with all other questions, was absorbed by the all-embracing issue of Negro slavery.

This issue had become acute after the Mexican War of 1846-48. Were conquests from Mexico—Texas, California, and the intervening Southwest—to be organized as free or as slave states? In 1848 former President Martin Van Buren (1782-1862) became the candidate of the new Free-Soil party, which advocated the exclusion of slavery from the new territories. He lost the election to General Zachary Taylor (1784-1850), the Whig candidate, but, by the Compromise of 1850, Congress admitted California as a free state (and, incidentally, abolished the slave trade in the District of Columbia). However, the Compromise also provided for the organization of territorial governments in the rest of the Mexican cession without any stipulation concerning slavery, and it stiffened the penalties for citizens who aided Negroes to flee from their masters.

The proslavery interests made further gains. The Missouri Compromise of 1820 had banned slavery forever in the Louisiana Territory north of 36°30'. In 1854, however, Senator Stephen A. Douglas (1813-61) of Illinois proposed, and Congress passed, the Kansas-Nebraska Act, which provided that the Nebraska country should be divided into two territories—Kansas and Nebraska—whose citizens would decide the issue for themselves. The result of this reversal of the Missouri Compromise was open war between free-soilers and slaveholders, who rushed into Kansas and set up rival governments. (It was assumed that the population of Nebraska, in the northern part of the area, would inevitably choose to ban slavery.) Some two hundred lives were lost in "Bleeding Kansas." Congress, unable to decide which government to recognize, did not admit Kansas as a state until 1861. (Nebraska was admitted in 1867.)

In 1857 the Supreme Court, under Chief Justice Roger Taney (1777-1864), threw its weight into the scales for slavery. In 1834 Dred Scott, a Negro slave, had been taken by his master from Missouri, a slave state, to Illinois, a state that had been carved out of the territory in which the Ordinance of 1787 had forbidden slavery. He was then taken to the Wisconsin Territory, where slavery had been forbidden by the Missouri Compromise. In 1846 Scott sued for his

freedom in the Missouri courts, arguing that he had been automatically emancipated by living in a free state and a free territory. The Supreme Court, on
appeal, denied his plea on the ground that his status as a slave was determined
by the laws of Missouri and asserted—thirty-seven years after its passage—that
the Missouri Compromise had been unconstitutional to begin with since Congress had no power to legislate on slavery, even in territories under its direct
control. Such power, the Court held, would in effect deprive a citizen—the
slaveholder—of his property—the slave—and therefore violated the Fifth
Amendment. The decision had the effect of aggravating an old wound. Northerners were alarmed by the danger not only of the spread of slavery, but of federal interference with the decision of free states to keep slavery outside their own
borders. For if slaveholders brought their "property" into free states, it would
become the duty of the federal government to protect that "property." The shoe
was now on the other foot: the North would now have to defend its right to be
free within its own states. Northern states passed "personal liberty" laws to protect Negro fugitives. The sentimental classic of Negro misery, Harriet Beecher
Stowe's *Uncle Tom's Cabin*, was read and wept over by hundreds of thousands of
Americans, and almost as many Europeans.

In October 1859 John Brown, a radical abolitionist who had been active in
the Kansas broils, invaded Virginia with a small band and attempted to seize
the United States arsenal at Harper's Ferry, with the object of distributing arms
in order to start an insurrection of the slaves. Several people were killed during
the raid. The state of Virginia hanged Brown for treason and murder. Conservative Northerners deplored the raid, but antislavery groups hailed Brown as a
martyred hero and redoubled their demands for the immediate freeing of the
slaves. The abolitionists were unpopular even in the North, and there were instances of mob violence against them. Many Northern businessmen and financiers who had close dealings with the South feared that any attempt to bring
matters to a head would endanger the economy of the Union. Both principal
parties—Democratic and Whig—had Southern as well as Northern supporters
and were chary of dividing their ranks by taking a strong stand on slavery.

If Northern leadership was cautious, Southern leadership was obstinate.
For a generation, the outstanding Southern politician had been John C. Calhoun. Before he died, in 1850, he developed a political doctrine that pivoted on
slavery. He felt that Nature condemned the Negroes to permanent inferiority
and that slavery was at the basis of great states and civilizations in the past.
Calhoun carried the doctrine of states' rights to extremes. He proposed that all
federal laws must be approved by the "concurrent majority" of the area or interest affected by them as well as by the majority of Congress, or the nation as
a whole. In other words, every group should have a veto power over federal legislation affecting it. Calhoun ended by proposing that two Presidents be elected,
one from the North and one from the South. One of them would be in charge of
domestic matters, the other of foreign affairs; which was to handle domestic and
which foreign matters was to be determined by lot. But each President would
have a separate veto over all laws. Slavery would then be quite secure.

Although few Southerners went as far as the doctrinaire Calhoun in drawing   *353* the logical implications of slaveholding, his uncompromising spirit proved contagious. Most Southern planters were content to stand on the right of the states to manage their own affairs without interference by the federal government and to preserve a strong position within that government to make sure that no interference occurred. On the notion that attack is the best defense, Southern apologists for slavery became radical critics of the capitalist industrialism of the free states of the North. Like the Marxists, they claimed that capitalism divided society into contending economic classes and that the proletarians were worse off than slaves. A Virginia planter, George Fitzhugh (1806-81), wrote a series of economic treatises arguing that slavery was perfect communism since the masters took responsibility for their wards, rewarding them not according to their labor but according to their need. Some Southerners even advised Northern factory owners to improve their system by turning their workers into legal slaves. Fitzhugh's position on Old World issues was consistent with his view of slavery: he asserted that the English Crown and Church were the natural protectors of the masses, as the Southern slaveowners were the natural protectors of the Negroes; English capitalists, like their counterparts in the American North, ground the faces of the poor; the House of Commons, a creature of the capitalists, was therefore a nefarious institution.

Sectional Division and Civil War

The decisive developments in the fifties were the greater growth in wealth and population of the free states as compared with the slave states and the division of the political parties along sectional lines. The Northern states had almost all the iron, coal, and copper resources developed in the country. The bulk of the industries and railroad lines were concentrated in the North, and the vast majority of new immigrants settled there. In 1860 the combined population of the Northern and Western states was twenty-two million; that of the South was nine and a half million. So long, however, as the leading political parties represented both Southern and Northern voters, the issue of slavery could not be resolved definitively. The rapprochement of North and West changed the relations of the parties.

Western farmers had long favored a liberal land policy, and Northeastern industrialists craved a protective tariff. For years the two regions had been divided on the question of centralization. The conservatives of the North wished to strengthen the authority and resources of the federal government while the Westerners wished to preserve local autonomy. It became clear, however, that the issue of slavery could not be settled without asserting the federal power. New railroads had brought the Northern and Western states into close commercial contact. Powerful interests in the two regions struck an alliance. In 1856 the Westerners endorsed the proposed tariff, with its implication of an active federal authority, and the Northern conservatives accepted free homesteads on the frontier. This compromise became the basis of the new Republican party, which

North vs. South, 1860

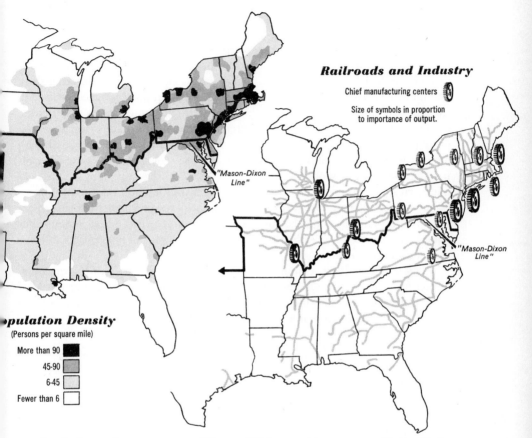

Railroads and Industry

Chief manufacturing centers

Size of symbols in proportion to importance of output.

"Mason-Dixon Line"

"Mason-Dixon Line"

Population Density
(Persons per square mile)

More than 90	■
45-90	
6-45	
Fewer than 6	□

consisted of a motley assortment of former Whigs, antislavery men, Know Nothings, industrialists, and farmers. The party platform opposed the extension of slavery but did not mention emancipation. The first Republican candidate for President, the frontier hero John C. Frémont (1813-90), lost the election of 1856 to Democrat James Buchanan (1791-1868), but he won nearly all the states of the North and Northwest.

The division between sections became deeper during the presidential election of 1860. The Northern Democrats supported free homesteads in the West and "popular sovereignty"—that is, permitting the settlers to decide for themselves the issue of slavery in their own states. The Southern Democrats feared the effect of these policies on the future of slaveholding. The two factions nominated two candidates for President, Stephen A. Douglas of Illinois and John C. Breckinridge (1821-75) of Kentucky, respectively. The Republican candidate was Abraham Lincoln (1809-65), also of Illinois. The remnants of the Whigs and Know Nothings nominated John Bell of Tennessee under the banner of the Constitutional Union party. The division of the Democrats, who together polled

360,000 more votes than the Republicans, resulted in the victory of Lincoln. Except for California, Lincoln carried only Northern states.

The outcome of the election underlined the need for a practical compromise if North and South were not to sever their bonds. Lincoln regarded slavery as immoral and inconsistent with the principles of natural rights. In 1858, when he ran unsuccessfully for senator, he asserted that " 'A house divided against itself cannot stand.' I believe this government cannot endure permanently half-slave and half-free." He was, however, more moderate than his eloquence suggested. Lincoln had entered politics as a Whig, supporting federal policies to stimulate economic activity. As a lawyer, he often represented railroad companies, the principal object of enterprise, investment, and speculation of the day. Although he was determined to prevent the further extension of slavery, he saw no prospect of abolishing it soon. He had not yet given up the hope that enlightened Southern states would voluntarily abolish the institution and that financial provision would be made for transporting the former slaves to settlements apart from white men, in tropical American islands or in Africa. Like many other Americans, Lincoln was willing to disburse federal funds to help the states compensate the slaveowners.

In December 1860, a compromise suggested by Senator John J. Crittenden of Kentucky proposed, among other things, that the dividing line of the Missouri Compromise—36°30′—be re-established as the line between slavery and freedom. This was acceptable to Southern legislators, but, since it meant that slavery was to be permitted not only in new states south of that line but also in territories previously closed to it, the Senate, on Lincoln's advice, rejected it. The crucial issue, then, was not the guarantee of slavery in states where it already existed but its possible extension. On this issue Southern leaders were in no mood to compromise. And they refused to abide by the results of an election that had gone against them. In the four months that elapsed between Lincoln's election and his inauguration in March 1861, seven states of the lower South—South Carolina, Mississippi, Florida, Alabama, Georgia, Louisiana, and Texas—repudiated the federal Constitution and seceded from the Union.

In his inaugural address, Lincoln pleaded with the South to acknowledge the principle of majority rule. One could not, he argued, expect a country to be unanimous, and the refusal of a minority to abide by the decisions of the majority could only lead to "anarchy or despotism." What issues would be easier to settle if the North and South separated? "Can aliens make treaties easier than friends can make laws? Can treaties be more faithfully observed between aliens than laws can among friends?" The "only substantial dispute" was that "one section of our country believes that slavery is *right* and ought to be extended, while the other believes it is *wrong* and ought not to be extended." But Lincoln assured the Southerners that his administration would not endanger the ownership of slaves where it already existed. "The government," he closed, "will not assail *you*. You have no conflict without being yourselves the aggressors." There were Southern leaders who were equally concerned that the South should not be the first to strike. Senator Alexander Stephens (1812-83) of Georgia, for example, opposed secession on the ground that it would put the South morally in the wrong. (He later became Vice President of the Confederacy.) But such voices were drowned by the extremists. South Carolina, which had been the first state to secede, again took the lead. On April 12, 1861, its soldiers opened fire on Fort Sumter, a federal arsenal in Charleston harbor, to prevent President Lincoln from sending supplies to the garrison. The fort returned the fire but was forced to surrender. The Civil War was on. Four states which had hesitated to leave the Union—Virginia, Arkansas, North Carolina, and Tennessee—now did so. Eleven states had seceded, while twice that number remained loyal to the Union.

The seceding states formed a new government, the Confederate States of America, and elected Senator Jefferson Davis (1808-89) of Mississippi as its President. The framers of the Constitution of 1787, hoping for gradual emancipation, had avoided the word "slaves" (they used "other persons") in stipulating that three fifths of the Negroes be counted in determining the number of representatives a state was to have in the lower house of Congress. The constitution of the Southern Confederacy asserted that slaves were property. It forbade the Confederate government to pass any law "denying or impairing the right of property in Negro slaves." It provided that citizens "shall have the right of transit and sojourn in any State of this Confederacy, with their slaves and other property; and the right of property in said slaves shall not be thereby impaired." The rules of laissez-faire economics were written into the constitution. The Confederate government was forbidden to grant bounties, to levy "any duties or taxes on importations from foreign nations," to "promote or foster any branch of industry," and to appropriate money "for any internal improvements intended to facilitate commerce." The Constitution of the United States did not provide for the acquisition and permanent administration of colonies, and in the Northwest Ordinance of 1787 the Republic had banished slavery from the territories under federal control. In contrast, the Confederate constitution declared that the government "may acquire new territory," and that everywhere slavery shall be "recognized and protected by Congress and the territorial government."

The South could afford to stand on the defensive; that was sufficient to show that it would not be coerced. But since the task of the North was to subdue the rebellious states, its strategy had to be aggressive. The objective had to be the West, whence the South drew much of its man power and supplies, and the lower Mississippi, whose control by the South blocked an important artery of trade for the Midwest. There was, however, too much division and hesitancy in the North to permit the adoption of an offensive strategy. The first skirmishes were in the area between two political objectives: the District of Columbia and Richmond, the newly chosen capital of the Confederacy.

The commander of the Northern armies in the East, General George B. McClellan, regarded the war as a gentlemen's duel directed toward a friendly compromise. He wished to concentrate the Northern forces in the East and conduct a war that avoided any appearance of conquest. He was opposed to any

President Abraham Lincoln visiting General George B. McClellan and his staff on the battlefield of Antietam, October 4, 1862. EASTMAN

interference with civilian activities in rebel territory and particularly with the institution of slavery. He warned President Lincoln that "a declaration of radical views will rapidly disintegrate our present armies."

The first year of fighting exposed the inadequacy of McClellan's strategy. The Southern armies won a succession of victories that placed Washington in danger, although they could not secure the prize, largely because of the Northern naval blockade, which prevented the South from exporting cotton and importing munitions and other supplies from Europe. The initial defeats of the North gave the impression—not only to the Southern leaders but also to foreign countries—that the South could not be coerced.

European Rulers and Peoples Divided on the War

Most European governments and ruling groups sympathized with the South. The British Prime Minister, Lord Palmerston (1784-1865), "desired the severance [of the Union] as the diminution of a dangerous power," particularly to British control of Canada. The Chancellor of the Exchequer, W. E. Gladstone (1809-98), declared that Southern leaders "have made an army; they are making, it appears, a navy; and they have made what is more than either, they have made a nation." Benjamin Disraeli, the leader of British Conservatives, declared that "the collapse of republican institutions must tell immensely in favor of aristocracy." Thomas Carlyle, an advocate of "hero worship" and leadership by the great, looked "with pity and awe . . . on the consummation of Constitutional Palaver and Universal Suffrage, and on poor Yankee brothers tearing one another in pieces about Nothing at all." Similar views prevailed among Continental conservatives. Otto von Bismarck, for example, wrote that he "instinctively" sympathized with the slaveholders, "as the aristocratic party."

Both France and Great Britain hinted at mediation or intervention. Emperor Napoleon III welcomed what he saw might be an opportunity to revive a French-oriented empire in America. He urged Great Britain to join him in an attack on the United States. Britain refused but agreed to assist him in a less direct offensive. In 1860 a liberal government under Benito Juarez (1806-72) had obtained control of Mexico, separated church and state, confiscated clerical properties, and suppressed the numerous religious orders. Prolonged domestic strife had weakened and impoverished the country, and Mexico suspended payment of the interest on the foreign debt, held largely by French and British investors. The loans, be it said, were highly profitable to the Mexican politicians and European financiers who had negotiated them. In the case of one loan of fifteen million dollars, only a million and a half ever reached the Mexican treasury. Napoleon III proposed to use Mexico's failure to pay interest as an excuse to seize the country. The United States was in no position to interpose anything but a verbal veto.

In December 1861, an army consisting mostly of French troops but containing also English and Spanish detachments landed in Mexico and occupied the port of Veracruz. Mexico promised to resume interest payments, and the

An American view of the delight with which the dynastic heads of the Old World anticipated the break-up of the Republic upon hearing the first news of the secession of the South. Among the figures caricatured are, from left to right, Pope Pius IX, Queen Victoria, Napoleon III, William I of Prussia, and Franz Joseph of Austria. From Harper's Weekly, *1860.*

WHAT THE TYRANTS OF THE OLD WORLD THINK OF SECESSION.
"Oh! ain't we Sorry!!!"

English and Spanish troops withdrew. But the French army marched into the interior, despite the feeble protests of the United States, and in June 1863 seized the capital, Mexico City. Conservative Mexicans proclaimed as emperor the Hapsburg Archduke Maximilian, a brother of Emperor Francis Joseph of Austria. In effect, however, Maximilian was a French agent.

The governments of France and Great Britain reflected the attitude of the dominant classes in Europe toward the United States as representing the principle of democracy. However, European liberals, democrats, and radicals supported the Northern cause. They were placed on the defensive at first by the victories of the South and by Lincoln's repeated insistence that slavery was not at issue. In 1862, for example, Lincoln asserted that his "paramount object in this struggle" was "to save the Union," not to destroy slavery. "If I could save the Union without freeing any slaves, I would do it; and if I could do it by freeing some, and leaving others slave, I would also do that. What I do about slavery and the colored race, I do because I believe it helps to save the Union; and what I forbear, I forbear also because I do not believe it would help to save the Union."

Nevertheless European liberals, like Northern abolitionists, felt that the position of the Negro was involved in the war, and the position of the masses of Europe as well. John Stuart Mill raised his influential voice for the defeat of the South. "It will be desirable," he wrote,

> . . . to take thought beforehand what are to be our own future relations with a new Power professing the principles of Attila and Genghis Khan as the foundations of its Constitution. . . . Unless we abandon the principles we have for two generations consistently professed and acted on, we should be at war with the new Confederacy within five years about the African slave trade. . . . The time might come when the barbarous and barbarising Power . . . would require a general crusade of civilized Europe, to extinguish the mischief which it has allowed . . . to rise up in the midst of our civilization.

Karl Marx regarded the war as a conflict to the death between "the system of slavery and the system of free labor." English workers in general supported the North, although the English textile industry depended on Southern cotton. A potent appeal was made by John Bright, the leader of the movement in England, for broader suffrage. At large popular meetings, Bright declared that the cause of European democracy was one with that of the American North. "Privilege," he declared,

> has beheld an afflicting spectacle for many years past. It has beheld thirty millions of men, happy and prosperous, without emperor, without king, without the surroundings of a court, without nobles, except such as are made by eminence in intellect and virtue, without State bishops and State priests, . . . without great armies and great navies, without great debt and without great taxes. Privilege has shuddered at what might happen to old

Europe if this grand experiment should succeed. . . . In the United States there has been an open door for every man—and millions have entered into it, and have found rest. . . .

My countrymen, who work for your living, remember this: there will be one wild shriek of freedom to startle all mankind if that American Republic should be overthrown.

Emancipation and the Strategy of Grant

The failure to bring the war to an end quickly led to a change of policy: both North and South were forced to draft men and to seek new sources of finance. The North now reaped the advantages of its greater population, wealth, and steam power. Twenty-two of the thirty-three states—two thirds of the total —remained loyal to the Union. The more numerous railway lines of the North enabled Northern generals to concentrate troops faster than could the Southerners.

In Lincoln's own party, a growing group of leaders—the Radical Republicans—insisted on a more energetic military strategy and on the immediate emancipation of the Negroes. Beginning in the spring of 1862, the President, now pushed and now seconded by the Radicals, gave the war a sharper turn. The powers of the federal government were expanded, particularly those of the executive, which, under the Constitution, held the military as well as the civil reins. The army had originally been recruited by volunteering and appeals to the states, but by 1862 volunteering had all but ceased, particularly after military defeats. Early in 1863 a conscription law was passed: men between 20 and 45 years of age were made liable to service, although exemptions were made, notably for married men and for those who could pay $300 or provide a substitute. More and more items were made subject to taxation. The President was empowered to commandeer railroads and telegraph lines. The Habeas Corpus Act was suspended in certain districts, even though the constitutional requirement for suspension was not always present. But although Lincoln was now and then driven to assume unusual powers, he had no dictatorial appetites. By using his authority sparingly, by keeping largely within constitutional limits, and by seeking Congressional approval for his actions (after the fact, it is true), Lincoln was able to wield wide powers without permanently injuring the rights of the individual.

The needs of the government for revenue speeded up the concessions to industry and finance that the Republican party had promised to its wealthier supporters. In quick stages the tariff was increased until the duties stood at 47 percent ad valorem. The government granted large subsidies to entrepreneurs to build transcontinental railroads. Capitalism was also encouraged by army contracts and bounties. The result was a striking efflorescence of industry. Finance was stimulated by the marketing of huge issues of bonds. Many big fortunes in both industry and finance were founded in the dark and often corrupt days of the war. At the same time, the government made the greatest concession to small farmers in American history. For a generation agrarian reformers had urged the free distribution of land to actual settlers. As late as 1860 President Buchanan had vetoed a bill embodying this demand. In 1862 Congress approved and Lincoln signed the Homestead Act, which provided that any settler could obtain 160 acres of Western land for $10—a fee for the surveying. All he had to do was to settle on the plot and cultivate it for at least five years. Although most of the land in the West was acquired by speculators, railroad companies, and other business groups, millions of acres provided homesteads for independent farmers.

Finally, the government repudiated the principle of slavery. In deference to Southern interests, the United States had not agreed to cooperate with the European states in suppressing the African slave trade. It now undertook to do so in a treaty concluded in April 1862 with Great Britain. The same month Congress abolished slavery in the District of Columbia, compensating the owners at $300 a slave. Slavery in the federal territories was abolished without compensation in June of that year. Congress promised financial help to loyal states which voluntarily ended the system and appropriated funds to experiment with the voluntary colonization of former slaves in Haiti or Liberia.

Efforts to start a colony failed. Lincoln's plea to the loyal border states to abolish slavery, with compensation provided by the federal government, fell on deaf ears. Using his prerogative as commander-in-chief of the army, and claiming military necessity, Lincoln issued the Emancipation Proclamation. He announced on September 22, 1862, that on the following January 1 he would proclaim the freedom of the slaves in rebellious states. In view of the fact that his writ was without effect in the Confederacy, the immediate practical consequences were small. Yet the Emancipation Proclamation made slavery henceforth impossible. The Thirteenth Amendment to the Constitution, ratified in December 1865, wiped out slavery everywhere in the United States, without compensation to the former owners. The Emancipation Proclamation made the Negroes friendly to the North. Although no rebellion of slaves occurred in the South, the North recruited more than 100,000 Negro soldiers. After Emancipation European governments found it difficult to justify a policy of friendship for the Confederacy.

The North matched military to political action. In November 1862, in the Eastern theater, Lincoln dismissed the dilatory General McClellan and tried one commander after another in a search for aggressive leaders. He found them eventually in the Western theater of operations. Generals U. S. Grant (1822-85) and W. T. Sherman (1820-91) had concluded that the war could not be won by conventional jockeying for position. Grant asserted that the utmost effort must be made to achieve "the complete subjugation of the South." He proposed "to use every means to weaken the enemy, by destroying their means of subsistence, withdrawing their means of cultivating their fields, and in every other way possible."

President Abraham Lincoln's own draft of the Emancipation Proclamation of January 1, 1863.

The Confederate government and its Eastern armies were cut off from supplies from Europe by the effective blockade of the southern Atlantic coast. Hence the line of supply from the Western hinterland, the Mississippi River and its mouth at New Orleans, was of vital importance to the Confederacy. If the Mississippi Valley was conquered, Sherman wrote to Grant, "I tell you the Atlantic slope and the Pacific shores will follow its destiny as sure as the limbs of a tree live or die with the main trunk! . . . Here [in the West] lies the seat of the coming Empire; and from the West, when our task is done, we will make short work of Charleston and Richmond and the impoverished slope of the Atlantic."

In a vigorous campaign in 1862, Grant began the conquest of the Western hinterland of the Confederacy. He picked off one by one the forts and the railroad terminals and junctions of the Tennessee River. As the Union armies moved into the Southern lands, they came upon forested and undeveloped areas where ordinary roads were rare and the few railroad lines provided the only lines of supply of the South. They always destroyed rails. They often satisfied their own needs for supplies by living freely off the population, in the manner of the French revolutionary armies.

While the resources of steam power were being wrested from the Confederacy, the North used them with telling effect. In April 1862, federal steamboats entered the mouth of the Mississippi and occupied the strategic port of New Orleans, the largest city in the South. The Confederacy was now prevented from receiving supplies from abroad through that port. At the same time, a fleet of Northern gunboats moved down the Ohio and the Mississippi and up the Tennessee rivers. However, a stretch of several hundred miles of the Mississippi was controlled by the Confederacy, principally through the strongly fortified river port and railway center of Vicksburg, Mississippi. The capture of this center was important politically as well as militarily. In the fall of 1862, Grant later reflected, "the North had become very discouraged. Many strong Union men believed that the war must prove a failure. The elections of 1862 had gone against the party which was for the prosecution of the war to save the Union if it took the last man and the last dollars. Voluntary enlistments had ceased throughout the greater part of the North and the draft had been resorted to to fill up our ranks. . . . There was nothing left to be done but to *go forward to a decisive victory*."

Grant, now commanding Union general in the Department of the Tennessee, launched a campaign which rivaled the strokes of Napoleon Bonaparte. A frontal assault on Vicksburg had proved vain. Grant marched an army on the opposite (western) banks of the river through difficult and marshy terrain to a point sixty miles below Vicksburg. The army then crossed the river in steamboats. Two large Confederate armies, and several lesser ones, challenged Grant's forces. Together they far outnumbered his troops. Violating conventional rules, Grant abandoned his supplies and marched with startling speed and striking strategic sense to engage each army separately. His forces were thus superior in numbers for each battle. In the first seventeen days of May 1863, he fought and won five battles and forced the largest of the Southern armies to retire into the stronghold of Vicksburg. Then he sat down before Vicksburg to starve the rebels out. On July 4, 30,000 Southerners surrendered; the key to the Mississippi was his. The eastern half of the Confederacy was cut off from the western, and supplies ceased to come either from the West or overland from Mexico and Europe. This was the turning point of the conflict.

The day before Grant's victory in the West, another Northern army had an essentially defensive success in the East. A Southern army had invaded Pennsylvania. It was checked, though not destroyed or even pursued sufficiently, at Gettysburg on July 1-3.

In the respite afforded by these victories, the numerical and economic superiority of the North began to make itself felt. War industries were constantly developed and railway lines extended. The South's natural resources of iron and coal were largely undeveloped, and the Confederates were poorly supplied with foundries and machine shops to extend and repair their rails and cars and to replenish their diminishing stocks of artillery, small arms, and ammunition. The North could raise domestic loans at will, although it sometimes had to pay as much as 15 percent interest, whereas the South found it difficult to raise money at home or abroad. The Northern army far outnumbered the Southern. Yet the popular mood in the North was hardly more sanguine than that in the South.

General Ulysses S. Grant, the victorious leader of the Union forces in the American Civil War. This photograph was taken by Mathew Brady at City Point, Virginia, in the summer of 1864. LIBRARY OF CON-GRESS

In 1864 the Democratic party adopted a platform for the Presidential election which declared that "after four years of failure to restore the Union by the experiment of war," it was imperative that "immediate efforts be made for a cessation of hostilities with a view to an ultimate convention of the States, or other peaceable means. . . ." It nominated the conciliatory General McClellan for the highest office. Lincoln was re-elected by a large majority in the electoral college, but by a small margin of popular votes.

Meanwhile, Grant's strategy had begun to yield fruit. In March 1864 he was placed in command of the armies of the Republic and proceeded to coordinate their movements. He drew in the armies scattered in the West and Southwest and arranged them in an arc stretching from the Army of the Potomac, in the East, commanded by himself, to the Army of the Tennessee, in the West, commanded by Sherman. The arc was to be bent from its western side until it enclosed the Confederate army in Virginia, cutting it off from the rest of the South. Grant applied pressure in the North, often by frontal assaults that cost him many more casualties than the enemy, but persisting in the knowledge that the North had reserves of men that the South lacked. While Grant was thus destroying the armed man power of the South, Sherman destroyed its supplies of both man power and food. He marched from Tennessee and in September took the capital of Georgia, Atlanta, the largest city then in Confederate hands. There he burned all the available supplies and factories and ripped up the railway lines. Duplicating Grant's strategy before Vicksburg, he abandoned Atlanta, cut his line of supplies, and marched all the way across Georgia to the sea, bringing the ravages of war home to the heart of the South. He thus cut the

365

The American Civil War 1861-1865

Battle of Gettysburg 1863

Grant's final advance; Lee's surrender at Appomattox April 9, 1865

Sherman's march to the sea 1864

Grant takes Vicksburg 1863

Free states

Loyal slave states

Confederate states

Area open to slavery by Dred Scott decision, 1857

Decisive Union campaigns

eastern half of the Confederacy again into halves. Savannah fell on December 22. He then turned northward to occupy the centers of the two Carolinas. In the spring of 1865, the Confederate Army of Northern Virginia, led by General Robert E. Lee (1807-70), was squeezed between the armies of Grant in the north and Sherman in the south. Lee surrendered to Grant on April 9 at Appomattox Courthouse. Five days later, John Wilkes Booth, a fanatical Southern sympathizer, assassinated the leader of the Union's great struggle, President Lincoln.

Reunion and Reconstruction

As a result of the Civil War, slavery was destroyed in the United States and the Republic acquired a secure foundation. The Supreme Court redefined the United States as "an indestructible Union of indestructible States." The plantation system collapsed along with slavery. No rival now stood in the path of industrial and financial capitalism, which had been stimulated by the needs and opportunities of the long war. The policies that capitalism favored were now to have freer play: protection of domestic industry, promotion of immigration of foreign labor, and official assistance for the development of transportation and communication—above all, for the construction of railroads.

The collapse of the Confederacy disclosed a scene of devastation and despair in the South. The emancipation of three and a half million slaves without compensation canceled nearly two billion dollars' worth of "property" values. The investors in Confederate bonds held worthless pieces of paper. Confederate currency was equally worthless. The plantation economy was disrupted. Rails, bridges, warehouses, wharves, and ships were in ruins.

The Negroes had a somber triumph. Intoxicated with the prospect of freedom, many of them deserted their plantations. They wandered about the country, taking jobs where they could, hoping that the government would provide them with land. Thousands of them died of starvation and disease in the months of disorder and dislocation following the collapse of the South.

The Freedmen's Bureau, established in 1865 and financed by the government, issued food rations to unemployed and displaced Negroes and whites, equipped and operated hospitals, transported Negroes to places where there was a demand for labor, resettled former slaves, established colonies for displaced persons, gave or leased small parcels of land to poor farmers, protected workers against rapacious landlords or employers, and set up courts to defend the interests of Negroes. The Bureau established the first large-scale system of education for the former slaves. With the help of private philanthropic and religious organizations, it gave financial assistance to many elementary schools and new universities and technical institutes, among them Howard, Atlanta, and Fisk Universities, and Hampton Institute. Teachers from the North assisted in the training of Negroes.

To raise the economic level of the Negroes required a gigantic, and expensive, program. For such a program the country was not prepared. A few daring Northerners proposed that the planters' estates be confiscated and distributed to the workers. "Forty acres and a mule" became the dream of the newly emancipated people. But no such measure could be carried through.

The Executive and the Congress were at odds over the method of restoring the Southern states to the Union. President Lincoln and his successor, Andrew Johnson (1808-75), proposed that the rebellious states be reinstated provided that the chiefs of the Confederate government retire from public life, repudiate the Confederate debt, and acquiesce in the legal emancipation of the Negroes. They hoped that the South would voluntarily extend the vote to a minority of the educated and propertied Negroes. President Johnson appointed military governors to supervise the reconstruction of the Southern states on his conditions. He issued pardons to many Confederate leaders. Within a year after the end of the war, most of the rebellious states had formed new governments and elected a sampling of the old leaders as governors, legislators, and members of the federal Congress. In a series of "Black Codes," the new legislatures virtually forced the Negroes back to work for their old masters and imposed a facsimile of the old discipline upon them: Negroes could not leave their plantations, carry firearms, hire themselves out, assemble together, or distribute "incendiary" literature.

The "Black Codes" angered many Northerners and strengthened the Radical wing of the Republican party, which opposed the presidential policy as timid and dangerous. The Radical Republicans, led by Representative Thaddeus Stevens (1792-1868) of Pennsylvania, proposed to enfranchise the Negroes, raise their economic level, and, by obtaining their political support, assure the continuance in power of the Republicans. They were supported by the emancipationists and by those who felt that legal freedom should be accompanied by economic rehabilitation and provision for the education and vocational training of the Negroes. The congressional elections of 1866 were fought on the issue of the treatment of the Negro. The Radicals won a majority in excess of two thirds, sufficient to override a presidential veto.

Congress proceeded to undo the presidential program and install its own. In 1868 it impeached President Johnson for "high crimes and misdemeanors"— *i. e.*, for dismissing a cabinet officer without the consent of the Senate. The impeachment failed by only one vote. Congress initiated and obtained the approval of a majority of states for two constitutional amendments. The Fourteenth Amendment of 1868 declared that "all persons born or naturalized in the United States, and subject to the jurisdiction thereof, are citizens of the United States and of the State wherein they reside. No State shall make or enforce any law which shall abridge the privileges or immunities of citizens of the United States; nor shall any State deprive any person of life, liberty, or property, without due process of law; nor deny to any person within its jurisdiction the equal protection of laws." The Amendment also prohibited the election to any future office of those who had held office in the governments of the rebellious states. The Fifteenth Amendment of 1869 protected the newly won franchise of the Negroes: "The right of citizens of the United States to vote shall not be denied or abridged by the United States or by any State on account of race, color, or previous condition of servitude."

Five generals were put in control of the South. The Negroes were given a full voice in the choice of officials and the making of laws. New governments were set up, with the assistance of Northern politicians, which accepted the congressional program. Many Negroes were elected to state and federal offices, although they did not win a controlling voice. The new state constitutions—the most liberal the South had ever had—brought that region into line with advances in the North and in Western Europe. They generally abolished property qualifications for voting and holding office, imprisonment for debt, and race distinctions in acquiring and inheriting property. They simplified and codified laws and provided for free schools.

The Radical program was applied under difficult conditions. There were Northern leaders who waved "the bloody shirt" and advocated vengeful policies, and Southerners who attempted to cancel the gains of the Negroes. Unscrupulous politicians from the North, known as "carpetbaggers," and local white "scalawags" persuaded Negro voters to support them for office and exploited their power for personal profit. The aftermath of the war was extensive political corruption in the North as well as the South, but many white Southerners blamed their plight on the reconstruction program, on the "incapacity" of the Negroes and the "vindictiveness" of the Yankees. The more fanatical among them banded together in secret societies, especially the notorious Ku Klux Klan and the Knights of the White Camellia. Masked and dressed in ghostly white costumes, Klan members terrorized the colored population, whipping, beating, and even murdering Negroes who dared to stand up for their rights as freemen, and even some whites who cooperated with Negroes. Armed bands patrolled some parts of the South day and night. The federal government struck back with energy. Congress enacted strict laws to punish intimidation at the polls. The President was authorized to suspend the writ of habeas corpus if necessary to suppress the "armed combinations." Conspiracy was to be treated as rebellion. Hundreds of arrests and convictions put an end to much of the violence, although attempts at intimidation continued. It became plain that the rights of the Negro could not be secured without the intervention of the federal government.

The New Image of American Democracy

The victory of the North had significant international results. It enabled the United States to force France out of Mexico and thus to drive a nail in the coffin of Bonapartism; it placed British rule in Canada and in Ireland on the alert; it inspirited liberal and democratic forces, particularly in England; and it generated a fresh respect for American strength and principles.

During the war the United States government had refused to recognize the Hapsburg Archduke Maximilian as Emperor of Mexico. Soon after the Confederates surrendered, it demanded that Napoleon's government recall the praetorian guard which supported the strange throne. The native liberals under Juarez rose against the imported potentate. In 1867 Napoleon yielded to the United States and withdrew his troops. Maximilian, abandoned, was overwhelmed and seized. The Mexicans tried and executed him. The authority of the Monroe Doctrine was re-established. The frustration of Napoleon's plans abroad intensified the opposition to his regime at home.

The effect on the British Empire was more subtle. British Canada consisted of five colonies, each with its own governor. There had long been talk of merging them, and the talk became more practical in the fifties, when the material progress of the United States was attracting Canadian interest. There were men on both sides of the border who hoped for a union of the two English-speaking areas. Their hope grew when the North won the Civil War and when Russia, in 1867, sold Alaska to the United States. Following the war, a group of Irish-Americans who had fought on the side of the North made adventurous plans to "conquer" Canadian areas for the United States; others recrossed the ocean to organize the secret society of the Fenians, whose aim was to make Ireland independent. In 1867 Ontario, Quebec, New Brunswick, and Nova Scotia were merged in a new "dominion," and eventually the rest of British North America was added to the confederation. In Ireland the immediate effect of intensified Irish-American activity was to increase official coercion, but liberal British leaders began to consider the compromise of home rule.

The reform movement in England was quickly revived in 1865 and 1866, under the leadership of John Bright. Early in 1866 the Liberal government proposed a moderate extension of voting rights, but the Conservatives defeated the measure, and with it the Liberal party. The country uttered a roar of protest. Hundreds of meetings demanded the reintroduction and liberalization of the measure. The agitation recalled the movement of the Chartists. Even the touch of force and illegality was not lacking. The government had closed the gates of Hyde Park, where a huge meeting of democrats had been called. On a sunny summer afternoon Londoners broke down the rails and thousands occupied the park to listen to fiery orations. The government capitulated; the meeting was unmolested, and reform became inevitable. The Conservative leader in the House of Commons, Benjamin Disraeli, with more cooperation from the Liberals than from his own party, introduced and passed a measure which gave the vote to every man who rented, in his own name, a dwelling in a town and to every substantial farmer. Although this was far removed from universal suffrage, the bulk of the urban lower-middle and working classes was enfranchised.

Lord Derby, Disraeli's own party chief, called the measure "a leap in the dark." Lord Robert Cecil berated his party's leaders for "surrendering" and the "comfortable classes" for lacking "stomach for a real struggle." He warned against the evils of the "American system": professional politicians, noisy electioneering methods, favoritism, corruption. To old Thomas Carlyle, who opposed the extension of the suffrage, democracy was nothing but "swarmery," of which the war on slavery was a sorry example. It spelled "new supplies of blockheadism, gullibility, bribability, amenability to beer and balderdash. . . ." It would be "the end of poor old England." Carlyle's only consolation was that the United States would "go to smash" first.

Most Europeans were impressed by the military energy and political resiliency of the Republic. Statesmen began to reckon with the United States as a potential rival. Disraeli acknowledged "the increasing influence of the United States upon the political fortunes" of the Old World. He admitted that the balance of power could "no longer be confined to Europe alone." In typically pessimistic vein, he predicted an America "of armies, of diplomacy, of rival states and maneuvering cabinets, of frequent turbulence, and probably of frequent wars"—in short, a typical "great power." Liberals and democrats were also impressed. Charles Dickens apologized to Americans for his criticisms of them in his early writings (see p. 239). John Stuart Mill reaffirmed his faith in the political ability of Americans: "Let them be left without a government, every body of Americans is able to improvise one and to carry on that or any other public business with a sufficient amount of intelligence, order, and decision. That is what every free people ought to be; and a people capable of this is certain to be free; it will never let itself be enslaved by any man or body of men, because these are able to seize and pull the reins of the central administration."

There was a fresh note of confidence among Americans. Ralph Waldo Emerson asserted America's claim to leadership of the West. "The office of America is to liberate, to abolish kingcraft and priestcraft, caste, monopoly, to pull down the gallows, to burn up the bloody statute book, to take in the immigrant, to open the doors of the sea and the fields of the earth,—to extemporize government in Texas, in California, in Oregon,—to make provisional law where statute law is not ready. This liberation appears in the power of invention, the freedom of thinking, in readiness for reforms."

America found its most powerful voice in Walt Whitman, who tried to blend liberty and individualism with democracy. His *Democratic Vistas* (1871) is a severe indictment of the political corruption and partisanship of "half-brained nominees, the many ignorant ballots, and many elected failures and blatherers." Nevertheless, he believed that the democratic ideal was valid and its future certain. The problem was to reconcile the claim of the individual with that of the mass. Whitman's sense of individuality was as strong as John Stuart Mill's. "Shall a man lose himself," he asked, "in countless masses of adjustments, and be so shaped with reference to this, that, and the other, that the simply good and healthy and brave parts of him are reduced and clipped away, like the bordering of a box in a garden?" Individuality was "the compensating balance wheel of the successful working of the aggregate machinery." The opening lines of his *Leaves of Grass* announced the poet's faith:

> One's-self I sing, a simple separate person,
> Yet utter the word Democratic, the word En-Masse.

Whitman repudiated conventional meter and rhyme. In a robust, loose, and entirely free verse, he sang the universality, naturalness, and variety of democracy. His democrats are strong, proud, and dignified individuals who love everything in Nature, from the grandest creature to the humblest.

> I speak the pass-word primeval, I give the sign of democracy,
> By God! I will accept nothing which all cannot have their counterpart of
> on the same terms.   . . .
>
> Whoever degrades another degrades me,
> And whatever is done or said returns at last to me.
>   . . .
> I see the European headsman,
> He stands mask'd, clothed in red, with huge legs and strong naked arms,
> And leans on a ponderous axe.
> (Whom have you slaughter'd lately European headsman?
> Whose is that blood upon you so wet and sticky?)
>   . . .
> I see not America only, not only Liberty's nation but other nations pre-
>   paring
> I see tremendous entrances and exits, new combinations, the solidarity of
>   races,
> I see that force advancing with irresistible power on the world's stage. . . .

18. *The Age of Liberalism*

After long travail, the Western world achieved stability. For nearly a century, many Western countries, notably those on the Continent, had been churned up periodically by domestic discontent or strife and by an international contest between liberalism and conservatism. During the Revolution of 1848 and the series of wars that soon followed it, the advocates of comprehensive change and the defenders of immobility had both been defeated. The field was taken over by cautious liberals, chastened conservatives, and the growing middle classes, whose craving for a calm order that secured property and freed enterprise became irresistible. Long-outstanding questions—particularly the consolidation of Italian and German states and of the American Republic—were resolved. The stage was set for the national state, for a high mobility of men, goods, and ideas, and for great industrial societies.

Coherence and Size: The National State

The centralized and homogeneous state, the result of a long process of evolution in Western Europe, became the goal for most energetic countries in the Western world and beyond. Traditional empires had often been little more than shapeless collections of discrete and diverse provinces. Now the various Germanic and Italian statelets, the heterogeneous lands of Austria and Hungary, were consolidated into firmer and larger entities. In all the new states and in many of the old, simple codes of law, uniform taxes, standardized measures and weights, and more or less uniform systems of local government unified varied provinces. The new means of transportation and communication and the economy associated with them brought together town and country, capital and province, region and region, port and interior. The new states were national, elevating the interests of cohesiveness above those of separatism, promoting swift and frequent exchange among their constituent parts, and nurturing a common language and culture as instruments and symbols of their functions and power.

But this general tendency toward more integrated states did not obliterate an old regional distinction. In Western Europe and the United States, liberalism became further confirmed and a tendency toward democracy became increasingly apparent. The fall of Bonapartism had restored republicanism in France. The victory of the North in the American Civil War had formally extended the rights of man to the Negroes. In both countries universal manhood suffrage was combined with strong representative institutions. The older constitutional state of Great Britain made a substantial step toward democracy by broadening the suffrage.

The countries of Eastern Europe adopted some of the forms but few of the principles of political liberalism. They accepted reforms promoting legal equality, freedom of economic exchange, and administrative efficiency, which had long been achieved in the Western countries. By making such concessions, the conservative regimes retained most of the substance of power. Behind a façade of constitutionalism, monarchs and noblemen retained executive, military, diplomatic, and bureaucratic leadership. They promoted a national language, culture, and religion but made these instruments of discrimination against minorities and liberal or radical critics.

Bismarck was the most successful practitioner of the art of merging conservative reality with liberal appearances. He demonstrated that where liberal groups and the middle classes were politically inert, monarchs and noblemen could preserve their position even though they made constitutional concessions. Such was the success of Germany that the constitution of the Prussian state and that of the Empire became the model for other countries in Central and Eastern Europe, and even for distant Japan. German liberals accepted a position of subservience. They prevailed in the adoption of free-trade policies and entertained the hope of introducing ministerial responsibility and increasing the power of the *Reichstag*. But since this hope depended on voluntary concessions by conservatives, their future prospects were highly uncertain.

There was one country, however, that persevered in both the forms of absolutism and the practice of repression. That country was Russia. Her defeat in the Crimean War was followed by the initiation of many reforms. These reforms, however, were administrative and judicial rather than political. Czarism did not propose to give up its monopoly of legislation and executive action and share power with an elected parliament. Yet in no Eastern country was Western culture assimilated more avidly than in Russia by the educated classes. Nowhere, therefore, did the contrast between the present and the possible appear so sharp. The result was that, at a time when revolutionary thinking ebbed everywhere in the Western world, it persisted in Russia.

The Mobility of Men and Things

Despite these regional differences, the reforms generally accepted in the Western world created an atmosphere favorable to busy activity in economic and intellectual life. Of serfdom and slavery only traces remained. In the Western world, only Brazil still sanctioned legal bondage, and there it was abolished in 1888. The vast majority of men had won freedom for their persons, their occupations, and their movements. In the Atlantic countries, men had for a long time been free to learn and engage in any trade they pleased and to go into any business. In the sixties, the German states abandoned the traditional guild restrictions and tests that limited this freedom. Most of the other states of Central and Eastern Europe took steps in the same direction.

It became easier to leave a country and resettle elsewhere. There were still some states—notably Russia and the Ottoman Empire—which required a person to obtain official permission to cross the boundaries and even, in the case of Russia, to change his residence within the country. Internal passports were used as a means of controlling and policing the population. But these were exceptions. Nearly all the Western states abolished passports. Frontiers were patrolled lightly. Once a man escaped the Russian and Turkish nets, he could roam freely over much of the globe. Millions of Europeans took to their legs.

The atmosphere was bracing for men who were prepared to enter new fields of endeavor in growing cities and colonial areas, to underwrite and manage commercial, industrial, and agricultural enterprises, and to collect and use the moneys of "sleeping partners," or inactive savers or heirs. In an earlier day the formation of companies had been associated with the grant of special privileges and monopolies and was, therefore, subject to the action of monarchs or legislatures. Early liberals wished to pit the individual's substance and ability against those of other individuals. They regarded collective capitalism as a kind of feudal "dead hand," which gave promoters and bankers with political influence an unfair advantage over the individual enterpriser fighting with his own capital only. From the beginning of the nineteenth century, this attitude was gradually abated. The first Napoleon had legalized the organization of companies, subject to certain rules. Later the constituent states of the American Republic had legalized companies for almost any purpose. A mere public announcement of the investors and the capitals involved was deemed sufficient to launch a collective enterprise. In 1825 England repealed her famous South Sea Bubble Act of 1720, which had been intended to protect unwary investors by prohibiting the collection of funds for speculative purposes. In the forties, when the hands of business were unshackled in many other ways, a company could be formed on mere registration. In most countries the principle of "limited liability" was gradually extended to all corporations. The emancipation of corporate business was regarded as but a generalization of the policy of noninterference with business and of the principle of individualism.

Another application of the principles of *laissez faire* and self-government by business resulted in the relaxation of bankruptcy rules. Failure to meet debts was traditionally regarded as a disgrace—indeed, as a crime, punishable in the typically harsh ways of the old order. Rigid bankruptcy rules and stringent prohibitions against the re-entry of bankrupts into business naturally inhibited enterprise, particularly of the adventurous and speculative sort. But the financial crises of the thirties and forties, which swept whole trades, countries, and even several countries at once, demonstrated that business failure was in most cases a social rather than a personal phenomenon. It was a risk which the creditor might be expected to share with the borrower. It came to be recognized that bankruptcy might be voluntary. A businessman might, sometimes in agreement with his creditors, wipe the slate of one enterprise clear and launch another, without prejudice and with hope of better fortune. The liquidation of his assets—the sale of his goods, etc.—became in such a case a matter not for government officials and courts but for his creditors. Only in Latin Europe and Latin America did the old legal principle that a debtor was always liable for his whole debt continue to be emphasized, although there, too, bankruptcies became more respectable.

The utmost freedom in this realm was achieved by the United States. Eventually it became possible, in certain states, for a man to be declared bankrupt even if he was not really insolvent, provided that he and his creditors could agree to clear the accounts by a partial fulfillment of his obligation. The failing debtor was not only permitted but encouraged to re-enter business. He was also relieved of the old punishment by imprisonment. At this point, business interests and humanitarianism met. It was argued that placing a man behind bars would prevent him from working and trading in order to satisfy his creditors. In the United States, again, freedom to the enterpriser was combined with generosity toward persons in financial straits. Bankruptcy proceedings were allowed to wipe out personal as well as business obligations, particularly in order to provide a refuge from unfair or usurious debts.

Individual enterprise became the general rule in economic relations, both within and between nations. The Western world experienced the greatest freedom of trade since the days of the Roman Empire. The integration of provinces into unitary states broadened the reach of local and domestic trade. Italy and Germany became single markets. Within the Austrian Empire trade barriers were broken down. The customs union between the two halves of the Hapsburg realm created one of the largest markets in Europe.

In foreign trade only England and Holland established absolute mobility. They preserved but a few tariffs, which were needed for revenue. The policy of reducing duties to moderate levels by mutual agreements, initiated by the Cobden-Chevalier Treaty concluded by England and France in 1860, became all but general. The United States pursued free-trade policies until the Civil War, when she raised duties. By continuing the rates after the war, she became one of the few highly protectionist countries, even while she was extending the most extreme form of *laissez faire* at home.

There was an unusual equilibrium of power. Most of the principal states—Great Britain, France, Germany, and the United States—were roughly equal in population—about thirty millions—in the sixties. Russia was more than twice as populous and, like the United States, uncommonly large, but the other powers made up the difference by greater capital wealth, arms, or prestige. The easy interchange of goods and traffic of men stimulated cooperative effort among countries. International movements came into fashion. The Crimean War and the Italian War of 1859 had disclosed a shocking—though quite common—neglect of sick and wounded soldiers. In 1864 sixteen European states met in Geneva and organized the International Red Cross, which most states joined subsequently. Ever since, the Red Cross has relieved much of the suffering of war (as well as of natural disasters), by caring for the sick and wounded and relieving the lot of prisoners. Eventually most of the countries of the world signed the Geneva Convention, which laid down the rules for the achievement of these and other humane goals. Similar national societies were organized to care for the victims of other catastrophes.

International conferences and bodies standardized postal rules and fees, set up uniform patent and copyright rules, and secured wide adoption of the metric system of weights and measures. Such conferences were commonly held in Switzerland. Thus the oldest free community in Europe became the seat and symbol of international effort. Another fashionable enterprise of the time was the "world exposition" for the display of advances in the industrial arts and the practical sciences. The first exposition was held in 1851 in London and was imitated by great cities of both hemispheres.

Finally, the international spirit affected the labor movement. At a meeting in London in 1864, a group of workers, reformers, and radicals, most of them French and English, organized the International Workingmen's Association, better known as the first International. In its opening address, drafted by Karl Marx, then a resident of London, the International announced that "all efforts" to "emancipate" the working masses had "hitherto failed from the want of solidarity between the manifold divisions of labor in each country and from the absence of a fraternal bond of union between the working classes of different countries." The organization proposed to supply this lack in order to attain "the protection, advancement, and complete emancipation" of the workers.

The Eminence of England

In the age of free trade and individualism, England stood at the height of her fame. Conservatives admired her reconciliation of aristocracy with capitalism, order with liberty, tradition with modernity. Liberals admired her superiority in political freedom and economic production. From all countries, particularly from Germany, economists came to England to watch the operations and try to discover the rules of industrial success. England's iron, coal, and cheap industrial goods bound both advanced and backward countries to her. The in-

376

creasing use of rails and locomotives, tools, machines, and cannon increased the demand for cheap wrought iron, which was malleable, and for the harder but more brittle cast iron. Of these products, in finished or unfinished form, England was the largest producer and the only considerable exporter. Until about 1870 most of the rails in the United States and all those laid in Russia, not to mention other countries, were English. The telegraph cables laid in the fifties and sixties were all made in London. In 1860, to take a more or less typical year, England contributed more than half the pig iron production of the world, or more than all the other countries together, and almost three times as much as the next two leading producers:

England	3,890,000 tons
United States	821,000
Germany	522,000
World total	*7,300,000*

England was the chief exporter of coal. Countries which, like Italy, lacked the "black diamond" entered into a permanent fealty. Even the United States, in the middle of the century, depended upon English coal; her own huge deposits had been insufficiently tapped. English ships, most of which were still using sails, laid up stores of coal in a chain of bunkering stations around the globe. In a day when frequent refueling was necessary, international steam-shipping became dependent on these stores, not only for commercial but for naval purposes: for England sold this coal to all comers. At the same time, Britain's position as the principal shipper was confirmed; the last substantial challenger was the famous American clipper ship. As sails gradually became replaced by steam, first in mail and passenger and then in freight traffic, the primacy of iron and coal delivered the seaways to Great Britain. The mercantile monopolies of old were succeeded by an industrial monopoly, more extensive although less political.

In commerce the story was the same. In 1840 England had had nearly one third of the estimated world trade; twenty years later she still had one fourth, but it was one fourth of a much larger and more competitive volume. France had only 11 percent, the United States only 9 percent. The value of English exports, not including exports to British colonies, rose from 63 million pounds sterling in 1854 to 92 million in 1860 and 148 million ten years later. England's piled-up wealth overflowed into American and Continental railroads, ships, and factories and into colonial enterprises. It sought virgin territory. Before 1850 English capital had been invested largely in Northern Europe and in America. After 1850, for a generation, a mighty stream poured into recently opened or developed lands, particularly in the Empire. In 1850 some 300 million pounds were invested outside the British Isles; twenty-five years later the figure was a billion pounds higher.

The widespread adoption of the gold standard in the 1870's, like that of free trade, was a testimony to the ascendancy of England. There were some countries, particularly those that had large silver supplies, that long persisted in bimetallism. To establish a single standard is to permit world prices to find their "natural" level in terms of the ratio of the entire gold supply to the entire stock of the world's goods. On the other hand, maintenance of the silver standard as well as the gold requires government action to redefine the ratio of gold to silver whenever the amount of either changes considerably. Such action may then be bent to other purposes, for by fixing different rates the government may favor one group in the population as against another—silver miners or gold miners, creditors or debtors, and so on. Many economic liberals, wishing to avoid political, sectional, or class interferences with prices, favored the single standard.

In the sixties and seventies most of the countries of Europe and Latin America demonetized silver. In 1867, under the leadership of France, the Latin Union, comprising most of the countries of Europe except Great Britain and Germany, adopted a common currency medium based on gold. Although the United States formally maintained bimetallism, it effectively favored gold. For a long time, the silver interests fought this tendency, seconded by politicians who wished to protect the consuming public and the debtors by fixing the value of the dollar in terms of silver (which was cheaper because there was more of it). But eventually the gold standard won out: the pro-silver Democratic party lost the presidential elections of 1896 and 1900, and in the nineties Austria, Russia, Japan, and India all abandoned silver coinage. The nineteenth century ended with the triumph of gold and of fluid international exchange.

In the mid-century, the position of Great Britain was distinctly imperial without being stridently imperialistic. The constant acquisitions, the alarums and defiances and posturings that are associated with imperialism were unnecessary, for Britain had no effective rivals. The old imperial powers of Spain and Holland had long since ceased to inspire envy; Germany was a new power and, like the United States, was absorbed in turn by domestic strife and domestic expansion; the French attempts to establish an empire in Mexico did not arouse fear, since Napoleon III always deferred to Britain in foreign policy and the Third Republic was too torn by domestic problems to present a danger. Only Russia's pressure on Turkey and the Mediterranean and on Central Asia, in areas pointing toward India, aroused serious concern. In opposing Russia, however, Great Britain had not only the assistance of France and other Western states but also the sympathy of liberals and radicals who regarded czarism as the principal reactionary force in Europe.

This unique position and the tendency of the time to manifest power in economic rather than political form combined to give the British Empire a benign appearance. But influence is not always overt. The political losses incurred when the colonies of Canada, Australia, and New Zealand obtained legislative autonomy from Britain and control over their fiscal and tariff policies were more than made up by the constant strengthening of their economic bonds with the mother country. From them and from colonies which were ruled from London, the British obtained their raw materials. England's raw cotton came from Egypt

—where beginning in 1876 the British and French condominium controlled the finances of the country—as well as from the United States; her wool came from Australia, India, and the African Cape; her silk came from India, although also from China; and her hemp from India. Colonial trade grew from 34 million pounds sterling in 1854 to 52 million in 1870. The railways of Canada, Australia, New Zealand, the Cape, and India were shipped—literally, rails and locomotives and cars, not to mention civil engineers—from Great Britain. Railways were shipped to foreign countries as well, but in the colonies the government guaranteed the investments, usually at the generous rate of 10 percent, and supplied deficiencies out of taxes. And since some of the railways were constructed for military and imperial as well as commercial reasons, deficiencies were not uncommon.

This was particularly true in India, where great care was taken for defense, and where the government in London took over the functions of the old British East India Company. The mercantilist monopoly of the Company was first relaxed in the economic field and then ended in the political. In 1813 the Company had lost its exclusive trade with India, and European settlers were admitted there for the first time. Twenty years later, in 1833, the monopoly of trade with China fell. Free and individual enterprise took the place of the exclusive operations of the great company-empire. And then the company-state itself fell. In 1857 its Indian troops in the north, east, and central areas mutinied, and for several months British dominion swayed violently in the balance. With the cooperation of Napoleon III, European troops were rushed across France to India. The English government put down the mutiny and took over control from the old Company, after safeguarding the interests of its stockholders and pensioning off its officials and agents.

The multifarious exactions of the Company were now simplified, pruned, and regularized, while indiscriminate looting by its "servants" was abolished. Company officials, who had always done business on their own account, now established firms to negotiate the interchange between India and other parts of Asia, and between Asia and the Western world. The "home charges," consisting of the sinecures, salaries, pensions, and commissions the English directors paid themselves out of Indian treasure and taxes, were systematized and expanded. Between 1854 and 1870 these charges rose from three and a half million to more than 10 million pounds sterling a year. The British government's policy of free trade ended the manipulations of customs prohibitions and differentials to favor British trade. But that trade and the commercial connections were so well established that India remained a good customer, not only for the newer products of the age of steam and iron, but even for cotton goods, of which she had once been a principal producer and exporter.

In one area, however, imperial position required more than economic penetration. The introduction of steam power had revived the use of the Mediterranean–Red Sea route to India and China, supplanting the route around the Cape of Good Hope. The question of the fate of the Ottoman Empire, which nominally commanded the route to the Far East, therefore became more acute. *379*

The Crimean War was one result of the revival of the Red Sea route. Egypt was virtually independent of the Sultan, she was rich, and, most important of all, she sat athwart the route. The British had already secured the strategic southern exit from the Red Sea by occupying Aden in 1837 and then nearby Perim in 1857. Both became coaling and cable stations. British companies proposed to complete the connection by building a railway across the Isthmus of Suez. The railway was finished in 1857, but twelve years later a French company completed a canal at Suez. The company, organized by Ferdinand de Lesseps (1805-94), had obtained a concession from the Khedive to cut the canal with Egyptian labor. The canal shortened the distance from London to Bombay—nearly 11,000 miles by the route around the Cape of Good Hope—by 4,500 miles. Other voyages were cut by as much as two thirds. Within a few years freight rates dropped to a fifth of their former levels. This striking saving in time and money enormously increased the traffic between Europe and Asia and did much to increase the importance of the Mediterranean area.

The canal could be used by all ships, and at the same rates, but control of the Suez Company was shared between the French investors and the Khedive of Egypt, to the distress of the British. In 1875, the Khedive, who had run deeply into debt, offered to sell the Egyptian shares. Prime Minister Benjamin Disraeli borrowed four million pounds, with his own word as security, bought the Egyptian shares, and made the British government the principal stockholder. English penetration of Egypt thenceforth proceeded without letup. "It was Napoleon who had recovered Egypt for Europe," wrote the British historian H. A. L.

Benjamin Disraeli buying from the Khedive of Egypt the shares that gave Great Britain virtual control of the strategic Suez Canal. Cartoon by Tenniel. © PUNCH

THE LION'S SHARE.

"GARE À QUI LA TOUCHE!"

Fisher. "It was Mehemet Ali, Napoleon's admirer and pupil, who had made of Egypt a modern state; it was De Lesseps, a French engineer of genius, who had in 1869 pierced the Suez Canal. All three were opposed by England." What French imagination and money wrought, England enjoyed.

Positivism and Liberalism

The Age over which England presided allowed free play to the mind and promoted scientific advance. A single year—1859—produced three classic works: Karl Marx's *Critique of Political Economy*, Charles Darwin's *Origin of Species*, and John Stuart Mill's *On Liberty*.

It was in the preface to the *Critique* (a book which at the time exercised little influence) that Marx stated the doctrine of historical materialism. The mode of production "determines, in general, political and intellectual life." When new material forces of production, and the social relations they engender, come into conflict with prevailing legal and political institutions, "there begins an epoch of social revolution," and "the entire colossal superstructure is more or less rapidly transformed." Eight years later, Marx predicted in *Capital* that wealth would become more concentrated and monopolistic, that it would inhibit production, and that labor would become increasingly impoverished and oppressed. "The centralization of the means of production and the socialization of labor reach a point where they prove incompatible with their capitalist husk. This bursts asunder. The knell of capitalist property sounds. The expropriators are expropriated."

He could hardly have written these words at a more inappropriate moment. Indeed, Marx himself had been astonished by the almost unbroken business prosperity of the fifties and sixties. In a letter in 1858, he wrote:

> Bourgeois society has experienced its sixteenth century a second time— a sixteenth century which will, I hope, sound the death knell of bourgeois society just as the first one thrust it into existence. The particular task of bourgeois society is the establishment of the world market, at least in its outlines, and of production based upon the world market. As the world is round, this seems to have been completed by the colonisation of California and Australia and the opening of China and Japan. The difficult question for us is this: on the Continent the revolution is imminent and will at once assume also a socialist character. Will it not be crushed in this little corner, if the movement of the bourgeois society is still in the ascendant in a much larger terrain?

For the moment "positivism" found more influence than Marxism. The French philosopher Auguste Comte (1798-1857), a disciple of Saint-Simon, had pictured three stages in the human experience. At the beginning of civilization man tried to explain and control his environment by appealing to supernatural fictions. He accepted the guidance of monarchs, who ruled by "divine right,"

381

and of priests, who discouraged the exercise of intellect by exaggerating the importance of feeling. In the second stage, theology was exposed as fictional, and man came to rely on abstract reason. He organized governments based on the idea of the "sovereignty of the people" and "natural rights." But philosophy, according to Comte, had proved as inadequate as metaphysics; the time was ripe for the final stage of positivism.

Positivism rested upon a synthesis of the sciences. Astronomy had built upon mathematics, physics upon astronomy, and the more complex sciences of chemistry and biology upon physics. Now "social physics," or sociology, was to build upon all of them. Man must turn his attention to the concrete and palpable phenomena of social, political, and moral life; he must observe, count, measure, and order them; he must discover the relations that, surely, exist among them; and he must bring them together under the great law that governs the social and moral as well as the material universe. Comte and his followers hoped that the accumulation of information, particularly of data susceptible of measurement and mathematical formulation, was the beginning of social wisdom. They enthroned the Fact.

In the final stage a new "industrial order" would succeed the traditional "military order." It would supplant the leadership of theologians and philosophers with that of industrial organizers and social scientists. Such a leadership might be quite authoritarian. Mill observed that reformers, such as Comte, "who have placed themselves in strongest opposition to the religions of the past, have been in no way behind either churches or sects in their assertion of the right of spiritual domination." Comtism "aims at establishing (though by moral more than by legal appliances) a despotism of society over the individual, surpassing anything contemplated in the political ideal of the most rigid disciplinarians among the ancient philosophers."

Mill's own writings were the most characteristic expressions of the liberal age. His *Principles of Political Economy* (1848) had been an exposition of the principles of Malthus, Ricardo, and Bentham. Translated into many languages, it became the bible of free-traders everywhere. Mill's vision was not bounded by free trade and utilitarianism. He supported political democracy, espoused the rights of women, and defended the interests of the lower classes. Although he felt that socialist proposals were not immediately feasible, he sympathized with their aim. Mill's *On Liberty* (1859), together with his *Representative Government* (1861) and *The Subjection of Women* (1869), is the best statement of the importance of freedom. Not since John Milton's famous attack on censorship, *Areopagitica* (1644), had so powerful an argument been made for unshackling the minds of men.

Mill lacked the poet's eloquence but made up for it by logic and comprehensiveness. He started from the proposition that "after the primary necessities of food and raiment, freedom is the first and strongest want of human nature." Only by making his own choices can man develop his perception, his judgment, and his moral sense. It is impossible to make choices, however, if only one pattern of action, thought, and taste is allowed. Diversity is essential to

382

Karl Marx BETTMANN   *John Stuart Mill* BROWN

progress; uniformity and conformity are death. "There is no reason that all human existence should be constructed on some one or some small number of patterns." The extreme of individuality is eccentricity, which has "always abounded when and where strength of character has abounded; and the amount of eccentricity in a society has generally been proportional to the amount of genius, mental vigor, and moral courage which it contained." Mill ascribed the advance of European nations, unique in history, to "their remarkable diversity of character and culture."

The true object of society and government, according to Mill, is to promote virtue and intelligence, and to do this they must nurture liberty. The representative system is one in which "the general standard of intelligence and honesty existing in the community, and the individual intellect and virtue of its wisest members" are brought most directly to bear upon government. Ideally all the people should share in the government. In any case, it is necessary to break up power as much as is consistent with efficiency, while centralizing the gathering and supplying of information to all parts of the society. Whatever its form, the government has the paramount duty to respect the autonomy of the individual.

> If all mankind minus one were of one opinion, and only one person were of the contrary opinion, mankind would be no more justified in silencing that one person than he, if he had the power, would be justified in silencing mankind. . . . The peculiar evil of silencing the expression of an opinion is that it is robbing the human race, posterity as well as the existing generation; those who dissent from the opinion, still more than those who hold it. If the opinion is right, they are deprived of the opportunity of exchanging error for truth: if wrong, they lose, what is almost as great a benefit, the clearer perception and livelier impression of truth, produced by its collision with error.
>
> . . . The sole end for which mankind are warranted, individually or collectively, in interfering with the liberty of action of any of their number, is self-protection. . . . His own good, either physical or moral, is not a sufficient warrant. . . . Over himself, over his own body and mind, the individual is sovereign.

No government has the right to coerce people for their own good. "Evil for evil, a good despotism, in a country at all advanced in civilization, is more noxious than a bad one; for it is far more relaxing and enervating to the thoughts, feelings, and energies of the people." Liberty is predicated on the capacity to use reason and to promote progress. "Those who are still in a state to require being taken care of by others, must be protected against their own actions as well as against external injury." That is the condition of children and of primitive or barbarous men. They must wait until they have become "capable of being improved by free and equal discussion." Even so, no "community has a right to force another to be civilized."

Liberty, Mill recognized, is a rare and fragile plant. A host of human passions and material forces constantly threaten to stifle it. Intolerance, self-righteousness, fashion, and power are dear to the heart of man. Habit and custom are constantly freezing life out of ideas and ideals. There is, indeed, "an incessant and ever-flowing current of human affairs toward the worse, consisting of all the follies, all the vices, all the negligences, indolences, and supinenesses of mankind." Mill wondered whether liberty is not peculiar to "periods of transition, when old notions and feelings have been unsettled and no new doctrines have yet succeeded to their ascendancy."

Recent developments raised special obstacles to freedom. The increasing influence of society, of public administration, and of public opinion was throwing the individual into the shade. There had been a reaction against the emphasis placed on reason by eighteenth-century thinkers and an "idolatry" of "Instinct" had arisen, "the most pernicious of the false worships of the present day." There were reformers who were willing to force improvement on "an unwilling people." Mill felt that the only unfailing source of improvement is liberty, since it provides "as many possible and independent centers of improvement as there are individuals."

The issue of liberty is not settled by establishing democracy. "The will of the people . . . practically means the will of the most numerous or the most active *part* of the people; the majority, or those who succeed in making themselves accepted as the majority; the people, consequently, *may* desire to oppress a part of their number; and precautions are as much needed against this as against any other abuse of power." It is not only through government that society may "tyrannize" over the individual: Mill demanded "protection also against the tyranny of the prevailing opinion and feeling; against the tendency of society to impose, by other means than civil penalties, its own ideas and practices as rules of conduct on those who dissent from them; to fetter the development, and, if possible, prevent the formation, of any individuality not in harmony with its ways, and compel all characters to fashion themselves upon the model of its own."

Liberty comes in spurts, as the result of outbursts of energy and deliberate choice and will. It grew in the wake of the Reformation, and during the Enlightenment. These impulses seemed spent, and there can be "no fresh start, until we again assert our mental freedom."

Men need not deceive themselves that truth always prevails and may therefore be left to shift for itself. "History teems with instances of truth put down by persecution. If not suppressed forever, it may be thrown back for centuries. . . . Persecution has always succeeded, save where the heretics were too strong a party to be effectually persecuted." "Mankind can hardly be too often reminded that there was once a man named Socrates . . . the head and prototype of all subsequent teachers of virtue" who was "put to death by his countrymen, after a judicial conviction, for impiety and immorality."

Evolution and Religion

While Mill's ideas summed up the hopes of the liberal tradition, those of Charles Darwin were destined to have a greater impact upon the future. No doctrine of the time made so much stir as Darwinism.

Evolution was an old—in fact, an ancient—idea. Since classical times, many philosophers had explained the world as the result of a process of development. Nineteenth-century theorists had described human history as a progressive change from simple to sophisticated societies. More recently, evolutionary thought had received expression in the philosophy of Hegel and in Auguste Comte's notion of the three stages of society.

In one of the classics of political economy, Malthus' *Essay on Population* (1798), English biologists found a suggestive idea. Malthus had pointed out that population increases geometrically while the supply of food increases arithmetically, and that a severe struggle for existence is the result of this fact. Alfred Russel Wallace (1823-1913) found here the "long-sought-for law that solved the problem of the origin of species." Animals propagate faster than men and their competition for subsistence is ferocious. Only a few, "on the whole the best fitted," survive and propagate themselves. Charles Darwin (1809-82) came independently to the same conclusion. He was groping for an explanation of the variations that occur in animal and plant species when he "happened to read" Malthus' *Essay* "for amusement."

In 1859 Darwin, who had been accumulating material on the subject for twenty years, spread it before the world in the *Origin of Species*. Probably no book published in the last two centuries has had a greater effect, both immediately and in the long run.

Darwin referred to the enormous fertility of plants and animals:

> What a trifling difference must often determine which shall survive and which perish. . . . Considering the infinitely various ways beings have to obtain food by struggle with other beings, to escape danger at various times of life, to have their eggs or seeds disseminated, &c., &c., I cannot doubt that during millions of generations individuals of a species will be born with some slight variation profitable to some part of its economy; such will have a better chance of surviving, propagating this variation, which again will be slowly increased by the accumulating action of natural selection; and

the variety thus formed will either coexist with, or more commonly will exterminate, its parent form. . . . This I believe to be the origin of the classification or arrangement of all organic beings at all times. These always *seem* to branch and sub-branch like a tree from a common trunk; the flourishing twigs destroying the less vigorous—the dead and lost branches rudely representing extinct genera and families.

Applying his theory to *The Descent of Man* (1871), Darwin concluded that man had evolved from "some less highly organized form," possibly but not necessarily the anthropoid ape. Man had inherited his psychic as well as his physical traits, for animals exhibit the powers of imitation, imagination, and reflection. Even the capacity for religious devotion is foreshadowed by the dog's worship of his master. There were, however, some features of men and animals for which Darwin found natural selection an insufficient explanation. He ascribed secondary sexual characteristics to the competition among males for females. Males who develop features that attract the ladies transmit them to their offspring. "Sexual selection" proved to be the weakest point of Darwinism.

The implications of evolution were at once heartening and disillusioning. There was advance in nature, but there were also brutality and fierceness. The ways of progress were not those of cooperation and kindness. The species moved ever upward, but the cost in waste and abuse of life was high. For the moment, however, the suggestion of ruthless and unremitting contention was overshadowed by the evidence of progress from formless to highly organized beings.

Yet this progress seemed to be a denial of the Biblical story of Creation. Darwin dealt traditional religion a sharper blow than any previous scientific discoverers. Copernicus, Galileo, and Newton had concerned themselves with the realm of astronomy, physics, and higher mathematics. Darwin's concern was with man himself. The favorite creature of God became merely the last in a line of animals. He was still, in Darwin's words, "the wonder and the glory of the Universe," but this was slim consolation. "With all his exalted qualities, with sympathy which feels for the most debased, with benevolence which extends not only to other men but to the humblest living creature, with his godlike intellect which has penetrated into the movements and constitution of the solar system— with all these exalted powers—Man still bears in his bodily frame the indelible stamp of his lowly origin."

The external supports of the dignity of man were falling away. Darwinists exposed the story of Creation as a poetic fable. A few verses of Genesis could hardly prevail against thousands of shells, marine specimens, and geological strata. Judaism and Christianity had once banished the pagan gods from Olympus and dispelled the world of fairies and elves. Now science banished the banishers, the angels and devils, the intercessors, atoners, and redeemers. For pagan deities, Judaism and Christianity had substituted an all-wise, all-merciful, all-powerful god. Now science offered "Nature," struggle, "survival of the fittest," and sexual selection as the sources of progress.

The orthodox were shocked, and the clergy counterattacked. In every Western country, a bitter and prolonged controversy was engaged between the two camps, on the platform, in the pulpit, in the press, and in millions of homes. The evolutionists accused the defenders of traditional religion of obscurantism, prejudice, and a blind refusal to hearken to the conclusions of objective investigation. Thomas Huxley (1825-95), an articulate scientist and vigorous controversialist, smote the defenders of orthodoxy hip and thigh. In Germany Ernst Haeckel (1834-1919), a prominent biologist, wrote powerful tracts in defense of Darwinism. The anti-evolutionists appealed to the authority of Scripture and taunted the evolutionists with having a preference for monkeys as ancestors. Disraeli proclaimed that he was "on the side of the angels."

The literal interpreters of the Bible were already under criticism from another quarter. For a long time scholars had been looking closely into the structure of the Holy Book. "Lower criticism" was engaged in establishing, by scrutiny of the varying and successive translations and copyings, the original text of the Biblical writings. "Higher criticism" attempted to ascertain, by comparison with evidence from other literary, historical, and archeological sources, the origin and development of the Bible. It was discovered that the Bible was not one but many books and fragments, put together by successive compilers. Some of the books were not written by their ostensible authors, and some were written much later than their ostensible dates of composition. Moses could not have written all the books traditionally attributed to him, nor David all the Psalms. In his sensational *Life of Jesus* (1835-36), the German theologian David F. Strauss had contended that many of the events in the Gospels, particularly the miracles, were myths current among later generations of believers. A brilliant French scholar, Ernest Renan (1823-92), wrote a series of works which treated the development of the Church as secular history, without appeal to dogma or supernatural assumptions. In his popular *Life of Jesus* (1863), he presented Christ as an extraordinary but entirely human figure, "an incomparable man."

Liberal theologians attempted to bring religious tradition and scientific advance into alignment, and often succeeded in strengthening the influence of the churches. Nevertheless, church affiliation began to diminish, and among educated urban groups there was a tendency toward agnosticism.

"Higher criticism" and evolution affected particularly Protestant denominations which emphasized devotional Bible reading. The Roman Catholic Church was placed on the defensive by political as well as scientific developments. In Italy, the victory of Sardinia in 1861 had swept out the princes of the Old Regime and threatened to end the temporal power of the Church. Moderate clergymen, particularly in Germany and France, concluded that the papacy should accept the constitutional reforms of the time, abate its dogmatic claims, and become, in short, liberal.

Pius IX, the papal *curia*, and their Jesuit advisers drew the opposite conclusion. They tightened the dogmatic and centralized power of the Church. In 1864 the Pope launched a thunderbolt at the whole of modern civilization. He reduced liberalism to eighty "errors." His exhaustive *Syllabus of the Principal Errors of Our Time* excoriated every doctrine and opinion of liberals, whether held by Protestants or by Catholics. Liberty of conscience, popular sovereignty, nationalism, education, separation of Church and State, civil marriage, divorce, *387* religious toleration—all these were condemned as dangerous errors. Error No. 19 reads: "Socialism, Communism, secret societies, Bible societies, Liberal-clerical societies; Plagues of this variety are reprobated in the strongest terms in various Encyclicals." It was an "error" to hold that "all the dogmas of the Christian religion are, without exception, the object of scientific knowledge or philosophy, and [that] human reason instructed solely by history is able, by its own natural strength and principles, to arrive at the true knowledge of even the most abstruse dogmas: provided such dogmas be proposed as subject matters for human reason." The final item proclaimed it an error to believe "that the Roman pontiff can and should reconcile himself to, and agree and align himself with, progress, liberalism, and modern civilization."

The Pope gained power at the expense of the bishops. The highest authority of the Church was the ecumenical council of bishops. Ecumenical councils had laid down new dogmas and even made and unmade popes. Organized by countries, the bishops had sometimes allied themselves with monarchies and reduced the influence of the popes. But now that the national churches were weakened by the advance of the secular state, the clergy felt the need of support from papal authority. Liberalism without made for Ultramontanism within the Church.

In December 1869 Pius assembled the Vatican Council, the first ecumenical council since the Counterreformation of the sixteenth century. For the first time no temporal rulers were invited to participate in the proceedings, a tacit admission that the secular and the ecclesiastical swords were now crossed. On July 18, 1870, the Council declared as "a divinely revealed dogma" that the Roman pontiff,

> when he speaks *ex cathedra*—*i.e.*, when, in his character as Pastor and Doctor of all Christians, and in virtue of his supreme apostolic authority, he lays down that a certain doctrine concerning faith or morals is binding upon the universal Church—possesses, by the Divine assistance which was promised to him in the person of the blessed Saint Peter, that same infallibility with which the Divine Redeemer thought fit to endow his Church, to define its doctrine with regard to faith and morals; and, consequently, that these definitions of the Roman Pontiff are irreformable in themselves, and not in consequence of the consent of the Church.

A group of German, Austrian, French, and American bishops opposed this assertion of absolutism in an age of growing parliamentarianism, but it proved a small minority.

The new claim of the papacy disturbed some Catholic laymen and alarmed European governments. The liberal Catholic historian Lord Acton (1834-1902) protested vigorously. The German theologian Johann Döllinger (1799-1890) resisted the doctrine of "infallibility" and was excommunicated. In 1870 a group of Germans, Swiss, and Austrians, calling themselves "Old Catholics," left the Church in protest against the doctrine. In 1867, when it restored civil marriage and introduced state education, Austria-Hungary had violated the concordat of 1855 with the Vatican. Upon the declaration of papal infallibility, Austria abrogated the concordat.

Charles Darwin   COURTESY OF THE ART INSTITUTE
OF CHICAGO, THE ALFRED STIEGLITZ COLLECTION

Pope Pius IX   BROWN

By a dramatic coincidence, the declaration of infallibility preceded by a few months the Pope's loss of Rome. In August 1870, during the Franco-Prussian war, Napoleon III withdrew the French troops which had been in Rome since 1849. Upon the capture of Napoleon at Sedan the next month the army of Italy attacked and took Rome. A plebiscite was held and Rome, annexed to Italy, became its capital. The Italian government passed a law granting the papacy full sovereignty over the Vatican, freedom of communication and diplomatic privileges with foreign peoples and governments, and as a compensation for the loss of income from papal territories, a large annual subsidy. Pius IX refused to accept the law, summoned all Catholics to refuse to hold office in the new state, and shut himself off as "the prisoner of the Vatican"—from which seclusion his successors did not emerge for more than a half century. All official relations between the Vatican and the Italian government were severed. Italy became the third country—after the United States and Belgium—to establish a completely secular state.

In the German Empire the hegemony of Prussia was written into the federal constitution, but not into the hearts of the non-Prussian constituents. Separatist tendencies were most apparent in the south and west, which contained the largest concentration of Roman Catholics. A sizable group of Catholic politicians were already functioning in the Prussian and German legislatures as the Center party. Bismarck was no more interested in liberal principles than was Pius IX, but he was supported by the National Liberal party, which had been outraged by papal pretensions. The Chancellor launched a campaign to adapt the Church to the new state system. The Jesuits were expelled from Germany. A series of "May Laws" passed in 1873 and others passed in the following two years provided for state supervision over the education of the clergy, made civil marriage obligatory, and dissolved many religious orders.

While Pius IX denounced Bismarck as "the modern Attila," Rudolf Virchow, a noted physiologist and positivist, hailed the campaign against the church as a *Kulturkampf*, or battle for civilization. Even though the German Chancellor was contending principally for unquestioned state power, his defenders justified his actions in terms of progress and freedom. For the age was liberal.

389

v *Steel,*

An old photograph of the Brooklyn Bridge, one of the early products of the Age of Steel. Suspended on cables made up of steel wires, the bridge connects the borough of Brooklyn with Manhattan Island. It is a fine example of the union of technology and good taste which was rare in the Age of Steel, whose progeny, while efficient and utilitarian, was generally ugly and even repelling. John Roebling (1806-69) designed the structure in the sixties (it was finished in 1893) and his imaginative conception was generalized in the doctrine "form follows function" of the American architect Louis Henri Sullivan (1856-1924). A building, Sullivan wrote, should "grow naturally, logically, and poetically out of its conditions . . . the real architect . . . must impart to the passive materials a subjective and spiritual human quality which shall make them live for other humans." It is only in the twentieth century, however, that a beginning has been made, in Western Europe and America, to adapt industrial products generally to the requirements of good taste.

Socialism, and Empire

19. *Steel and the World Economy*

In the liberal age of the mid-nineteenth century, the Western world acquired a political framework that endured for a half century, until the Russian Revolution of 1917. That framework made for substantial domestic stability and international exchange. It made possible developments that changed the face of the Western world—indeed, of the world as a whole—and set the stage for technological and scientific advances so striking as to suggest a second and more important "industrial revolution." There were sharp pulsations of economic prosperity and depression and yet an almost constant increase in material wealth. Western practices—and Western capital—spread throughout the world. A world market evolved, with great interdependence of the various continents and yet with a central position for Western countries. New areas in Africa and other continents were penetrated and explored. Socialist and populist movements arose. And, finally, economic, military, and naval rivalry increased, and new alignments of powers emerged.

Steam Power Makes the World Smaller

Some of the new developments resulted from the application of industrial methods evolved in the first half of the century. Steam power, for example, was put to work on a spectacular scale. Not only provinces but whole continents were brought together. Engineers and workmen pierced mountains, threw bridges across rivers, bored tunnels under them, and cut isthmuses.

In the United States, two companies, generously supplied with loans and land grants by the federal government, succeeded in spanning the continent. The Central Pacific Company laid tracks eastward from Sacramento, California. The Union Pacific Company built westward from Omaha, Nebraska. In May 1869 the two roads were joined by golden spikes near Ogden, Utah. The venture was enormously profitable to the railroad builders, as well as to the nation.

Physical obstructions in the heart of Europe were overcome. Twenty-two short tunnels were bored and sixty viaducts and bridges built in order to lay rails over the Alps through the Brenner Pass. Austria and south Germany were thus brought close to Italy and Mediterranean ports. In 1871 the first long tunnel was opened under Mont Cenis, to connect France with Italy. About ten years later, the Saint Gotthard Tunnel, one of the engineering feats of the century, was completed in Switzerland. The tunnel, bored through nine and a half miles of rock, rose and descended within the rock by spirals. It provided the best route between Germany and Italy, which countries, among others, contributed toward the cost of construction. Northern and Southern Europe, the Atlantic and the Mediterranean regions, became one. Another link by water—the Suez Canal—connected the Mediterranean with the Red Sea and, through them, the North Atlantic with the Indian Ocean, and Europe with the Middle and Far East.

Communication went hand in hand with transportation. The telegraph initiated and sped the shipment of goods and facilitated commercial as well as diplomatic negotiations. The processes of electroplating and wire-making produced winged messengers that outsped the locomotive and the steamship. From the sixties onward, thick nets of telegraph wires began to spread over Western Europe and the United States, and a looser net over other areas. Several cables were laid at the bottom of the English Channel, the North Sea, and the Atlantic Ocean which made contact between England, the Continent, and North America almost instantaneous. A telegraph line joined the United States with Alaska, and another united Russia and eastern Siberia; a short cable between

Federal Land Grants to Railroads
(to 1872)

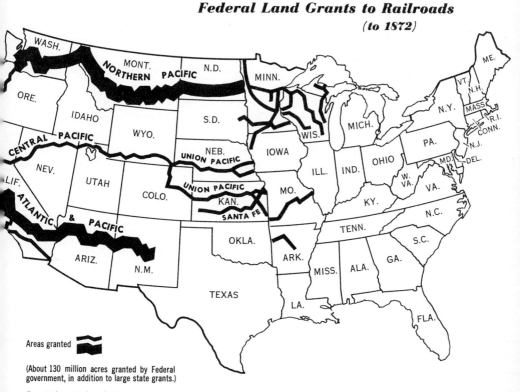

Areas granted

(About 130 million acres granted by Federal government, in addition to large state grants.)

Present-day state boundaries shown

Alaska and Siberia then connected the two lines. The farthest ends of the two hemispheres were thus placed in rapid communication with each other.

Freight and passenger rates dropped. Mails became faster and cheaper. The relation between distance and the cost of postage was abolished: a uniform rate was introduced within and between countries. Through the organization of the International Postal Union in 1874 at Bern, Switzerland, the whole world became a single mail area. International postal rates for letters, post cards, and printed matter were made uniform, each signatory country guaranteeing safe and expeditious transmission of foreign mail.

Swift commercial and personal communication became a matter of course. The experience of Great Britain is typical. When the penny post was introduced, in 1839, the annual mail jumped at once from 75 million to 196 million letters. In 1870 Englishmen mailed 648 million letters, in 1900 more than two billion, and in 1914 nearly three billion. Post cards were introduced in 1870 and in the year 1914 nearly a billion were mailed. At the beginning of the nineteenth century every Englishman was writing an average of two or three letters a year. At the end he was writing a letter a week and a card every three weeks.

Combined with the use of cheap wood pulp—instead of cotton or linen—for paper and speedier printing machines, the telegraph and cable (later supplemented by the telephone) brought into being the modern popular newspaper of mass circulation. It became possible to print and distribute millions of copies of the same newspaper at a price that the humblest person could afford. Important events and fashionable scandals in one country or continent were quickly conveyed to millions of readers in the cities of another.

Science and Steel

To the new means of swifter communication were added new industries and sources of power, intricate machines and novel scientific devices.

Experiments in electricity, begun in the eighteenth century, culminated in striking practical achievements. The carbon arc light and the incandescent lamp made gas lighting obsolete. They provided steadier, less dangerous, and less odoriferous illumination for homes and offices than gas or kerosene. A flood of light turned night into noon in the homes of the rich and the central streets of great cities. Electric motors and dynamos yielded a new source of power. The first of their many triumphs was to replace animal power in urban traction. The horse was unhitched from the tramcar, which was now moved by electricity. This was the second great defeat for the draught horse, which had been ousted from traction over long distances by the steam locomotive. The breeding of work animals diminished, and the horse population of the world eventually dropped by the tens of millions.

The vulcanization of rubber, discovered by Charles Goodyear (1800-60) in 1839, had opened a large realm of production. It began modestly with rubber coats and galoshes, went on to bicycle and carriage tires, and the end is not yet in sight. The proliferation of rubber goods may be measured simply by the demand and supply of crude rubber. World production, which in 1870 stood at a mere 10,000 tons, reached 70,000 tons in 1910.

Progress in distilling crude oil yielded a variety of valuable by-products: lubricating fluids, paraffin, kerosene, and naphtha. Some of the by-products became useful as fuel for new engines and dynamos, taking the place of coal as coal, a half century earlier, had taken the place of wood and coke. The oil wells of the world yielded 2000 barrels in 1857, almost 6 million in 1870, 30 million in 1880, and 328 million barrels in 1910.

The application of the internal combustion engine, which was developed largely in Europe, laid the foundation of the new automobile industry. In the first decade of the century, American inventors and mechanics tried to produce a cheap "horseless carriage." By 1914, Henry Ford, using assembly-line methods, had finally produced an automobile within the reach of many middle-class persons. More than a half million passenger vehicles were made in that year. The motor age had dawned.

But it was steel that left the deepest imprint on the age. It was an age characterized by the proliferation of machines, and of machines that bred machines. For these cheap steel was imperative. Most metals are neither hard enough for durable tools nor tensile enough for the tiny parts which must be interlocked and precisely dovetailed to form precision tools and machines. Copper and bronze are too soft; cast iron is hard enough, but it is also brittle; gold and silver are not only too soft but rare and costly. Steel had all the necessary characteristics, but it was expensive to produce.

Fine steel was no new discovery. Smelting and tempering steel and forging knives and swords were ancient crafts. But the craftsman had to have fairly pure iron ores, and these were rare. The problem was how to make fine steel in abundance. The solution was speeded by the least beneficent of gods, and the steel industry has always shown a due gratitude to Mars. Rifled cannons had been developed before the mid-century. Stronger metal was needed to resist the pressure of revolving cannon balls. The Crimean War of 1854-56 had stimulated the demand for it. The war was just over when an English inventor, Henry Bessemer, hit upon a process for the manufacture of cheap steel. A blast of air, passed rapidly through the molten pig iron, oxidized and reduced carbon and silica and turned the crude metal into steel. An American, William Kelly, had discovered the same process somewhat earlier but had neglected to exploit it. Bessemer eventually collected ten million dollars in patent rights. A few years later a German-born Englishman, William Siemens, and a Frenchman, Pierre Martin, using coal gas as fuel, were able to produce large quantities of steel in "open hearths." Within a dozen years the price of steel was halved. Bessemer, Kelly, Siemens, and Martin had introduced the promising—and horrific—age of steel.

The importance of their discoveries can hardly be exaggerated. It can be compared only with that of the introduction of the steam engine. Indeed, the development of cheap steel had results that were vaster and deeper, and they materialized more promptly. More than any other single factor, cheap steel was responsible for the industrial glories and martial terrors of the contemporary world. It was responsible for the extreme mechanization of industry, transport,

Henry Bessemer's invention of a process for making steel cheaply was one of the crucial developments of the second Industrial Revolution. This engraving of 1875 shows two Bessemer converters, one being filled and the other "blowing." BETTMANN

and munition-making that prepared the ground for mass comforts and mass conflict. Machine technology, myriads of labor-saving devices, sleek engines of destruction—cheap steel is behind all of them, and steel became ever cheaper. The price of American steel rails, for example, dropped from more than $100 per ton in 1870 to less than $30 at the turn of the century. The range of production and destruction widened marvelously: sewing machines, tractors, construction girders, bicycles, shoemaking machines, better textile machines, woodworking machines; small arms, battleships, armorplate, heavier and more deadly ordnance; above all, machines that made machines. The substitution of iron and then of steel for the wooden plough saved as much labor, human and animal, on the land as the substitution of modern machines for craft tools saved in industry. Reapers, threshers, harvesters, and other farm machinery made a mechanized industry of agriculture and multiplied the food resources of mankind. The hardness of steel, married to the dependability and versatility of steam power, produced extraordinarily cheap transportation both by land and by sea. The older brittle iron rails, not to speak of the wooden rails, had placed severe limits upon the size of freight cars and the size and speed of locomotives. Heavier freight could move on the less vulnerable steel, and move much faster.

Greater loads plus greater speed equaled cheapness. The new steel steam freighters could afford to charge low rates. For the first time in history, the most distant continents could compete on a large scale for one another's markets in heavy and bulky goods, raw materials, and grains. Naval and merchant vessels were henceforth made of steel. By the opening of the new century, Great Britain, still the largest shipbuilder, was producing six steel-bottomed ships for each one made of iron or wood. Many industries came to depend, directly or indirectly, upon the steel industry. In highly developed countries, the enterprises that produced steel and steel products soon formed one of the largest aggregates of wealth.

The use of modern technology spread both extensively and intensively. There was hardly a country in the Western world and in the parts of the globe most directly under Western influences that did not introduce, in one measure or another, mechanized methods in industry and agriculture, in transportation and communication. Industrialization was not uniform, however, even within the same country. It became concentrated in areas that were blessed with the necessary materials, skilled workmen and competent managers, ready capital, and accesibility to world markets. In such areas, often moderate in geographical extent, networks of factories, machine production, mines, and railroads were woven, creating a highly urbanized life and yielding high production for distant markets. To the original crowded seat of industry in the English Midlands were added several favored regions in Belgium, northern France, Bohemia, Russia, Japan, and, above all, the rich east-central region of the United States and the Rhine basin of Germany.

In the production of Bessemer steel, iron ore containing much phosphorus could not be used. Most of the large iron deposits of the Continent were high in that element, but much of the British ore was fairly free of it, and this circumstance promised to extend British supremacy from the age of iron to the new age

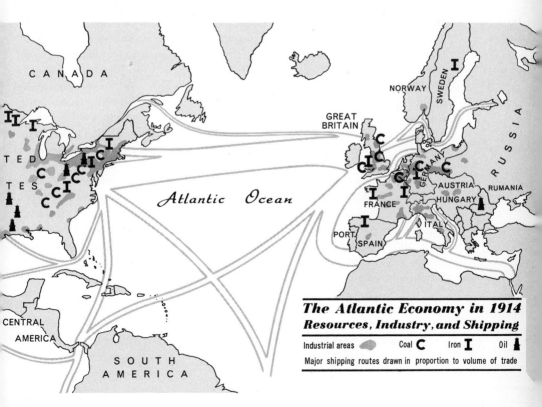

The Atlantic Economy in 1914
Resources, Industry, and Shipping

Industrial areas ●   Coal **C**   Iron **I**   Oil ⬆

Major shipping routes drawn in proportion to volume of trade of steel. In 1878, Sidney Gilchrist Thomas (1850-85) and his cousin, Percy C. Gilchrist (1851-1935), introduced a chemical method of removing the phosphorus from iron ore, thus making some of the largest deposits in the world available to steel manufacturers. The effect of their innovation—called the Thomas-Gilchrist process—was to enrich the United States and Germany, create competition for England, and embitter the relations between France and Germany.

Industrial America and Germany

The Mesabi range of Minnesota contained the largest supply of phosphorus and nonphosphorus iron in the world. The exploitation of that region, and of the rich coal deposits of Pennsylvania and adjoining states, transformed the industrial character and position of the Republic. The United States became a leading steel producer. Large oil deposits were discovered in a number of states. Steel and oil, combined with American inventiveness, free land, cheap labor, and tariff protection, supplied and produced the largest single market in existence.

Protection, an already established policy, was increased. The tariffs which had once been defended as a needed source of revenue and as a shield for infant industries against foreign rivals became a high tax on the consumer. Nor did the capitalists share the proceeds of this tax with the workers; they fought their demands at every step, and frequently in the most brutal way. If the consumer was a farmer his plight became especially invidious. The country exported food and so could not protect its agriculture in the international market, even had it wished to do so. In short, American surpluses were sold at low competitive prices, but its manufactures at highly protected prices. Industrialism was in the saddle.

The achievements of Germany were equally impressive. To its military and political power, the Hohenzollern Empire added the wealth of a modern industrial plant.

Germany's victory over France in 1870-71 bore a close relation to her industrial growth. The war indemnity collected from France in the early seventies stimulated investment—indeed, overstimulated it. Lorraine had been both stake and battleground between the two countries. Germany had annexed it for reasons of prestige and future military strategy; now it became also an industrial prize. For Lorraine, together with adjoining Luxembourg, contained the largest deposits of high phosphorus iron on the Continent. Its iron and the coal of the Ruhr and Saar valleys supplied the basic materials for heavy industry. National competition made a reconciliation between the two countries, already difficult, virtually impossible.

German industry grew even faster than American. Aside from a few countries which were also becoming industrialized and hence were highly protected, there were many outlets where competition was free: Latin America, huge parts of Asia, and, nearer home, Southeastern Europe. Industry profited from the better tools and machines of new plants and from the adaptability of the fresh salesman to the taste of his customers. German exports grew apace; at the same time the German markets were increasingly reserved for native agriculture and industry. Germany was thus able to benefit from the fairly free international market and her own restrictive national policies. She became in one generation an urbanized and industrial country. In 1871 nearly two thirds of her population lived in rural areas; by 1890 more than half lived in towns and cities, and the trend continued.

New Agricultural Techniques

The extension of the means of transportation and the mechanization of production affected agriculture as decisively as they did industry, although somewhat later. A long "agricultural revolution" was reaching a climax. In the eighteenth century new methods of cultivation and animal breeding had been developed, in England and elsewhere, and commercial agriculture had been instituted on a large scale. Throughout the nineteenth century many agricultural implements and machines, such as the mechanical reaper and thresher, were invented in England and the United States. New fertilizers were introduced, particularly the artifical superphosphate of lime and nitrate of soda, and the guano deposits of Peru. A multitude of devices—seeders, cultivators, harvesters, and still better reapers and threshers—now improved and facilitated every step in the process of raising grains. Slowly the gasoline engine began to replace human and animal power in most of these operations. Railroads and steamships carried an increasing volume of farm products to more and more distant markets. The traditional small-scale agriculture of Western Europe and the eastern United States was made more productive.

Even more significant was the impetus these mechanical advances gave to the development of regions of large-scale cultivation. In Europe, Russia was the largest such region. Overseas, agricultural and pastoral domains were carved out of the frontier lands of North and South America, of Australia and New Zealand. The most important and spectacular instance was the first conquest and settlement of the Western "frontier" of the United States. In the last three decades of the nineteenth century, American farmers took possession of as much land as their ancestors had settled in nearly three centuries of colonization and settlement. In the sixties the Western frontier had stood at about the geographic center of the North American continent, near the 100th meridian. A few settlements, established in the forties and fifties, were scattered along the Pacific Coast. Between these two frontiers lay a vast plain and the Rocky Mountains. Over the prairies roamed perhaps 300,000 Indians, about twelve million buffaloes, which supplied them with food and clothing, and, to the south, large herds of cattle, amounting to several million heads, originally bred by Spanish colonists.

The occupation of this area—and the removal of its native inhabitants—was accomplished in three successive and overlapping waves of migrants: miners,   *399* cattle rangers, and farmers. In 1859, a decade after the California gold rush, rich deposits of gold and silver were discovered in Nevada and Colorado and, later, also in Montana, Idaho, Wyoming, and Arizona—to use the names of the states which were eventually established in those regions. From both East and West, prospectors and adventurers hurried to stake out land claims. The smaller prospectors generally sold out to companies and investors, which accumulated large fortunes.

The next, and wider, surge was that of the cattlemen. The region between the 100th meridian and the Rockies, and between Manitoba in Canada and Texas, became a paradise of rangers and cowboys, a paradise without fences, without farms, without rents, and without sheriffs. The southern regions were used for breeding grounds. Cowboys would round up herds of thousands, even tens of thousands, of cattle and drive them hundreds of miles to be fattened up on Northern grasses. At ten to fifteen miles a day, the "long drive" ran into weeks. When they were heavy enough for the market, the herds were driven to railroad depots for transportation and slaughter in Western abattoirs. Refrigerated cars and ships then delivered them for consumption in the cities of the Eastern states and of Europe.

The seventies and the early eighties were the golden age of the cattle industry and of the cowboy. Then came difficult times, the result of overproduction, of foreign tariffs, and, most of all, of the irresistible spread of great agricultural enterprises. The ancient struggle of herder and farmer was re-enacted on a stupendous scale. The railroads that were taking away cattle brought back people. The Homestead Act of 1862 awarded 160 acres free to bona fide settlers after five years of continuous residence. Railroad companies and land agents scoured Eastern cities for prospective pioneers, tempting them with offers of free transportation and loans.

There were obstacles to permanent settlement. The Great Plains lacked timber, building stone, and water: they had long been regarded as uninhabitable. But two developments virtually decided the struggle against the wide-ranging cowboy: the invention of barbed wire in 1874-75, which made it possible to enclose farms against the ravages of wandering herds of cattle; and the manufacture of cheap windmills, which were used to pump ground water for irrigation. The age of the "long drive" was over. The wire that enclosed farms also enclosed cattle ranches. Western lands passed, for the most part, to the farmer. Tens of thousands of settlers poured in. The movement often assumed the proportions of a stampede. For example, on April 22, 1889, the government threw open former Indian lands in the Oklahoma territory to settlement; a bugle sounded the signal at noon; a crowd estimated at twenty thousand surged over the borders; using every sort of conveyance, they rushed in and occupied perhaps two million acres in a few hours.

The newly settled farmland comprised an area more than twice as large as the combined territory of the British Isles and Scandinavia. Between 1860 and 1900 twelve new states were added to the Union, bringing the total to 45. A whole new empire had been won. It was an empire created by the lavish hand

The Advancing Frontier in the United States

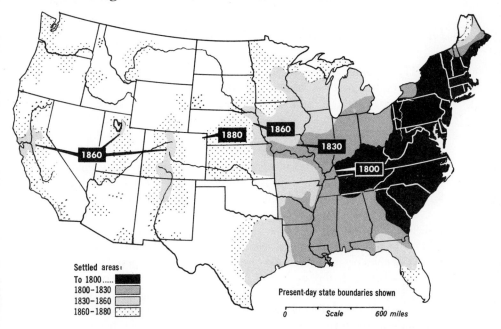

Settled areas:
To 1800.....
1800–1830
1830–1860
1860–1880

Present-day state boundaries shown

Scale: 0 — 600 miles

of Nature, the new technology, and human energy, inspired by the old European dream of wealth and leisure through land ownership. "In the Old World," the economist N. S. B. Gras has observed,

> land of itself was desirable, because it would produce a revenue and give the owner a life of leisure. Land was rented to the farmer or the peasant cultivator who paid a rental that enabled the landlord to live comfortably in the town or the metropolis. In America this was not the case, at least not at first when free land was plentiful. Only gradually, first in the east and then in the west, has it been possible to find a tenant. Accordingly the immigrant, peasant or artisan, coming to get rich, remained to labor. A mistake had been made, but America was settled.

Although most of the land was taken up by real-estate companies and railroads, a good many small farmers secured a holding.

Between 1850 and 1900, annual American production of wheat rose from 100 million to 600 million bushels, of corn from 592 million to 2662 million bushels, and of cotton from 2 million to 10 million bales. The increase in the production of grain was more than enough to supply the needs of the increased population; it helped to feed not only the new cities of the East but the old, and growing, cities of Europe. It made it possible not only for Americans but also for Englishmen and Germans to shift to industrial occupations and urban living. The success of American agriculture thus furthered the growth of industry in Europe as well as in the United States.

The Pace of Population and Migration

The mobility of the agrarian classes and the multiplication of industrial centers resulted in a remarkable growth and shift of population in the world at large, but particularly in the United States and Germany. In the last quarter of the century, the population of the United States grew from 45 million to 76 million. By 1914, it reached almost 100 million. From about 45 million in the mid-seventies. Germany's population rose to 56 million in 1900 and nearly 70 million in 1914. The story was repeated, in proportionately smaller degrees, everywhere, in agrarian as well as in industrial areas. The latter grew the fastest, for the increase of population in the villages was often channeled to the cities.

In the second half of the nineteenth century, the population of the globe rose from 1200 million to 1600 million, and that of Europe from about 300 million to 476 million. The growth of European populations was greater than that of peoples originating in Asia or Africa. The world population of European origin—whether living in Europe itself or in settlements overseas—reached nearly 700 million by 1914. The increase of Europeans and their settlement in many parts of the globe help to explain why the continent of Europe was more dominant at the turn of the century than it had ever been before.

As significant as the growth of population—indeed, closely related to its growth—was its increased mobility. Millions of villagers moved to towns, townsmen to large industrial centers, Europeans to overseas countries. The poor peasant lad, the restless provincial, the prospectless craftsman or journeyman, the unemployed proletarian, the unsuccessful businessman, the adventurous youth, the political or religious dissenter—a whole slice of mankind—packed up, entrained, and embarked. They could not always become rich—although fabulous tales of American riches circulated in Europe—but they could attain a better future, if not always for themselves, at least for their children. Steamship company representatives and employment agents scoured the more populous and poorer areas of the globe to direct the vast traffic to routes and countries in which they had an interest. They did not restrict themselves to Europe. Poor Chinese and Indian coolies appeared in the employment markets of the Americas and the expanding settlements of Africa.

Never before had so many men migrated. From 1840 to 1880, twenty to twenty-five million Europeans left home. Eight and a half million of them flocked to the United States. After 1880 the tide rose higher. There were years in which a million people and more entered the United States. Altogether, between 1870 and 1914, twenty-two million Europeans were added to the American population.

This massive movement changed the face of Europe as well as that of the United States. In the earlier decades of the century the Irish and the English had furnished the greater part of the transoceanic current. In the fifties and sixties they were joined by masses of immigrants from Germany and the Scan-

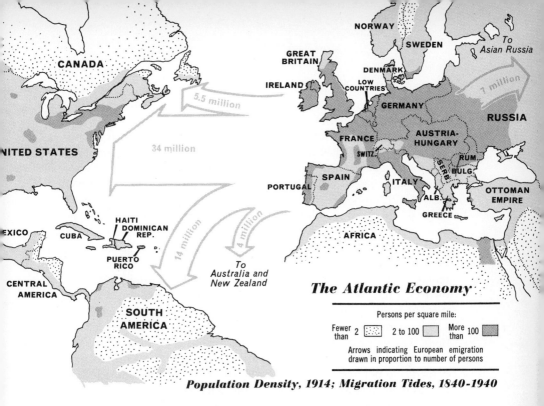

The Atlantic Economy

Persons per square mile:
Fewer than 2 / 2 to 100 / More than 100

Arrows indicating European emigration drawn in proportion to number of persons

Population Density, 1914; Migration Tides, 1840-1940

dinavian countries. Later the people of Italy, Austria-Hungary, Russia, and the Balkan countries began to supply the bulk of the immigrants. In 1910 Southern and Eastern Europe accounted for three fourths of the immigrants to the United States. For many of the new immigrants, the move meant a change not only from the Old World to the New but from patriarchal villages to urban life. New bonds between the Old World and the New were forged as millions of families in Southern and Eastern Europe threw off American branches.

Immigrants passing the Statue of Liberty in New York harbor. CULVER

The new immigrants were generally poorer and less skilled than the old. Most of them were Catholic, Greek Orthodox, or Jewish in a country Protestant in origin and attitude. Many of them came from semifeudal countries long dominated by aristocratic and absolutist regimes. The immigrants did not become assimilated easily. They tended to maintain their nationality groupings in seeking employment: Czechs and Poles mined coal, southern Italians built roads and houses, Jews sewed clothes and engaged in petty trade, and Scandinavians logged and lumbered. The immigrants clustered in homogeneous settlements, forming "little Italys," "little Polands," and Jewish centers. Yet the new homes were not quite the same as the old. The tearing away of ancient associations and the breakup of families; the attempt to strike fresh roots, psychological as well as material; the exchange of the security of custom for the unfamiliar and the remote; the inevitable misunderstanding between European immigrants and their children; the frequent and painful changes of location and occupation—these were the normal incidents of migration.

The immigrant's feeling of strangeness, which often persisted for generations, was reciprocated by the older American stock, which held political office and was usually in a better economic position. Many of the immigrants were herded into political organizations by self-seeking politicians who pretended to defend them against the prejudice of the older Americans. The immigrants were easily persuaded to barter their votes for small favors. The educated men among the immigrants were similarly separated from the cultivated American community. It was sometimes a generation before immigrant professional classes took their places alongside their native-born counterparts.

Transplantation was a spiritual experience. There was a glory in renouncing the familiar and the constricted for the adventure of risk, hope, and hardship, but there was often tragedy too. The United States, and all new countries, reflected this glory and this tragedy.

Major Sources of American Immigration

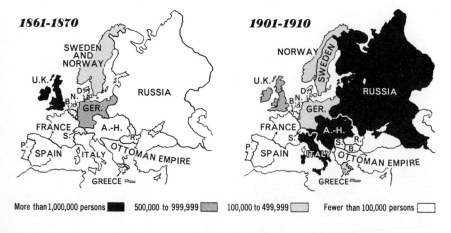

1861-1870

1901-1910

More than 1,000,000 persons ■   500,000 to 999,999 ▢   100,000 to 499,999 ▢   Fewer than 100,000 persons ▢

The Great Corporation and the World Economy

The increase of migration was, in the long run, the most significant human aspect of the Age of Steel. Of more immediate practical consequence, however, was the growth of wealth and the evolution of big business. In 1914 the national income of Great Britain was £2,165 million ($10,305,000,000), or nearly double the figure for 1880. The national income of the United States grew nearly five-fold in the same period, rising to over $30,000 million. Since the population also grew faster in the United States than in England, the average per capita income was merely doubled. In lesser degrees, France and Germany also registered increases.

It was industrial wealth that was advancing most rapidly. For example, the value of American agricultural products dropped from one third of the national income in 1850 to 22 percent in 1910. In the same period the value of the industrial product rose from 19.6 to 27.6 percent. The increasing complexity of machinery enlarged the scale, and the costliness, of industrial enterprise. Factories, shipyards, and other businesses employed more and more men per unit. Larger units called for larger outlays of capital, and industry reached far afield for financial sources. The capitalist or industrialist before the middle of the century had been typically an individual, or one of a small group of partners: he had been financier, manager, owner, and not infrequently inventor, all in one. He was now largely displaced in the first role by the investor and banker and in the others by the large impersonal corporation.

The demand for capital attracted thousands of investors who poured their money into the market, where it was directed toward enterprises at home and abroad (and occasionally into the pockets of bankers and brokers). The investor was remote from the scene of investment and usually innocent of a working knowledge of its operation, its industrial application, and its effect. Divorced from managerial functions, he became an abstract character, a name attached to a stock, like the facsimile signature of a minister of finance on a banknote. Active ownership was virtually abolished; the directors, the hired managers, and especially the bankers and the investors came to occupy the commanding seats of capitalism. In the United States the law specifically permitted the nonowning managers to acquire a power and control independent of the original investors, quite like the liege lords of feudal days. Industrial capitalism became subservient to financial.

The apex of the new financial structure was the corporation of corporations, the so-called holding company, which produced no goods but owned a controlling interest in several other corporations. Adventurous stock manipulators and ambitious industrialists conceived imperial projects: to combine railroads or steamship lines; to control raw material sources and transportation in addition to industrial production in a certain field; to corner all the available sources of crucial materials, such as rubber or oil; to monopolize this and reach the top of that. In the United States, for example, Andrew Carnegie assembled a veritable empire of iron ore and steel mills, Cornelius Vanderbilt and J. P. Morgan secured control of important railroads, and John D. Rockefeller built up a virtual monopoly of the oil industry.

Control of the aggregations of both capital and capital goods passed into fewer and fewer hands, and the controllers—who were not necessarily the investors—grew more and more powerful. Horizontal trusts, vertical monopolies, agreements to divide up markets and raise and maintain prices artificially, demands that prices at home be protected so that those abroad could be reduced to undercut the competitors, renewed demands reminiscent of the half-forgotten mercantilist age that the government support imperial adventures and international competition—all these marked the new age of corporate and financial capitalism. Perhaps properly, in no industry did size, integration, and concentration play so large a part as in the industries of steel, steel products, oil, and rubber. In Britain, and even more in the United States and Germany, a small number of huge corporations and combines effectively bestrode production in the most crucial fields and placed their rivals, not to speak of their employees, at a great disadvantage.

From these developments, integrated national economies, as well as a world economy, emerged. Large-scale industry and railway networks melted provinces and sections into homogeneous systems of production and distribution. "Giganticism" often made for greater efficiency, although there were cases in which it proved uneconomical and wasteful. It accented the distinctiveness of individual countries and stimulated national interest and pride. Trade between countries and continents grew along with trade among the sections of the same country. The possibilities of consumption for undeveloped countries and of production for those that had industrial resources were simultaneously enhanced. As capital and savings heaped up in industrial areas, repeated reinvestments in the same enterprises flattened the rates of profit and interest into a plateau, when it did not actually depress them into a valley.

The less developed countries, or those which were in process of being developed, had a greater thirst for capital, and paid more for it, in labor or in materials. The possibility of extraordinary gains beckoned investors. European capital took wing to all points of the compass. It moved to countries which were industrializing, developing their domestic markets, and, while land-blessed, hungry for labor and capital. Capital also went to unindustrialized but otherwise rich and populous countries, such as China. And it went also to areas, notably in Africa, which, while poor as markets for industrial goods, were rich in some particular material (rubber, for example, in the Congo) and also in the resource of cheap, unskilled labor. Here capital materialized in the form of rails and locomotives, there in the form of pipelines, textile machines, or electrical equipment. Rubber, oil, gold, as well as the more humdrum grain and cotton, hemp and wool, and lumber, were drawn from freshly tapped interiors to the cosmopolitan seaports, finished in European industrial centers, and distributed throughout the world.

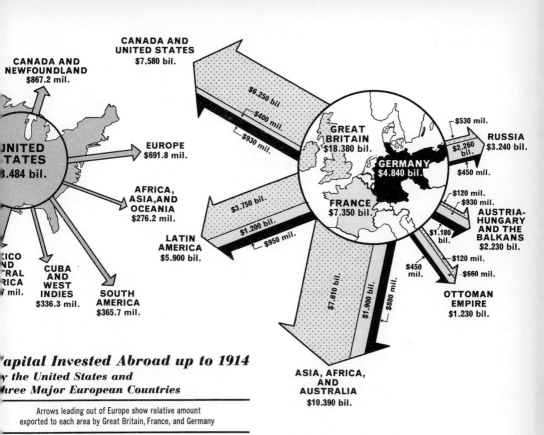

CANADA AND
UNITED STATES
$7,580 bil.

CANADA AND
NEWFOUNDLAND
$867.2 mil.

$6.250 bil.

$400 mil.

$930 mil.

GREAT
BRITAIN
$18.380 bil.

$530 mil.

RUSSIA
$3.240 bil.

UNITED
STATES
3.484 bil.

EUROPE
$691.8 mil.

GERMANY
$4.840 bil.

$2.260
bil.

$450 mil.

AFRICA,
ASIA, AND
OCEANIA
$276.2 mil.

$3.750 bil.

$120 mil.
$930 mil.

FRANCE
$7.350 bil.

$1.200 bil.

AUSTRIA-
HUNGARY
AND THE
BALKANS
$2.230 bil.

$1.180
bil.

LATIN
AMERICA
$5.900 bil.

$950 mil.

$120 mil.

ICO
ND
RAL
RICA
mil.

CUBA
AND
WEST
INDIES
$336.3 mil.

SOUTH
AMERICA
$365.7 mil.

$450
mil.

$660 mil.

$7.610 bil.

$1.900 bil.

$880 mil.

OTTOMAN
EMPIRE
$1.230 bil.

apital Invested Abroad up to 1914
y the United States and
hree Major European Countries

ASIA, AFRICA,
AND
AUSTRALIA
$10.390 bil.

Arrows leading out of Europe show relative amount
exported to each area by Great Britain, France, and Germany

It was the export of capital, principally from Europe, that made possible these world-wide operations. By 1914 Great Britain had invested twenty billion dollars abroad, over six billion in the United States and Canada; France had eight billion dollars' worth of foreign and colonial investments and loans and Germany had six and a half billion. Several billion dollars more were represented by the investments of Dutch, Swiss, Belgian, and other European capitalists. Asia, Africa, and Australia accounted for the largest share of this European wealth overseas. American foreign investments were beginning to catch up with those of Europe. In 1897 they had amounted to only 684 million dollars, but by 1914 they exceeded three billion. As yet the foreign investments of the United States were surpassed by European holdings in American enterprises, but the Republic was moving from a debtor toward a creditor position.

The political interest created by the investment of capital was different from that produced by activities in selling, buying, or exchanging goods, whether raw or finished. In order to pursue trading, legal permission, the assurance of economic freedom and financial responsibility, and a reliable trading class were sufficient. The investment of capital, however, meant the export to a borrowing country of machines, rails, locomotives, and other capital goods, and also of skilled personnel to mount and run them. A continuing connection was thereby established. This was perhaps particularly true in cases in which investment   *407* took the form of railroad building and the construction of public utilities, for these required the grant of franchises by the government. The stage was set for financial competition, colonial expansion, national rivalries—in short, for imperialism.

Speculation, Depression, and Prosperity

The course of the Age of Steel was dramatic. Like a capricious river, it ran now smooth and straight, now rapid, turbulent, and devious. The opening of new fields of economic activity in the sixties and early seventies encouraged speculation. Increasing free trade among nations (with the notable exception of the United States), government expenditures in the wars of the period, and the unification of Italy, Germany, and the United States stimulated adventurous enterprise and investment. In Germany an additional stimulus was created by the large sums paid by France as indemnity for the war of 1870. Stock speculation on European and American markets grew ever more daring and irresponsible. Stock swindles and corrupt relations between financiers and politicians became commonplace.

The day of retribution dawned in 1873, when a depression of international dimensions broke out. It brought to an abrupt end a quarter century of fairly continuous expansion—an unusually long period without serious business crises. A financial crash in Vienna initiated the depression. The inflated stock exchange of Berlin and then of other cities echoed the Austrian crash. The American stock market, which depended upon Europe for credit, resounded with sharp declines in stock values.

Thousands of businesses on both sides of the Atlantic were hurt severely. The leading investment and brokerage house in the United States, Jay Cooke and Company, went into bankruptcy. Waves of failures spread in concentric circles and inaugurated two decades of sharp depressions, relieved by spasmodic recoveries. Prices dropped, both in industry and in agriculture. A short period of deflation and suffering was followed by a wave of speculation and renewed enterprise, stimulated by the rise of new industries. In the early eighties there was another depression, not so severe as the first but more prolonged. This alternation of ups and downs continued for nearly a generation, until the mid-nineties.

European agriculture suffered not only from the fall in prices but also from a series of bad harvests and from the competition of overseas grain. From the seventies to the mid-nineties, grain prices dropped steadily until they were cut in half. Irish and English agriculture experienced the decline long predicted by the critics of free trade in grain. Continental agriculture suffered as much from glut as from want. The rich soil of Russia and Rumania yielded large supplies for the world market. This market was then flooded by the grain and meat produced on the millions of acres opened to cultivation and grazing in the United States, and soon after in Canada, Argentina, and Australia. European agriculture recoiled before this competition. A series of droughts, crop failures, and animal epidemics turned the retreat into a rout. Germany and France lost half their sheep. In many areas, and especially in England, the acreage under cultivation and the number of cultivators diminished sharply.

The agricultural depression crossed the Atlantic more slowly than the financial crash. American agriculture at first did well but then began to suffer from the fall of prices due to the constriction of European markets and its own fabulous production.

After the mid-nineties stability was largely restored. There followed two decades of recovery and advance during which the fall of prices was arrested and unemployment dropped. Economic competition within and among countries became somewhat less sharp. There was greater opportunity for domestic reform, for reform often costs money, and the Age of Steel had augmented impressively the financial resources of nations and states.

20. *Socialism and Populism*

The spasmodic changes and dramatic contrasts of the Age of Steel were reflected in society and politics. In the generation of depressions, laissez-faire policies fell under a cloud. There was social unrest throughout the Western world. This was aggravated, in several countries, by financial scandals and the revelation of corrupt relations between financiers and public officials. State intervention came into fashion. Reform movements, new parties, and class conflicts, not untouched by violence, arose in many countries, agrarian as well as industrial, parliamentary as well as absolutist. Industrial labor was organizing on a large scale. When economic conditions improved, toward the turn of the century, these movements blended into a broad tendency of gradual reform.

State Intervention and Collectivism

The successes of capitalistic organization in industry, and the human suffering that seemed inseparable from them, suggested the need for protective action by large groups, even whole societies. The decades of depression dramatized the inequality of the burden of economic progress. Labor bore much more of it than capital, agriculture more than industry. Every time prices dropped, unemployment rose. When employment resumed, it was often partial and spasmodic. The spread of industrialization brought a repetition, in many areas, of the earlier experiences of English proletarians: exhausting hours of work, inadequate wages, exploitation of women and children, and unhealthy and degrading conditions in factories and cities.

The agricultural depression of Europe was more continuous than the industrial and financial depression. The small independent farmers were the hardest hit. Wherever the farmers were not established securely, individual holdings decreased and tenancy rose.

Outbursts of individual violence testified to the passing of revolutionary tactics, although not to a weakening of widespread social unrest. Since effective police and military measures made street uprisings difficult, desperate doctrinaires sometimes resorted to assassination as a means of political protest. In 1878 an anarchist shot and wounded Emperor William I of Germany. Three years later the American president, James A. Garfield (1831-81), was shot and mortally wounded by a demented fanatic. In 1893 a more ambitious rebel tried to blow up the whole Chamber of Deputies of France. He failed, but in the following year, an anarchist stabbed to death President Sadi-Carnot (1837-94). At the turn of the century, in quick order, assassins took the lives of Empress Elizabeth of Austria-Hungary (1837-98), King Humbert I of Italy (1844-1900), and President William McKinley of the United States (1843-1901). These deeds were done by isolated individuals. Only in Russia and in Ireland, where political issues were sharp, did assassination become the policy of organized groups, aimed at lesser officials as well as heads of state.

Such acts, although symptomatic of popular distress, usually had little social effect. It was the growth of reform movements that eventually ameliorated conditions. Earlier, liberals had hoped that social improvements would follow automatically from unrestricted individual competition. Now scholars and statesmen, moralists and radicals, agreed on the need to regulate or direct the operations of the economy in one way or another. Their proposals ranged from moderate legislation to help proletarians to social ownership and management of industry. Economists became increasingly critical of the doctrine of *laissez faire*, with its fixed "laws" that were presumed to hold for any society, and turned to evolutionary and historical methods of analyzing social needs and the responsibilities of government. The "historical school" stressed the impor-

Woman and child working in an American knitting mill. EASTMAN HOUSE

tance of tradition and national aims and peculiarities. If society was an organism, as the members of this school contended, and not a mere statistical assemblage of individuals moving at will, then action in the interest of the collectivity was justified.

Many Protestant clergymen, particularly in the United States and Great Britain, urged social action on religious grounds. The movement of Christian socialism thrived. In 1891 Pope Leo XIII (1878-1903), successor to the conservative Pius IX, issued the encyclical *Rerum Novarum* ("Of New Things"), in which he counseled a benevolent attitude toward the victims of industrialism. Property rights, social inequality, and suffering, he asserted, were all "natural." Yet class conflict was wrong, for "capital cannot exist without labor, nor labor without capital." Workers must abstain from violence and capitalists from exploitation. It was "shameful and inhuman to treat men like chattels to make money by." Wages must be fair; "the rich must refrain from cutting down the workmen's earnings, whether by force, by fraud, or by usurious dealings."

The extension of suffrage in industrial countries gave the working classes some leverage. The old parties exerted themselves to attract the new voters. Conservative and landed interests, perceiving an opportunity to win popular support against industrial and financial groups, put the tradition of paternalism to modern uses. It was, however, among liberals that social policies gained the most favor. The concentration of wealth threatened the principles of political equality and liberty. Why not apply the ideals of fair play and equity, the methods of political, legal, and administrative reform, to economic questions?

Two Americans distinguished themselves among the social critics. Edward Bellamy (1850-98) dressed utopia in industrial clothes. His fantasy *Looking Backward, 2000-1887*, published in 1888, eventually sold a million copies in the United States and was translated into many languages. It pictured the city of the future—the new Boston—as an efficient cooperative community, deriving the advantages of science and industry and avoiding the waste, scarcity, and invidiousness of capitalism.

Of more lasting significance was *Progress and Poverty* (1879), a comprehensive indictment of landlordism. Its author, Henry George (1839-97), described the masters of the land throughout the ages as fat and selfish drones. Whenever a country grows richer and more populous, George pointed out, the value of the land rises automatically. He advocated a fiscal reform which, in a more modest form, had been proposed by David Ricardo: a "single tax" upon that part of the landowners' income from rent which is due not to their own efforts and contributions but to the general improvement of society. The "unearned increment" would thus return to the society which created it, to be used for public improvements and services. It would make other taxes unnecessary. The economic system would remain otherwise uncontrolled, competitive, and individualistic. The "single tax" movement won many adherents.

Hegel and Marx

Of the social doctrines that survived from the first half of the century, that of Karl Marx alone found a wide response. In the preface to *Capital* Marx declared himself "frankly . . . a disciple of that Great Thinker" Hegel. Indeed, much of Marxism derives directly from Hegelianism (see pp. 212-13).

Following Aristotle, Hegel had insisted that reason and freedom became real only as they were embodied in action and achievements. As mere thought or desire they were nothing. Hegel asserted the power of reason, not only to explain, but also to shape and dominate the practical world and the course of history. It seemed to him that, from the beginning, the universe and every significant part of it had been penetrated and would eventually be governed by the "World Spirit." Hegel's World Spirit, or God, was the essence of reason acting in full consciousness of itself and of its relation to the environment. Deliberation and action were to Hegel true freedom.

Previous thinkers had distinguished between subject and object, the mind and the outside world. Some of them, suspecting that our senses and our understanding deceive us, had posited a truer reality, an inner meaning, behind the appearance of things. This was the realm of God, the source of ultimate value. Hegel's "dialectical idealism" threw a bridge between subject and object, and between both of them and God. Nothing can be understood, he claimed, nothing can exist, in the absence of its opposite. Good implies evil, cause implies effect, agent implies act, form implies content, and vice versa. Every event is the result of the clash of contraries. But the clash never issues in clear victory or defeat; rather, it leads to a conjoining of contraries, to a reconciliation in a higher entity which submerges their original differences. The process is then repeated, and results in ever closer approximations to perfection.

The stages of social evolution are those of the growth of man. Childhood, youth, and manhood, Hegel pointed out, are distinct stages, yet also links in a chain. The true character of an individual resides, not in any one stage, but in the direction taken toward reason. The direction is present in the seed, but it is fulfilled only in the last stage. The passage from one stage to another is the result of an inner conflict between contrary tendencies, the thesis and the antithesis. Neither tendency prevails, but the two are merged into a higher entity, or synthesis. Freedom is developed through the clash with discipline. The child gives up a primitive and capricious freedom (thesis) for the discipline of education (antithesis). The resulting synthesis is the triumph of disciplined freedom. The further antithesis of the exigencies of law then makes its appearance. The resulting synthesis is the rise of the orderly freedom of the citizen.

Like man, society evolves from infancy to maturity. The stages of history are the Oriental, the Classical, and the Modern. The first political form is despotism; the second, an uneasy equilibrium of democracy and autocracy; the third, modern monarchy. Each stage of development is initiated by a revolution. *413*

The cause of change is critical thought, and the process is one of conflict and acceptance of a higher view of things.

In each great epoch a leading nation carries the torch of the World Spirit. The missionary nation, Hegel believed, had the right to assert its superiority over other nations. Only the history of such a nation is significant; the experience of other nations is irrelevant to progress, and they are therefore—and in Hegel's language the characterization was a malediction—"unhistorical." China and India, for example, were condemned to lie, "as it were, still outside of the world's history." This theory proved a most powerful weapon in the hands of conquerors and imperialists. With Herder and Fichte (see pp. 188; 188-189), Hegel introduced the age of "advanced peoples" and "backward peoples," of "civilized nations" and "benighted tribes."

Hegel accepted Thomas Hobbes's description of international relations as a perpetual state of war. He went further than Hobbes in holding that war is not only inevitable but desirable. There can be no judge among states, he claimed; the only test of right is the ultimate judgment of posterity. "The history of the world is the world's court of justice." Unfortunately, by the time the court convenes, the criminal is gone.

This was the philosophy that Karl Marx engrafted upon the political thought of France and the economic thought of England. The aim that Marx set himself was the abolition of poverty. Where Hegel ascribed progress to the rational spirit potential in man from the beginning, Marx ascribed the solution of man's economic problems to his attempts to master the physical environment. The stages of Hegel's "Idea" became in Marx's work the stages of man's control of the environment, or a hierarchical series of "methods of production." Industrial production, he believed, would do away with the plague of poverty. Moral, intellectual, and political questions would be solved quite incidentally, since they were reflections of economic questions, or, in short, of poverty. In this supernal hope, Marx reflected the influence of the utopians.

For an explanation of how progress would be brought about, Marx appealed to French political thought and experience. French thinkers had recently been suggesting that history is the result of the division of people into social classes and the conflicts between those classes. The French Revolution of 1789 seemed to Marx the model instance of the assumption by a vigorous class—in this case, the bourgeoisie—of the leadership of the urban and rural masses—that is, of the nation—and its achievement, not only of political dominance for itself, but of a higher stage of evolution for society as a whole. Marx cast the proletariat in the same role in the next revolution. The leading nation of Hegel became the leading class of Marx. Slaves to the machine, degraded in their human dignity, deprived of the joys of family life, likely to be thrown out of work in commercial crises, and yet essential to the operation of industry, the proletarians had every interest in reforming the economic order and alone held the possibility of doing so. The rise of Chartism in England demonstrated that the proletariat was capable of political action. Marx concluded that the modern proletariat must lead society toward socialism by doing battle with the bourgeoisie. As capitalist exploitation reduced small owners to wage earners, the proletariat would become virtually synonymous with the nation. By destroying capitalist rule, it would put an end not only to its own miseries but also to social division, national oppression, imperial exploitation, and the rule of the few over the many.

Marx emphasized the role of the proletariat on ethical as well as Hegelian grounds. The proletariat was not only the future leader of mankind; it was also the most conspicuous victim of capitalism. Marx agreed with English classical economists in tracing "value" to labor—manual or mental—operating upon the resources of nature. He differed from them in his view of how economic "value" was distributed among the various classes. A portion of this "value," he contended, comes back to its creator in the form of wages, to assure the maintenance and reproduction of the labor force. Another part is withdrawn for repairs and the replacement and expansion of capital goods. Under cover of this withdrawal, the capitalist abstracts a share for his own profit, a profit to which he is not entitled by any contribution that he has made. This is "surplus value." Marx's description of the plight of the proletariat under the wage system, amply documented from English experience, became a classic.

Although he accepted the ideals of French and Anglo-American liberals, Marx differed in his conception of politics. To them politics was a tool for safeguarding the individual and guiding the course of society; to him it was an automatic reflection of economic forces. To them freedom was a fragile plant that needed much care; to him it was the fruit of a deep-rooted historical tree. He did not share their suspicion of the appetite for power and their conviction of the dangers of too much organization and centralization. Marx did not fear that a highly integrated economic order would necessarily be incompatible with a large "realm of freedom." The dialectical mode of thinking accustomed him to combine contraries and opposites, such as freedom and authority, spontaneity and order, and to identify them—indeed, often to confuse them. Hence he did not find it necessary to provide for a political organization during the transition period of the proletarian dictatorship. Nor did he feel a need to explain why a future "administration of things," which was highly disciplined and required the exercise of authority, was not a "state," or how society could prevent its authority from spilling over beyond the economic realm.

Marx's intransigent opposition to private capitalism and his conviction of the "scientific" validity and inevitability of his prognosis made a strong appeal. In the *Communist Manifesto* he warned that capitalistic industry, by creating a class of proletarians, had produced "its own grave-diggers." The downfall of the bourgeoisie and the victory of the proletariat were "equally inevitable." In *Capital* he asserted that "capitalist monopoly becomes a fetter upon the method of production" and predicted that "the expropriators" would be "expropriated." Marx painted the future in glowing terms. Plentiful production would make calculated distribution unnecessary: "to everyone according to his needs."

When in the course of social evolution, class distinctions have disappeared, and when all the work of production has been concentrated into the hands of associated producers, public authority will lose its political character. Strictly speaking, political power is the organized force by one class in order to keep another class in subjection. When the proletariat, in the course of its fight against the bourgeoisie, necessarily consolidates itself into a class, by means of a revolution makes itself the ruling class, and as such forcibly sweeps away the old system of production—it thereby sweeps away the system upon which class conflicts depend, makes an end of classes, and thus abolishes its own rule as a class. The old bourgeois society, with its classes and class conflicts, will be replaced by an association in which the free development of each will lead to the free development of all.

The doctrines of Marx prevailed over those of the utopians, who had concentrated their attention either on "perfect" small communities or on the spiritual transformation of man. Like the liberals, Marx took the world for his province and trusted to the operation of economic forces. In an age when Europe dominated the other continents, Marx linked the fortunes of socialism with the spread of the European system of machine production. In an age of science, he based his conclusions on a materialist view of social evolution and distinguished his doctrine as "scientific socialism." Finally, in an age when the urban masses were growing rapidly in numbers, importance, and self-consciousness, he singled out the proletariat as the "hero" of society. Marx managed to absorb and combine some of the most potent forces of the nineteenth century. As the century drew to a close, "socialism," a term which had rich and varied connotations, became virtually synonymous with "Marxism." There was hardly a country in the Western world that did not have a Marxist party. On the Continent, the doctrine of Marx acquired a cultural as well as political influence, and in the twentieth century it became the official ideology of states inhabited by well over one third of the human race.

Marxism came into its own only after a long hibernation. In essentials, it was complete in the 1840's, but the first Marxist parties were not organized until thirty years later. Meanwhile the political atmosphere and the character of the economy and of the middle classes had changed. In consequence, Marxism was no sooner applied than it was revised. The prosperity of the fifties and sixties and the advance of constitutional principles suggested to Marx that, in the more advanced parliamentary countries, peaceful reform rather than violent overthrow might prove to be the road to socialism. But his conviction that capitalism would eventually break down and that the governments would cooperate to suppress socialist efforts, in the spirit of the Holy Alliance of his youth, persuaded him that, sooner or later, the struggle would take a violent form.

Yet revolution had gone out of fashion. The governments had become less vulnerable as well as more agreeable, for they had strengthened their techniques of order and repression. Marx's collaborator, Friedrich Engels, in 1895 admitted that "history has proved us wrong. . . . A real victory of an insurrection over the military in street fighting . . . is one of the rarest exceptions." The growing disposition of the governing classes to alleviate social distress diminished the coldness that the *Communist Manifesto* ascribed to the capitalist state. Democratic gains, though modest, suggested that the state was not merely an "executive committee of the bourgeoisie." The economic recovery of the nineties and the first decade of the new century further belied Marx's pessimistic prognoses.

These developments prompted socialists to modify some of the assumptions and conclusions of the master. The German revisionist Eduard Bernstein (1850-1932), in *Evolutionary Socialism* (1899), cited statistics which refuted the prediction of the *Communist Manifesto* that the middle classes would descend into the ranks of the wage-earning class, leaving a small band of capitalists to face the proletariat, the overwhelming majority of the nation. The middle classes were, in fact, growing, not only in absolute numbers but relatively to other classes. The proletariat was not a majority even in the more industrialized countries. It was not suffering from constantly "increasing misery." This meant that socialism could not be exclusively proletarian. To muster a parliamentary majority, the socialists had to develop a program that would attract the support of lower-middle-class and professional groups. Bernstein concluded that the dependence upon a capitalist catastrophe and the vision of a full-blown socialist society must be abandoned; that emphasis should be placed on political and economic amelioration through trade union and parliamentary action. There were, however, many socialists who, although aware that a violent onslaught on capitalism was out of the question for the moment, supported an "orthodox" interpretation of Marxism and hoped for the day when the bourgeoisie might be overthrown. Consequently, two rival tendencies and wings of Marxism arose: the evolutionary, or revisionist, and the revolutionary.

Social Reform and Trade Unionism

Although collectivist doctrines and reform proposals varied over a wide range, they reinforced each other in producing a common effect, which was sometimes called state or municipal socialism. Many states and communities accepted the responsibility for promoting public welfare, improving urban living conditions, and protecting the weaker elements of society, notably by expanding educational and public health facilities.

Several factors combined to compel the rapid spread of popular education: the increase of taxable wealth, the need of modern industry for literate workers, and the need to inculcate national and patriotic ideals, through the teaching of history, in the recruits of the mass armies which came into vogue in the seventies and eighties. Great Britain and France expanded their formerly partial educational enactments into a complete national system in 1876 and 1881, respectively. Free and universal elementary education soon became the rule in most other countries.

Advocates of "municipal socialism" worked for slum clearance, improved   *417* housing, and reduction of the cost of public utilities. Many cities built and ran their own plants to supply gas and later electricity and provided transportation.

Scientists began to work on the problems of epidemic disease. Cities, regions, and whole countries had often been ravaged by cholera, plague, and typhoid. Tuberculosis was widespread. It was not known until the eighties that microbes carried these and dozens of other communicable diseases. It was not even clear that filth and excrement were related to dangerous disease, that the improvement of transportation and the concentration of large populations in cities were a greater boon to the microbes than to the passengers and city-dwellers. Then a young French chemist, Louis Pasteur (1822-95), demonstrated that most human and animal diseases are carried and produced by a large variety of microbes. The destruction of microbes and the establishment of conditions unfavorable to their multiplication and movement became the principal defense of health. It was found that inoculation with mild microbe cultures could increase bodily resistance to disease in the future. Enlightened communities and governments began to undertake a variety of programs, particularly in the capitals, large cities, and crowded industrial centers. They established sewer systems and clean water supplies and sought to prevent seepage from one to the other, which had hitherto been common. Many states provided clinics for treating the poor compelled dairymen to pasteurize their milk (that is, to heat it in order to kill harmful bacteria), and vaccinated the whole population at public expense.

By the end of the century, cholera, plague, and typhus had been brought under control in the more advanced countries, and attention was being directed to the widespread ravages of tuberculosis and to the problem of infant mortality. In 1882 a German chemist, Robert Koch (1843-1910), isolated the microbe of tuberculosis and opened the way for the treatment and cure of the disease. The reduction of infant mortality took longer to accomplish, since the problem involved not only disease factors but also the economic status, housing, and employment of the mothers.

One of the most striking expressions of state initiative was social legislation. This legislation was of two kinds. One kind, known as labor legislation, dealt with abuses of and hazards to workers while on the job: accidents, dangerous machines or methods, unhealthy materials or locales, fire dangers, and the like. The pioneer in labor legislation was Great Britain, which had begun earlier in the nineteenth century to take small steps toward improving conditions in textile factories and mines in so far as they affected women and children. In the last third of the century, these measures were extended to cover all workers employed in these and other industries. In 1862 it was enacted that wages were the first charge on employers' credit. In 1864 and 1867 the laws which prohibited inhuman conditions in textile factories were applied to factories generally. In 1906 it was provided that employers must compensate workmen injured while working and must pay a pension to the survivors of employees who were injured fatally. Finally, in the first year of the new century, the Factory and Workshop

Act consolidated and stiffened the enforcement of the whole body of labor legislation.

The example of England was followed, and on some points anticipated, by other European countries and by various states of the American Republic. In 1884 Germany enacted a law compelling employers to insure their workers against accidents occurring while they were on the job. Three years later another law placed limits upon the employment of women and children, and upon the length of the working day in certain industries. By the end of the century there were few countries which had not enacted, if not always seriously enforced, some labor legislation.

Another type of legislation—social insurance—dealt with the hazards of sickness, disability, and old age. Germany led the way by passing in 1883 a sickness insurance bill, which compelled employers and employees to contribute to a fund from which modest payments were made to sick workers for a maximum of thirty weeks. The following year an accident insurance law was enacted. A third measure, passed in 1887, provided insurance against old age and invalidism. The state as well as employers and employees contributed to a pension fund. At 70 years of age—later 65—a workingman would be entitled to a small pension in proportion to his own contribution. The scope of these provisions was gradually extended, and the insurance laws were codified in 1911.

Similar measures were passed, though on a less comprehensive scale, in Austria-Hungary and other countries. France regulated voluntary health insurance societies. After the turn of the century, she enacted a series of laws providing for pensions to the aged. In 1909 England provided small pensions to be paid entirely out of funds raised by general taxation. She established labor exchanges to supply information on employment opportunities. The epoch-making National Insurance Act of 1911 covered all workers against illness and provided payment for prevention as well as cure. In trades subject to severe fluctuations, the workers were insured against unemployment. Laid-off workers received benefits for fifteen weeks. The cost of both systems was shared by the state, the employers, and the wage earners.

The principal difference between the English and the German insurance systems was that in England the state's contribution to the insurance funds was generally larger. The taxation measures which supplied the necessary money had the effect of diminishing the extremes of economic inequality. Finally, wherever possible, the government built upon existing voluntary cooperative efforts, whereas in Germany the element of legal compulsion was stronger.

Legislation dealt generally with the emergencies of labor and with the miseries of the weaker elements of society. The day-to-day problems of the majority of workers remained the concern of the workers themselves, who drew together increasingly in trade unions. Austria legalized labor organizations and collective bargaining in 1867, Germany in 1869, Great Britain in 1871, and France in 1884. By the end of the century the right of association was formally secure in most countries. Efforts to organize labor were often more successful in years of prosperity, when workers were able to obtain employment and hence pay dues, than in periods of depression. It was chiefly the skilled workers of the more established trades who were organized at first. By 1914 there were more than four million organized workers in Great Britain, three and a half million in Germany, and about two and a half million in the United States.

Populists and Progressives in America

The United States lagged behind England and the Continent both in social legislation and in unionization. Probably nowhere was the tradition of *laissez faire* so deep-rooted. Although protectionism became an established policy during and after the Civil War, the "hands-off" tradition remained a strong force in domestic affairs. The division of functions among federal, state, and municipal governments diffused responsibility for social action, and the extraordinary tide of immigration delayed the coalescence of popular movements. Although much of the labor force was native-born, employers exploited the presence of foreign-born industrial workers to divide the working class and balk the efforts of reformers. Judges often "enjoined," or warned, unions against striking or picketing and then punished the workers, not for breaking a law, but for "contempt of court." These tactics slowed the growth of unions.

The first large national labor organization, the Knights of Labor, was

Contemporary newspaper drawing of a clash between strikers and police in New York during a strike of street-railway workers in 1886. From Frank Leslie's Illustrated Newspaper, *March 13, 1886.*

established in 1869; it admitted both skilled and unskilled workers, both local organizations and individuals, and it developed a broad program of reform. After a flurry of success, it gave way to the more powerful and more exclusive American Federation of Labor, led by Samuel Gompers (1850-1924), a cigar maker who had emigrated from England. The AFL was made up of existing trade unions, most of which were craft groups—the so-called aristocracy of labor. From its beginnings in the eighties, the AFL dominated organized labor for nearly two generations. It held aloof from ideologists and reformers, accepting neither their leadership nor their programs. It shunned collectivist doctrines and political activity, although its members were urged to support local political candidates who were sympathetic to labor. The emphasis was on the immediate interests of the unionized workers.

The American Socialist Labor Party, organized in 1877, was one of the earliest Marxist organizations in the field. Its leader was Daniel De Leon (1852-1914), a university lecturer who took the revolutionary view of the doctrine. In 1901 the more moderate elements withdrew and organized the Socialist party. The two parties exercised a feeble influence. They attracted some followers from among the recent immigrants, particularly those of German and Russian origin, but made little dent on the mass of workers. They were overshadowed by the appeal of single-taxers, municipal reformers, and, above all, agrarian populists.

The American farmers were in a stronger political position than the city workers, for they controlled many state legislatures. Yet they were denied their share of the wealth that they had been instrumental in producing. The introduction of agricultural machinery required the investment of capital, and farmers went into debt to obtain it. The tendency to produce a single crop for the market deprived the producer of the security against the vagaries of the market afforded by more diversified agriculture. The competition of the large commercial farms strained the capacities of the small farmer. And while farming was highly competitive, in the manufacture of farm machinery, transportation, and packing, the trend was toward large organizations and monopolies. The prices of the things the farmer bought rose, and those of the things he sold dropped. They dropped faster, moreover, than productivity rose. After routing his European rivals, the American farm producer began to feel the competition of Canadian and Argentinian farmers. Tenantry and sharecropping, already widespread throughout the South, made their appearance elsewhere, even in the newer lands of the West.

In the seventies, the farmers organized educational "granges," to stimulate technical improvements and economic cooperation. In a few years a million and a half farmers joined thirty thousand local granges. Although the movement was ostensibly nonpolitical, grievances were freely aired, particularly against the railroads, whose high freight rates were widely resented. Some of this sentiment was mobilized behind the new Greenback party, which proposed to raise prices by inflating the currency. The rebellion grew in the eighties, when the Great Plains suffered a drought. The grangers gathered in large "alliances," which merged to form the People's (Populist) party in 1891.

The Populists demanded that United States senators be chosen by the citizens instead of by state legislators, and that the citizens be empowered to initiate and enact laws by direct referendum. They asked that the federal government take over and run the railroads and the telegraph and telephone companies, advance loans to farmers, and store perishable crops. Their suggestion that silver be coined freely, so as to effect a rise in prices, appealed to debtors in both town and country. The Populists proposed to shift the fiscal burdens to the rich by levying a tax on incomes. They reached out a hand to industrial labor by endorsing the eight-hour day, demanding the restriction of immigration, and condemning the use of spies and detectives by employers in labor disputes. In the hope of bringing together the poor classes of both races, they appealed for support to the Negro tenant farmers of the South, encouraging their aspirations for political equality.

The Populists were more successful in agricultural states than in the nation as a whole. They elected many state legislators, obtained laws restricting the local powers of railroad companies, and won over large segments of the Democratic party in the South to their ideas. In 1896, they endorsed William Jennings Bryan (1860-1925), the Democratic candidate for president.

"Free silver" became the simplified summary of the demands of Democrats and Populists. Since the mines were pouring out generous amounts of silver, its coinage would bring a rise in agricultural prices. This was no more artificial than indirectly raising the prices of industrial goods by protective tariffs, but many Democrats as well as Republicans were alienated by the proposal: it was not clear to them how the United States could go off the gold standard unless other countries also did so. Industrialists and financiers raised huge campaign funds to influence the public and branded the free-silver men "radicals" and even "anarchists." A slight improvement in economic conditions, combined with the discovery of large gold deposits in South Africa and Australia, lifted prices. The result was that the conservative Republican candidate, Governor William McKinley (1843-1901) of Ohio, obtained more than seven million popular votes and 271 votes in the electoral college. Bryan garnered only a half million fewer popular votes but since they were less strategically distributed among the various states his vote in the college was only 176. Populism had demonstrated its popular appeal, but it had failed to prevail over the forces of finance and industry.

For the Negroes, the failure of Populism was particularly tragic. Many of them had been intimidated into voting against Populists. Those who dared to vote Populist aroused the fear of the white population that Negroes might acquire political influence. In the end the Southern Negroes were removed from politics altogether. The process of disfranchisement, begun in the late seventies, was now completed. State after state in the South passed laws requiring property, fiscal, residence, and educational tests so difficult that virtually the whole Negro population was excluded from the polls. The result was that the various classes of whites in the South accepted a single-party system, since any opposition to the Democratic party would naturally be tempted to seek the support of Negroes by enfranchising them. Thus race discrimination hurt both races by depriving the South of normal contests between vigorous rival parties.

As Populism went down, Progressivism came up. At the turn of the new century, a host of publicists—particularly the "muckrakers" Ida M. Tarbell, Lincoln Steffens, and Upton Sinclair—documented the indictment of plutocracy. They showed how the trusts grew fat through corrupt practices, how selfish business interests and complaisant politicians conspired to misgovern cities for their own benefit. Progressive politicians became active in reforming municipal government, which had become a byword of corruption. They were able in many cases to arrest the extortions of privately owned utilities, improve water supplies, and enforce sanitation rules. Some cities—notably Galveston, Texas, and Dayton, Ohio—abandoned government by politicians and parties altogether, substituting commissions of nonpartisan administrators or professional city managers. Reformers of both parties were elected to state legislatures and even to executive seats. The result was a tide of laws to regulate railroad rates, improve housing conditions, and scrutinize the practices of corporations. The processes of democracy were safeguarded by the introduction of the secret ballot, legislation by popular referendum, recall of legislators by dissatisfied constituencies, and direct primary elections at which the voters could choose the party candidates for office. The state of Wisconsin became the principal laboratory of reform, under the leadership of the Progressive Republican Governor (later Senator) Robert M. La Follette (1855-1925).

Progressivism then ascended to the federal level. The larger issues of protectionism, the regulation of businesses which crossed state lines—that is to say, of most big business—and monopoly and concentration could be dealt with only at that level. Since the Republican party controlled the federal government, the issues led to a controversy within that party. The principal figure in the controversy was Theodore Roosevelt (1859-1919), who succeeded to the presidency in 1901, when McKinley was assassinated by a deranged anarchist.

Roosevelt was a patrician who disdained the new plutocracy. He had an almost boyish exuberance and seemed to be the incarnation of American energy. He pursued a bold foreign policy and, by assailing the "malefactors of great wealth," earned the applause of reform groups. During his administration the Department of Justice brought suit against the Northern Securities Company, which sought to concentrate control of Northwestern railroads; the Supreme Court in 1904 ordered dissolution of the Company under the terms of the Sherman Anti-Trust Act of 1890, which forbade "any attempt to monopolize . . . any part of the trade and commerce among the states. . . ." Despite this and other defeats, monopolies continued to grow. The prevention of adulteration of prepared foods and patent medicines was begun in 1906, when the Pure Food and Drug Act was passed. Roosevelt attempted to obtain a "square deal" for coal miners by inducing the mine operators of Pennsylvania to make concessions to striking workers. Rebates to favored railroad companies were forbidden in the Elkins Act of 1903, and the principle of railroad regulation by the government was written into law in 1906.

423

Roosevelt was succeeded in 1909 by William Howard Taft (1857-1930), also a Republican but one who lacked Roosevelt's interest in aggressive reform. Perceiving an opportunity to return to the presidency but unable to win the Republican nomination against Taft, in 1912 Roosevelt accepted the most radical planks of the Progressive program, snatched the leadership of the Progressives from La Follette, and ran for office as a third-party candidate. By dividing the Republicans, he made possible the election of Woodrow Wilson (1856-1924), the second Democratic president since the Civil War.

Wilson, an admirer of the British Constitution, wished to enlarge the opportunity for leadership by the American president and to reduce the sharp separation between the executive and legislative functions in the federal government. As President of Princeton University he had tried to abolish the privileges of the "aristocratic" clubs. As Governor of New Jersey he had fought the political bosses by espousing a program of civic and social reform. Wilson had campaigned for the presidency on a platform which called for improvement of the conditions of the small and debt-ridden farmer, the small businessman, the consumer, and, to a degree also, the workingman. He wished to curb economic privilege and vivify individual competition. "The New Freedom" was his name for a program compounded of both individualism and state intervention to remove economic abuses.

Wilson brought in with him a Democratic majority in both houses of Congress, which soon passed the Underwood Tariff, lowering rates on most items about 10 percent and extending the list of goods admitted free of duty. As a result of the pressure of progressives over several years, the Constitution was amended in February 1913 to permit the levy of federal income taxes and again in May 1913, to provide for the popular election of Senators by the voters of the states instead of by state legislatures. The Underwood Tariff included a provision for a graduated tax on annual incomes above $20,000. Congress imposed controls in order to reduce speculative methods. The Federal Reserve System, virtually a new Bank of the United States, came into being in 1913. In the following year the Sherman Act was supplemented by the Clayton Anti-Trust Act, which increased the prohibitions of illegal corporation practices and exempted labor and agricultural organizations from prosecution under antitrust laws. The Federal Trade Commission was established to investigate and secure the aid of the courts in checking "unfair methods of competition in commerce." Easy credit was extended to farmers in 1916 through the Farm Loan Act. Seamen's conditions, long notorious for their misery, were improved. Railroad men were granted an eight-hour day. In Wilson's first term (1913-17) a fresh breeze blew through the corridors of the American government.

Irish Populists and British Labor

The problems of the Age of Steel were intensified in England by her dependence on imported food, the long-standing dispute with Ireland, and the sensitiveness of an old empire to new challengers.

For a generation after the abolition of the Corn Laws in 1846, British agriculture had prospered, but by the seventies, when grain prices began to plummet, the policy of free trade had become firmly established. The interests of industrial exporters in keeping world markets as accessible as possible, and the interests of the urban population in keeping its food bills down, were too strong to countenance a revival of the Corn Laws. The government tried other measures of relief. It gave small strips of public lands to poor farm laborers. It encouraged small holdings. It removed prohibitions against the killing of game and gave farmers compensation for improvements they had made on rented lands. Henceforth landlords and not tenants paid the tithes.

In Ireland economic distress in the villages, exacerbated by old religious and political grievances, assumed the proportions of a crisis. Irish farmers and laborers suffered from harsh and absentee landlordism as much as from sinking prices and values. Henry George's attack on landlordism in *Progress and Poverty* found strong support in Ireland. The Tenant-Right League, formed in 1850, had demanded "three F's": "free sale of occupation rights by tenants at will, fixity of tenures, and fair rents." A more aggressive organization, the Land League, was formed in 1879. Its numerous followers enforced their arguments by intimidating landlords and their agents in order to prevent evictions. They invented the "boycott"—complete severance of all relations, economic and social, with their opponents. Several especially brutal landlords and even some high government officials were assassinated.

The Irish rebellions were largely "made in the United States." The League received financial support and much of its inspiration from Irish-Americans, who did not forget that famine and English misrule had driven them from their homeland. The American supporters, in fact, had sometimes been more unyielding than the natives. They formed the Fenian Brotherhood in 1858 in New York with the aim of overthrowing English rule of Ireland. In 1867, as we have seen, they tried unsuccessfully to attack England indirectly, by plotting an invasion from northern New York State into Canada.

Since the British House of Commons was often divided almost evenly between Liberals and Conservatives, the contingent of Irish members held the balance of power. They threatened to stop all legislative activity by obstructing debate and abusing parliamentary rules unless Irish troubles were attended to. William Gladstone, leader of the Liberal party, had made himself spokesman of a broad program of reform. In 1869 the "Irish" (Anglican) Church was disestablished and partially disendowed; this meant that Irish Catholics were no longer forced to support a state church of which they were not communicants.   *425*

Beginning in 1870, a series of "land laws" was passed, providing that evicted tenants were to be compensated, as in England, for improvements made on the land. The "three F's" were written into the statute book in the Land Act of 1881. Tenants could not be evicted unless they failed to pay rent. An official commission reduced rents to a fairer level. Later funds were voted—by Conservatives as well as Liberals—to supply easy credit to tenants who wished to purchase their farms. The government spent a hundred million dollars to replace large estates with small holdings. These measures undermined landlordism in Ireland while they compensated the former owners and their agents generously. They brought a large measure of relief to villages. On the whole, however, substantial farmers were in a better position to take advantage of the land laws than poor tenants or laborers. Nor were the Irish in a mood to be grateful, especially since self-government was denied them.

In the largest of the British Isles, industrial labor had increased its pressure for favorable legislation. In the mid-century, unions of long standing combined in national federations in trade after trade. They formed councils in large cities in order to concert the local efforts of all organized workers. In the sixties these councils began to meet every year in national trade union congresses, which represented between a million and a million and a half organized workers. Such associations were legal, but striking was sometimes deemed by judges an infringement on the property rights of employers. The strikers' freedom of action was limited by the fact that the House of Lords, the court of last resort for interpreting points of law, was a conservative body.

While the workers concentrated on building their unions, there were groups of reformers who became active politically. The Social Democratic Federation was organized in 1881 along Marxist lines, but its influence was negligible; England was stirred, rather, by native voices or the kindred American voices. The American Henry George converted more Englishmen than did Karl Marx, who lived in London from 1849 until his death in 1883. To Christian idealism, which had an old history in England, was added aesthetic socialism. The art critic John Ruskin (1819-1900) and the artist-poet William Morris (1834-96) were appalled by the ugliness as well as by the cruelty of the factory and slum. They preached the values of art and craftmanship and the ethics of social justice.

The most characteristic form of English socialism grew out of an idealistic society, the Fellowship of the New Life, formed in 1883 in London by Thomas Davidson (1840-1900), a peripatetic American philosopher of Scottish origin. In the winter of 1883-84 a majority of the Fellows joined with a brilliant group of economists, historians, and writers to form the famous Fabian Society. The leading figures were the Anglo-Irish critic and dramatist George Bernard Shaw (1856-1950) and a prolific team of social historians, Sidney Webb (1859-1947) and his wife, Beatrice Webb (1858-1943). Their patron saint was the Roman general and consul Quintus Fabius Maximus, who refused to confront the Carthaginian general Hannibal in direct battle but preferred to wear him out by indirect maneuvers. The Fabians addressed themselves to the whole educated community, and particularly to the influential groups in society and politics.

They loosed a flood of tracts, histories, and economic studies analyzing and criticizing the practices of capitalism. They proposed an ameliorative program, capable of indefinite expansion, involving municipal reform, local socialism, scientific administration and government, and state control over working conditions. The Fabians were distinguished in two ways from other socialists: like the utilitarians (see p. 225), they were interested in devising new administrative and political techniques, and they followed in the British tradition of aristocratic and educated leadership. Beatrice Webb wrote that the common people should be "served by an elite of unassuming experts, who would appear to be no different in status from the common man." Membership in the society was small, but its influence was pervasive and cumulative.

Other radicals took more direct action. In 1893, a group of members of the Social Democratic Federation founded the Independent Labor party, with the aim of electing representatives to the House of Commons on a moderate socialist program. The paths of reformers and unions converged.

In the closing years of the century a "new unionism" was born, sired by rising prices and wages. In Great Britain, as elsewhere, trade unions had traditionally included only skilled and better paid craftsmen. Their members showed the familiar human tendency to distinguish themselves from their "inferiors," the workers of mere brawn. But now the unskilled workers were forming large organizations of their own. At the end of the eighties a great strike resulted in the organization of a dockmen's union, and a large miners' union came into being.

In 1900 several trade unions joined with the Independent Labor party, the Fabian Society, and other organizations to form the Labor Representation Committee, which was renamed the Labor party six years later. The party was federal in structure, the constituent organizations retaining their identity within it. The bulk of the support came from unions, while the leadership was supplied by the relatively small socialist organizations. Its program was but mildly socialistic and distinctly un-Marxian. Avoiding the ideology of "proletarian dictatorship," class strife, and revolution, the party advocated "socialization of the means of production, distribution, and exchange, to be controlled in a democratic state in the interests of the whole community, and the complete emancipation of labor from the domination of capitalism and landlordism, with the establishment of social and economic equality between the sexes." Its immediate aim, however, was social and economic improvement under the capitalistic system.

In 1906 the Liberal party won an overwhelming victory, and remained in office for eleven years. The Labor party elected 29 of its 50 candidates to the House of Commons. Spurred by the Labor contingent, the Liberals engaged in broad reforms, including measures to compensate workers injured on the job, legalize picketing, and exempt unions from suits for damages resulting from strikes. In 1909 the annual budget included funds for small pensions to the aged poor, along with large sums for naval expansion. The Liberals proposed to raise the additional moneys needed by steeply increasing land and inheritance taxes, but the Conservatives, who had the support of the landed rich, threw out the budget in the House of Lords. This raised a constitutional issue, since the House of Commons had traditionally been virtually sovereign in money matters. Two elections were held in 1910, with the result that the Liberals, although reduced in numbers, retained a parliamentary majority and won the support of Irish Nationalists and of the Labor party. The latter party increased its representation to 40 members. During these elections, David Lloyd George (1863-1945), the Chancellor of the Exchequer, appealed for popular support by virulently attacking the aristocracy, the rich, the landlords, and, incidentally, established institutions as well—particularly the House of Lords.

The Lords accepted the budget after the first election of 1910. However, the Liberals and their allies now pressed for a broader measure to reduce the powers of the House of Lords. The government introduced the Parliament Act, which the Lords accepted only after the second election of 1910 had confirmed the Liberal majority, and the ministry, with the support of the King, had threatened to create enough new peers to overcome the opposition. Under the new law, the House of Lords was no longer to veto money measures, and its veto upon other bills might be overridden by the lower house acting in two successive sessions. The life of a parliament was reduced from seven to five years, a measure traditionally regarded as unfavorable to conservatism, and the House of Commons voted a salary of 400 pounds a year to its members. The privileges of the amateur—that is, of the well-to-do—politician were waning. In December 1911, as if to cap its social program, the Liberal party sponsored, and Parliament approved, the National Insurance Act.

Continental Socialism

The radical and proletarian movements of the Continent, in distinction from those of England and the United States, were much influenced by Marxism. In France, Italy, and Spain, anarchist and syndicalist tendencies qualified the strength of Marxism, but elsewhere it became the principal expression of radicalism. The trade-union movement of England, France, and the United States was older than Marxism. In newly developed industrial areas, it was socialists who were often instrumental in organizing the workers, and their leadership was therefore taken as a matter of course. In Germany, Austria-Hungary, and Russia, Marxists had a political function as well—they strove to extend liberal institutions and the power of representative bodies—a function which in the Atlantic countries had formerly been fulfilled by the middle and professional classes.

Nowhere was the variety of social doctrines so rich as in France. The anarchism of Proudhon and the militant revolutionism of Blanqui (see pp. 277-78), still had sizable groups of adherents. By the nineties, a half dozen socialist parties could be counted.

The first Marxist organization in France was barely two years old when it split, in 1882, into revolutionary and moderate groups. The *Parti Ouvrier* represented Marxist orthodoxy. The rival *Parti Ouvrier Socialiste Révolutionnaire* (called "possibilist") relied on the gradual introduction of collectivist measures. Before long, the latter party itself split into two organizations. A fourth group of "independent socialists" prepared and promoted legislation for the socialization of public services and the wider distribution of property.

These groups fought over the soul of the proletariat. However, after participating in a revolution every generation without permanently elevating their position, the workers had become disillusioned with political action. They suspected that the advocates of such action were middle-class and professional persons who craved office and power. Hence they gravitated toward syndicalism, a movement that relied for both immediate improvements and a new society on the efforts of the unions (*syndicats*) themselves. The syndicalists advocated aggressive strikes, sabotage, boycotts, and, as a revolutionary measure, a "general strike" of all the workers of the country instead of a war on the barricades. For the future, they proposed an "economic federation" of unions and labor exchanges on the local level, and the voluntary association of these local federations on a national level. The political state, under which a minority of legislators, executives, and administrators were entrusted with the duties of government, would disappear. There was more than a touch of anarchism in syndicalism.

Another touch was added by Georges Sorel (1847-1922). Sorel, an engineer and writer, felt that socialism was growing stale and European capitalism cowardly. He argued in *Reflections on Violence* (1908) that the mere image of a general strike which would bring down the old order at a single blow was in itself potent enough to rekindle the enthusiasm of the working class. Such a strike need never actually occur; it would be a "myth" whose function was to restore to the oppressed classes their former combative will.

Sorel generalized his theory of violence as an anodyne for society at large:

> Proletarian violence not only makes the future revolution certain, but it seems also to be the only means by which the European nations—at present stupefied by humanitarianism—can recover their former energy. This kind of violence compels capitalism to restrict its attentions solely to its material role and tends to restore to it the warlike qualities which it formerly possessed. A growing and solidly organized working class can compel the capitalist class to remain firm in the industrial war; if a united and revolutionary proletariat confronts a rich middle class, eager for conquest, capitalist society will have reached its historical perfection.

Such a middle class, Sorel felt, existed in America. Only the American capitalist was still a warrior by nature. "It was he who had created the extraordinary greatness of the United States." In the overseas Republic "are found the indomitable energy, the audacity based on a just appreciation of its strength, the cold calculation of its interests, which are the qualities of great generals and great capitalists."

Syndicalism vied with socialism for the allegiance of the French workers.   *429*

French labor exchanges performed functions as important as those of unions. Supported by municipalities, the exchanges provided library facilities and meeting places for employers and employees. The first federation of exchanges was inclined to follow the leadership of the moderate Marxists, while the federation of unions collaborated with the revolutionary Marxists. However, when a comprehensive organization of unions and exchanges was formed in the nineties— the *Confédération Générale du Travail* (C.G.T.)—syndicalist tendencies prevailed.

While the labor and socialist movements diverged ideologically, their practical efforts were often complementary. The C.G.T. practiced the methods of the "class struggle" and "direct action," and the moderate socialist groups secured for labor the benefits of collaboration with middle-class groups and helped to safeguard republicanism during the Dreyfus affair. (see pp. 444-45).

In other Continental countries, notably Germany, Marxism and trade unionism joined forces. A rival of Marx launched the first political organization of the German working class. Ferdinand Lassalle (1825-64) was a state socialist. He accepted David Ricardo's "iron law of wages"—if wages rise, the working population promptly increases, causing wages to drop again—which condemned the proletariat to intermittent penury. He appealed to the state to counteract the operation of this "law" by supplying credit to enable workers to organize factories of their own to compete with those of the capitalists. To influence the state to do so, Lassalle believed, it was necessary to increase the political power of the masses. He persuaded Bismarck, who was then engaged in the constitutional struggle with Prussian liberals, that popular suffrage would weaken the middle classes. In the early sixties Lassalle launched a frenetic campaign to organize unions and political associations. He founded the Universal German Workers' Association in 1863.

Following in the path of Lassalle, the adherents of Marx proceeded to organize proletarian groups in south Germany. In 1869 they drew local unions and societies together in the Social Democratic Workers' party. This party and Lassalle's Association joined in 1875 to form the Social Democratic party. The principles of the new party were a mixture of the class-struggle doctrine of Marx and the state-minded program of Lassalle, but the leadership fell largely to Marxists. The Social Democrats polled a half million votes and sent a dozen deputies to the *Reichstag*.

Disturbed by the spread of socialism, Bismarck secured the passage of social-insurance measures, hoping that this would reconcile labor to the existing order. At the same time, however, he obtained legislation forbidding socialist meetings and publications. By declaring a state of siege in any area, the authorities could expel individuals from it. These antisocialist laws were enforced sternly. However, persecution, imprisonment, and exile proved stimulants rather than deterrents to the socialists. By 1890 the Social Democratic party had much increased its popular poll and its representation in the *Reichstag*. When Bismarck resigned, in 1891, the antisocialist legislation was repealed. In 1907 the Social Democrats and the Centrists combined to defeat a proposal to increase the army. Chancellor Bernhard von Bülow (1849-1929) promptly dismissed the *Reichstag*

English comment, from an 1878 issue of Punch, *on the effort of Bismarck to arrest the growth of the socialist movement by the enactment of a law denying freedom of speech, press, and assembly to the advocates of socialism.* © PUNCH, LONDON

and called new elections. In a savage campaign he accused these groups, particularly the Social Democrats, of lack of patriotism. The Social Democrats returned in much smaller numbers, more than ever persuaded that they could not attain a stable influence unless the parliamentary system were strengthened and ministerial responsibility introduced. In 1912, however, the party regained —indeed, surpassed—its former position, increasing its representation in the *Reichstag* to 110 members and becoming the largest single party in the country.

In neighboring Austria-Hungary, socialism encountered ethnic obstacles. The incidence of industry was distinctly spotty. A few national groups developed industrial and professional classes, while others remained agrarian, pastoral, and provincial. In Austria, where the national mosaic was most complex, more than a third of the Germans and Czechs and a quarter of the Italians were engaged in industry, but only 15 percent of the Poles, 5 percent of the Serbo-Croatians, and 3 percent of the Rumanians. About 90 percent of the Rumanians, Serbo-Croatians, and Ukrainians were engaged in agriculture and forestry. The Social Democratic party and even the trade unions were organized by national units tied together by loose bonds. At its Congress at Brno in 1898, the party adopted a program which called for abandonment of the traditional "historic" provinces and the substitution of new units characterized by a high degree of ethnic homogeneity. The rights of the remaining minorities within the new areas were to be protected by new legislation.

The Austrian socialists were strongly influenced by the German party, which became the keystone of a movement embracing many countries in Continental Europe. In 1889, representatives of the various national parties met in Paris and formed a loose federation, called the Second International Workingmen's Association. The First International had succumbed in 1876 to the struggles between Marxists and anarchists. It had included individual members as well as organizations, and its program was broadly humanitarian. The Second International consisted only of national parties.

Within it, as within the constituent parties, the controversy over revisionism raged. German revisionists, inspired by Eduard Bernstein, proposed a frank policy of gradual improvement within the existing order. Many French socialists also contended for a moderate Marxism; some of their leaders accepted posts in bourgeois cabinets. Orthodox Marxists were led by the German writer Karl Kautsky (1854-1938). Kautsky conceded that developments since Marx's day belied the master's conviction that revolution was imminent. Nevertheless, he insisted that Marx's premises and aims remained valid, and that it was necessary to combine, somehow, efforts for immediate reform within the existing order with a militant readiness to overthrow capitalism.

A war of exegesis was begun. The protagonists combed the copious writings of Marx and Engels for supporting authority. The issue remained uncertain, for even as the practices of the socialist parties became increasingly reformist, the orthodox managed to preserve the letter of the Marxist "law." In 1901 the German party condemned the "heresy" of reformism. In a three-day debate at a congress of the Second International in 1903, Jean Jaurès (1859-1914), leader of the French socialists, pleaded for a realistic policy of collaboration with non-Marxian reformers, while the leader of the German socialists, August Bebel (1840-1913), insisted on adherence to the teachings of the master. Jaurès, a brilliant orator, had the better of the argument, but the majority, under the strong influence of the German party, voted against revisionism.

Narodniks and Bolsheviks

There was one country in which revolutionism was more than verbal. That country was Russia. In the first half of the nineteenth century, when the rest of the Continent, Western Europe in particular, was experiencing periodic outbreaks, Russia was relatively quiescent and czarism was the very Gibraltar of reaction. In the second half, Western European radicalism and liberalism lost its militant edge: with the exception of the short-lived Paris Commune of 1870 (which was occasioned by war as well as by social discontent), there had been no serious challenge to authority since the turbulent years of 1848-49. In Russia, however, there arose an opposition movement that grew stronger with the years, engaged occasionally in violent attacks, and eventuated in the first two revolutions of the twentieth century. The center of European revolution was shifting slowly from France to Russia.

This shift was due to the increasing vulnerability of czarism. Russia remained the only power in Europe that refused constitutional concessions. The people of no other large country were treated so highhandedly by their rulers. The majority of Russia's educated and professional classes—the intelligentsia— strove to align Russia with the cultural aims and political institutions of the

West. The term "intelligentsia" came to imply not only a commitment to the things of the mind but an active interest in liberal and scientific progress. The peasantry, although legally emancipated in 1861, remained desperately poor and sporadically rebellious. And, beginning in the nineties, the advance of industry created a small but concentrated urban proletariat without the means of free expression and organization. Finally, domestic discontent was deepened by a series of blows to the diplomatic and military prestige of czarism.

The Russian opposition found early expression in literature. Since the press was censored and political organization forbidden, fiction became a forum of discussion and debate. In the fifties and sixties a galaxy of novelists painted a critical picture of the state of their country. In *Oblomov* (1859) Ivan Goncharov (1812-91) satirized the sloth, inefficiency, and good-humored irresponsibility of the gentry. It took a third of the long novel to drag Goncharov's aristocratic protagonist out of bed. Oblomov's own hero was, significantly, an engineer of German extraction, the embodiment of industriousness and responsibility. In *Fathers and Sons* (1862) Ivan Turgenev (1818-83) depicted the rebelliousness of educated youth. The protagonist, Bazarov, was a "nihilist," who described his ideal as "a man who does not bow down before any authority whatever [and does] not take any principle on faith, whatever reverence that principle may be enshrined in." Bazarov regarded science as the principal instrument of progress. Feodor Dostoevski (1821-81) delivered the answer to *Fathers and Sons* in *Crime and Punishment* (1866). Dostoevski rejected extreme individualism and rationalism as presumptuous and immoral. The salvation of Russia, he contended, lay in Christian brotherhood and in the humility and the goodness of her people. Dostoevski depicted dramatically the revolutionary and reactionary types. Leo Tolstoi (1828-1910), in his great novel *War and Peace* (1864-69), created a brilliant pageant of the old nobility of Russia and a nostalgic evocation of the early years of the century, when young nobles and officers, and the entourage of Czar Alexander I, hoped to establish a free society. The novel was an indictment of military and political leadership: The great generals and leaders, the noise-makers of history, flatter themselves when they think they have the slightest effect upon events. It is the humble and peaceable work of the people at large, and great impersonal forces that shape life and promote progress.

In the seventies and eighties, Russian opposition took the form of populism. Taking Russia as a whole, it was an open question whether the land settlement of the sixties (see p. 336) had made the hard life of the Russian masses a little better or a little worse. The agrarian depression was an added affliction. In 1868 famine wasted the southeastern areas of European Russia. The villagers of the region of Samara, on the Volga, hungered for three years on end. Later, famine struck other Volga districts as well. Discontent erupted in open disorder. Cossacks swept through the disaffected regions, hanged peasants by the hundreds, and razed dozens of rebellious villages.

The plight of the peasants aroused the intelligentsia, whose spiritual leaders were Alexander Herzen (1812-70), Nicholas Chernishevsky (1828-89), and Peter Lavrov (1823-1900). Chernishevsky, a publicist and economist, was the   *433* "father" of the Narodniks (populists). A strong believer in cooperation, Chernishevsky criticized "social Darwinism," the application—more accurately, misapplication—of Darwin's biological theory of "natural selection" to social and economic phenomena. By stressing the competitive aspects of evolution, social Darwinism exalted the importance of struggle, force, and competition—whether of individuals, peoples, or races—in the progress of mankind. Social Darwinists set a great value on success and successful men, who were often merely the strong and the selfish. Chernishevsky hoped that a new socialist society might be built upon the old village commune, which had originally characterized all European societies and still survived in Russia. The commune would enable Russia to avoid the stage of capitalism. Lavrov, a teacher and social philosopher, believed in the power of ideas, and of the dedicated intellectuals who carried them, to improve society. He advocated the organization of a small and disciplined party composed of "critically thinking individuals." This party of "leaders" would attract a following of convinced idealists, and together they would guide the masses toward socialism.

The ideas of Lavrov and Chernishevsky took practical shape in the formation of small revolutionary circles, where idealistic youths met to read forbidden books and discuss forbidden subjects. They organized political demonstrations in universities, boycotted the lectures of reactionary professors, and "struck" classes in protest against the government. On one such occasion, in 1861, several students were expelled from the University of St. Petersburg for voicing sympathy with the grievances of the peasants.

From Herzen, an exile who edited influential periodicals which were smuggled into Russia from Western Europe, came the call "*V Narod*"—"Go to the people." In the seventies, several thousand students swept out of universities and cities into the villages. They taught the illiterate, nursed the sick, worked side by side with village craftsmen, and tried to bring the peasants to a consciousness of their rights. But the peasants proved unresponsive and suspicious, and the government was brutal. Hundreds of agitators were rounded up and imprisoned. One trial of 193 youths lasted four years. The courts finally decided that only 40 of them were "guilty," but meanwhile 73 had either been driven insane by savage treatment or killed themselves in protest or despair.

Such proceedings appalled public opinion. Obstinate revolutionaries continued to "go to the people," agitating for a drastic redistribution of the land. Others took more violent courses. In 1879 terror became systematized. An organization called the "Will of the People" plotted the assassination of ministers, governors, and generals who distinguished themselves by brutality. It made several attempts to take the life of Alexander II. In 1881, six bomb throwers waited for his carriage at successive corners, and one of them found his mark. The new Czar, Alexander III (1881-94), inaugurated a regime more reactionary than that of his predecessor.

Gradually populism retreated, giving ground to socialism. In 1901, the old leaders of the Narodniks organized the Social Revolutionary party. The membership adhered variously to ethical, religious, romantic, idealistic, and quasi-utopian socialism. The party tolerated a small group that persevered in terrorist activity. It attracted industrial workers and professional men as well as peasants, yet its stress was upon agrarian reform.

The rapid introduction of industry in a few large urban centers, under official auspices, was followed by trade union activity and radical agitation. The Social Democratic party, Marxist in its orientation, was founded in 1898. From the beginning it was torn by differences. Its trade-union following wished to wrest concessions from the employers, moderate members worked for a constitutional regime as a prelude to socialism, and extremists engaged in conspiratorial tactics. In 1903, extremists and moderates split into factions which became known, respectively, from a crucial vote taken at a party congress, as Bolsheviks, or majority men, and Mensheviks, or minority men. The Mensheviks, who, despite their name, were the larger group, followed the Western tradition. They held that since her economic development was immature, Russia needed a period of growth under capitalist auspices. They proposed a liberal democracy and educational opportunities to prepare the ground for an eventual socialist order. The Bolsheviks, led by Nicolai Lenin (1870-1924), pointed out that Russian industrialization was highly intensive. The average size of the plants, for example, was larger than in the West. This was understandable for a country which had arrived late on the industrial scene and naturally imported the latest equipment, suitable for large plants. The Bolsheviks concluded that a capitalist-liberal regime was superfluous; czarism might be replaced at once by a socialist state, which would complete the modernization of the economy; one of Marx's stages might be skipped. Yet the Bolsheviks appreciated that, for such an adventure, the technical and diplomatic assistance of the advanced countries, at least of adjacent Germany, was essential.

Bolshevik organization was as important as Bolshevik doctrine. To the aristocratic and military establishment of czarism, the Bolsheviks opposed a dictatorial, hierarchical, and conspiratorial party. Although a professedly orthodox Marxist, Lenin reached some strikingly "heretical" conclusions. He held that the workers were interested, not in socialism, but in the improvement of their conditions under capitalism. He rejected a democratic party as "nothing more than a useless and harmful toy." Lenin gathered around him a small group of professional revolutionists. By raising divisive issues, he winnowed out the "softs" from the "hards" and imposed his will on his comrades. The handful of men at the top appointed the leaders of the rank and file.

Lenin approved the practice of defaming opponents and critics within and without the party. He advocated tactics that were "calculated to evoke . . . hatred, aversion, and contempt, calculated not to convince but to break up the ranks of the opponent, not to correct the mistake of the opponent but to destroy him, to wipe his organization off the face of the earth." The resources of wealth of the existing regime were to be met, when necessary, by "expropriation." Gangs of Bolsheviks were authorized to rob banks and trains carrying specie. A local Bolshevik of Georgia, Joseph Stalin (1879-1953), distinguished himself in these operations.

The danger of Bolshevism was recognized by other revolutionaries. The Polish-German socialist Rosa Luxemburg (1870-1919) wrote that "the ultra-centralism advocated by Lenin is not something born of a positive creative spirit but of the negative sterile spirit of the watchman." The Russian Leon Trotsky (1877-1940) characterized Lenin's system simply as "ego-centralism." "The organization of the party takes the place of the party itself; the Central Committee [the executive body of the party] takes the place of the organization; and finally the dictator takes the place of the Central Committee. . . ."

Revolutionary developments were accelerated by national discontent. The peoples of the Baltic, Poland, the Ukraine, and Georgia resented the imposition of autocratic Russian rule. Among the Finns, a broad movement of passive resistance underlined the determination to preserve old rights which were constantly being whittled down by the government. Jewish workers and professional men in western Russia organized their own socialist party—the *Bund*—which added to Marxist planks the demand for an end to the invidious treatment of their people. The greatest source of disaffection was Poland, which had risen in arms against Russian rule three times in the nineteenth century, the last time in 1863. In 1893 a Polish Socialist party was organized which combined the aim of restoring Polish independence with an anticapitalist program. A broader movement was initiated by the National Democrats, which brought together urban and rural elements and tried to soften the old differences between farmers and gentry. The party prescribed the use of the Polish language and the avoidance of things Russian. It refused to merge into the larger stream of the Russian opposition, suspecting that a parliamentary regime would be as determined to maintain the unity of the Empire as was the czarist government. For the eventual aim of all Polish groups was independence.

The multiple tensions of Russia and the survival of an absolutist state employing repressive policies forced her radical and even her liberal critics into revolutionary paths. Elsewhere, populism and socialism accommodated themselves to the pervasive atmosphere of reform within existing institutions.

21. *Big Business and Power*

The rise of collectivist thinking was one of the most significant and lasting results of the Age of Steel. Of more immediate consequence, however, was the impact of industrialization upon the position of the leading classes and states of the Western world.

The depressions of the seventies and eighties occasioned a political reaction against liberal policies and tendencies, particularly on the Continent. The middle classes grew strikingly in wealth, influence, and ambition and began to reach out for a substantial share of the power exercised by the traditional ruling groups of Europe. New industrial states rose to eminence, and the competition for markets, resources, and investment opportunities grew intense. Colonial expansion and imperialistic rivalries became the order of the day. The countries that had agricultural as well as industrial wealth forged ahead of less favored lands. The growth of domestic markets and the sharpening of international competition led to protectionism. The policy of excluding the products of foreign countries by tariffs and other trade restrictions accentuated national jealousies and rivalries.

The Magnate and the Nobleman

Within the ranks of the middle classes there arose a group of powerful and audacious corporation magnates, masters of industrial and mining empires, and international financiers. The size of fortunes grew spectacularly. The Krupps of Germany and the Rockefellers and Mellons and Morgans of the United States amassed fabulous riches. At the turn of the century there were four or five thousand Americans who were "worth" a million dollars or more. Although there were individual Europeans as wealthy as any American, the American millionaire became the model of the modern rich.

The new captain of industry and finance was a towering figure who had a bare family resemblance to the capitalist of old. He was distinguished not only by his rapid success and greater possessions but also by his ambition and daring. He had left behind the conventional doctrines of prudence and gradual accumulation. He delighted in great risks, vast combinations, and extravagant triumphs. He did not feel the attachment of the old merchant to fair competition among equals under agreed-upon rules. His was the strategy of maneuver, monopoly, and subjugation.

The new magnate often enjoyed the flattering implication of social Darwinism: life is struggle and the fittest survive; success is prima facie evidence of superiority. He carried his public responsibilities lightly, ascribing the less lovely aspects of the social battle, including the human cost, to the inexorable decree of science and nature.

Riches and the number of the rich grew faster than the rate at which new men could be assimilated to the traditional governing circles. Although here and there a European magnate vied with the noblemen for the social spotlight—typically, by outspending them—on the whole the magnates were content to be "recognized" by their "betters" and to snub, in their turn, the victims of the race they had won.

The old elite was charmed by money though repelled by its begetters. Even in the most august circles, it is true, a few individuals—such as King Edward VII of Great Britain (1901-10) and Emperor William II of Germany (1888-1918)—befriended self-made men who had made much money. Yet the two classes did not merge. Gentlefolk were snobbish and on the defensive. Industrial and financial magnates put the wealthiest noblemen in the shade, except for those who, like a few titled Englishmen, had discovered coal or iron on their estates or owned the land on which crowded industrial centers rose. European noblemen suffered, along with farmers, from the agricultural depression of the eighties and nineties and from the competition of American grain. But America also exported heiresses, and marriage with American fortunes became the standard gambit of reduced titled families.

While waging a rear-guard action for economic advantage, nobles and landlords entrenched themselves behind their old ramparts. They still occupied, in most European countries, the leading executive, diplomatic, military, naval, and bureaucratic positions. Their advantage of position was now more profitable than ever since the material resources of the state were much enlarged, thanks to the industrial and financial advances. As monarchs and aristocrats used their executive and legislative influence to secure larger appropriations for the diplomatic, military, and naval services and to enhance the status of these services, they naturally contributed to a more emphatic assertion of state power, to aggressive policies, and to national and imperialist rivalries. The great capitalists had free rein in industrial and financial policy. They had a large voice in determining economic policy without incurring the obligations of public accountability. They expected the state not only to protect their domestic interests but to promote actively their foreign investments. To the traditional ruling groups the capitalists brought wealth and adventure; in return, they received official support and social sanction for their aims and methods.

Big Business in America

In the United States, which lacked an established aristocracy, the capitalists won the most comprehensive victory. Their principal former rivals—the plantation owners of the South—had been ruined in the Civil War. Politicians deriving chiefly from prominent New England and Southern families had manned the important offices of the federal and state governments since the founding of the Republic. Although comfortably situated, this group was rooted neither in great wealth nor in political privilege. Within a generation, the new men in industry and finance had elbowed their predecessors out of power and supplanted them in many leading positions. The Democratic party, which had dominated American politics before the Civil War, yielded place to the newly organized Republican party. This party fell increasingly under the influence of big business.

Higher and higher rose the tariffs which protected great industry against even the weakest foreign competitors. More and more sacred became the enclosure within which plutocracy had entrenched itself. Until the ratification of the Sixteenth Amendment to the Constitution in 1913, it could not be touched by income taxation. It could not be challenged by organized labor: executive and judiciary almost invariably threw weight into the scales of capital in its struggle with labor. The Fourteenth Amendment of 1868, intended to secure the rights of the former slaves, declared that no state shall "deprive any person of life, liberty, or property"; by defining the corporation as a legal person, the Supreme Court made this Amendment a weapon for the defense of big business and finance against the efforts of legislators to curb their abuses and regulate their practices. State and federal troops were dispatched to put down strikes and demonstrations, although on occasion they fraternized with the men. Capitalists organized armed teams of detectives and thugs to wage war against labor.

Through the control of political machines, small groups of politicians established an oligarchy in political life, as the industrialists had done in economic life. In exchange for political favors to the industrialists and financiers, machine politicians received economic advantages. The seventies and eighties in particular had been punctuated by scandals involving state legislators, congressmen, and highly placed executives. Railroads, industrial combinations, and monopolies often purchased whole majorities of legislative committees and even legislatures. American municipal government became a symbol of failure and corruption; its reform became one of the principal aims of the Progressives (see p. 423).

The rule of big business had harsh effects on the Negroes. Businessmen had combined with conservative politicians to arrest their progress during the Reconstruction period (see p. 422). Financiers, industrialists, and railroad corporations sought special privileges, franchises, and contracts from Southern legislatures. Southern merchants, manufacturers, and politicians craved the help

The Tammany Tiger, symbol of the corrupt political organization that dominated and degraded the government of New York City, by the American cartoonist Thomas Nast (1840-1902), one of the pioneers of modern political cartooning. BETTMANN

of Northern capitalists to rebuild communication and transportation and initiate new enterprises. Their influence grew at the expense of that of the old "aristocracy" of cotton planters. Both groups were concerned lest the Negroes, Northern workers, and Western farmers—all restive under conditions of economic depression—join in an alliance which might threaten to control both state and federal governments.

In 1872 Congress removed the political disabilities of many officials of the Confederacy, and the Democrats soon regained control of most of the state governments. In 1876 they nearly won the presidency. The Democratic candidate, Samuel J. Tilden, obtained 184 electoral votes; the Republican candidate, Rutherford B. Hayes, obtained 166; an additional 19 votes from three Southern states were claimed by both parties. Hayes needed all of the disputed ballots in order to secure 185 votes, which would give him a majority of one. It is now generally agreed that these 19 votes should have been counted for Tilden. Southern leaders, however, drove a bargain with the Republican leaders of the North. Hayes was conceded the disputed votes and became President. He withdrew the federal troops from the South and supported federal appropriations for "internal improvements" in that region.

Southern legislators and Northern capitalists traded favors, concessions, credits, and contracts. The Negroes paid the price of the bargain. The federal government abandoned its efforts in their behalf and turned them over to the mercies of the upper classes of the South. "White supremacy" triumphed. In a series of "Jim Crow" laws, Southern states denied the Negroes access to "white" theaters, restaurants, parks, railroad cars, and barbershops. The federal Supreme Court approved the establishment throughout the South of separate schools for Negroes, provided that they were "equal" to the schools for white children. These schools were in fact seldom "equal." The plight of the Negroes was underscored by mob attacks and lynchings.

The Negroes forfeited most of the gains they had made on the morrow of the Civil War. Some of them migrated to Northern states, but most of them stifled their ambitions and hopes. The leading spokesman of the Negroes was Booker T. Washington (1859-1915), founder and principal of the Tuskegee (Alabama) Normal and Industrial Institute, a school for training Negro teachers and craftsmen. Washington counseled his people to accommodate themselves to the new conditions, to concentrate on acquiring modest economic skills, and to abandon—at least for the time—the ideal of equality with white men.

Irish Home Rule and British Conservatism

The problems of the United States were those of a rapidly growing industrial power; those of Great Britain derived from a threat to her long-established international position. Great Britain had attained the pinnacle of her prestige in the age of *laissez faire*. No country had done more to spread the gospel of free trade. England was the principal industrial producer of the world and the dominant naval power. As early as the seventies, she began to feel the competition of the new industrial countries, particularly of Germany. In the eighties she also felt the effects of the wave of protectionism. The doors of other countries were closing tighter and tighter, while hers stood invitingly open to foreign imports. British agriculture was hit hard by overseas competition and bad crops. Now that a number of other states had become strong and rich enough to seek investment opportunities and colonies overseas, the British Empire faced the first serious competition as a world power since the days of Napoleon I.

These developments had the effect of a party revolution. British political parties are the processors and cushioners of change. In the preceding century, the turn against the French revolutionists had been signaled by a split in the old Whig party; the transition to free trade in the forties had been smoothed by a division in the Conservative party; now the challenge to the British position was reflected in a division in the Liberal party. Laissez-faire policies had put the Liberals in power, and the party was still officially wedded to them. Tariffs appealed particularly to the agricultural interests, whose influence was constantly diminishing. Commercial and shipping groups wished to keep the course of trade as fluid as possible. To the man in the street, protection evoked the specter of dearer food, and dearer food suggested the nightmare of the hungry forties.

A "radical" element in the Liberal party had been striving to revise the party program in the direction of social and constitutional reform. Its leader was Joseph Chamberlain (1836-1914), a wealthy hardware manufacturer of the *441* industrial center of Birmingham. But the growing prospects of expansion and exploitation overseas, as well as the competition of other countries, suggested other solutions and greater possibilities of power. Chamberlain shifted the emphasis to imperial remedies: a well-knit empire, with mutual voluntary trade preferences by mother country and colonies. Behind a strengthened rampart of economic understandings and naval defenses, supplemented by convenient alliances, the British Empire, he believed, might refresh its economic strength.

The Irish question provided Chamberlain's opportunity. Although the English government was enacting agrarian legislation and had disestablished the Episcopal Church in Ireland (see p. 425), Irish demands for political autonomy remained unsatisfied. In 1886, Prime Minister Gladstone, leader of the Liberal party, introduced the first Home Rule Bill, providing for a separate two-chamber legislature for Ireland. Irish legislators were no longer to sit in the British Parliament, which was to relinquish its power over Ireland except in military, naval, trade, and navigation matters. Chamberlain and his followers feared that Irish autonomy would expose a vital flank of the Empire to the attack of a future enemy and weaken the movement to draw the colonies closer together. They insisted on the retention of the Union of 1801, which had merged the parliaments of the two islands. Seceding from the Liberal party, the Unionists combined with the Conservatives to defeat Gladstone's bill. Their defection weakened the Liberal party, which lost the ensuing election. In 1892, Gladstone waged and won another election on the issue of home rule. The following year, with the help of Irish members, he carried a second Home Rule Bill in the Commons. But the House of Lords defeated it. Not a few Englishmen drew from this the conclusion that no far-reaching reforms were possible unless the power of the House of Lords was curbed. In 1911, on the occasion of the struggle over the budget, this power was diminished (see p. 428). And in 1914 a Home Rule Bill was finally passed, under Liberal auspices. But the outbreak of the First World War led to the passage of another measure postponing the operation of home rule until the end of the war.

The Empire had always been closer to the Conservative heart than to the Liberal. It became clear where the Liberal Unionists belonged. Chamberlain and his group joined the Conservatives to form the Conservative-Unionist party. In 1895 the enlarged party was returned to power. Chamberlain became Colonial Secretary. In Africa, Asia, and Oceania, he encouraged the most daring annexationists.

The Trials of the Third French Republic

On the Continent, the strains of industrial competition and depressions occasioned attacks on political liberalism as well as on laissez-faire policies.

The Third French Republic fought a long battle for its life. In the National

Assembly, elected by manhood suffrage in 1871, the Bourbonists, Orleanists, and Bonapartists together held a substantial majority. For four years they refused to give the Republic a constitutional basis, hoping for a compromise that would unite them in support of a candidate for the throne. Finally they agreed that the Bourbon pretender, the childless Comte de Chambord (1820-83), would reign first and that the younger Orléans candidate, the Comte de Paris (1838-94), would succeed him. But one insuperable obstacle remained: the Bourbon count would not abandon the white flag of his forebears in favor of the tricolor, which, since 1789, had become associated with martial victory, patriotic ardor, and also with republicanism. Moderate monarchists, exhausted by the interminable quarrels, concluded that a republic was "that form of government which divides us least" and lent their support to a number of "organic" measures for republican government, known as the Constitution of 1875. The chief executive, or president, was to hold office for seven years. There was to be a senate chosen by local assemblies elected for the purpose. The Chamber of Deputies was to be chosen by universal suffrage. The cabinet was to be responsible to the Deputies.

Within the next several years broad reforms were made. Divorce, long opposed by the Church, was legalized; an elaborate system of public schools, from the primary to the university level, was established; and instruction in public schools was secularized. July 14, the date of the first defeat of the Bourbons—the fall of the Bastille—was made a national holiday, and the capital was again, as in 1789, transferred from the royal palace of Versailles to the republican atmosphere of Paris.

However, new issues raised by recent developments in finance and industry enabled the enemies of the Republic to renew their attacks. Agricultural stringencies made the peasants restive. The depressions of the seventies and eighties made employment insecure. Finally, a series of financial scandals was disclosed. In 1887 President Jules Grévy resigned when his son-in-law was caught selling medals of the Legion of Honor. The most spectacular scandal was the failure of the Panama Company, which had been formed in 1879 in order to realize the old dream of shortening the route between Atlantic and Pacific ports by piercing the isthmus connecting Central with South America. So many thrifty peasants and burghers bought stock in it that the project assumed the aspect of a national enterprise. In 1889 the Company was declared bankrupt and the life savings of many small investors were wiped out. It was disclosed that unscrupulous financiers had milked the treasury of the Company dry, with the connivance of high-placed politicians whom they had heavily "subsidized."

Monarchists blamed the Third Republic for the scandals. In 1888-89 there was a flurry of "Bonapartism." General Georges Boulanger (1837-91), a nationalist suspected of dictatorial ambitions, began to intrigue for a personal *coup d'état*, in the manner made familiar by the events of 1799 and 1852: a show of force, a promise of glory, and plots with irresponsible politicians. Boulanger had become popular by improving the living conditions of his soldiers. He

443

received the support of patriots—notably Bonapartists and royalists—who felt that he was the man to restore the military prestige of France by leading a war of revenge against Germany. But Boulanger, although he lavished promises on every discontented group and was repeatedly elected as a deputy, did not have the agility and drive of the two Napoleons. More important, this time the republican government was willing to fight for its life. In 1889 it made preparations to try the General for treason. Boulanger lost heart and fled the country, to the surprise of his friends as well as his enemies. He was condemned *in absentia*, and two years later, for personal reasons, he committed suicide.

The difficulties of the liberal regime were aggravated by the opposition of the Clericals, a party of antirepublican Catholics who worked to preserve the influence of the Church in society. Comte Adrien de Mun (1841-1914), an army officer and the lay leader of the Clericals, declared boldly: "Between the Church and the Revolution [*i.e.*, the liberal Republic] there exists open incompatibility. The Church cannot perish and therefore it will kill the Revolution." Militant clergymen organized religious processions and public pilgrimages, reminiscent of the days of Bourbon ascendancy. They demanded that non-Catholic Frenchmen be deprived of citizenship. Through the press, they launched venomous attacks upon Freemasons, Protestants, and Jews.

The conflict between the Church and the first two groups was old, but political anti-Semitism on a large scale was novel. The Jews had welcomed the political freedom of the Republic and the economic opportunities of the period. As a pacific and commercial people, they symbolized to extreme traditionalists the "weaknesses" of republicanism. Most of them were in moderate or lowly circumstances, although small groups shared in the growing influence of industrialists and financiers. A few individuals had been involved, along with many non-Jews, in the financial scandals.

In the eighties and nineties the enemies of liberalism and republicanism joined forces under the banner of anti-Semitism. The ground had been prepared by newspapers and pamphlets which, since the last days of the imperial regime, had charged that the Jews had organized an international conspiracy to dominate and corrupt the Christian world. The movement came to a head in 1894, when Captain Alfred Dreyfus (1859-1935), a junior officer attached to the General Staff and member of a wealthy Jewish family, was accused of selling military secrets to Germany. The chief witness against him was a Major Henry, chief of intelligence. He was promptly tried and convicted by a court martial— which met in secret, as is the custom of courts martial. Degraded from his rank and sentenced to imprisonment for life, Captain Dreyfus was transported to the notorious penal colony of Devil's Island, off the coast of French Guiana.

Most classes of society accepted the verdict of the military court. Many Radicals, workingmen, and socialists at first hesitated between indifference to a family quarrel among aristocrats and capitalists and a readiness to believe in Dreyfus' guilt. It was left to the intellectuals to join battle. Persistent rumors and suspicious incidents strongly suggested the probability that Dreyfus was innocent. Georges Clemenceau, physician and republican editor; Émile Zola, Anatole France, and Joseph Reinach, men of letters; and Jean Jaurès, socialist editor, historian, and orator, formed a staunch brigade which demanded a new trial.

In order to allay the rising suspicion, the General Staff published a facsimile of the list of secrets that had been used to convict Dreyfus. When this list was examined by experts, it became apparent that the handwriting was not that of Dreyfus. By 1896 the new chief of the secret service, Colonel Picquart, had reached the same conclusion, but he could not persuade his superiors to correct the miscarriage of justice: the conviction of the real culprit—later revealed as another officer of the General Staff, Major Ferdinand Esterhazy— would mean exposure of the questionable actions of the army leadership in condemning Dreyfus. The Colonel was "exiled" to a distant African post. Major Esterhazy was tried before a court martial, which acquitted him in face of the most damning evidence. Zola thereupon published *J'accuse*, an eloquent open letter to the President of the Republic, charging seven high officers with conspiring to conceal the facts about the case. "I accuse . . ." he concluded, "the First Court Martial of having violated all human rights in condemning a prisoner on testimony kept secret from him, and I accuse the Second Court Martial of having covered up this illegality by order, committing in turn the judicial crime of acquitting a guilty man with full knowledge of his guilt."

A sketch of Captain Dreyfus at his second court martial in 1899.

J'accuse brought the affair to a boiling point. Zola was himself accused and convicted of libel in a sensational trial, which was followed attentively by the whole civilized world. Shortly after Zola's trial, Henry, now a lieutenant colonel, confessed to having forged one of the documents used to convict Dreyfus, was imprisoned, and then cut his throat. The Dreyfusards rallied their forces. In 1899 republican groups combined to force the resignation of a promilitary cabinet and formed a strong cabinet under the leadership of René Waldeck-Rousseau (1846-1904).

The court of appeal had ordered another court martial, but the new trial body reasserted the guilt of Dreyfus and sentenced him on September 9 to ten years' imprisonment. However, it concluded that there were "extenuating circumstances" for his actions. This was as much as to say that there were occasions when a man might betray his country! Ten days after the strange verdict, President Émile Loubet (1838-1928) pardoned Dreyfus. The Dreyfusards, still unsatisfied, accumulated more evidence, and in 1906 the court of appeal annulled Dreyfus' conviction and restored him to his military rank. The government decorated him and promoted him to the rank of major. His principal defenders were also vindicated. Colonel Picquart, who had been retired, was restored to active service, and Zola, who had died in 1902, was given final rest in the Pantheon.

The results of the Dreyfus affair were far-flung. The government strengthened civilian control over the military. Republicans succeeded monarchists in high military office. In 1905 the term of service in the army was reduced from three to two years. The Clericals were also humbled. In 1902 most of the religious orders were dissolved; the rest were subjected to official control. The clergy was forbidden to teach in state-supported schools, and eventually only a small minority of children attended religious schools. Finally, in 1904, the parliament enacted a law ending the association of the state with the Catholic or any other church. The Concordat of 1801, negotiated by Napoleon, was denounced. Public worship was to continue, however, and churches and other religious edifices and property were to be controlled by the clergy. Liberal and social reform became the order of the day.

The Eminence of Germany

The rapid advance of industry gave a new dimension to the military and diplomatic position of Germany. She held a central position on the Continent, one leg planted in the conservative political society of Eastern Europe, the other in the liberal society of Western Europe. For several years after the foundation of the Empire in 1871, Germany continued the policy of compromise with Western practices that had characterized the period of "unification." Her adherence to free trade was confirmed: the last important duty, on pig iron, was allowed to lapse in 1874. Liberal reforms that enhanced the integration and centralization of the Empire were speedily accepted: the adoption of a uniform monetary system based on the gold standard, paid for by the indemnity imposed on France; the establishment of a uniform code of relations between employer and employee; and the institution of a simplified code of civil and criminal procedure. The reform of the civil code was begun, though it was not completed until 1897.

The National Liberal party, which represented business and industrial groups and had supported Bismarck's wars, proposed to turn Germany into a parliamentary state by using the power of the *Reichstag* to pass on the budget. Under free-trade principles, the imperial income was restricted; it depended largely on the contributions of the individual states. Military expenditures absorbed nine tenths of the budget. Bismarck wished to have the *Reichstag* approve a permanent minimum figure for the size of the standing army: since the cost per soldier was fixed, the government would become virtually independent of the *Reichstag*. The National Liberals insisted on annual approval, but at the last minute they accepted a compromise of a vote every seven years. Bismarck then proposed to obtain a permanent revenue by indirect taxation and the establishment of state monopolies for the processing and sale of tobacco, beer, and brandy. The National Liberals were willing to make concessions provided that they received representation in the cabinet, hoping that they might thus advance the prospects of responsible ministries.

Developments in the mid-seventies suggested to Bismarck a decisive solution. The depression and the fall of prices hit German agriculture hard, and aristocratic landowners were pressing for a tariff on foreign grain. A substantial number of manufacturers abandoned their adherence to free trade and demanded protective duties on imports from abroad. Duties on agricultural and industrial goods would provide a reliable revenue. During the same years two political developments disturbed Bismarck. The *Kulturkampf*, by stimulating the advance of the Catholic Center party, had increased rather than diminished the opposition to the regime. The new Social Democratic party gave signs of growing influence.

Bismarck dealt with all these problems by a single stroke. He broke with the National Liberal party by abandoning the *Kulturkampf* and espousing protection. His advocacy of protection endeared him to the conservative and aristocratic landlords and a group of industrialists, and his withdrawal of anticlerical legislation appealed to the Center party.

In 1878 two unsuccessful attempts were made on the life of the old Emperor, William I. Bismarck promptly dismissed the *Reichstag* and called for new elections. He beat the drums of dynastic patriotism, blamed the attempts on the atmosphere of liberalism, and demanded the curtailment of constitutional freedoms. The elections weakened the National Liberals and strengthened conservative groups.

The new *Reichstag* enacted a tariff law which conferred a high degree of protection to both agriculture and industry. Landlords voted for duties on iron, while manufacturers reciprocated by voting for duties on grain and meat. Imports of textiles, timber, and a host of luxuries were taxed. Subsequent measures raised the walls around the domestic market. The income of the government from these sources increased in proportion: it was tripled in twenty years. Asserting the power of the state in another direction, the *Reichstag* inaugurated Bismarck's broad program of social legislation and passed the anti-socialist law. This law represented more extreme interference with fundamental liberties than any state with pretensions to constitutionalism had hitherto undertaken.

The socialists and the liberals were not the only victims of the new turn. The *Reichstag* voted large appropriations to buy out Polish farmers and landlords and supplant them with Germans. Leading Alsace-Lorrainers who evinced a sympathy for the French connection were persecuted and exiled. Bismarck did not hesitate to condone or derive advantage from the anti-Semitism which was rising in the eighties. He spoke of a *Kulturkampf* against Jews and looked with complaisance upon a movement led by the court preacher, Adolf Stöcker (1835-1909), to oust them from public and civil life. The Conservative party officially accepted the program of anti-Semitism; in a country where order was worshiped, a synagogue was burned and a "ritual murder" trial allowed to come to court.

Liberalism, divided and confused, ceased to be a political force. Bismarck hectored the opposition in the *Reichstag*, while the conservatives and industrialists sped to do his bidding. Active independent spirits left politics. Absorbed in private pursuits, they came to look upon Bismarck as a wizard and to admire politics from a distance as the art of successful deceit. They became armchair strategists of *Realpolitik*. In the American Midwest, liberal German immigrants raised their voices against the dictatorship of Bismarck, as Irish immigrants in the East twisted the British lion's tail.

The world at large, however, was dazzled by Germany's might and fame. Her economic progress cast the first shadow on the splendor of England. The United States was making equal progress, but she was situated three thousand miles away from the continent which was the heart of the world, and the influential classes of Europe still regarded Americans as upstarts and provincials. Germany, by contrast, seemed all gloss. Her army was reputed the most splendid in the world. In an age of faith in science, Germany gave the example of a priestly devotion. Experimentation and research, theory and industrial application, were organized by elaborate specialties and their results combined systematically. Teamwork and a narrow, intricate, and interwoven division of labor were introduced in all fields of abstract, practical, and even humanistic learning. The spirit of specialization seized the whole realm of knowledge and taste. History was studied by examining limited subjects intensively; art, by describing in detail the lives, techniques, and subjects of the artists; literature, by amassing facts and classifying them. The proper "scientific" account of any subject was taken to be a collection of detailed descriptions of the separate parts of that subject. The ideal of the professional and the expert carried all before it. The first responsibility of the expert was to his vocation. The seminar of the highly specialized professor trained him, the footnoted thesis attested him, and the doctoral degree crowned him. As learning moved further and further from the broad philosophic view, experts in agronomy, beer-making, and salesmanship, as well as in economics and literature and ethics, became Doctors of Philosophy.

There were serious dangers in this narrowing of disciplines. It precluded that consideration of values and of larger relations among analyzed parts which are traditionally associated with learning. In the end there was a loss of perspective and even of meaning. This was particularly harmful to the civic spirit. The Germans became disposed to leave public affairs to "experts": politics to the Chancellor and the bureaucracy, military affairs and policy to the General Staff, and foreign policy to professional aristocratic diplomats. For the moment the practical achievements of the Empire stilled doubt. The assurance and power that Germany derived from the monarchical and aristocratic system inspirited industrialists and businessmen. The wealth she derived from modern technology raised the self-confidence of her ruling groups to the point of arrogance. She seemed to combine the stability of old institutions with the energy of modern industry. Had Germany discovered the secret of reinforcing authority with efficiency, tradition with modernity? Had Bismarck found the magic key that the Bonapartes had looked for in vain?

The fame of Germany spread wide. The ruling classes of new states in Central Europe and of distant Japan modeled their constitutions upon those of Germany rather than the older constitutions of France and the United States. German learning, research, and professionalism influenced the whole Western world. The German university system was imitated by many countries, notably by the United States and Japan. There were English and American scholars who, inspired by the theory of evolution to search into the distant origin of institutions, traced liberal forms and practices to the primeval forests of the ancient Germanic tribes. They concluded that these tribes had, in the early migrations, brought the customs of freedom and elective institutions from Germany to England and that the descendants of the Anglo-Saxons then carried them across the Atlantic Ocean. The more enthusiastic devotees of Anglo-Saxondom proposed a modern alliance of the three branches of the "Teutonic" or "Nordic" race—the Germans, the English, and the "Nordic" Americans— which could assume a beneficent guardianship over the globe.

Eastern Reaction and Russian State Capitalism

The process of industrialization, which enhanced the prestige of Germany, was less rapid in the neighboring empires of Austria-Hungary and Russia, where it tended to deepen liberal and national opposition movements.

In Austria, the privileged German minority supported the policy of a centralist government, but it also desired constitutional reform and anticlerical policies. Since liberalism came to be associated with German hegemony, the   *449* rulers experimented with concessions to the non-German nationalities in order to preserve their control over the machinery of the state. Francis Joseph took advantage of the periods of depression in the seventies to check the influence of parliamentary parties and ministries. In 1879 he installed a conservative administration in Austria, under the leadership of Count Eduard von Taaffe (1833-95). While Taaffe revived the influence of the aristocracy and the clergy, he was willing to make concessions to the non-German elements, particularly the Czechs. He relaxed the rules insisting upon the use of the German language in administrative and local offices and admitted Slavs to the middling posts in the public service.

This policy of mild toleration angered the German nationalists, who resorted to extreme ideologies. An aristocratic demagogue, Georg von Schönerer, aroused the Austrian villagers and small townsmen by castigating both capitalism and Hapsburg rule. He appealed to popular prejudices by singling out the Jews for attack and by demanding their elimination from political life. Another demagogue, Karl Lueger, was repeatedly elected Mayor of Vienna on a platform of anti-Semitism. Many a Jew lost his place in the public service. After the turn of the century, a young man from the Austrian provinces, shiftless and passionately prejudiced, watched the attacks on the Jews of Vienna with a sinister rapture. His name was Adolf Hitler.

German agitation led to Taaffe's resignation in 1893. One more attempt was made, in 1897, to grant the Czechs full equality with the Germans in Bohemia, but the violent tactics of the German nationalists brought parliamentary life to a virtual standstill.

Nowhere was the reaction against liberalism so extreme as in Russia. After the assassination of Czar Alexander II in 1881, a systematic repression was instituted. The leader of this repression was Constantine Pobiedonostzef (1827-1907), son of a village priest, tutor of Alexander III, and mentor of the last czar, Nicholas II. From 1883 to 1905 he was the Procurator General, or the lay head of the finances and administration of the powerful state church.

Pobiedonostzef might be characterized as a conservative nihilist. To him, liberal leaders were self-seeking men, parliament was a device for the dishonest manipulation of corrupt power, the free press a means for disseminating lies, and the jury system an invention of unscrupulous lawyers for deceiving the people. Reason and knowledge were false guides. Progress was delusive; inertia was the soul's rest. Untaught and rude feeling, mystical groping, submission to force, and fatalistic obedience to external authority were the proper lot and mood of man, a mood that popular education would undermine and destroy.

The difference between authority and reason, according to Pobiedonostzef, was the difference between East and West. The East was light and truth, the West darkness and error. Western civilization, having accepted the false principles of reason and individuality, had become hypocritical and decadent. Western religions—whether Protestant or Roman Catholic—were infected by the same principles and were inferior to Eastern Orthodox Christianity. Roman

Catholicism exalted the Church and was not properly related to the State; Protestantism was too individualistic; only Eastern Orthodox caesaro-papism was valid. Russia must barricade herself against Western tendencies.

The views of Pobiedonostzef struck the keynote of the reign of Alexander III and that of his son, Nicholas II (1894-1917), who succeeded him. Under these two reigns, the political and administrative concessions of Alexander II were whittled down. A more severe censorship was introduced; none but nonpolitical and thoroughly conservative publications were tolerated. The universities lost much of their former autonomy and most of their liberal professors and students. The jurisdiction of local administrative bodies was restricted, and the influence of the nobility over them was increased.

The most repressive measures were reserved for those groups in the population that were distinguished from the dominant classes by their religion and tradition as well as by their station in life. By attacking minorities, the government hoped to earn the good will of the Eastern Orthodox majority. Forcible attempts were made to "Russify" the various nationalities within the Empire, to destroy the study and use of their languages and the practice of their religions. The Great Russian language became the literary badge of absolutism. It took the place of native languages in the schools of Poland, the Ukraine, and elsewhere. The government harried Roman Catholic clergy and believers in Poland, Lutherans in the Baltic provinces, Mohammedans in the south. It encouraged conversion to Eastern Orthodoxy. Within the Orthodox Church, dissenters were persecuted and exiled. One of the harried sects—the Dukhobors—found refuge in Saskatchewan in Canada.

No people suffered more than the Jews. Several million of them were pressed together in a Pale of Settlement, restricted to fifteen provinces of western Russia, whose territory was frequently reduced. Within the Pale, they were forbidden to reside in villages. Thousands of artisans who had been permitted to settle in Moscow were thrust back into the Pale. The *numerus clausus* was established: no more than 5 to 10 percent of the students in the secondary schools of the Pale could be Jews; no more than 2 to 3 percent in the universities. But the government was not satisfied to segregate and stifle the Jews. Pobiedonostzef's solution was simple: "One third will be converted, a third will emigrate, and a third must perish."

The government proceeded on all three lines. It inspired, and even organized, violent attacks on Jews. In 1881 a series of pogroms broke out with official connivance. Police plied mobs with alcohol and incited them to assault, murder, and burn. Jewish communities were thrown into panic, and thousands of Jews stampeded to the nearest open door, the lightly patrolled Austrian border. Many of them finally arrived in the United States, after a brief period during which various European countries, and sometimes their own leading Jews, tried to divert the stream of refugees from their borders. Added to the thinner streams issuing, for similar reasons, from other Eastern countries—notably Hungary and Rumania—the flight from Russia inaugurated a huge wandering which lasted for several decades. A million Jews left Central and

Eastern Europe in the eighties and nineties, and another million in the first decade of the new century.

The Jews who remained, as well as many of those who fled, responded to the rising anti-Semitism by embracing in large numbers the cause of Zionism. A Hungarian journalist, Theodor Herzl (1860-1904), was shocked by the Dreyfus case into the conviction that the Jews could not continue to exist as a people if they remained scattered in many countries. They must gather together, return to Zion, and found a state of their own. In 1897 the first Zionist Congress was held in Basel, Switzerland; the bulk of the followers of the new movement were Eastern Jews, notably those of Russia and Poland.

Serious as they were, the ethnic stresses of Russia were overshadowed by the industrial problems. The government instinctively inclined to the side of the masters. It hampered the organization of unions, forbade strikes, and enforced but feebly the legislation protecting factory workers. It ensured the home market to native manufacturers by surrounding it with a high tariff wall.

There were many landed noblemen and imperial bureaucrats who did not welcome the prospect of an industrialized and urbanized society, with its accompaniments of middle-class influence and proletarian unrest. Under the regime of serfdom itself, capitalist enterprise had begun and developed. The emancipation of the serfs had created a fluid labor market and furthered industrial growth. In the eighties, textile and metallurgical firms multiplied. The insistent example of other countries showed that commercial and industrial wealth was an indispensable ingredient of modern power, military or imperial. Was it possible, the traditionalists wondered, to avoid the political dangers of the rise of a numerous capitalist class?

The financial situation offered a possible answer to this knotty question. Like other undeveloped countries, Russia needed foreign capital. Domestic accumulations were insufficient to supply the needs of industry, and internal unrest, combined with the reactionary and anti-Western orientation of the government, reduced Russia's political prestige and financial standing in the international markets. The shocking outrages against minorities were reflected in the rise of interest rates. But if industry needed the cooperation of the government in obtaining foreign credit, the government needed industrial production to ensure its ability to raise future loans. Russia could pay for imports of money and manufactured goods only by exports. Her chief exports were foodstuffs, livestock, and lumber, and the value of these goods was reduced by the descent of agricultural prices and a series of disastrous crop failures. The continued flow of credit could be assured only by the development of productive enterprises in transportation and industry as well as in mining, forestry, and agriculture.

The government had always taken a direct hand in business, operating mills and mines and raising crops for export. State capitalism was now extended. Under the leadership of Count Sergei Witte (1849-1915), the Ministry of Finance (which included the departments of commerce and industry) became, in the early nineties, a center of loan flotation and industrial planning. It stimulated private industry by loans, subsidies, concessions, and large government orders. It encouraged aristocrats and landowners to invest their surpluses in new enterprises. The state became the competitor, as well as the promoter, of private capitalism. It planned, financed, and operated factories, mines, and railroads. Private construction and operation had been the vogue in Russia as in many other countries. The state had stimulated railroad construction by valuable concessions—such as guaranteed profits and free depots—which matched in generosity and in temptations to speculation and corruption the land grants made to companies by the American government. Now, however, the government itself went into the business of transportation. Paying fat prices, it bought many private railroad lines. It laid down thousands of miles of new track, to minister to military as well as economic needs. At the end of the century it owned and operated 60 percent of the railroads in the country, and in 1914, 80 percent. City and village, Russia and the outside world, were brought closer together.

The government encouraged foreign bankers and investors to ship their capital—often in the form of machinery and capital goods—by guaranteeing returns and paying high rates of interest. It often borrowed only to lend to native capitalists. The government entered the liquor business. It made the manufacture and distribution of alcohol a state monopoly, and exploited the misery of the Russian peasant. "Man must have work, rest, and recreation—one must replace the other," a peasant complained. "There is very much of the first, very little of the second, and absolutely nothing of the third except drunkenness." The increase of drunkenness brought the treasury great profits and enabled it to float more loans.

These efforts had a startling and rapid effect. Within a generation, railroad trackage increased two and a half times. In the nineties alone, 16,000 miles of track were laid. Industrial output more than doubled. The number of textile spindles rose rapidly. Coal and iron deposits were exploited on a large scale, particularly those of the rich Donets region. In 1913 Russia produced ten times as much coal and fourteen times as much iron as she had produced in 1885. Her foreign trade rose two and a half times. While Russia still lagged far behind the highly industrialized countries, a half dozen districts assumed the appearance of heavy industrialization. The urban population grew, although before 1914 it was still outnumbered by the peasantry three to one. If, therefore, one looked at the quality and size of plant and at the whir of urban life, it appeared that Russia was rapidly becoming industrialized; if one compared her production with that of Western countries or considered the predominance and backwardness of her agrarian life, the story was quite different.

Rapid industrialization in Russia, as in France and the United States, resulted in speculative finance, political corruption, and shady "deals," involving in some cases members of the high aristocracy. The essential difference between Russia and Western countries, however, was that neither protest nor punishment was possible in Russia, for she lacked a free press and an elected parliament.

Russia became the most heavily indebted country in the world. The national debt stood at almost twelve billion dollars in 1895 and at eighteen billion in 1914. Less than one third of the debt in 1895 was owed to foreign creditors, but nearly half of the larger sum owed in 1914 was. If one adds the credit extended to private railway companies, industrial firms, and municipal bodies, Russia's foreign debt in 1914 stood at fifteen billion dollars. Even while she was turning away from the West politically, Russia was becoming more bound to it financially. The trade balance became generally favorable; that is to say, Russia imported less than she exported. But the difference was not sufficient to pay for the mounting charges of the debt, with the result that further loans had constantly to be made. The upshot was that the financial condition of the country was worse in 1914 than it had been at the beginning of industrialization.

The Russian Revolution in Rehearsal

The introduction of industry, the consequent growth of the middle classes, and the concentration of factory labor—even though they were stimulated by the government—strengthened the opposition to czarism. In addition to the socialist parties (see p. 434), there arose a party of the advocates of constitutionalism. Leaders and officials of the local elected councils established by Alexander II had for many years carried on an informal campaign for reform. In addition to the improvement of local conditions—particularly school services and roads—they demanded a share in the drafting of legislation bearing upon their functions, the establishment of a national representative body, and individual rights. In 1903, council leaders joined liberal capitalists, professional men, advanced writers, and enlightened landlords to form the "Union of Liberators," whose ideal was a liberal monarchy of the British type.

Faced by a manifold opposition, the government resorted to fantastic devices. A group of secret police officials, supported by Pobiedonostzef, conspired to take over the leadership of the working class from the socialists and use the proletariat to frighten the capitalists. They dispatched renegade revolutionaries and other dubious characters to proletarian quarters. One of them, a priest, Father Gapon, earned popularity in St. Petersburg as the friend of labor. The police poured secret funds into the support of labor newspapers. "Police socialism" proved to be too clever by half. Strikes were easier to call than to call off. In a few cases, strikes organized by the Czar's police had to be put down by his army.

After the turn of the century unrest increased in the villages as well as in the cities. Peasant disorders multiplied. Yet the government resisted all demands for concessions. It became plain that only external pressure could shake the autocracy. That pressure was applied, quite irrelevantly, by Japan. Russia's aggressive policy in Asia (see Chap. 22) led to war with the Asian empire in February 1904. The government proved as inefficient in fighting abroad as it was in governing at home. In May the armies of Czar Nicholas were defeated at the Yalu River near the Liaotung Peninsula, and the Japanese besieged Port Arthur. The opposition at home was emboldened: the Czar found himself virtually at war with his own people as well as with the Japanese. In July terrorists assassinated the reactionary Minister of the Interior, Vyacheslav Plehve. The Czar appointed a more conciliatory successor and relaxed police measures somewhat, but the effect was hardly to silence the critics. In September and October the Russian army, ill equipped and miserably led, was defeated in two great land battles south of Mukden, the capital of Manchuria. Nicholas, in a desperate effort to retrieve the situation in the Far East, dispatched his Baltic fleet to the Pacific. Simultaneously, Russian liberals called a congress to extort reform from the government. The congress, which met in St. Petersburg in November, demanded the immediate concession of parliamentary institutions.

Both struggles reached a climax in January 1905, when Port Arthur surrendered to the Japanese and the first great workers' demonstration gathered in St. Petersburg. Thousands of people, led by Father Gapon, marched to the palace to present a petition to the Czar. They were received with a volley of shots. Seventy workers were killed and several hundred injured. A wave of strikes swept the country. The Czar yielded, promising to call an assembly to advise him on reform of the government and to concede personal liberties.

By summer the position of the government had deteriorated further. The

A Soviet artist's depiction of "Red Sunday," January 22, 1905. Demonstrators bringing a petition to Czar Nicholas II were fired upon—and seventy persons were killed—by troops waiting for them in front of the Winter Palace in St. Petersburg. The demonstration was led by Father G. Gapon, a secret police agent. SOVFOTO

Czar's Baltic fleet was annihilated upon its arrival in Tsushima Strait in May 1905. In July and August there were disorders in many towns and cities, and a full-scale mutiny broke out in the Black Sea fleet. Fortunately for czarism, Japan was as strained economically by her victorious exertions as Russia was humiliated by her defeats; both participants desired a prompt peace. So did the United States, which disapproved of Japanese penetration in China. In August 1905 the Treaty of Portsmouth was arranged under American auspices.

Upon opening peace negotiations with the Japanese, the Czar conceded to his subjects a Duma (parliament). The Duma was to be elected by restricted suffrage and to have only the power to deliberate and advise on legislation. This was not enough, and in October there occurred an extraordinary event which recalled in spontaneity and universality, though not in violence, the famous "days" of the French Revolution. Russia went on strike. Not only workingmen and professional men but also judges and lesser government officials, even shopkeepers, refused to work. The Czar was forced to promise, in the October Manifesto, a broadly democratic suffrage and participation by the Duma in legislation. He canceled all redemption payments due from the village communes for land sold to them in 1861. The peasant was no longer to be flogged by officials or punished by forced labor when he fell behind in taxes. Many liberals, known as Octobrists, accepted the concessions, but a large group insisted on the convocation of an assembly that would write a new and advanced constitution. This group formed a separate Constitutional Democratic party, called the Cadets.

After the October Manifesto, the wave of revolution receded. The government brought back troops from the silenced fronts, obtained loans from foreign financiers, and, to divert the populace from attacking the Czar, encouraged criminal and fanatical elements to harass the Jews. While official rowdies massacred hundreds of innocent people in the winter of 1905-06, reliable regiments put down an insurrection of proletarians in Moscow.

The first Duma, elected by universal manhood suffrage, met in 1906 and vainly demanded that ministers be made responsible to it, that all civil and religious disabilities be removed, and that the land be expropriated in favor of the peasants. It unanimously censured the government, which did not, however, resign. The Czar punished the Duma by sudden dissolution. Two hundred members tried to imitate the "Oath of the Tennis Court" taken by the Third Estate of France when Louis XVI locked it out from its assembly hall in June 1789. They met in Viborg, Finland, and called upon the people of Russia to stop paying taxes and supplying recruits to the army. They warned foreign creditors that they disclaimed responsibility for any debts extended to the government.

The Russian deputies did not, however, attempt to organize a boycott or an uprising against the government. The French deputies had challenged the King to use force. When Louis showed intention of doing so, the people of Paris rose and destroyed royal power in the capital. But when, after the dissolution of the Duma, its building was surrounded by troops, the people of St. Petersburg did not rise. The government obtained a large loan from France.

The Czar now reneged on his promise that all adult males would be permitted to vote: he disfranchised millions of peasants and diminished the representation of non-Russian nationalities. Despite government pressure on the voters, the second Duma was more radical than the first. Nevertheless, the deputies were reduced to talking and complaining, since the Duma had little real power.

Meanwhile Prime Minister Peter Stolypin (1862-1911) tightened the screws of authority. He set up secret courts to deal summarily with critics, invoked the death penalty for persons who insulted officials, deprived universities of their rights of self-government, and turned out the more articulate liberal professors. The Czar publicly pardoned hooligans and officials who had been convicted of inciting mass murder of Jews. Tens of thousands from the ranks of the opposition found their way to the gallows, the hardly less fatal hard-labor prisons, and the cold and distant wastes of northern Siberia.

To his program of repression Stolypin shrewdly yoked a rural program. The village system ensured a rough equality, even if it was too often the equality of common poverty. Stolypin's plan was to divide the peasantry by elevating a portion of it above the mass, thus establishing a class of substantial and enterprising peasants which, he hoped, would become a conservative weight in the countryside. It was decreed that peasants could leave the commune and set up their own compact farms for individual ownership and cultivation. Each new farm would be owned, not by the household members together, as was customary, but by the head of a household (actually, the oldest male relative of a group of related families). All the members but the chief lost their rights in the holding. In short, common ownership and work through village and household was to give way to individualism.

Stolypin's land reforms initiated a painful and prolonged revolution in the villages. His repressive policy produced immediate results in the embitterment of urban classes and the intelligentsia. Attempt after attempt was made on the life of the minister, sometimes with the connivance of the secret police, which, along with other powerful elements of the bureaucracy, looked upon Stolypin as too "enlightened" and "radical." In 1911 Stolypin was assassinated in a Kiev theater in the presence of the Czar. The Russian Revolution was not over—it was merely simmering.

In Russia, as in Austria-Hungary, the problems of the industrial age deepened the longing for liberal institutions. In the countries of Western Europe, these problems were met largely by economic reform. Within the bounds of a common objective arising from similar industrial characteristics, the enduring differences between great regions of the Western world asserted themselves. However, while the domestic consequences of industrialization varied from region to region, and sometimes from country to country, international relations entered upon a period of uniform and increasing tension.

457

22. *Imperialism and Rival Alliances*

The effect of the Age of Steel upon international relations was portentous. Economic development was highly uneven. Advanced industrial states secured a great advantage over other states, and the countries of Europe and North America over other continents. The result was national self-assertion among the Western powers and rivalry for overseas colonies.

The Spirit of Aggression

Many of the tendencies of the time, and a good many of the conflicts, were channeled into imperialism: the overflow of financial surpluses abroad, the search for markets and resources, the intervention of the state in economic questions, the ambitions of big business, and the fashion of aggressive action. Navalism and militarism flourished. In *The Influence of Sea Power upon History* (1890) and *The Influence of Sea Power upon the French Revolution and Empire* (1892), the American Captain Alfred Mahan (1840-1914) argued that naval strength was essential to the quest for trade, wealth, and international prestige. The great struggles for imperial power had been decided by navies, he claimed. Mahan evoked the age of mercantilist rivalry, particularly the golden age of the British navy and its heroes—above all Admiral Nelson, who had defied and defeated the great land captain Napoleon Bonaparte. Mahan drew the moral that ambitious countries ought not only to build large navies but also to secure naval stations and strategic harbors on the great shipping lanes and in the narrower seas and straits of the world. His views captivated naval and diplomatic circles everywhere, especially in Japan and Germany, avid newcomers in the race for naval glory.

As Britain was the naval model, Germany set the military fashion. In short campaigns she had defeated two of the principal European powers, Austria and France. The Continental states hastened to imitate her military organization. They introduced universal conscription, organized large armies around a cadre of aristocratic officers and professional noncommissioned officers, and founded staff schools to train organizers and leaders of war. They poured great treasure into the equipping of ever larger conscript armies and ever more destructive—and expensive—artillery. They established general staffs to prepare plans of campaign, elaborated to the last detail, for besting any possible combination of enemies. Fighting was one of the oldest occupations, but organized and professional planning for war was novel. These activities naturally encouraged the stance of pride and defiance.

The vogue of social Darwinism threw the halo of progress around contests for national supremacy, as it had "justified" unrestrained competition among individuals. Whoever rises to the top of the heap demonstrates his worth. The "lower" races or passive peoples were doomed to defeat by the "law" that only the "fittest" will survive. If social Darwinism justified the struggle for the wealth of colonial peoples, religion sanctified the struggle for their souls. For every anthropologist who rose to the challenge of strange cultures, there were dozens of missionaries who threw themselves eagerly into the work of "salvation." The new means of transportation, the new methods of medicine, the spread of literacy, and the new techniques of printing enabled missionaries to make contact with the most isolated of tribes. But the inevitable misunderstandings between native chieftains and priests and the resentment aroused by the merchants and soldiers who came along with the missionaries often made it necessary to invoke the secular arm.

Religion and science endowed expansion with the aura of altruism and heroism. The *ism* was born: empire became imperialism, an ideology, a propaganda, and—for martial temperaments—an ideal.

In each country imperialism borrowed its nuance from the prevailing mood or culture. American expansionists stressed the moral duty to improve the lot of less fortunate peoples. During the Spanish-American War President William McKinley told how he had got down on his knees and prayed for divine guidance. It came to him that it was God's will the United States should annex Pacific islands in order to "educate" their inhabitants, to "uplift and civilize and Christianize them, and, by God's grace, do the very best we could by them, as our fellowmen for whom Christ also died." French imperialists felt that their country should share her civilization with other peoples, and not in Europe alone. Premier Jules Ferry urged the obligation to extend the range of influence of French language, culture, and "genius" as well as that of French economy and arms. German leaders asserted the power and the glory of the German name. Emperor William II, who was fond of blustering and speeches, became a loud propagandist of imperialism. As though the Chinese and Japanese were about to invade Europe, he declaimed against the "yellow peril." He sent off an expedition to China in 1897 with a public injunction that contained a fearful simile: the Germans must behave in Asia as the Huns had behaved in Europe. Nationalists in both Germany and Austria spun a Pan-German scheme, comprehending the kindred peoples and enclaves from the

Baltic coast to the Black and Adriatic Seas. This empire of Mittel-Europa would dominate the Continent and then would win world hegemony. To Russian expansionists, the merger of Russia with Asia was a more intoxicating prospect than the older Pan-Slav dream of merger with the peoples of Central Europe and the Balkans. English imperialists stressed the hard "obligation" of the British to discipline the "lesser breeds without the law." Such was the appeal of Rudyard Kipling:

> Take up the White Man's burden—
>   Send forth the best ye breed—
> Go bind your sons to exile
>   To serve your captives' need;
> To wait in heavy harness
>   On fluttered folk and wild—
> Your new-caught, sullen peoples,
>   Half devil and half child.
>
> Take up the White Man's burden—
>   And reap his old reward:
> The blame of those ye better,
>   The hate of those ye guard.

The First Steps of Empire

The penetration and exploration of new areas in Asia, Oceania, and Africa provided the opportunity for imperialists. The opening of five ports to trade in 1842 proved the beginning of contacts with China that increased with the years. The many archipelagoes and isolated islands of the vast Pacific Ocean attracted merchants and shippers. The interior of the African continent, hitherto unexplored, first began to attract adventurers in the early nineteenth century. They soon reached Lake Chad, the mouth of the Niger, the upper Nile, and a few of the great lakes and mountains. In the fifties and sixties the Scottish missionary David Livingstone (1813-73) crossed the continent from Angola to Mozambique, explored the Zambezi River, and discovered Lakes Nyasa and Chilwa and Victoria Falls. When Livingstone was given up for lost, the English explorer Henry M. Stanley (1841-1904) was commissioned by the New York *Herald* to find him. Stanley not only fulfilled his assignment but later traced the course of the Congo River. These were only the most successful of a group of explorers, including Frenchmen, Germans, Portuguese, and Arabs as well as Englishmen, who laid bare the interior of Africa.

For some years imperialism was covert. It blossomed in the hothouse of diplomacy and adventurous finance. "Deals" were negotiated in the antechambers of foreign offices and embassies, in admiralty and military centers, in the inner sanctums of investment bankers, and in the haunts of speculators.

460

In dark jungles and remote isles, primitive chieftains affixed inadvertent X's to harmless pieces of paper that the European strangers later said were treaties which made them masters.

There seemed to be enough opportunity to go around. This was especially true in Africa. Great Britain, already in possession of several coastal colonies, extended her dominion. To Britain's annoyance—for she was unaccustomed to rivalry—Bismarck picked up a piece of coast here and the mouth of a river there, in support of German enterprisers. In 1884-85 Bismarck presided in Berlin over a Conference on African Affairs attended by representatives of fourteen governments, including that of the United States. The Conference recognized the Congo Free State, which had been organized by King Leopold II of Belgium in 1876. In effect, it sanctioned the recent acquisitions of Germany and other powers, set up rules under which further annexations might be made, and pledged the powers to help to suppress slavery and the slave trade. Within a decade, coastal and interior areas amounting to millions of square miles had been taken over. France assembled an empire of four million square miles, including the wastes of the Sahara and older colonies in the north; Britain one only slightly smaller. Nearly a million square miles became German, and 800,000 Portuguese; only one thirteenth of Africa remained under native rulers, the object of future appetites and quarrels.

The vast expanse of waters, archipelagoes, and islands that comprise

An American criticism of one of the most notorious examples of imperialistic exploitation, that of the Congo Free State by King Leopold II of Belgium. Leopold's rule was notorious for its cruelty to native labor and avidity for profit, in this case from crude rubber. Reproduced from a pamphlet by Mark Twain, King Leopold's Soliloquy, *Boston, 1905.*

Oceania was almost entirely distributed among the powers. Their value was sometimes strategic, sometimes economic, and sometimes merely imaginary. Great Britain took the islands of Fiji, Gilbert, Ellice, the southwest Solomons, and Santa Cruz. She divided the New Hebrides with France. Germany annexed northeast New Guinea, western Samoa, the Carolines, and the Palau Islands. The United States annexed eastern Samoa and Hawaii. These were the more important and larger groups. Over the others, wide nets were drawn. In the mid-eighties, Germany, Great Britain, and France established "spheres of influence" over large stretches of water dotted with tropical and subtropical islands. Germany assumed control over a large area of Micronesia and western Melanesia; France over southern Melanesia and a small part of Polynesia; and Great Britain over the largest area, from southeast Melanesia and Micronesia to Polynesia. The natives of the islands were too weak, gentle, bemused, or amazed by the energetic strangers to offer or even contemplate effective resistance.

On the Asian mainland the powers nibbled at the vast periphery of the Celestial Empire. Russia had obtained partial control over Manchuria. In Indochina, over which China claimed an ancient overlordship, represented by annual tributes of the constituent states, Britain had annexed the kingdom of Burma. France had acquired Annam, Cambodia, and Tonkin. In 1883 China tried to force the withdrawal of France. She failed, and the bulk of eastern Indochina became a French protectorate.

Despite the substantial expansions of the European powers, public opinion at home was at first wary of aggressive policies. In 1880 the German *Reichstag* rejected a government proposal to subsidize a company for trading in the Pacific, largely on the ground that such a subsidy was a prelude to colonialism. Four years later Bismarck observed regretfully that there was still lacking in Germany "an impulse from the nation itself" toward acquisitions overseas. In the early eighties, the people of the Sudan, led by the fanatic Mahdi, rebelled against Egyptian rule. The British government determined to persuade the Egyptians to withdraw. When a British-led force sent to assist in the evacuation was surrounded by the Sudanese, relief was slow in coming: the British government suspected the besieged leader, General Gordon, of opportunism. And when General Gordon was killed, it wrote off the incident without "punishing" the Sudanese.

It was by presenting the annexations as *faits accomplis* that early imperialists won the approval of the public and parliaments; and even then not always without difficulty. Many annexations were made, and subsequently approved, before imperialism had been announced and defended as a deliberate policy. In the nineties, however, more or less covert activity became no longer adequate or possible. In industrial countries, surplus capital and surplus goods were accumulating. Protectionist policies intensified trade rivalries. As the craving for empire grew, the means of satisfying it diminished. The bulk of Africa and of Oceania had been apportioned among the powers. Since many of the annexa-

462

tions had been improvised, it could hardly be expected that the powers would remain satisfied with their shares. The territories that were still open became the objects of rivalry. The powers became covetous of one another's territories and often cast a common glance at the holdings of weaker states.

A new act of the drama of expansion was opened. Informal compromises were succeeded by open disputes. If rivals were to be defied successfully, military and especially naval forces must be strengthened and public and parliamentary support invoked. From the screened tent of diplomacy, the expansionists emerged into the open forum of politics, publicity, and ideology. When they could not discover, they invented reasons to explain why expansion was not only an economic benefit and a political right but a moral and biological duty.

The variety of interests, ambitions, and sentiments that went to make up imperialism explains why small powers as well as large succumbed to it, why countries that had to borrow capital shared in it as insistently as those that had surpluses, why sterile patches of land and valueless coasts were appropriated with eagerness, and why individuals and classes with no palpable interests overseas entered into the spirit of the thing enthusiastically. In a span of six years, beginning in 1898, three wars and several lesser conflicts broke out in America, Africa, and Asia.

The United States in the Caribbean and the Philippines

Imperialism presented a special problem to the United States. After the purchase of Alaska from Russia in 1867, the possibilities of expansion on the North American continent seemed to be exhausted. The long drive to the Pacific coast had been motivated by the ideal of a republic large and strong enough to maintain itself and to exercise influence in a world of monarchical empires. In the past expansion had meant political assimilation: new lands were to be governed from Washington only until they had a population large enough to create additional states, equal in status to the older members of the Union. However, the occupation of overseas territories or islands inhabited by peoples lacking the habits of political freedom would present both constitutional and psychological obstacles. The acquisition and rule of subordinate "colonies" were not provided for in the Constitution. Yet many ambitious politicians, segments of the capitalist class, diplomats, and naval officers proved susceptible to the fever of expansion. Followers of Mahan, they were intent on strengthening the position of the Republic in the Pacific Ocean and in the Caribbean Sea and the approaches to the Panama isthmus joining North and South America. If the long-projected canal connecting the Atlantic and Pacific Oceans was cut, the area would become even more important.

In the mid-nineties the Monroe Doctrine was restated with exaggerated emphasis. In 1895 a boundary dispute between Venezuela and British Guiana suggested the possibility that British troops would be dispatched to the Western

463

Hemisphere. President Cleveland threatened war unless Great Britain agreed to submit the question to arbitration. Secretary of State Richard Olney made the inflated declaration that "today the United States is practically sovereign on this continent [which denoted both North and South America], and its fiat is law upon the subjects to which it confines its interposition." Great Britain demurred to the claim but, after reflection, agreed to Cleveland's demand. An international commission in 1899 awarded Great Britain most of the land in dispute, but meanwhile the only power whose naval force could frustrate American ambition virtually surrendered her own further ambitions in the Western Hemisphere.

The British decision was made in light of a dispute with Germany. The Emperor had ostentatiously declared his sympathy with the Boer Republic in South Africa, which had repelled an informal invasion by British troops. It was thought, not without reason, that Germany contemplated establishing a "protectorate" over the Boers. In view of this challenge to British predominance in South Africa, English statesmen thought it prudent to secure the "rear door" in America.

Soon after this diplomatic victory for the United States, conditions in Cuba presented an opportunity for American expansionists. The disaffection of the Cubans, under Spanish rule, had led to a bitter civil war in 1895. The Spanish forces resorted to ruthless tactics and atrocities of an unusual kind and dimension: they established huge concentration camps into which thousands of natives were herded, under conditions of famine and disease that killed them in the tens of thousands, and they did summary justice to captured rebels. These acts lost nothing in the reporting of the American "yellow press" and inflamed public opinion. For a century, American statesmen had proclaimed the United States as the heir of Spanish power. "Filibustering" expeditions of private citizens and smuggling arms to Latin-American rebels had become traditions. Now the United States formally protested the atrocities. A liberal cabinet came to power in Spain and made promises of reformation. However, American expansionists would not be cheated of their chance, which came on February 15, 1898, when the U.S.S. *Maine* was mysteriously blown up in the harbor of Havana. President McKinley and the businessmen who supported the Republican party were indifferent to a war with Spain, but the President and many Congressmen were afraid of defying the expansionists and a public opinion that they judged to be determined on war. McKinley omitted mention of the Spanish concessions in a belligerent message to Congress delivered on April 11, 1898. Congress responded by declaring war on April 20.

The Americans easily defeated the forces of Spain in Cuba and the Philippines, where the Spanish Pacific fleet was stationed. At a crucial moment, when the American navy, under Admiral Dewey, was preparing to attack the Spanish in the harbor of Manila, a British and a German squadron of ships stood by. The former assumed an attitude of sympathetic observation; the latter watched with the apparent intention of intervening in favor of the Spanish if the chances of battle turned against the Americans. So, at least, did the American officers in

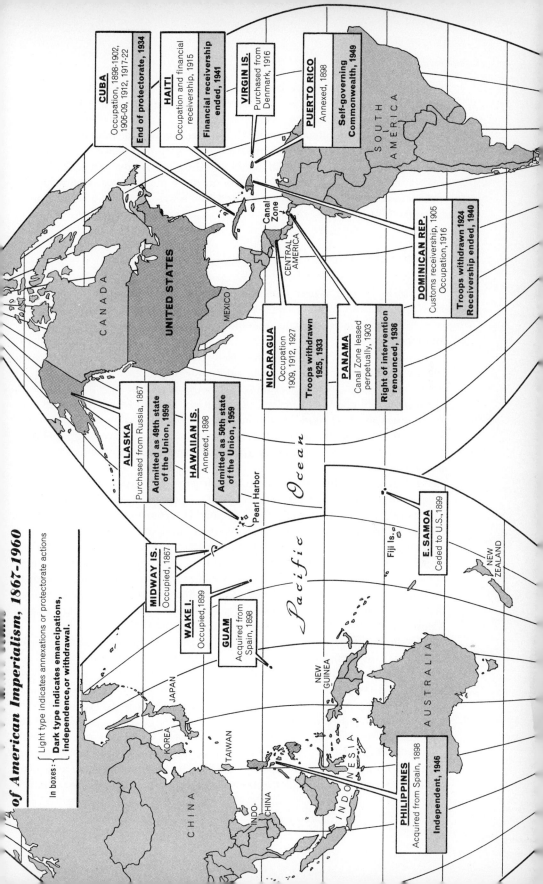

of American Imperialism, 1867–1960

In boxes:
- Light type indicates annexations or protectorate actions
- **Dark type indicates emancipations, independence, or withdrawal.**

CUBA
Occupation, 1898-1902, 1906-09, 1912, 1917-22
End of protectorate, 1934

HAITI
Occupation and financial receivership, 1915
Financial receivership ended, 1941

VIRGIN IS.
Purchased from Denmark, 1916

PUERTO RICO
Annexed, 1898
Self-governing Commonwealth, 1949

DOMINICAN REP.
Customs receivership, 1905
Occupation,1916
Troops withdrawn 1924
Receivership ended, 1940

NICARAGUA
Occupation 1909, 1912, 1927
Troops withdrawn 1925, 1933

PANAMA
Canal Zone leased perpetually, 1903
Right of intervention renounced, 1936

ALASKA
Purchased from Russia, 1867
Admitted as 49th state of the Union, 1959

HAWAIIAN IS.
Annexed, 1898
Admitted as 50th state of the Union, 1959

MIDWAY IS.
Occupied, 1867

WAKE I.
Occupied,1899

GUAM
Acquired from Spain, 1898

E. SAMOA
Ceded to U.S., 1899

PHILIPPINES
Acquired from Spain, 1898
Independent, 1946

CANADA

UNITED STATES

MEXICO

CENTRAL AMERICA

Canal Zone

SOUTH AMERICA

Pearl Harbor

Pacific Ocean

Fiji Is.

NEW ZEALAND

CHINA

KOREA

JAPAN

TAIWAN

INDO-CHINA

NEW GUINEA

INDONESIA

AUSTRALIA

command interpret the attitude of the Germans. The American fleet destroyed the Spanish, but an uneasy concern over German aims lingered in the memory of American diplomats.

Although the public at large had supported the war for humanitarian and patriotic reasons, it was the expansionists who made the peace. In the treaty signed at Paris in December 1898, Spain withdrew from Cuba and ceded Puerto Rico, Guam, and the Philippine Islands to the United States. The principal approaches to the Caribbean were secured. Cuba was to be occupied temporarily by the United States.

Rivalries in Africa and the Boer War

Save in Liberia, where American Negroes had established a small state, the United States manifested no interest in Africa. European powers, however, were determined to consolidate and enlarge their gains of the eighties. Germany envisioned an empire stretching across the width of the southern part of Africa, encompassing South-West Africa, which she already possessed; southeast Africa, then Portuguese; and the intervening lands in the interior, which as yet belonged neither to Portugal nor to Germany. Russia proposed to begin in Abyssinia, which she could claim to "protect" as a lonely Christian kingdom of Africa, in the manner she had made traditional in the Balkan Peninsula. From there Russia would expand westward, not stopping until she reached the broad Atlantic. But since she did not yet control Abyssinia, the vision was highly abstract.

The plans of other powers were more feasible and hence more dangerous. Britain, which controlled the Cape Colony, hoped to cut an axial swathe the length of the continent, from the Cape of Good Hope north to Egypt. A proposed Cape-to-Cairo railroad would do double duty: it would justify the acquisition of the intervening domains, and, when completed, it would bind them together. Cutting across this project was the French plan. Starting from the colonies she already held on the west coast, France would proceed across the widest part of the continent to the east coast along the Red Sea and Indian Ocean. Through the sandy Sahara this broad base would then be connected with France's Algerian colony on the Mediterranean Sea.

Exclusive influence in Abyssinia and the Sudan was essential to both the French and the British plans. In 1889, with the blessing of Great Britain, Italy had obtained an ambiguous treaty from Emperor Menelek II (1889-1911) of Ethiopia. As Italy read it, the treaty gave her a protectorate over Ethiopia. As the Emperor read it, his country was still independent. In 1895 and 1896 the Emperor validated his interpretation by defeating Italian armies. Behind the dispute of these two states raged the rivalry between Great Britain and France.

In 1898 the Anglo-French quarrel broke out more directly, in the Sudan. A French military explorer, Captain J. B. Marchand, penetrated the area south of Egypt and raised the tricolor at the small but strategic town of Fashoda. The

SP. MOROCCO

MADEIRA
(Port.)

CANARY IS.
(Sp.)

RIO DE ORO

MOROCCO

ALGERIA

TUNISIA

LIBYA

EGYPT
(Occupied by British, 1882)

20°N

FRENCH WEST AFRICA

ERITREA

FR. SOMALILAND

BR. SOMALILAND

ANGLO-
EGYPTIAN
SUDAN

LEONE

GOLD
COAST

NIGERIA

ABYSSINIA

LIBERIA

TOGO

KAMERUN

EQUATORIAL AFRICA

ITALIAN
SOMALILAND

Fernando Po
(Sp.)
RIO MUNI

Equator

BR. EAST
AFRICA

European Control
Before 1880

FRENCH

BELGIAN
CONGO

PEMBA
ZANZIBAR } (Br.)

KABINDA

GERMAN
EAST
AFRICA

Niger R.

Nile R.

ANGOLA

RHODESIA

(Port. 1484)

Congo R.

Zambezi R.

(Port. 1505)

Boers

MOZAMBIQUE

MADAGASCAR

22°S

GERMAN
S.W. AFRICA

BECHUANALAND

22°S

Walfish Bay
(Br.)

UNION OF
SOUTH AFRICA

Exploration of the Interior

CAILLÉ
1827-28

NACHTIGAL
1869-74

NGO
RK
95

Niger R.

Nile R.

BARTH
1850-55

Congo R.

Victoria

STANLEY
1871-77

Zambezi R.

LIVINGSTONE
1841-1873

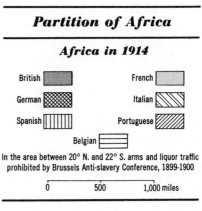

Partition of Africa

Africa in 1914

British

French

German

Italian

Spanish

Portuguese

Belgian

In the area between 20° N. and 22° S. arms and liquor traffic
prohibited by Brussels Anti-slavery Conference, 1899-1900

0   500   1,000 miles

British moved up the Nile into Sudan and threatened to dislodge the French. The local commanders referred the quarrel to Paris and London. Joseph Chamberlain, the British Colonial Secretary, was ready to go to war rather than yield the claim. It was a hard choice for France. Germany had been more sympathetic to French colonial ambitions than Britain had been. However, as payment for her neutrality in a French-British war overseas, Germany expected France to confirm the loss of Alsace-Lorraine and to dismantle her border fortifications as a guarantee against future defiance. In the choice between an African colony and Continental independence, the interests of France in Europe prevailed over her interests in Central Africa. Fashoda was yielded, war was averted, and the road was opened for French-British agreement on other differences.

Successful in the Sudan, British imperialists rushed to fulfill earlier plans in the far south. There a bitter quarrel had been brewing for a long time. When the Cape Colony was ceded by the Netherlands to Britain at the Congress of Vienna in 1814, its population of European origin consisted principally of Boers (peasants of Dutch stock). The Boers chafed under foreign rule and objected particularly to the activities of English missionaries in behalf of the colored natives. When Britain abolished slavery in 1833, the Boers, who regarded the institution as economically necessary and also as justified by the Bible, took an extraordinary step. Beginning in 1835, ten thousand families "trekked" northward in oxcarts and established two pastoral states of their own in the Transvaal. Eventually the two states were united under the name of the South African Republic. Britain alternately accepted and rejected this solution until finally in 1881 she recognized the independence of the Republic, but under her own formal suzerainty. Thus matters stood when English diggers and adventurers flocked into the Transvaal in order to exploit its mining riches: diamonds had been discovered in 1867 and gold in 1886. Differences soon developed between the mining and agricultural communities, particularly over the Boers' refusal to grant the franchise to the English for fear of being outnumbered and outmatched. These differences were exploited by the English imperialists, led by Cecil Rhodes (1853-1902), who had made a vast fortune in diamond mining and who became Prime Minister of the Cape Colony. Rhodes was obsessed by the vision, first, of an enlarged British Empire, and then of world domination by the "superior" Anglo-Saxon race. His avidity was unlimited: "I would annex the planets if I could." Rhodes' British South Africa Company in 1889 obtained huge grants of land, with the right of government, on the borders of the Boer state. In 1895 Rhodes and his followers conspired to organize a private invasion of the republic. The imperialist Joseph Chamberlain had just become Colonial Secretary, and they knew they had a friend at court. A force of about six hundred men, under the command of a colonial official, Dr. L. S. Jameson (1853-1917), crossed the border of the republic in December 1895 with the intention of overthrowing the government. But the Boers promptly surrounded and captured the group, and the British punished its leader by imprisoning him for a year. The scandal of the Jameson raid further worsened relations with the Boers, and, in 1899, convinced that Britain was determined to subdue them, they declared war on her.

The conflict between the world-wide empire and the small republic was long and difficult. The Boers' stand aroused the sympathy of the world—including a large part of the British public—and stimulated the ambitions of Britain's rivals. Germany officially announced her sympathy with the Boers. In 1902 the British finally prevailed in South Africa, offered fair terms to the Boers, and annexed the South African Republic as the Transvaal colony.

Another development, in a more sensitive area, underlined the potentiality of conflict. For some time German financiers and diplomats had been developing an interest in the Balkan and Asian provinces of Turkey. In 1899 a German syndicate obtained a concession from Turkey to build a railway across Asia Minor to Baghdad. A future extension of several hundred miles would bring the railroad to the Persian Gulf, which opens into the Indian Ocean, the sea route to India. "Berlin-to-Baghdad" raised visions of future German armies and naval equipment moving across Central Europe and Asia Minor to challenge Britain's command of the sea. Although her financiers participated in the railroad loans, Great Britain became apprehensive.

"Spheres of Influence" in China

Of all the opportunities for profitable penetration, none seemed more tempting than that presented by China. Her internal strains exposed China to the ambitions of three powers in particular. Great Britain had forced China to open ports to trade, and the British navy dominated Asian waters. From the sixties on, Russian pressed deeper into Asia. At first the direction was southeast. Local military commanders, frequently acting on their own initiative, annexed much of Central Asia, including the legendary cities of Samarkand, Tashkent, Khiva, and Bokhara. Russian attempts to subdue Afghanistan, on the northwest border of India, were frustrated by the British, who invaded the country in 1878-79 and assumed control over her foreign relations.

Russia met similar disappointments in Europe. In 1877 she won a military victory in another war against Turkey, and her armies advanced within sight of Constantinople. Again Great Britain intervened by threatening war, and Russia's gains were whittled down (see p. 473). In the eighties Russian attempts to control the newborn kingdom of Bulgaria were unsuccessful. Her European policy had foundered.

Russia shifted her pressure to northeastern Asia. There she crossed the path of another ambitious empire. Ever since the sixties, when Japan had decided to transform herself on European models, her industry, commerce, and shipping, all based on modern technology, had grown apace. She became pre-eminent in the manufacture of inexpensive goods, for the cost of labor was the lowest in the industrial world. Japan's interest in obtaining markets on the mainland, combined with her traditional militarism, produced an especially virulent imperialism. In 1876, imitating the earlier action of England and the United States, Japan induced Korea, which had sealed herself against the world, to open her ports to trade. Japan and several Western countries obtained extraterritorial rights. Japan's penetration into Korea led to war with China in 1894-95. To the surprise of the world, Japan defeated the huge and once formidable "Celestial Empire," acquiring Formosa, the Pescadores Islands, and the northern peninsula of Liaotung. China gave up her old claim of sovereignty over Korea and acknowledged Korean independence.

Japan proceeded to intervene in Korea to establish her domination. In this effort she was challenged by Russia. Seconded by France and Germany, Russia intimidated Japan into returning the Liaotung Peninsula to China. Russia had begun to construct the Trans-Siberian railroad in 1891. Its terminus was Vladivostok, on the Pacific. The northward bulge of Manchuria made a large detour necessary. In 1896 China granted Russia the right to build and police a more direct railroad link with Vladivostok across Manchuria: the journey from St. Petersburg to the Pacific could now be made in eight days. Russia came into virtual control of Manchuria, and in 1898 she obtained a twenty-five-year lease of the valuable Port Arthur, farther south in the Liaotung Peninsula. Unlike Vladivostok, Port Arthur was not icebound in the winter months and so was more suitable as a naval base.

Was China to be partitioned? There was a moment of hesitation. British officials suggested to the United States a joint demand that China be kept open to the trade of all countries equally. The United States did not object to the principle but was chary of entering into "entangling alliances," as she had been in 1823 when George Canning had suggested common action against a proposed expedition by Spain to win back her former colonies in Latin America. As in 1823, the United States later issued a declaration along the lines suggested by England, but the so-called "Open Door Note" sent by Secretary of State John Hay in 1899 to the capitals of Britain, France, Germany, Russia, Italy, and Japan proved more theoretical than the Monroe Doctrine. For in the meantime the powers had acted. By offers of loans, open threats, and other pressures, they forced China to make a series of concessions which placed her economically and politically in bond to Europe. In 1897 Germany sent a fleet to China to avenge the murder of two missionaries. The fleet returned, having secured, in token of future respect for Christianity, the lease of the harbor of Kiaochow. The Chinese government considered it safer to distribute its concessions among several rival powers than to concentrate them in the hands of one. Professions of friendship proved as profitable as threats of war: the forced lease of Kiaochow to Russia was followed by the apparently voluntary leases of Kwangchowan to France and of Kowloon (opposite Hongkong) and Wei-hai-wei to England. Influence in Korea was to be divided between Japan and Russia.

The powers then proceeded to claim whole regions of China, particularly the hinterlands and great river valleys of their leased ports, as "spheres of influence." The investors, bankers, and exporters of each country were to have a

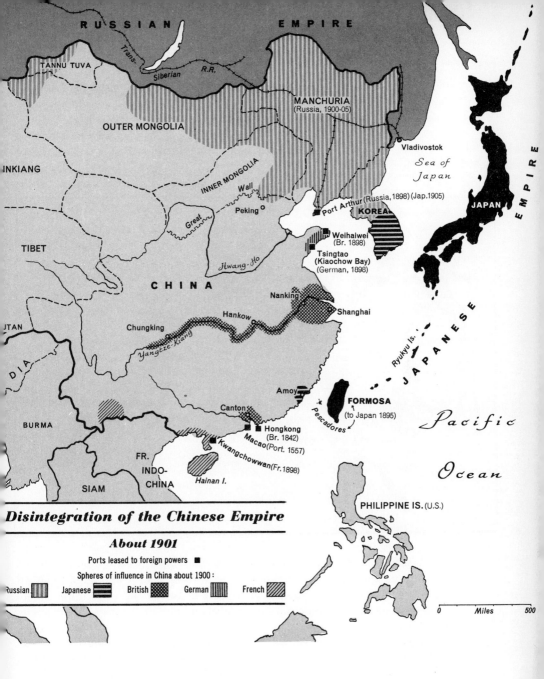

Disintegration of the Chinese Empire

About 1901

Ports leased to foreign powers ■

Spheres of influence in China about 1900:

Russian | Japanese | British | German | French

monopoly of whatever concessions of railroad construction, loans, and trade were made in the respective spheres. By the end of the century every great power possessed leased ports and held privileges of investment over large zones stretching far into the interior of China. In 1900 the Chinese government encouraged a "spontaneous" rising, organized by a secret society the Westerners called the "Boxers," to oust the "foreign devils" from the country. The Boxers besieged the foreign legations in Peking. A joint expedition of German, Russian, British, Japanese, American, Austrian, French, and Italian troops defeated them the following year and imposed a large indemnity on the government.

A Chinese view of the imperialistic attacks of foreign powers. This is a poster of the "Boxers," the patriotic group that in 1900 attempted unsuccessfully to oust the "foreign devils" from China.

While most of the powers managed to share in the distribution of spheres, the ambitions of the two neighboring empires of Russia and Japan clashed directly in the northern regions, particularly in Korea and Manchuria. Japan drew the logical conclusion from this rivalry and moved closer to Great Britain, Russia's old antagonist in Asia. The Anglo-Japanese alliance of 1902 provided for the cooperation of the two navies if either fought more than one other power in the North Pacific. Two years later, Japan attacked Port Arthur, without troubling to issue a declaration of war. When the Czar dispatched his Baltic warships halfway around the globe to the Pacific, Britain assumed an unfriendly attitude toward Russia. The German Emperor, vaunting his friendship, extorted a draft of a secret treaty of alliance from Czar Nicholas II. Russia, however, insisted on taking into her confidence France, her only reliable diplomatic friend. Germany objected, and the project of an alliance fell through. The Japanese were successful on both land and sea. With the mediation of the United States, Russia agreed at Portsmouth, New Hampshire, to a treaty which acknowledged

Japan's paramountcy in Korea and awarded the lease of the Liaotung Peninsula to Japan.

Russia's adventure ended in humiliation. Except for Italy, defeated by the Abyssinians in 1898, she was the first modern power to lose a war to a non-European state.

The Formation of Rival Alliances

The staccato series of wars at the turn of the century had the quality of rehearsals. In each case two states were engaged, and around them the other states formed a ring of spectators, watching the combatants and each other, taking the measure of potential enemies and looking for friends in time of trouble. Before long the principal powers and lesser states had ranged themselves in two opposing combinations.

The alliance system preceded the imperialist conflicts. It had its roots in the anti-Western orientation of Germany and the conservative Concert of Europe in the first half of the nineteenth century. Bismarck had exacted no territorial concessions from Austria in 1866, but he annexed Alsace-Lorraine five years later, after the Franco-Prussian War. In 1873 Germany, Austria, and Russia drew together in the Three Emperors' League, isolating France, now republican, and anathemizing radicalism, of which the Paris Commune of 1871 had been the latest example.

The new "Holy Alliance," however, was not so stable as the old had been. Austria's losses in Germany and Italy led her to concentrate her efforts to expand in the Balkan Peninsula. There the Hapsburg Empire crossed the path long trodden by Russia. The Three Emperors' League lapsed. In 1878, when Russia, having defeated Turkey, was constrained by the powers to give up some of her gains, it was Bismarck who presided over the Congress of Berlin, which assigned Bosnia-Herzegovina to Austria-Hungary. Russia sulked, remembering that but for her neutrality during the Austro- and Franco-Prussian Wars there might have been no Hohenzollern Empire. Bismarck protected himself by concluding the Dual Alliance with the Hapsburgs: if Russia attacked either Germany or Austria-Hungary the partners would fight together. If France attacked Germany, the Hapsburgs would remain neutral, but if Russia joined France in such an attack, Austria-Hungary would join Germany.

Attracted by Germany's prestige, and resentful of the French occupation of Tunis in 1881, Italy joined Germany and Austria-Hungary, and the Dual became the Triple Alliance. The three powers agreed to fight together if any of them was attacked by two other powers—that is to say, by France and Russia. The Alliance, concluded in 1882, was to be renewed every five years.

Bismarck for a time contrived to keep open "the bridge to St. Petersburg," for the czars had no taste for a *rapprochement* with the "red republic" of France. In 1881 the Three Emperors' League was revived, yet differences persisted. In 1887 Russia declined to renew the League and signed a secret Treaty of Reinsurance with Germany. Germany expressed sympathy with the Czar's Balkan ambitions and with his desire to obtain a grip on the Turkish Straits. The two empires would maintain neutrality if either was at war with another power; but if Germany attacked France, or if Russia attacked Austria-Hungary, the partner's hands were not bound. The last provision made it possible to argue that the Reinsurance Treaty was not inconsistent with Germany's obligations to Austria-Hungary under the Dual Alliance. Given Bismarck's ability to disguise provocation as defense—as illustrated in the Franco-Prussian War—and to perceive a concealed attack in another power's defense, the two alliances signified that he had maneuvered Germany into an extraordinary position. If matters were properly handled, Germany could count on being assisted in an emergency, but she could decide for herself whether to assist any of her allies, and which to favor. There was always the possibility that other powers might exhibit a similar agility. Hence German hegemony required superior legerdemain.

To complete his system, Bismarck proposed an alliance to Great Britain. But a formal treaty which would automatically involve Britain in war in certain circumstances stood little chance of acceptance by Parliament and the British public. (Bismarck thought it a weakness in constitutional states that their rulers could not conclude secret treaties.) However, by coming to an understanding about naval affairs with Italy and Austria-Hungary, Great Britain appeared to be an informal partner of the Triple Alliance.

Germany pushed her advantage hard. She exercised economic as well as diplomatic influence. In order to force Russia to accept more German imports, Bismarck, in the late eighties, inhibited Berlin bankers from granting the credits the Czar needed sorely. Long-isolated France was ready with investment funds. Laying aside her conservative scruples, Russia floated loans in Paris. Her new course was sped by events in Germany.

In 1888 Emperor William died, at the age of ninety-one. Awed by Bismarck's successes, he had allowed the Chancellor to exercise a virtual dictatorship. His successor, Frederick III, was more sympathetic to constitutionalism than his father had been, but he ruled for only three months. The new emperor, William II, was articulate, febrile, ambitious, and somewhat neurasthenic. He craved popularity and wished to cut a political figure. This was impossible so long as Bismarck, who was not used to sharing power, was Chancellor. Bismarck demurred when William insisted on repeal of the measures forbidding socialist meetings and publications and on the broadening of social services. The two men differed also on the alliance with Russia, which William regarded as inconsistent with the Austrian alliance. Bismarck's talent for playing off one power against another created tension; there was always the possibility that some of the neighbors might combine in order to avoid being manipulated. The true alternative was relaxed relations, particularly with France, and avoidance of militarist provocation. But William II chose to retain the essence of Bismarck's diplomacy and merely precipitated its consequences by simplifying it. He dismissed the Chancellor early in 1890.

The Reinsurance Treaty with Russia was expiring; William refused Russia's proposal to renew it and drew closer to the Hapsburgs. Russia turned more decisively toward France: in a convention signed in 1891, the two countries promised to consult if war threatened or if either was attacked. Subsequent agreements bound them to assist each other in case of a German attack. The agreement was to last as long as the Triple Alliance.

This development presented a knotty problem—indeed, a problem eventually insoluble—to the German General Staff: a war on two fronts. The combined armies of France and Russia were larger than those of Germany and Austria-Hungary. Simultaneous campaigns in the east and the west were out of the question. This suggested that it was a mistake to rely on military force alone to secure Germany's position in the future. But the influential aristocratic and military cadre was not ready to make the sacrifices implied by a rational revision of policy, and its prestige was too high to be challenged.

The imaginative Count Alfred von Schlieffen (1833-1913), who was chief of the General Staff in the crucial years 1891 to 1905, devised an adventurous plan which proposed, in effect, to transmute a war on two fronts into two campaigns in tandem: a lightning attack and victory in France, via Belgium (although Germany had joined with other powers in guaranteeing Belgian neutrality), followed later by a swift lunge at Russia. The initiative must always be Germany's, both campaigns must be completely successful, and the whole war must be short. Otherwise Germany might repeat the experience of Napoleon, who had conquered most of the Continent but eventually received the *coup de grâce* from Britain. The General Staff had little fear of the small professional British army, which they regarded as only an auxiliary to Britain's naval power, best suited for descents from the sea and inland raids. If British soldiers ever landed in north Germany, Bismarck had mocked, he would have them arrested. Germany was also reassured by the long-standing differences of Britain with France and Russia. The fact was, however, that Great Britain was abandoning her traditional foreign policies. The evolution of powerful alliances made it impossible for her to maintain, in "splendid isolation," a balance and division among the Continental states. She attempted to secure her position in the Atlantic by agreeing to American terms in the Venezuelan boundary dispute and to strengthen her position in the Pacific by signing a defensive alliance with Japan in 1902 (see pp. 463 and 472).

English liberals inclined toward friendship with France, and many conservatives, including Lord Salisbury, Prime Minister of England from 1895 to 1902, distrusted the German leadership. But advanced imperialists were attracted by the energy emanating from Germany and by racist doctrines which suggested the superiority of the Anglo-Saxon and Germanic peoples and the desirability of their cooperation against "lower races." Britain, however, wished support against Russian designs in Asia, and this was not forthcoming from Germany. Moreover, the British envisaged a broad and informal alignment of colonial policies, whereas Germany preferred to bind Great Britain to the Triple Alliance. Finally, Britain craved security, above all through the preservation of

Colonial Empires Before the First World War

RUSSIAN EMPIRE

ALASKA

ALEUTIAN IS. (U.S.)

Pacific

KOREA

JAPANESE EMPIRE

CHINA

MIDWAY IS.
(U.S.)

HAWAIIAN IS. (U.S.)

Hongkong
(Br.)

FORMOSA

WAKE I. (U.S.)

INDIA

BURMA

PHILIPPINES
(U.S.)

MARIANAS

GUAM
(U.S.)

MARSHALL IS.

Ocean

GOA
(Port.)

Pondicherry
(Fr.)

CEYLON

INDO-
CHINA

MALAY
STATES

CAROLINE IS.

BISMARCK
ARCH.

GILBERT IS. (Br.)

DUTCH EAST INDIES

ELLICE IS. (Br.)

MARQUE
(Fr.)

Indian

SOLOMON IS.
(Br.)

Ocean

NEW
HEBRIDES
(Br. & Fr.)

FIJI IS.
(Br.)

SAMOA
(Germ.)(U.S.)

SOCIETY IS.
(Fr.)

AUSTRALIA

NEW
CALEDONIA
(Fr.)

TONGA IS.(Br.)

TASMANIA

NEW ZEALAND

British	United States	French
German	Portuguese	Danish
Spanish	Italian	Dutch
Belgian	Japanese	

her naval predominance, while Germany was intent on becoming a sea power. In 1898 Germany launched a naval-building program and two years later, at the height of the Boer War, passed a large navy bill. Its preamble stated that Germany must possess "a fleet of such strength that a war against the mightiest naval power would involve risks threatening the supremacy of that power." In plain language, this meant that Germany's goal in building a navy was not necessarily to defeat Britain in naval warfare but to intimidate her into making constant concessions by threatening to put her dominance of the seas to a test. Sea warfare is notoriously more subject to chance and accident than land warfare. Germany was wagering, in effect, that Britain would not incur the risks of such a test.

Great Britain declined to play her assigned part. She was determined that her navy—once larger than all others combined—must exceed the German navy by 60 percent. And she attempted to reach a diplomatic understanding with France. At Fashoda in 1898 France had chosen to yield in the Sudan in order to maintain her ability to withstand German pressure in Europe. This opened the way to other compromises with Great Britain and then to a broad understanding. The Entente Cordiale of 1904 provided for British-French consultation in international questions and implied an obligation to act in concert. Great Britain was to have a free hand in Egypt, and France in Morocco.

In 1905, France concluded an agreement with Morocco that gave France a virtual protectorate, and Germany seized the opportunity to test the new Franco-British Entente. Emperor William landed suddenly in Tangier and proclaimed his interest in Moroccan independence. He insisted on a conference of the powers involved, which was held in Algeciras early in 1906. A compromise resulted: France was to police the Morocco-Algerian border and was to share control within Morocco with Spain. Throughout the negotiations, the French were supported firmly by Great Britain—indeed, by all the European powers except Austria-Hungary, which took the German side. Germany's other ally, Italy, sided with France.

While the Entente weathered the German challenge, France was disturbed by the imperial differences between her ally Russia, on the one hand, and Great Britain and Japan, on the other. After the Russo-Japanese War, however, Russia agreed to a compromise with Great Britain. In a convention signed in 1907, the two parties agreed that Persia was to be divided into two spheres of influence, with a neutral belt between them. This closed the circle, and the Triple Alliance of Germany, Austria-Hungary, and Italy faced the Triple Entente of England, France, and Russia.

American Isolation and Involvement

The formation of these rival combinations, both of them with overseas interests, raised the prospect of a conflict of unusual dimensions and a redistribution of colonies around the globe. This prospect placed hard choices before the

United States. The heart of the Republic was divided: recent expansion involved her more deeply than ever in international issues, yet in many parts of the country an isolationist mood was growing.

From the beginning of her existence—with the exception of the treaty with France during the War of Independence—the United States had avoided "entangling alliances." The Monroe Doctrine, which barred Europe from conquests in the Western Hemisphere, implied a reciprocal obligation on the part of the United States not to intervene in European affairs. But the attitude of Americans toward Europe had undergone several changes since 1823. As a result of the victory of the North in the Civil War and subsequent economic advances, America's sense of distinction from Europe became deeper and acquired a moral edge: Americans felt that they were not only different but superior.

The traditionally defensive attitude of the American toward European culture was weakening. In humorous travel books, Mark Twain (1835-1910) poked fun at the manners of Europe. Americans, he felt, did not have to apologize for themselves; they were simple, but they were good. Mark Twain repudiated the traditional obeisance to the sources of civilization. Copies of artistic works seemed to him brighter than the originals. Famous places left him cold. "It is popular to admire the Arno. It is a great historical creek with four feet of water and some scows floating around." Twain's philistinism was half pose, yet it was significant.

The rich American traveler of the novels of Henry James (1843-1916) was drawn to the Old World by the magic of art and refinement. But his confrontation with the cultivated European, especially the aristocrat, was that of two essentially different worlds. The aristocrat was sophisticated and well bred, but he was also insincere and even immoral. If the American was provincial and gauche, he was also innocent and full of good will. He had made money by daring and hard work, and the idle European aristocrat captured his imagination and then deceived him.

The sense of distinction was heightened by the arrival in America of millions of immigrants from Southern and Eastern Europe. For almost three centuries, the American colonies and then the Republic had had strong bonds with Western and Northern Europe. In the long run, the great migration of the turn of the century strengthened the tie to Europe by adding a bond with the peoples farther east. Immediately, however, the new immigrants, who differed from the majority of natives in economic status, religious affiliations, and cultural and political backgrounds, made many Americans more conscious of their own tradition.

Since most of the immigrants settled in the industrial areas of the Northeast while the Midwest remained largely native and agrarian, the distinction between the new and the old Americans acquired a sectional connotation. And so, although the era of Western expansion was coming to a close and the frontier of free land vanished in the nineties, the image of the "true" American as a Westerner became sharper. This image was greatly strengthened by Frederick

Jackson Turner's epochal essay *The Significance of the Frontier in American History* (1894). In this and other writings Turner acknowledged the contributions of the immigrant, but he insisted that the uniqueness of American civilization had its source not in Europe or on the Atlantic coast, but in the experience of Western settlement.

> To the frontier the American intellect owes its striking characteristics: that coarseness and strength combined with acuteness and inquisitiveness; that practical, inventive turn of mind, quick to find expedients; that masterful grasp of material things, lacking in the artistic but powerful to effect great ends; that restless, nervous energy; that dominant individualism, working for good and for evil, and withal that buoyancy and exuberance which comes with freedom—these are the traits of the frontier, or traits called out elsewhere because of the existence of the frontier.

The effect of all these tendencies was to increase America's political and cultural isolation. Other tendencies, however, were pulling in the opposite direction. Henry James, self-exiled in England, dreamed of a synthesis of American idealism and European taste. The rise of liberal and democratic movements in Western Europe strengthened the transatlantic interest of American progressives. Among groups concerned with international developments and diplomatic affairs there developed a leaning toward Great Britain. Investments, annexations, and strategic expansion overseas swept the United States into the broad current of world politics, and the prospect of a change in the balance of power was disturbing. The Republic had filled out her continental domain in a world whose oceans were patrolled by the British navy. In 1900 Secretary of State John Hay declared that "if the existence of the British Empire should be called into question there is no knowing what constellation might then make its appearance among the powers."

Since the Civil War, British statesmen had removed one outstanding difference with the Republic after another. In 1872 they had agreed to the United States damages for the depredations of British-built Confederate raiders, including the *Alabama*, during the Civil War. In 1895 they yielded to the insistence of Secretary of State Olney that the controversy over the boundary between Venezuela and British Guiana be submitted to arbitration. Six years later they agreed to the abrogation of the Clayton-Bulwer Treaty of 1850, which provided that any canal built in Central America would be jointly controlled by England and the United States; under the Hay-Pauncefote Treaty of 1901, the United States might build, control, and, by implication, fortify such a canal. The claims of the United States for boundary lands lying between Alaska and Canada were recognized by Britain in 1903; Canadian opinion was sacrificed to American. In short, Britain was giving the United States virtually a free hand in the Western Hemisphere.

The ambitions and behavior of Germany, on the other hand, caused concern in America. Expansionists and navalists could not forget that the German fleet had behaved in what seemed to them an unfriendly way during the recent war with Spain. The United States hoped to buy the Virgin Islands from Denmark in order to safeguard the entrance to the Caribbean Sea; would Germany act first? German nationalists stressed the "unity" of the Germans wherever they lived; there were many Germans in Brazil; did this portend future German intervention in the Western Hemisphere? While England had given positive tokens of her friendliness, the goal of Germany's diplomacy was apparently to preserve her freedom of action in future or unsettled questions.

There were Americans, mindful of an old friendship, who wished to draw France as well as England into an "Atlantic system." The Entente Cordiale reassured them. Some even envisioned a union of all the liberal countries bordering on the Atlantic. "Sweden, Norway, and Great Britain," wrote the historian Henry Adams (1838-1918), "belong to our system, not to Eastern Europe. . . . Somebody, at the beginning, cut Europe in halves along the Vistula." Adams depicted an Atlantic system based on industrial resources:

> We want our Atlantic system—which extends from the Rocky Mountains on the West, to the Elbe on the East, and develops nine-tenths of the energy of the world—to control France and Germany as far as it goes. Germany tried, and has always tried, to be independent and she faces east, south, and west, jumps over our head, and intrigues with every bankrupt beachcomber, to maintain a continental system like Napoleon's independent of ours. The law of mass is against her thus far, and, except in Silesia, she has no real balance to her Western strain. All Western Germany is American, Atlantic, and antimilitary. We need only to work with it. . . .

American policy reflected the conflicting tendencies of international involvement and isolation. At the Algeciras conference, President Theodore Roosevelt, while attempting to play the role of peacemaker, consistently supported the Anglo-French Entente and was determined to help France "get what she ought to have." He intervened more actively in European affairs than any president had done before. The United States Senate restated the old policy of aloofness from European issues at every occasion. It was becoming clear, however, toward which side the United States inclined.

The division of the powers of the Western world into rival groups was complete. The alignments were shaped by diplomatic and military aims, by the character and ambition of ruling groups, and, here and there, by political traditions. They were shaped, above all, by considerations of international prestige, colonial profit, and imperial hopes and fears.

The alliance system had large consequences. It made war more likely and more imminent and greatly expanded its potential scale. The powers must henceforth act in groups instead of individually. They could not afford to act alone. They could not remain neutral if a confederate were involved in war. Even peace was more likely than a limited war.

VI *War and Revolution*

*The First World War (1914-18) brought to an end a long period of
domestic peace and gradual political progress. The immediate effect of the War
was frenetic social convulsion and civil strife, particularly in the defeated
states of Central and Eastern Europe. The democratic republics that followed
upon the collapse of the three continental empires were assaulted by dictatorial,
terroristic, and revolutionary movements. This dramatic poster—"Vote
Communist"—was displayed during the elections in Vienna, Austria, in
1920. The revolutionary proletarian is carrying the "red" flag and a
flaming torch, ready to set fire to the established order of society. He is
trampling upon the Parliament, for whose seats he is appealing to the voters
in a democratic election!*

23. *The Military Deadlock*

The First World War was an extraordinary event. It concentrated in four years an almost unprecedented destruction of lives and property. Yet it was not its scale alone that distinguished it. For this was no conventional military or naval duel, no mere quarrel over territory, colonies, or prestige. It was— or turned out to be before it was over—a revolution in the guise of a war. It tested the political structures of the Western world, precipitated the dissolution of all the Continental empires, initiated a vast competition of social ideals and systems, and changed the temper of Western civilization.

Violence in the Air

The immediate antecedents of this conflict were the economic and colonial rivalries, the friction of bristling alliances, and the military and naval race between the great powers. Yet the broader antecedents, and some of these developments themselves, reached to deeper strains and unresolved issues in Western society and culture. It was his awareness of the pressure of these strains that led the English statesman and writer John Morley to remark that the British system was "verging on the humor of 1848." He might have said it of the whole of Europe. The unrest was not confined to one country, one class, or one sex.

As the first decade of the century wore on, the symptoms of deep restlessness accumulated. There was an incongruity between the reform tendencies of the time and the rising threat of international strife. Industrialization and centralization intensified national sentiment and competition, while developments in communication and transportation and the exchange of staple goods among countries and continents fostered internationalism. The disposition to defiance, which had become pronounced in diplomacy in the nineties, infected domestic politics and even intellectual life.

Among "advanced" writers and artists the disturbing theories of the German philosopher Friedrich Nietzsche (1844-1900) came into vogue. Nietzsche abhorred conventionality, moderation, and placidity. Kindness, modesty, and altruism, he claimed, were the morality of slaves. "The good, the true, and the beautiful" were not, to him, an ideal, but an illusion that spelled decadence. We need not saints but heroes, he wrote; there will be no progress until an elite of talented, selfish, power-loving, proud, and harsh Supermen—the "Big Blond Beast"—trample down the weak mass of mankind and fulfill themselves.

Not many who agreed that conventional values were too much "milk and water" could stand the "red meat" of Nietzsche. There were writers who looked for ways of safeguarding the inheritance of civilization and adapting it to the conditions of a materialistic society. But others became increasingly critical of scientific, rational, positivist, and peace-minded attitudes and were attracted by theories that stressed instinct, willfulness, and dynamism. The vogue of social Darwinism reinforced the bent for struggle.

It was not only esoteric literary and philosophical circles that caught the mood of defiance and aggressiveness. The women's suffrage movement, for example, organized violent agitation, particularly in Great Britain. Women harassed obstinate politicians and even assaulted them physically. They broke shop windows in fashionable streets. From a secret office in Paris, Englishwomen plotted the burning of churches, railway stations, and mailboxes. Hundreds of women were arrested and imprisoned.

Conservative and aristocratic elements grew impatient with the methods of peaceful persuasion. In France, for example, the opposition to republican institutions, smarting under the comprehensive defeats which followed the out-

Sir Max Beerbohm (1872-1956), the English essayist and cartoonist, commented bitterly on a dilemma of the twentieth century:

The Principle of Good: "How is it that you always seem to get the best of it?"
The Principle of Evil: "Because I'm *active*, my dear!"

From Observations,
London, 1925.

come of the Dreyfus affair, assumed belligerent forms. A group called the *Action Française* advocated a *coup de force* against the Republic and obtained the enthusiastic support of many royalists, aristocrats, army officers, priests, and young men of good family. It organized meetings, marches, and demonstrations and formed a special guard, the *camelots du roi*, consisting of drilled and uniformed young men who acted as defenders of the demonstrators.

British conservatives and military men moved even further along the road of defiance during the debates on Irish home rule in 1913-14 (see p. 442), introduced by the Liberal Prime Minister Herbert Asquith (1852-1928). The Protestant countries in Ulster, the northern part of Ireland, fearing absorption into a predominantly Catholic state, began to drill a volunteer army to resist the introduction of home rule. The southern counties replied in kind. The Conservative party in England supported the Ulster volunteers. Some of its leaders proposed to submit the measure to a popular referendum and to use such a referendum as a precedent for eventually nullifying the Parliament Act of 1911, under which the House of Commons could pass laws over the veto of the House of Lords. The Liberal government assembled arms in northern Ireland and prepared to quell any rebellion. A number of army officers preferred to resign rather than obey orders to act against the Ulstermen. The issue was eventually compromised, and the government gave assurances that Ulster would be excluded from the operation of the home-rule law. But English army officers had barely skirted mutiny, and Conservatives had barely avoided civil war.

The disposition to forceful action affected the labor movement also, although most workers were reconciled to gradual reform through peaceful means. The price of staples was rising, and thus it was becoming difficult for families on low wages or fixed salaries to make ends meet. Here and there the moderate policies of unions and socialist parties and the oligarchical tendencies of some of their leaders aroused discontent. These tensions found expression in the spread of syndicalism. From 1906 on, French and Italian workingmen and farmers engaged in spectacular stoppages. Railway strikes in France and Italy were particularly serious, for the roads had become vital to economic and military pursuits. In both countries, the government invoked military discipline. The strikers, and only they, were mobilized as soldiers and ordered to go back to work, on pain of court martial. The fact that in France this measure was approved by former socialists in the cabinet did not soften the aversion of syndicalists toward politicians.

Between 1910 and 1912, hundreds of thousands of British workmen went out on equally spectacular strikes. Some of them were "unauthorized" and local, spontaneously organized by the workers themselves, and directed almost as much against the traditional trade-union leadership as against the employers. Miners, dockers, textile workers, seamen, and firemen engaged in protracted struggles, in which rioting was not uncommon.

In 1905 an organization named the Industrial Workers of the World had been formed in the United States. The I.W.W. proposed to organize workers by whole industries rather than by crafts, as the American Federation of Labor was doing. It rejected the politics of compromise and practiced "direct action" to abolish the wage system. In 1912, the "Wobblies" successfully led a militant strike of textile workers in Lawrence, Mass. The authorities took stringent measures. "Criminal syndicalism" was outlawed in a number of states, and labor organizers were harried and imprisoned, often in defiance of the constitutional guarantees of individual freedom.

The Tensions of the Continental Empires

In France, Britain, and the United States, domestic shocks were absorbed by political springs. The possibility of constitutional changes kept alive the hope of future advances. The Continental empires, on the other hand, adhered to absolutist and aristocratic forms in the face of the mounting opposition of liberals and moderate conservatives as well as radicals, national minorities as well as socialists, capitalists as well as proletarians.

The domestic disease of Austria-Hungary was such that relief only induced more spasms. In 1897 the tariff union, which was, aside from the common army, the last bond existing between the two halves of the monarchy, had been renewed with difficulty. The magnates of Hungary proposed to control their half of the imperial army by substituting Hungarian for German as the language of command. The Emperor brought them to book with a threat to establish universal suffrage and thus give the Slavs and Rumanians political preponderance in Hungary. The unity of the army was preserved at the expense of the minorities.

In the Austrian half of the Empire, the government, yielding to the pressure of the Social Democrats, introduced universal manhood suffrage in 1907. But the constituencies of the legislature were divided among the nationalities. Although the Germans were granted more seats than their numbers warranted, they constituted a minority and could be outvoted by the Slavs in combination with the Italians or the Rumanians. The multiplicity of parties and their inability to cooperate frustrated the formation of governments supported by a majority. Ministries appointed by the Emperor functioned without parliamentary sanction. Under an article of the constitution, emergencies (which did not exist) were proclaimed in order to justify the substitution of decrees for legislation. Early in 1914, the parliament was virtually dispensed with.

The sense of impasse became pervasive. The borders of the Empire could not contain the swelling disaffection. Nationalist agitators in the adjacent kingdoms of Italy, Rumania, and Serbia clamored for union with their "unredeemed" brethren under the Hapsburgs. Since the first two countries were allied to Austria-Hungary, their governments were disposed to restrain the violent nationalists, or "irredentists." The ruling groups of Serbia felt no such inhibition. They conceived ambitious plans to detach the Hapsburg areas of Croatia, Slovenia, and Bosnia-Herzegovina and form a great Yugo (or South) Slavia. Plots were hatched under the acquiescent eyes of Serbian leaders. The

487

response of the leaders of Austria-Hungary was to project a speedy reckoning with Serbia in order to intimidate the domestic dissidents.

To the manifold divisions of the Hapsburg realm was added the final touch of dynastic danger. Francis Joseph, who had come to the throne in 1848, was in the ninth decade of his life in 1914. He was becoming a romantic myth that magically bound his heterogeneous realm together and made the present an indistinguishable part of the traditional past. It seemed impossible to conceive of the "eternal" emperor without an empire, but what of the empire when the emperor was gone? He had outlived his consort, Elizabeth—long separated from him and then assassinated by an anarchist—and his only son, Rudolf— dead in a suicide pact with his mistress. His nephew and heir, the Archduke Francis Ferdinand, was a dour militarist with strong clerical leanings. The Archduke disliked the Hungarian magnates, whose virtual independence weakened the unity of the Dual Monarchy. It was reported that he wished to convert Austro-Hungarian dualism into an Austro-Hungarian-Slav trialism and revive the League of the Three Emperors in order to safeguard conservatism. These tendencies were certain to antagonize Hungarians, Western-oriented liberals, and socialists. The possibility of a reconciliation with the Slav elements disturbed, above all, those who wished to establish a great Yugoslavia, consisting of Serbia and the south Slav districts of the Hapsburgs.

In Russia, as in Austria-Hungary, the domestic scene was hardly reassuring. The Russian government had turned back the revolutionary tide of 1905, but in doing so it had disillusioned even moderate reformers and friendly critics. In industrial centers strikes multiplied. Cossack troops and ordinary soldiers intervened repeatedly to quell disturbances. When the miners struck in the Lena gold fields in 1912, the troops attacked the strikers and killed 162 of them.

The prestige of czarism was sinking steadily. Nicholas II was a man of modest intelligence and narrow views. A uxorious husband, he was dominated by the strong-willed Czarina, Alexandra, who was a religious neurotic. Both fell under the influence of a charlatan, the peasant-monk Gregory Rasputin (1871?-1916). By the use of hypnotic suggestion, Rasputin apparently healed the heir to the throne during attacks of the hereditary disease of hemophilia. This feat, and Rasputin's peasant shrewdness, impressed the imperial pair, who took the former as evidence of miraculous powers and the latter for a higher wisdom. Before long the monk was manipulating appointments, obtaining favors for his friends, dismissing officials, and even helping to shape state policy. Aristocrats and members of the imperial family protested in vain against his sinister influence. The highest official circles became permeated with pessimism. Early in 1914, the Minister of the Interior, Durnovo, warned the Czar that if Russia went to war and was defeated—and defeat was more likely than victory—the country would be "flung into hopeless anarchy, the issue of which cannot be foreseen." Indeed, "social revolution in its most extreme form is inevitable."

Germany alone seemed outwardly calm in an age of rising tension; there were no great strikes, as in France, or threats of revolution, as in Russia, or fear of dismemberment, as in Austria-Hungary. The labor movement was apparently immune to syndicalism; national minorities maintained the decorum of loyalty. Appearances, however, were somewhat deceptive. Liberal democracy remained an unfulfilled promise. Chancellors ruled by *ad hoc* bargains with conservative groups. A semi-absolutist monarchy and higher bureaucracy governed with but a formal obeisance to parliamentary procedure. The imperial government was determined not to submit to the pressure of public opinion. In 1912, as we have seen, the Social Democrats became the largest single party in the *Reichstag*, and constitutional reform was one of their dearest aims.

Emperor William took heroic stances but was basically weak. He had neither the iron of the absolute monarch nor the flexibility of the liberal ruler. Initiative slipped from his hands into those of his military, bureaucratic, and diplomatic officials. But these officials did not always integrate their aims and policies. Careful observers wondered whether the most powerful country on the Continent had in fact coherent leadership. Durnovo asserted that the Hohenzollerns as well as the Romanovs risked revolution if they went to war. "No matter how strange it may appear at first sight, considering the extraordinary poise of the German character, Germany likewise is destined to suffer, in case of defeat, no lesser social upheavals."

The Opposition to Militarism and Imperialism

Serious as were the domestic strains of some of the states, the international dangers—to all of them—were more pressing. For some conservatives and imperialists, patriotism became chauvinism, and chauvinism xenophobia. Natural attachment to one's country or people became alloyed with envy and dislike of other countries. The duty of defending the country against an invader became the duty of forestalling invasion by attacking a presumed enemy. A Christian minister extolled war as "God's red rain." Hilaire Belloc, the English writer, mocked the pacifists:

> Pale Ebenezer thought it wrong to fight,
> But roaring Bill (who killed him) thought it right.

In *Germany and the Next War* (1913), the Prussian General Friedrich von Bernhardi argued that war was a "biological necessity," that unwarlike nations do not deserve to survive, and that bellicosity bespeaks superiority. He concluded that Germany would fight and win.

The fever spread to some liberals and socialists. There were reformers who felt that the masses had acquired a stake in the economic position of their respective countries and that this position must be defended against attack from without. A minority went so far as to justify the defense of imperial interests. Liberal politicians gravitated toward posts that dealt with social questions and concerned themselves less with diplomatic, naval, and military matters. They tended to support the professional and traditional groups and the army general staffs, which threatened dire consequences if their counsel was not followed.

Most liberals and socialists, however, worked to stem the tide toward destruction. They condemned appeals to "national honor," "racial superiority," and "military heroism" as atavistic echoes of primitive prejudice and unreason. *The Great Illusion* (1910) was the expressive title of the most widely read antiimperialist work of the time. Its author, the English publicist Norman Angell, denied the current prejudice that war made for the survival of the fittest. "The struggle between nations is no part of the evolutionary law of man's advance . . . the idea resides on a profound misreading of the biological laws. . . . Physical force is a constantly diminishing factor in human affairs. . . ." Angell refreshed the old argument of eighteenth- and nineteenth-century free-traders: that colonies do not make a country rich, that prosperity cannot be secured by war.

The capitalist world itself was divided on the issue of whether aggressive policies were profitable. Many financiers and industrialists profited from prohibitive tariffs and imperial privileges. But there were substantial commercial and shipping interests which had a stake in peace and freer trade between countries and continents. Shippers, importers, and distributors profited more from the volume and frequency of exchange among the great countries than from colonial business, which was in most cases a modest item in the balance of trade. German shippers knew that they would be the first to be sacrificed in a war against the British navy and did not relish the prospect.

But the business community did not challenge the powerful imperialist groups that cooperated with aggressive militarists. Consequently, imperialism and capitalism were often confounded in a single condemnation. It did not escape notice that militarists and imperialists tended to be conservative in domestic affairs. J. A. Hobson, an English economist, described imperialism as a latter-day aspect of capitalist evil. He charged in *Imperialism* (1902) that capitalists had extended the system of exploitation to "inferior" races overseas. The accumulation of surplus goods and capital, due to the insufficiency of distribution and consumption, required the extension of the realm of capitalism. It was the search for investment that motivated modern imperialism. Imperialist expansion, Hobson's argument ran, was the culminating phase of capitalism and suffered from the same moral and economic deficiencies that socialists had criticized in the earlier commercial and industrial phases. Hobson's view was accepted by many socialists, notably by Lenin, as a correction or supplementation of the theory of Marx.

A sizable number of socialists were pacifists on principle. The French socialist leader Jaurès labored to remove the obstacles to a reconciliation between his country and Germany. He proposed—and in this he was supported by German socialists—that autonomy be granted to Alsace-Lorraine, and that conscript armies be made responsive to popular control. Instead of standing armies led by cadres of conservative and aristocratic officers, there would be a popular militia. The whole people would be trained, like the Swiss, and keep their arms at home. The government would no longer monopolize the hardware of coercion.

The question remained whether the socialist parties could stop a war once it had broken out. Most of them had rejected the "general strike" of the syndicalists as a tactic of revolution, but such a strike seemed to many the only practical step in case of war. It would paralyze at once the industries without which war cannot be carried on: munitions factories and transport. The proposal that the strike should be called in a country which provoked or started a war was energetically debated at the Congress of the Second International at Stuttgart in 1907 and defended by the French, British, and Dutch parties. The German party, supported by most of the other Continental parties, defeated the proposal. Many German socialists believed, in the tradition of Marx and Engels, that the destruction of czarism was necessary to European progress. "We German Socialists," wrote Engels in 1891, "have the duty of maintaining the position won by us in the van of the workers' movement, not only against the internal but against the external foe. If Russia is victorious we shall be crushed. . . . If the Russians start war against us, German Socialists must go for the Russians and their allies, whoever they may be, *à outrance*."

There were other radicals, however, who could not be reconciled to militarism by any considerations of revolutionary strategy. French syndicalists, for example, did not shrink from tampering with the loyalty of conscripts. The symbols which were objects of veneration and worship to nationalists and militarists—the flag, the uniform, the colorful parades—became to them objects of execration. Patriotism itself was held up to contempt. The editor Gustave Hervé stigmatized the national flag as "a rag planted on a heap of dung."

While the general staffs were hopefully calculating that the large conscript armies and improved armaments would bring victory in an offensive, there were observers—many of them civilians—who predicted that modern techniques would instead strengthen the defenders. The war of the future, they contended, would be one of slow attrition rather than of swift and decisive blows. The defenders would fight from trenches, and war would assume the character of a huge siege. Long before victory could be attained, the countries would succumb to economic bankruptcy and moral collapse.

The governments made a few efforts to ease international tensions. Early in the armaments race, its high cost led Czar Nicholas of Russia—a country deep in debt—to issue a call for a conference to limit armaments. Twenty-six states met at the Hague in 1899 but could not come to an agreement. However, they established a Permanent Court of Arbitration consisting of a panel of distinguished jurists from which states could choose arbiters. A substantial number of minor issues were settled by the Court. The Hague conference adopted rules of war for the protection of civilians, neutrals, prisoners, and wounded soldiers. They forbade, for a period of five years, bombardment from the air and the use of asphyxiating gases and "dum-dum" bullets—bullets that expand upon striking. At a second conference, called by President Theodore Roosevelt in 1907, the United States and Great Britain proposed the compulsory arbitration of disputes, but a majority of the states represented, led by Germany, objected. However, the machinery of voluntary arbitration was strengthened.

In 1913 and 1914, the American secretary of state, William J. Bryan, negotiated treaties with thirty nations providing for a "cooling-off" period when disputes arose. The signers pledged themselves to submit disputes to permanent investigating commissions and to wait for a year for the result. Meanwhile they were neither to start war nor to increase their armaments. Great Britain, France, and Italy signed the Bryan treaties, but Germany refused.

The Galloping Crisis

European tensions had for some years been moving toward a climax. Since the powers felt that they could not afford any injury to an ally or any success of a state belonging to a rival camp, every international incident broadened into a general quarrel. In 1908 revolution had taken place in Turkey. The "Young Turks," a group of energetic professional men and army officers who wished to modernize the Ottoman Empire, compelled Sultan Abdul Hamid to accept a constitutional regime. At the end of the year a parliament met in Constantinople, the ancient capital of Byzantine and Ottoman despots. Since the Young Turks wished to strengthen the central administration and the authority of the state, the Christian minorities were displeased by their ascendancy. The powers with Balkan interests were quick to exploit the situation. Austria-Hungary and Russia agreed secretly, the former to annex Bosnia-Herzegovina, which she had administered for thirty years, and the latter to secure free passage for her warships through the Straits. For such a change in the rules governing the Straits the consent of Turkey and Great Britain was needed. Before it could be obtained—incidentally, it never was—Austria-Hungary proceeded to collect her half of the bargain.

The alliance system came into play. Germany had not been consulted by her ally and disapproved of the annexation; nevertheless, she felt bound to support Austria-Hungary. Italy, the third partner in the alliance, was regarded as unreliable. Germany demanded, therefore, that Russia approve the annexation. The German and Austro-Hungarian military leaders thought the time propitious for settling scores with the Entente, but the Czar's government, weakened by the recent defeat in Asia and revolution at home, was unready to pick up the challenge. It submitted to the "humiliation" but determined to be better prepared in the future. A long-range program of military improvements, including the construction of strategic railways, was financed with French credits. It was to be completed by 1917, which turned out to be an interesting year indeed.

When disturbances in Morocco in 1911 led the French to occupy the capital at Fez, Germany took the opportunity to put pressure on France. The German gunboat *Panther* appeared at Agadir, the best potential naval base on that coast, and encouraged the natives to resist the French. Great Britain became concerned lest Germany seize a Mediterranean as well as an Atlantic naval base in Morocco. A compromise was reached. France was to retain a free hand in Morocco, but she ceded to Germany a part of the French Congo and another small strip of land in Africa.

Then the Balkan problem flared up again. In a brief war against Turkey in 1911-12, Italy wrested Tripolitania in North Africa from her. In 1912 Serbia, Greece, and Bulgaria attacked Turkey. In short order, they conquered and divided up a substantial part of the center of the peninsula, inhabited by Slavs, Greeks, and Macedonians. Serbia's share was a strategically situated strip of the western coast of the Adriatic. Italy and Austria-Hungary protested Serbia's intrusion into waters they considered their own. Austria used the threat of mobilization to intimidate Serbia and began to defy Russia, which loomed behind Serbia. But Russia, although she mobilized her army, was still unready to go to war. Serbia reluctantly yielded her new gains in the Treaty of London in 1913, but she asked her allies to reshuffle the recent distribution in order to award her other territory. Bulgaria, whose army had shown the greatest energy in the war against Turkey, had obtained the major share of the conquest and was loath to yield any part of it to Serbia. In 1913 Serbia joined with Greece and with Turkey herself to force Bulgaria to disgorge. While the new allies attacked from the south and west, Rumania invaded Bulgaria from the north. Overwhelmed, the isolated state gave up most of her recent acquisitions to her neighbors.

After the victory of Serbia, the diplomats and militarists of Vienna became more than ever persuaded that they must humble Serbia in order to intimidate their own South Slavs into continued obedience. Archduke Francis Ferdinand, heir to the Hapsburg throne, was scheduled to pay a visit of state to Sarajevo, the capital of Bosnia-Herzegovina, in an attempt to repair the dubious loyalty of the inhabitants. A secret Serbian terrorist organization, the "Black Hand," decided to assassinate Francis Ferdinand in order to provoke a crisis and perhaps a rebellion. The plot, it was alleged, was known to members of the Serbian cabinet, but the ministers had not felt it their duty to inform Austro-Hungarian officials. On June 28, 1914, a Serbian terrorist shot and killed the Archduke and his wife as they were driven through the streets of Sarajevo.

The outrage aroused widespread sympathy for the Hapsburg emperor. Serbia could have been compelled to offer substantial guarantees of her behavior in the future. The leaders of the Empire, however, projected an ultimatum which if accepted would humiliate Serbia and if rejected would provide the excuse for attaining the same end by force. They hoped to deal with Serbia singlehandedly and avoid a war with Russia, but they were prepared to take all risks which seemed necessary for the preservation of the Dual Monarchy.

The Austrian leaders laid their plans carefully. For nearly four weeks they labored to collect evidence of Serbia's complicity in the murders. With some difficulty, they obtained the consent of the Hungarian ministers to their dangerous course. The German General Staff felt that the sooner war broke out,   *493* the better the chances of victory. But there were *two* German policies. The Kaiser and his chancellor, Theobald von Bethmann-Hollweg (1856-1921), hoped that Austria-Hungary might exact revenge without provoking the interference of other powers, but they did not dare to challenge the military chieftains. They therefore gave their consent to Austria's proposal of an ultimatum, without demanding to see its text in advance.

While these secret arrangements were going forward, the other powers took stock of the situation. The Czar would stand by Serbia, even if it meant going to war with Austria-Hungary, but he hoped to avoid a clash with Germany. France strengthened his position by assuring him of instant support. Great Britain was determined not to allow Germany to defeat France or to occupy Belgium or Holland. Only the United States did not feel called upon to decide on her course.

In every country, the calculations of generals and admirals narrowed the margin of accommodation. The German Chancellor hoped that Belgium might be spared invasion lest Great Britain be aroused, but he was informed that such an invasion was essential to the plan of strategy devised by Count von Schlieffen (see p. 475). Great Britain and France had agreed in 1912 to transfer the French Atlantic fleet to the Mediterranean, in order to defend both French and English interests and thus make it possible for the British to add their Mediterranean fleet to their North Sea fleet, to provide the maximum defense against a German attack. Thus the northern French coasts would be undefended unless the British joined in the war. Even if Germany promised to refrain from steaming warships into the English Channel, her land armies could proceed to Paris.

The Czar expected to mobilize his army against Austria-Hungary but not on the borders of Germany. Strategic considerations forced him to change his mind. The railways of Russia were built to transport troops *to* the Western borders but not *along* them. If troops had to be transferred from one part of the border to another, they would first have to be withdrawn inland; this would take time. If the army was dispatched against Austria-Hungary and then had to be redeployed to cover the German border as well, the loss of time would give the German army an advantage. The military therefore insisted that, even if the controversy involved only Austria-Hungary, Russia must mobilize against Germany as well. Such a mobilization aroused German military leaders, particularly since their strategy depended upon swift attack. The technicalities of mobilization ruled out a cooling-off period. The military men felt that the first blow might be decisive. They preferred the risk of war to the risk of a delayed mobilization.

Such was the impasse that Europe was approaching in the month of July 1914. On July 23, Austria-Hungary, although lacking conclusive evidence against Serbia, dispatched an ultimatum, which demanded not only explanations and apologies but vigorous action to punish the plotters and to put an end to propaganda and activity against Austria. The Empire further demanded that Austrian officials be allowed to participate in investigations into the assassination plot. Serbia accepted most of the conditions. The Kaiser thought the reply satisfactory, but Austria-Hungary rejected it without consulting him and mobilized for war. Great Britain proposed a conference of powers, but Austria rejected all overtures for a compromise, and Germany did not insist. On July 28, Austria-Hungary declared war on Serbia.

European public opinion became alarmed. The assassination of the Archduke and his wife had occurred a month earlier, and the declaration of war came as a surprise. In the great European cities, the socialists held meetings and demonstrations of protest. As late as July 16, the French Socialist party had reaffirmed its support, in case of war, of a general strike, particularly in the arms, munitions, and transport industries. But a strike could hardly be called unless the enemy country was embarrassed by a strike of its own. On July 29-30, at an emergency meeting of the Bureau of the Second International at Brussels, the French socialist leaders tried in vain to persuade their German comrades to agree to common action. At home they were denounced as traitors by the jingoist press. The *Action Française* had written on July 23: "We have no wish to incite anyone to political assassination, but M. Jean Jaurès may well shake in his shoes! . . . A fanatic . . . may desire to settle by the experimental method the question whether anything would be changed in the invincible order of things" if Jaurès were killed. A deranged young man took the hint. On July 31 Jaurès was shot in the back and killed.

The next day the war was on in full scale. Germany, less sensitive to public opinion than the Western powers, declared war on Russia on August 1, on France on August 3, and on Belgium (*after* invading her) on August 4. The inva-

An Allied view of the German invasion of Belgium in 1914. Germany violated a treaty of 1839 guaranteeing Belgian neutrality. From Punch, *August 12, 1914.*
© PUNCH, LONDON

BRAVO, BELGIUM!

sion of Belgium brought the British around. Several members of the Liberal cabinet of Herbert Asquith resigned rather than acquiesce to intervention. On the ground that Germany had broken the treaty of 1839, in which she and other powers had pledged themselves to respect Belgian neutrality, England declared war on Germany on August 4. Since Austria-Hungary had not been attacked, Italy contended that she had no obligation to join her allies and stood aside for the time being. Japan joined England in declaring war on Germany, on August 23. By the end of 1916, more than thirty countries in all continents were engaged in war. Not since the French revolutionary and Napoleonic wars had so many powers been involved in a single conflict.

Fifteen million men donned uniforms in August 1914. They were assembled in depots, placed on trains and disposed along the fronts. In eight to ten days they were ready to attack. There was no hitch in the long and carefully laid plans, no defiance, no disobedience. In Great Britain a minority of the Labor party remained pacifist throughout the war, and some of its members and leaders were jailed. The socialist delegation in the German *Reichstag* voted 78 to 15 to deliver the whole bloc of 93 votes in support of the war credits requested by the government. Other social-democratic parties, in France and Russia as well as Germany, followed suit, though often with misgivings and after heated controversy. In exchange for this support, the imperial regimes refrained from harassing their domestic critics; the liberal governments even gave them minor positions in the war cabinets.

The people fell into line. Patriotic demonstrations were held in the principal avenues and squares of capital cities. Newspaper editorials breathed devotion to allies and defiance to enemies. The parliaments resounded with patriotic orations and calls to sacrifice. Yet speeches, editorials, street demonstrations, and official proclamations are not entirely reliable guides for judging public attitudes. The people were nowhere consulted on the dreadful issue; the parliaments of the imperial states were not invited to sanction the declarations of war. The literature of the war discloses that there was much private puzzlement and reluctant acceptance of the decrees of fate. The adventure of war made a striking, though momentary, appeal to men beset by routine or private responsibilities. It was impossible, in any event, to stop the triple juggernaut of military discipline, martial law, and chauvinistic hypnosis. The effect of mobilization was massive and electrifying.

Aristocratic officers led a democratic soldiery to battle. In every country, but especially in the Continental empires, military rank corresponded to social rank, while the system of conscription made the armies a large sampling of the broad masses of the population. The commanders carried on the traditional rivalry for territorial conquest, prestige, and dynastic glory. Their strategy applied the code of the duel on a gigantic scale. This was typified, above all, in the philosophy of the German General Staff: the surprise attack, the outflanking gesture, the rapid stroke to the heart of the opponent.

Military and Naval Deadlock

Upon the outbreak of war, Germany seized the initiative with the Schlieffen plan, which called for two successive campaigns, in France and in Russia. The bulk of the German army would be concentrated in the west, where it would outnumber and quickly defeat the French army. The smaller, eastern army would stand on the defensive, even yielding ground to the Russians if necessary. It was assumed that the Russians would be slow in mobilizing and attacking and thus would be able to inflict little damage before the victorious soldiers of the western army joined their comrades in the east to defeat her.

The plan to concentrate first on a swift defeat of France and only then to attack and invade Russia hung on a delicate chain of assumptions: that the German army had sufficient men to advance on a front extending from Switzerland to the English Channel; that supplies could keep up with a hurried march through Belgium and northern France; that France could be overwhelmed in the space of six weeks on a schedule timed to the hour; that Russia would be slow to attack; and that the political leaders of Germany could afford to sacrifice East Prussia if necessary. It assumed also that, after defeating France, the German army could turn around and bring Russia to her knees in a short time. Yet the Russian army was larger than the German, if not so well trained, and it could withdraw into distant and cold interiors, as Napoleon had tardily discovered.

At first, in August 1914, the plan worked with precision. The German armies overwhelmed Belgium and swept into northern France on schedule. The initial strategy of the French miscarried. Convinced that the Schlieffen plan required more standing-army troops on the front lines than the Germans had, the French mobilized in the northeast on the German border, leaving the Belgian front relatively undefended. At the outbreak of the war, therefore, the main armies did not face each other at all. The German advance in the north compelled the French commander-in-chief, General Joseph Joffre (1852-1931), to shift his troops, an expensive and slow operation. Fortunately for the French, the Schlieffen plan was bungled. Owing to the paucity of troops on the right wing and the fact that supplies failed to keep pace with the rapidly advancing soldiers, a gap opened between the two armies at the extreme end of the right arm. This gap could be closed only by wheeling in the last army on the wing toward its neighbor, thus bringing the German armies to face Paris on one side instead of surrounding it. The order to close the gap was given by a subordinate officer sent out from distant military headquarters with power to overrule the officers in the field. At the battle of the Marne in September, the French stopped the German advance. Paris was saved and defeat averted. The Schlieffen plan for quick victory in the west had failed.

In the east, the Germans fared better, although not according to plan. During the outflanking operation in the west, the Czar had responded to a

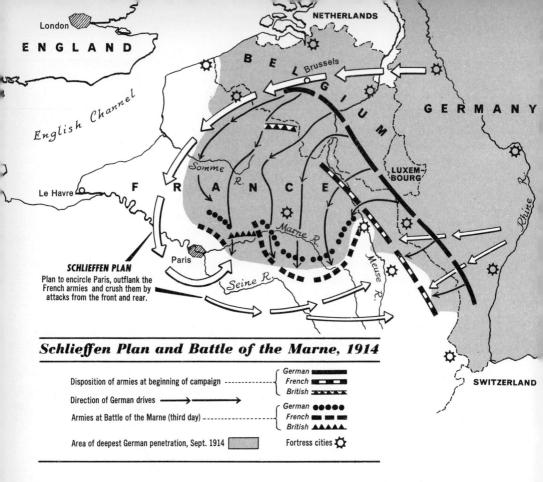

Schlieffen Plan and Battle of the Marne, 1914

SCHLIEFFEN PLAN
Plan to encircle Paris, outflank the
French armies and crush them by
attacks from the front and rear.

Disposition of armies at beginning of campaign	German	
	French	
	British	
Direction of German drives	German	
Armies at Battle of the Marne (third day)	French	
	British	
Area of deepest German penetration, Sept. 1914	Fortress cities	

French appeal for a diversion by sending two ill-prepared armies into East Prussia. Under the Schlieffen plan, Prussian territory might be yielded in order to ensure a victory in the west. But to the imperial German government the implied loss of prestige was inadmissible. Two corps were detached from the west and were en route through Germany while decisive battles were fought by the German armies of the east, under the command of Generals Paul von Hindenburg (1847-1934) and Erich von Ludendorff (1865-1937). The invading armies were repelled in August and September 1914, in the battles of Tannenberg and the Masurian Lakes. The Germans took nearly a quarter of a million prisoners and penetrated into Russian Poland.

By 1915 the war had assumed a new aspect. The long western front from the Channel to the Swiss border stagnated. The soldiers went down into an enormous open graveyard of trenches, protected by machine guns and barbed-wire entanglements. Behind a curtain of heavy artillery fire striking at the enemy, both sides made futile but bloody sorties against almost impregnable obstacles.

The Germans held the western front and transferred their energies eastward. They helped Austria-Hungary to repel the Russian invaders, who had penetrated into Galicia and Bukovina. Farther north, they launched a powerful offensive which shook Russia: they captured the Russian provinces of Poland,

Lithuania, and Courland, with the capitals of Warsaw and Vilna and the strategic fortress of Brest-Litovsk. Turkey, which had entered the war on the side of Germany in November 1914, closed the Dardanelles, thus breaking the connection by sea between the Western Allies and Russia.

In May 1915, on the promise of large slices of Austria and colonial gains, Italy joined the Entente and declared war on Austria. In the fall, Bulgaria joined Germany and attacked Serbia, which lost most of her territory to her old rival. By the end of 1915 Germany and her allies were in control of Central Europe, most of the Balkans, and a large part of Eastern Europe and the Baltic coast. Yet the war went on. Russia had reeled, although not collapsed, and the Western Allies had been placed on the defensive; but they persevered. The military leaders refused to admit that conventional offensive strategy had failed; such an admission would have implied the need to negotiate a peace, without spectacular gains. Effort after bloody effort was made to break the stalemate in the west. The costs were enormous, and the gains minimal. A French offensive at Artois, for example, purchased three miles of ground at the price of 400,000 dead or wounded men.

In 1916 the protagonists again tried their fortune on the obstinate western front, and the determination to win by conventional methods led to a deteriora-

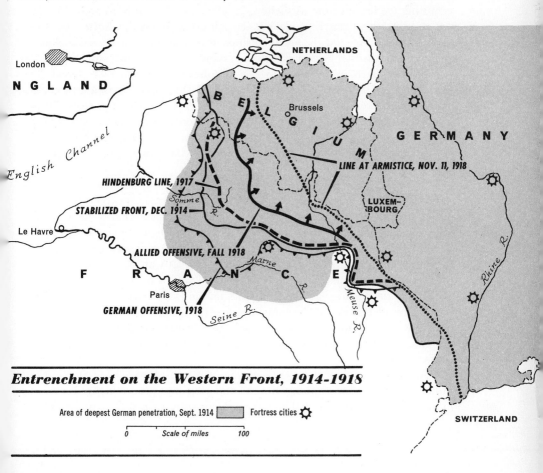

Entrenchment on the Western Front, 1914-1918

Area of deepest German penetration, Sept. 1914   Fortress cities

0   Scale of miles   100

tion of warfare into mass assassination. Germany decided to attack the old fortress of Verdun, hub of the front, not in the hope of taking it but in the expectation that the French would spend themselves holding it. Germany lost 300,000 men, France 350,000—and France could afford such sacrifices much less than Germany. A large-scale British-French attack farther to the north—the battle of the Somme—gained seven miles at the exorbitant rate of nearly one million casualties, Allied and German.

In the east, Rumania entered the war on the side of the Allies in August 1916, but after some initial gains her army was defeated by a vigorous German campaign, and more than half of the country was occupied. But this victory had no effect on the war as a whole.

The naval war was eventually also a stalemate. The British and French swept all German surface vessels, both naval and mercantile, from the seas. They seized most of the German colonies within a few months of the outbreak of the war. Japan occupied German islands in the Pacific Ocean. In Europe, the Allies declared a blockade of Germany. The British unceasingly patrolled the English Channel and the waters from northern Scotland to the Scandinavian peninsula. Thus, instead of blockading the German coast, they assumed indirect control over the whole North Sea. The German High Seas Fleet was wary of venturing too far out from its shelters, let alone into the open oceans. The result was that the two fleets kept glaring at each other across the North Sea. Only once, in May 1916, did the German ships issue from their protected shelters to challenge the British Grand Fleet off Jutland. The two sides still dispute the victory. The Germans proved superior in gunnery and drew more blood. The tonnage loss of the British was twice as high as that of the Germans, and British casualties were more than twice as high. Yet the German fleet did not persevere to a decision but retreated to its shelters and did not emerge to fight again. On points, so to speak, the British had come off second best, but since the fleet survived to continue its watchful patrols of the seas, the battle of Jutland was in effect a British victory.

From the early months of the war the British navy, assisted in the Mediterranean by the French, had been able to cut off the central powers from the outside world. Britain considerably extended her interception of neutral shipping, much to the annoyance of such important trading countries as the United States. She declared as contraband, subject to seizure, many goods that had previously been regarded as free to move in time of war—food, for example—thus nullifying the rules of neutral shipping. Trade with neutrals like Holland was strictly limited to peacetime amounts, on the assumption that imports could be transshipped by rail to Germany and Austria-Hungary. These measures gave the Entente a decided advantage, since they could tap the whole world for supplies. But this advantage was whittled down considerably by submarine warfare.

At the outbreak of the war Germany used her submarines to attack naval rather than merchant shipping. But the undersea craft proved highly vulnerable to attack by warships, and they were subsequently turned principally against merchantmen. Early in 1915, Germany declared a submarine blockade of the British Isles, which was contrary to custom. Much shipping, both British and non-British, was lost. The unprecedented sinking by submarines of unarmed merchantmen and passenger vessels, without warning and without provision for the lives of passengers and crews, added a special horror to the war. When the Cunard liner *Lusitania* was sunk, in May 1915, with the loss of 1198 lives, 139 of them American, the United States warned Germany against repeating "anything so obviously subversive of the principles of warfare." In September Germany promised to desist from unrestricted submarine warfare, to give warning before sinking ships, and to provide for the safety of the lives of noncombatants.

An advertisement inserted by the German Embassy in the New York Sun *for May 1, 1915, advises American travelers against sailing on the* Lusitania. *The sinking of this ship by a German submarine six days later led to a diplomatic crisis with the United States. Germany subsequently promised to stop sinking liners without warning and without providing for the safety of noncombatants.*

This pledge was repeated in May 1916, after a U-boat torpedoed an unarmed French vessel, the *Sussex*, in the English Channel; the casualties included several Americans. German submarines continued to do great damage to Allied shipping, especially in the fall of 1916. In the month of October alone, they destroyed 148,000 tons of British and 164,000 tons (124 ships) of non-British shipping. The Allied fleets were fairly helpless to arrest these losses. Nets, mines, and depth bombs were tried, but, although they did much damage, they proved but weak tools against the agile craft that could move in three dimensions. Meanwhile the shipping situation grew alarming. In December 1916, 167 Allied and neutral ships were destroyed, and the food as well as the industrial supplies of Great Britain were placed in jeopardy.

War Weariness Grows

The course of the war confounded the experts on both sides. The predictions of financial collapse in case of a prolonged war were not realized. Neither was the expectation that military and naval strokes could achieve victory. The long and costly preparations, the carefully laid strategic plans, and the subtle diplomatic contrivances had contributed to the outbreak of the war but were helpless to bring it to an end. The military and naval leaders knew how to fight but they did not know, with the tools and ideas at their command, how to win. Armies of millions of men and navies of thousands of tons had clashed, and the echo rang hollow.

A mood of weariness and disillusionment and a longing for peace swept over Europe. The enormous losses in the field, the sufferings of civilians, particularly in the devastated areas, and the evident inability of the war commands to bring about victory combined to produce demands for a reasonable compromise. Substantial opposition groups everywhere questioned not only the conduct of the war but the wisdom of its aims.

The "cave dwellers" of the Western front in the First World War. A more or less primitive trench shown during a pause in the fighting. Some trenches were elaborately built, with wooden "sidewalks," overhead bridges, and barbed wire fences. Beyond the trench to the right is "no man's land."
CULVER

There was increasing protest among radicals. A number of socialist leaders in England went to prison or were ostracized as pacifists. While the official Socialist parties remained "patriotic," a growing wing became increasingly dissident. As early as September 1915 a group of thirty-eight socialist and labor leaders from eleven belligerent and neutral countries had assembled at Zimmerwald, Switzerland, to protest the continuance of the war. The conference adopted a manifesto calling on the working classes to repudiate chauvinism and the capitalist rulers and thus to end the slaughter. A revolutionary minority, led by Nicolai Lenin, who was living in exile in Switzerland, went further. It asserted that it was the business of the proletariat to work for the *defeat* of its own country! Only thus could it destroy capitalism as well as warfare. The workers should "turn the imperialist into a civil war," and a new International should be organized to prosecute this daring policy. The following year, at Kienthal, also on neutral Swiss soil, another small conference endorsed Lenin's position. Although these conferences represented small minorities of socialists, they gave expression to a growing disaffection with the war, particularly in Central and Eastern Europe.

To silence grumbling, elicit further sacrifice, and steel the popular will became a principal task on the home front of the warring nations. The military chieftains, who had been given free rein when the war broke out, could only repeat the familiar offensives, with the prospect of repeating the familiar holocausts. The new task tested the belligerents' resources of imagination and the flexibility of their institutions. Upon its fulfillment hung the survival of the embattled states of Europe.

24.   *Defeat and Revolution*

The World War had begun in 1914 as a military and naval enterprise. Within two years it had become as much a contest in economic resources and efficiency, in political leadership, and—for the Continental empires—in the stability of the state and society. Only a careful exploitation of industrial capacity, raw materials, scientific resources, and man power could ensure the continued prosecution of the war. Only a renewal of the confidence of hard-driven peoples could provide the necessary psychological and moral support.

Economic and Psychological Warfare

Up to a certain point, it was easier to supply the economic needs than the political. The governments issued regulations concerning the kinds and amounts of goods to be exported or imported and set up controls to allocate raw materials to war industries. They directed the production of factories, discouraged the output of consumers' goods, and arranged for the distribution of food to the army and civilian populations. They set limits to prices and occasionally checked or taxed excessive profits. Great Britain, which depended for food as well as raw materials on imports from overseas, regulated even the space on ships. The Western allies replenished their stocks from neutral countries, particularly from the United States. Germany, effectively blockaded and prevented from receiving supplies from overseas—except from Scandinavia—imposed the widest controls and gave the sharpest stimuli to domestic production, on farms and in factories. She introduced food rationing as early as 1915, two years before France and three before Great Britain. Raw materials were assembled and distributed by official fiat. Scientists and laboratory technicians outdid themselves in devising synthetic substitutes for petroleum, nitrates, textiles, and even for certain foods, such as sugar. In Germany, as in other industrial countries, mass produc-

504

tion, standardization of products and of machine parts, greater efficiency, and further applications of electric power to industrial plants were being promoted more effectively by death and destruction on the battlefield than they had been by consumption in peacetime. Under the spur of "war socialism," Europe was experiencing a technological revolution.

The ownership of industry was everywhere left in private hands, but its scale was enlarged. In order to promote efficiency and to eliminate conflicts and divided counsels, the governments encouraged the consolidation of plants, the merger of companies, and the sharing of raw materials and markets by competing firms. This tendency was especially marked in Germany, where the movement toward cartels and syndicates was already well under way. In compensation for war controls and as a reward for ready compliance with them, the governments guaranteed minimum profits on the huge contracts they awarded. The chiefs and owners of industry, shipping, and finance grew rich to abnormal degrees. At the same time, labor found that the increases in pay readily granted by employers and allowed by the governments did not always catch up with the rise of prices. In the midst of cooperation, and under the appearance of social harmony, the cleavage between classes was sometimes more accentuated than attenuated.

Domestic organization was not enough. Since national boundaries often stood in the way of war planning, the diplomatic and military alliances became economic alliances. In moments of emergency, the Central Powers shared a little of their food and more of their industrial supplies. They prepared plans to establish a free-trade union to include their allies, Bulgaria and Turkey. An integrated Mittel-Europa which would control the greater part of the industrial and agrarian wealth of the Continent outside of Russia and would be dominated by German industry became one of the war aims of the Central Powers. The future plans of the Western Allies were less grandiose, but their immediate cooperation was more extended and effective. They set up common control over their stocks of gold in order to preserve the strength of their currency and of their purchasing power. They organized joint purchasing agencies abroad to avoid costly competition with one another, and together bought and allocated shipping space and supplies of wheat and meat, not to mention the all-important war materials.

The political and psychological problems were more complex. At the beginning of the war, the belligerents attempted to maintain morale by means of propaganda and censorship. Germany insisted that the Allies, particularly England, wished to crush her out of sheer hatred and envy. The Allied Powers accused Germany of breaking treaties by invading neutral Belgium, harboring ambitions to dominate the world, and conducting war in barbarous fashion.

The conflict was not only international. On every home front a struggle was engaged in, now open, now latent, between military and civilian leaders, between conservatives and liberals, or between aristocrats and democrats.

Civilian Control in France and Great Britain

Characteristically, the contest took military form in France and naval form in Great Britain. In the spring of 1917, several corps of the French army refused to obey further orders to attack. The mutiny was suppressed. Behind the front, "defeatists" worked for a compromise with the enemy. Patriotic politicians formed a great coalition—the *Union Sacrée*—and turned to a man of tenacious will and surpassing shrewdness to head it: Georges Clemenceau (1841-1929) became Premier and Minister of War. Clemenceau rooted out the falterers; several high-placed personages, including some former ministers, were tried for treason and imprisoned. He exercised a closer surveillance of the plans of the generals, checked their proclivity for staging sorties and attacks that held no prospect of success, and encouraged the troops by frequent visits to the front. War, Clemenceau remarked, is too serious a business to leave to the generals.

A more direct showdown with the martial mind took place across the Channel. The cabinet of Herbert Asquith was inclined to accept the counsel of the British military and naval commanders and was unprepared to deal with the new psychological and economic necessities. But a few statesmen, notably David Lloyd George, had early perceived the real character of the war. In December 1916, Lloyd George, who was War Minister in Asquith's cabinet, demanded a more determined and more concentrated civilian control of the war effort and proposed that a four-man "war cabinet" be created to gather all the reins. With the support of a ministerial and parliamentary majority, he forced Asquith and his friends out of power and became Prime Minister at the head of a coalition government of Liberals, Conservatives, and a few Laborites.

The most significant effect of the political change was the triumph of common sense in the evolution of naval tactics. The Admiralty had not been able to devise a defense against the German submarines, which in one month alone—April 1917—destroyed 875,000 tons of Allied shipping. A group of naval officers had proposed a revival of the old convoy system, used commonly in the eighteenth century but rarely deemed necessary in the nineteenth in view of Britain's control of the seas. Under the new convoy system, merchant ships would be assembled in large fleets and escorted by naval craft. If the convoy was attacked, proponents of the plan argued, the warships could proceed against the submarines; even if some ships were sunk in the engagement, the others would escape, since the submarines could be driven away by more heavily armed surface vessels. But the Admiralty gave strong reasons for rejecting the idea of convoy: the speed of the merchant fleets would be reduced to that of the slowest vessels; holding ships to wait for others to load and join them would mean delays; and, above all, it was considered necessary to hold the principal fleet together against the possibility of another irruption of the German navy (which, incidentally, never occurred). The Admiralty conceded that the merchant losses were alarming and that they might eventually force Great Britain to her knees, but they were unwilling to risk the imperial fleet. It was Lloyd George who cut the Gordian knot; he insisted on the institution of convoys, which proved to be the first successful answer to submarine warfare.

In such political figures as Clemenceau and Lloyd George the Western Allies found shrewd, energetic, and flexible leadership. While they drove their peoples to great sacrifices, they avoided rashness and mollified criticism. Clemenceau was as stern with monarchist and conservative critics as with pacifists and radicals. The British government brought food prices down and made concessions to democracy by enfranchising women householders over thirty years of age and wives of householders over thirty-five, extending free education, and restricting child labor in factories. Promises were made to effect home rule in Ireland and reforms in the Indian government.

Decomposition in Austria-Hungary

The leaders of the Western governments were invested by the parliaments with wide discretionary powers. The rulers of the Austro-Hungarian, German, and Russian empires were beset by a problem as old as the French Revolution. For a century they had successfully resisted the introduction of effective parliamentary government. In the aftermath of the Revolution of 1848 they had made formal concessions to liberal ideas while preserving monarchical and aristocratic control over the apparatus of the state and over policy. As the war dragged on, their prestige sank while that of the liberal opposition rose.

The socialists and national minorities swelled the chorus of criticism. In Austria-Hungary the war brought to a head national disaffections of long standing. The Empire had gone to war principally in order to discipline the South Slavs. However, instead of an easy triumph over Serbia, she suffered a series of humiliating defeats at the hands of Serbia's ally, Russia. These defeats were retrieved only by the assistance of Germany. In 1915 the Germans repelled a Russian army which had penetrated deep into Austria-Hungary. The following year, when Rumania declared war and conquered much Hungarian territory, German armies turned the invaders back and went on to occupy more than half of Rumania, including the capital, Bucharest. In the process the Empire fell increasingly under the influence of her stronger ally.

Hungary, meanwhile, made herself virtually independent of the Hapsburg emperor. In 1915, when food was scarce, she closed the frontier to stop the flow of grain to the other half of the Dual Monarchy—in effect, blockading Austria! To persuade Italy to renounce the Triple Alliance and intervene on their behalf, the Western Allies promised her a large slice of Austria. To ensure Rumania's intervention, they promised to recognize her claims to Transylvania, then held by Hungary, and to Bukovina, held by Austria.

Torn by national animosities, the Hapsburg armies showed little tenacity or reliability. Whole regiments of Slavs developed alarming ambitions to become prisoners of war of Russia, their ethnic "brother." Abroad, committees of leading Czechs, Slovaks, and South Slavs put forward bold demands for separation and independence. For a long time, the Western Allies refused to sanction these demands, in the hope of detaching Austria-Hungary from Germany. But as Austria's helplessness became apparent, they underwrote the national claims.

In the fall of 1916, the long-delayed crisis broke out. The reactionary premier of Austria, Count Stürgkh, intimidated the national groups by imprisoning their leaders and even executing some of them. On October 21, he was assassinated as a "demonstration of protest" by Friedrich Adler, the son of the chief of the Social Democrats. A month later Emperor Francis Joseph died, at the age of eighty-eight. With him a whole epoch, and Austria herself, seemed to die. His grand-nephew and successor, Charles I (1916-18), tried to save his desperate legacy by attempting to allay domestic descontent and take the Empire out of the war. He convened the parliament for the first time in three years, only to find that the Czechs demanded a federal union of free states, the Poles independence, the South Slavs an autonomous realm of their own. The Emperor granted amnesty to political prisoners, but he could not satisfy the many overlapping claims. Hungary was uncompromisingly opposed to any concessions that threatened territory she ruled, whereas the representatives of the Croatians, Serbs, and Slovenes combined to work for an independent South Slav state.

In April 1917 Count Ottokar Czernin, Foreign Minister of Austria-Hungary, informed his master that "the burden laid upon the population has assumed proportions that are unbearable," that "our military strength is coming to an end," and that, therefore, it "will be most important to begin peace negotiations at a moment when the enemy has not yet grasped the fact of our waning strength." The Emperor made secret overtures to the Entente. He was ready to acknowledge the right of France to Alsace-Lorraine and to satisfy Serbia's claim to a strip of the Adriatic coast, Russia's claim to Constantinople, and Italy's demand for Italian districts of the Istrian peninsula. Italy, which wanted Trieste as well, found the offer inadequate. But the greatest obstacle to a negotiated peace between Austria-Hungary and the Entente was Germany. She warned Charles that if he quit the war German armies would occupy his empire.

What with the pressure of the national groups, the threats of Germany, and the growing disaffection of Hungary, the dynasty was all but paralyzed. Since Austria-Hungary had lost the power to decide whether to fight or not, it may be said that the Hapsburg Empire ceased to be an independent state in 1917.

The First Russian Revolution

Russia sped faster to a more dramatic climax. Her armies were bested several times by the Germans, and her losses in casualties and territory were great. Along with the civilian population, the Russian armies suffered as much from the incapacity and corruption of their leaders as from the blows of their enemies. Food and clothing became scarce. Transportation and distribution were inadequate to supply grain to the front. The means of defense, let alone those of attack, were lacking. The army was short of the most elementary weapons—rifles and ammunition. Soldiers often had to wait for their own comrades to fall in order to get a rifle. The closure of the Dardanelles and the German watch in the Baltic Sea made it impossible for the Western Allies to supply Russia with arms.

Although the cooperation of all elements of the population was essential to the war effort, the government became less and less disposed to take counsel with leading parties and classes. Any organized activity, it felt, would draw attention to the conduct of affairs. Arbitrary rule became more pronounced. In September 1915, the Czar himself assumed command of the armies in the field. The influence of palace cliques and backstairs intriguers became paramount. Nicholas appointed to the highest places men notorious for their incompetence, corruption, or contempt of public opinion. Prominent among his advisers was the monk Gregory Rasputin (see p. 488), who used his extraordinary influence at the Court to install his creatures as ministers and commanders.

It seemed so incomprehensible that the government's policy should become most rigid when it needed to be most flexible that suspicions of treason arose. The Court, and the imperial couple themselves, were accused of plotting deliberately to weaken Russia and sell her to the Germans. It was whispered that the reins of power were slipping into the hands of the unstable and superstitious Czarina, born a German princess, who dominated her husband. It was noticed that reactionary ministers were often recruited from the Baltic nobility, which was largely German in origin and preferred the German language and family names. Suspicion undermined the loyalty of the most exalted aristocrats and military leaders and infected even those in the inner circle of the Court. Con-

The Russian monk Gregory Rasputin surrounded by admirers, some of whom belong to aristocratic and court circles. As a friend and adviser of the imperial couple, Rasputin exercised a sinister influence during the last years of Czarism. The photograph was taken shortly before the outbreak of the Russian Revolution in 1917. EUROPEAN

servatives were concerned lest the whole social order become involved in the
retribution that was apparently preparing for the heads of the dynasty. In December a group of aristocrats assassinated Rasputin. There were plots afoot to
organize a palace coup, seize and depose Nicholas II, and substitute a member
of the Romanov family better fitted to preserve the integrity of the Empire.

Before the high-placed rebels could act, czarism collapsed. On March 8,
1917, a series of demonstrations and strikes broke out in St. Petersburg (renamed
Petrograd at the beginning of the war). On March 10 regiments stationed in
the capital, including even the long-faithful Cossacks, refused to obey orders to
fire on the demonstrators and mutinied. None of the traditional supporters of
czarism would stand by it except for a handful of police, who kept up desultory
shooting for a few days. The almost bloodless revolution spread quickly to other
cities. On March 11, the day after the mutiny, the Duma refused to obey an
imperial command to adjourn. From his headquarters at Pskov, the Czar tried
to flee for shelter and support to the armies on the front but was denied transportation by rebellious railwaymen. On March 15 he abdicated in favor of his
brother Michael, who refused the crown with the statement that he would
accept it only from an elected assembly of the Russian nation. After a reign of
303 years, the Romanov dynasty was gone.

Together with czarism, a host of burdens disappeared: aristocratic privilege, religious and clerical persecution, humiliation of national minorities, police
snooping, harsh penalties for political expression and activity, and, to a large
extent, social invidiousness. The collapse had involved no great struggle, and an
exhilarating sense of good will and fraternity filled the air. All the hopes and
questions of the Russian people, muzzled for so long, found expression. Gathering spontaneously in large and small groups, at the front, on city streets, and in
village squares, the people plunged into discussions and debates. Soldiers,
sailors, town workmen, and peasants held countless meetings, passed resolutions,
and formed organizations. Under the leadership of Social Democrats and Social
Revolutionaries these informal exchanges and organizations promptly assumed
a political shape. First in Petrograd, then in other cities, and finally in the villages and at the front, informal popular assemblies elected delegates to form
broader councils, or soviets.

After the people moved, the leaders came. Under czarist rule, many radical
and liberal politicians had been put behind bars or had fled abroad. Now the
gates of the prisons swung open and tens of thousands of political prisoners
poured out. Those of the exiles who could overcome the difficulties of war travel
made their way home.

The new government was indirectly the creation of the spontaneous democracy that had come into being. The only political institution that survived the
autocracy was the Duma. As an elective body—last chosen by a highly restricted
suffrage in 1911—and as one that had been excluded from effective influence, it
did not share the opprobrium of the old regime. The Duma was none too eager
to assume the responsibility for steering the nation in such critical times. But
the pressure of the masses in the streets and of the Petrograd soviet, which was

formed on the first day of the Revolution, induced the Duma to form a provisional government from among its members. The new cabinet was headed by Prince George Lvov (1861-1925), an enlightened aristocrat, and consisted of liberal landlords, capitalists, lawyers, and publicists. The Minister of Justice, Alexander Kerensky, (1881-   ) was its only socialist member. The radical parties were more active and influential in the soviets than in the Duma and the government.

The provisional government lost no time in bringing Russia into line with the liberal system of the West. The freedoms of the press, of speech, of assembly, and of association were duly proclaimed. There was to be complete equality before the law. Legal and political distinctions based on religion, nationality, or language were erased. The official religion lost its superior position; Roman Catholics, Protestants, and other dissenters were placed on a par with the adherents of the Eastern Orthodox Church, and anti-Semitic enactments disappeared. The Little Russians, the White Russians, the Baltic peoples, and the dozens of small nationalities rose to equality with the Great Russians. Poland recovered her independence, and Finland and Estonia their autonomy. Arbitrary arrests ceased and capital punishment was abolished. The government confiscated the monastic and imperial estates. It projected agrarian reform and a distribution of lands, upon compensation to the owners and after a careful census of both land and people. This reform and the writing of a new permanent constitution were to wait upon the convening of a national assembly elected by universal manhood suffrage under conditions of free discussion and political activity. These elections, in turn, were to wait upon the conclusion of peace. Meanwhile the government proposed to persevere in the struggle against the Central Powers until final victory.

The Western Allies were pleased to deal with a liberal regime in Russia. They hoped that with the corrupt and inefficient czarist regime out of the way the energies of Russia might be gathered more effectively for military exertions. A constitutional order in Russia would validate the Allies' claim that they were fighting reactionary imperial powers.

Military Dictatorship in Germany

Events in Germany gave color to this claim. While the Empire was as successful as the Western countries in rationalizing industrial production, she was as obstinate as the other Continental empires in resisting responsible government. In the third year of the war, the German people were weary of the stalemate. The Social-Democratic party had not been unanimous in its support of the war, even in August 1914, and the dissenters had meanwhile grown from a minority to a large company. Increasing numbers of Centrists and Liberals joined this group in proposals for a negotiated peace and renunciation of imperialist ambitions and retaliatory punishments. Simultaneously, they renewed their demands for responsible government.

It is hard to say which of these proposals was more unpalatable to the ruling groups. They preferred to give the military another chance to extricate them from the dilemma. In August 1916 the two successful commanders of the eastern front were placed in charge of the western front as well. Field Marshal von Hindenburg became Chief of Staff and an abler strategist, General Ludendorff, became Quartermaster General. To these men, military compromise meant humiliation abroad and political capitulation at home. Under their code, defeat was preferable to accommodation. By threatening to resign, Hindenburg and Ludendorff, who had come to be thought of as indispensable, checked any temptation of the government to yield on imperial and domestic issues. Even Chancellor Bethmann-Hollweg acknowledged their virtual dictatorship—in effect, that of General Ludendorff. The rise of this military dictatorship had great bearing upon the relations between Germany and the United States, for Ludendorff proposed to carry on the naval war in a manner intolerable to the Republic.

American Hesitation and Intervention

At the outbreak of the war in 1914, the United States had promptly declared her neutrality. President Wilson urged Americans to be neutral in thought as well as deed. In a message to Congress in August 1914 he pointed out that the people of the United States were drawn "chiefly from the nations now at war" and that the temptation to take sides would lead to "divisions among us." As "the one great nation at peace," the United States should hold herself "ready to play a part of impartial mediation."

The President had no illusions about the reasons for the war; it was due, he said, to "England's having the world and Germany's wanting it." But he was increasingly disturbed by the possibility of a German victory. There was uncertainty regarding the reach and direction of German ambitions. As the head of a republic that had a small military establishment and abhorred conscription, Wilson opposed a diplomacy based on force. A German victory would strengthen militarism. Wilson's position coincided with that of many influential Americans, who felt that only a pacific world could provide the conditions under which the United States might continue her accustomed life. The reduction of armaments in the future, the substitution of democratic governments for militaristic and imperialistic monarchies, and the settlement of disputes by international organization became for many Americans the real issue of the war.

There was much discussion of ways and means by which these objects might be attained. Various projects for international cooperation were formulated and discussed. One of these was that of the economist Thorstein Veblen (1857-1929). In 1795, during the French revolutionary wars, the German philosopher Immanuel Kant had proposed the formation of a league, consisting of republican states, to secure the peace. In 1917, in *An Inquiry into the Nature of Peace*, Veblen suggested a modern version of such a league. The principal members would be the North Atlantic countries, including not only the United States, Britain and her English-speaking dominions, and France, but the Scandinavian countries and the Netherlands as well. "By and large, these peoples have come to the tolerant attitude that finds expression in the maxim, 'Live and let live.' " Veblen considered them mature enough "to have abjured dynastic ambitions of dominion."

Around this nucleus of democratic nations, Veblen explained later, would be ranged the peoples of Central and Eastern Europe—freed from dynastic rule—and then the still less developed colonial peoples overseas. While the degrees of influence would differ, the relations among the three groups were to be no longer exploitative and imperial. The league was to follow the pattern of the United States, in which states, territories, and "outlying possessions" exercise different degrees of autonomy and sovereignty. There were to be no economic discriminations and privileges, the resources of every part of the globe would be accessible to all peoples on an equal basis, trade was to be free, and diplomacy was to become "open" and public.

Public interest in projects of international organization grew as the European conflict dragged on and the United States became increasingly concerned over its outcome. During the first two years of the war the American people were not prepared to intervene. The large German-American and Irish-American elements were naturally hostile to England. Liberals considered Russia the head and front of reaction, intolerance, and absolutism. There were whole regions, particularly in the Midwest, which were isolationist in feeling. President Wilson won re-election in November 1916 on the slogan "He kept us out of war." Yet public opinion had veered strongly in favor of the Western Allies. The unprovoked attack on Belgium, the reports of German brutality, the sense that Germany represented a contemptuous aristocratic and militaristic force, and her very efficiency and energy had made many friends for the Allied cause.

Moreover, the United States had become involved in the conflict economically. Since Britain and France were sweeping German merchant shipping from the seas and blockading German ports, American producers could deliver only to the Allies. There had been, in 1913-14, some fear of an economic recession in the United States, and after war broke out the government encouraged Allied purchases by approving the flotation of loans. These loans were supported by the sale in the United States of American securities held by British and French subjects. In short order, the ownership of many enterprises which had been financed with European capital—notably railroads—passed into native hands. The old "colonial" position of the American economy passed into history; the wheel turned and Western Europe became the debtor of the United States. This gave the Republic a stake in an Allied victory. Secretary of State Bryan protested repeatedly against the flotation of foreign loans, but he was powerless to stop it.

Finally, the United States was affected, as in previous European conflicts, by the strategic and maritime consequences of the war. The government acted to secure the position of the United States in the Caribbean Sea. If Germany conquered or dominated Holland and Denmark, she might claim the strategic islands held by these states at the northeastern entrance to the "American Mediterranean" and the approaches to the Panama Canal. In 1916, Denmark was induced to sell the Virgin Islands to the United States, for fifteen million dollars. The conduct of the war at sea involved the United States in disputes with both sides. England and France exercised a greater control over neutral commerce and shipping than had ever before been attempted. The long-range blockade, the long contraband lists, and the restriction of neutral imports were extraordinary measures. Viewing these as violations of international law, the United States protested vigorously and repeatedly, without effect. She had been more successful in persuading Germany to abandon unrestricted submarine warfare (see p. 501), which violated the letter as well as the spirit of the law.

In January 1916, in the hope of bringing about a negotiated peace, President Wilson had sent his personal emissary, Colonel Edward M. House of Texas, to offer the mediation of the United States. Her mediation would make her a participant at the peace table and give her a voice in the settlement. If Germany rejected it, the United States would move closer to the Allies and perhaps enter the war on their side. But before House's mission bore fruit, Germany seized the initiative. In December 1916, fresh from victories in the Balkans, Germany asked President Wilson to inform the Allies that she was prepared to attend a peace conference. Wilson inquired of both sides what terms they would entertain. The answers were incompatible. Wilson insisted, without effect, that there must be a "peace without victory," a reasonable compromise between equals, and, above all, one without indemnities and annexations.

The attempts to reach a negotiated peace having failed, the war took a sharper turn. On January 31, 1917, Germany announced the immediate resumption of unrestricted submarine warfare. Since a thrust on land was out of the question for the moment, Ludendorff decided that it was necessary for Germany to strike harder at Britain's shipping and thus to deprive her of industrial supplies and of food. The German navy drew the outlines of a broad zone of two to three hundred miles around the coasts of Great Britain and France. This zone was to be the graveyard of Allied shipping. No ship was to be allowed to pass through this zone, regardless of whether it was neutral or belligerent, passenger or freight, carried legal goods or contraband. It would not be warned, inspected, or allowed to provide for the safety of its crew or passengers. It would be sunk on sight. A large pack of submarines stood poised to enforce the grim decree. The civilian leaders, including the Chancellor, opposed this measure, fearing that it would antagonize the neutral world, particularly the United States. They were overruled. The military leaders characteristically discounted a state which was not organized to strike by force at any moment; they trusted to win before the United States could organize her man power or industrial potential.

514   On February 3, promptly after Germany resumed unrestricted submarine

warfare, President Wilson broke off diplomatic relations. In March an attempt by Germany to propel Mexico into an attack on the United States came to light. The German danger seemed to be nearer than was suspected. President Wilson ordered the arming of merchant ships. Finally, on April 2, he asked Congress to declare war on Germany, asserting that the United States was contending

> . . . for the ultimate peace of the world and for the liberation of its peoples, the German peoples included; for the rights of nations, great and small, and the privilege of men everywhere to choose their way of life and of obedience. The world must be made safe for democracy. Its peace must be planted upon the tested foundations of political liberty. . . . No autocratic government could be trusted to keep faith or observe its covenants. . . . Does not every American feel that assurance has been added to our hope for the future peace of the world by the wonderful and heartening things that have been happening within the last weeks in Russia?

Four days later Congress complied with his request.

At first it seemed that the United States might have intervened too late. The German submarines were sinking Allied and neutral ships at a rate which, if continued, was certain to starve out Great Britain in a few months. In April 1917, more ships were destroyed than the whole world could normally replace in that time. But this proved to be the climax. The newly introduced system of convoying, supplemented by devices for detecting and destroying undersea craft, and a huge shipbuilding program in the United States began slowly to turn the tide. The losses began to diminish, month by month. Considerable tonnage was still being sunk, but it was now submarines that were being destroyed faster than they and their crews could be replaced.

The intervention of the United States strengthened the opposition within Germany. The leader of the Center party, Matthias Erzberger (1875-1921), protested against the submarine campaign and pressed for another attempt to negotiate. He had become aware that Germany's principal ally, Austria-Hungary, was on her last legs. Secret committee meetings of *Reichstag* members exposed the expectations of victory as groundless. Centrists and Social Democrats drafted a peace resolution, but Hindenburg and Ludendorff threatened to resign if such a resolution was passed. Squeezed between the two sides, Bethmann-Hollweg resigned as Chancellor and a creature of the Army Headquarters, Dr. Georg Michaelis, took his place; the predominance of the military became complete. On July 19, the *Reichstag* nevertheless resolved, by a vote of 212 to 126, to strive "for a peace of understanding and the permanent reconciliation of the peoples." The resolution further stated that "forced acquisitions of territory and political, economic, or financial oppressions are inconsistent" with such a peace. Although this statement revealed a split within the German state, its immediate practical effect was nil. The new Chancellor tried to cover the breach with the military dictators by declaring that he supported the resolution "as I understand it." Nevertheless, it was clear that while the *Reichstag* proposed, the dictators disposed. Michaelis made a few political concessions, by appointing *Reichstag* deputies to minor ministerial posts. The Kaiser made a vague promise to broaden suffrage laws in Prussia—sometime after the war.

Lenin and the Bolshevik Revolution

The German military leaders had one more string to their bow. They had detected weaknesses in the Italian military position and were projecting an offensive to improve the Austrian position on that front. While the *Reichstag* was debating the peace resolution, they were turning back a Russian offensive, and this event opened prospects of a definitive victory in the East, which would enable them to add eastern to western troops and make possible still another, and greater than ever, offensive in the West. In this reckoning, the German General Staff was much assisted by domestic developments in Russia, notably by the rise of the Bolsheviks. In the belief that the multiplication of sects and schisms and the repatriation of defeatist politicians would undermine the fighting will of the Russian army, the German Command had facilitated the return to Russia of a group of exiled radicals, among them the Bolshevik chief, Nicolai Lenin, in April 1917. Thus the German General Staff had made a substantial contribution to the Russian Revolution.

The war cast a shadow over the morning glow of the Russian Revolution. The French Revolution had had three years of peace in which to shape its principal reforms. The domestic renovation of the American Revolution was accomplished in the individual states, while the quarrel with Great Britain was being fought to a conclusion by common forces. It was only after victory and a decade of experiment that a definitive federal constitution was drafted and adopted. With the exception of the Paris Commune, the many revolutions of the nineteenth century had occurred in times of international peace. In the Russian Revolution, however, the question of war and peace and of relations to other European states—allies and enemies—further complicated the domestic problems.

The difficulty of extricating the country from the war was compounded by the weakness of the provisional government. The disappearance of czarism left a political vacuum. There were two foci of activity. The moderate conservative and liberal parties functioned in the Duma and the cabinet. The radical and socialist parties were in a minority in the Duma but exerted major influence in the soviets. The lack of a strong political authority gave unusual scope to the spontaneous will of the masses. The government's proposal to continue the war and to postpone solution of the constitutional and agrarian questions struck the ordinary peasant and soldier as a mysterious deception. The war had been represented by liberals and radicals as imperialistic in aim: why, then, not put an end to it at once? The German workers had been represented as antimilitarist and anticapitalist; why, then, not fraternize with them and turn the fighting front into a meeting of comrades? The villagers had often risen against their masters and had always considered the land, drenched with their sweat, as their very own; now that the government of the masters had fallen, why not take the land? But if the peasants present in the village were to do themselves justice at last, what about the peasants absent in uniform? Must they not repair home at once to assure themselves a share in the great divison? And what about that socialist transformation that many city workers had come to associate with the Revolution?

In this psychological gap between the government and the masses, the soviets spoke with telling effect. Their members were fresh from contact with the men who had elected them. They avoided, perhaps shrewdly, a claim to govern the country themselves. As early as March, at the outset of the Revolution, a fissure opened between the Petrograd Soviet and the government. Intent on democratizing the army, the Soviet issued the so-called Order No. 1, which stripped the officers of all but strategic functions and transferred the control and administration of army units to committees elected by both soldiers and officers. Since the Soviet had not only recognized but urged the assumption of power by the provisional government, this order was, strictly speaking, invalid, and was indeed countermanded by the government. The order was nevertheless obeyed widely, if not uniformly. The integrity of the centralized and hierarchical command was broken.

On the heels of the military issue, there arose the broader issue of peace. The feeble attempts at a negotiated peace made by Germany and the United States just before the outbreak of the Revolution had failed. Russia's only hope of a prompt cessation of the fighting lay in suing Germany for a separate treaty. Since Germany held the upper hand, she was likely to make stiff terms. Such a remedy might be worse than the disease, but the man in the street does not always appreciate the importance of political boundaries: many Russian peasants felt that they could do with a farm back home without also being the ostensible master of a stretch of Europe from the Baltic to the Black Sea. There were, of course, men who experienced every geographic diminution of their country as a personal tragedy. And there were many liberals and radicals who were just as much concerned over the prospect of the battening of an imperial Germany as over the reduction of a democratic Russia. The upshot was that no prominent political party save the Bolsheviks could reconcile itself to the price of a petition for a German peace.

The provisional government let it be known, in April 1917, that it meant to honor the treaties that bound Russia not to make a separate peace and promised her considerable acquisitions in case of victory. The Petrograd Soviet, however, in common with war-weary elements abroad, favored a peace without transfers of territory or retaliations. On May 1, the labor holiday, it massed a huge demonstration of protest. Riots broke out in the capital. The Foreign Minister, Paul Miliukov, was compelled to resign. The cabinet was reshuffled; the socialist Alexander Kerensky became its most powerful member, the Minister of War; the Soviet for the first time agreed to participate in the govern- *517* ment; three Mensheviks and three Social Revolutionaries took office. The Revolution thus moved to the left. The government announced that it favored the re-establishment of a general peace "without annexations or indemnities and based on the right of nations to decide their own affairs."

Kerensky labored to reanimate the will to fight. In June he traveled along the whole front and made impassioned appeals to the troops to retrieve the glory of Russian arms. At the end of the month, the armies opened a large-scale offensive in Galicia. The first few weeks brought encouraging success. Then difficulties developed. Troops sometimes stopped in mid-battle to debate the strategy suggested by their officers. German troops arrived to support the Austrians, and the Russians were routed at several points. Whole regiments broke and fled, often after murdering their officers. All the recent and past gains of Russian arms in the Hapsburg Empire were abandoned, and Russia lay wider open to invasion than ever.

The dilemma of the war was simplified: was military exertion any longer possible, whatever its aim or justification? Conservative groups felt that the Revolution was impeding the war by disintegrating the army and that the Revolution would therefore have to be checked and reversed. In September, General Lavr Kornilov (1870-1918), Commander-in-Chief of the Russian forces, advanced toward Petrograd at the head of a Cossack army, determined to overthrow the provisional government and to establish a dictatorial regime. Kerensky, now Prime Minister, obtained large discretionary powers. With the support of the various parties, including the most radical, and of the soviets, he defeated and imprisoned Kornilov.

Kerensky soon faced a more formidable challenge in the Bolshevik party and its dominating figure. Nicolai Lenin's father was a Great Russian school official and his antecedents on his mother's side were Baltic Germans. Lenin came by his revolutionary tendencies naturally. When he was eighteen, his older brother Alexander was executed for participating in a plot to assassinate Czar Alexander III. "His brother's execution," wrote Leon Trotsky, "indelibly stamped on his consciousness, helped to determine his later life." Thenceforth, Lenin fairly vibrated with a single aim: to tear up the existing order by the roots. He had a rough-and-ready mind and a highly utilitarian attitude regarding ideas and words: they were weapons in the social war. He distrusted aesthetic pleasure and abhorred gentleness: ". . . you must not stroke anyone's head—you might get your hand bitten off."

While Lenin's intellectual and spiritual resources were modest, his political endowment was extraordinary. He had a superb sense of reality, enormous shrewdness, and an unbending will to power. The trappings and glitter of office left him cold: he was entirely unassuming in his personal life and conduct. It was only the substance of power that he loved. Lenin belonged, in short, to the race of drastic doers, men who tend not to consider the ultimate consequences of their acts. They do not always know what to think, but they know what to do.

Lenin, who had been trained as a lawyer, was quite pedantic in his insistence on supporting his arguments and crushing his adversaries with texts from

Marx and Engels. He was, however, more captivated by Marx's fiery temperament and zeal for revolution than by his doctrines. We have seen (p. 435) that he repudiated Marx's emphasis on the proletariat as a force for socialism and his view that only highly developed countries were in a position to abolish capitalism. For all his Hegelianism, Marx had tried to assimilate into his system the liberal democratic ideas of Western Europe. Lenin, although he lived for many years in Switzerland and briefly in England, remained a stranger to Western ways. His true provenance was the Russian tradition: dependence upon an energetic elite for political leadership; unquestioned discipline of parties designed for secret and conspiratorial action; stress upon centralized authority; exaggerated respect for "science"; and belief in the transcendent importance of the deed.

This was the man who had for many years been shaping the Bolshevik party into an instrument of action obedient to the will of a central committee. He perceived, in the summer of 1917, that the moment had come to use that instrument for the largest political purpose: to make the party the state.

As we have seen, Lenin was among those Marxists who refused to support the war. Past experience suggested to him that czarism could be overthrown only if it suffered defeat. Lenin's formula for Russia was therefore defeat and revolution. When the war broke out in 1914, he saw no immediate prospect of realizing his hopes. Lenin returned from Switzerland to Russia in April 1917, a month after the fall of czarism. He promptly shocked his own supporters, who had agreed with other socialists to back the provisional government, by calling for a fight *à outrance* against the new regime. In his famous "April theses," he declared:

> . . . owing to the capitalist nature of this government, the war on Russia's part remains a predatory imperialist war. . . . Without the overthrow of capital it is *impossible* to conclude the war with a really democratic, non-oppressive peace. . . . The peculiarity of the present situation in Russia is that it represents a *transition* from the first stage of the revolution, which, because of the inadequate organization and insufficient class consciousness of the proletariat, led to the assumption of power by the bourgeoisie,—to its second stage which is to place power in the hands of the proletariat and the poorest strata of the peasantry.
>
> This transition is characterized, on the one hand, by a maximum of legality (Russia is now the freest of all the belligerent countries of the world); on the other, by the absence of oppression of the masses, and finally, by the trustingly ignorant attitude of the masses toward the capitalist government, the worst enemy of peace and socialism. . . . Not a parliamentary republic [is needed] . . . but a republic of soviets of workers', agricultural laborers', and peasants' deputies. . . . Abolition of the police, the army, the bureaucracy. All officers to be elected and subject to recall at any time, their salaries not to exceed the average wage of a competent worker. . . . Not the "introduction" of socialism as an immediate task, but

519

the immediate placing of the Soviet of Workers' Deputies in control of social production and distribution of goods.

Contact with Russian conditions confirmed Lenin's views. He perceived that the real seat of power lay in the soviets, that the people were exhausted by the war, and that the highest trump card in the game of politics was peace. Lenin's mastery over his party was such that he prevailed upon it to promise to stop the war, although he had no assurance that Germany would agree to satisfactory terms.

Two other issues were made to his hand. The collapse of czarism had led not only to the disorganization of the army but to the collapse of authority in the villages. Many peasants acting alone, many villages acting as units, were dispossessing landlords; many peasant soldiers, rifles slung across their shoulders, struck out for home, determined not to be left out in the informal distribution. A wide extension of small-scale farming was in prospect. This was contrary to the socialized and large-scale agriculture advocated by the Bolsheviks, in common with other Marxists. In order to obtain popular support against the government, Lenin promised to satisfy the peasant's craving for land immediately, without specifying the real aim of the Marxist program.

On the constitutional question he pursued a double tactic. On the one hand, he called for the election of the Constituent Assembly, although the Bolsheviks had dim prospects of victory in a general election held under free conditions; the Social Revolutionaries had always been the more popular radical party in the village. However, by making it appear that the government did not trust the people, the Bolsheviks placed it on the defensive. The elections were scheduled for November 25. On the other hand, Lenin called for the transfer of "all power to the soviets"—in which bodies his followers succeeded in obtaining posts of leadership.

The reason Lenin and his followers did not flinch from a peace which portended the surrender of much Russian territory to the Kaiser, an agrarian reform that did not jibe with Marxist plans, and elections in which other parties stood a better chance to win was that they believed in the imminence of a general European revolution. Their own uprising would merely be a contribution to the revolution of industrial countries farther west.

In July 1917, while the army was recoiling before the pressure of the Germans, riots broke out in the capital. Workers and soldiers rebelled spontaneously and rushed into the streets, shouting the Bolshevik slogans of immediate peace and power to the soviets. The Bolsheviks followed rather than led in this uprising. The government suppressed the rising and imprisoned several Bolshevik leaders. Lenin fled and went into hiding in a nearby village across the Finnish border.

In the summer and fall of 1917, the condition of Russia approached anarchy. Army units melted away at the front through wholesale desertion. In a number of cities the people rioted for food. The position of the provisional government became precarious. The Bolsheviks' slogan of peace rapidly gained

A striking photograph of Lenin in action. From an improvised platform, the Russian leader is addressing a crowd, in a square in Petrograd in the spring of 1917. Below him, at the right, his principal aide in the Bolshevik revolution of the following November, Leon Trotsky, stands as if on guard.
FPG

Street riot in Petrograd in July 1917. In November, the Bolsheviks adopted the tactics of carefully planned and organized military coups, carried out by selected, armed, and drilled "Red Guards" officered by professional revolutionists. SOVFOTO

them adherents among the soldiers and workers of the capital and other large cities. In October, shortly after the Kornilov attack had been put down with their help, the Bolsheviks won over a majority of the Petrograd Soviet. From his hideout in Finland, Lenin nerved his party to action. He was confident that the time was also ripe for a German revolution and expected that a coup in Russia would hurry it. There were reports of widespread disaffection in the German navy. "We stand on the threshold of world proletarian revolution," he wrote. An all-Russian Congress of Soviets was scheduled to meet in Petrograd on November 7. Lenin's plan was to seize power and present the Congress with a *fait accompli*.

The insurrection was prepared by the Military Revolutionary Committee of the Petrograd Soviet. Both Soviet and Committee were headed by Leon Trotsky, a brilliant organizer, orator, and pamphleteer. Trotsky had long been critical of the dictatorial tendencies of Bolshevism, but captivated by Lenin's political assurance, he had recently joined the Bolshevik party. In planning the coup, Trotsky departed from the classic model, the French Revolution of 1789. That had been a more or less spontaneous movement of the masses, directed or assisted by energetic leaders. Its weapons were informal, its battleground was the public street, and its aim the seizure of the seats of political power, royal courts, and ministers' palaces. Since 1848, however, no similar rising had been successful.

Trotsky turned from the examples of Danton and Robespierre to those of Napoleon Bonaparte and Auguste Blanqui, who had attempted—the first successfully, the second in vain—a secret conspiracy for a military stroke by officers or politicians with armed troops at their command. The stroke was to be directed not only at political centers but also at telephone, telegraph, and post-office buildings, railroad stations, bridges, and power stations. The long preparation of a party of professional revolutionists was the real source of the new strategy of overthrow. The military *coup d'état* spelled dictatorship; the popular barricade war of old implied continuing contact with the masses. The new coup was to be made by a conspiratorial party which could then rule by armed force, without reference to democracy. The disciplined members of the Bolshevik party were to be the cadre of the revolutionary army; the party's Central Committee was to be the general staff; and its dominant figure, Lenin, was to be the leader. They were to become, respectively, the exclusive ruling elite, the authoritarian government, and the dictator. The revolution and the dictatorship of the twentieth century were born.

The Military Revolutionary Committee installed its agents in the arsenals of the capital and obtained the support of several regiments of the garrison and of naval units in the nearby port of Kronstadt. The garrison began to accept the orders of the Soviet in preference to those of the provisional government, which had proposed to transfer some of these troops to the front. Selected groups of determined workers were also organized, armed, and drilled. The insurrectionary army counted about 25,000 men. The government and the various socialist parties were aware of the preparations of the Bolsheviks, but they were neither prepared nor willing to use force against another socialist party.

During the night of November 6 the rebel troops and workers' "Red Guards" took positions around the Czar's Winter Palace, where the government had its headquarters, and the centers of communication, transportation, power, and railway traffic. Gunboats moved up the River Neva from Kronstadt. After a brief struggle, the government buildings were seized. Most of the members of the government were arrested; some of them fled. Kerensky left the capital and tried unsuccessfully to march troops to recapture it. In Moscow, the fighting lasted a whole week.

On the evening of November 7, while the Congress of Soviets was holding its first session, the Bolsheviks took control of Petrograd. Lenin had arrived from Finland in disguise—with a bandage over his face as though suffering from toothache. He tore off the bandage, appeared before the Congress, and announced: "We shall now proceed to construct the socialist order." The Mensheviks, the Social Revolutionaries, and the Jewish Bund vigorously protested the "military conspiracy" against the provisional government and Lenin's "policy of adventure." The Congress passed a Menshevik resolution for cooperation among all socialist groups to put an end to the fighting and form a broad government, but the Bolsheviks ignored it. Unwilling to sanction the violent proceedings of the Bolsheviks, the representatives of the Mensheviks and Social Revolutionaries withdrew from the Congress, leaving the field to their enemies.

A "Committee to Save the Country and the Revolution" was organized, which denounced "the use of force against the government of revolutionary Russia" as "an unheard-of crime against the country." It called upon citizens to reject "the authority of violence" and to strike. But it would not launch a civil war by calling the citizens to arms. The Bolsheviks prevailed because their opponents would not meet force with force.

After the other socialist groups had withdrawn, the Bolsheviks obtained the sanction of the Congress of Soviets for a new provisional government. The Congress delegated local administration to local soviets and central control to the Council of People's Commissars, which was headed by Lenin and consisted entirely of Bolsheviks. A month later the Left Social Revolutionaries, a group which had approved of the coup and split off from the Social Revolutionary party, joined the Council. The majority of the Council, however, remained Bolshevik. Both the Congress and the temporary government acknowledged that ultimate sovereignty would rest with the Constituent Assembly. The Congress insisted that the elections be held as scheduled—on November 25—and called upon local electoral officials to ensure "the freedom of the voters and fair play."

In order to cajole the peasantry and gain time to consolidate their regime, the Bolsheviks dropped their own land program in favor of that of the Social Revolutionaries: upon Lenin's motion, the Congress voted a sweeping decree which confiscated, without compensation, the estates of landlords, the Crown, 523 churches, and monasteries. Livestock, implements, and farm buildings were confiscated along with the land, which was to be taken over by peasant committees and eventually distributed on a basis of equality. Small farms were left to their owners. Small-scale farming had won out. All decisions, however, were made subject to final revision or approval by the impending Constituent Assembly.

In a series of decrees, the Bolsheviks turned over control of large businesses and factories to committees of employees, nationalized privately owned railroads and ships, took over all banks, put an end to stock transactions, made foreign trade a state monopoly, and established an eight-hour working day. They repudiated the huge debts contracted by the czarist and provisional governments. About half the debt was held by Russian citizens and the other half by foreign governments, bankers, and investors. French investors, many of them small property holders, were badly hit. The Bolshevik Revolution cost France $2,200,000,000.

The government decreed the abolition of the aristocracy and of inheritance. It separated church from state and turned over control of church buildings to committees of worshipers. Religious instruction in the schools was ended, and divorce was made free at the request of either party. As a symbol of the new regime, the government adopted the Gregorian calendar—the one in use in the rest of the world—and abolished the Julian calendar, which was thirteen days behind the "new style" reckoning. The date of the Bolshevik Revolution was October 25 old style but November 7 new style.

Eighteen days after the Bolshevik Revolution, on November 25, the Russian people voted for the Constituent Assembly in a free election. They gave 25 percent of the vote to the Bolsheviks and their allies, the Left Social Revolutionaries, and 62 percent to their rivals, the Social Revolutionaries and the Mensheviks. Only 13 percent voted for nonsocialist parties. Out of 707 deputies, 370—a clear majority—were Social Revolutionaries; only 175 were Bolsheviks and 40 Left Social Revolutionaries. The vote was in effect a repudiation of the November Revolution and of the Bolshevik government. But when the Constituent Assembly met, on January 18, the government refused to resign and proposed blandly that the Assembly abdicate its powers and confine itself to drafting "a general statement of the fundamental bases of a socialist reconstruction of society." The Assembly insisted on the right to govern and legislate. When the delegates arrived for their second session, on January 19, they found the hall locked and surrounded by Red soldiers. A demonstration of citizens in support of the Assembly was fired upon, and several persons were killed by the troops.

Lenin offered lame excuses. He contended that the soviets were "revolutionary mass organizations" and therefore "immeasurably superior to any other parliament in the world. . . . The people at large have not yet realized all the implications of the November Revolution." His government argued that although the elections were held after the November Revolution, the Social Revolutionaries had made up their lists of candidates before the Revolution and that therefore the Assembly belonged to "the old order." "At the time of voting for the Social Revolutionaries, the people were not in a position to decide between the Right Wing—partisans of the bourgeoisie—and the Left Wing—partisans of socialism. This accounts for the fact that the Constituent Assembly, the crown of the bourgeois parliamentary republic, stands in the way of the November Revolution and the Soviet government."

The Council began to call itself the Soviet government and enacted a constitution which abandoned the practice of election based on geographic districts. Representation was to be by economic classes. The bourgeoisie was excluded, and sovereignty was to rest formally with representatives elected separately by peasants and urban workers. In practice, however, it rested with the Bolshevik. By rapid degrees, the government repressed political freedom and raised a powerful apparatus of coercion, intimidation, and terror. It closed down opposition newspapers, imprisoned or executed leaders of dissenting parties, and forbade all political activity and organization save that of the Bolsheviks and Left Social Revolutionary parties. It tightened its control over the army, abolished the old system of justice, and set up "people's courts," where justice was dispensed in accordance with the interests of the party. In December the Bolsheviks placed the capstone in the system of repression. They organized the Cheka, a secret police with wide powers of arrest, trial, and execution. The Cheka, later known as the G.P.U., became the government's right hand of terror.

The experiment was launched: a socialist government controlled by a minority party, resting on military and police power and relying on the acquiescence of the masses. The success of the experiment depended, in the opinion of the Bolsheviks, on the consolidation of their power in the rural areas (for as yet their writ ran mainly in the large cities), on the outbreak of revolutions abroad, and, above all, on their ability to extricate themselves from the war.

The Treaty of Brest-Litovsk and the Fourteen Points

While the Bolsheviks were disposing of the Constituent Assembly, they negotiated for a separate peace. They had asked Germany for an armistice, which was granted on November 28. On December 22 two incongruous commissions met at Brest-Litovsk in Poland to work out details of the peace: on one side a galaxy of high-ranking German and Austrian generals and diplomats; on the other, plain-uniformed Bolshevik officials symbolically flanked by a soldier from the ranks, a sailor, a peasant, and a worker. The Germans demanded the cession of all the lands that Russia had acquired since the seventeenth century. The Bolsheviks refused and tried to use the negotiations as the basis for an appeal to German workers to rebel. (In January, coincidentally, German munitions workers went on strike and made political as well as economic demands. But the strike did not spread.) The German delegation told the Russian negotiators to accept its terms or fight. Lenin was convinced that the

Bolshevik government could not maintain itself unless it submitted, but he could not prevail upon his comrades or the Left Social Revolutionaries in the cabinet to accept the stiff German terms. The majority preferred waging a "revolutionary war"—irregular guerrilla warfare—to signing an "imperialist" peace. Trotsky, who had meanwhile become the head of the peace delegation, devised an original formula: Russia would neither sign a treaty nor fight! The Germans were dumbfounded, but when they recovered their reply was brief. They denounced the armistice and on February 18 resumed the offensive on a wide front. As they advanced on Petrograd, Lenin threatened to resign and form an opposition group in favor of peace. He finally won over a majority of his party. The Social Revolutionaries refused to go along and resigned from the government.

The Treaty of Brest-Litovsk was finally signed on March 3, 1918. The price, which the Germans had raised in the interim, was high. Russia lost more than a quarter of her population, arable land, and railway mileage. Germany established control or tutelage over a half million square miles and sixty million people. She established "protected" states in the Baltic, Poland, and Armenia. Russia agreed to pay an indemnity of 150 million dollars and to extend commercial privileges to Germany. Ambitious plans were projected to put German princes on new thrones in Lithuania, Courland, Latvia, Estonia, and Finland, and an Austrian archduke on a prospective throne in the Ukraine.

The Ukraine, where the native General Skoropadsky had set up an independent government, had earlier signed a separate peace treaty. German and Austro-Hungarian troops occupied the country in order to ensure the shipment of badly needed foodstuffs. In May, Germany imposed the Treaty of Bucharest upon Rumania, which guaranteed her a monopoly of Rumanian grain exports for nine years and of oil exports for ninety years. Her Hungarian and Bulgarian allies received slices of Rumanian territory. Germany was lord of Eastern Europe.

The separate peace with Germany was a breach of Russia's treaty obligations. The Allies not only refused to listen to Bolshevik appeals for a general cessation of hostilities but refused to recognize the new government. To force their hands, the Bolsheviks opened the archives of the czarist government and published the texts of the secret treaties it had made with the Allies. For the first time, the man in the street learned of the projected territorial and colonial distribution. England was to seize the German colonies and share with France some of the Asiatic possessions of Turkey, notably Syria and Arabia. Russia was to get the Straits, Constantinople, and Armenia from Turkey. According to the secret Treaty of London, signed in 1915, Italy was to have a part of the Tyrol, Trieste, and Istria from Austria-Hungary, as well as a share of the Turkish possessions in Africa and in Anatolia, on the coast of the Aegean Sea. Rumania was promised half of Hungary and a smaller slice of Austria; Serbia, a larger part of southern Austria-Hungary.

The secret treaties were published in England and the United States, where they made a poor impression indeed: it appeared that millions of men were dying to consummate a vast real-estate transaction. To allay discontent, Lloyd George appeared before the British Trade Union Congress and prettified the war aims by calling for the independence of oppressed nationalities. He alluded vaguely to an international organization to prevent future wars.

Old World statesmen were too deeply committed to conventional diplomacy to enter the lists with Lenin as the exponents of an idealistic policy. The task fell to the willing hands of President Wilson of the United States. Like most informed observers, Wilson had been aware of the existence of territorial agreements, but he had evidently not been shown the text of the secret treaties, and he would not have relished the courtesy. To avoid any appearance of approval, he designated the United States as an "associate" and not an "ally."

On January 8, in an address to Congress, he announced a peace program known as the Fourteen Points: navigation on the seas in war and in peace was to be free; economic barriers between nations were to be removed; armaments were to be reduced; colonial claims were to be adjusted, with the agreement of the colonial peoples themselves; Russian territory and freedom were to be restored; Belgium was also to be restored to the Belgians; Alsace-Lorraine was to be returned to France; Italian frontiers were to follow the lines of nationality; the peoples of the Ottoman and Hapsburg Empires were to secure autonomy; Poland and the smaller independent states were to be restored. Above all, "open covenants of peace openly arrived at" were to take the place of secret diplomacy and secret agreements. A "general association of nations" was to watch over international peace, prevent future wars, and thus make costly and dangerous armaments unnecessary. It would provide for "mutual guarantees of political independence and territorial integrity to great and small states alike."

Wilson became the spokesman of peace without revolution, as Lenin was the spokesman of peace through revolution.

The Collapse of Germany and Austria-Hungary

While the American and the Russian contended for the souls of men, Germany profited from her military triumph in Eastern Europe. Ludendorff withdrew large armies from the east and prepared a great offensive in the west. For the first time since 1914, Germany had a preponderance of troops. This advantage had to be quickly exploited, for by summer, when Americans were expected to arrive in force, it would vanish.

Ludendorff devised an intricate plan. He would mount a series of offensives at various parts of the western front so that the Allied defenders would disperse their forces. But he would exploit only one of these offensives. Which it was to be was determined in advance and confided only to the inner circle of the command. The plan leaked out, and the Allied hosts were disposed accordingly. But their danger was not over, for Ludendorff did not follow his own plan. When he launched his attack, in March, it turned out that one of the secondary offensives was more successful than he had expected. It breached the front at its most sensitive point, where the French and British armies joined. Quick to press his advantage—too quick, as it turned out—Ludendorff followed this secondary offensive instead of the one he had planned and thus forfeited the advantage of preparation. Alarmed, the British generals wished to retreat toward the Channel, while their French comrades wished to rush southward to protect Paris. In short, they were about to tear up the front and abandon the common effort.

Courage was needed, and the civilian leadership supplied it. Lloyd George and Clemenceau vetoed the generals and looked for a commander as daring as themselves. They found him in Ferdinand Foch (1851-1929). With the consent of President Wilson, they appointed Foch Commander-in-Chief of all the Allied armies, including the American. Until that moment of danger, unity of command had been impossible because of the mutual jealousy of the Allies, and of their generals.

Foch acted at once to blunt the German attack. He plugged the holes and prepared counterattacks. As in 1914, the Germans were short of reserves and supplies. The Americans began to arrive in substantial numbers, took over a small portion of the front at Chateau-Thierry in June, and managed to stop the German advance. Soon the initiative passed to the Allies; they counterattacked at the second battle of the Marne. On August 8 Ludendorff privately conceded defeat and asked the Kaiser to arrange a peace. The war went on for three months more before a proposal could be worked out.

The allies of Germany collapsed first. In each case, defeat was accompanied by the overthrow of the government and the monarch. Bulgaria signed an armistice on September 30; her Czar, Ferdinand, clung to his throne for four days more before abdicating in favor of his son. On October 30, Turkey capitulated, and the Sultan, though not overthrown at once, plunged into a serious conflict with rebellious officers who wished to continue the war to save Turkey the costs of surrender. And when, next, Austria-Hungary signed the long-wished-for armistice, on November 3, the Hapsburg signature had virtually ceased to have meaning. During October, the Czechs and Slovaks had declared their common independence, and so had the Yugoslavs; in the centers of the Dual Monarchy, Vienna and Budapest, revolutionary committees had assumed the conduct of affairs with the helpless acquiescence of the government; in Transylvania, an elected assembly proclaimed adherence to the Kingdom of Rumania; the Italians were marching upon the Tyrol and Dalmatia, upon Trieste and Fiume; the Polish provinces in the northeast were gravitating inevitably toward the Polish state which was rising phoenixlike from the ashes of war. All the various lands of the oldest dynasty of Europe were accounted for in a roll call of dissolution. On November 12 Emperor Charles II laid down the numberless dignities of his House. The dynasty died at the ripe age of 636 years.

The powerful Hohenzollern dynasty died with less grace. During September and October, the German government negotiated with Wilson but was finally, on November 11, driven to accept the harsher military terms of General Foch. As in Russia in 1917, mutiny had broken out. On November 3, the naval crews refused to put to sea on a desperate sortie contemplated by the officers as a gesture of defiance. Soon the north of Germany was aflame with disobedience. On November 7, a rising in Munich forced the King of Bavaria to abdicate. Strong pressure had for some time been exerted upon the Kaiser to give up his kingly and imperial crowns in an attempt to save the dynasty, for a young grandson might have been accepted as a successor. But William persistently refused. His generals complained that the army would no longer follow them. Unable to wait longer, the liberal Prince Max von Baden, who had been appointed chancellor as a concession to the Center and Social Democratic parties, on November 9 announced the abdication which William had not proffered. The Kaiser fled to Holland, bringing to an end an imperial dynasty of forty-seven years.

Of the three great conservative states that had dominated the Continent since the fall of Napoleon I, Germany had become a republic, Russia was Bolshevik, and Austria-Hungary lay scattered in pieces. The three Continental empires had in effect destroyed one another. Germany suffered greater casualties on the far-flung eastern front than in the west. Russia made a substantial contribution to the disintegration of the Hapsburg Empire by undermining the loyalty of the Slavic nationalities of Austria-Hungary and wearing down her military energy. In compensation, Germany virtually battered czarism out of existence. On the other hand, the leading Atlantic powers had fought together and won after a terrible ordeal. France barely escaped defeat in 1914, and England in 1916. It was France and her Russian ally that had provided the stage of fighting, with enormous human and material loss. The French nation was bled white. The British Empire won at a prohibitive cost; she could hardly afford another such triumph. The United States suffered the least, but gave up, at least temporarily, her traditional isolation. Only the Far Eastern world earned clear profits. Japan enhanced her position in the Pacific, and India obtained a promise of autonomy.

The overwhelming fact was that while the war was over, the European Revolution had only begun. What started as a quarrel between competing imperial powers ended as an introduction to far-reaching changes in the structure of Western civilization. The victorious powers could redistribute colonies, shift boundary stones, and penalize the losers. But could they bring order and stability into the fragmented estate of the Hapsburgs? Could they deal with the social revolution initiated in Russia? Could they fulfill the promise of a peaceful international order? None of the problems that Western civilization faced when the war broke out in 1914 was so baffling as those it faced as the year 1919 dawned.

25. *The Versailles Settlement and the League of Nations*

The peoples of the Western world stacked arms and counted their losses. For several years seventy million men had been under fire. Ten million of them died a violent death. Twice as many were maimed in body or mind. There was hardly a family in Europe that did not lose a member or a friend. Most of the casualties were young men in their twenties and thirties, or even in their teens. There was great destruction of capital and property. Thousands of dwellings, barns, and factories were ruined, machines and tools and vehicles destroyed, stores of food and goods and livestock wasted or wiped out. The loss left a gaping hole in the Western economy. The population felt it in the scarcity of necessaries and in increasingly high prices. Estimates of the damage are astronomical. More than 180 billion dollars were squandered in direct expenditure of fighting, and a sum nearly as large—152 billion dollars—measured the incidental damage to civilian property. If anyone had proposed in 1914 that five hundred million people should go on a four-year holiday, producing nothing and living on past accumulations, he would have been dispatched to an insane asylum. But such a fantastic holiday would have left Europe no poorer in material wealth, let alone in mood and spirit.

The war demonstrated that under modern conditions aggression is a double-edged instrument which cannot be limited to the aims of the user. It exposed the failure of the professional mind in the largest affairs, notably in military and diplomatic relations. It proved the need for closer contact between public opinion and the shapers of policy. And it showed that social thinking, planning, and direction are indispensable to the achievement of any considerable public purpose. National boundaries and chauvinistic policies had proved inadequate for fruitful production and interchange. In the fire of necessity, national states had begun to melt into larger associations. The scale of this association was suggested by the cooperation of the two coalitions. France and Great Britain on the one hand, Germany and Austria-Hungary on the other, had pooled war materials and resources as well as men and had regulated and shared imports and, to some extent, even production for the common purpose.

It is human to hope that great sacrifices will have a reward in a higher morality and rationality. Did not peace deserve as much cooperation as war? Was it too much to expect that the leaders of a successful war would shape a lasting and satisfying peace?

Clemenceau, Wilson, and Lloyd George

The Peace Conference met in Paris in January 1919. Its formal functions —the presentation of the completed treaty to the German delegation and the signing ceremony—were staged in the Hall of Mirrors at Versailles, where the Germans had proclaimed their Empire in 1871. The Paris Conference formulated the terms imposed on Germany. The treaties with Germany's confederates— Austria, Hungary, Bulgaria, and Turkey—were signed later at St. Germain, Trianon, Neuilly, and Sèvres, respectively.

The Conference presented the aspect of a Parliament of Man. Hardly a movement, a national or political interest, but was represented in the conference rooms or at least in the antechambers. Beyond, public opinion played a large role; editors, newspapermen, and party leaders voiced approval or disapproval at every step of the proceedings. Seventy plenipotentiary delegates spoke for the victors, who comprised twenty-seven states. The Conference was the first great European congress attended by the states of America, Africa, Asia, and Oceania.

The defeated powers were not invited to participate in the negotiations, although their written comments on the treaties were received and considered. Russia also was absent, although she had borne the brunt of some of the most massive onslaughts of Germany. By signing a separate peace she had forfeited her membership in the alliance and the profits promised her in secret treaties with France and Great Britain. Constantinople and the Straits again eluded her. The Bolshevik government was not recognized by the Allies; there were, in fact, hostilities between them. The conferees often had to turn from the problem of drafting the treaties to that of dealing with revolutionary attempts, particularly in Central Europe. Like Banquo's ghost, the Russian Revolution hovered around the conference table.

The decisions of the Conference were made largely in private discussions and negotiations of the Council of Ten, a body consisting of two representatives each from the United States, Great Britain, France, Italy, and Japan. The voices that carried the greatest weight were those of President Wilson, Premier Clemenceau, and Prime Minister Lloyd George. The "Big Three" dominated the Conference.

The 77-year-old Georges Clemenceau of France was chosen to preside over the Conference. Clemenceau was fully aware of the common interests of the North Atlantic countries. As a young man, he had lived in the United States for three years. In the early nineties, when conservative British statesmen had distrusted France and wooed Germany, Clemenceau had worked for a Franco-British understanding. He may have been the first to speak of an "entente cordiale." Clemenceau was sensitive to the relation between political and diplomatic compatibility; he had originally opposed the alliance between France and Russia on the ground that "there could be no real sympathy between the Republic and an autocrat."

Clemenceau's first concern was for the security of France; yet he knew that France alone could not assure the peace of Europe. He proposed an alliance in which France, Great Britain, and the United States would cooperate in applying stringent measures designed to prevent another attack by Germany. Together they would contain the forces of both militarism and extreme radicalism. Unlike the Triple Entente, the alliance would contain, now that the United States had supplanted Russia, only constitutional countries.

President Wilson became, for a shining hour, the eloquent spokesman of a more idealistic but also more difficult and uncertain project. He had arrived in Europe in December 1918—the first American president to leave the country during his incumbency—as the herald of a new world order, peaceful, liberal, and progressive. During the last year of the war he had excoriated militarism and imperialism. His Fourteen Points were the manifesto of the new order. The exhausted peoples of Europe put their trust in Wilson more than in their own leaders and rulers. No other American leader ever possessed the magnetic attraction that Wilson did in the winter and spring of 1918-19. To Europeans, he seemed to be the leader of the whole Western world.

His proposal of a League of Nations was indeed startling, for it involved a new pattern of international relations. Wilson's League grew out of the thinking of many enlightened men—both in America and in Europe—since the bellicose years of the turn of the century. Secret diplomacy, excessive armaments, aggressive policies, rival alliances, and *Realpolitik*—the politics of intrigue, selfishness, trickery, and threat—were to be abandoned. The principles of parliamentary government and the open forum of debate, persuasion, and compromise were to be projected from the domestic to the international scene. The League of Nations was to include the states of the world that were determined to be friendly and sincere in their dealings abroad—ideally, all the states of the world. By earnest cooperation, this grand combination, Wilson believed, could discourage or withstand the efforts of those who would break the peace.

Wilson's plan, like Clemenceau's, had a national as well as a cosmopolitan root. It was in the interest of the United States to maintain her newly won international position without disturbing her national habits, abandoning her policy of a small peacetime military establishment, and entering the circle of conventional European diplomacy and armaments. For Clemenceau the chief problem was German aggressiveness and the survival of France as the heart— so he thought of his country—of the liberal civilization of the West. For Wilson, it was the general issue of international anarchy. Clemenceau trusted to the

The "Big Three" of the Paris Peace Conference. Premier Georges Clemenceau of France pointing out the sights of Versailles to President Woodrow Wilson of the United States and Prime Minister David Lloyd George of Great Britain during the Peace Conference of 1919.
BETTMANN

combined influence of three states both liberal and strong. Wilson staked the future on a daring extension of international law.

The British Prime Minister shared neither Wilson's international nor Clemenceau's Atlantic vision. David Lloyd George was the first politician of modest social origins (he was the son of a Welsh schoolteacher and never attended a university) to penetrate to the front rank of political leadership in modern Britain. A brilliant improviser and opportunist, he was quick to sense the mood of men, whether they were few gathered around a conference table or many massed in front of the speaker's rostrum. He had a rude eloquence and an infinite capacity for adjustment and maneuver.

Lloyd George's energy and shrewdness stood Great Britain in good stead in ensuring victory. But the tasks of peace in a distracted world were more complex. They called for imagination and large views. Here Lloyd George was less successful. Imaginative in intrigue, he was unsure of principle. He had called an election barely a month after the Armistice and whipped up the dogs of revenge, promising the voters to make Germany pay the whole cost of the war. He was returned to power at the head of a "coalition" government which consisted principally of Conservatives and controlled five sixths of the seats in the

533

House of Commons. The bulk of the Liberals and the Labor party had refused to follow his leadership.

Although Lloyd George had been a critic of the Boer War and of colonial and naval ambition, he had quickly assimilated the aims of imperialism. In matters of grand policy, he adhered to traditional policies: the balance of power, playing off one Continental state against another, preserving British ascendancy overseas. He perceived not only German strength but also French hegemony as a threat to British power. His resourcefulness and opportunism made him a dangerous opponent. Toward the end of his life, he used to hum his own version of the Negro spiritual: "Nobody knows the trouble I've *been*." Clemenceau knew.

The German Settlement

At the Conference, Clemenceau held an initial advantage over his colleagues: he had worked out in advance a detailed set of proposals, which frequently served as the point of departure for the discussions. He presented territorial, financial, military, and naval terms that would reduce the chances of success of another invasion of France, for Clemenceau doubted that the character of the German state and its international methods and manners were likely to improve quickly.

By hard bargaining, Clemenceau won the agreement of Lloyd George to his territorial demands and the acquiescence, sometimes reluctant, of Wilson. Under the terms of the Treaty of Versailles Germany returned Alsace-Lorraine to France and ceded the Saar coal district. When Prussia seized Schleswig from Denmark in 1864, she had promised to allow the population to vote on the final settlement. The promise, which had not been kept, was now honored. Plebiscites were held in two zones. The population of the larger zone voted in favor of Denmark; that of the smaller, in favor of Germany. A small portion of Upper Silesia was ceded to the newborn state of Czechoslovakia. Most of the provinces of Posen and West Prussia, which had been seized by Prussia in the eighteenth-century partitions of Poland, were returned, in order to give Poland access to the sea. The Allies thus cut a "corridor" separating East Prussia from the rest of Germany and leading to Danzig, which became a free port. Altogether, Germany lost 13 percent of her territory. She lost nearly seven million (or 10 percent) of her people, mostly non-German in speech or sympathy, two thirds of her iron deposits (which lay in Lorraine), nearly half her coal, and much of her other subsoil resources. She retained the bulk of her industrial establishment.

Germany atoned for the losses caused by submarine warfare by giving up all but one tenth of her merchant fleet. She was forced to surrender all her submarines and most of her warships—all but a half dozen battleships of 10,000 tons, a half dozen cruisers, and a dozen destroyers and torpedo boats. Her officers scuttled the forfeited fleet instead of surrendering it, but the second greatest navy in the world was nonetheless gone.

Germany lost her entire colonial empire: over a million square miles scattered about in Africa and in the Pacific, with twelve million natives, much rubber, and a handful of German colonists. Her legal privileges and trading concessions overseas were all wiped out. The trade of her former colonies was to be open to all countries. The holdings and investments of German citizens abroad were forfeited. They represented one tenth of Germany's capital wealth.

The Treaty stated that "Germany accepts the responsibility of Germany and her allies for causing all the loss and damage to which the Allied and Associated Governments and their nationals have been subjected as a consequence of the war imposed on them by the aggression of Germany and her allies." This "war guilt" clause was resented by the German delegation. Its leader, Count Brockdorff-Rantzau, asserted that "in the last fifty years Imperialism has poisoned the international position of all European states. The policy of revenge, the policy of expansion, and the flouting of the rights of self-determination have contributed to the crisis." The clause was nevertheless retained, but the Allies asked Germany to pay only for the "damage done to the civilian population" and for the entire loss suffered by Belgium. Since the precise amount of reparations was a matter of controversy among the Allies— the United States asked no reparations for herself and suggested a much smaller total sum than France did—its determination was referred to a special commission, which was to report by May 1, 1921. Meanwhile, Germany was to make a first payment of five billion dollars in addition to all her large merchant ships, coal, building materials, and other goods. These terms were severe but less so than those imposed by Germany on Russia at Brest-Litovsk the year before.

In order to ensure the future security of France, Clemenceau demanded that the Rhineland be set up as an independent buffer state. Lloyd George feared that such a step would diminish the influence of Great Britain as an arbiter of contending powers. Wilson argued that the proposed League of Nations, by checking aggression, would give France sufficient protection. Clemenceau disagreed, since the obligations of the states under the proposed League would be moral and voluntary; there would be no executive or armed force to maintain the peace. The most that he could obtain was a compromise. The Rhineland was demilitarized, and so was a zone of thirty miles on the eastern bank of the Rhine. Allied troops would occupy the important bridgeheads for fifteen years. Conscription was abolished in Germany, the army was limited to 100,000 volunteers, and the General Staff was disbanded. The manufacture and import of war materials were limited. Finally, Lloyd George and Wilson promised France a guarantee of assistance in case Germany attacked her without provocation. The House of Commons approved the guarantee by unanimous vote.

These were the terms, and the immediate consequences, of the treaty with Germany, signed at Versailles on June 28, 1919.

Rival Alliances of First World War, 1918

Allied Powers and associates

Central Powers and associates

German colonies that were transferred later to Allies under League of Nations mandate

W. SAMOA (N.Z. mandate, 1920)

FIJI IS. (Br.)

NEW CALEDONIA

BISMARCK ARCH. (Australian mandate, 1920)

SOLOMON IS.

GILBERT IS. (Br.)

CAROLINE IS.

MARSHALL IS.

MARIANAS IS.

GUAM (U.S.)

German Islands (Jap. mandate, 1920)

Kiaochow Bay (To Japan, 1914)

AUSTRALIA

NETHERLANDS EAST INDIES

PHILIPPINE IS.

CHINA

JAPAN

Asia

U.S.S.R.

CEYLON

INDIA

AFGHAN-ISTAN

PERSIA

ARABIA

ADEN

OTTOMAN EMPIRE

ETHIOPIA

Indian Ocean

MADAGASCAR

GERMAN EAST AFRICA (Br. mandate, 1920)

North Pole

GERMANY

AUSTRIA-HUNGARY

BULGARIA

ITALY

FRANCE

SPAIN

PORTUGAL

GREAT BRITAIN

Africa

Ocean

TOGOLAND (Br. and Fr. mandate, 1920)

CAMEROONS (Br. and Fr. mandate, 1920)

SOUTH-WEST AFRICA (U. of South Africa mandate, 1920)

ALASKA

CANADA

North America

UNITED STATES

MEXICO

CENTRAL AMERICA

GUIANAS

BRAZIL

South America

Atlantic

Pacific

Ocean

National Self-Determination

On the whole the allies of Germany lost more than she did. The Hohen-zollerns and Romanovs lost their thrones along with the Hapsburgs, but, unlike Germany and Russia, the Austro-Hungarian Empire fell apart altogether. The disintegration of Austria-Hungary presented the Western Allies with a problem in constructive statesmanship. For four centuries the leading dynasty of Europe had assembled a congeries of heterogeneous provinces and imposed a certain coherence upon their interrelations. After the Revolution of 1848 that coherence had steadily weakened until little was left of it. Monarchical rule had failed: the alternative was republican federalism. There was need of autonomy for the nationalities in their cultural and local affairs within a parliamentary order strong enough to preserve the established lines of movement of goods and men in that region.

For several reasons, however, this solution did not seem feasible in 1918. There was no personality or party that represented enough elements to provide a binding center for such a system. The inability of some of the nationalities to secure equality had driven their leaders to claim complete political independence. In their efforts to weaken Austria-Hungary, the Allies had accepted the help and committed themselves to the cause of these national leaders. The French hoped that new states created out of former Hapsburg territories would prove grateful friends on the flank of Germany. These tendencies coincided with the doctrine of national self-determination espoused by Wilson.

This doctrine, originally based on the liberal principle of government with the consent of the governed, had become transmuted into the quite different doctrine of the right of each ethnic group, however small or specialized economically, to establish a separate state of its own. Wilson shared with many Americans the impression that national self-determination was the European counterpart of American democracy. From the view that minority groups ought to be treated with fairness, that they ought to have cultural autonomy, and that small nations and states should not be dominated by large, they passed to the view that nationality ought to become the basis of new states. It so happens that nowhere in Europe is it more difficult to draw lines which would enclose each nationality into its own exclusive pocket and which would coincide, even roughly, with lines of economic viability. However the boundaries were drawn, every area would contain several minorities of considerable numbers alongside a "dominant" nationality. Only by jumping like a knight on the chessboard could one assemble realms with fairly homogeneous populations; but then the states would not be compact, and in modern times compact they must be.

Four states were carved out of the imperial body by the treaties of St. Germain (signed Sept. 10, 1919) and Trianon (signed June 4, 1920): Austria and Hungary, much reduced, the new state of Czechoslovakia, and the revived state of Poland. Czechoslovakia was to consist of Bohemia, Moravia, most of

Austrian Silesia, and part of lower Austria. Most of the Polish territory was retrieved from Russia and Germany; from Austria, Poland received Galicia. Three neighboring countries also received large accessions from Austria: Rumania obtained Bukovina; Yugoslavia (an enlarged Serbia) won Bosnia and Herzegovina and the Dalmatian coast of the Adriatic; Italy received southern Tyrol, Trieste, and Istria and rounded out her horn on the Adriatic.

The "succession states" received almost as much from the other partner of the Hapsburg realm, Hungary. Croatia-Slavonia went to Yugoslavia. The Banat area was divided between Yugoslavia and Rumania. Rumania also received the large province of Transylvania. Slovakia became part of the new state of Czechoslovakia. A small strip on the border between Austria and Hungary was transferred to the former. Hungary was reduced by three quarters of her former size. Austria was forbidden to be united to Germany. There were now German minorities in all the succession states and Hungarian minorities in nearly all. Three million Germans were given to Czechoslovakia because they inhabited principally the mountainous areas essential to a strategic defense against Germany; when Rumania was awarded most of the Rumanians in Hungary, two million Hungarians and Germans had to be thrown in too. Finally, Austria and Hungary were to pay reparations and sharply reduce their military establishments.

Bulgaria, the smallest of the allies of the Central Powers, presented the least difficulty to the peacemakers. Under the terms of the Treaty of Neuilly, signed on November 27, 1919, western Thrace and its Aegean coast, which the Bulgarians had wrested from Turkey in 1913, were now transferred to Greece. Smaller cessions were made by Bulgaria to Yugoslavia and Rumania. Bulgaria was to pay 445 million dollars in reparations and reduce her army.

Turkey was the only defeated country that defied the terms of the victors. There the armistice was followed by the beginning of a domestic revolution that eventually led to a renewal of the fighting with Greece and to the overthrow of still another imperial government. By the Treaty of Sèvres, which was accepted by the Sultan on August 20, 1920, the Straits were to be internationalized and the Sultan was to surrender control over lands inhabited by non-Turkish peoples. In Europe, only Constantinople and Adrianople and the district around them remained Turkish. The Armenians and the Arabs were to form independent states. Great Britain was to have the mandates, under the new League of Nations rules (see p. 541), over Mesopotamia and Palestine, and France the mandate over Syria. Greece received not only the greater part of Thrace in Europe but the administration of Smyrna and its hinterland in Asia Minor for five years, after which a plebiscite was to be held to decide whether they were to be Greek or Turkish.

Before the Treaty was drafted and signed, however, the impending dismemberment of Turkey had aroused the vigorous opposition of Turkish nationalists and reformers. Since the turn of the century, liberals and Western-minded army officers had been striving to modernize their country. They had attained their aims only partially in the Young Turk Revolution of 1908. They rose now

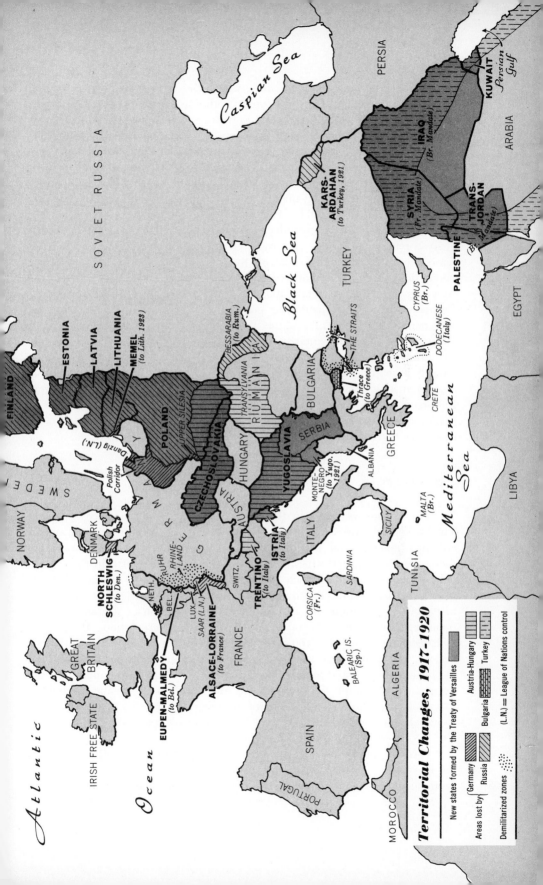

Territorial Changes, 1917–1920

not only to assert the national dignity and the territorial integrity of their country but to reform its government and administration. When a Greek army had landed in 1919 to occupy Smyrna, with the sanction of the Allies, nationalists and army officers in Asia Minor led by Mustapha Kemal Pasha (1881-1938) proclaimed a provisional government and, after prolonged fighting in 1920-22, finally routed the Greeks. The result was that the Allies softened the terms of peace in a new treaty signed at Lausanne on July 24, 1923. Turkey recovered a part of Thrace; there were to be no reparations; and the capitulations, which granted special legal rights for foreigners in Turkey, were abolished, while Turkey promised to introduce reforms to assure them justice in her courts. Smyrna remained Turkish and, by a separate agreement, Turkey and Greece resorted to a drastic method of solving their minority problems. They exchanged populations: over a period of several years, about 1,250,000 Greeks moved from Asia Minor to Greece, while 400,000 Turks moved from Greek territory in Europe to the Turkish districts of Asia Minor. This procedure set a portentous precedent. After the signing of the Treaty of Lausanne, Kemal Pasha and his followers abolished the sultanate and proclaimed a republic. The last Sultan, Mohammed VI, fled his capital on a British ship. The new government launched an ambitious program of political and clerical reform. Thus a fourth empire foundered as a result of the revolutions that followed defeat. The Ottoman Empire went the way of the Hapsburg dynasty, with which it had vied for predominance in Southeastern Europe since the sixteenth century, and of the more recent creations of the Romanovs and the Hohenzollerns.

The League of Nations

The various treaties of 1919-20 were only one part of the peace settlement. The other part—the organization of the League of Nations—was meant not only to supplement the treaties but to compensate for their compromises and shortcomings by introducing a new method, and a new spirit, in the conduct of international relations. Such, at least, was the meaning of the League in the mind of its founder, the President of the United States. The leaders and governments of Great Britain and France did not share Wilson's optimism, although popular opinion did. "If you would have a new spirit among the nations, "Clemenceau observed, "you must begin by having a new spirit within the nations." He worked hard to settle the war issues first, leaving the question of the League to later and separate discussions. But Wilson was adamant. He was determined to commit the twenty-seven Allies to the League, and he could do so only if the provision for it was made an integral part of the treaty which they would all sign. No league, no treaty! Wilson prevailed, and the first part of the Treaty of Versailles outlined the new organization.

Part I of the Treaty opened with the declaration that the "High Contracting Parties . . . agree to this Covenant of the League of Nations" in order "to promote international cooperation and to achieve international peace and security, by the acceptance of obligations not to resort to war, by the prescription of open, just and honorable relations between nations, by the firm establishment of understandings of international law as the actual rule of conduct among Governments, and by the maintenance of justice and a scrupulous respect for all Treaty obligations in the dealings of organized peoples with one another." The principal instruments of the League were to be an Assembly, consisting of representatives of the member states, and a Council, consisting of permanent representatives of the five largest victorious powers—the United States, Great Britain, France, Italy, and Japan—and four (later increased to nine) members elected periodically by the Assembly. Except for procedural matters, the decisions of both Council and Assembly had to be unanimous. The larger body was designed for discussion and debate and the smaller for more active functions. The Council was charged especially with preparing plans for general disarmament and with mediating disputes as they arose, designing and publishing recommendations for peaceful settlement and for action against aggressors or breakers of recognized treaties. If a recommendation for the settlement of a dispute was not unanimous, the member states reserved the right to act according to their individual lights. If it was unanimous (except for the parties in the dispute), the members bound themselves not to make war on the party that accepted the recommendation of the Council. But this commitment was essentially a moral one, for neither Council nor Assembly possessed the means to enforce it. In the final analysis, therefore, the authority of the League rested upon the concerted good will and discipline of its members.

The League was to be the instrument for realizing the more idealistic aims of the peace treaties. It was to supervise plebiscites in disputed territories. In order to protect minorities, the Allies insisted that the new states sign special treaties guaranteeing fair and equal treatment to all their subjects; the enforcement of these treaties devolved upon the League. Wilson opposed the outright annexation by the Allies of the former German colonies. The victorious states were to be the mandatories of these colonies, and they were responsible to the League for their proper management. Colonial peoples were to rise to autonomy and finally to independence by a series of steps.

Given the crucial position of the Council, it was apparent that, in the initial stages at any rate, the full support of the large states was essential to the success of the League. But the lukewarm attitude of the European powers did not bode well; the full support of the United States became all the more necessary.

The Tragedy of Woodrow Wilson

The scene shifted from Paris to Washington. On June 28, President Wilson signed the Treaty of Versailles on behalf of the United States. He also signed a treaty with England and France, pledging mutual defense against German attack in the future. The next day he sailed home to obtain the approval of the Senate, without which no international engagement of the United States is valid. But Wilson did not command the political power that Clemenceau and Lloyd George did. In the Congressional elections of November 1918 he had made an unfortunate appeal to the voters to elect Democratic candidates, thus giving the impending peace negotiations a partisan aspect—and the American electorate often supports the opposition party in elections that fall midway in presidential terms. Wilson had not taken the precaution of including leading members of the Republican party in the Paris negotiations and so committing them to the result. The upshot was that Wilson faced an inimical Republican majority in the Senate, led by Henry Cabot Lodge of Massachusetts (1850-1924), Chairman of the Foreign Relations Committee.

Senator Lodge was bent on destroying, or at least compromising, the prestige of the Democratic President and party, in preparation for the Presidential election of 1920. He was engaged in a difficult maneuver. If the Treaty of Versailles and the League of Nations were to be approved by the Senate, it would have to be done in such fashion as to shed credit upon the Republican party; if they were to be rejected, the odium would have to be made to fall upon the Democratic party. Lodge had the support of groups that were opposed to international commitments. There were senators from the Western and Midwestern states to whom all thought of collaboration with European powers was anathema. German and Irish immigrant groups combined to assail a settlement which profited France and Great Britain. Liberals and radicals thought the peace terms vindictive and the League a mere cabal of the victorious powers.

The Republican leadership proposed to attach a number of reservations to the Treaty—for example, that the United States could withdraw from the

"SEEIN' THINGS"

A critical American comment on the Senate's exaggerated fears of American membership in the League of Nations. Cartoon by Nelson Harding in the Brooklyn Daily Eagle, *February 28, 1919.*

League at will, that Congress had to approve the acceptance of mandated territories, and that the transfer of German rights in Shantung to Japan was disapproved. The proposed reservation that led to the most heated controversy was the amendment attached to Article X of the Covenant. That article read: "The Members of the League undertake to respect and preserve, as against external aggression, the territorial integrity and existing political independence of all Members of the League. In case of any such aggression, the Council shall advise upon the means by which this obligation shall be fulfilled." The reservation stated that the United States would not be bound by Article X "unless, in any particular case, the Congress, which, under the Constitution, has the sole power to declare war or authorize the employment of the military or naval forces of the United States, shall by act or joint resolution so provide." Given the eagerness of the European powers to obtain the cooperation of the United States, Wilson could probably have persuaded the cosignatories to accept these reservations. But he was as rigid and touchy as Lodge was partisan, and he rejected them. The two leaders never met to attempt to adjust their differences.

Under the American Constitution, national elections are held at fixed intervals; it is not possible to dismiss Congress and call a special election to decide particular issues. The President therefore resorted to another expedient. In September 1919, on the eve of the Senate vote on the Treaty, he went on a speaking campaign across the continent in order to mobilize public opinion against the "little band of willful men" in Congress. He exhorted large and often enthusiastic audiences to bring pressure to bear to prevent the "nullification" of the Covenant and the peace terms of the Treaty. His argument was that the League offered a "95 percent guarantee" for maintaining the peace and that it was essential to the future of American democracy:

> . . . if the United States should conceivably . . . stay out of the League of
> Nations, it would stay out at its own cost: we would have to see, since we
> were not going to join our force with other nations, that our force was
> formidable enough to be respected by other nations. We would have to
> maintain a great Army and a great Navy. We would have to do something
> more than that: We would have to concentrate authority to be able to use
> the physical force of the nation quickly upon occasion. All of that is
> absolutely undemocratic in its influence.

In three weeks, President Wilson delivered nearly forty addresses in two dozen cities. After the exhausting negotiations in Paris, the effort proved too much for him. On September 26, he suffered a nervous collapse and a partial stroke of paralysis. With him fell the leadership necessary to save the Treaty. His illness made him still more stubborn. When the Republicans in the Senate moved for acceptance of the Treaty with the reservations appended to it, Wilson asked the Democrats to vote in opposition. Consequently, the Republicans were unable to muster the two-thirds vote stipulated by the Constitution for such actions. On November 19, the Treaty of Versailles and the League of Nations failed of confirmation by a vote of 55 to 39.

Ill and incapacitated, the President tried expedient after expedient to apply pressure on the Senate to reconsider its vote and eliminate the reservations. In the prolonged discussion that followed, it became apparent that a majority of Democrats as well as Republicans, considerably more than two thirds of the Senate, and an overwhelming majority of newspapers favored acceptance of the reservations. But Wilson hoped that the elections of November 1920 would justify him and confound his enemies. The Senate reconsidered the Treaty in February 1920 and approved a similar though somewhat milder set of reservations. But Wilson again advised the Democratic Senators to defeat a treaty so encumbered. Nearly half of them nevertheless voted to ratify the Treaty with the reservations attached to it, but the other half combined with the handful of Republicans who were irreconcilably opposed to it and together they prevented American adherence to the Treaty or to the League.

Congress thereupon tried to establish peace by a joint resolution which simply repealed the declaration of war and reserved to the United States "all the advantages accruing to it under the Treaty of Versailles." This claim to advantages without obligations enraged the President. He vetoed the resolution as "an action which would place ineffaceable stain upon the gallantry and honor" of the Republic. He declared in withering terms that, by rejecting the Treaty, "we have . . . in effect declared that we do not care to take any further risks or to assume any further responsibilities with regard to the freedom of nations or the sacredness of international obligations or the safety of independent peoples. Such a peace with Germany . . . is inconsistent with the dignity of the United States, with the rights and liberties of her citizens, and with the very fundamental conditions of civilization." Eventually, in 1921, the United States signed separate treaties with Germany, Austria, and Hungary.

The Wilsonian adventure was over. The United States had fought the war but dissociated herself from the peace settlement which her own representatives had helped to shape. The American people were puzzled and uncertain. The Midwest was indifferent to European affairs; the Far West looked toward the Pacific rather than toward the Atlantic; the various immigrant groups were concerned with European issues but often took opposite sides. The long bridge that was needed to rejoin America and Europe could be built only by sensitive compromise and in long-range enterprises. After a brief encounter, the United States and Europe still stood back to back.

While the American Senate was debating the Treaty, Germany ratified it, in July 1919, and the European Allies in the following October. The League of Nations was duly convened and organized on January 10, 1920. By the end of the year it had forty-four members, a majority of the self-governing nations of the world. The headquarters of the League were in neutral Switzerland. In Geneva, on Lake Leman, arose an impressive set of buildings, which had the distinction of being the first official home of humankind. In the Assembly, small nations and large, Latin-American, African, and Asian as well as European, were represented equally. But the great powers that were members of the League had joined half against their will, and large and defeated states—Germany and

Russia—had not been admitted to membership. The country whose chief had created the international organization was conspicuous by its absence. The League was born an orphan with poor prospects in life.

The failure of Wilson's work involved also the failure of Clemenceau's. He had obtained the signature of Wilson and Lloyd George to a treaty providing for assistance against a German attack. After the Senate had refused to ratify the Treaty of Versailles, there was no point in submitting for ratification the three-power treaty which was auxiliary to it. Great Britain withdrew her own promise. France felt that she had been deserted. She had to rely upon her own energy to enforce the Treaty of Versailles.

The Atlantic plan of Clemenceau and the international plan of Wilson went aglimmering. The world was to jog along much as before and take its chances with the future. The difficulty was that the world was never to be the same again.

26. *Socialism, Communism, and Fascism*

The peace treaties were drafted and signed, but the aftermath of war was almost as bitter as the war itself. The "social peace" enforced everywhere during the war ended, and all the internal tensions that had accumulated in Europe erupted in an epidemic of violence. For four and a half years the clash of arms had rung on large fronts; it now reverberated on smaller but more numerous battlefields, in factories and mines, on city streets and at railroad junctions. This second "war" lasted almost as long as the first.

Unrest and Conservatism

The World War encouraged a disposition to violence. In the sudden relaxation of peace, the influence of authority receded everywhere, particularly in the former Continental empires, whose collapse left a vacuum of power. Previously peaceful workers and farmers were now hardened men of arms—often, indeed, in Central and Eastern Europe, men *with* arms. Some of them gathered in veterans' organizations which came under extremist leadership. Professional officers had exercised public authority too long to accept easily the anonymity and modesty of civilian life once they were demobilized.

When hostilities ended, in 1918, most countries experienced a brief economic boom. Control of raw materials, production, and prices was lifted and the channels of exchange were reopened. The hunger for consumer goods which had not been produced during the war at first stimulated production and trade. Prices and employment rose together. Soon, however, the effect of the war made itself felt; trade slackened and employment fell. During the war, governments and employers had made concessions to labor by recognizing union leaders and organizations in official dealings and agreeing to wage increases or price limitations. These concessions and controls, and the rationing of necessary goods, had provided a modicum of security for the industrial masses. They were now gradually withdrawn. The sudden demobilization increased the supply of labor while the cessation of war production diminished the opportunities for work. The "full employment" of the war—whether at the front or at home—was over.

Radicalism grew in intensity. Strikes could again be called, and were. Unions raised their demands. Nearly every government had pledged the worker-soldiers an improvement in the standard of living, and the promissory notes were now presented for payment. Disillusionment with the war and with the prospect for a healthy international order strengthened the more advanced wings of the Socialist and Labor parties. The example of Russia was potent. There was much sympathy with the Bolsheviks, whose deeds at home in suppressing other parties were neither well known nor sufficiently appreciated. In some countries, dockers and other transportation workers refused to cooperate in shipping military supplies to counterrevolutionary armies in Russia. The Bolsheviks seemed to have discovered the key to the modern revolution and were more than willing to teach others how to use it.

The victorious countries eventually weathered the postwar difficulties. In the defeated countries, however, extreme parties, military adventurers, and political gangs rioted, staged coups, and tried, sometimes successfully, to overthrow governments. In Germany, Russia, and Hungary, civil strife assumed the scale of campaigns by organized armies. Russia, which had had two revolutions in 1917, endured a civil war which lasted for three years. A series of campaigns, in which her former allies participated directly or indirectly, were engaged over the question of the spread of Bolshevism. From the Rhine to Vladivostok, there was hardly a country or a region for which the end of the fighting did not mean the beginning of internal disorder. The change from war to peace seemed to be a change from military and imperial contests to issues that went down to the roots of government and society: Shall the overthrown monarchies be replaced by democratic republics or by dictatorships? Shall capitalism be curbed or abolished? Shall the land be distributed free to the peasants? Shall socialism be established by force?

The victorious countries were not immune to the pressures of labor and radicalism. In England and France, union leaders took advantage of the resumed freedom to strike. In November 1918 the Labor party of England had withdrawn from the wartime coalition government and adopted a socialist program. For the first time, it proposed the nationalization of railways and mines, the participation of workers in the management of industry, and the assurance of a minimum standard of living to all men. This was a mild and constitutional program, without Marxist overtones, but it was the most advanced program that the Labor party, or any other large English political party, had ever sponsored. In France, the *Confédération Générale du Travail* launched a series of strikes, many of which succeeded in bringing about a rise in wages. Its membership swelled to two and a half million workers. There were plans to call a general strike, which syndicalists hoped might be a prelude to the overthrow of capitalism. A strong wing of the Socialist party advocated a revolution à la Lenin.

Of the large Western countries, the United States had suffered least in the war. Yet even there radical movements grew somewhat in intensity. The Socialist party won several state offices in New York. In 1919 a large strike broke out in the steel industry.

Beneath the wave of radicalism there was a strong undertow of conservatism. In each of the victorious countries, elections held immediately after the war had weakened liberal and labor parties and strengthened the conservative groups. In France the coalition of all parties—the *Union Sacrée* of the years of crisis—broke up into liberal-socialist and conservative-nationalist blocs. It was the conservative bloc that was returned to power after the elections of 1919, under the leadership of Clemenceau. Its policy was to combat socialism and collect a large indemnity from Germany. The British general election of December 1918 returned a largely Conservative "coalition" government, under Lloyd George. Labor captured only 61 seats out of approximately six hundred, although it became for the first time the leading opposition party.

In the United States, the Democratic party had lost control of both houses of Congress to the more conservative Republicans in 1918. Two years later the Republicans won the presidency as well, with the election of Warren G. Harding. The resistance to radicalism stiffened as the economy revived. American industrial magnates combined with politicians in an attack upon the "reds" which quickly degenerated into violence and hysteria. Strikes and picketing led to clashes between workers and troops. The federal Department of Justice hunted radicals and the Post Office hindered the circulation of even liberal publications. In 1920 the state of New York went so far as to expel socialists elected to the legislature, in violation of constitutional principles.

The British government countered radicalism with many promises and a few measures of reform. Old-age pensions were increased somewhat to meet rising prices, rents were restricted, hours of work in mines were reduced, and industrial courts were established. Although a royal commission supported the Labor party's recommendation that the mines be nationalized, the government ignored the proposal. The French government, relying on anticipated indemnities from Germany, made lavish pledges to compensate war victims and their dependents and to reconstruct destroyed areas. A new law limited the hours of work per day to eight. The strike threats were dealt with boldly. Thousands of railway men were dismissed from their jobs and the *Confédération Générale* in the end hesitated to call its vaunted general strike. Its membership dropped quickly to the original 600,000 of prewar days.

In comparison with the condition of the victors, that of the defeated countries bordered on anarchy. Government finance collapsed in the former Hohenzollern and Hapsburg Empires, and with it the value of their currency. The disintegration or sudden demobilization of huge armies, the slackening of military discipline as well as of political authority, the mood of defeat and anger, and the dim prospects of new careers combined to produce a condition of disorder. Soldiers came home to find less security and food than they had had at the front. Instead of public recognition they met disillusionment, even reproach. Thousands of professional officers and noncommissioned officers had no place in states compelled by treaty to diminish their armies. These officers were drawn particularly from aristocratic or conservative classes which felt themselves threatened not only by socialism or Bolshevism but even by liberal republicanism. Finally, adventurers, soldiers of fortune, unscrupulous politicians, and criminals perceived in the atmosphere of desperation and disorder an opportunity to snatch power by ruse, violence, and demagogy.

Ancient institutions foundered, monarchies disappeared, aristocracies fell or retreated, and old bureaucracies lost their grip on administration, taxation, and justice. The conservative parties stood on the defensive. Ever since the sixties, when aristocrats and monarchs had accepted the forms of constitutionalism, they had done everything in their power to dilute its substance. The result was that liberalism had not struck deep roots. There were only a few regions, such as Czechoslovakia, where the professional and middle classes were committed to liberal policies.

This was the legacy of the imperial regimes. Their political successors were, broadly speaking, two groups of parties which had been critical of militarism and advocated political and social reform. Like French democracy in 1792, these parties came into their own in a time of crisis. The Center party of Germany and the Christian (Catholic) Socialist party of Austria were active in securing democratic and republican constitutions and welfare measures for the poorer classes. In Italy the Catholic party, renamed the Popular party in 1919, was led by an able organizer, the priest Luigi Sturzo (1870-1959), who advocated radical agrarian reform. These parties were particularly strong in rural districts. In the urban districts, whether Catholic or Protestant, the leading groups were often the Socialist or Social Democratic parties. In Germany and in most of the other defeated and succession states, the socialists formed the largest single party and often shared the reins of government with other reform parties. Since the middle classes were weak or intimidated by monarchical and aristocratic groups, the socialists had become the principal carriers of liberal democracy. In the course of time, their social program had become one of broad reform. But the collapse of the conservative monarchies and the success of Bolshevism inspired a strong wing of socialists to revive the program of radical opposition to capitalism and to adopt revolutionary tactics. A serious split loomed in the socialist movement.

Communism vs. Socialism

The Second International (see p. 431) had been all but shattered by the war. A conference to reconstitute it was held in Berne, Switzerland, early in 1919 and attended by delegates of most of the socialist parties of Europe, including the non-Bolsheviks of Russia. The conference rebuked the Social Democratic party of Germany for its failure to take a more critical position on the war policies of its government, notably for its failure to protest the treaties of Brest-Litovsk and Bucharest and to press for the return of Alsace-Lorraine to France. It endorsed the League of Nations and proposed that the delegates be chosen by parliaments rather than appointed by governments. It insisted that the League impose mediation and arbitration in all disputes whatever, "including those considered to be of vital interest to the power or honor of the States."

The majority of the conferees wished to repudiate Bolshevism, to reaffirm the principles of liberal democracy, to make socialization conditional upon the agreement of a majority of the people, and to subject any future socialist government to democratic control. Kautsky protested that Bolshevism created "a new militarism." Arthur Henderson (1863-1935) of England, who had visited Russia, said, "I have been able to observe that Bolshevism is nothing but oppression, violence, and terror." To the German socialist Eduard Bernstein the Bolsheviks were "the true counter-revolutionaries in Russia; they will kill the revolution." A strong wing, however, contended that information about Russia was scanty and that condemnation of Bolshevism would encourage reactionaries, justify intervention in Russia, and dishearten revolutionary elements in other countries.

The result was that no vote was taken. The following August, at another conference, held in Lucerne, the machinery of the new International was launched and a constitution adopted. But the old fissures reappeared. This indecision discouraged both wings, and at the next congress, held in Geneva in 1920, attendance was so reduced that no further meetings were called. Member parties were split down the middle. Russia refused to accept the visit of a commission of inquiry. No funeral oration was spoken, but the Second (socialist) International was dead. As it went down, the Third (communist) International, or Comintern, came up.

On January 24, 1919, two days before the Berne conference met, Lenin had issued an invitation to all socialist parties to send representatives to Moscow for the purpose of forming a more radical organization. He insisted that "the world revolution" had made "rapid and enormous progress" and pointed to "the danger which this revolution runs of being strangled by the alliance of capitalist states organized against the Revolution under the hypocritical flag of the League of Nations. . . . This is the epoch of the decomposition and break-up of the world capitalist system, which will mean the break-up of European culture in general, if capitalism, with its irreconcilable antagonisms, is not destroyed. . . . The present task of the working class is the immediate seizure of State power."

The Moscow conference was held early in March. The Western parties that were loyal to Berne did not put in an appearance. The representatives of those Western factions sympathetic to the Bolsheviks found it difficult to travel to Moscow. The conference was attended by two dozen representatives of parties in Eastern and Central Europe and Scandinavia. The Spartacists, the extreme radical group in Germany, instructed their representative to prevent a split in the labor movement by opposing the formation of a rival international.

He was, however, won over by the contagious enthusiasm of the Eastern radicals.

On March 10 the conference issued a manifesto "To the Proletarians of the Whole World," which was later described as a "second *Communist Manifesto*." The latter-day rebels claimed the full inheritance of Marx and Engels. "In spite of all," they insisted, "the development at bottom went the way forecast" by the first *Manifesto*. "The epoch of the last decisive battle came later than the apostles of the social revolution expected and wished. But it has come."

Homage to Marx and Engels did not preclude modification of their theories. The original *Communist Manifesto* had implicitly accepted liberal democratic institutions; the new one proposed to replace them with the Soviet system. "Communism . . . repudiates the possibility of winning over the parliaments; its aim is to destroy parliamentarianism." The Communists were to establish "scouting parties in the parliamentary institutions of the bourgeoisie in order to facilitate this task of destruction." The old *Manifesto* had pleaded for cooperation with all popular parties and for the adjournment of revolution until the proletariat formed a majority of the nation; the new broke decisively with all radicals who did not accept the policy of immediate overthrow. The first *Manifesto* had conceived of the revolution as a chain of independent revolutions in each country; the second ignored national boundaries and placed control of the revolutionary movement in the hands of the Russian Bolsheviks. Under the rules—the "Twenty-one Points"—formulated at the second congress, held in July 1920, the central committee of each party exercised a close supervision not only over ordinary members but particularly over officials and leaders. The party press—periodicals and other publications—was strictly controlled, and the editors were allowed no freedom of criticism, dissent, or deviation from the policy of the party. Communist members of any parliament were equally subject to the orders of the central committee. The open or legal organization was matched by an "illegal apparatus," ready to act at "the decisive moment" of revolution.

The individual parties were instructed to worm their way into trade unions, cooperatives, and other organizations of working people, forming within them "cells" of members "completely subordinated to the party." They had to break with meliorist or evolutionary tendencies and to remove comrades tainted with such tendencies from "all the responsible posts in the labor movement (party organization, editorship, labor unions, parliamentary factions, cooperatives, municipalities, etc.)." On this ground, the International proscribed such prominent socialists as Filippo Turati and G. Modigliani of Italy, Karl Kautsky of Germany, Rudolf Hilferding of Austria, Morris Hillquit of the United States, Jean Longuet—the grandson of Karl Marx—of France, and Ramsay MacDonald of Great Britain. It engaged in periodic" purges" of leaders and comrades who had fallen from grace.

Finally, the International assumed control over its constituent parties. Their very name was not their own. They all had to call themselves "Communist Party of such and such a country, section of the Third International. . . ." Programs of action had to be submitted for approval to the next congress of the International. Each party had to pledge itself to "render every possible assistance to the Soviet Republics in their struggle against all counter-revolutionary forces."

By compelling the old parties to take an unequivocal stand on the Twenty-one Points, the Third International split radical and labor organizations everywhere. In every country of Europe, America, and Asia, sizable segments of the Marxist movement formed separate parties and assumed the name and policy of Communism. Many parties remained open to anyone who professed to be a Communist, but the membership was always directed by an inner core of "professional" revolutionists. The influence of the International varied in inverse proportion to the distance from Moscow. France, England, and the United States were little affected. The Communists captured the bulk of the American Marxists, but they were a small group to begin with. They attracted few members in England. They won over a majority of the French party, but revolutionary possibilities were not good in France.

The Independent Labor party of England voiced the reaction of Western socialists to Bolshevism in a statement of December 1919:

> The weakness of the Socialist movement cannot be made good by Revolution, which with a Dictatorship may succeed for a time, but which in the end has to base itself on public acceptance. . . .

The statement then criticized the Soviet system:

> . . . the electors vote for a man as an engineer, or a miner, etc., and he governs as a citizen. . . . The Socialist elector whose intelligence is equal to building up the Socialist State must vote as a citizen and not merely as a workman belonging to a certain trade, and with a full knowledge of all that Socialism means. . . . The Soviet System necessitates a method of indirect election so that the central governing authority has no direct responsibility to the people for its acts.
>
> The elimination of the bourgeois parasitic class will take place by economic means as we approach to socialism, and it cannot be done effectually in any other way.

Russia was no example for other countries:

> What has happened in Russia has been done in a country whose economic structure was smashed by war and by revolution, and under famine conditions, and how it would have worked under any other conditions it is impossible to say.

The party denied the necessity of a "proletarian dictatorship" as a transition from capitalism to socialism. In most democratic countries, the statement asserted, an attempt to establish such a dictatorship would lead only to the "massacre [of socialists], not to revolution."

In Germany and Italy, Austria and Hungary, Socialists and Communists confronted each other not only with words but with arms. There, as in Western countries, the Communist parties were often minority groups, but they were stimulated by the presence of greater opportunities and encouraged by political disintegration. Russia provided both inspiration and funds. Within a few months after the Armistice, the activists made good their threat of revolution.

The Weimar Republic

The first German government formed after the abdication of the Kaiser consisted of the two largest factions of the Socialist party—the Majority Socialists, who advocated social reform and the eventual socialization of industry by liberal democratic methods, and the Independents, who hesitated between reform and revolution and between parliamentarianism and dictatorship. In the elections for a constituent assembly held two months later, in January 1919, the Majority Socialists won nearly 40 percent of the votes and the more radical Independents polled only 5 percent. A third and smaller group—the Spartacus party, named after the leader of a slave rebellion in ancient Rome—refused to participate in the election. The Spartacists, who later assumed the name of Communists, advocated revolutionary action against capitalism.

Hoping to impel the Majority Socialists toward an energetic policy of socialization, the Independents resigned from the government and joined the Spartacists in opposition. The Majority Socialists thereupon formed a coalition with the Center and with the newly formed Democratic party. The fruit of this collaboration was the constitution adopted at Weimar on July 31, 1919.

The new constitution made an uneasy compromise between federalism and centralism, legislative and executive power. Its drafters shored up the central power in order to counteract the weakening effect of the loss of territory and of the appearance of centrifugal tendencies. The *Reichsrat*, the upper chamber of the federal legislature, was to consist of representatives of the states in proportion to their size and population. But, unlike the American Senators, the *Reichsrat* delegates were not to be elected but appointed from among the cabinet officers of the constituent states. The constitution assigned broad functions to the states but empowered the central government to "advise" them how to carry out federal laws.

The elections to the *Reichstag*, or lower chamber, were by universal suffrage. The constitution adopted proportional representation instead of the Anglo-American system of single-member constituencies. The citizen voted not for a person but for a party list. The total votes of a party determined the number of seats it won, but the allocation of seats was made by the party organization, which set up the order of its candidates. The individual deputy had no way of appealing in his own name to the voters, and the voters no power to punish or reward their representatives. The citizen was theoretically compensated for the lack of direct contact with legislators by the power of initiative and recall, but this power could at best be used seldom, and only in matters of national concern. The proportional system ensured the representation of minority parties, but it made for coalition governments and dispersed and obscured political responsibility.

A comprehensive bill of rights guaranteed the inviolability of the home and the secrecy of mail, telephone, and telegraph communications, as well as freedom of the press and speech. The constitution took the novel step of supplementing individual with social rights. Citizens were guaranteed the right to education and to employment, even if protecting these rights involved making inroads on the right of private property and enterprise. The power of the state was considerably expanded. The constitution assigned duties as well as rights to the individual and rights as well as duties to society and the state. The right of citizenship was based not, as in older models, largely on birth, but on conditions which were to be set, and could be changed, by the legislature. In emergencies, the executive—a president elected for seven years—also might change the conditions of citizenship.

Article 48 was destined to acquire a sad fame: "If public safety and order in the German Commonwealth is materially disturbed or endangered, the National President may take the necessary measures to restore public safety and order, and, if necessary to intervene by force of arms. . . . To this end he may temporarily suspend, in whole or in part, the fundamental rights" of personal liberty—free speech, the inviolability of the home, the privacy of communications, freedom of association, and even private property. In older, liberal countries, such actions had occasionally been condoned when there was common agreement that an emergency actually existed, but no such blanket power had been given in advance to the executive alone. Article 48 concluded with the promise that "the details will be regulated by a national law." The promise was never fulfilled, with the result that no safeguards were erected against abuse of power. The Article did state that the president must inform the *Reichstag* of his action at once, but otherwise discretion was left to him.

From the beginning, the German republic had to fight for its life against extremists of the Left and the Right. As in Russia, soviets, or councils, were elected at the end of 1918 by workingmen and soldiers and soon came to exercise much influence on affairs. As in Russia, the socialist leaders formed a government only after the councils of the capital had given their approval. But there the resemblance ended. In Russia, the Bolsheviks were able to ingratiate themselves with the soviets; they made their coup after they had obtained a leading position in the councils. But the German Communists—the Spartacists —never obtained the predominant influence in the councils, which on the whole supported the non-Communist policy of the Majority Socialists. Nor did they, like the Bolsheviks, obtain the support of substantial bodies of organized soldiery. The result was an attempted coup with Communist aims and French revolutionary methods of mass demonstration and street warfare.

In January 1919, two weeks before the election of the Constituent Assembly, the Spartacists assembled 200,000 workers and converged upon the

Chancellery in Berlin. At the last moment they hesitated to issue the order to attack. The government was better prepared; it had come to an agreement with army officers in various parts of Germany to organize "spontaneously" bands of ex-soldiers, adventurers, and conservative youths. These so-called Free Corps took over the campaign against the reds. More interested in destroying radicalism than in protecting republicanism, the Free Corps seized the Spartacist leaders, Karl Liebknecht (1871-1919) and Rosa Luxemburg (1870-1919), and handed them over to reactionary officers, who murdered them. The Free Corps descended upon the proletarian quarters of Berlin and exacted many lives. The Spartacist movement collapsed, but the government's alliance with military elements persisted.

Communist adventurism and reactionary violence had become a pattern of politics. In Munich a socialist leader, Kurt Eisner, had organized a radical regime upon the abdication of the King of Bavaria in November 1918. His hope was to undermine conservative institutions and prestige rather than to consolidate a proletarian dictatorship. By late February 1919, opposition to his regime had increased, and Eisner decided to resign. He was on his way to the Diet to do so when he was murdered by a reactionary Junker. The act aroused proletarian protests throughout Germany. The federal government came to depend still more heavily on militarist forces to crush whatever revolutionary threats survived. In the month following Eisner's murder, troops dispatched from the capital easily snuffed out the Soviet Republic in Bavaria. The Communists, encouraged and financed by the Third International, went so far as to hire criminals to increase revolutionary "opportunities" by adding to the disorder and disturbance, particularly in the vital industrial region of the Ruhr, but the federal government prevailed. The cost was a resurgent militarism and the sacrifice of 15,000 lives, which naturally deepened the divisions in the ranks of the Left.

How strong the Left could be when its ranks held together was soon demonstrated. On March 14, 1920, a group of monarchist officers marched Free Corps into Berlin, seized the government buildings, and sent the ministers flying from the capital. The government, removed to Stuttgart, appealed to the laboring masses to paralyze the country:

> Strike! Lay aside your work and throttle this military dictatorship. With every means, fight for the preservation of the republic. Cease all dissension. There is only one way to prevent the return of William II. Paralyze the economic life. Let no hand stir, let no proletarian help the military dictatorship. Let there be a general strike along the whole line. Proletarians, unite!

The response was virtually unanimous. All the various factions of the Left rallied and enlisted the sympathy of middle-class and liberal groups as well. Transportation, industry, and public utilities ceased to function. The insurrection collapsed without the firing of a single shot. Within a week the conspirators fled and the government was back in Berlin. Militarism, standing alone, proved helpless, a lesson which was not lost on the more perceptive officers.

This was the moment when a united non-Communist Left might still have retrieved the opportunity to pursue a common program. But the government declined to use this great power to turn about and destroy the political influence of the military and the Free Corps. In the first election under the new constitution, in June 1920, the Independents gained votes at the expense of the Majority Socialists. Together, the two parties mustered fewer votes than in the preceding year. The middle-class parties, headed by the Center, formed a new government, and the socialists never returned to power. By the agreement of all parties, however, the socialist Friedrich Ebert (1871-1925) remained President of the Republic until his death in 1925.

The Inflation Revolution in Germany

The Weimar Republic survived the direct attacks from the Left and the Right in 1919-20. But worse troubles were ahead. The economic tensions which characterized the whole Western world in the following years were intensified in Germany by the huge government debt and the reparations bill. The imperial government had financed the war less by taxes and more by loans than other governments had. The Allied victims of a German triumph were to repay the sums that Germany had borrowed from her own citizens. But Germany did not triumph, and she now owed, in addition to the war debt, reparations to the European Allies. The total of the reparations debt was not set until May 1921, but under the Treaty of Versailles, as we have seen, Germany was to pay five bil ion dollars on account. She was also to make deliveries of coal, machines, and timber to France, ships to Great Britain, and livestock to wasted Belgian farms.

In March 1921, Germany announced that she had paid the interim bill, but the Allies valued the goods at less than half the amount due and declared Germany in default. The zone of occupation was enlarged and taxes were imposed on German exports to Allied countries. The reparations total was then fixed at 132 billion gold marks, of which 52 percent was to go to France, 22 to the British Empire, 10 to Italy, 8 to Belgium, and the remaining 8 percent to smaller Allied powers. Payments were to be made by fixed annuities of 2 billion marks and 26 percent of the value of exports.

There were economists who believed that Germany could not pay these large sums without destroying her value as a buyer and producer and thus harming the Allied countries as well as herself. As events proved, the Allies were not averse eventually to scaling down the sums. Germans were divided on the issue of "fulfillment." Liberal and democratic groups felt that an honest effort should be made to meet the bills as far as possible, and that such an effort would strengthen the bid for future reductions. Nationalist, militarist, and reactionary groups protested against fulfillment, although they did not believe that the country was in a position to defy the Allies. How were the costs to be apportioned among the various classes? How was Germany to regain economic stability? The answer to these questions was contained in one of the most re-markable economic revolutions of modern times.

The charges of debt and reparations could have been met fairly only by heavy taxation bearing proportionately upon the classes possessed of wealth. The German government resorted instead to the printing press, on the advice of in-dustrialists and financiers. These groups preferred inflation to taxation, not only because they did not wish to pay high taxes, but also because they saw in infla-tion a means of rapid enrichment. As the value of the German mark tumbled, private credit dropped with it, and capitalists transferred much of their holdings abroad. German currency disappeared beyond the clouds. In June 1923 an American dollar was worth 150,000 paper marks; in November it brought 4,200,000,000,000. Money figures became meaningless. Wages went up too, but not so fast as the value of the mark came down. Between the time a house-wife left for a store with enough money to buy the necessary groceries and the

Runaway inflation in Germany. A two-billion mark note of 1923.
(A billion, according to the German system, is a million million.)
THE CHASE MANHATTAN BANK MUSEUM OF MONEYS OF THE WORLD

time she reached the counter, the price was likely to have flown out of sight. For the working classes the distress amounted to near-starvation. Members of the middle and professional classes who had fixed salaries or incomes were even worse off. The value of mortgages, government bonds, insurance policies, sav-ings accounts, bank deposits—everything that bore a fixed interest—was wiped out.

The rural population suffered less than the urban. As industrial production waned, country people refused to give up their produce to the townsmen. In some regions, the normal exchanges between village and town deteriorated or ceased entirely. The farmer paid his mortgages with diluted currency, and the price of both his real property and his produce fell. But even the modest farmer did better than the formerly substantial middle-class person. And he still could eat.

The only gainers from this catastrophe were the speculative capitalists. Inflation made it possible for producers to undersell their foreign competitors abroad. Manipulators on the stock market and dealers in foreign exchange grew enormously wealthy. Real-estate operators bought the land and buildings of impoverished holders. Manufacturers acquired the plants of their less agile rivals. One capitalist, Hugo Stinnes, assembled an industrial empire of dozens of factories and mines. The *Reichsbank* granted large credits to business and industrial firms, which used them to extend and improve their plants, and then paid off their debts with depreciated money. Such loans were virtually gifts from the national treasury out of the property of less fortunate owners. The result of the inflation was that Germany became a society consisting largely of two classes, the very rich and the very poor. She preferred ruining her middle classes and starving the workers to paying for the war.

In December 1922 the reparations committee declared Germany in default on coal and timber deliveries. A cabinet of businessmen and industrial experts, headed by Wilhelm Cuno (1876-1933), suspended all deliveries to the Allies. Raymond Poincaré (1860-1934), who had become Premier of France in 1922, was determined to force Germany to pay. In January 1923 a Franco-Belgian army marched into the Ruhr district, the industrial heart of Germany, and proceeded to siphon off coal production without the sanction of the other Allies. The aim was not merely to collect reparations. Among the supporters of the conservative bloc in office in France was the *Comité des Forges*, an association of powerful metallurgists. The *Comité* wished to prevent a possible combination of German coal-mine owners and the Swedish iron-ore magnates that would reduce the value of the iron produced in Lorraine.

The German government called on the people of the Ruhr to engage in passive resistance and to cease producing. It promised to indemnify both employers and workers. There was some popular response to this call, and the French army imprisoned and exiled a number of inhabitants. But the resistance was not fully effective, and the mines continued to operate. The French squeezed out goods worth 490 million gold marks in a little over a year and a half, but they had to spend 184 million to do it. Having assumed extraordinary obligations in the Ruhr, the German government speeded up the printing of money and bloated the currency to the bursting point.

The crisis provided a field day for extremists. The Communists plotted revolution. Among the many other extremist groups that arose in the wake of the war was the Nationalist Socialist German Workers' party, better known as the Nazis (from *Nazional*). The Nazis were a small band which professed socialist ideals but stressed chauvinism and authoritarianism and blamed the ills of

Germany on the Jews. Their leader was Adolf Hitler (1889-1945), a product of prewar Austrian provincial anti-Semitism, who had served as a corporal in the German army. After demobilization, Hitler worked as a spy and propagandist for the army. In 1923 he received the support of General Ludendorff in a plot to seize the government of Bavaria. On November 9, 1923, the wartime dictator and the Austrian corporal, at the head of several hundred Nazis, marched from a beer hall in Munich toward the center of town. Near the royal palace, government troops opened fire and scattered the rebels. Ludendorff was taken prisoner but shortly released; Hitler received a five-year prison sentence, of which he served less than a year. The "Beer Hall *Putsch*" had failed.

The French occupation of the Ruhr aroused opposition not only in Germany but also abroad, for it smacked of imperialism. Poincaré's policy displeased Great Britain, whose leaders hoped that Germany might be revived as a customer and weakened as a competitor if the inflationary measures which enabled her to undersell countries with more stable currencies were ended. Britain had often implicitly encouraged German reluctance to meet the reparations payments and sought to obtain an agreement by which both German reparations and Allied debts to the United States would be wiped out. While the American government refused to agree to cancel the debts of the Allies, American investment houses were eager to extend credits to Germany, provided that reparations were scaled down and the mark stabilized. Thus France was isolated. Purchases of French goods slowed down. It was the franc's turn to tumble.

Both the French and the German people had had enough of the game of defiance. In May 1924, Poincaré and the conservatives were decisively defeated by the *Cartel des Gauches*, a coalition of liberal and democratic parties. Edward Herriot (1872-1957), the leader of the Radical Socialists, became Prime Minister. He reversed the militaristic policies of his predecessor. In the same month, a general election weakened the extreme parties across the Rhine.

A reparations committee under the chairmanship of Charles G. Dawes, an American banker, worked out a compromise in 1924. It fixed reparations payments on a rising scale from one to two and a half billion marks a year. Allied agents were to supervise German revenues, with discretionary power to change the payments. Germany was granted a foreign loan of 800 million gold marks, most of which was subscribed in the United States. These measures pulled Germany out of bankruptcy. The inflated currency was replaced by a new *Rentenmark*, secured theoretically by a mortgage on all the land and industry of the country, exchangeable for one trillion of the old marks. This deflation confirmed the repudiation of the internal debt, both public and private, and the destruction of the savings and capital of the *rentier* class accomplished by the inflation.

Civil War in Russia

While the turmoil in Germany was compounded of nationalistic and military as well as economic elements, the struggles of Russia had the aspect of an international conflict between social orders. Capitalists, landlords, aristocrats, and military groups bitterly fought not only the attempts to spread Bolshevism to Central Europe and Germany but the consolidation of Bolshevism in Russia herself. The Western Allies encouraged and assisted anti-Bolshevik efforts. Civil war in Russia, revolutionary coups and overturns in Hungary and Austria, and a full-scale war in Poland were the principal incidents of this international struggle. In the process, new movements of a decidedly militaristic and chauvinistic nature struck root on the Continent.

The Bolshevik government emerged from the war with Germany early in 1918 only to find itself engaged in civil war. Its power was at first restricted to the great cities, and its claims were challenged in many parts of the country. In the Ukraine, the large "White" army, consisting of czarist officers and Cossacks, established an independent government under General Anton Denikin (1872-1947) which penetrated to within 250 miles of Moscow. In Siberia, legions of Czech soldiers, formed from among Austro-Hungarian prisoners of war, started marching toward the Pacific, meaning eventually to join the Allies in Europe; in the collapse of authority in Russia, they seized control of most of the Trans-Siberian Railway. Admiral Alexander Kolchak (1875-1920) commanded an anti-Bolshevik Russian force in Siberia. In the Baltic areas and elsewhere, smaller forces were in the field against the Bolsheviks.

The Allies, hoping to regain Russia as an ally, assisted the anti-Bolshevik forces with money and supplies. President Wilson was reluctant to intervene, but Japan's insistence on penetrating into Siberia forced him to change his mind, lest the Japanese gain control of northern Asia and place China under subjection. Between April and August 1918, the Japanese landed 60,000 troops in Vladivostok, the Americans 8000, and the other Allies smaller contingents. A smaller British force landed in the port of Murmansk on the Barents Sea to protect war materiel from falling into the hands of the Germans, who were in a position to extend their occupation.

The Bolsheviks responded to this emergency with a three-pronged campaign against the counterrevolution. In the course of 1918 they tightened their grip on the economy, improvised a new army, and prepared to launch the Third International in order to stimulate sympathy abroad and foment revolutions in nearby countries.

They had begun their domestic reforms by giving workers a voice in management. This measure, the abolition of the profit system, and the drop in prices all but stopped production and generally unsettled conditions. As the fighting countries had introduced "war socialism," the Bolshevik government appealed to "war communism." It nationalized without compensation all plants employing more than ten workers and using mechanical power. It hired managers and placed them under the supervision of party officials. Labor was mobilized and assigned to jobs by command. The peasants were compelled to give up their surplus food at fixed prices. The government bought all goods and then sold them in its own stores and cooperatives. It rationed consumption, favoring industrial workers and soldiers. As the supply of goods diminished and the government increased its printed money, prices were so inflated as to make money all but valueless. Most transactions took the form of primitive barter. Business was virtually at a standstill.

To replace the old army and its officer corps, the government called into being the "Red Army," under its strict control. The first soldiers of this army were volunteers. Soon, however, the Bolsheviks took a leaf out of the traditional book: they imposed conscription on all adult males and abolished the election of officers. Many officers of the imperial army returned to service. At the side of the officers stood political commissars who watched their conduct and indoctrinated the troops. Within a year and a half, the Red Army had five million men, although it used only a tenth of these in active fighting. In Leon Trotsky the army found an energetic and imaginative commander.

It was, however, favorable circumstances as much as military effort that saved the Bolsheviks. Their enemies could not combine and synchronize their efforts, for the liberals and socialists among them were at odds with the conservative and military elements. A rival government was formed in Siberia, but it soon fell under the control of the reactionary Admiral Kolchak, who ousted the socialist ministers. The peasants had resented the food requisitions of the Reds, but they resented even more the attempts of some of the Whites to return their farms to the landlords. The Whites developed also an extreme chauvinistic propaganda and indulged in robbery and massacres of minorities, particularly Jews. The intervention of the Allies was sporadic and fitful. With neither the will nor the ability to mount a great offensive of their own, they gave money and supplies to the Whites. French sailors sent to the Black Sea mutinied in protest; British dockers refused to load supplies going to Russian Whites. The Allied intervention was on a smaller scale than the war of Austria and Prussia against revolutionary France in 1792 or the campaign of Russia against the Hungarian republic in 1848.

In the circumstances, the Bolsheviks won an easy victory. They had the advantage of interior fighting lines and the support of patriotic officers who resented the intrusion of the foreigners. In a disconnected series of local battles on a dozen swiftly moving fronts, the Red Army disposed in 1919-20 of most of the White armies and governments. It drove back the northern White army which threatened Petrograd. Kolchak's army, which had advanced into eastern Russia, was defeated and the leader executed. The Reds pushed the southern White army into the Crimea, on the shores of the Black Sea, whence French ships took 135,000 officers and refugees into exile. The Allies quickly withdrew their troops from Russian soil; by the end of 1920, only Japan retained a foothold in Vladivostok.

The last confrontation between the hosts of capitalism and those of Communism occurred in Poland. Polish nationalists were ambitious to restore the ample boundaries of 1772, which included much of the Ukraine and White Russia. Karl Marx had supported these claims in the day when czarism was the heart of European conservatism. In the spring of 1920, Poland declared war on Russia and, in association with White Russian generals, opened a full-size campaign. Slicing quickly into the Ukraine, the Poles captured the Ukrainian capital of Kiev and the Lithuanian capital of Vilna. The Bolsheviks counterattacked effectively. By August they in their turn stood at the borders of Poland. There they had to choose; they could obtain a favorable peace guaranteeing their frontier, or they could try to take Warsaw and assist the Polish Communists and other radicals in setting up a "proletarian dictatorship"; with luck, perhaps they might revive the revolution in Germany and Hungary.

Hardheaded politicians, like Lenin, were chary of this adventure, which would evoke active intervention by other states. The more romantic revolutionaries prevailed. A new drive brought the Russian army to the outskirts of Warsaw. It also brought a French military staff posthaste to Poland to direct the defense. Meanwhile, no radical group in Poland thought the moment when the country was being invaded propitious for a revolution. Their political hopes frustrated, their lines strung out too thinly, their supplies lagging, the Russians faltered. They were repulsed, and the Poles again penetrated Russia's borders. The two sides had discovered the limits of their strength. The disputed territory was divided between the contenders. Both sides were dissatisfied with their partial gains and yet relieved of their greatest fears. On March 18, 1921, Poland and the Soviet Union signed the Treaty of Riga. The White generals, the last in the field, abandoned their resistance to the Bolsheviks and went abroad to plot future campaigns.

With the end of the Polish war and the uprisings, "war communism" passed into history. Under its regime the Russian economy had deteriorated sharply. Production figures had dropped to less than a fifth of prewar levels. The government could not distribute efficiently the little that was being produced. The old personnel of managers, foremen, engineers, and bureaucrats either were not cooperating, in resentment of their reduction to the rank and wages of workingmen, or had insufficient authority to enforce their counsel. Whether the breakdown was due primarily to the ravages of a long war and civil strife or to the difficulties inherent in the sudden introduction of extreme Communism, the effect was overwhelming. Denied industrial goods and suspicious of the highly inflated rubles issued by the government, the peasants resisted, often by force, the requisition of food. They resorted to the most effective of defenses: they produced only as much as they needed for their own consumption, thus starving the cities. In the summer of 1920, a bitter drought ravaged the rich fields of the southwest; most villages now had no more food than the nearby cities. American relief organizations fed millions of people for months but could hardly make up for the huge lack. In the winter of 1920-21 there were peasant outbreaks which assumed the proportions of near-rebellions, and industrial strikes broke out. In the spring of 1921, the sailors of Kronstadt rose against the government. (It was Kronstadt, ironically, that in 1917 supplied part of the military force with which the Bolsheviks had ousted the Kerensky government.) The rising was suppressed, but "war communism" was at an end.

Its place was taken in 1921 by the New Economic Policy (NEP)—a blend of individual enterprise and state supervision. To stimulate agricultural production, the government made large concessions to the peasants. Wholesale requisitions gave place to a moderate land tax, first paid in produce and later in money. The rest of the produce might be sold in the open market, at competitive prices. Peasants were soon allowed to lease land and hire labor. They could thus rise, by industry and shrewd management, above the level of the mass.

The government permitted enterprisers to open stores and set up small factories. The larger plants were withdrawn from the control of their working forces. The government retained the direction of the heaviest and largest industries. It organized trusts in steel, textiles, and other industries, much in the fashion of capitalist combines, except that they were more comprehensive and held official monopolies in their field. Banking, credit, and foreign trade were also kept within the sphere of the government. Other plants were leased by individuals for private operation and profit. Both government and private plants were to compete in the market for labor, materials, and customers. They were to sell their products in the market and charge competitive prices even to government agencies. This meant that the labor as well as the price market must be fluid. The military organization of labor was brought to an end, along with equal pay. Workmen would henceforth be paid according to skill or amount of labor expended, or by piece. Unions, too, had to be refurbished and strengthened in order to give their members bargaining power *vis-à-vis* their new employers.

All this made it necessary to restore freedom of trade and a stable currency. The new currency was based, in the conventional way, on a stock of precious metals and notes which would bring in money at a stated future date. The government ceased printing money indiscriminately and sought to deflate and stabilize prices by curtailing its functions, lowering its expenditures, and trying to cut the cost of production—that is, by cutting wages.

Dictatorship of Left and Right in Hungary

Although they had to retreat on the economic front, the Bolsheviks had made good their political control of Russia. Their comrades abroad had a more difficult time. The Third International dispatched agents, armed with propaganda literature and money, to stimulate revolutions in nearby countries. Russian leaders went to the scene of action to nerve the rebels and in many cases to impose on them the strategy and aims of the International—in effect those of the Bolshevik government, which controlled the International. The activists fomented riots all over Central Europe, but their strongest attacks were mounted in Hungary and Germany.

The government which Count Michael Karolyi (1875-1955) of Hungary formed in November 1918 consisted of liberals and socialists. Its aim was to introduce political and agrarian reform. But although Karolyi distributed his own 50,000 acres to his peasants, other aristocrats did not follow his example. He shrank from confiscation and from using dictatorial measures against the enemies of democracy, whether these were landlords or Communists. The soviets of Budapest pressed for more daring social measures. His socialist colleagues abandoned Karolyi and joined forces with Communist groups. When the Allies decided to turn Transylvania over to Rumanian occupation, Karolyi protested and in March 1919 resigned. The Communist Bela Kun (1885-1937) became Premier with the assistance of the socialists. Kun had been in Russia during the Bolshevik Revolution and had been instructed by the Third International to organize a "proletarian dictatorship." He showed the socialists the door, announced the expropriation of the land and the nationalization of industries and banks, subjected the press to government control, and imprisoned opposition leaders. The revolution fanned out: Hungarian troops penetrated into Slovakia; Communists incited outbreaks in Austria.

The manifold attempt miscarried. Kun's terrorist regime had aroused the wrath not only of the powerful gentry and middle classes but also of Allied generals in the area. Rural and urban conservatives, aristocrats, and army officers set up a rival government in French-held territory and improvised an army under the leadership of Admiral Nicholas Horthy (1868-1957), who had commanded the small Austro-Hungarian navy. In August 1919, with the consent of the French government, a Rumanian army marched into Budapest and overthrew Bela Kun, who fled to Vienna.

Three months later, Horthy's adherents set up a reactionary government. They unleashed a "White terror," in which hundreds of Communists, socialists, and liberals were tortured and murdered. In March 1920, in an election held under conditions of political repression, a conservative majority repudiated the republic, proclaimed Hungary a kingdom, and designated Horthy to act as regent, presumably until the throne was filled. However, two attempts of the former Emperor-King Charles to reclaim his crown in 1921 were vetoed by the Allies and frustrated by Hungarian forces. An admiral without a navy—for Hungary was now landlocked—remained provisionally the regent of a monarchy without a king.

Communists and democrats had both failed. Their divisions gave intransigent conservatives an opportunity to create a regime more reactionary than Hungary had had in the recent past.

The Rise of Italian Fascism

Italy had fought on the winning side in the war, but her internal condition resembled that of the defeated countries. Only the quick action of the Allies had saved her army from rout by the Austrians in 1917. After the war, the unpopularity of the military became so great that the army had to permit its officers to wear civilian clothes off duty. Ex-officers, restless veterans, and patriotic young bloods felt "humiliated." Their mood was brought to the boiling point by the opposition of the Allies to Italian demands at the Paris conference. Italian nationalists insisted on a slice of the Dalmatian coast, including the port of Fiume; they wanted Albania, at the Adriatic entrance from the Mediterranean, in order to control the smaller sea; they wanted the largely German-speaking southern Tyrol for reasons of military strategy. The Allies retorted that these demands contravened the Fourteen Points, that Fiume was Yugoslavia's only feasible outlet to the sea, and that some of these territories were not Italian in speech or feeling. They conceded fewer of the former Hapsburg territories than they had promised Italy in the secret London Treaty of 1915.

The result was a movement that was at once a mutiny, a nationalistic orgy, and a romantic adventure. In September 1919 the flamboyant poet and aviator Gabriele d'Annunzio (1863-1938) placed himself at the head of a body of armed volunteers and seized the port of Fiume from the small Allied garrison that held it. For fifteen months, he successfully defied his own government and the great powers. He promulgated a constitution under which the state was based on a grouping of the population into ten "corporations." Nine of the corporations consisted of the various trades and professions. "The tenth has neither art, nor number, nor title," D'Annunzio proclaimed. "Its coming is expected like that of the tenth muse. It is reserved to the mysterious forces of the people in toil and attainment. It is almost a votive figure consecrated to the unknown genius, to the apparition of the new man, to the ideal transfiguration of labor and time, to the complete liberation of the spirit over pain, over blood and sweat. . . . In the pauses of music is heard the silence of the Tenth Corporation." The style was strained, but the hint was broad enough: the "unknown genius" was D'Annunzio. The poet-soldier assumed the classic stance. He revived the Roman salute of the outstretched arm and the frequent harangues of the "legionnaires." Nevertheless, the Allies assigned Fiume to Yugoslavia, and in January 1921 the Italian government nerved itself to deal with the leader. D'Annunzio threatened to embark his legionnaires and march on Rome, vowing to die for his state, but he quickly retired to his "eagle's nest" on Lake Garda. Yet his adventure was more than *opera buffa*. It exposed the weakness of the government, the disintegration of military discipline, the potency of appeals to romantic glory, and the value of ritualism in politics. It demonstrated the need for positive leadership by the democratic parties.

Such leadership rested with two parties. Catholic groups formed the Popular party, advocating agrarian and social reforms. After the elections of November 1919, this party sent 103 deputies to the legislative chamber. The Socialist party, with 160 deputies, was the largest single group in the chamber but was short of a majority. Its habit of noncollaboration with middle-class parties stood in the way of its assuming office. Events in Russia and, nearer home, in Hungary and Germany had stimulated the ambitions of the Left Wing. Yet most Socialists were unwilling to break entirely with liberal democracy.   *565*

In October 1919 the party adopted a program calling simultaneously for adherence to the Third International, which meant revolution, and for participation in elections, which meant reform. To avoid a split, the party paid a high price. It practiced sabotage in parliament, mechanically voting against every government measure. Some of its members engaged in revolutionary activities, while others, by standing aside, prevented these activities from coming to a head. Extensive strikes were called and many were successful. Railway men, factory workers, even government employees stopped working. In the fall of 1920 the fever was at its highest. The metal workers of northern Italy remained in their mills—in effect, occupying them. They tried to continue producing without the cooperation of the owners and managers, but efficiency soon dropped. The government brought workers and employers together under a promise to organize coordinated control by the two groups. The factories were evacuated.

At this crucial moment, the Socialist movement at last was split. When it had applied for admission to the Third International, the Russians had insisted that it acknowledge the total authority of Moscow. At a congress held in Leghorn in January 1921, the majority of the Italian Socialists voted to join the International but rejected its dictation in the internal life of the Italian party. A minority split away to form the Italian Communist party, which joined the International without this qualification. A like-minded minority seceded from the trade-union movement to form a federation of Communist unions.

The division of the radicals and the failure of the metalworkers' strike disposed of the danger of revolution. But strikes engendered fear among the propertied classes, and the antics of D'Annunzio suggested novel means of exploiting it. Embittered ex-Socialists, uprooted ex-combatants, restless and unemployed professionals, young people who had missed war service and regretted it, and politicians who combined an appreciation of mass psychology with a readiness for *condottiere* tactics and the *coup d'état* combined to form a new type of party. The Fascists derived their name from *fasces*, the bound bundle of rods that had symbolized the authority of the ancient Roman republic. Their leader was an ex-radical who had been long a stormy petrel in the Socialist movement and had become a nationalist during the war. His name was Benito Mussolini.

Mussolini (1883-1945) was an opportunist of histrionic ability. What he lacked of D'Annunzio's poetic appeal he made up in brutal forcefulness and ambition. His first platform of 1919 was socialistic in tone. He proposed, for example, to let the workers run the railroads. Within two years, the platform became respectably capitalist; even the post office was to be turned over to private enterprise. But Mussolini and his Fascist followers were less interested in programs than in getting and holding office. "Our program is simple," Mussolini announced. "We wish to govern Italy. . . . It is not programs that are wanting for the salvation of Italy, but men and will power." He organized *Fasci di Combattimento*, "fighting bands," frankly dedicated to intimidating radicals and liberals and to creating and exploiting public disorder. Fascist gangs broke up meetings of Communists, Socialists, and trade unions. They beat up their opponents and even murdered some of them. They counted upon the impotence of the government, the acquiescence of the police, and the private satisfaction of the frightened middle classes. In order to impress the crowd, the Fascists devised a colorful ritual: black shirts, huge military parades, and stiff salutes with outstretched arm.

Beginning in February 1921, the Fascist gangs engaged in open warfare with organized Socialist and Communist squads in the streets of Italy. Fascist coups overturned the governments of several municipalities. In October 1922, Mussolini forced a showdown by gathering 40,000 uniformed men in Naples and marching them through the streets. He announced a march on Rome. The ruling groups and middle classes were not entirely displeased to note the strength of this new scourge of the Left. As the Fascists trickled into the ancient capital, the capitalist and military groups, speaking through the King, enthroned Fascism by refusing to call out the regular troops to protect the existing government and by inviting Mussolini, whose party held a small fraction of seats in the Chamber, to take over the reins. Parliament voted Mussolini dictatorial powers for one year. It virtually abolished itself by agreeing to give him two thirds of the seats if he could gather a plurality—not a majority—in the forthcoming elections. This he did by having the opposition candidates beaten up by his gangs, by appointing or suborning the men who counted the ballots, and by hamstringing the press. He won 4,700,000 of the 7,700,000 votes cast and left the whole opposition with but a tiny minority in

Benito Mussolini, the Fascist dictator of Italy, reviewing a parade of the "Sons of the She-Wolf," an organization of boys of six to eight years old. Fascism inculcated the "virtue" of unquestioning obedience and encouraged a martial attitude in the young. ACME

parliament. In order to make his grip upon the country permanent, he raised his reign of terror to an official status, harrying and imprisoning dissenters and curbing public life and expression.

Mussolini assumed the title of *Duce*, or "leader." He attempted to give his regime the appearance of novelty and idealism by proclaiming the abolition of "liberal capitalism" and individualism and establishing a "corporative state," a mixture of syndicalism and fascism. In theory, economic life was to be directed toward just social ends by organizing all occupations and professions into "syndicates" (later called "corporations") representing the employers, workers, and the state. The "corporative state," which was initiated in 1926 and developed over a number of years, actually weakened organized labor, favored capital, and, above all, worked to the advantage of the Fascist party. For the party, by appointing the state representatives of all "corporations" and the officials of trade unions and by nominating the members of the parliament, which ostensibly represented the "corporations," won jobs, sinecures, and other economic advantages, as well as exclusive political power, for its members.

The spasm of violence was over. Lenin's dream of an international revolution, Wilson's hope of American participation in a League of Nations, and Clemenceau's project of an Atlantic alliance all evaporated. The extension of constitutionalism, initiated by the American and French Revolutions, was arrested. In a few countries—Germany, Austria, and Czechoslovakia among them—democratic republics succeeded imperial regimes. A number of other countries, however, introduced dictatorships or semidictatorships of the Right, to which the Italian name "Fascism" was increasingly applied.

Fascists and Communists agreed in rejecting individual freedom and parliamentary politics. Both sought monopoly of power by one party—in effect, by a small group of leaders who controlled the party by undemocratic means. Both practiced terrorism: arbitrary arrest, imprisonment, and execution. While the Communists were intent on developing collective production and distribution, the Fascists retained the old economic order in substance. Much of their support came from landlords and capitalists who saw in Fascism a means to check at once social reform, union labor, and radicalism.

Finally, while the Communists used the language of traditional Marxism and professed ideals of freedom, democracy, and internationalism, the Fascists rejected traditional values and practices. For the monarchs of traditional conservatism they substituted Caesars; for hereditary aristocrats, demagogic oligarchs. They engaged in leader-worship. They appealed to national prejudices and passions. Everywhere, save in Italy, they were virulently anti-Semitic.

Different though they were in their professions and final aims, Fascism and Communism together undermined liberal and democratic values and institutions and introduced the techniques of absolutism, arbitrariness, and force. The two movements were the most portentous legacy of the First World War.

27. *The Whirl of the Twenties*

The nineteen-twenties were a counterpoint of energy and doubt, stability and rebelliousness. In comparison with the long period of domestic order which preceded the First World War, they were unsettled and disturbed. But they seemed a welcome respite after the great outbursts of violence and revolution. Many men chose to regard the war as a temporary interruption of an age of progress and conventional ambitions and behavior. Conservative politicians hastened to resume prewar policies. In the effort to recapture the spirit of a bygone, though recent, age, much energy was generated. It was a febrile energy that tended to overreach itself. There was excessive speculation in investment and finance and sharp competition in industry.

Beyond the centers of business and power, however, there was restlessness. A broad tendency to challenge conventional thinking and accepted standards had been gathering force for some years before the outbreak of the war. It now became pronounced. There was much idealism and a strong undercurrent of pessimism and skepticism. Novelty and experimentation—in the arts, in political thinking, in personal conduct, even in dress—became the order of the day.

The Rebellion of Culture

The twenties teemed with heterodoxy. The example of Russia, the rise of Communist parties elsewhere, and the prominence of socialists in the regimes that succeeded the Hohenzollern and Hapsburg Empires gave Marxism a fame and a practical influence that it had not had before the war. Among academic and literary groups the doctrine of economic determinism gained many followers. Another doctrine, less popular in its appeal, was hardly less influential among intellectuals: this was the theory of psychoanalysis. At the turn of the century, a Viennese physician, Sigmund Freud (1856-1939), had developed a method of diagnosing and treating mental disorders based on "free association" and analysis of dreams. Freud ascribed some of man's most potent drives and conflicts to repressed experiences and unconscious motivation. He regarded sex as a central element in psychology and the earliest emotional experiences of the infant, particularly in relation to his parents, as decisive factors in the evolution of his personality. Freud's treatment of neuroses took the form of dredging up repressed and forgotten events and experiences in the patient's formative years to expose the roots of irrational behavior.

By the twenties, psychoanalysis had come to have a deep impact on every enterprise that was concerned with the motives of action and with man's view of himself. It shed a new and sympathetic light on emotional conflicts and "maladjustment." It placed new emphasis on the role of the personality and psychological forces in society, politics, and history. By stressing the continuity between infancy and maturity, the neurotic and the normal, primitive and civilized mores, it encouraged artists to abandon conventional subjects and forms for abstraction, "surrealism," and expressionism. Surrealist painters borrowed fantastic shapes and images from the world of dreams and nightmares; their works frequently revealed an obsession with the atmosphere of death, disease, and destruction. Surrealism was the most novel aspect of a movement toward "expressionism" which had begun long before the war. Many artists, novelists, and poets had turned from the "academic" methods of description, imitation of nature, and the evocation and communication of familiar feelings and impressions. They gave expression, instead, to inner visions, personal images, private feelings, and half-conscious perceptions. The terminology of

An example of surrealist painting. Illumined Pleasures (*1929*) *by Salvador Dali (1904-   ).* THE MUSEUM OF MODERN ART, THE SIDNEY JANIS COLLECTION

Freud—Oedipus complex, the id, the libido, the superego—became literary idiom. The distance between avant-garde and popular culture widened. Novelists and playwrights abandoned conventional plot and dialogue for "the stream of consciousness." Painters and sculptors represented the world as they imagined it to appear to the eyes of children, African tribesmen, or mathematicians. Not since the days of the fantastic Dutch painter Hieronymus Bosch (1450-1516) had the artistic imagination been so unrestrained.

Scientific developments similarly tended to leave accustomed paths. Earlier mathematicians and physicists had challenged the traditional foundations of modern science. They questioned the axioms of Euclid and constructed alternative geometries in which parallel lines met and the sum of the angles of a triangle was more or less, but never quite, equal to the 180° calculated by the ancient Greek. Although the principles of these geometries differed, there was no way of demonstrating which was the "true" geometry. In 1905, the German-born physicist Albert Einstein (1879-1956) had propounded the theory of relativity. Einstein repudiated the accustomed conceptions of space, time, and matter: there is no absolute motion or absolute rest; time and motion are relative to an observer's position.

All these tendencies, at first the concern of small groups of scientists and artists, now entered the consciousness of the wider public. The world and man himself suddenly seemed considerably less "reliable" and coherent. The old categories of scientific logic, artistic form, and social motivation gave way to new and more controversial categories.

The League of Nations and Disarmament

The most significant manifestation of the new attitudes was the virtually universal revulsion against militarism. The recent exhibition of brutality and irresponsibility on an international scale discredited traditional diplomacy and foreign policies. A spate of novels exposed the immorality and spiritual vacuity of warmaking and warmakers.

Secret diplomacy and imperialism fell into sharp disfavor. It was said that all Europe's postwar troubles were due to the destruction of her best young men during the trial at arms. It was said that the Western world was in danger of declining. People talked of "the lost generation" and said that the older generation had failed the younger. Many writers, artists, and scientists repudiated nationalistic ideologies and became strenuous advocates of peaceful policies and international-mindedness. In the victorious countries, this attitude led, curiously, to pro-Germanism. "Revisionist" historians and writers laid much of the blame for the war on the Allies; some of them pronounced Germany less responsible for initiating it than France or Russia. They castigated the Versailles Treaty, particularly the "war guilt" and reparations clauses. By concentrating their attack on Western leadership, they inadvertently built up the image of an innocent and martyred Germany.

The hope of exorcising international conflicts had found expression in the League of Nations, the most imaginative enterprise of its kind in history. Within a decade after its establishment in 1919, fifty-four states, containing the bulk of the human race, had become members of the League. The United States remained outside, but Germany joined the organization in 1926 and the Soviet Union in 1934.

The League took a series of steps for the preservation of peace. In 1920 it established the Permanent Court of International Justice at The Hague. The Hague Court of Arbitration, formed in 1907, continued to function as a panel of distinguished jurists from which states could choose arbiters to decide their disputes. The new Court consisted of fifteen permanent judges and held regular sessions. About forty states—most of the members of the League—accepted its jurisdiction as binding upon them in what were called "justiciable" cases. These were cases that involved the interpretation of treaties, questions of international law, or breaches of international custom. For other cases, appeal to the court was optional. The Presidents of the United States from 1920 to 1932—Harding, Coolidge, and Hoover—were in favor of joining the Court, but isolationists prevailed upon the Senate to refuse. Yet prominent American judges sat on the tribunal.

Next, the League proposed a procedure for checking aggression. This was embodied in the Geneva Protocol of 1924, which required that the states submit all disputes either to the Permanent Court or to a special committee of arbiters. The country which refused to submit its dispute or claim to arbitration or which, having submitted it, refused to abide by the decision was designated the aggressor. It then became the duty of the other members to proceed against it, under Article 16 of the Covenant, by economic pressure and possibly military measures as well.

The Geneva Protocol was the first attempt to devise measures to arrest aggression. Its critics argued that the Protocol sanctioned existing territorial arrangements since it forced those who challenged these arrangements to prove the justice of their case and refused them the appeal to arms. Yet no more satisfactory method than that outlined by the Protocol had been framed. Only seventeen governments ratified it. The British feared that the Protocol might entangle them in Continental disputes. New Zealand and Australia had a more concrete objection: they suspected that their policy of restricting immigration to Anglo-Saxons might, upon challenge, be adjudged contrary to international propriety by a court consisting largely of jurists from other countries. The United States once again stood aside, concerned over the effect the Protocol might have upon the Monroe Doctrine and her strong position in the Western Hemisphere.

Upon the failure of the Protocol, other attempts were made to prevent future wars in Europe and particularly challenges to the settlement of the peace treaties. The most notable of these was the series of Locarno Treaties of 1925, in which the Continental states bound themselves in a defensive network. France, Germany, and Belgium guaranteed their common borders and the demilitarization of the Rhineland. Great Britain and Italy reinforced this promise as outside guarantors. France and Germany agreed to submit disputes to arbitration, as did Czechoslovakia and Germany, and Belgium and Germany. The groundwork was laid for Germany's admission to the League, which was accomplished, after some delay, in September 1926.

It was in Eastern Europe that the danger of conflict seemed greatest. The states that had lost land and population pressed for a revision of the peace treaties. As Serbia and Rumania had once tried to "redeem" their conationals in Austria-Hungary, so Germans and Hungarians now took up the cry of "redemption." In 1920, Czechoslovakia and Yugoslavia had signed an agreement to ensure Hungary's observance of the territorial settlement. The following year Rumania joined Czechoslovakia, and the Little Entente came into being. Later France signed defensive alliances with the Little Entente and with Poland. France thus became the pivot around which the security systems of Eastern and Western Europe revolved.

The feverish search for security produced another and broader series of treaties, by non-European as well as European states. About a hundred agreements to arbitrate stated issues and 250 treaties to cover cases of dispute arising under these agreements were signed in the twenties. Three years after Locarno, the United States and France, which had always been at peace with each other, signed the Kellogg-Briand Pact, agreeing to renounce war "as an instrument of national policy." The American public, so often deeply disappointed by previous failures of their government to join in the declarations and organizations of peace, acclaimed the Pact with enthusiasm. Virtually all nations insisted on sharing the renunciation. It was the first general agreement that Soviet Russia was invited to sign, and she did so promptly. Altogether sixty-one states signed the Pact, more than had joined in any other such agreement. If moral engagements alone were sufficient, the peace of the world was secure.

The League was fairly effective in settling a number of minor issues. In 1921 it settled a dispute between Finland and Sweden over the possession and government of the small group of Aaland Islands in the Baltic Sea. When Poland seized the city of Vilna from Lithuania, the League was unable to bring the two states to arbitration, but it asserted the right of Lithuania to the city of Memel, which was occupied by Poland. The League conducted a plebiscite in Upper Silesia in order to divide it between Germany and Poland. By threatening to invoke sanctions, the League was successful in compelling Yugoslavia to desist from attacking Albania. It settled a dispute between Great Britain and Turkey over the region of Mosul, rich in oil.

The peace treaties had bound the signers to reduce their armies, navies, and weapons. A preparatory commission for a disarmament conference, appointed by the League in 1925, met for the first time in 1926 and held many sessions thereafter without achieving results. The commission drafted a convention showing the categories of armaments and apportioning a share to each country. But figures themselves were not indicated; when a conference was finally convened to supply the crucial quotes, in 1932, the military and economic climate had changed considerably, and no agreement could be reached. Meanwhile, those aspects of disarmament on which the great powers could agree were dealt with in negotiations outside the auspices of the League. In 1922, at a naval-disarmament conference in Washington, the United States, Great Britain, and Japan accepted a ratio of 5:5:3 for their capital ships and agreed to a ten-year naval holiday during which no ships were to be built. The three states saved much in naval expenses; indeed, they scrapped two million tons of shipping in excess of the ratio. But neither they nor other naval powers, notably France and Italy, also a party to the agreement, could agree on the limitation of cruisers and other naval vessels or on the proposed abolition of the submarine.

Recovery and Speculation

There was more promise in economic life than in diplomacy. In the mid-twenties, after the dislocations of war and revolution, trade conditions became more fluid, prices steadier, currencies more stable. The depression of the early years of the decade was overcome. Real wages rose moderately but fairly generally. Employment increased nearly everywhere. In most industrial countries, production caught up with prewar figures. Agricultural countries actively promoted the development of industry. New industries arose. Chemical products and synthetic goods made their appearance on a large scale. The amalgamation of industrial firms, promoted during the periods of war and inflation, diminished competition, frequently to the disadvantage of workers and consumers, but it often improved efficiency. Many firms, particularly in Germany, improved the organization of their labor power, simplified methods, standardized materials and products, adopted newer techniques and machinery, and improved distribution and marketing.

Yet the recovery was spotty. It benefited the industrial more than the agrarian population, and industrialists much more than their employees. Farmers everywhere remained relatively depressed. When the extraordinary demands of the military ended, food prices dropped sharply. Organized labor lost ground after reaching a peak of trade-union membership in the early, and depressed, twenties. In 1919 the organizations affiliated with the International Federation of Trade Unions counted 25 million members in 21 countries. Adding the unaffiliated unions, the total reached perhaps 42 million in 30 countries. By the late twenties the membership of the Federation had dropped to 13 million. Although the membership of unaffiliated unions brought the total to 45 million, some 10 million of these belonged to "official" unions controlled by governments or employers. The spread of such organizations weakened unionism, as did the bitter division between socialists and Communists. In Russia the unions forfeited their role as bargaining agents for their members and became government agencies for regulating wages and disciplining labor. In Fascist Italy they became the pawns of party manipulators.

The recovery was further qualified by restrictive national economic policies on the one hand and private overspeculation on the other. Protectionism was general, and some countries strove to attain economic self-sufficiency. The world was being closed off into compartments. This was true of populations as well as of goods. The United States and other newly settled countries drastically limited immigration. They ceased to be the refuge of the masses of the Old World.

Two developments aggravated the condition of international exchange. Before the war Russia had been an important market for surplus capital and an active participant in commercial and industrial exchanges. After the Bolshevik government repudiated the foreign debt and confiscated private estates and industrial property, foreign investors and bankers became chary of throwing good money after bad. Russia could not obtain loans; she could only engage in barter, sending grain, gold, precious art collections, and other valuables to pay for her imports. The United States replaced Great Britain as the world's creditor and banker, but her trade policies were not calculated to facilitate exchanges. Her own market was shut off from foreign products by higher and higher tariff walls. Debtors could not pay in goods, which is the normal and fertilizing method, but had to send their gold instead. The metal was moving in only one direction, draining debtor countries and surfeiting the United States.

While the interchange of goods was inhibited by nationalistic trade policies, international finance flourished. There was much speculation in the stock exchanges. Stock prices rose rapidly, far more so than production figures warranted. Speculation outran industry. There were two countries in particular where inflated financial activities were especially marked. In Germany there was much buying and consolidating of enterprises, not always in order to improve production but to resell quickly at a profit to middlemen and manipulators. To a large extent, recovery was financed by foreign loans, principally American, granted in connection with the reparations settlement. In the United States, the recovery assumed the dimensions of a boom. A share of the United States Steel Corporation sold for less than $100 in the early twenties and brought $279 in 1929. Nor was this stock among the most inflated.

In this atmosphere tinged by speculation, the big businessman was in his element. The collapse of the three Continental empires had dealt his aristocratic rivals a great blow. The nobleman's losses in one region were reflected in his lowered prestige everywhere else. The spectacle of exiled Russian aristocrats reduced to taking homely jobs removed the sheen from the escutcheon of nobility. Marcel Proust constructed the mausoleum of European aristocracy in his great novel *Remembrance of Things Past*. It was symbolic that one of his heroines, Mme. Verdurin, a bourgeoise who had been snubbed for decades by high society, after the war married not one but, in quick succession, two men of the purest blood and most ancient lineage. As the aristocrats retreated, businessmen moved forward. In nearly every country, industrialists and financiers acquired political influence and high office as well as social esteem.

American "Normalcy" and Heterodoxy

In the United States, where the business classes did not have to contend with a titled nobility, the efflorescence of the business spirit was especially notable. The Republican party, as we have seen, returned to power in 1921 and retained its ascendancy throughout the decade. Within it, the influence of big business was stronger than it had ever been. After the storm of the war and Wilsonian idealism, the president, Warren G. Harding, called for a return to "business as usual" and "normalcy." "What we want," he asserted, "is not heroics but healing; not nostrums but normalcy; not revolution but restoration; not surgery but serenity." Harding's administration gave corporate capitalism free rein. Republican-dominated courts watered down the effect of legislation governing the activities of corporations and monopolies. The tariff was raised to the highest levels ever reached.

Profit-making infected politics. Albert B. Fall, Secretary of the Interior, "leased" the oil resources of the nation to his friends, accepting several hundred thousand dollars for this favor, and became the first American cabinet officer to be jailed on criminal charges. But Vice President Calvin Coolidge (1872-1933), who became president upon Harding's sudden death in 1923 and was elected himself the next year, remarked that the official corruption was no concern of the head of the government. His philosophy was brief: "The business of America is business."

Economic life was indeed active. Several new industries made remarkable advances: motion pictures, radio, household appliances, and especially automobiles. The number of cars in use trebled in the twenties; the figure for 1930 was 27 million. The rise of this industry stimulated a host of other enterprises: road building; garages for servicing and repairing; bus transport; trucking; and thousands of sales agencies.

Advertising spurred buying and easy credit. Installment terms were generous. Manufacturers and stores sold their products, and customers avidly bought, on the presumption that payments would continue over a span of years rather than months. As Americans bought goods on easy installment terms, so they bought stock "on margin," paying but a small sum down, promising to pay the remainder instantly on call, but expecting to sell soon at a profit. Millions of small investors—middle-class and professional people, small merchants, and people who scared up money from their friends or relatives—became stock gamblers along with experienced and adventurous capitalists. The leaders of business persuaded the public, and even themselves, that the United States had discovered the key to continuous prosperity and that there would never again be depressions.

The speculative atmosphere obscured weaknesses in society. In America as elsewhere, the benefits of prosperity were distributed unevenly. Agricultural prices did not keep pace with the cost of industrial goods. While the power of capital was growing, that of labor was stagnating, even declining. Courts frequently "enjoined" workers from striking and government agencies harried union organizers and leaders as "reds." The membership of the American Federation of Labor, the dominant combination of unions, dropped from its highest point of four million in 1920 to less than three million ten years later. Transportation, building, mining, clothing, and printing accounted for the bulk of the unionized workers. The rest of American labor remained unorganized, including the great enterprises of steel, automobiles, textiles, and merchandising, not to speak of the public-service, clerical, and professional occupations.

The country lacked federal legislation against the hazards and crises of capitalism. Social services were local, private, and limited in character. If prosperity had continued, these neglects might have been tolerated; the pressure for social reform and labor organization was not strong. Yet the dominance of big business and of the Republican party did not go without challenge. Senator Robert M. LaFollette ran for president in 1924, the candidate of a third party, the new Progressive party. With the support of liberals, Midwestern Progressives, and socialists, he polled five million votes.

American literature became distinctly critical. A lively group of writers made *The American Mercury*, a magazine edited by H. L. Mencken (1880-1956), a citadel of heterodoxy. With great verve, they tilted at pompous businessmen, aggressive patriots, Puritans, and religious fundamentalists. They had a field day in 1925, when John T. Scopes, a high-school biology teacher in Tennessee, was arrested for violating a state law forbidding the teaching of evolution in tax-supported schools. In the famous "monkey trial" that followed, William Jennings Bryan, thrice a Democratic candidate for the presidency, joined the prosecution. He defended the letter of the Bible against the Darwinian exposition of Scopes's lawyer, the agnostic Clarence Darrow. Scopes lost the case. Enlightened opinion was shocked, both by the trial and by the spectacle of an eminent politician leading an attack on science.

Next to religious fundamentalism, prohibition was the favorite target of liberals. The Eighteenth Amendment to the Constitution, ratified in 1919 under the pressure of religious groups, prohibited the manufacture, sale, and transportation of alcoholic liquor. The "noble experiment," as it was characterized by President Herbert Hoover (1874-   ), proved on the whole a failure. It led to informal war between "bootleggers" and government agents. The urban population, particularly in the Eastern states, resented prohibition as an example of sumptuary legislation. Many citizens, particularly young people, took to drinking as a protest against authority. It became fashionable to patronize "speakeasies," or illegal bars.

The novelist Sinclair Lewis (1885-1951) drew the caricature of the provincial American, the restless American woman, and, above all, the philistine American businessman. His *Babbitt* (1922) became a best-seller and a household word. Babbitt not only craved money and material things but thought of them

577

as spiritual values, as the best expressions of the national ideal. He shied away from introspection, sensibility, and social criticism as treasonous to the "American" spirit.

What Lewis and *The American Mercury* did for the whole literate community, the economist Thorstein Veblen and the philosopher John Dewey did for the professional and academic groups. Veblen has been called the American Marx. Like Marx, he attacked capitalism as an obstacle to rational production. But Veblen's socialism was not Marxian. Whereas Marx depicted human history as a series of conflicts between social classes and between economic systems, Veblen depicted it as a continuing conflict between "generically human" and predatory instincts. "Idle curiosity" and the "instinct of workmanship,"according to Veblen, were creative impulses, responsible for scientific knowledge, industrial progress, and beauty. The urge to exploit, to extort, or to use force to get something for nothing—characteristic of capitalism, in Veblen's view—made for intellectual sterility, inertia, and oppression. In modern times, technicians, engineers, economists, and men of science generally, together with the working people, embodied the instinct of workmanship, while businessmen, salesmen, advertisers, and, above all, financiers represented the spirit of guile, exploitation, and vested personal interest. Whereas Marx trusted to the industrial proletariat to reshape society, Veblen proposed to transfer the leadership of the economy from the businessman and financier to the technician and man of science.

Veblen's thought was a blend of European culture and American experience. The son of Norwegian farm people who had migrated to Wisconsin ten years before he was born, Veblen was brought up in an immigrant environment whose language and culture were Norwegian. He had an unusual command of foreign languages and a broad knowledge of the European countries. Yet his absorption with technology was distinctly American. His very quality as an "outsider" enabled him to see the problems and promises of American life in a fresh perspective.

More indigenous voices had articulated a philosophy which came to be regarded as distinctively American. The mathematician Charles S. Peirce (1839-1914), the psychologist William James (1842-1910), and the philosopher John Dewey (1859-1952) developed the pragmatic, or instrumentalist, view. To the pragmatist, the world was an unfinished creation which could grow and improve along with man himself. The greatest instrument of this double process was the scientific spirit and method. The validity of all goals and ideas must be tested, like that of scientific theories, by their effectiveness in the external world. The striving of liberalism and democracy to improve the environment and men themselves was scientific in character. Dewey observed that "freedom of inquiry, toleration of diverse views, freedom of communication, the distribution of what is found out to every individual as the ultimate intellectual consumer, are involved in the democratic as in the scientific method." Pragmatism reflected the bent for action, change, and growth that characterized America. It challenged the notion that the world was a finished creation into which man had to fit himself somehow and that ideals and standards were eternal verities which he had but to decipher and accept. Such a view might be suitable to the rigid and static character of Europe, but not to the dynamism of America.

Pragmatism made for a vibrant and searching attitude toward public problems. It justified the efforts of liberals to improvise methods for dealing with the problems of industrial society, of lawyers to bring to bear empirical data upon the interpretation of old maxims, and, above all, of educators to prepare the young for a society based on the values of science as well as democracy. Dewey emancipated the American child. He conceived of education as a process in which the initiative, purpose, and effectiveness of the individual play the same essential role as in life itself. Formal discipline, learning by rote, and emphasis on the mastery of accumulated information were to be abandoned. Under Dewey's influence, many a school weakened its formal curriculum and introduced the "project method," in which groups of children undertook tasks that engaged their interests, curiosity, and abilities. "Learn by doing" was Dewey's motto. Later educators found that it required much common sense in its application.

While the influence of pragmatism accented the distinctiveness of America, the contacts and mutual influences of the Old World and the New multiplied in the twenties. The World War, and American intervention, had worked a change of attitude on both sides of the ocean. Americans reversed the experience of Columbus: they discovered the Old World. The experience was both disturbing and exhilarating. Some Americans could not get home fast enough. They still thought of the Old World as effete and corrupt. To Lewis' Babbitt, Europe was the home of both snobbishness and radicalism, "artiness" and mass poverty. In the interior of the United States, "isolationism" became pronounced, although contrary forces were at work on the Atlantic seaboard. Foreign policy reflected this difference. The United States had loaned to the Allies nearly eleven billion dollars' worth of weapons and goods. Most Europeans, and many Americans felt that this debt should be written off as a contribution to the common effort and as a counterbalance to the reduced German reparations. Since the United States was not a party to the Versailles Treaty and had from the outset renounced reparations for herself, the Republican administration refused to combine the issues of reparations and debt. "Uncle Shylock" became a common phrase in European journalism. In a series of agreements with individual Allied countries, however, the United States greatly reduced their debts and stipulated small annual payments spread over a long period.

The fact was that Americans were being drawn more and more into international activities. Although the United States remained out of the League of Nations, American citizens participated unofficially in the activities of the League's subsidiaries, such as the International Labor Organization. Americans played prominent roles in the reparations settlement and in credit and monetary conferences, and on the World Court. Merchants and engineers as well as bankers were active in European businesses.

A significant segment of American intellectuals accepted the artistic and literary values and products of European culture. American publishers brought out many translations of Continental authors. American buyers and connoisseurs encouraged expressionist painters in France. Many young American writers and artists stayed on in Europe after the war, or visited it later, to refresh themselves at the artistic springs of the Old World. The Left Bank of Paris in particular became the home of the American as well as the European avant-garde of culture.

At the same time America projected a new and more potent image to the European mind. American authors were finding a large reading public in Europe. In 1930 Sinclair Lewis became the first American to win the Nobel prize for literature. The fame of Walt Whitman as the poet of democracy grew apace. Soviet Russia for a time adopted Dewey's "project method" in education.

Despite the isolationism of American foreign policy, the memory of Woodrow Wilson's tragic struggle for a new diplomacy and a united world remained fresh in the minds of Europeans. Above all, Europe was impressed by the debut of the Republic as a great power, her demonstration of industrial capacity in the organization of the war effort, and the two-million-man army she had sent abroad. Various countries imitated American methods of mass production. German manufacturers introduced Henry Ford's "assembly line" technique. The planners of Soviet Russia adopted the United States as a model and hired American engineers to construct power dams and initiate Russian managers in advanced methods. "We must reach and overreach the Americans" became a Bolshevik slogan. America became synonymous with industrial efficiency.

The British General Strike and the Devaluation of the Franc

British domestic policy resembled that of the United States in its business-minded orientation. In 1922 the Conservative party, which had been part of the coalition government presided over by Lloyd George, the Liberal leader, withdrew from the partnership and forced an election on party lines. Its chief, Andrew Bonar Law (1858-1923), a former iron merchant, advocated "tranquillity" as President Harding advocated "normalcy." The Conservatives won a majority in the House of Commons while the Liberal party declined severely. Then a new opposition arose—a development that did not take place in the United States. The Labor party, with 142 seats, supplanted the Liberals as the principal rival of the Conservatives.

In economic development, Britain differed much more sharply from the United States. The war had confirmed and made painfully manifest a decline that had set in long before. By disposing of her American bonds and other foreign holdings in order to purchase military supplies, Great Britain had cut deep into her income from overseas investments. She never recaptured her former financial eminence. Her share of world trade continued to drop—from

17 percent in 1913 to only 14 percent in 1929. It had been 33 percent a century earlier. British industrial plants, being older, were less efficient than those of the United States or Germany. The coal-mining industry, in the nineteenth century one of the pillars of British prosperity, slipped into permanent distress. It suffered from falling exports, lower prices, and superannuated techniques. In the country at large, unemployment declined from the worst moments of the early twenties, but a large residue persisted obstinately. There were never fewer, and usually more, than a million idle men. The "irreducible million" became a persistent feature of British life. "If we go on pottering along as we are, we shall have grave unemployment with us to the end of time," declared Stanley Baldwin (1867-1947), a retired iron manufacturer and mine owner who succeeded Bonar Law as Prime Minister in May 1923. For a solution, Baldwin fell back on the policy of protectionism. He proposed to combine tariff legislation with imperial preference and promised that he would not tax imported food. On these issues, his party called an election at the end of 1923. Long wedded to the principle of free trade, and suspecting that protection was an inadequate solution for the problems of the country, the electorate deprived the Conservatives of a majority but left Labor and Liberals also minorities.

The Liberals assisted Labor, whose 191 seats outnumbered theirs, to form a government. The first Labor regime, under Ramsay MacDonald, a former journalist, did not introduce the capital levy, nationalization of industry, and other radical measures which the party had been proposing for some time. On the ground that the voters had repudiated protection, it lowered some tariff duties. It was most active in efforts to smooth international relations, and it was in this field that it was eventually defeated. Although disapproving of Soviet propaganda, the MacDonald cabinet recognized the Soviet government officially and entered into negotiations for trade exchanges. The rapprochement with Russia enabled Labor's opponents to raise the issue of the "Red peril," and, in an election in October 1924, the Conservatives won a thumping majority of well over 200 seats. Stanley Baldwin again became Prime Minister. The Liberal party was reduced to only 42 seats and was all but destroyed. The Labor party remained the principal opposition and alternative to the Conservatives.

The economic problem proved recalcitrant, particularly in the coal industry. The miners struck for higher pay, and other unions joined them in sympathy. In May 1926 Great Britain witnessed its first general strike. Two and a half million workers—railway men, transport workers, printers, builders, and others, in addition to the miners—stopped work. The government improvised essential services with the help of volunteers. It used troops to guard and operate power stations and transport. The unions were not prepared to take revolutionary steps and called off the strike after nine tense days. Only the miners remained on strike. Six months later they surrendered to the operators. Parliament then outlawed sympathetic strikes and reduced the power of trade unions over their membership. But the government was unable to solve the problems of the slowly bleeding industry, to reduce unemployment substantially, or to find a remedy for the reduced position of the country in the international market.

A street scene during the British general strike of 1926. London strikers being dispersed by police. WIDE WORLD

Across the Channel, in France, political life also tended toward conservatism. But the French economy was less dependent upon the world market than the British. It had an equable balance between agriculture and industry, and between small and large, individual and corporate, enterprise. After the war, the rich agriculture of France resumed its normal course. The rebuilding of devastated industrial areas provided an opportunity to improve both plants and machinery. The ores of Lorraine enabled steel production to reach unprecedented levels. Textile and automotive products made France a serious contender in the international market. By the mid-twenties she was exporting half again as much as she had before the outbreak of the war.

However, the large war debt, Germany's failure to pay reparations, and the inability of the government to balance its budget or raise new loans induced a financial crisis. The franc declined to about one twelfth of its prewar value. A National Union cabinet, including six former prime ministers and headed by former president Raymond Poincaré, was formed in 1926. It secured new taxes and economies and a provision for a sinking fund. It stabilized the franc at four cents—one sixth of its prewar value—thereby repudiating four fifths of the national debt. The *rentier* class was hard hit and became bitterly opposed to further devaluation.

The Achievements and Trials of the Weimar Republic

Despite worse financial troubles, France's largest neighbor to the east registered more striking economic advances. Germany recovered her former leadership in the chemical, electrical, and optical industries. By 1925 her steel production had shot up to prewar levels. German coal re-entered the international market. By the end of the twenties, one third of Germany's industrial product was finding its way to other countries. Her merchant marine, almost entirely wiped out by the war and the terms of peace, flourished mightily.

Germany's tonnage almost equaled the prewar figure. In 1929 her luxury liner *Bremen* wrested from the British the speed record for a transatlantic voyage. There were unusual expenditures for housing, slum clearance, and other civic improvements and social projects. People asked themselves whether Germany had lost or won the war.

There was one sobering qualification to these advances. Germany financed her peacetime activities as she had financed the war, largely by loans. American financiers lent her large sums, which she used to pay reparations and to launch new enterprises and combine old ones. She lent some of the borrowed money to Central European, particularly Austrian, banks and industries. Many of these American and German loans were granted for short terms. This created a sensitive financial relation, for if any creditors called in their loans, the markets of several countries might be disturbed in quick order.

In the field of labor, the German revolution had achieved some of the great aims of the Social Democrats: the eight-hour day, unemployment relief, and fair wage rates. But the eight-hour day remained secure only in trades with strong unions. Real wage rates, after rising in the mid-twenties, began to decline. The unions became conservative, intent on preserving their past achievements and protecting their funds and properties. As in other countries, their political influence diminished.

The Weimar Republic registered great success in the cultural realm. Under its liberal constitution, the Germans enjoyed complete freedom of expression and conduct. Berlin vied with Paris as a center of art. Germans produced marvels of innovation in music, stagecraft, and motion pictures. Avant-garde movements thrived. Perhaps the most significant of these was the Bauhaus school of industrial arts, founded in Weimar by the architect and urban planner Walter Gropius (1883-   ) in 1919. For a generation, Englishmen, Americans, Dutchmen, and Frenchmen had experimented with functional architecture and new industrial designs. An American architect, Louis Sullivan (1856-1924), had struck the keynote of this movement with his formula "Form follows function." Spurred by Germany's need for new housing and improved industrial products to recapture her former markets, the Bauhaus applied this formula and developed forms of beauty congruous with the materials and requirements of industry. It broke down the compartmentalization of the crafts and fine arts. It challenged the overprofessionalization that kept schools of painting and sculpture separated from schools of architecture, and design separated from engineering. In its laboratories and studios, architects and engineers worked side by side with industrial designers, painters, and sculptors. The practical result was a wealth of "modernistic" furniture, functional homes and factories, tubular chairs, indirect lights, novel advertising layouts and posters, new printing type faces, and new industrial products. The fame of the Bauhaus spread far beyond the borders of Germany.

In cultural life as in economic life, there were shadows as well as lights. Indeed, nowhere were the contrasts of the twenties sharper than in Germany. Some of the literary, artistic, and moral tendencies of the time were disturbing.

There were artists who made a cult of inexpressibility, poets who sang the virtues of unreason and recklessness, and others who indulged in decadent practices and poses. None of the paradoxes of culture, however, could match the conflict latent in politics.

Conventional and avant-garde interiors of the twenties. At the left, a corner of a typical living room. At the right, the functional furniture and modernistic decoration of the Bauhaus, *the German experimental school of design, whose products achieved international fame. The* Bauhaus *style combined the various arts—architecture, sculpture, painting—with technological processes and materials. The Director's room in the* Bauhaus *building at Dessau.* CULVER

Since 1918, Germany had been governed by cabinets supported principally by the Social Democratic and the Catholic Center parties. Between them, the socialists and Communists accounted for a majority of the electorate, but they were at daggers drawn. The socialists moved toward compromise with capitalism, while the Communists, intent on the destruction of the existing regime, flirted with violent, and even Fascist, elements. The extremes of Right and Left discovered a mutual attraction. The greatest danger to the republic came from demagogic conservatism. The National Socialist (Nazi) party was conducting a propaganda campaign against liberals and socialists, against the Treaty of Versailles, against Western civilization, and, most of all, against the Jews, whom they blamed for Germany's troubles. Adolf Hitler, leader of the Nazis, was released from prison after serving less than a year for his part in the Beer Hall *Putsch.* In 1925-27, he published *Mein Kampf,* a violent tract of racial egoism and hatred, which he had composed while in prison. In it, he insisted that Germany must rule the world, that the "biologic elite" of "Aryans" must rule

Germany, and that those who stood in the way—lesser races or dissenting classes —must be physically annihilated.

While Hitler's following was as yet small, more respectable opponents of the republic were numerous and influential. The aristocratic Junkers, officers, and diplomats and the great industrialists and financiers were reconciled neither to the Weimar regime nor to the settlement of the Versailles Treaty. The military caste, although it had exercised virtually dictatorial control over Germany during the war, blamed her defeat on the "home front" and craved a return engagement. They and their fellow conservatives were royalist in sympathy, although the prospect of restoring the Hohenzollern dynasty was dim. Monarchists without a monarch, they were open to adventurism. These groups were not sufficiently strong to control *Reichstag* majorities or form cabinets, but they held substantial power within the government and bureaucracy. In 1925, Field Marshal von Hindenburg, an old man of seventy-seven who made no secret of his continuing devotion to the Hohenzollerns, was elected President.

The leading politician of the republic during the twenties was Gustav Stresemann (1878-1929), who was Chancellor in 1923 and thereafter held the post of Foreign Secretary in every cabinet from 1923 until his death in 1929. Stresemann was an organizer and manager of associations of industrial and business firms. He was the leader of the People's party, supported by many big businessmen. During the war, Stresemann had been a strong annexationist and imperialist. He then turned to republicanism. He pursued the tactics of reconciliation, took his country into the League of Nations, acquired the reputation of "a good European," and in 1926 shared the Nobel peace prize with Aristide Briand, coauthor of the Kellogg-Briand Peace Pact. Yet his predilections seemed to remain monarchical and militaristic. While serving as a leading minister of the republic, he conducted a dutiful correspondence with the former crown prince. He winked at the quiet efforts of the military authorities to prepare the ground for the rearmament of Germany.

Stresemann was not alone in abetting these efforts. Defense ministers also acquiesced. The army general staff was informally continued under another name; new arms were tested in Russia, with the cooperation of the Bolshevik government, which was eager to nurture a countervailing power to the Western European states; and a tough cadre of commissioned and noncommissioned officers was assembled against the day when Germany would reintroduce a conscript army and emerge in new armor to resume an old battle. So great was the respect—amounting sometimes to awe—in which Germans, including many Social Democrats, held the officer corps that no protest was made against the violation of the pledged word of the nation.

Equally portentous was a cultural gap between Germany and the countries to the west. The war dramatized this gap, and the propaganda on both sides exploited it. The leading conservative and professional classes of Germany had been animated for a century by a conception of culture—*Kultur*—which was quite different from the idea of civilization that prevailed in the rest of the Western world. They inherited this conception from a long line of thinkers and writers, notably from Hegel and Fichte. It was a conception that predisposed them to reject the emphasis on individual rights, equality, humanitarianism, and internationalism. Rationalism seemed to them cold and dry, and the bent for empiricism grubbing and materialistic. German conservatives craved a warmer, more romantic, and more elevated philosophy in which history and "idealism" played a larger role than abstract reason and empiricism, and in which the individual was melted into the state and the state became indistinguishable from society. They idealized Germany as an organic entity, created by a long and continuous evolution and inspired by great goals peculiar to herself. In this view, good and evil, right and wrong, freedom and authority, were so entwined that discrimination and choice became difficult. The result was a pervasive tendency to justify whatever existed in the present or had happened in the past, to admire the exhibitions of power in the rise of Prussia and Germany, and to conclude, with Nietzsche, that "might is right."

In 1922 the theologian and sociologist Ernst Troeltsch (1865-1923) summed up the mutual antagonism of German and Western culture:

> Those who believe in an eternal and divine Law of Nature, the equality of man, and a sense of unity pervading mankind, and who find the essence of humanity in these things, cannot but regard the German doctrine as a curious mixture of mysticism and brutality. Those who take an opposite view—who see in history an ever-moving stream which throws up unique individualities as it moves and is always shaping individual structures on the basis of a law which is always new—are bound to consider the West European world of ideas as a world of cold rationalism and equalitarian atomism, a world of superficiality and Pharisaism.

While praising German culture for its social idealism, its strong sense of community, and its enrichment of historical learning, Troeltsch condemned it for deifying the state and exalting Prussian militarism, for nurturing the spirit of inequality and caste, for pursuing pure detail and relativistic interpretations in historical research to the neglect of ethical and philosophical considerations, and for its tendency "to brutalize romance and romanticize cynicism." Troeltsch urged his compatriots to rise from nationalist to international views, to keep humanity as a whole and the future in mind when investigating the past, and to accept the Western sense of the value of the individual and his rights. His counsel fell on deaf ears.

The thought of Oswald Spengler (1880-1936), a teacher of science who drew upon the history of many societies to launch a broad attack on liberalism and democracy, was better suited to the conservative mood. In his widely read and translated *Decline of the West*, published in 1918 and revised in 1923, Spengler argued that cultures, like plants, go through the stages of youth, maturity, and decay. Yet each culture is unique and highly mysterious; men of one culture cannot understand those of another. In their youth and maturity, cultures are led by healthy peasants living by intuition, and by creative priests and noblemen. Then comes "civilization," the age of decay, with its abstract thinking, objective science, large cities, internationalism, and humanitarianism. This stage ends in the dictatorship of the powerful over the inert masses.

There were a few German conservatives who made their peace with republicanism, among them the novelist Thomas Mann (1875-1955). During the war Mann had published, in *Observations of an Unpolitical Man* (1918), a severe attack on liberal values. But the violent and reactionary tendencies of educated youth shocked him into a defense of the republic. In a public address in 1923, he indicted monarchical and militarist prejudice, the apolitical and excessively professional attitude of many Germans, and the incompetence of the former imperial regime. He attacked Spengler for promoting aggressive nationalism. Walt Whitman's democracy and humanitarianism seemed to Mann a better guide for German youth.

Yet Mann did not escape national and romantic biases. He justified every ideal by appealing to German traits. Hans Castorp, the unintellectual hero of Mann's novel *The Magic Mountain* (1924), rises to the highest insights by confronting death, disease, and evil in a Swiss sanitarium for tuberculars and learning that these are inevitable accompaniments of life and idealism. *The Magic Mountain* was enormously popular in Germany and helped to bring Mann the Nobel prize for literature in 1929. A decade later the novelist undertook to explain to Americans the meaning of his book. "*The Magic Mountain*," he wrote, "is a very German book. 'There are,' Hans Castorp once says, 'two ways to life: one is the regular, direct and good way; the other is bad, it leads through death, and that is the way of genius.' The German reader recognized himself in the simple-minded but shrewd young hero of the novel. He could and would be guided by him." In the end, while his political commitments were rationalistic and liberal, Mann believed in instinctive "wisdom" and romantic action.

Central Europe and Turkey

Though defeated in war and reduced in size, Germany had remained a substantial and united country. She retained many of her industrial and agricultural resources, and this made eventual economic recovery possible.

The aftermath of defeat was far more serious for other empires. Austria-Hungary had fallen apart into small competing and jealous states, and Russia had lost considerable territory to five new states and several old neighbors. The region that lay between Germany and Russia, and between the Baltic and the Mediterranean Seas, accounted for nearly a fifth of the area of the Continent. Its population of 106 million was divided among thirteen states. Only Poland, with about thirty million people, was comparable in size with the more considerable states of Europe. This political subdivision resulted from the attempt to put an end to national oppression by introducing the principle of self-determination. However, in a region of inextricably mixed peoples it was impossible to draw any boundaries that enclosed only compact and homogeneous peoples. The result was that the minority problem was, in a manner of speaking, decentralized. Each state now had a large sampling of minority groups. Twenty-two million out of 106 million people belonged to such groups. Germans and Hungarians joined the ranks of minority subjects in such countries as Czechoslovakia, Rumania, and Poland. The solution of the national problem therefore depended on a liberal and equitable treatment of their minorities by the new states.

Distribution of Minorities in Central and

Eastern Europe in the Twenties

(SOURCE: *Encyclopaedia Britannica*, 13th ed., supplementary vol. II, pp. 931-32)

Country	Majority	Minorities
Albania	817,800	Some thousands of Greeks
Austria	5,360,000	Jews, 270,000
		Czechs, 245,000
		Serbs-Croats-Slovenes, 117,500
		Hungarians, 88,500
Bulgaria	3,441,000	Turks and Tartars, 454,700
		Gypsies, 115,700
		Rumanians, 78,000
		Greeks, 48,300
		Jews, 43,500
		Various, 676,000
Czechoslovakia	8,760,000	Germans, 3,123,000
		Magyars, 745,000
		Ruthenes, 461,800
		Jews, 180,800
		Poles, 75,800
		Various, 260,000
Estonia	969,900	Russians, 91,200
		Germans, 18,000
		Swedes, 7,800
		Jews, 4,500
		Various, 15,000
Finland	3,500,000	Swedes, 380,000
		Russians, 6,000
Germany	61,000,000	Danes, Poles, and Wends
Greece	5,157,000	Rumanians, 486,700
		Albanians, 162,000
		Jews, 110,000
		Turks and Tartars, 59,000
		Various (Slavs, etc.), 500,000
Hungary	7,147,000	Germans, 551,200
		Slovaks, 141,800
		Jews, 60,000

		Serbs-Croats-Slovenes, 53,900
		Rumanians, 23,700
Italy	41,000,000	Germans, 280,000
		Slovenes, 250,000
		Croats, 150,000
		French Vaudois, 85,000
		Albanians, 80,000
		Greeks, 25,000
Latvia	1,159,300	Great Russians, 91,500
		Jews, 79,300
		Little Russians, 66,000
		Germans, 58,000
		Poles, 52,200
		Lithuanians, 25,500
		Estonians, 8,700
Lithuania	2,702,000	Jews, 153,700
(including Memel)		Poles, 65,600
		Russians, 50,500
		Germans, 29,200
Poland	17,667,000	Ruthenes, 4,220,000
		Jews, 2,520,000
		Germans, 1,550,000
		Russians, 1,135,000
		Lithuanians, 72,750
		Various, 50,000
Rumania	11,576,000	Magyars, 1,650,500
		Ukrainians, 1,100,000
		Germans, 804,000
		Ruthenes, 793,800
		Jews, 770,000
		Bulgars, 251,000
		Turks and Tartars, 230,000
		Serbs, 62,300
		Various, 579,000
Turkey	8,518,000	Greeks, 220,000
		Jews, 68,600
		Armenians, 40,000
		Gypsies, 23,500
		Various, 2,413,000
Yugoslavia	9,971,600	Germans, 518,400
(Serb-Croat-		Magyars, 472,400
Slovene State)		Albanians, 441,500
		Rumanians, 229,000
		Bulgars and other Slavs, 174,000
		Italians, 12,800
		Various, 212,000

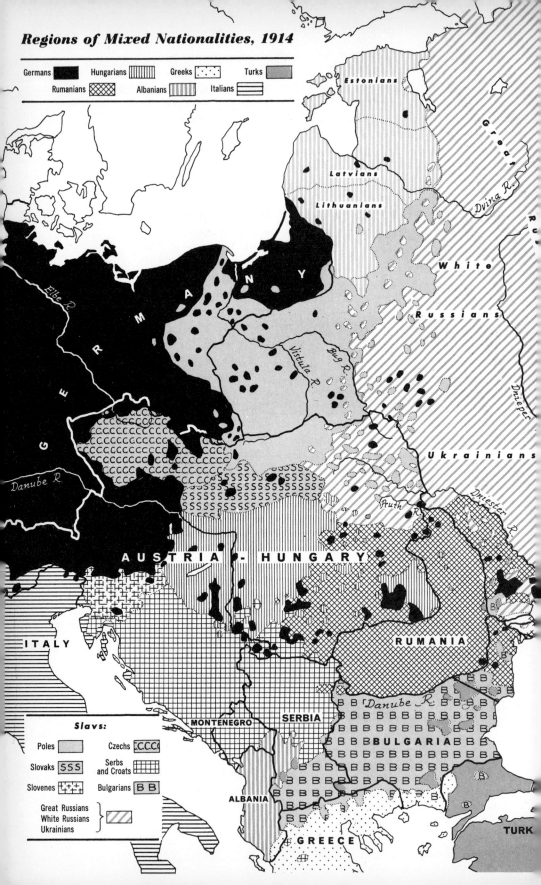

Regions of Mixed Nationalities, 1914

Germans ▉   Hungarians ▐▐▐   Greeks ⁛   Turks ▨

Rumanians ⊠   Albanians ▨   Italians ▤

Estonians

Latvians

Lithuanians

Great Russia?

Dvina R.

Dnieper

White

Russians

Ukrainians

GERMANY

Elbe R.

Vistula R.

Bug R.

Danube R.

AUSTRIA - HUNGARY

Pruth

Dniester R.

ITALY

RUMANIA

B

Danube R.

MONTENEGRO

SERBIA

BULGARIA

Slavs:

Poles ▨   Czechs CCCC

Slovaks SSS   Serbs and Croats ▦

Slovenes +++   Bulgarians BB

Great Russians
White Russians   ▨
Ukrainians

ALBANIA

GREECE

TURK

Such treatment, however, was hard to come by. Nearly everywhere the minorities suffered from a variety of economic and political disabilities or discriminations. Czechoslovakia's fair minority policy made her a shining exception. Poland governed her German subjects with mildness, but on the other hand she bore down hard on Ukrainians, White Russians, and Jews.

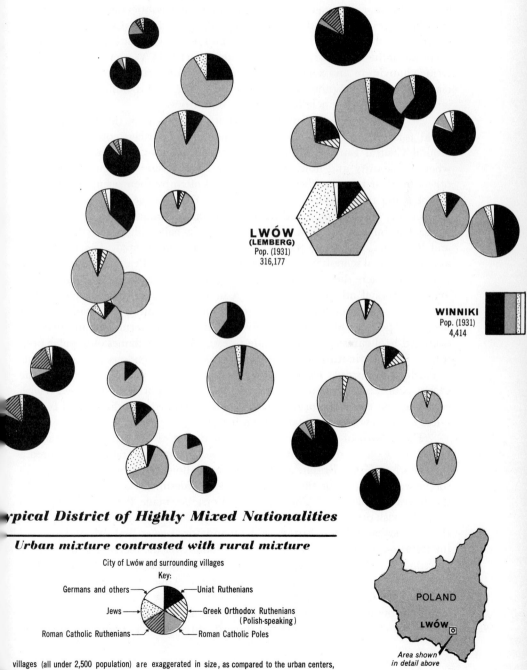

LWÓW
(LEMBERG)
Pop. (1931)
316,177

WINNIKI
Pop. (1931)
4,414

ypical District of Highly Mixed Nationalities

Urban mixture contrasted with rural mixture

City of Lwów and surrounding villages
Key:

Germans and others ——————— Uniat Ruthenians

Jews ——————— Greek Orthodox Ruthenians
(Polish-speaking)

Roman Catholic Ruthenians ——————— Roman Catholic Poles

POLAND

LWÓW

*Area shown
in detail above*

villages (all under 2,500 population) are exaggerated in size, as compared to the urban centers,
⸱rder to show the national distribution, but are drawn to a scale that compares them with each other.

There was hardly an issue, whether territorial, economic, or cultural, in which national suspicions were not brought into play. Where, as often happened, landlords and peasants belonged to different nationalities, the land problem became most acute. The urban population often belonged to minority groups, while the peasantry formed the official "nation." It was the village that in some of the countries supplied the "official language" and a large class of semi-literates, white-collar clerks, professional men, and politicians, who aspired to the offices, privileges, and emoluments of the new national states. In the circumstances, the more enlightened urban and liberal elements did not generally exert the influence that their counterparts exerted in Western countries. Extreme chauvinism and xenophobia were often stimulated by opportunist politicians. Textbooks magnified the most trivial "glories" of the official nations and ignored those of their neighbors or their minorities.

No people suffered more from national excesses than the Jews. Out of a world total of 14 million, fully half lived in the thirteen countries grouped around Central Europe. Unlike the other nationalities, the Jews were everywhere a minority and nowhere a majority. They were distinguished from all others by their religion, their traditions, and often by their occupations. In an age of rising peasant power, they were an urban people, although the small towns many of them inhabited resembled villages or market places rather than cities. The bulk of the Jews—about four and a half million—lived in Poland and Rumania, and there they were harried and persecuted. The universities and professional schools imposed severe quotas on them. Peasant youth streamed into towns, where they competed with the Jews for work, business opportunities, and professional advancement. Since a university degree was the passport to positions in the professions, the intimidation and beating of Jewish students became a permanent feature of university life. The governments in effect encouraged hooliganism. A semiliterate priesthood fed the flames of popular prejudice by indoctrinating their ignorant flocks with horrendous tales of the role of the Jews in history. *The Protocols of the Learned Elders of Zion,* a forgery of the czarist police, first printed in Russia in 1903, was purported to disclose a Jewish conspiracy to rule the world. It was widely translated and distributed by agitators who knew it for the fabrication it was.

The growth of anti-Semitism stimulated that of Zionism, which had become an organized movement at the turn of the century. The Zionists scored a success when Great Britain asserted, in the Balfour Declaration of 1917, that she viewed "with favor the establishment in Palestine of a national home for the Jewish people. . . ." The Treaty of Versailles made Palestine, along with other Turkish provinces, a mandated territory, and in 1922 the League approved the designation of Great Britain as the mandatory power. But Britain restricted immigration severely, and Zionists were at odds over the methods of developing Palestine. A European group led by Dr. Chaim Weizmann (1874-1952) advocated an energetic cultural and political policy, while an American group led by Louis D. Brandeis (1856-1941), Associate Justice of the Supreme Court, favored economic investment and development.

In an effort to abate national discord, three Balkan countries resorted to the drastic means of exchanging populations. In the early twenties, Greece and Turkey had exchanged minorities (see p. 540), whose resettlement was financed with the help of a loan from the League of Nations and donations of American organizations. Greece made a similar but smaller exchange of population with Bulgaria. If this solution had been applied elsewhere in the region, it would have required the resettling of twenty-two million people.

Common sense suggested flight to some members of discontented minority groups. But the doors of receiving countries began quickly to close. In 1921 the United States limited immigration. The quotas assigned to the various countries were based on the national origins of the American population of 1920. The number of immigrants immediately fell from 805,228 for the fiscal year ending June 30, 1921, to 309,556 for the following fiscal year. The quota was further reduced until it was fixed, in 1927, at 150,000 persons. Since Western and Northern Europe had contributed the bulk of the population in the past whereas the pressure for migration to America was now stronger in Southern and Eastern Europe, the effect of the quota system was to restrict immigration from the latter regions especially severely. The United States was not the only country that limited immigration.

Other overseas countries imposed various restrictions, such as the possession of capital or knowledge or training in particular skills. On the Continent, only France, which had lost a considerable part of her working force in the war, encouraged entrants. From the mid-twenties on, Germany discouraged immigrants from Eastern Europe. The national problems of the new states were aggravated by their economic difficulties. Only Czechoslovakia and Poland had large-scale industrial centers. Rumania had valuable deposits of oil. With these exceptions, the region was predominantly pastoral and agricultural. The landlords generally dominated the villagers, most of whom were poor peasants or landless laborers. While the farm lands were more crowded than those in Western Europe, the yield was much smaller. In many places the wooden plough was still in use. Raising the level of the farmer required a complex program to reduce the density of rural population by siphoning off labor to urban occupations, to train the remaining farmers in modern means and methods of cultivation, to extend credit for farm machinery, and to provide free land. Neither governments nor landlords proposed to carry out such a program. The peasants demanded that the large estates be broken up into small farms. Peasant parties arose throughout the region.

A few countries promoted peasant proprietorship. Czechoslovakia and Yugoslavia distributed land bought from landowners to thousands of peasants. On a smaller scale, Rumania also increased independent farming. Elsewhere, by raising the cry of "Red" and promoting dictatorial governments, landowners arrested the movement. Poland soon stopped the process of breaking up large estates. In Hungary, even the few estates divided during 1919 were returned to their owners. There and elsewhere cooperative marketing and purchase were discouraged as "communistic." The discontent of peasants was often deflected by demagogues toward antagonism to the urban population and the Jews.

Next to the condition of the peasantry, trade restrictions presented the most serious economic problem of the region. The new boundary lines did not encourage economic exchange. The Hapsburg Empire had had two free trade areas, Austria and Hungary; the two became six as a result of the rise of Czechoslovakia and Poland and the Empire's losses to Rumania and Yugoslavia. The Danube now flowed through six countries separated by currency and tariff walls. The industries of Czechoslovakia found markets in Western Europe but lost their former free outlets in Austria. Hungary was as badly placed to sell its foodstuffs as Czechoslovakia its finished goods. The economic position of Austria was the sorriest of all. Two thirds of her six and a half million people squeezed a poor living from an infertile, though beautiful, countryside, and the rest lived in Vienna, a metropolis that had lost its *raison d'être* as the commercial, financial, and administrative center of an empire. The countryside was Christian Democratic while Vienna had a Social Democratic government. This Social Democratic government developed an energetic program of housing reform, but it could not solve the basic difficulty: there was no need for one Viennese to manage and supply every two peasants. League of Nations loans eased the condition of Austria, but only temporarily.

These discords were hardly favorable to basic reform. Only two countries undertook significant improvements. One of these was liberal Czechoslovakia, the other dictatorial Turkey.

Czechoslovakia introduced not only the forms but the practices of liberal democracy. Her constitution was modeled on that of the United States, except for the federal feature. As in most Continental countries, there were many parties, but the Czechs managed to weld them into effective governing coalitions. Two able statesmen, Thomas Masaryk (1850-1937) and Eduard Benes (1884-1948), provided leadership through their presidencies. Czechoslovakia had a fair balance of modern industry and competent farming. She provided the population with a more efficient government than it had ever had. She had an energetic commercial and industrial class, a liberal class of professional and educated men, and a disciplined and modest people.

Turkey went through the first revolution since the Mohammedan conquest five centuries earlier. It was a French-style revolution, but in a country whose social and political pattern was more archaic than the Old Regime of Western Europe. The reformers were a tightly knit group of officers and professional men led by a dynamic figure. He was Mustapha Kemal Pasha, an officer whose energy had frustrated the British invaders of Gallipoli in 1915-16 and rolled back the Greek invaders of Asia Minor in 1922. In 1923, as President of the provisional national government, he had wrested the only negotiated treaty from the Western Allies.

Kemal was determined to make Turkey the equal of Western countries in efficiency, strength, and dignity. Before a decade passed, he and his followers had turned Turkey upside down. They swept away the cobwebs of Ottoman despotism and a host of autocratic and traditional institutions, as well as the picturesque customs which had dazzled romantic Europeans for centuries. Kemal forbade the wearing of the red fez which had become inseparable from the very idea of a Turk and discouraged the veil which had always covered the faces of Turkish women. He abolished polygamy and introduced divorce. Women became the legal equals of men in matters of property, education, marriage, and divorce.

An effort was made to encourage industrial and technological development and commercial exchange. The peasant secured full tenure in his land. The Sultan, who had been the Caliph, or religious head, of the Mohammedan world as well as the Turkish ruler, was exiled; Kemal separated the two functions, then abolished the caliphate. The capital was removed from Constantinople (later Istanbul), a labyrinth of corruption and intrigue and a strong Greek commercial center, to the ancient but humble town of Angora (later Ankara) in central Asia Minor. Kemal introduced parliamentary forms but exercised a mild dictatorship in order to bring the recalcitrants into line. He prescribed male suffrage and free and compulsory primary education, and replaced the Turkish script with the Latin alphabet. He adopted wholesale the tools and trimmings of Westernism: the metric system, the Gregorian calendar, international time, and family names.

Kemal's revolution impressed the world as much as his military victories. It made Turkey the only defeated country that was stronger and more self-confident, though much smaller, than before the war.

The advances of Turkey and Czechoslovakia were exceptional. Other countries made neither political nor economic progress. While parliamentary forms were generally introduced, the regimes were in effect dictatorial and authoritarian. In Hungary, Admiral Horthy and his followers directed an apparatus of police control and repression. A similar group, led by army officers under Marshal Joseph Pilsudski (1867-1935), ruled Poland with an iron hand inside the velvet glove of constitutionalism. In Rumania, a constitutional monarchy, the governing party called itself "Liberal" while its leader, Ion Bratianu (1869-1927), effectively kept other parties out of power by fixed elections, intimidation, and manipulation of the courts. Like Rumania, Yugoslavia was a constitutional monarchy, but she was ruled by a clique of Serbian politicians who excluded Croatians from office. Finally, in 1929, King Alexander (1921-34) proclaimed a royal dictatorship.

The multiple tensions of Central Europe—political, economic, and national—found vent in a literature of frustration. The cultural centers of Vienna and Prague radiated a mood of despair. Their inhabitants had seen more trouble than those of Western Europe—the dissolution of an ancient empire, revolutions, mob outbreaks, national persecution—and, unlike the Russians, they were free to publish their hurt and their fear for the future—not only their own future but that of the whole Western world.

The Austrian novelist Robert Musil (1880-1942) drew a frightening picture of social decay and incoherence. In his uncompleted novel, *The Man Without Qualities*, he traced the moral and intellectual decline of the modern world to social deterioration, political ineptitude, and "an out-and-out intoxication, a very fire of matter-of-factness." The symbol of his age to Musil was the slide rule, carried in the breast pocket "like a hard white line over the heart." To Musil mechanical, statistical, and material explanations stifled the sublime elements in human experience.

In the play *R.U.R.* (1920), the Czech dramatist Karel Capek (1890-1938) announced the victory of machine over man. His "heroes" were a new race of machine-made "robots," who walked, talked, and performed physical tasks but had no imagination, feelings, or sexual desires. In order to distract the robots from combining to attack mankind, their manufacturer proposes to divide them by endowing them with national prejudices. Each country would produce machine-men of "a different color, a different language. They'll be complete strangers to each other. They'll never be able to understand each other. Then we'll egg them on a little in the matter of misunderstanding and the result will be that for ages to come every robot will hate every other robot of a different mark." However, before the robots can be "nationalized," they rise in rebellion and destroy the whole human race. Fortunately, the engineer who produced them had recently changed their character, endowing them with irritability. This made them human, and they proceeded to fall in love and reproduce themselves. Man vanished, but technology and science provided a reasonable facsimile.

Franz Kafka (1883-1924), a native of Prague who wrote in German, distilled the essence of human rootlessness, incoherence, and incommunicability. The hero of *The Trial* (1935) is arrested without cause; the charge is unknown even to the judges and counsel. The only defense of the accused is his attitude toward the situation in which he finds himself, and although he is innocent— indeed, he cannot find out what he is accused of doing—the best he can hope for is a suspended sentence. In Kafka's *Amerika* (1935) there are only sumptuous hotels and cheap slums. The nameless hero of *The Castle* (1936) arrives in a village dominated by a mysterious castle to claim the post of surveyor, to which he believes he has been appointed. He is informed, on the one hand, that there is no work for a surveyor and, on the other, that his claim is just and he ought to press it. It turns out to be impossible to locate the responsible official in charge and obtain a definite answer to what is, after all, a very simple question. The hero cannot even communicate satisfactorily with the villagers, whose relation to the castle is as mysterious as his own. Thus, Kafka seems to say, man wears himself out in the fruitless effort to make contact with his fellow men.

Kafka ordered his manuscripts to be burned after his death, and Musil never finished his sprawling novel. Their work reflected a region in dissolution.

The Rise of Stalin and the Five-Year Plan

To the east of this region lay a country where national problems had been attenuated even while political dictatorship was intensified. Russia had lost much territory in the war, but she was still by far the largest country in Europe. Her losses had removed many of her former subject nationalities. The Bolshevik rulers were determined not to repeat the error of the czars, who had increased disaffection by persecuting minorities. They were careful not to seem to discriminate in favor of the Great Russians. Joseph Stalin, who was Commissar for Nationalities as well as Secretary General of the party, and himself a Georgian, encouraged the use and development of minority languages. Yet Russia was riven, like the capitalist countries, by political and economic tensions.

Lenin died in 1924, at fifty-four. He supplied Communist Russia with its first saint. His body was embalmed, like that of an Egyptian pharaoh, and placed on permanent display in a mausoleum in Red Square in Moscow. Millions made the pilgrimage to the shrine, crossing themselves in awe as they stared at his face. Yet Lenin suffered no defeat in life as sharp as his defeat in death. He had no answer to the question of succession, and his party ignored his warnings and preferences.

Lenin's repudiation of the republican and parliamentary principle deprived the Communist state of an orderly process of succession and made dictatorship or oligarchy inevitable. Lenin's own dictatorship was somewhat obscured by his demeanor. Although his powers were as substantial as those of the absolute czars, he was modest in his bearing and personal wants. He worked, like a modern ward politician, by exercising personal influence on a small body of compeers.

The ruling party was an oligarchy, controlled by a small group at the top, usually the twenty-odd members of the Central Committee, with the support of a larger cadre of local and administrative officials. These officers were virtually nominated from the top, with confirmatory elections from below. Decisions were never submitted to an open vote of the party as a whole, not to mention the citizenry. A leader who could nominate or influence the members of the Central Committee could become a dictator. Indeed, the original committee of the party had been assembled by Lenin before the November Revolution.

During the last two years of his life Lenin was ailing, and two members of the Central Committee—Leon Trotsky and Joseph Stalin—began to measure themselves for his mantle. Their relationship had always been rasping. In a political "testament," Lenin singled out Trotsky as the abler man. He feared, however, that Trotsky had a "too far-reaching confidence and a disposition to be attracted by the purely administrative side of affairs." Lenin's comment on Stalin was portentous.

> Stalin has concentrated an enormous power in his hands; and I am not sure that he always knows how to use that power with sufficient caution. . . . Stalin is too rude, and this fault, entirely supportable among us Communists [!], becomes insupportable in the office of General Secretary. Therefore I propose to the comrades to find a way to remove Stalin from that position and appoint to it another man who in all respects differs from Stalin only in superiority— namely, more patient, more loyal, more polite, and more attentive to comrades, less capricious, etc. This circumstance may seem an insignificant trifle, but I think that from the point of view of preventing a split and from the point of view of the relation between Stalin and Trotsky . . . it is not a trifle, or it is such a trifle as may acquire a decisive significance.

Although he seemed to prefer Trotsky, Lenin could not designate a successor nor a method for ensuring the moderation of the Communist oligarchy. He could only suggest that the Central Committee of the party be increased in size in order to recruit fresh talent.

Upon Lenin's death, Trotsky and Stalin locked horns. Maneuvers behind the scenes, intrigues among a small group of leaders, and the manipulation of bureaucratic and press support were the weapons of their war. In this struggle, Trotsky betrayed political ineptitude while Stalin proved supple as well as unscrupulous. He placed his followers in strategic positions and demoted or removed his opponents. These opponents were not always the same, for he entered into deals first with one faction and then with another. By 1925-26 he had emerged as the principal figure in the Communist party and government. The consequence of the struggle was that the restraint upon public opinion in general was now extended to the members of the party. The last vestige of freedom within the party disappeared. Trotsky was removed from his post as Commissar of War, and many other opponents of Stalin were also thrown out of office and of the party. Front-rank leaders who had carried out the Revolution gave place to obedient officials, bureaucrats, and administrators, bound to the new dictator.

Stalin, which means "of steel," was the assumed name of Josef Vissarionovich Dzhugashvili. He was indeed hard and all of a piece. Yet there were complexities and even contradictions in him. Born in Georgia, he became a Great Russian patriot. Trained to become an Eastern Orthodox priest, he reduced Marxism to a catechism. He drew the most extreme conclusions from the doctrine and applied them with the utmost literalness. He was as savage to the unseen millions he consigned to death in the Arctic purgatories of Siberia as he was rude to his closest comrades and intimates. Alone of the leading Bolsheviks, he had spent no considerable period abroad and was untouched by Western culture.

Stalin inherited the basic dilemma of the Bolshevik Revolution. That Revolution had been made with the expectation that more advanced countries—above all, Germany—would overthrow capitalism, give Russia technical and financial assistance without turning her into a dependency, and help to prevent the remaining capitalist countries from combining against her. By the mid-twenties, however, it had become clear that the revolutionary wave produced by the war had ebbed. Marx's assumption that a revolutionary regime could not maintain itself in an isolated country, especially if that country was backward economically, and that the capitalist countries would crush the experiment was still to be tested.

The economic dilemma was even more serious. Industrialization was held to be a condition of socialism, but the introduction of modern industry could be speeded up only through the help of foreign credits and technical advice. The fact that the Bolsheviks had repudiated the Russian foreign debt and were directing an international organization for the overthrow of capitalism made conditions anything but attractive to foreign investors. Moreover, the

Lenin and Stalin photographed in 1922. SOVFOTO

re-establishment of friendly relations with non-Communist countries seemed to be incompatible with the maintenance of exclusive control by a party which made the fear of capitalist enmity and "encirclement" one of the chief justifications of its dictatorship. Thus the interests of the party required the isolation of Russia, and the defense against a presumed eventual capitalist attack required the rapid development of industrial and military resources.

These aims were summed up in the controversy over the New Economic Policy which had been begun by Lenin in 1921. It became apparent in the mid-twenties that the NEP, under which the country had regained some stability, would have to be either extended or curtailed. The NEP provided for a mixed economy. Industry, banking, and transportation were in the hands of the state, while agriculture was largely in the hands of individual farmers, and a substantial amount of private trading was permitted. Under this regime the number of private entrepreneurs ("nepmen") and richer farmers ("kulaks") increased, as did the pressure for greater economic freedom.

One wing of the Communist party, led by the leading Bolshevik theoretician, Nikolai Bukharin (1888-1938), was inclined to yield to this pressure. It proposed to satisfy the demand for consumers' goods by imports from abroad and extend the power of the peasants to lease land and hire labor. Another opposition group, led by Trotsky, wished to put an end to individualistic agriculture. Having overthrown aristocratic institutions, Russia, they claimed, must

599

proceed without delay to root out capitalistic tendencies and to press for intensive industrialization, as a basis for the establishment of complete communism. Such an effort was bound to fail in the end, however, unless the revolution spread to other countries. While prosecuting a "permanent revolution" at home, Russia had to induce revolutions in capitalist countries.

Stalin recoiled from both of these programs. Bukharin's course implied an easing of the dictatorship and Russia's assimilation to the Western pattern of economic development. Trotsky's stress on international revolution made the destiny of Russia dependent on events elsewhere. Stalin combined the interests of the dictatorship with those of nationalism: he asserted the possibility of building "socialism in one country." After defeating Trotsky, he appropriated his program of rapid industrialization and applied it with a characteristic literalness.

To force Russia to become—overnight, as it were—an industrialized and urban country was an enterprise from which most of the Bolshevik leaders, even Lenin himself, had shrunk. Nor were the implications of Marxism encouraging on this point: political measures reflected rather than initiated economic development; force was the "midwife," not the mother, of new societies. Marx had predicted that socialism would be the outcome of industrialization but that it was the "historical role" of the capitalists to develop industry. That is, the exploitation necessary to transform an agricultural into an industrial country would be perpetrated by capitalists. The abolition of capitalism would then "purge" mankind of the perpetrators and the memory of oppression. Under Stalin's plan, however, a socialist government, representing a small proletariat, would act the role of exploiter. Assuming that it succeeded in industrializing Russia by dictatorial means, freedom could be obtained only by putting an end to the "socialist" government. However, Stalin did not appreciate theoretical niceties and was not deterred by social cost or by future political consequences. "This cook," Lenin had said of him, "will prepare only peppery dishes." Stalin's first dish was the Five-Year Plan.

Under this plan, the trading privileges of the NEP would be ended. Forced domestic savings would take the place of foreign capital. The people were to be compelled to work harder, produce more, and consume less. The farm surpluses thus produced would be exported to pay for the much-needed machinery and technical skill. As a result of the revolution, 95 percent of the land was under the control of individual owners. Most of these holdings were now to be amalgamated into collectives or state farms. This would facilitate the collection of the surplus, the allocation of the produce assigned to consumption, and the mechanization and rationalization of cultivation. The government would regiment labor, allocate raw materials, direct the building of new plants, and, above all, lay the foundation for heavy industries, at the expense of the production of consumers' goods. Industrial production would be increased by 130 percent. The largest increases were provided for in the production of coal, iron, oil, electrical power, and farm machinery. The area under cultivation was to be increased by nearly 25 percent in five years.

The Five-Year Plan was launched in 1928. In order to reconcile the population to the hardships and deprivations involved, the government appealed to patriotism, to the fear of attack, and to the hope of eventual betterment. Where argument failed, it resorted to the whip. The present generation was to be sacrificed on the altar of the future. No government of a large country had ever embarked upon so deliberate and comprehensive an industrial revolution. No government had imposed so difficult a regimen upon its people, except in times of war or national emergency. The Five-Year Plan set Russia upon the course of a frenetic industrialization and "isolationism" and tore many of her bonds with the rest of the Western world.

The launching of the Five-Year Plan, a mixture of economic radicalism and political regression, completed the counterpoint of experiment and conformity that characterized the 1920's. The Western world as a whole, like Russia, had much unfinished business. It had adjourned many an old problem and was gingerly testing many a new idea. The decade of the twenties was a time of transition. The poles between which it oscillated were nowhere more apparent than in economic life. After beginning with a depression and staging a striking recovery, the decade ended in a thundering crash.

VII   *The Ordeal of Liberty*

Der Zweifler (The Doubter), *1937, by the German sculptor Ernst Barlach (1870-1938).*

28. *The World Depression and the Western Democracies*

The depression which began in 1929 was the worst economic crisis the Western world had ever experienced. Its impact, reach, and consequences set it apart from the earlier depressions that had punctuated the career of capitalism. It affected agricultural as well as highly industrial countries, countries that had won the war of 1914-18 as well as those that had lost it. Unemployment reached the largest scale known to modern history. In some countries the consequences of the economic crisis were hardly less than revolutionary, and every country was affected by the international tensions that it produced.

The Crash of 1929

The depression began in the United States. The excessive speculation of the mid-twenties, the sensitiveness of the financial market, and protectionist policies, which made it difficult to improve trade relations with the rest of the world, were straws in the wind. Since influential financiers, economists, and politicians had assured the community, and convinced themselves, that prosperity had no limits, the decline seemed to come out of the blue. In March 1929, President Herbert Hoover (1874-   ), who had made his reputation as an expert in industry and technology, told the American people, "In the larger view, we have reached a higher degree of comfort and security than has ever existed before in the history of the world. . . . We are steadily building up a new race, a new civilization. . . . I have no fears for the future of our country. It is bright with hope."

Six months later American finance and investment caved in. In September stock prices stood at the highest point in history. They were highly inflated, and some stocks brought ten times more than they were worth. In October the market broke: there was a stampede of sellers. Millions of shares changed hands and prices plummeted downward. Within a few days, many rich men lost much of their wealth, and smaller investors were wiped out by the hundreds of thousands. Those who had bought largely on credit could not supply the money suddenly required for keeping possession of their holdings. Eventually seventy-four billion dollars in stock values—much of it, it is true, speculative—disappeared.

Not only financial but industrial and commercial loans were called in. Consumption and buying began to lag. Many businesses gasped for the breath of credit. It was two years before the full effect was felt. National income was cut virtually in half. Wages dropped even more, although profits of solvent firms stood up better. Employment dropped sharply. A sizable proportion of the masses sank into daily want.

Soon the depression spread abroad. The falling off in buying affected European countries. The fever of speculation had already drained Europe of funds and credits in search of inflated profits; now the crash caused investors and financiers to withdraw their funds from any industry or country that seemed in trouble. The atmosphere was filled with rumors and nerves were tense.

Early in 1930, the Assembly of the League of Nations considered a proposal to create an economic federation of Europe. No agreement could be reached. Meanwhile Germany and Austria discussed a treaty abolishing customs duties on their common frontier. The fears of the resurgence of a greater and militant Germany were revived, and the World Court voided the treaty.

In May 1931 it was discovered that the largest bank of Vienna—the Kredit Anstalt für Handel und Gewerbe—could not meet its obligations. Among its

During the great depression, encampments of unemployed sprang up in many parts of America. They were named "Hoovervilles" after the incumbent President. These desolate shacks, on the shores of the Hudson River in New York City, form a sharp contrast to the comfortable apartments and Riverside Church in the background. KEYSTONE

creditors were financial houses in Western countries and the United States, and its investments were scattered all over Central Europe. After the collapse of the Hapsburg monarchy in 1918, the failure of the Kredit Anstalt was the greatest blow to the economic unity of the succession states and to the importance of Vienna as an investment center.

The effect was felt promptly in Germany. Several great financial and commercial firms failed in the summer. As foreign investors called in their loans and sold their German holdings, the *Reichsbank* itself became shaky. For a time, all banks were closed, and so was the stock market. Reparations payments were jeopardized, which disturbed the expectations and hence the operations of other governments.

Then the paralysis spread across the Channel. As the ranks of the unemployed swelled, trade declined, and the receipts of taxation were reduced, the British government found it increasingly difficult to make ends meet. The balance of foreign trade worsened, and gold flowed constantly to the United States and France. Government commissions warned of trouble ahead unless stringent measures were taken. There was growing unrest in the country due to falling employment and wages, and even the beginning of a naval mutiny. Holders of government bonds sold heavily. Finally, in September 1931, pressed to the wall, the British government suspended the gold standard. The pound fell from its normal level of about $4.80 to approximately $3.50. Other currencies were also falling; by 1933 half the countries of the world, including the United States, had followed suit in abandoning the gold standard. The psychological effect was even greater than the economic. The gold standard, particularly its embodiment in the English pound, had for a century been the symbol of stability impressed on the world largely by the once-dominant British Empire and economy.

France closed the circle of crisis. Less industrialized than England and endowed with a more balanced and self-sufficient economy, France was able to resist the first onslaught of the depression. Her banks had been gathering up the gold of less steady countries. But the effects of the diminution of world trade and foreign tourism were inescapable. In the winter of 1931-32, both exports and imports dropped, unemployment rose, and the charge of relief payments was heavy on the national exchequer. The budget showed a large deficit, and in December 1932 France refused for the first time to pay the installment, or even to make a token payment, on her debt to the United States.

Finally, even Russia, which stood outside the prevailing system of international relationships, did not remain unaffected. When the depression deepened, the first Five-Year Plan was in full swing. The Plan contemplated the sale of agricultural products and other raw materials abroad in exchange for industrial imports. As world prices dropped, so did the value of Russian exports. The government tightened the screws of the domestic economy by decreasing consumption still more and exacting still more effort of the toilers.

By 1932 the crisis had become general. In many countries, national income fell off by 40 percent from the levels of 1929. Thirty million men were idle. This

Massive unemployment in Great Britain. A scene outside a labor exchange : men crowding in to register in the hope—often vain—of securing work. WIDE WORLD

figure includes only fairly industrial countries which kept statistics. It does not include Asia, or the many millions who were working only part time. It is estimated that enforced idleness trebled from 1929 to 1932.

The depression worsened the position of Europe among the continents, changed the relation between industrial and undeveloped countries, and induced a crisis of leadership. By the early twenties, Europe's share of world trade had dropped to 45 percent from the 60 percent it had held before the World War. The beginnings of industrialization in "backward" regions reduced the markets of countries exporting finished goods. Economic imperialism became more difficult. The governments of the more advanced industrial countries were democratic, but the direction of economic affairs had been left to business leaders who bore no responsibility to the community for their decisions. Would the owning and managing classes permit a democratization of economic policies? Were the popular parties in a position to take over the management of affairs? Could the various countries adjourn their disputes to act together on a common problem?

Business leaders and conservative politicians could propose only conventional palliatives. They hoped to ride out the storm by measures of economy and deflation at home and by international agreements on disarmament, reparations, and war debts. The Republican administration in Washington laid responsibility for the depression on Europe. There were budgetary difficulties everywhere, and this suggested the desirability of an agreement to reduce military and naval expenses. In 1930 the United States, Japan, and Great Britain agreed, in the London Naval Treaty, to limit their naval building by accepting fixed ratios for the various arms and shops. But they could not prevail upon France and Italy to join them. Italy insisted on parity with her neighbor, who was willing to grant it only if the other powers undertook to check aggressors, which they refused to do. General disarmament had been promised in the Treaty of Versailles as a measure of amity; it now became even more desirable as a measure of economy. In February 1932 the Disarmament Conference, long prepared by the League of Nations, finally convened. Germany demanded equality, but France rejected this demand. The Americans proposed reduction of all arms by one third. The European powers wished to distinguish between defensive and offensive arms, but they could not agree on how to make the distinction. For example, the submarine was rated by the United States and Great Britain as offensive and by France as defensive. When Great Britain finally proposed a draft treaty, with discriminating reductions, Germany objected and withdrew from the conference and from the League of Nations altogether.

Economic efforts fared no better. In the Summer of 1931, when the financial crisis had broken out on the Continent, President Hoover secured a one-year moratorium on payments of foreign-government debts and reparations. Since the United States was the largest creditor, the relief was welcome, though temporary. At the same time, a conference of bankers agreed to a "standstill agreement," under which Germany would not be called upon to honor private foreign debts for six months. The larger issues remained unsettled. Germany never resumed the payment of reparations, but the United States refused to consider forgiving the debts owed to it by other governments. After the year's grace, Great Britain paid the usual installment but suggested a revision of future payments. France and a number of other countries defaulted. The structure of war debts crumbled.

It remained only to attempt to stabilize currencies and trade. With this object, a World Economic Conference met in London in the summer of 1933. The United States agreed to join only if the debt question was avoided. It was proposed to restore the gold standard, in order to stabilize prices and to facilitate exchanges. To this the United States objected, and the Conference adjourned without results.

While these international efforts were going forward, domestic measures were taken which followed a common pattern. The various governments reduced their budgets by slashing administrative salaries and relief payments. This encouraged businessmen to follow similar tactics. Tariffs were generally raised, and in some cases the governments applied controls over imports and exports. The export of gold and capital was often forbidden. But direct interference with the processes of production and domestic investment was generally avoided.

Radicalism, Reform, and Fascism

The widespread distress aroused political criticism and popular unrest. Reports of the advances of the Russian Five-Year Plan suggested a glaring contrast to the continuing decline in capitalist countries. The Soviet government announced that the Plan was being completed in only four years and would be followed by another, and more ambitious, Five-Year Plan. On the Continent, Communist membership and following grew rapidly. In countries where Marxism had never exerted much influence, there was a sudden interest in the works of the founders, and many a liberal was won over to economic planning. Communism found hard political sledding in Great Britain and the United States, but Marxist ideas acquired a vogue in professional and academic circles.

Whether in Europe or America, the "man in the street," particularly when he was there in search of work, was often enticed by utopian, demagogic, or Fascist appeals. Hardly a country but sprouted movements to "go back to the land," to substitute social credit for capitalist finance, to divide the wealth, or to organize consumers and small producers into cooperatives. Some of the proposals recalled the imaginative projects of the 1840's.

If the range of ideas and movements was wide, the practical alternatives were narrow indeed. Laissez-faire policies were discredited and lost many of their former supporters. For the Communists, the prospects of direct action were more unpromising than ever. For one thing, conservatism had found in certain Fascist movements as violent an embodiment as Marxism had found in Communism. For another, the Soviet Union, which regarded the rise of Fascism as a threat, ordered the moderation of Communist tactics. Communists therefore supported the meliorative measures advocated by liberals and enlightened conservatives. Other dictatorial movements, however, assumed variously the shapes of monopolistic capitalism, militarism, landlordism, and clericalism. Whatever the form, they shared a contempt for individual freedom, for the forum of public discussion, and for parliamentary institutions, and they all placed emphasis upon nationalism. The alternatives of action were reduced to two: a reformation of the economic realm within the liberal system, or the overthrow of that system. In broad terms, it may be said that the countries of Western Europe, with the exception of Italy, adopted the first of these alternatives and the countries of Central and Eastern Europe, the second.

The war and the subsequent revolutions left several dictatorial governments in their trail. Fascist movements on the Continent exploited the antagonism of the peasantry—everywhere a majority of the population—toward urban liberalism and radicalism, popular prejudices against foreigners and Jews, and the conservatism of aristocratic and landed proprietors. With every year of the depression Italian Fascists and German Nazis found new imitators of their uniforms, their provocative demonstrations and violent street brawls and fights,   *609* their appeals to chauvinism, and their demagogic promises of a utopian social order.

In Austria, Engelbert Dollfuss (1892-1934), Chancellor and leader of the Christian Socialist party, dissolved by decree all the other parties in 1934. When he attempted to take away the arms collected by the Social Democrats, the workers of Vienna rose in fierce rebellion. The proletarian quarter—graced by modern housing erected by the Social Democratic regime of the city—fittingly became the battleground. Bombarded by artillery, for four days the workers maintained an obstinate and unequal struggle. They were forced to surrender after three hundred lives had been lost. A new constitution made Austria a "corporate" state with clerical overtones.

In Yugoslavia, political tension developed over the efforts of the more advanced region of Croatia to maintain its autonomy within a federal government. The politicians and King Alexander wished to tighten the centralized system and their own domination over the enlarged country. The thirties were punctuated by dictatorial regimes, concessions to parliament so slight that the Croatians boycotted it, and fitful attempts to bring the two sides together.

In Rumania, the Transylvanians produced more enlightened politicians than the Old Kingdom. Their chieftains, Juliu Maniu and Vaida Voyevod, presided for a few years over liberal governments. But the jealousy and enmity of the politicians of the Old Kingdom and their tradition of corruption and illegality led to the formation of a number of regimes which governed in defiance of parliamentary forms. In Bulgaria, agrarian and military difficulties rather than political problems led to a similar alternation between semiliberal and dictatorial governments.

To a lesser extent, Fascist and demagogic movements appeared also in Western Europe and North America. A deserter from the British Labor party, Sir Oswald Mosley, formed the British Union of Fascists, which attempted to provoke clashes with Communists in the streets. Neither the Fascists nor the Communists won a single seat in Parliament. French Fascists found allies in old militarist and royalist groups; the *Action Française* became more active, and ex-soldiers organized a movement to uproot radicalism and establish a dictatorial regime. In Canada "social credit" parties swept the western provinces. In the United States Dr. Francis Townsend gained the ears of hundreds of thousands of distressed people, particularly the elderly, by his proposal to cure the depression by giving each unemployed person over sixty a monthly pension of $200. Reverend Charles E. Coughlin, a Roman Catholic priest of the automobile center of Detroit, attracted a large radio audience with his invectives against bankers, radicals, and foreigners and his exhortations to inflate money and isolate the United States from the rest of the world. But the man who came closest to embodying the American prototype of the Fascist dictator was the Governor (later United States Senator) of Louisiana, Huey P. Long (1893-1935).

Long was an effective demagogue who made extraordinary promises of social improvement. His motto was "Every man a king," and he proposed to "share the wealth" and give every family an income of $2,500 a year. His popularity induced a subservient legislature to grant him virtually dictatorial powers over Louisiana. Long surrounded himself with a gang of "storm troopers" and reached out boldly for influence in adjacent states. He swayed a large section of the Democratic party in the South. In 1935, he was assassinated by a citizen with a private grudge.

The "Popular Front" in France

The need to arrest the worst effects of the depression in France was long frustrated by the reluctance of the parliament to take strong measures. The middle classes were extraordinarily sensitive to direct taxation, and politicians were loath to antagonize them. The danger of dictatorship, the example of countries that were succumbing to it, and the flirtation of some politicians with Fascism made parliament chary of endowing ministers with decree power to act decisively.

In 1933 a speculator and adventurer, S. A. Stavisky, disappeared after swindling many small investors of millions of francs. It was charged, although never proved, that he had operated with the connivance of corrupt politicians and an indifferent police. Reactionary and Fascist groups exploited the scandal, blaming it on the system of liberal democracy. Riots broke out in several cities. On the night of February 6, 1934, a crowd gathered threateningly before the Chamber of Deputies, which was guarded by troops as well as police. Fighting ensued, more or less accidentally. Seventeen demonstrators were killed and six hundred wounded. The defenders counted one dead and sixteen hundred wounded.

As a result of the Stavisky riot, a "national government," comprising six former premiers, was formed to secure the republican institutions and avert the threat of civil war. But when the danger was past and falling trade again brought financial instability, the government proved unable either to resort to forced economies or to soften the blows of the depression. In the elections of 1936, a "Popular Front" of Radical Socialists, Socialists, and Communists won a majority in parliament. Leon Blum (1872-1950), leader of the Socialists, headed the new cabinet. Although they refused to join the government, the Communists supported its policies.

Labor was now emboldened to assert its claims. The means it used were novel and daring. Hundreds of thousands of workers struck, not by staying away from the factories, but by occupying and "sitting down" in them day and night, squatting around the idle machinery. In the past such occupation, despite its peaceful character, would have invited forceful measures. Now the government induced the employers to come to terms. Wage increases, annual vacations with pay, and other concessions were granted. The parliament passed legislation providing for a forty-hour week without reduction in pay and for collective labor contracts. Industrial disputes were to be submitted to mediation and arbitration. In order to check militaristic tendencies, the munitions industries were nationalized. The employers were compensated on terms set by impartial arbiters.

The National Government in Great Britain

In Great Britain the depression occasioned a transformation of party life. In the summer of 1931, business groups and economic experts pressed the Labor government to reduce the budget by cutting social services. The majority of the ministers, supported overwhelmingly by the Labor party, declined to accept these drastic measures and resigned in protest. Prime Minister Ramsay Mac-Donald, followed by a handful of Laborite colleagues, thereupon joined with the Conservative party and the small group of Liberals to form a "national coalition government." Expelled by the Labor party, MacDonald formed a new National Labor party. The old Labor party touched the nadir of its postwar fortunes. Its membership in the House of Commons dropped from 289 to 52 in a chamber of 615 seats. In 1935, the party regained about a hundred of the lost seats, but the Conservatives still had a healthy majority of 247 members.

The coalition carried out a policy of retrenchment in social services. In 1932, after nearly a century, Britain abandoned the policy of free trade, enacting the Import Duties Act, which provided for a minimum duty of 10 percent *ad valorem* on imports. Industries received official grants on promise to improve their techniques. Subsidies were advanced to maintain agricultural prices. In order to reduce the waste of unrestrained competition, industries were encouraged to agree to fix prices and wages and to share markets. Road building and railroad improvements were undertaken with the support of official funds. Finally, slum clearance and the construction of new housing were stimulated by the appropriation of large sums by the government. The country began to recover slowly; unemployment dropped. But the government rejected the proposals of the Labor party and Lloyd George for economic planning and a bolder program of public works.

Roosevelt and the New Deal

Measured against the advances in the twenties, the impact of the depression was particularly severe in the United States.

The onset of the depression found President Hoover and his fellow Republicans unprepared to meet the disaster. Hoover recognized the evils of financial speculation and considered legislation to correct them. But he could not persuade business leaders and Republican legislators to accept any restraints on the stock market. He was determined to allow prices and wages to find a "natural" lower level, whatever the cost in business bankruptcies and unemployment. He believed that the self-regulating mechanism of *laissez faire* was "healthy" in the long run.

In 1930, an impatient electorate returned a Democratic majority to the lower house of Congress. Congress set up a government agency to extend credit to needy business firms and home-loan banks to help home owners and farmers who were unable to meet their debts. It proposed public works to reduce unemployment, but Hoover interposed a veto; relief was left to private charity, which, soon exhausted, proved sadly inadequate, and to local and state governments. Various states—notably New York, under the governorship of Franklin D. Roosevelt (1882-1945)—relieved the unemployed, pensioned the aged poor, and engaged in public works. But only the federal government could mobilize the resources of the country. President Hoover still assured the country that "prosperity is around the corner." "Around the corner" conditions were worse. In the winter of 1932-33 the economy sank to its lowest point. A quarter of the labor force—about 13 million people—were out of work.

Disillusioned, public opinion turned away from the customary centers of influence: manufacturers' councils, chambers of commerce, conservative politicians, bar associations, and the bulk of the press. It looked for guidance to groups more sensitive and responsible socially and more critical and fertile intellectually. It turned, above all, to the opposition Democratic party. In the presidential election of November 1932, the Democratic candidate, Franklin D. Roosevelt, defeated Hoover and the Republicans by the overwhelming majority of 472 to 59 electoral votes. Hoover carried only six of the forty-eight states. The Democrats won control in Congress and most state offices.

In the four months that elapsed before the inauguration of the new administration, employment and business activities plunged to unprecedented depths and the financial structure of the country folded up. Bank failures multiplied in geometric progression. A run to withdraw deposits caused still more failures. When Roosevelt was inaugurated on March 4, 1933, there was hardly a bank in the country that was not either closed or operating under severe restrictions by state governments.

President Herbert Hoover (left) rides with his successor, Franklin D. Roosevelt, to the inauguration in 1933. UNITED PRESS

In this economic graveyard, the "New Deal" was born. The New Deal was a movement to "reshuffle the cards" of economic power and political position in order to give the various social classes a fair chance in the game of life. It commanded the services of an able leader and an intellectual general staff. Roosevelt belonged to the nearest American approximation of a European aristocracy: a group of distinguished families with a long record of public service. He was a fifth cousin of President Theodore Roosevelt. From his class Roosevelt inherited a critical view of the *nouveaux riches* of big business. Toward the poor and distressed his attitude was that of *noblesse oblige*. Although he had been crippled in the prime of life by infantile paralysis, he possessed much stamina and courage.

Roosevelt assembled a "brain trust" to draft reform legislation and drew into the public service new elements to give it effect. The New Dealers were typically university professors, economists, social workers, political theorists, and journalists. During his presidential campaign in 1932 three professors of Columbia University—Raymond Moley (1886-   ), Rexford G. Tugwell (1891-   ), and Adolph A. Berle, Jr. (1895-   )—helped Roosevelt to draft a broad program of reform. Among the most active in developing it and carrying it out were Harry L. Hopkins (1890-1946), an administrator of relief who became the President's closest advisor; Harold L. Ickes (1874-1952), Secretary of the Interior; Henry A. Wallace (1888-   ), Secretary of Agriculture; and Frances Perkins (1882-   ), Secretary of Labor and the first woman member of an American cabinet. Anna Eleanor Roosevelt (1884-   ), wife of the President, was an active promoter of humanitarian reform.

The New Dealers drew their inspiration from the treasury of the American past: Jeffersonianism and Jacksonianism, which had held the promise of fulfilling the ideals of democracy and equality; populism, which had urged the cause of the average man, particularly of the poor farmer; more recently, the progressivism of the Theodore Roosevelt and Woodrow Wilson eras, which had fought the oligarchical tendencies of big business; John Dewey's pragmatic approach to society; and Thorstein Veblen's philosophy, which contrasted the efficiency of the technician and the worker with the wastefulness of business and speculation.

To these strains were added European influences. American public opinion was struck by the contrast between the falling economy of the United States and other capitalist countries and the success of the first Five-Year Plan in Russia. Under cover of sympathy for liberal aims, Communists wormed their way into positions of trust in many organizations, both public and private, and exerted an influence out of proportion to their numbers. Concealing their connection with the Communist party, they won the cooperation of a small proportion of idealistic Americans. In the presidential election of 1932, the Communist party polled its largest vote: 103,000 out of a total of about 40 million votes cast. Of greater import than communist activity was the general realization that European countries, because of their long-established system of social insurance, were better able to face the exigencies of a depression than the United States.

Finally, economists were questioning the traditional view that, in times of depression, the government should behave like other enterprises and pull in its belt. They argued that government borrowing and spending on projects that gave employment would spur the economy. The outstanding advocate of this policy of "unbalanced budgets" was the English economist John Maynard Keynes (1883-1946).

Roosevelt set the mood of the new regime in his 1933 Inaugural Address:

> The only thing we have to fear is fear itself—nameless, unreasoning, unjustified terror which paralyzes needed efforts to convert retreat into advance. . . . The rulers of the exchange of mankind's goods have failed through their own stubbornness and their own incompetence, have admitted their failure and have abdicated. . . . They know only the rules of a generation of self-seekers. They have no vision, and when there is no vision the people perish. The money-changers have fled from their high seats in the temple of our civilization. We may now restore that temple to the ancient truths. The measure of the restoration lies in the extent to which we apply social values more noble than mere monetary profit.

The new Chief Executive declared that if new laws designed to arrest the paralysis were not enacted, "the need for undelayed action may call for temporary departure from [the] normal balance [of] executive and legislative authority." If Congress did not act promptly he would ask for "the one remaining instrument to meet the crisis—broad executive power to wage a war against the emergency as great as the power that would be given me if we were in fact invaded by a foreign foe."

The warning was unnecessary. The President and his "brain trust" launched a veritable avalanche of reform, with the eager cooperation of Congress and the stunned acquiescence of the business community. Supplemented or modified by further legislation, the New Deal accomplished three lasting results: it established the responsibility of the federal government for relieving social distress, initiated a federal policy of preventing the more extreme fluctuations of the business cycle, and redistributed national wealth and power in a democratic direction.

The New Dealers attacked the curse of unemployment from several sides. The Public Works Administration projected and erected public buildings, often in collaboration with state and local governments. The Works Progress Administration heavily subsidized a host of projects that employed skilled as well as unskilled workers. A significant feature of the W.P.A. was the support of cultural and artistic activities. It put to work needy artists, writers, actors, archivists, and scholars and financed the writing of regional histories, the embellishment of public buildings, experiments with new plays, and the composition and performance of music. The number of people thus employed temporarily by the government ran into millions. The Civilian Conservation Corps engaged hundreds of thousands of young men in reforestation, road-improvement, and flood-prevention projects. For others relief was provided. Most of it was dis-   *615*

An example of the achievements of one of the agencies of the New Deal —the Tennessee Valley Authority. A stretch of the Tennessee River, near Knoxville, Tennessee, is shown before and after the TVA built one of its many dams, making practical navigation of the river possible, producing cheap electricity, providing employment, and vivifying the economic life of a previously much-neglected region.
TVA

bursed in cash, but in some cases the government bought up large quantities of surplus food and distributed it free to people in need, thus relieving both the glut of the producers and the want of the consumers.

Farm prices dropped sharply after the onset of the depression and the diminution of demand for produce in both Europe and America. In order to bring supply into closer relation to demand and so raise prices, Congress passed the Agricultural Adjustment Act, which subsidized farmers to withdraw land from cultivation. Serious droughts in 1934 and 1936 further reduced the surplus. The government made loans which enabled many a farmer to escape from tenantry to ownership.

A few states had experimented with measures to ensure workers against enforced idleness and to protect the aged poor. In a sharp and sudden reversal of policy, the federal government established national coverage against these social ills in the comprehensive Social Security Act of 1935. A tax on payrolls supplied the funds for unemployment benefits, to be regulated and administered by the states, which could adopt individual measures so long as they met minimal conditions of fairness and adequacy. Workers past the age of sixty-five received moderate pensions.

The New Dealers strove to repair the neglect into which important services and large regions had fallen under the regime of *laissez faire.* Corporate enterprise had done little to bring electricity to the humbler farmers and the more remote rural areas. The federal government built generating plants and power lines in rural areas and distributed power at low cost. The Tennessee Valley Authority revivified a large region comprising sections of seven states which had fallen into poverty. Huge dams and generating plants began to turn out electricity and fertilizer at low cost. The floods that plagued that area were brought under better control. Apart from affording work for thousands of workmen and engineers, the project raised the standard of living of many communities. The government had given a startling demonstration of regional planning.

The New Deal curbed speculation and investment abuses. Gambling in stocks by means of small payments on account became illegal; the purchaser of a stock had to pay at least half its price. New issues of stock were scrutinized carefully to protect unwary investors. These measures eventually restored normal banking and investment and revived business confidence. The Glass-Steagall Act of 1933 insured small depositors against loss from bank failures. After examining the condition of the banks, the government reopened most of them promptly.

Modifying the laissez-faire system on yet another side, the New Dealers made strenuous efforts to stabilize prices. By adjusting the amount of money in circulation, the interest on government bonds, taxation rates, and government expenditures, they hoped to diminish unwelcome fluctuations of the economy. Fiscal policy became a lever of social action. Since this lever could be exercised only within the bounds of the domestic economy, the effect of the New Deal was to discourage international exchange. When the World Economic Conference of 1933 attempted to stabilize world prices by agreeing on a common money standard, President Roosevelt refused to cooperate.

Broadening their aims, the New Dealers attempted to redress the balance between labor and capital and between agriculture and industry. By graduating inheritance, luxury, and income taxes steeply, reducing the share of the wealthiest groups in the national product, and using government funds to raise the level of the lower classes, they reduced somewhat the gap between economic groups. In the decade beginning in 1929, the share of wages and salaries in the national income rose from 65.5 percent to 68.2 percent, while rents and dividends dropped from 11.5 to 10.1 percent and corporation dividends from 7.4 to 6 percent. The New Dealers built up the position of the industrial workers and farmers as a counterweight to the power of capital. They reduced hours of work, thereby increasing employment somewhat, and set minimum wages. The Wagner Labor Relations Act of 1935 established the right of workers to organize and to bargain collectively with employers through their elected representatives. Labor leaders were thus enabled, with the open or tacit support of the government, to unionize the great steel, automotive, and textile industries and to extend the organization of other industries. Since the American Federation of Labor had proved slow in promoting organization and was committed by the preponderance of its membership to craft unions, a new association was set up in 1935—the Congress of Industrial Organizations—which proceeded to organize whole industries, in disregard of craft distinctions. Total union membership rose from three million to nine million in a few years. For the first time in American history, industrial labor could compete with some approximation of even strength with powerful corporations and trusts in the basic industries.

The New Dealers ended the dominance of the Republican party. Since its formation on the eve of the Civil War, that party had elected twelve out of fifteen presidents and had come to be regarded as the permanent majority party. The Democratic party had been traditionally dominated by Southern conservatives and Northern city bosses. Roosevelt now drew to its support the bulk of organized labor and Midwestern farmers. In addition, he commanded the allegiance of most of the professional classes. With this broader base, the Democratic party went from victory to victory; it remained in control of the presidency and most of the Congresses for twenty years.

The electorate endorsed the New Deal with enthusiasm at the first opportunity. In 1936 Roosevelt was re-elected for a second term, carrying all but two of the states (Maine and Vermont). Congress remained overwhelmingly Democratic. Only in the third branch of the government, which is not elected by the voters, was there brewing a threat to the New Deal. In 1935-36 the United States Supreme Court invalidated as unconstitutional some of the more advanced New Deal projects, notably the National Recovery Administration of 1933. The NRA was an attempt to eliminate unfair competition and to raise prices by limiting production. These aims were to be achieved by the framing of codes in every field of business and industry by boards representing management, labor, and the public. The Court also declared the Agricultural Adjustment Act unconstitutional.

These decisions were reached by a 5-4 majority. As soon as Roosevelt was re-elected in 1936, he proposed to neutralize the conservative majority by the enactment of a law that would give him the power to appoint up to six additional judges if those incumbents who were over seventy years of age refused to retire. There was a great outcry, among Democrats as well as Republicans, against this "court-packing" suggestion. Roosevelt abandoned his proposal, but eventually voluntary resignations and a shift in the opinion of the Court brought the judiciary into line with the evident desires of the country. Reversing an old decision, the Court validated a law fixing minimum wages and then endorsed the principal labor, agrarian, and social-insurance measures of the New Deal. But the Court had effectively stopped the attempt to introduce a measure of economic planning to the United States.

The New Deal changed the face of the Republic, but without basically altering the system of private enterprise. It reduced unemployment but was unable to wipe it out. It raised the national income only moderately. It could not maintain an even tempo of economic recovery; in 1937 the United States experienced another, though milder, recession. Yet the New Deal started the economy, which it found at dead point, moving generally upward, and it mitigated the worst evils of the depression. It ended the reign of unrestricted *laissez faire* in the domestic economy. Above all, it refreshed the spirit of democracy. It put an end to the unchallenged domination of government by the great capitalists and their political instruments. Not since the days of Andrew Jackson had American democracy been so vibrant. There was, in the thirties, a significant revival of historical interest in Jackson and Jefferson.

The New Deal aligned the United States with Western Europe in social policy. The American people came to think of the government as an instrument for social enterprise and welfare. The young, the educated, and the public-spirited found in the New Deal a cause worthy of their energies. Proto-Fascist demagogues lost their following as the morale and condition of the population improved. The New Deal took the wind out of their sails at a time when dictatorship and Fascism were spreading in Continental Europe.

29. *Hitlerism and Stalinism*

The decade of the New Deal was also the decade of Hitlerism and Stalinism. The world-wide depression, which in America evoked a comprehensive reform within the framework of liberal democracy, was exploited by German Nazis and conservatives to destroy the Weimar Republic and replace it with a dictatorship of unexampled ferocity. In Russia the early years of the depression coincided with the evolution of the first Five-Year Plan. Joseph Stalin drove the Russian people toward industrialization and agricultural collectivization. Extreme factions in other countries fell under the spell of the Nazis or the Communists, and a crisis which had begun as economic ended by becoming a deeper crisis of political organization and international relations.

The Rise of Nazism

The wound inflicted by the tragic inflation of the early twenties was still open in Germany when the crash came in 1929. The middle and professional classes, which had lost much of their property and social position, were smarting from their fall. Many of the members of these groups nursed a sense of injured dignity and resentment against society. The old strain was now compounded by depression and unemployment.

The German economy, more dependent upon credit than the economies of other countries, was more promptly affected by the flight of both foreign and domestic capital. Many banks closed their doors, and business bankruptcies multiplied apace. Unable to renew loans, industry reduced production. Three million workers were without jobs in 1930, five and a half million the next year, and six million the following year.

Since its inauguration, the Weimar Republic had generally been governed by cabinets supported by the People's party, the Social Democrats, and the Centrists. Since the groups further to the Right were openly or tacitly antirepublican, the survival of the new system rested on the agreement of these "Weimar parties." The question of how to deal with the depression divided them. The People's party and the Centrists supported the conservative and deflationary approach; the Social Democrats opposed the implied cuts in relief and social disbursements and withdrew from the government. Dr. Heinrich Bruening (1885-   ), a leader of the Center, became Chancellor in March 1930. He was often unable to muster a majority in the *Reichstag* for his measures. Encouraged by Hindenburg, he resorted to the privilege of issuing decrees allowed the president by Article 48 of the Constitution (see p. 554). The Chancellor reduced payments to the unemployed, diminished the civil service, and enforced many an economy. The government became in effect a presidential dictatorship. At the same time, economic distress made the voters susceptible to extremist appeals. In the elections of September 1930 the moderate parties lost ground. The Social Democrats remained the largest single party, but the Communists increased their vote from 3.25 million to 4.5 million and their *Reichstag* contingent from 54 to 77 deputies.

The elections brought into prominence a party which had languished in the twenties. As late as 1928 the Nazi party had still only 60,000 members, most of them south Germans. Now it had the second largest representation in the *Reichstag*. In the election of September 1930, the Nazis vaulted from a mere dozen to 107 seats. Nazism was distinguished by its ideology, its organization, and its tactics. It rested on a primitive racism. It divided mankind into a hierarchy of races as distinct from one another as animal species and singled out the "Aryans" as the "master race." Among the Aryans the Germans were pre-eminent, and among them, a self-appointed elite formed the "natural leaders." The leadership of Germany therefore implied the right to control the "Nordic" race (which included the Anglo-Saxon and Scandinavian peoples) and through it all the other, "inferior" races.

The party was organized in a strictly authoritarian fashion. The self-appointed leaders designated subleaders who had unquestioned authority over their subordinates. "He who wants to be the leader bears, with the highest, unrestricted authority, also the ultimate and the most serious responsibility," Adolf Hitler wrote in *Mein Kampf.* "Only the hero is chosen for this. . . . Progress and the culture of mankind . . . are not the products of the majority but rest exclusively upon the genius and energy of the personality." While this doctrine reserved for Hitler the office of national "hero" or "personality," it made room for lesser leaders, the chieftains of every local group or subdivision of the party.

The Nazis exploited their electoral success promptly. They assembled a strong cadre of leaders and subleaders, orators and toughs, journalists and strong-arm experts, and recruited a private army of brown-shirted Storm Troopers. They extended their operations into the populous industrial centers of northern and western Germany, where they mounted a campaign to attract various classes through contradictory promises and demagogic appeals to popular prejudices, to dazzle the masses by militant demonstrations, to intimidate their opponents by physical as well as political attacks, and to seize the streets and undermine the authority of the state. The Nazis staged spectacular parades in the centers of great cities through which thousands of uniformed members goose-stepped to the blare of martial bands. In huge meeting halls Storm Troopers stood at stiff attention, when they were not beating up hecklers in view of thousands of Germans. The audience sang nationalistic songs with brutal overtones. Suddenly the *Führer*—the "Leader"—would appear, preceded by uniformed guards.

Hitler was a frenetic orator who magnetized his audience by repeating provocative challenges and popular shibboleths. At first he spoke haltingly, but as soon as he established contact with the mass he whipped himself into a contagious frenzy. His phrases shot out like bullets, staccato, angry, violent: the trouble with the modern world was too much liberty, too much reason, too much kindness, too much pacifism, too much internationalism; the plight of Germany was the fault of the wicked Allies and their *Diktat* of Versailles; Germany never lost the war but was betrayed by cowards, liberals, and Marxists; behind these men, and behind the Allies themselves, stood the "international Jews," who were corrupting the "Aryans," above all the Germans themselves; the French are hateful because they are degenerate through intermarriage with Negroes; the Latin peoples and the Slavs are inferior and fit only for slavery. Germany must subjugate the Slavs, conquer Europe, and dominate the world.

Hitler and his followers revived on a larger scale the violence of the years immediately following the war. The Storm Troopers broke up opponents' meetings, started street brawls, and assassinated political enemies. Other paramilitary organizations, notably the veterans' organization, the *Stahlhelm*, were only slightly less violent in their demonstrations. The Communists retaliated with bodies of informal troops, but the government was chary of taking the strong measures required to restore order, since the Nazis posed as patriots. There had always been a weakness in Germany for illegal acts committed in the name of patriotism or militarism. Chancellor Bruening presided over a bacchanalia of rioting and outrage.

The Alliance of Nazis and Conservatives

While the Storm Troopers were destroying public order, the Nazi leaders pledged to every group in society its heart's desire. To the unemployed they promised work; to the workers, socialistic measures; to the small enterprisers and shopkeepers, the abolition of large firms and department stores; to the indebted farmers, the end of "usurious" bankers; to the capitalists, the suppression of Marxist radicalism and trade unionism; and to professional misfits, the jobs of their abler rivals.

Nazi ideology appealed to a variety of sentiments, prejudices, and ambitions. The contempt of the Nazi leaders for reason and moderation seduced inexperienced youth, romantic adventurers, and semiliterate malcontents. It cajoled many folk by exalting them as members of a mistreated but superior "master race." Similarly, it promised party workers and fighters the privileges and emoluments of a master group within the nation. It attracted ambitious but unsuccessful men on the fringes of the professions, *déclassé* members of the middle and upper classes, men who could not succeed by conventional methods, and, above all, resentful members of the petty bourgeoisie. To those who felt superior to the ordinary mass, the Nazis held out the vision of a natural elite better than the hereditary aristocracy. The degradation of Germany's neighbors and rivals to an inferior status was unction to the soul of nationalists. Hitler's interminable speeches on sex and race mixture created an erotic, even pornographic, atmosphere that titillated the immature and attracted persons of unconventional morals and tastes.

But the biggest and most remarkable fish caught in the Nazis' net was German conservatism. On the surface, Nazi demagogy and traditional conservatism had little in common. However, industrialists, financiers, Junkers, aristocratic officers, and diplomats—the most powerful groups in Germany—had much unfinished business. The electoral success of Hitler persuaded them that they had found the means to finish it. They had never reconciled themselves to the Weimar Republic or to the territorial, military, and naval settlement of the Versailles Treaty. In a country where many segments of the population had the habit of obedience to authority and where many of the most energetic and intelligent spirits were apolitical, the leading groups carried unusual weight and bore a heavy responsibility for careful statesmanship. Yet the German conservative class was extremely selfish. It did not flinch from a compromise with Hitlerism. Even the few conservatives who made their peace with the republic could not bring themselves to accept liberal principles. Others tried to rescue conservative values by violent and radical means.

The most influential "revolutionary conservative" had been Arthur Moeller van den Bruck (1876-1925), who came from an old Prussian family of military men and officials. He was a rebel in every sense save one: he accepted the traditional patriotic view that Germany was entitled—indeed, destined—to subjugate Europe and adjacent areas. In Moeller's hands, the Superman of Nietzsche became the Supernation. He did not believe in the theory of racial differences but felt that it was a useful myth which could inspire Germans to heroic efforts. In *The Third Reich* (1923), Moeller described Germany as a "young," "proletarian," and overpopulated nation which, given the will, could prevail in a war over the effete, sated, and "old" Western nations. He worked for an alliance with Russia, an "infantile" country that could be persuaded to seek its fortunes in Asia, leaving Europe to the Germans. Although Moeller rejected the traditional reverence of his class for Throne and Altar, he claimed leadership for the adventurous scions of aristocratic and rich families grouped around a masterful chieftain.

Doctrines such as Moeller's threw a bridge between the conservatives and the Nazis. Each conservative group found a reason to cross that bridge. Aristocratic and influential families naturally measured themselves for the role of the elite exalted by the Nazis. Monarchists who could not agree to restore a monarch and nationalists who smarted at the defeat of 1918 relished the Nazis' attacks on the republic. Militarists and imperialists expected that the aggressive nationalism of the Nazis would wipe out the pacifism and internationalism associated with liberal and socialist principles. The reckless Schlieffen spirit was still alive in the German General Staff, which had retained its prestige despite its failure in the recent war. The Staff planned another engagement and hoped to ensure victory by avoiding the "mistakes" of the war, notably the attempt to fight on two fronts simultaneously. The rise of the fire-eating Nazis seemed to them a heaven-sent opportunity to revive Germany's military glory.

Industrialists were quick to perceive in the Nazis political mercenaries who would help them to curtail the influence of unionism and radicalism. Under the Weimar government German industry and finance had been freer to combine in huge monopolies and cartels and had received greater and more practical favors from the state than industry and finance elsewhere. But this circumstance, instead of suggesting tolerance for the more modest beneficiaries of state intervention, provided industrialists with greater means and organization for attacking them. The schemes developed in the twenties for social assistance for the indigent, the ill, the unemployed, and the aged—more elaborate and expensive than the systems developed in any other country—could not be undermined without weakening unionism and socialism, and these could not be weakened without abolishing freedom of opinion and of the ballot. The dictatorial program of the Nazis seemed to industrialists, therefore, all to the good.

The tactics of the Nazis were as violent as those of the Communists; their promises more generous than those of the socialists. But the Nazi leaders gave private assurances that their radical promises—and the word "Socialist" in the name of their party—need not be taken seriously. In a speech before important industrialists in Düsseldorf, Hitler endorsed private enterprise and capitalist leadership in economic life. The result was that scions of powerful, rich, aristocratic, and even royal and imperial families flocked into a party generally regarded as demagogic and irresponsible, and that conservatives placed money and power in the hands of the Nazi leaders. The Nazis had always received subsidies from individual industrialists, such as Fritz Thyssen, who was reputed to be the richest man in the country. After their success in 1930 they received the wider support of the owners of heavy and large industry.

The industrialists were influential in the Nationalist party, whose chief, Alfred Hugenberg (1865-1951), was a powerful newspaper proprietor and inveterate enemy of the republic. That party, the *Stahlhelm*, and the Nazis soon formed a common front. With these supports, the Nazis marched from victory to victory. In the presidential election of March 1932, Hindenburg was re-elected for a second term by 19 million votes, but Hitler received the impressive endorsement of 13 million ballots. In an election for the *Reichstag* later in the same year, all extremist groups made further gains, but the Nazis accumulated 230 seats, which made them, at last, the largest single party in the country.

Their added votes came from middle-class groups, for the proletarian vote was still divided largely between the Social Democratic and Communist parties, in a ratio that increasingly favored the latter.

Despite their success, the Nazis did not have a majority in the *Reichstag*. They were helped to power by a series of intrigues among army officers, diplomats, and industrialists. When Chancellor Bruening hinted at the desirability of agrarian reform in Prussia to assist the unemployed, Hindenburg dismissed him from office in May 1932 and installed an unsavory diplomat of the Center party, Franz von Papen. Von Papen (1879-) assembled a cabinet of nationalists and conservatives. He encouraged the Nazis and struck at their enemies. He rescinded the prohibition against the demonstrations of the Nazi Storm Troopers that Bruening had recently imposed; public outrages and disorders multiplied. In a sudden coup, Von Papen forcibly removed the Social Democratic prime minister of Prussia and other officials as well. Intimidated, the Social Democrats refrained from calling a general strike.

Von Papen called new elections for the *Reichstag* in November 1932. The Communists gained a few seats, and the Nazis lost ground—34 seats—for the first time since their sudden rise in 1930. It appeared that they had passed their peak. Hindenburg nevertheless invited Hitler to accept the chancellorship, provided that he could assemble a majority in the legislative body. When Hitler

"1932," painted in 1959 by the American artist Jack Levine, showing President Hindenburg of Germany and Adolf Hitler. A retrospective evaluation of the character and relationship of the two leaders.
THE ALAN GALLERY

was unable to meet this condition, Hindenburg appointed General Kurt von Schleicher (1882-1934), an ambitious officer who hoped to establish a military and "social" dictatorship. Schleicher's strategy was to make mild socialistic concessions to obtain the support of trade unions and the radical wing of the Nazis, thus splitting Hitler's following. While he plotted, his rivals plotted more effectively. Hugenberg promised Hitler the votes of the National party, thus assuring the Nazis of a majority, and Von Papen prevailed upon Hindenburg to renew his offer of the chancellorship to Hitler. In January 1933, Hitler became Chancellor, presiding over a cabinet which consisted largely of the followers of Hugenberg and the friends of Von Papen and Hindenburg.

The Character and Mentality of Adolf Hitler

Hitler's National party supporters counted on exploiting him and retaining the substance of power. They may have been betrayed by their snobbish contempt for the lowborn Austrian corporal, by their inability to imagine that he could fail to defer to his betters. They were not alone in underestimating Hitler. His hysterical oratory, his appeals to the lowest instincts of his listeners, his irrational and contradictory promises, his threats to exterminate his enemies, to subjugate whole races and wipe out whole peoples, his lack of education and breeding created the impression of an unstable character who could not possibly mean everything he said, let alone do it. The fact was that Hitler was tenacious, shrewd, and consistent.

His mentality, however, was rigid and narrow. He could grasp no meaning except the most literal. What was opinion or impression to others was inflexible law to Hitler. His logical processes were drastic. No conclusion, however startling, suggested to him that he might take a second look at his premises or his "facts." As he lacked skepticism or nuance, Hitler lacked charity and fellow feeling. He had an equal contempt for the masses and for the respectable and aristocratic classes. To him, the great majority of men were stupid, forgetful, lazy, cowardly, and base. The masses were inert, sentimental, and cringing in their adoration of brutality and their submissiveness to impudent strength. Mendacious themselves but petty in soul, they discounted small lies but would believe any lie that was big enough and therefore beyond their experience. Hitler was not committed to the human race. "Plainly," he remarked, "I belong by nature to another species."

Above all, Hitler admired cunning. He read the history of civilization as a triumph of craft. The advances and inventions that raised man above the animals were a series of "tricks and ruses" by which the highest races "got around" and exploited nature, the animal kingdom, and the inferior races as well. Hitler thought of his opponents as foxes, and he meant to outfox them.

Many writers at the turn of the century had preached the inequality of races; the exaltation of the idea of struggle and will had been a rising phenomenon of Western literature and philosophy; anti-Semitism had been used as a po-

Adolf Hitler. This photograph is from the collection of Eva Braun, whom the Führer married on the eve of his suicide in 1945 and who committed suicide with him in the Berlin bunker. U.S. ARMY

litical tool in Eastern European countries and, for a time, even in France. But in the prism of Hitler's mentality, the racial question assumed a grotesque shape. He regarded the conflicts between peoples as the crudest kind of evolutionary struggle. Competition, destruction, and the domination of the strongest and most brutal was still for him the law of their relationship. The Aryan race, especially its German branch, was responsible for all true progress and culture.

Why, then, had the Germans been unable thus far to establish dominion over all the other races of the world? Because, Hitler said, a tiny people, by superior craft, had frustrated the great race for thousands of years. In Germany and elsewhere, the Jews had established their mastery (which Hitler took for granted as an actual fact) by corrupting the culture, keeping their own stock pure but deteriorating the other stocks. They had given the world Christ and disarmed mankind by inducing it to worship meekness and peace and robbing it of its natural weapons of hatred and force. They had promoted—notably by launching the French Revolution—the equality of peoples and the dignity of the individual, thus challenging the hierarchy of races, the subjection of the individual to his nation, and the principle of aristocratic leadership. By devising the system of capitalism, finance, corporate enterprise, and international trade, they had undermined the true economy of national self-sufficiency and territorial wealth. After turning the heads of the middle classes, the Jews had spread Marxism in order to corrupt the virtues and instincts of the working classes.

627

A few invisible "Elders of Zion" in the great capitals of Berlin, Moscow, London, and New York pulled the strings, simultaneously, of finance, diplomacy, liberalism, and Marxism, in order to keep the Germans from supplanting them as masters of the world and from rescuing world culture.

Hitler concluded that the Jews must be exterminated. The Aryan race must be purged of the "unfit," the weak and the mentally ill. A new German aristocracy must be recruited from the last reservoir of unpolluted blood—the peasantry. This aristocracy would distinguish itself from the mass as the wild beast from domesticated animals. "A violently active, dominating, intrepid, brutal youth—that is what I am after," Hitler asserted. "There must be no weakness or tenderness in it. I want to see once more in its eyes the gleam of pride and independence of the beast of prey."

Hitler's doctrine was a mixture of pseudo-science and nationalism. The concept of a "pure" race assumes that blood is the carrier of civilization and talent. Yet nurture is as important in human development as heredity, and mixed peoples have often been superior to pure breeds. There are, in fact, no "pure" races. To say that a single race has been responsible for all the creative ideas flies in the face of the facts. And there is no criterion by which one would be justified in arranging the races on a hierarchical scale. Their culture, outlook, environment, circumstances, and achievements have been too varied to permit it. That peasants are healthier than city folk or have purer blood is a romantic illusion. To say that national or racial success is due to physical aggression and conquest is to ignore the fact that trade and industry, ideas and religions have often brought greater and more lasting victories. Hitler's "Elders of Zion" were the product of the imagination of czarist police agents; and the *Protocols of Zion* had been exposed as a forgery.

Yet no amount of evidence or reasoning could prevail against Hitler's beliefs. Once an opinion or a prejudice found lodging in his mind, nothing could shake it. Such was the mentality of the man whom the German conservatives made Chancellor in January 1933.

The Nazi State

Hitler lost no time in making his power absolute and applying his program, by degrees, first within Germany and then outside. He had two weapons against his conservative confederates in the cabinet: he did not mean to keep his promise to consult them before making any important political changes, and he was ready to use the executive power against his friends as well as his enemies. He called a new election for the *Reichstag* in full-dress Nazi style. As Prussian Minister of the Interior, the Nazi Hermann Goering (1893-1946) placed Nazis in control of the Prussian police force and ordered it to cooperate with the Storm Troopers. Throughout Germany, the constitutional guarantees of freedom were nullified. The meetings of opposition parties, particularly of the socialists and

Communists, were broken up; speakers were assailed or arrested and their followers dispersed. Communist publications were banned. The Nazis then resorted to a sensational stroke to destroy the Communist party. In late February, just before the election, fire gutted the *Reichstag* building, and Hitler threw the blame, without a shred of proof, on Communists. Hundreds of Communist leaders were arrested and thrown into jail. Their deputies were driven from the parliament.

Despite these provocations, the electorate went to the polls and again refused to give the Nazis a clear majority. Hitler's party polled 17 million votes out of 39 million and won 288 seats. The Nazis were still outnumbered in popular vote, although not in *Reichstag* seats, by the "Weimar parties." But when the Nationalists added their 52 deputies to those of the Nazis, a majority was secured. Further, so weak was the attachment of the other groups to republicanism that a law destroying parliamentarianism was passed by a huge majority. The law conferred upon Hitler the power for four years to legislate by decree on any subject. The only thing he could not do was reduce the powers of the presidency or abolish the *Reichstag* "as an institution." But in effect, the *Reichstag* had abolished itself. Only 94 voices in the *Reichstag*, all Social Democratic, registered objection. To the end, the Social Democrats remained the chief liberal party in Germany.

The conservative leaders were soon pushed out of the government and replaced by obedient Nazis. Joseph Goebbels (1897-1945), who became Minister of Propaganda, considered no lie too harsh or patent to be distributed by the German press or radio. Heinrich Himmler (1900-45), chief of the Nazi practorian guard (the SS, or *Schutzstaffel*) and the Secret Police, was a man of mediocre ability and bottomless insensibility. These men and other Nazi leaders fulfilled some of the aims of the conservatives by promptly snuffing out individual freedom, emasculating trade unionism, routing Marxism, executing the radicals within their own ranks, expanding the army and navy, and resuming an aggressive foreign policy. But the new regime did not follow the established pattern of conservative, Fascist, or reactionary regimes. It turned out to be corrupt and violent beyond the expectations of the men who had enthroned Hitler.

The government seized the headquarters, treasuries, properties, and presses of the labor movement. It deprived the unions of the power to represent the workers in negotiations and contracts with employers. "Trustees" of labor named by the government took over these functions. The Nazis had no economic program. They did not challenge the system of private property and did not carry out their old promises to restrict large-scale enterprises, particularly department stores. They artificially diminished unemployment by banishing women to the home and thus making room for more male workers. They increased the hours of labor and taxed the workers for social services. The standard of living of the masses declined substantially. The Nazis established labor camps for idle youth. They forbade the export of capital and restricted imports. They confirmed the action of previous governments in refusing to pay reparations. Those party members and leaders who favored socialistic legislation were de-   *629* moted, imprisoned, or exiled. All these steps weakened labor. Finally, federalism was destroyed; Hitler issued a decree assuming the power to name the governors of the states.

The universities and schools were purged not only of radicals and liberals but of all teachers sufficiently independent to be critical; Germany lost many of her outstanding scholars, intellectuals, and scientists, and the quality of her schools deteriorated. The same process was applied to the press, publishing, radio, theater, and every other cultural and artistic movement. Legal and medical practitioners who were not Nazis suffered the same fate. In every activity and profession, in every field of human endeavor with hierarchical prerogatives, in every enterprise that commanded wealth and property, Nazis took over the positions of power, profit, and dignity. The removal of liberals and other dissenters made room for men whose chief distinction lay in adherence to the party. In every nook and cranny of life, the Nazis elbowed themselves into office, jobs, loot, bribes, patronage, and advantage. Nazism gave the leaders of local and regional party organizations the authority of little autocrats and the right to exploit their power at will.

The "Brown Army" of Storm Troopers, led by the notorious Captain Ernst Roehm (1887-1934), demanded the weapons and rights of regular troops, thus arousing the jealousy of the professional officer caste. In order to conciliate the professionals, Hitler ordered, on June 30, 1934, the assassination of Roehm. Nazi leaders seized the occasion to pay off old scores against their enemies. They murdered General von Schleicher, his wife, and, by Hitler's account, seventy-four other persons. It is estimated, however, that nearly a thousand persons were murdered by the goverment without warning, without trial, and without explanation in the "Great Blood Purge." Hitler appeared before the *Reichstag* and announced that he had acted as the "justiciar" of the people. He was judge and executioner as well as ruler.

All pretence to justice or law was dead in Germany. Secret police, spies, and informers abounded. Opponents of the regime—even lukewarm liberals, radicals, and recalcitrant conservatives—labor leaders, journalists and writers, and any men who aroused the envy or the hatred of Nazi bigwigs were arrested without warrants and incarcerated without trial. Snatched from their homes and their families in the dead of night, they were whisked off to secret concentration camps and subjected to brutalities, sadistic assaults, exploitation, and, in thousands of cases, premeditated starvation and assassination. The concentration camps became veritable human abbatoirs. Unspeakable tortures and "experiments" on body and soul were perpetrated by brutalized and criminal guards, carefully selected from among the hardened hooligans that the Nazis had attracted from the beginning. A simple announcement to the family that their father or son had died of diseases of which they had had no inkling, or while "trying to escape," with no indication of offense committed or penalty deserved, closed the matter.

The Nazis treated the churches with somewhat less daring. Independent-minded Protestant ministers were removed and arrested. Nazi pastors proposed to the churches that they reject the Old Testament, abandon the cross for the Nazi swastika [卐], an ancient tribal symbol, and repudiate the divinity of Christ and the substance of Christianity. The churches, although complaisant in political matters, were recalcitrant in theological doctrine. But the influence of these attempts was considerable. The Nazis weakened the religious schools and drew the bulk of the young people, both Protestant and Catholic, into the Hitler Youth Movement.

Nazi propaganda specialized in spectacular public demonstrations and mass meetings, in order to create a mood of national unity, military obedience, and hero worship. Here the Führer, Adolf Hitler, is being hailed by uniformed youths, with the prescribed gesture of the outstretched right arm, at a rally held in 1938 at Nuremberg, Bavaria, the scene of the principal pageants of the Nazi party. UNITED PRESS INTERNATIONAL

Hitler's coadjutors in racial matters, Heinrich Himmler and Walther Darré (1895-1953), the party's agrarian experts, were trained agronomists and animal breeders. Neither they nor Hitler saw any difference between the eugenics of the barnyard and bull pen and that of human society. Herded into the movement of Hitler Youth, the boys and girls of Germany were marched, drilled, and indoctrinated. They were taught to extol the body, to train their muscles, and narrow their minds. In order to increase the population forcibly, young girls were publicly urged to bear children, without love and without marriage. Several "orders" were set up to raise a hardened elite: hundreds of tall, blond, and blue-eyed young stalwarts were gathered in spacious castles, where they lived a disciplined and athletic life, filled their minds with hatred of liberalism and humanitarianism, and mated with patriotic girls to breed more stalwarts, blond, tall, and blue-eyed.

The Nazi leaders proposed to sterilize all persons suffering from hereditary diseases and to dispatch those who suffered from incurable physical or mental ailments. Feeble old people were removed to special homes, ostensibly for special medical treatment, but they began to die with suspicious promptness. While "scientific" propagandists tried to convince the Germans of the desirability of euthanasia, the government was already practicing it.

The most comprehensive example of Nazi methods and aims was provided by the treatment of the Jews. At first their persecution seemed to revive, on a larger scale and in a more organized form, the mob tactics of czarist anti-Semitism. The Storm Troopers and such of the Germans as were eager to join them were encouraged to attack and despoil the Jews and promised immunity by the authorities. The police were ordered to refrain from intervening to protect the lives and property of the victims. An orgy of beatings in the street, invasions of homes, looting of Jewish stores and factories, and firing of Jewish properties and synagogues was let loose in the most important centers of Germany. The German population stood by. Abroad, protests were voiced, but the governments held aloof. The United States, however, did recall her ambassador. On April 1, 1933, the Nazi regime ordered a general boycott of all Jewish business and simultaneously barred Jewish doctors and lawyers from practice. There was a rush for the frontier, but only a tiny minority of Germany's 500,000 Jews were able to escape, including some of the wealthy who were willing to leave a share of their property to Nazi officials.

In 1935 the Nuremberg decrees were issued: a Jew was defined as any person who had one Jewish grandparent. The fact that he might have been a Christian from birth, the child of Christian parents, made no difference. So defined, the Jews were deprived of citizenship, forbidden to marry a German or to employ a German woman under 45, and, with very few exceptions, removed from all offices and privileges in the government, the army, the professions, and finally also business. Eventually the theaters, cafés, restaurants, and even the streets were virtually denied to them. Those Jews who were critical or independent-minded or who were liberals or radicals were removed to concentration camps, where their treatment was always worse than that of other inmates. The casualties were heavy.

Forced Industrialization and Collectivization in Russia

The domestic outrages of Hitlerism were a prelude to foreign aggression. Germany was to be merely a laboratory for initiating an international reign of "blood and soil." Nazi propaganda was directed in the first place against the

Soviet Union. German-Russian relations indeed worsened even while the domestic policy of each country converged upon dictatorship. For the rise of Hitlerism coincided with the rise of Stalinism.

Joseph Stalin, the Bolshevik dictator, had one overriding aim: to strengthen Russia's power in the world and ensure the continuance of Bolshevik rule (see p. 598). In a speech to industrial executives in 1931, he delivered a patriotic defense of speedy industrialization:

> . . . those who fall behind get beaten. But we do not want to be beaten. No, we refuse to be beaten. One feature of the history of old Russia was the continual beatings she suffered for falling behind, for her backwardness. She was beaten by the Mongol khans. She was beaten by the Turkish beys. She was beaten by the Swedish feudal lords. She was beaten by the Polish and Lithuanian gentry. She was beaten by the British and French capitalists. She was beaten by the Japanese barons. All beat her—for her backwardness, for cultural backwardness, for political backwardness, for agricultural backwardness. She was beaten because to do so was profitable and could be done with impunity. . . .
>
> We are fifty or a hundred years behind the advanced countries. We must make good this distance in ten years. Either we do it, or they crush us.

As we have seen, the first Five-Year Plan, adopted late in 1928, was declared fulfilled in 1933, and a second Five-Year Plan was decreed. In 1938 a third Plan went into effect. By the end of the thirties, Russia had begun to assume the aspect of an urban industrial state. There were thousands of new factories, and the number of factory workers had doubled. Nearly half the population had become urban. Russia produced three times as much oil, four times as much coal, five times as much steel, seven times as much electricity, and ten times as many machine tools as she had on the eve of the first Five-Year Plan. In 1930 Russia had 35,000 farm tractors; in 1938 she had 470,000. Under the supervision of the American engineer Charles Cooper, Russia built the Dnieprostroi, the largest power dam in Europe. The connection with Asia was strengthened by double-tracking the Trans-Siberian railway and connecting it with the Central Asiatic (Turkestan) line. Many of the new factories and steel plants were located east of the Volga and the Urals, beyond the reach of invaders from the west.

The achievement was substantial. From having been one of the smallest industrial producers of Europe, Russia now vied with France and overtook her and even Germany in several fields of production. Yet the pace of the Five-Year Plans gave a deceptive impression of their success. The emphasis on heavy industry and the neglect of light manufacturing had a lopsided effect on the economy. The ambitious goals of the successive plans were seldom wholly fulfilled—indeed, they seem often to have been intended as a psychological stimulus to exertion. The quality of the goods produced was inferior. Industrial productivity in general was still low—only one quarter that of the United States and one third that of Germany. The standard of living was correspondingly low, and it had not been raised by the fever of industrialization.

Further, the human and moral cost of the plans was high. In the industrial areas they spelled forced overwork. The unions ceased to protect their members and became mere transmission belts for the orders of the employer—the state. Piecework was introduced and harsh penalties were eventually decreed for absenteeism. Russia became an industrial barracks. Strikes were out of the question, and failure to perform with maximum success was punished as sabotage and treason. When Alexei Stakhanov, a miner in the Donets basin, mined 102 tons of coal in a single shift (more than ten times the normal quota), the government lionized him and called on the workers to emulate him. "Shock troops" of Stakhanovites, often provided with especially favorable working conditions, were used to set an example of harder and faster work. Since bonuses were given for unusual output, inequality increased.

The greatest sufferers from the rigors of the Five-Year Plans were the peasants of Russia. In the decade that elapsed between the Revolution and the first Five-Year Plan, the peasant was on the point of achieving the position won by the French peasant as a result of the Revolution of 1789. While the title of the land rested in the nation, the Russian peasant was in effective possession. There were 5 to 8 million small farms, some 16 million middling ones, and nearly two million farms owned by *kulaks* (the more prosperous farmers, who hired some labor and sold their surpluses in the market). Since the *kulaks* were growing in number and, many Bolsheviks believed, in wealth as well, the development of something approaching capitalistic agriculture, Lenin's nightmare, was a possibility. The peasants were eating better; the *kulaks* sometimes held back surpluses in protest against the official policy of setting high prices for industrial goods while keeping the price of farm produce low; and the government dumped grain abroad in order to finance Communist movements. In consequence, there were endemic food shortages in the cities. When harvests were bad, famine threatened.

The Bolsheviks did not propose to preside over a country of independent farmers, with all that implied for the limitation of their power over the economy, the labor force, and the distribution of the national income. The largest visible source of capital for investment was agricultural surpluses, provided that the state could get its hands on them. Marx had contended that Western landlords and capitalists had expropriated small property owners and thus procured the capital for launching industrial enterprises. Why could not the Soviet government also engage in "primitive accumulation"? Stalin and his colleagues decided to expropriate the rich farmers, precisely the class they regarded as a potential threat to their regime. They would then gather both large and small farms into huge collectives and state farms, supplant animal with mechanical power, and decrease the swollen agricultural labor force. The government would then increase industrial man power and drive it to work harder, reduce the consumption of both farmers and city workers, and invest the surpluses thus accumulated in capital goods and new industries.

When the first Five-Year Plan was launched, there was an attempt to use only mild coercion, such as higher taxes for the wealthier peasants, to induce peasants to merge their farms, implements, and animals into collectives. The pace turned out to be slow, and it was decided, in January 1930, to press for immediate collectivization at all costs and particularly to destroy the class of *kulaks*. The immediate result was catastrophic. The craving for private possession was deep-rooted, and the peasants fought for their farms bitterly. When they heard that their animals as well as their land would be pooled into collectives they slaughtered some 18 million horses, 30 million head of cattle, 100 million sheep and goats, and countless pigs. For years afterward, Russia was short of meat. The peasants sometimes rebelled openly. More often they resorted to sabotage or passive resistance. It was to no avail. The recalcitrants were deported and the village population was starved into submission by the "man-made" famine of the early thirties.

The peasants who were classified as *kulaks* especially felt the scourge of Bolshevism. The line of demarcation between *kulaks* and non-*kulaks* was vague, and many middling peasants suffered along with the relatively well-to-do. Their lands and tools were confiscated and melted into collectives, and they and their families were scattered to the four winds. Some were shot, others deported en masse to Siberian work camps, and still others turned adrift to shift for themselves with their families. The *kulak* families numbered perhaps ten million people. No large class had ever been destroyed so quickly. The rest of the peasants became virtual serfs on the collectives. Their life was somewhat eased in 1935, when they were permitted to own a few animals and fowls and to work small kitchen gardens.

Meanwhile, however, Russia had been brought to the verge of starvation. In 1931-33 famine struck many areas, especially those which had been collectivized most rapidly. The horrors of infanticide, epidemics, and even some cases of cannibalism accompanied the famine. It is estimated that collectivization and famine cost at least five million lives. Nor could the world come to the help of the famished peasants, since the government denied the existence of the famine, continued to export grain, and barred foreign visitors from the affected regions. By 1935, however, there was sufficient food to justify the abolition of rationing. Two years later Russia had a bumper crop.

Private farming was gone. Eighty percent of the land had been collectivized, 15 percent was cultivated by state farms, and barely 5 percent consisted of peasant holdings. Efficiency did not improve so rapidly as these figures might suggest, and the huge state farms were not successful. But eventually the harvests picked up, and both the produce and the labor force were now under the control of the state.

Stalinist Conservatism and Terror

The price of forced collectivization and industrialization was cultural and political as well as economic and moral. It was not enough to displace and kill peasants and to sweat industrial workers. Stalin carried on his domestic "war" on a broader front. He wrenched the Communist party and the country from Western moorings, nurtured conservative and nationalistic ideologies, and unleashed a comprehensive terror against all critical, doubting, or independent minds in all classes, equally within and without the party. He removed all the Bolshevik leaders with commitments or sympathies for Western culture. His principal colleagues were, like himself, Communists whose experience was wholly native and who were antagonistic toward the "softer" ways of the West. The character of the party and of the ruling class was changed. The majority of the party had consisted of proletarians; it now consisted of non-proletarians. But these were no longer professional men, intellectuals, and revolutionary conspirators and politicians; they were the new and practical Soviet "intelligentsia" of business executives, farm managers, factory foremen, engineers, bureaucrats, and army officers.

The government closed Russia more and more tightly against Western travelers and Western influences. It encouraged the revival of traditional practices in education and family life. Schools abandoned the progressive techniques of the American philosopher John Dewey and returned to drill, memorization, and the mastery of factual information. Divorce was made more difficult and birth control discouraged. Avant-garde movements in the arts and letters were banned. Novelists, poets, and painters were required to stop experimenting with new forms and subjects and to confine themselves to depicting in bright colors the achievements and the aims of the Communist party. The government did not hesitate to rewrite the history of the Russian Revolution in order to expunge the contributions of Trotsky and exaggerate the role of Stalin. Marxism was denuded of its libertarian, humanitarian, and critical tendencies and became a formal dogma, the source of texts, slogans, and shibboleths adapted to every shift of official policy.

Stalin set the tone of theoretical discussions with such assertions as this:

> We are in favor of the withering away of the State, and at the same time we stand for the strengthening of the dictatorship of the proletariat, which represents the most powerful and mighty authority of all the forms of the State which have existed up to the present day. . . . Is it "contradictory"? Yes, it is "contradictory." But this contradiction is a living thing, and completely reflects Marxist dialectics.

Stalin became not only the infallible interpreter of Marx but a veritable demigod in his own right. He exacted adulation from the party and the people, as a matter of policy as much as from personal vanity. His bust was in every

Soviet propaganda poster: the dictator Joseph Stalin as a loving father of his people. The mothers and children around the poster are attending a sports parade in Moscow in 1936. The artist has been careful to omit from Stalin's face all signs of his secretiveness, suspiciousness, and obduracy. SOVFOTO

shop window, his portrait in every office. Hardly a speech, a book, or a pamphlet but opened with an invocation to the "great genius," the "greatest statesman of all times," "the Sun." No czar in modern times had exacted such extravagant obeisance.

But the principal means of Stalin's policy was not psychological. He covered the land with a close network of secret police, spies, and prosecutors with virtually unlimited power to arrest, imprison, torture, and execute without trial anyone suspected of opposition, criticism, or even lack of sympathy with the regime. Informing was encouraged, and children were set to spy on their parents. Not only critics, saboteurs, and enemies of the regime but often quite innocent people were rounded up at night, forced to confess or invent improbable crimes, and shot or shipped off to hard labor. Their families were made hostages. The victims came from all ranks. Labor camps in Siberia and many other parts of the country served the double function of disposing of masses of suspects or

637

potential opponents and supplying slave labor to execute difficult tasks, such as building canals and railroads in icy regions or mining coal and gold. It has been estimated conservatively that there were five to six million slave laborers.

The purge reached to the top. In a series of spectacular trials in 1936-38 many leading Bolsheviks were "liquidated." Did Stalin regard his former colleagues in the government and party as potential threats to his power? They were, indeed, old hands at conspiracy. Before Stalin destroyed his comrades physically they were compelled—by torture, by continuous interrogation for days and even weeks under blinding lights, by threats to their families and friends—to destroy themselves morally and politically. They confessed to extravagant and incredible crimes: plotting to overthrow Bolshevism and restore capitalism, plotting the assassination of true Communists, spying for foreign imperialists, and selling out the country to Nazis and Japanese. Bukharin, Grigori Zinoviev, the former chief of the Third International, Lev Kamenev, the former president of the U.S.S.R., dozens of other front-rank leaders, and thousands of lesser officials and bureaucrats died as self-confessed renegades and traitors so that their memory and fame could not serve as inspiration to opponents of Stalinism. Those who refused to condemn themselves publicly were executed in secret. Of the old leadership only Stalin and Trotsky survived, and the dictator pursued his chief rival implacably. In 1929 he had exiled Trotsky from Russia and then harried him from Turkey to France, from France to Norway, from Norway to Mexico. All Trotsky's children died mysteriously. In 1940, a comrade who had posed as his follower broke Trotsky's skull with an ice ax as Trotsky sat at his desk writing a biography of Stalin.

Meanwhile Stalin had purged the army officers corps. Marshal Mikhail Tukhachevski, the professional chief of the Soviet defense forces, was tried secretly with several other high military figures for treason and executed in 1937. Within a short period more than half the colonels and generals and 10 percent of the lower officers—perhaps 20,000 men in all—were arrested, and several thousand of them were executed.

Stalin ruled supreme. He had accelerated a movement of industrialization that had been started in czarist times by Count Sergei Witte (see p. 452). The cost ran into millions of lives. The opposition was dead or smothered. Smothered also was much of the intelligence, the gentleness, the dignity of Russia. In this condition, Russia faced an external danger that was to test her last ounce of will and strength: the imperial designs of Nazi Germany.

30. *The Tragedy of Appeasement*

"Today Germany, tomorrow the whole world." This cry of the Nazis was not an empty slogan. The policies Hitler pursued at home were part of a larger pattern. Indeed, Hitler did not expect to solve Germany's problems at home. He proposed to solve them abroad, particularly in Eastern Europe.

The Scheme of Planetary Conquest

Hitler was no sooner installed as Chancellor than he accelerated the rearmament of Germany. His government secretly increased the standing army beyond the limits set by the Versailles Treaty. It built new airfields, ostensibly for commercial reasons, and used them for military exercises. It used commercial aircraft to train fighting crews. Shipyards began busily to turn out naval craft.

These measures were not intended merely to restore the equality of Germany with other powers. Before Hitler came to power he had adumbrated, in *Mein Kampf* and myriad speeches, a scheme for organizing Europe around Germany as a center, and the other continents around an Aryan Europe. Germany would extend over Central Europe, the Balkan Peninsula, the Baltic areas, the Ukraine, and, indeed, most if not all of European Russia. She would monopolize the industrial plant of this large empire. The indigenous urban populations, the middle and upper classes, the professional groups, the teachers and journalists and politicians—in short, all the articulate, literate, and trained groups, accustomed to exercising influence, exerting power, or commanding wealth—regardless of political orientation, would be exterminated. The agrarian populations would be reduced in numbers and fecundity by overwork, a lowered standard of living, and denial of the most rudimentary sanitary and medical services. They would become the virtual slaves of landlords recruited from the peasantry of Germany. Above the layer of German colonists, a small elite of agrarian and political chieftains would live in modern castles, with the latest weapons of war always close at hand.

The eastern hinterland would supply Germany with food and raw materials, cheap and mute labor, room for her growing population, and a testing ground for her large army. Controlling directly two thirds of Europe, Germany would not find it hard to dominate the rest. With the exception of Italy, which was redeemed by Fascism and slated to become a subordinate partner of Germany, the Latin peoples would lose their sovereignty and their military independence. The principles of authoritarianism and racism would be applied within their own much reduced borders.

Incorporated in Germany, northern France and the Netherlands would supply the industry and the Atlantic seaboard so useful to world empires. The British, who, like the Scandinavians, were Nordic kinsmen of the more resplendent Germans, would assume a position suitable to the character of poor relations. A Nordic league subordinated to Germany would complete the organization of Europe. The British would help to administer the great reaches of Asia and of Oceania. Their Empire, correlated with the larger German holdings, would be preserved: this would be their compensation for fitting into the New Order. The Mediterranean world and most of Africa would be organized directly by the Germans or indirectly through Italian imperial brokers. There remained only America. Groups of German origin in the United States and in Latin America would be stimulated to take the lead in introducing congruent domestic and international policies. Associated with other Aryan elements, they would introduce totalitarian governments, yield Germany valuable markets and even additional colonies, and bring the New World into the New Order. The colored races and peoples of America, Africa, and Asia would become, like the Slavs, raw material of labor.

This was the most ambitious dream of planetary empire outside the covers of extravagant fiction, which Adolf Hitler was fond of reading. The dreams of an Alexander, a Napoleon, a Genghis Khan, were pale by comparison.

The Response to Nazism

Although Hitler's scheme was known in its broad outlines, it was discounted both at home and abroad as a harebrained fantasy intended largely to arouse German chauvinism. His open avowal and daring application of immoral policies evoked a crisis of conscience beyond the borders of Germany.

The shock of the Nazi revolution was swifter than that of the Russian Revolution of 1917. The earlier revolution had occurred in confused and extraordinary circumstances, amid a world at war. News reports were scanty, censored, and unreliable. The Nazi triumph occurred in the full light of publicity, in a world at peace and served by a busy press, photographic services, and cinematographic witnesses. The deeds of the Nazis scandalized the Western world. The abrogation of the rights of the individual and of free political life, the arbitrary arrests and imprisonments and the horror of the concentration camps, and the harrying of liberals, radicals, trade unionists, and Jews drained the credit of Germany as a civilized country.

A considerable segment of opinion felt that Nazism was of general concern, fearing—not without reason—that the German movement would inspire imitation, by direct pressure as well as by example. Like-minded groups were indeed established and inspired, and became active and vocal, in most countries. In countries, such as the United States, where there were large groups of German origin or tradition, pro-Nazi elements repeated the slogans, incitations, and rituals of their compeers at "home." With a little modification, some of the demands of the Nazis were echoed by small native groups as well. Another, and perhaps more serious, ground for concern was the fear that extreme nationalism and militarism, given the means and opportunity of success, would lead to war, and that a war involving large countries could not be localized.

Yet there was great reluctance to intervene or even to apply pressure upon the Nazi regime. Among liberals and socialists, the tendency toward reform, pacifism, and "revisionism," and among conservatives, the opposition to Communism and socialism blunted the reaction to Nazism. A strong wave of anti-militarism and anti-imperialism had been gathering throughout the twenties. The rise of the Nazis, by accenting the fear and possibility of war, further deepened the desire for peace. The peace movements were particularly strong among youth, above all among educated and urban youth. At Oxford University, to cite one striking example, a meeting of the debating society adopted a resolution stating that the participants would refuse to fight "for King and Country." Any tendency that implied aggression or even counteraggression was sharply discountenanced. An investigation by the American Senate brought to light the self-interested action of munitions manufacturers and "salesmen" in provoking profitable war incidents. Loud was the outcry against the "merchants of death," who were saddled with much responsibility, not only for negotiable squabbles in Latin American and other small countries, but for the outbreak and conduct of the First World War. The memory of the harrying of liberals and radicals in some countries during the war did nothing to recommend war as a means of safeguarding the rights of men. Since many of the charges of German *Schrecklichkeit* (frightfulness) in the First World War were exposed as propaganda, there was a strong disposition to discount reports of Nazi atrocities, which were incredible enough to begin with. The Versailles settlement was criticized as vindictive. Liberal-minded men urged its revision and criticized particularly Franco-Polish "imperialism," which had cut Germany into two unequal parts and torn from her the trade of Danzig and the coal mines of the Saar district.

The movements of "revisionism," pacifism, and domestic reform were particularly strong in precisely those circles—liberal, socialistic, intellectual, literary—which were the direct targets of Nazism, and which were most critical of it. They were at the same time the circles traditionally least disposed to appeal to strong diplomatic and military measures. As liberals were reluctant to challenge the Nazis in the realm of force, many a conservative was reluctant to challenge them in the realm of ideas. The anti-Communist emphasis of the Nazis had a wide appeal. By proclaiming himself the enemy of all forms of liberalism, Hitler exploited the tradition of conservatism from Burke, Chateaubriand, and de Maistre on.

Under the circumstances, the conscience of the Western world had to content itself with measures of private or public generosity that could be exercised safely within the boundaries of a single country. Refugees were received with sympathy in a number of countries. France and Holland in particular were hosts to political and religious exiles. The United States and Great Britain interpreted with some liberality the laws against mass immigration. Turkey, which at the end of the fifteenth century had welcomed many a Jewish exile from Spain, repeated her generosity by staffing a whole university with scholars evicted from Germany as non-Aryans or self-exiled from the regime of intolerance. In these and other countries, private organizations and individuals found work for displaced professional men.

A movement to boycott German goods was launched in the United States after the Nazis' open attack on Jewish business. Its effect was limited, however. There were many verbal protests, even of a semiofficial character, but statesmen were careful to employ the accents of sorrow rather than anger. Nazi hoodlums, in their enthusiasm for indiscriminate violence, occasionally attacked foreign tourists, and protests evoked the customary bows of apology.

French and Russian Efforts to Resist Hitler

To the trend of passivity only the countries that felt themselves immediately threatened formed an exception. Although the French, like people in other Western countries, were pacifistic and antinationalist in opinion and mood, they were also more sensitive to the danger of German rearmament. In 1934 the Foreign Minister, Jean Louis Barthou (1862-1934) made a series of visits to Central European capitals, attempting to weld the policies of the Little Entente—Czechoslovakia, Rumania, and Yugoslavia—into agreement with those of France. These countries had a common interest in resisting the rising propaganda for revision of the Versailles settlement. There were difficulties, however, with Poland. The dictatorial government of that state feared Germany less than it feared Russia, toward which power France was moving in seeking support against a German threat. Hitler's desire to forestall a crisis before the completion of German rearmament made it possible for Poland to conclude what seemed to be a favorable ten-year nonaggression pact with Germany. But the loss to France was more than made up by her rapprochement with Italy and with Russia.

Hitler often hailed Mussolini as his model, and the Duce reciprocated with an avuncular interest in Nazism. But Mussolini was disturbed by Germany's designs on Austria and feared German rivalry in the Balkans. In 1934, when

Austrian Nazis tried to seize the government in Vienna and melt Austria into Germany, Italy mobilized and threatened to intervene. The following year Italy and France reached an agreement on outstanding issues. Italy was to still her demands for Tunis in exchange for concessions elsewhere in Africa. There was a hint that France would not stand in the way of Italian ambitions in Ethiopia.

No state reacted more sharply to the triumph of the Nazis than the Soviet Union. The shock was particularly stunning since Germany had earlier shown partiality to the revolutionary regime in Russia. The two countries had signed a treaty of friendship and trade at Rapallo in 1922. Both countries smarted under the arrangements of the peace treaties. The German army had found in Russia the testing ground for new arms and the training ground for skilled personnel which it was denied at home by the provisions of the Versailles Treaty; the Russians profited by observing the methods of the German army. Hitler ended this arrangement brusquely in 1935. Apart from anti-Semitism, anti-Communism had always been the principal motif of Nazi propaganda. Indeed, the attacks on Jews, as also on liberals and socialists, were often based on their imputed weakness for Communism. Nazi leaders openly proclaimed that they coveted Russian territory, especially the Ukraine, at once a fertile and a sporadically disaffected region of the Soviet Union.

Soviet Russia met the threat by executing an ideological about-face. The Communist International had labored to weaken the liberal, democratic, and capitalistic regimes by any means, including acquiescence in the rise of reactionary and dictatorial movements. On the theory that Nazism was the "last stage of capitalism," the German Communist party had refused to collaborate with the Social Democrats to stem the advance of Hitler. The disillusionment was Russian as well as Communist, for the German Communists formed the largest and most influential of the Communist parties, if we except the Russian party itself. The existence of a strong Communist party in Germany had been something of a guarantee against a German attack on the Soviet Union.

The Communist International now decided to woo socialists and liberals unblushingly and to support parliamentary regimes. At a special congress of the International in 1935, Chairman Georgi Dimitrov sounded the new keynote: ". . . in the face of Fascist danger, Communists may . . . participate in election campaigns on a common platform and with a common ticket of the anti-Fascist front. . . ." In every country the raging Communist lions became bleating lambs. They formed "popular fronts" with anti-Nazi groups. Communists discovered that they were the heirs of the liberal tradition. In the United States they characterized Communism as "twentieth-century Jeffersonianism." Under a new constitution adopted in 1936, Russia ceased to be a state based on the representation of functional groups of workingmen, particularly proletarians and farmers. Universal suffrage was reintroduced, and so was election by districts. There was to be a parliament and a cabinet of ministers responsible to it.   *643*

An elaborate "improved" bill of individual rights was adopted. The retention of a single political party, the absence of rival candidates at elections, and the restriction of the rights to adherents of the regime largely nullified the constitution. The hierarchs of the Communist party doubled as the elected officials and ministers of a parliamentary system.

The U.S.S.R. launched a long-range plan to strengthen its military arm. Officers suspected of sympathy with their German counterparts were watched and often removed. In order to stimulate patriotism, the Soviet government published new official histories praising the heroes, czars, warriors, and patriarchs of the past. The administrative machinery was tightened. Diplomatic fences were mended. Russia and France broadened negotiations for a trade treaty into political discussions which eventuated, in 1935, in a mutual-assistance pact. Russia signed a similar pact with Czechoslovakia and became indirectly associated with the Little Entente. In the preceding year, as Japan and Germany moved out of the League of Nations, Russia moved in and became a permanent member of the Council. For the first time since 1917 Russia acquired international respectability.

The effectiveness of the Russian and French efforts to meet the German threat hinged indirectly on the policies of Great Britain and the United States. At crucial moments France hesitated to act without the support of Great Britain. Not least of the difficulties of the situation was that while Continental states were drawing together to confront the German danger, Britain and the United States were engaged in a race of isolation.

The British Conservative party, which virtually controlled the national coalition government, was determined to avoid war and hoped that the Nazi fury would spend itself upon the Soviet regime. The National Laborites, headed by Ramsay MacDonald, were committed to international action but were yoked to a majority of Conservatives. The Labor party, in opposition, was restrained by a pacifist wing, led by its chairman, George Lansbury (1859-1940). Lansbury went so far as to visit Hitler in the hope of converting him to moderate views. Even Conservatives who were sensitive to any threat touching the imperial position of Great Britain retreated into acquiescence. Winston Churchill, for example, asserted that Great Britain should diminish her commitments on the Continent, particularly to France. He rejoiced that "the fierce passions that are raging in Germany have not found, as yet, any other outlet but upon themselves." His counsel was seconded by the former Liberal prime minister, David Lloyd George.

There were American leaders who felt that the interests of the Republic required cooperation with other powers, particularly the former wartime allies, against any disturbers of the peace. These leaders included President Roosevelt himself and many prominent Republicans, such as Henry L. Stimson (1867-1950), a former Secretary of State. But such men were helpless before the determination of the mass of politicians, and evidently of the electorate, to avoid involvement. Antiwar sentiment found expression in unprecedented "neutrality" legislation, which the President did not dare to veto. In 1935 the Congress passed a law, strengthened twice in the succeeding years, prohibiting the sale of munitions to belligerent states. Ignoring the efforts of international arbitration and the Kellogg-Briand Pact, these acts drew no distinction between aggressors and defenders, or between former allies and other states. They threw overboard the historic insistence on the right of neutrals to trade with states at war or with other neutrals.

The policies of the United States and Great Britain made it more difficult for France and Russia to build a front against Nazi aggression.

Aggression and Rearmament

Such was the international atmosphere that Hitler exploited, with much adroitness. He had before him the example of successful aggression in Asia.

Japan had for some years been making strenuous efforts to secure a strong economic and strategic position on the Asian mainland. In resisting this pressure, Chinese Nationalists had resorted to a boycott of Japanese goods, while attempting to invigorate the military and administrative apparatus of their country. As the struggle sharpened, the Japanese military, encouraged by imperialistic industrial and financial elements, took matters into their own hands. In 1931, without troubling to declare war, they had occupied Manchuria. The Chinese intensified their boycott and succeeded in reducing imports from Japan by 80 percent. The Japanese countered by seizing Shanghai, China's most valuable port, and its environs. They declared the "independence" of Manchuria (renamed Manchukuo), set up a creature of their own as emperor, and supplied him with Japanese advisors.

This assault upon China and the prospect of her disintegration or further subjection to Japan disturbed the other powers with Asian interests. The American Secretary of State, Henry L. Stimson, attempted to secure the cooperation of other powers, notably Great Britain, and of the League in checking Japan, which had violated the Covenant of the League as well as the Kellogg-Briand Pact. In order to forestall any concessions, Japanese army officers assassinated several of their own leading politicians, including the Premier himself, Inukai. Generals and admirals then organized a new cabinet which combined a dictatorial regime at home with aggressive imperialism. When Great Britain declined to take joint action with the United States, the Republic declared that she would refuse to recognize illegal acquisitions. A special commission named by the League brought in a report intended as a compromise: Chinese sovereignty would be restored in Manchuria, but the economic interests of Japan would be respected. Japan refused to accept the report and in March 1933 (shortly after Hitler became Chancellor of Germany) gave notice of resignation from the League of Nations. It was the first withdrawal of an important power from the international organization.

It was not to be the last. The ineffectiveness of the League, the unwillingness of great powers to enforce the observance of solemn agreements, and Japan's successful defiance encouraged the Nazis to do likewise. During the Japanese crisis, the Disarmament Conference was reaching its futile climax. Chancellor Bruening and, after him, Hitler had insisted that Germany could not agree to a general reduction of arms before she attained "equality"—before, that is, she had *increased* her arms. In May 1933, while the conferees tried and discarded one formula after another, Vice Chancellor von Papen was inspired to deliver a eulogy of war and martial virtue. In the fall, seven months after the Japanese representative had stalked out of a meeting of the League, Germany withdrew from both the Disarmament Conference and its parent body at Geneva.

Hitler exploited the divergence between French and English policies. In June 1935, while France was wooing Italy with the promise of colonial concessions, he concluded an agreement with Great Britain that conceded him a fleet 35 percent the size of Britain's own. Meanwhile encouragement had come from the Saar. In January 1935 a plebiscite was held by the League to decide whether the inhabitants of the district would rather join Germany or France or would prefer to continue to be governed by League administrators. The Nazis staged an energetic nationalistic campaign, and 90 percent of the voters opted for Germany. On March 1, the Saar was German again. On March 15, France lengthened the military service of a few groups in order to replenish the army, depleted by the low birth rate of the war years. Striking the pose of an injured party acting in self-defense, Hitler announced the next day that he would henceforth disregard the provisions of the Treaty of Versailles which limited the German army to 100,000 men. He reintroduced conscription and set the period of military service at one year. (The next year he raised it to two years, doubling the size of the army.)

The powers made a gesture of protest. The diplomats of France, Great Britain, and Italy conferred at Stresa and complained that "the method of unilateral repudiation adopted by the German government has undermined public confidence in the security of a peaceful order." France could not persuade the others to agree to sanctions in the event of further repudiation. Within a year of the announcement of German rearmament, Italy imitated in Ethiopia the Japanese aggression in Manchuria.

The depression had worsened the economic condition of Italy and the fiscal condition of her government. The population continued to increase by 400,000 persons a year, and the impact of anti-immigration legislation in overseas countries in the twenties was felt all the more because of the constriction of employment. The tourist trade and remittances from emigrants to their relatives at home dropped severely. Fascism had no remedy to offer, but it boasted of its armed might and painted glowing pictures of a revived "Roman Empire." The disagreeable fact was that the principal imperial venture of Italy, in 1896, had culminated in her defeat by Ethiopian troops at Adowa. Modern weapons had since widened the gap between African tribesmen and European warriors. Perhaps the time had come to wipe out the blot of Adowa.

At the end of 1934, border troops had clashed in a disputed area between Italian Somaliland and Ethiopia. Italy demanded reparations and an apology.

The League of Nations was attempting to arbitrate the issue of responsibility when France and Italy announced that they had come to an agreement on colonial divisions. Great Britain joined France in offering Italy a free hand in the economic development of Ethiopia. On October 3, 1935, an Italian army invaded the country without a declaration of war.

Public opinion in Europe and the United States was outraged. At the end of 1934, in a remarkable referendum held in Great Britain, more than eleven million persons had expressed strong support of the League of Nations and of sanctions against aggressors. The United States government was minded to cooperate with the League while Germany ostentatiously sided with Italy. The League now voted to impose sanctions: a large majority of its members bound themselves to supply Italy no arms, credits, loans, or materials valuable for war. But they quailed before the most crucial prohibition. Italian airplanes, ships, and trucks could not do without foreign oil, and the powers could not bring themselves to apply the "oil sanctions." The French premier, Pierre Laval (1883-1945), and the British foreign secretary, Sir Samuel Hoare (1880-1959), agreed to "cede" much of Ethiopia to Italy. There was a loud public outcry: Sir Samuel was compelled to resign, Laval was severely criticized, and their concession was annulled. However, in the spring of 1936, the Italian armies overwhelmed the tribal levies of Ethiopia. The country was annexed, her emperor, Haile Selassie, fled, and the king of Italy assumed his title.

In March, after the controversy on sanctions had reached fever pitch, Hitler chose to strike again. He denounced the Locarno Pacts and marched his troops into the Rhineland, which had been demilitarized by the Treaty of Versailles. Hitler was ready to withdraw his troops on a show of opposition, but the governments, particularly Great Britain, were still not prepared to act. France made a strong but futile protest, and the Council of the League found Germany guilty of treaty-breaking. The British government asked Germany whether she would henceforth respect existing international arrangements. Hitler did not answer.

The logic of events aligned Germany with Italy and Japan. All three states had defied the League and liberal opinion, all three were dictatorial, all claimed to be "have-not" powers in a world pre-empted by older empires. In October 1936, the "Rome-Berlin Axis" was forged. Germany and Italy announced that they would henceforth coordinate their policies. Since the outstanding difference between them had been Italy's objection to the union of Austria with Germany, it was assumed that, in exchange for German support in the Mediterranean and in Africa, Italy would waive that objection. The following month Germany and Japan, joined a year later by Italy, drew together under the ostensible banner of common opposition to Communism. They agreed, in the Anti-Comintern Pact, to cooperate against Communist activities and propaganda.

In three years Hitler had set Germany on the road to renewed power and had torn up the treaty that signalized her defeat. The old wartime allies had not acted together to stop him, and the League of Nations had failed a crucial test. For the moment, in 1936-37, the Atlantic powers, as well as Russia, had enough domestic problems to distract them from the contemplation of future dangers. Stalin was purging the Communist party of its old leadership. A mild recession in the United States gave pause to the New Dealers. France was equally absorbed with a wave of "sit-down" strikes. With the encouragement of the New Popular Front government, employers were persuaded to grant increases in pay and paid annual vacations. Britain was rocked by a dynastic scandal. King Edward VIII, who succeeded to the throne in January 1936, proposed to marry an American woman, Mrs. Wallis Simpson, who had been twice divorced. The Church of England and the Conservative party could not condone a marriage which, by its implications, would require a change in the strict Church custom concerning divorce—for the king of England is head of the Church—and the consequent modification of its social standards. Edward VIII was persuaded to abdicate in December 1936, and his brother succeeded him as George VI (1936-52). (Edward, who became the Duke of Windsor, married Mrs. Simpson six months later.) The atmosphere was tense during the abdication crisis; no British king had ever before abdicated "voluntarily."

The Spanish Civil War

Abroad, there was no surcease from tension. In July 1936 an event occurred that was to divide the Western world into opposite camps. The Spanish Civil War broke out.

For a century or more, the course of Spanish affairs had moved outside the main stream of European life. In 1823 efforts of Spanish revolutionists to establish a constitutional government had been frustrated by an invading French army, dispatched with the consent of the conservative Concert of Europe; but subsequent changes of regime, coups, and civil wars had started hardly a ripple on the surface of international affairs. Spain's defeat by the United States in 1898 and her lack of participation in the World War had diminished her importance to the vanishing point. Such influence as she retained she owed to her position as the cultural center and inspiration of the Latin American republics, her former colonies. The image of Spain abroad was that of a benighted and retarded country, populated by an impoverished peasantry in the grip of proud and old-fashioned landlords, clerics, and military men.

Since 1923, Spain, still ostensibly a monarchy, had been in fact a military dictatorship under General Miguel Primo de Rivera (1870-1930). The opposition blamed the king, Alfonso XIII (1886-1931), as well as the dictator for the absence of freedom. In 1930 Alfonso ousted De Rivera and held municipal elections, which were overwhelmingly republican. The King left the country, without abdicating, and a republican constitution was adopted. Long-overdue land and clerical reforms were initiated. Radical, conservative, and moderate governments alternated in office until February 1936, when, following a general election, a coalition government was formed similar to the Popular Front in France.

The antirepublican opposition became restive and kept the country in turmoil.

Political violence became endemic. Rich Spaniards shipped their capital abroad. A recently formed party, the Falange, emulated the provocative tactics of the Fascists and Nazis. The officers' corps, which was bound by strong family and social ties to the landowning class, plotted to engineer a restoration of the monarchy. The various conservative groups drew together.

On July 17, 1936, army officers raised the banner of rebellion in Spanish Morocco, with the support of their Moorish troops, and touched off a series of prearranged risings in the chief garrison towns of Spain. The Nationalists, as the insurgents called themselves, controlled the bulk of the small regular army, the air force, and half the navy, although the sailors were generally Loyalist in sympathy. General Francisco Franco (1892-   ) assumed leadership of the rebellion. The republic commanded few regular troops, but it improvised a militia and organized regiments of trade unionists. It was short of trained personnel, but it had the support of the peasantry, the urban proletariat, and the liberal professionals and intellectuals. Catalonia and the Basque country, traditionally regionalist in sentiment, had been granted autonomy and remained Loyalist. In the circumstances, the rebels, though they achieved considerable successes, were unable to destroy the republic. By November they held half of Spain, but Madrid, the capital, the port of Barcelona, the gold reserve of the country, and the principal industrial centers remained in the hands of the legal government.

In the hope of averting an extension of the conflict, the French government prevailed upon 27 other countries, including Germany and Italy, to agree not to intervene. A Non-Intervention Committee was organized to help to enforce the agreement and began to act in London in September. From the outbreak of the rebellion, however, Germany and Italy had begun to assist the Franco forces. Their assistance was at first limited principally to aircraft, but then it snowballed. Fascist Italy, fresh from her triumph over the tribes of Ethiopia, perceived another opportunity to earn easy "glory" and to enlarge her power in the western Mediterranean. The Nazi regime was determined to destroy a liberal republic. Late in 1936, Italy and Germany began to pour "volunteers" and materials into the distraught peninsula. In a few months Italy had dispatched an army estimated at from 50,000 to 75,000 trained men, with the necessary equipment, trucks, guns, and ammunition. The Germans sent airplanes, technical equipment and personnel, and guns. They tested their new weapons by savage bombardment of Loyalist cities. The dictatorial government of President Antonio Salazar (1889-   ) in neighboring Portugal provided political as well as material help.

Militant liberals and radicals of many countries came to the aid of the Spanish republic. Some 40,000 volunteers, about 3000 of them American, joined the Loyalist armies. Their idealism, however, was counterbalanced by their lack of training, and eventually also by their differences of political opinion, especially as the Communist influence grew stronger. Soviet Russia sent food, money, and arms to aid the Loyalists, but her ships were often attacked by Italian submarines and her shipping capacity was limited. Russia also contributed technical personnel and political agents, who exploited the occasion to increase the influence of Communists in the embattled government.

Other governments acted with extreme caution. The Western powers stopped Italian submarine attacks on Russian ships, but they did not check military and air intervention. The Loyalist government, as a legal and recognized regime, was entitled under international law to purchase arms abroad, but Britain and France refused to permit the shipment of war supplies to either side. The American Neutrality Act of 1935, which forbade the sale of munitions to belligerents, was extended to cover both parties in a civil conflict as well.

The Spanish conflict rapidly polarized the ideological issue of the thirties. On the field of battle German Nazis and Italian Fascists as well as Spanish monarchists and clericals confronted Spanish and non-Spanish liberals, socialists, anarchists, and Communists. Elsewhere pro-Loyalists debated with pro-Nationalists and vied in raising funds and contingents of fighters.

"Guernica"—a mural painted in 1937 by the Spanish artist Pablo Picasso (1881-   ). It commemorates a town in Spain that was ravaged by Nazi bombers during the Civil War. THE MUSEUM OF MODERN ART

The Policy of Appeasement

Even as liberals and radicals steeled themselves to meet the challenge of Nazism, conservative groups moved toward an accommodation with the dictatorial powers. "Appeasement" became the official policy of the Western states, and particularly of Great Britain in 1937, when Neville Chamberlain succeeded Stanley Baldwin as prime minister and leader of the Conservative party.

Neville Chamberlain (1869-1940) was the son of Joseph Chamberlain, the aggressive Colonial Secretary at the turn of the century. Like his father, he was a businessman turned politician. As Colonial Secretary, the elder Chamberlain had striven to bolster the economic and imperial position of Great Britain by taking the offensive in colonial expansion and protectionism. His son was confronted by Nazi Germany, more defiant than the imperial Germany that had faced his father. Neville Chamberlain and like-minded Conservatives proposed to mollify Germany by making concessions to her and to attempt to deflect her expansionist drive toward Eastern Europe and that of Italy toward African regions.

Since France was wary of taking a strong stand without the agreement of   *651*

Britain, the policy of the Chamberlain government became in effect the policy of the Western powers. There were, in Great Britain as elsewhere, conservatives who distrusted the dictatorial regimes too much to accept the policy of appeasement. Anthony Eden (1897-   ), the British Foreign Secretary, resigned his office in protest against a pact in which Great Britain made colonial and other concessions to Italy without insisting that the Fascist legions be withdrawn from Spain. Winston Churchill, shaken out of his passive response to the rise of Hitler by the display of Nazi fire and air power in Spain, became the Cassandra of the House of Commons: from its back benches he predicted dire consequences unless Britain speedily took a firm stand. But neither the dissenting votes within the conservative ranks nor liberal opinion could change the course of Chamberlain, who was encouraged by the widespread craving for the continuation of peace. In the United States, President Roosevelt attempted to arouse the country to a sense of the totalitarian danger. In 1937 he urged in a speech at Chicago that the aggressors be "quarantined" in order to prevent war. But neither Congress nor American opinion—let alone the Western European governments—were prepared to follow him.

To Stalin the passivity of the Western powers seemed a confirmation of the conspiracy against Russia which had been dramatized by the conclusion of the Anti-Comintern Pact. He tightened his control over Russia against the day of trouble, intensifying the purges. Hitler stiffened his grip over Germany's military and political apparatus. He was determined to surround himself with officials for whom his word was law. Early in 1938 he summarily dismissed the minister of war, General Werner von Blomberg, upon his marriage to a woman beneath his station and of dubious reputation—a marriage, incidentally, that Hitler had attended. He forced the resignation of General Werner von Fritsch, commander-in-chief of the army, on trumped-up charges of homosexuality. More servile creatures, Generals Wilhelm Keitel and Heinrich von Brauchitsch, became Hitler's chief military coadjutors. Hjalmar Schacht yielded his post as minister of economics to a more pliable Nazi, Walther Funk, and the conservative Constantin von Neurath gave up his post as Foreign Minister to the Nazi Joachim von Ribbentrop.

The Führer was ready to act. On November 5, 1937, he had summoned his military and diplomatic chiefs in secret session and told them plainly that he intended to annex Austria and Czechoslovakia in the very near future and then to conquer slices of Poland and southern Russia. He anticipated no resistance from the Western powers, and none from Russia without their aid. Since Germany's armaments were at the moment superior to those of her possible enemies and might not continue to be superior, she "had nothing to gain from a prolonged period of peace." The military chiefs expressed some concern over the military strength of Czechoslovakia and France and the possibility of the intervention of other powers, but Hitler dismissed their fears.

The Seizure of Austria and Czechoslovakia

In March 1938 Hitler provoked a quarrel with Austria. On the 15th, without warning, a German army poured into Austria and occupied the country. No resistance was offered; a strong element welcomed Nazi totalitarianism and annexation (*Anschluss*) to Germany. The racial laws, the concentration camps, the abolition of political parties, the harrying of radicals and liberals, the installation of Nazi politicians in office—all the signs of Hitler's rule—were reproduced promptly in the land of his birth. There were only mild protests from the other powers.

Before the annexation of Austria, the Nazi government had launched a propaganda campaign against Czechoslovakia, charging that Russian planes were using Czech airports and that the German minority in the mountainous area of the Sudeten was being persecuted. Although the charges were false and were officially and repeatedly denied, the Nazis reiterated them with increasing frequency. The Sudeten Nazi leader, Konrad Henlein, demanded autonomy for the Germans in the area. Hitler significantly promised to "protect" German minorities everywhere. The Czechs were prepared to defend themselves against an attack, but after the occupation of Austria they were surrounded on three sides by German arms. They had become virtually an enclave in a hostile country. Their fate rested, therefore, principally upon their allies and friends. Russia pledged her word to come to their assistance if France did, but France waited upon the decision of Britain. That decision was to appease Germany.

Hitler's followers proceeded to provoke disorders in Sudetenland. The Czech government stood ready to grant regional autonomy, but the Nazis refused, playing for higher stakes. The British fleet was assembled, a million Frenchmen were mobilized, and Neville Chamberlain proposed a conference. On September 15, 1938, he met Hitler at Berchtesgaden, in Bavaria. Hitler insisted on the annexation of German areas on the basis of self-determination. Both Chamberlain and the French premier, Edouard Daladier (1884-   ), advised the Czechs to yield. After an agonizing hesitation, the Czechs did so.

Hitler then raised his ante: he must annex more territory and at once, without consulting the population. The Czechs were not to remove any property or installations from the territory to be surrendered; plebiscites were to be held later in additional territories with German minorities. The sudden change angered the prime ministers of France and Great Britain, but, intent on preserving peace, they prevailed upon Mussolini to arrange another conference with Hitler. On September 29, the four statesmen assembled at Munich for the most momentous meeting since the conference at Versailles in 1919. Most of Hitler's demands were granted. Germany promptly annexed about ten thousand square miles and three and a half million inhabitants of Czechoslovakia; only one fifth of the people were Czechs; plebiscites were not held. Germany won the right to build a road across Czechoslovakia to Vienna. Thus the Czech republic

The four-power conference held at Munich in September 1938, which gave Hitler the Sudeten area of Czechoslovakia. Left to right: Chamberlain, Daladier, Hitler, Mussolini, and Ciano, the Italian foreign minister. In center rear is the German foreign minister, Von Ribbentrop. ACME

was made helpless to resist the appetites of other aggressive neighbors. Poland seized the Teschen area, containing a quarter of a million people, a majority of whom were not Poles, and Hungary grasped a strip of border containing a million people. The agrarian and backward region of Slovakia obtained full autonomy; the influence of the Czechs was broken within the remnants of their former state. In a few weeks the most successful republic born of the First World War was reduced by a third of its population, her defenses were removed, and her internal integrity was violated.

In the Western countries, popular reaction to the dismemberment of Czechoslovakia was a mixture of relief and dread. War had been averted. Hitler had declared that the Sudeten area represented his last territorial demand in Europe. His colleagues assured foreign diplomats of their pacific intentions. Neville Chamberlain came back from Munich waving a piece of paper, signed by Hitler and himself, expressing the desire of Germany and Great Britain never again to go to war with each other. But there was no concealing the fact that the position of the powers had been rearranged and that the Versailles settlement had been destroyed. Great Britain was again haunted by the fear that one of the Continental powers would dominate Europe.

In Germany, the last vestiges of doubt had fallen away: military and political leaders bowed before the "genius" who conquered countries without firing a shot. Half a dozen states hastened to do Germany's bidding at a nod. In Czechoslovakia, President Beneš resigned and left his country. A new government was organized, the Communist party was dissolved, and anti-Semitic legislation was initiated. Hungary resigned from the League of Nations, signed the Anti-Comintern Pact, and curtailed the opportunities of Jews in the professions and business. The Prime Minister resigned when it was disclosed that one of his grandparents, although baptized as a Christian, had been a Jew to the age of seven. Germany's Axis partner also fell into line. The 70,000 Jews of Italy fell under the ban of racial legislation. Fascism had previously not been anti-Semitic, and the tolerant attitude of the Italian people qualified the brutality of these decrees. Yet thousands of Jews whose families had resided in Italy for centuries lost their positions, and many of them ate the bread of exile.

Germany's new-found strength in Central Europe endangered the position of Russia and France. Russia's exclusion from the Munich conference was tantamount to notice that her desires and her fate were of no concern to the Western European powers. It was of little account that she declared herself relieved of treaty obligations to France. The position of France was hardly better. Italian politicians felt encouraged to demand publicly that France cede Tunis. The victory of the Spanish Nationalists placed a dictatorial sentinel on the flank of the Pyrenees, for it was in this same winter that the Spanish republic gave up the ghost. Franco's troops overran Catalonia, took Barcelona, and drove the bulk of the Loyalist troops across the border into France, where they were interned. France, Great Britain, and the United States recognized the new government. Franco imprisoned and executed many of the Loyalists, canceled the land-redistribution and anti-clerical laws, forbade labor unions, and put an end to civil marriage and divorce and to secular public education. He made his obeisance to the powers that had put him in power: on the model of Mussolini, he became a Duce and made Spain a "corporative" state. He left the League of Nations and in April announced Spain's adherence to the Anti-Comintern Pact.

In the winter of 1938-39, Germany enjoyed "the top of sovereignty." How she would use it had already been determined by her leaders but was not known for certain by others. A year after the *Anschluss*, on March 15, 1939, in defiance of formal promises to respect the Munich settlement, Germany crossed the borders and overran the remainder of Czechoslovakia. The day before, the Czech president, Emil Hacha, had been called to a conference with Hitler. He had been intimidated by the threat that the German air force was poised to destroy the cities of his country, shouted down and insulted by Hitler until he fainted, revived by a Nazi doctor, and constrained to sign a statement placing "the fate of the Czech people . . . trustingly into the hands of the Führer." Torture of heads of states had been made into a technique of diplomacy.

The snuffing out of a helpless country by degrading as well as aggressive means exposed Hitler's hand. Chamberlain painfully admitted that he had been duped by the German Chancellor. It became plain that no agreements could be made with the German government; there was no security in making concessions, since the terms under which they were made would not be respected. It also became plain that the absorption of Austria and the annexation of Czechoslovakia were merely links in a long chain of which the end disappeared over the horizon. Hardly a week had passed after the occupation of Czechoslovakia

German tanks crossing the German border into Czechoslovakia in March 1939, encountering no resistance—and no welcome. The weather is chilly, both actually and figuratively. WIDE WORLD

before the German government frightened Lithuania into giving up "voluntarily" the port of Memel. Not to be left behind, the other partner of the Rome-Berlin Axis dispatched an army across the Adriatic in April and annexed Albania, in contravention of the recent Anglo-Italian agreement.

Hitler stepped up his demands. He asked Poland to agree to the cession of Danzig to Germany and the construction of an extraterritorial rail and motor road across the Corridor. Poland refused, and Germany annulled the nonaggression pact of 1934. Great Britain, alarmed, introduced conscription. The King and Queen paid a visit to Canada and the United States—the first time a reigning British monarch had crossed the ocean—in order to stimulate support for obviously impending troubles. France speeded up her plans for mobilization, and parliament voted the cabinet unprecedented powers of governing by decree.

A feverish attempt was made to patch up a system of alliances. France and Great Britain pledged support to Poland, Rumania, and Greece in case of attack. They signed mutual-assistance treaties with Turkey. And then they made a belated and ineffective effort to come to an understanding with Soviet Russia. Their task was made more difficult by Poland's refusal to admit Russian troops in case of a war against Germany.

For his part, Stalin hoped, as the leaders of Great Britain and France had hoped earlier, to avoid involvement and to deflect the direction of Nazi conquest away from his borders. There was room for compromise. On August 23 the world was astounded by the news that the two sworn enemies—Soviet Russia and Nazi Germany—had signed a pledge not to attack or join in an attack upon each other for at least ten years. Secretly they also agreed to divide up Central

Europe. Russia was to control or occupy eastern Poland and the Baltic states, with the exception of Lithuania, which was eventually to go to Germany, together with the bulk of Poland. Bessarabia was assigned to the Russian "sphere."

Everywhere in the world, the Communist parties changed sides. At a signal from Moscow, they abandoned their opposition to Hitler and denounced the Western Allies as imperialistic. Hitler demanded a free hand in Poland; Chamberlain warned that Britain would defend Poland against aggression, and President Roosevelt urged Germany and Poland to settle their quarrel peaceably; Poland agreed but Germany did not reply. All efforts to stop Hitler were futile. On September 1, 1939, without a declaration of war, Germany invaded Poland by land and air. Two days later England and France declared war on Germany. The Second World War had begun.

31. *The Conquests of the Axis*

Twenty-five years after the outbreak of the First World War, Germany was again fighting France and Great Britain. She again had an eastern enemy as well; but this time it was Poland rather than Russia. In 1914 Germany had shared with other countries the responsibility for unleashing war. She was now the sole deliberate aggressor. The stakes were higher. To the familiar goals of conquest and empire, there was now added an ideological aim. It was highly likely that the countries defeated by Germany would have to adapt themselves to Nazi policies in domestic as well as international affairs. On the other hand, Nazism could hardly survive defeat.

The Blitzkrieg in Poland and France

The military situation also was different, but only superficially so. It was again imperative for Germany to achieve a swift decision, for a long war still exceeded her capacity. Hitler had hoped to avoid a two-front war; he had calculated that the Western Allies would not declare war, and now that they had, he was convinced that they could not or would not prosecute it seriously. The General Staff had therefore prepared a campaign against Poland while remaining on the defensive in the west. It was determined to avoid at all cost the stalemate and drawn-out fighting of the First World War and thought it had found the means to do so in the strategy of the *Blitzkrieg* (lightning war). The *Blitz* would begin with a concentrated air attack upon the forts, communications, troop concentrations, supplies, and air force of the enemy. Secret agents would break up communications, tear up rails, and blow up bridges. Parachutists disguised as natives, in violation of international law, would attack forts and troops in the rear. While the area behind the lines was being softened up, border lines and fortified areas would be forced. In previous wars a large army had formed a solid line on a wide front and advanced along it. Now, at a few selected points, a group of tank divisions would rush forward and penetrate deep into enemy territory. The tank units would slice into the opposing army and sever the territory into "pockets." Pairs of tank lines would form into pincers, surrounding the isolated troops. Infantry would follow in armored trucks, occupy the ground, and deploy to destroy them. Both tanks and infantry would advance under the protection of air fleets.

Poland became the first testing ground of the *Blitzkrieg*. At dawn on September 1, 1939, swarms of German bombers attacked the civilian population in the cities, put railways and other centers of transportation and communication out of commission, damaged airfields, and destroyed Polish airplanes before they could leave the ground. Simultaneously, several armored divisions crossed the border and lunged forward, outrunning the motorized infantry in their wake. One armored group "bit off" the industrial areas of western Poland, and the other closed a vise around the capital of Warsaw. The Polish armies, stunned by the manifold attacks, surrendered. The people of Warsaw withstood a short siege against attacks from the air and the ground but capitulated on September 27.

Russia collected the reward promised in the Nazi-Soviet Pact. On September 17 she ordered her troops into eastern Poland, on the pretext of protecting the local minorities of White Russians and Ukranians. She thus obtained dominion over the eastern half of the country, with thirteen million inhabitants; Germany ruled the more populous and industrial western half, with twenty-two million inhabitants. Posen and the nearby areas were incorporated into the Reich, while the rest of western Poland was organized as a "protectorate," under a German administration. Thus in less than a month one of the large states of Europe was swallowed up by two larger ones.

Her immediate aim accomplished, Germany offered peace to the Western Allies. England and France had stood by in startled impotence while Poland was being annihilated. While they were unwilling to purchase what they felt must be only an uneasy truce between conquests, they were not prepared to

On November 11, 1939, Armistice Day, the British cartoonist Low published this comment on Hitler's offer of "peace" after his destruction of Poland.

DIDN'T I OFFER THEM PEACE ?

undertake an offensive of their own. After a brief advance, the French army had ensconced itself in the Maginot Line, a long, well-equipped, and massive chain of fortifications along the German border. Slowly a British army was assembling in northern France. Belgium and Holland, hoping to escape involvement in war, were afraid to coordinate military measures with each other or with the Allies. On the other side of the Rhine, opposite France, the Germans had constructed a line of forts and pillboxes called the Siegfried Line, or West Wall. This line was now manned ready for defense. But no attack came. The inactivity of the winter 1939-40 led observers to speak of a "phony war."

Eastern Europe was less quiet. After the partition of Poland, Stalin hurried to strengthen Russia's defenses. The Baltic was now her "sphere of influence," and in September and October Estonia, Lithuania, and Latvia felt constrained to sign treaties which permitted Russia to establish fortified stations on their soil. They virtually ceased to be independent. Finland refused terms that were tantamount to annexation, and on November 30, 1939, Russian armies attacked her. They were checked by an obstinate defense, and it was not until March 12, 1940, that the great disparity in numbers prevailed. Finland ceded the Karelian Isthmus, the naval base of Viborg, and several islands in the Gulf of Finland. Meanwhile Russia had become the only country to be expelled from the League of Nations as an aggressor. The Allies had shipped military supplies to the Finns and had come close to breaking relations with Russia. They soon had troubles of their own in Scandinavia. On April 9, 1940, German troops invaded and occupied Denmark, which could offer no resistance. On the same day, a large German fleet appeared suddenly before the Norwegian ports from Oslo to Narvik and overwhelmed the small body of unsuspecting defenders. Norwegian troops, assisted by small bodies of troops landed from British and French craft, fought a rear-guard action in the interior, while the British navy inflicted great losses on the German fleet. The struggle was brief and futile. The Germans made good their hold on the entrance to the Baltic: through Norwegian ports, they could enter the open seas. The British could not close the North Sea to them as they had in the First World War. German air and sea craft were now in a position to attack the northern route of communications between the Western powers and Russia. Since Hitler had long before determined to attack Russia eventually, the Scandinavian enterprise was essential to his plan.

The effect on France and Great Britain was electric. Premier Daladier was overthrown, and Paul Reynaud (1878-   ) succeeded him. The Chamberlain government was discredited, and Winston Churchill became prime minister in a coalition government, which included Labor leaders and Liberals as well as Conservatives.

Churchill took office on the day—May 10—when Germany launched her thunderbolt against Western Europe. She struck simultaneously at Holland and Belgium and a week later at France. Her bombers and parachutists seized bridges over rivers and canals and attacked railroad installations and forts. Fierce air raids were loosed on city populations. The Germans drew a square enclosing the center of Rotterdam and, sending wave after wave of bombers, razed it to the ground. This outrage, which had no clear military purpose, was meant to intimidate other peoples as well as the Dutch. Armored columns snipped the thin defenses of Holland. In vain the Dutch opened their dikes. In five days the resistance ceased, but the government fled to London to continue the war from there.

Meanwhile, German armored columns forced the defenses of Belgium. Assisted by French and British troops, the Belgians were able to hold out a little longer than the Dutch. A Franco-British army assembled in the north of France to receive the principal German attack, which was expected to come through Belgium. In 1914, the Germans had attempted to envelop the whole enemy army in one wheeling movement: standing on the defensive on the center and left of the front, they had used the bulk of their army on the right flank to describe a wide arc through Belgium and northern France. Now, however, they surprised the Allies by coordinating an attack on the center of the line with one on the right. An armored corps sped southwest, through Luxembourg, and pierced the front at Sedan, where the fortifications of the Maginot line were weak. Not waiting for the infantry, the tanks rushed from town to town without much opposition. On May 20, only ten days after the offensive had begun, they reached the Channel coast at Abbeville. The Allied front had been severed. Racing back along the coast, the German armored troops took Boulogne and Calais. On May 28 King Leopold of Belgium capitulated without consulting his allies. Pressed from the west by the German right wing, an Allied army of more than 330,000 men, two thirds of them British, the rest mostly French, was cornered on the beaches of Dunkirk. The Germans failed to seize the opportunity to destroy and capture them. In an improvised operation, Britain evacuated the army on warships and thousands of small private craft, which were rushed over from the island. Although the troops left behind a treasure of equipment, they lived to fight another day.

The next campaign was more decisive. The French strategy, apart from diverting an army to meet the attack in the northwest, was to hold the Maginot Line, in the expectation that the new war, like the First World War, would be one of attrition and immobility. French troops were therefore spread over the long frontier, forming a solid front. The many tanks were scattered among infantry divisions instead of forming an independent force. There were not enough antitank guns, and the air force was weak. As the Germans had intended, raids on cities forced much of the population onto the roads, where they impeded the movement of troops and exposed themselves to merciless raking by fire from German airplanes. German tanks started southward on June 5 and enveloped Paris. The great city fell on June 14. Meanwhile, another German tank army had raced south behind the Maginot Line and reached Lorraine. On June 10 the Fascists attacked France from the southwest. An Italian army pushed forward but was held to petty gains by a smaller French army. President Roosevelt declared, "The hand that held the dagger has struck it into the back of its neighbor."

The French government made desperate efforts to stave off complete disaster. The High Command was changed, but it proved impossible to mount a counteroffensive. Premier Reynaud appealed to England and the United States for immediate help—particularly airplanes and destroyers. Anticipating that she would soon need every soldier and weapon for her own defense, England declined. She tried to prevail upon France to continue the struggle from her North African possessions, for the French fleet was undefeated. As a token of England's loyalty, Churchill made a dramatic proposal for "an indivisible union": England and France would become one country, with dual citizenship. "The constitution of the Union will provide joint organs of defense, foreign, financial, and economic policies. . . . The two parliaments will be formally associated." But the moment was hardly propitious for the realization of Saint-Simon's dream of a Franco-British nation. From the United States came warm words of sympathy and concern, but no help.

The French government and political leaders were divided as well as desperate. Their ordeal was more than military. Liberals and socialists, perceiving in defeat a mortal threat to republicanism and democracy, joined in Britain's plea that the government escape to North Africa to continue the war from there. They were seconded by certain officers, notably General Charles de Gaulle (1890-   ), who adhered to the tradition of military boldness and defiance. On the other side, favoring capitulation, were men of the Right, who had chafed under the liberal policies of the Third Republic and wished to restore a conservative social order, and the ranking military and naval leaders. Chief of the Rightists was the octogenarian Vice Premier, Marshal Pétain, who had made his reputation in the First World War as an opponent of offensive strategy. After several days of political maneuvering and intrigue, the men of the Right prevailed. On June 17 Reynaud resigned and Pétain became pre-

Hitler exultantly performs a dance at Compiègne, France, after imposing his armistice terms on the French Republic in 1940. Compiègne was the scene of the armistice negotiations after Germany's defeat in 1918. WIDE WORLD

mier. He at once asked for an armistice. The Germans granted it, on June 22, under harsh conditions. The whole of northern and western France, from the Atlantic to the Pyrenees, and including Paris—three fifths of the country—was to be occupied by German troops. France was to pay the costs of the occupation. Her army was to be demobilized and all weapons turned over to the victor. The navy was to be interned but not used by Germany. The return of French prisoners of war was to await a treaty of peace.

The Third Republic had lost more than a war. Pétain abrogated the constitution and made himself "Chief of State." From the town of Vichy, a famous watering resort, he ruled, with the assistance of politicians like Laval, who favored a Fascist society in France, and conservative generals and admirals. He annulled the freedom to speak and to publish and acquiesced in "racial" legislation against the Jews. General De Gaulle fled to London, where he raised the standard of Free France. "We have lost a battle, not the war," he broadcast to his compatriots, and proceeded to organize a rival government, army, and underground opposition, with the support of England, which severed relations with Pétain's government.

The Battle of Britain and American Involvement

The fall of France appalled the civilized world. Since the Revolution, France had been the chief center of liberal ideas in politics, society, and art. With her fell the shield before the breast of England and Russia and the blinkers that gave the United States the illusion of security.

England anticipated a German invasion of the island. Hitler toyed with the idea and made ambitious plans for "Operation Sea Lion," but he was not prepared to carry them out. He launched instead an air attack with the object of breaking Britain's will to fight, while instructing the German military leaders to prepare for an invasion of Russia in the following year.

The Battle of Britain began in July. For a month German bombers raided the Channel ports and shipping. Then they tried to destroy airfields, with only moderate success. Finally, they rained destruction upon the civilian population. London in particular was bombed almost uninterruptedly in September and October. On November 10, 1940, the city of Coventry was virtually razed to the ground.

But neither material loss nor psychological strain cowed the islanders. There was no panic. Public services continued to function. Germany's planes failed to master the skies. After a year of preparation, new British planes were coming off the assembly line in large numbers. Some of the models were more maneuverable than the German planes. The invention of radar enabled the British to detect the approach of an invading fleet and to measure its size. At the point of meeting, the defenders were often superior to the attackers. The German losses exceeded the British. In November the attacks slackened, although night bombing of cities continued until the following summer.

Destruction from a fire-bomb raid near St. Paul's Cathedral in London during the Second World War. In another raid the Cathedral was damaged severely. BRITISH INFORMATION SERVICES

Scene in a London underground converted into an air-raid shelter in the Second World War. The tracks were torn up and platforms built on the cross ties. BRITISH INFORMATION SERVICES

By the end of 1941, nearly a hundred thousand civilians had been killed or seriously injured. But the defenders had won the Battle of Britain. The war continued under water. German submarines took a heavy toll of shipping. Throughout the winter of 1940-41 Britain stood alone, virtually besieged in her island, pressed in the Mediterranean and in Africa, and unable to counter-attack. But she was beginning to receive help from across the ocean.

The fall of France and the peril of England swerved the course of the United States. The fears of the Republic during the First World War were revived in sharper form. Germany had shifted her submarine bases to French ports on the Atlantic and multiplied her depredations on shipping. If she now obtained bases in northwestern Africa as well, she could extend her operations to the South Atlantic.

In May 1940, while Germany was flaunting her might in the air over the forts and cities of Western Europe, President Roosevelt announced his government's intention to build up to fifty thousand planes a year, or ten times the prevailing production. In September he turned fifty destroyers over to Great Britain in exchange for a semicircle of eight naval and air bases, reaching from Newfoundland to the West Indies. Britain gave private assurance that, in an extremity, she would send her government and fleet across the ocean to carry on the struggle in cooperation with the United States. Congress appropriated 17.5 billion dollars for armaments and passed a bill to conscript men between the ages of 21 and 36 for one year of military training.

Would the American people approve this gradual involvement in the war? The European crisis coincided with the quadrennial presidential election. The Republicans nominated Wendell Willkie (1892-1944), a corporation lawyer, pledged to restore "free enterprise." The Democratic party broke precedent and nominated Roosevelt for a third term. Both candidates made pacific gestures, yet both stood ready to meet the German challenge by force. The isolationist elements, concentrated largely in the Republican party, organized and heavily subsidized the "America First Committee" to defeat Roosevelt. Their efforts were seconded by a motley aggregation of provincial-minded Midwesterners, last-ditch anti-New Dealers, religious pacifists, antiwar radicals, and a growing group of anti-Semites and pro-Nazis in German immigrant areas.

While the presidential campaign was being fought out, in September and October, German fire was raining down upon English cities, ports, and factories. Americans of both parties organized the influential Committee to Defend America by Aiding the Allies. The political coalition that had won power in 1932 was cemented by the European danger. The Southern wing of the Democratic party represented a region whose white population was more largely Anglo-Saxon in origin than that of any other section; it therefore reacted with an instant sympathy for England. Liberal and labor groups were concerned over the growth of Fascist and Nazi tendencies. Negroes resented the inferiority to which the racist propaganda of the Nazis condemned them. Immigrant groups —particularly Jews and Poles—were exercised over the fate of their coreligionists and conationals conquered by Germany. Finally, many of those who opposed the New Deal and the innovation of a third presidential term regarded Roosevelt as better equipped to meet the international crisis than Willkie, who had never held elective public office. Roosevelt won by a reduced though still impressive majority, and his party retained control of Congress. "Isolationism" was defeated.

In a message to Congress after his re-election, the President announced his determination to give "full support to all those resolute peoples everywhere who are resisting aggression" and to ensure that "the democratic cause shall prevail." He brought the liberal democratic ideal up to date and summed it up as the Four Freedoms: "freedom of speech and expression . . . freedom of every person to worship God in his own way . . . freedom from want—which, translated into world terms, means economic understanding which will secure to every nation a healthy peacetime life for its inhabitants . . . freedom from fear—which, translated into world terms, means a world-wide reduction of armaments to such a point and in such a thorough fashion that no nation will be in a position to commit an act of physical aggression against any neighbor—anywhere in the world."

The government opened economic warfare against the Axis. It froze funds deposited in the United States by citizens of occupied countries to prevent the conqueror from using them. It prohibited the export of war supplies by firms with German or Italian connections. It acquired "stockpiles" of strategic materials, such as rubber, tungsten, platinum, and copper, and made "preclusive" purchases to prevent Germany from acquiring them. Since England's funds for purchasing supplies were exhausted by early 1941, the American government took a further step: in March 1941, Congress approved a plan to "lend-lease" munitions and other goods to any country "whose defense the President deems vital to the defense of the United States." There was to be no repetition of the loans, and failure to repay, of the First World War. To protect the ships carrying supplies abroad, the United States occupied Iceland as a base of attack on undersea craft, convoyed the outgoing merchant fleets far out into the ocean, and finally approved the arming of merchantmen and firing on submarines. A virtual Anglo-American alliance took shape. In the summer and fall of 1941, the United States moved close to undeclared war. In September American and German craft exchanged fire.

The German Invasion of Russia

The increasing involvement of the United States had no effect upon military affairs on the Continent, where German armies stood poised to invade Russia. The fate of France and that of Russia were bound together. The Nazi-Soviet Pact of 1939 had exposed France to the full weight of the German sword; the debacle of France exposed Russia to the same sword. Had the Pact been as much a mistake for Russia as it had been a misfortune for the Western states?

Russia had watched the falling fortunes of France with mounting concern. She tried to redress the balance in June 1940 by occupying the Baltic states, divesting Rumania of Bessarabia and Bukovina, and resuming diplomatic relations with Yugoslavia. She regained nearly all the ground lost since the fall of czarism, but this hardly made her more secure. Germany won the adherence of Slovakia, Hungary, and Bulgaria to the Axis camp. In November 1940, at a conference in Berlin between the German and Russian foreign ministers, Russia was invited to turn her attention eastward, toward Iran and India (where she might become embroiled with England), leaving the Balkans to Germany. But Russia insisted that her orbit be enlarged to include Finland and that she be allowed virtual control over the Dardanelles. Both countries prepared to fight. Russia reaffirmed her sympathy for the South Slavs, and the German army prepared another, and larger, *Blitzkrieg*. In order to obviate any difficulty on the flank, the Germans overran Yugoslavia in April 1941, securing the towns; partisan bands retired to mountain fastnesses to wage guerrilla warfare. Next the Germans occupied Greece, which had repelled an invasion by

Italy the preceding fall. Turkey was being cautious but not unfriendly. The Balkan Peninsula was under German control.

On June 22, 1941, Hitler began his attempt to conquer Russia. On June 24, 1812, Napoleon had set out on the same errand. Both conquerors commanded vast armies and had the assistance of allies of doubtful reliability. Both calculated that the summer months would be favorable to their military operations. Hitler possessed, in the tank, a mobile fortress that Napoleon did not dream of. Air fleets were now doing the work of the cavalry. But logistics had become a more serious problem. While fodder and food could be requisitioned in any rural area, oil and gas had to be transported thousands of miles. Modern war proved wasteful of heavy munitions: the proportion of suppliers needed—both in industries at home and in transport—to fighters was much greater than of old. The Russian winter was even more dangerous to the internal-combustion engine than to men and horses. While Napoleon had sliced into Russia at a single point—and made better time—the Germans sent in three armies and covered three broad fronts. Like Czar Alexander I, Stalin ordered the destruction of food stocks and fixed installations—dams, factories, bridges, rails—in the path of the enemy. Like Kotusov, Stalin's generals decided to withdraw their armies into the wide interior.

At dawn on June 22, without advance warning, three and a half million German soldiers lunged forward—in the north toward Leningrad, in the center toward Moscow, and in the south toward Kiev. The first few weeks seemed extraordinarily successful. Russia stood virtually alone in defense. Great Britain and the United States had promised aid, but they could not bring it quickly enough. The northern German army delved deeply into the Baltic provinces, reaching the outskirts of Leningrad and surrounding it early in September. The principal obstacle on the road to Moscow, Smolensk, had been taken by the central army six weeks earlier, on July 16. The tanks of that army turned southward to cooperate with the slower southern army in an attempt to surround large Russian armies and to achieve the conquest of the Ukraine.

The Russian armies retreated after destroying food stores and industrial installations and organizing bands of "partisans" to harass the enemy behind the lines. The Germans took Kiev on September 19 and then surrounded and captured an army, but the bulk of the Russian forces escaped them. Hitler announced prematurely that "the enemy is broken and will never rise again." The central German army resumed its advance toward Moscow, after a diversion of two months, and the Russian government was removed to Kuibyshev, five hundred miles to the east. But "General Mud" and then "General Winter" made their appearance. Russia lacked the good roads that had made the rapid conquest of Holland, Belgium, and France possible. Caterpillar tracks took the German tanks through the mud, but the wheeled vehicles of infantry and supply bogged down. It was December 6 before the German army was in sight of Moscow. By then the mud had become ice, the snow was thick, and the temperature low. Attempts to surround the capital from the south and north miscarried. Suddenly the German army was on the defensive. So confident had the government been of a speedy victory that the troops had not been supplied

Russia—Invasions from the West and Russian advance in Second World War

Napoleon's invasion, 1812 ——→

Limit of Allied intervention,1918-19 —·—·— Deepest German penetration { 1918 ----- 1941 ∿∿∿ 1942 〰〰〰

Russian territory occupied 1918-19 and 1941-42 [shaded]   Direction of Russian drives, 1942-45 ⇐

Areas beyond Russia's prewar western boundary taken by May 8, 1945 ·········· [shaded]

Boundaries as of Aug. 1939

0   400 Mile

with warm clothing. Under winter conditions, Russian infantry and cavalry were more effective than German tanks and armored trucks. Whereas the *Blitzkrieg* had, in its forward stage, exacted relatively few casualties of the invaders, the winter campaign was costly.

Judged by its own aims, the German campaign was a failure. The Russian armies had not been destroyed, Moscow and Leningrad were not taken, and the war was not over. Hitler dismissed his leading generals, including the commander-in-chief, Field Marshal von Brauchitsch, named himself commander-in-chief, and appointed his own chief of staff, superior to the chief of staff of the army. The military elite had lost its last remnant of autonomy.

Contemporary opinion was stunned by the sweep of the *Blitzkrieg* and by territorial and tactical triumphs. Germany held two fifths of European Russia, including the Crimea and the fertile fields and industrial centers of the Ukraine. Germany also ruled the Baltic countries, Poland, Czechoslovakia, Austria, Yugoslavia, Greece, Holland, Belgium, Luxembourg, and nearly half of France. German troops moved about freely in Rumania, Hungary, and Bulgaria. Spain had refused to enter the war but sent a legion to fight on the Russian front. Sweden was neutral and unsympathetic but, surrounded by pro-Nazi Norwegian and Finnish governments, could not afford to deny Germany the valuable metal of her mines. Switzerland was neutral but armed to defend herself in terrain unsuitable to tanks and air warfare. Italy was an ally. Three hundred million Europeans were "integrated" into the "New Order" of the "Thousand-Year Reich." The program of *Mein Kampf* seemed to have been realized in Europe.

Across the Mediterranean, the road lay open to Africa. Eastward, it led to Asia Minor and to India. The western coast of Africa had ports from which the Atlantic "lifeline" of Britain might be cut. Italy inaugurated the African war in August 1940 by conquering British Somaliland and invading Egypt from Lybia. The British counterattacked and soon drove the Italians from both areas. The Germans came to the assistance of their allies with divisions, commanded by General Erwin Rommel (1891-1944), that had been trained for desert warfare. After a seesaw of advances and retreats, Rommel's army drove into Egypt in the summer of 1942. It reached El Alamein, only seventy miles from Alexandria, before it was stopped by the British.

Japanese Aggression and American Intervention

The conquests of Germany encouraged her partner in Asia. In September 1940, Japan, Germany, and Italy signed the Tripartite Pact. They promised to cooperate if any of them went to war with a country still neutral, which meant the United States or Russia. The following April Japan signed a neutrality pact with Russia; the two countries promised to respect each other's territory and to remain neutral if the partner was attacked by other powers. With the consent of the Pétain regime, the Japanese army penetrated into French Indochina. There was to be a "New Order" in Asia which would replace European with   *669*

This photograph shows a part of the loss inflicted on the American navy in the surprise attack by Japan on Pearl Harbor, Hawaii, on December 7, 1941. The two ships at the left were severely damaged. The U.S.S. Arizona, which is aflame, was sunk. WIDE WORLD

Japanese hegemony. Control of Dutch Indonesia and China was clearly part of the plan. However, any push southward might expose the left flank to the action of the American Pacific fleet, based on Hawaii. The Japanese therefore felt it necessary either to obtain the consent of the United States or to immobilize her fleet. But the United States, although absorbed with the German challenge in the Atlantic, refused to agree to such an extraordinary extension of Japanese power, above all to the control of China. She indicated her disapproval by stopping the export to Japan of scrap iron, much needed by Japan to make up for her lack of iron mines. Japanese and American diplomats were conferring on December 7, 1941, when a fleet of Japanese bombers took off from carriers, swooped out of the sky, and crippled the American Pacific fleet, riding unsuspectingly at anchor in Pearl Harbor, Hawaii. Two battleships were sunk, three put out of service, and three others, as well as a host of cruisers and destroyers, badly damaged. A day later, the Japanese attacked American, British, and Dutch naval and air bases in the Philippines, Guam and Wake Island, Hong Kong, and Malaya. On December 8 the United States Congress declared war on Japan, and on December 11 Germany and Italy declared war on the United States. In the next few weeks Japanese fleets entered the principal ports of China, Indochina, and Dutch Indonesia. They quickly took possession of Hong Kong, Siam, Malaya, Singapore, Burma, the Philippines, Indonesia, much of China, and numberless islands in the intervening waters, reaching down to the horizon of Australia and New Zealand.

Germany and Japan divided the mastery of the European and East Asian continents. Could they make good their vast gains? The opposing powers were only half prepared, but that only meant that their strength would have to increase in the near future. Large as were the areas over which the members of the Axis exercised direct control, the areas and populations of their rivals and their combined resources and industrial potential were considerably greater. Everything, therefore, hinged on the question of which group of powers would be more successful in organizing its industries, galvanizing its peoples, winning the sympathy of other countries, and coordinating its strategy.

The "New Order" of the Axis

The Axis powers gave every appearance of discipline and efficiency. Their dictatorial and oligarchical regimes professed to embody the undivided will of their nations. They advocated a "New Order" in Europe and a "co-prosperity sphere" in Asia, mocking the countries of the opposing alliance as decadent and divided.

Yet appearances were deceptive. Germany and Italy did not dovetail their military or economic operations. Germany did not inform Italy of her decision to attack Czechoslovakia and Poland, nor did Italy forewarn Germany of her attacks on Albania and Greece. Germany joined Japan in the war on the United States, but Japan did not join Germany in the war on Russia. No material aid was sent to Japan from Germany or received from Japan by Germany.

None of the Axis powers permitted opposition parties and leaders to share in the direction of the war or the definition of its aims. Japan was ruled by the more aggressive wing of the military and naval castes, which kept civilian political leaders at arm's length. In Italy, antagonism to German influence and dissatisfaction with the defeats in Greece and North Africa produced a growing malaise, which affected monarchists, conservatives, and even Fascists. Germany presented a paradox of increasing centralization and increasing incoherence. Hitler had established absolute control over military and diplomatic affairs. In 1941, he obtained from the *Reichstag* the power to override at will all courts of justice, thus becoming by formal grant the total ruler of the nation. Yet Hitler virtually severed his ties with the country. He never showed himself to the soldiers at the front, never visited a bombed city quarter, seldom addressed the *Reichstag* or any other group, seldom held cabinet meetings. Meanwhile, the administration of affairs was beset by overlapping jurisdictions, the arbitrary behavior of local leaders, and competition for graft and position. Deputy Führer Goering was assembling foreign industries and mines into a private economic empire and pillaging art treasures; at the same time, lesser minions of the party were lining their pockets with whatever lay handy in conquered countries.

The Axis powers labored under industrial difficulties. Japan possessed a limited plant. She reached the peak of her production in 1939, two years before she attacked the United States. From 1940 on, her industry suffered from shortage of materials, and the product of her metallurgical, chemical, machine, and textile factories declined. Her steel capacity was one eighth that of the United States and her coal supply one sixth. She was dependent for raw materials on distant lands. The freezing of her funds by the United States and Great Britain in July 1941, before the attack on Pearl Harbor, dealt her a heavy blow. Much of her oil and metal (in the form of scrap) had come from the United States. By exertions extending over a period of years she had been able to build and equip an army, a navy, and an air force of great striking power, but her plant was not equal to replenishing that power if a substantial part of it were destroyed.

Germany's position was quite different. She possessed one of the greatest industrial plants on the globe, and the conquest of Europe supplemented her capacity. She obtained oil from Rumania, Hungary, and southern Russia; iron ore from France and Sweden; and other materials and supplies from Finland, Spain, Norway, the Ukraine, Yugoslavia, and Greece. Her agricultural position was better than it had been in the First World War. She squeezed grain out of the Balkans, the Ukraine, and France, potatoes and sugar out of Poland, and dairy products out of Holland and Denmark to feed both her civilians and her military forces. The blockade and other forms of economic warfare did not affect her as much as they had in the First World War.

The deficiencies of Germany, both material and moral, were nevertheless serious. In the thirties, Germany had stockpiled much iron ore, wool, and cotton. The first *Blitzkrieg* campaigns did not consume much material. The casualties of the first two years of war (1939-41) were only one seventh as great as those of the first two years of the First World War (1914-16). But Germany had planned for short campaigns rather than for a long war. In the fall of 1941, confident of the success of the *Blitzkrieg* in Russia, she reduced war production and increased the output of consumer goods. It was not until after the first defeats that a Ministry of Armaments Production was organized—in February 1942—and empowered to allocate materials and coordinate production.

The results were impressive but not sufficient. Skilled man power was poorly organized. When the British blockade made normal coastal shipping impossible, a greater burden was placed on the railway system of the Continent. Although Germany looted locomotives and rolling stock from subject countries, she could not cope successfully with this transportation problem, especially when she had stretched her supply lines deep into Russia. (The oceanic lines of supply of the Allies were much longer and often dangerous, but the American shipbuilding industry eventually produced enough vessels to overcome this difficulty.)

Exploitation and Genocide

The Axis powers controlled a large and rich area with a population of over six hundred million people. But they could exploit it fully only with the cooperation of the peoples of Europe and East Asia. The aims and methods of Axis imperialism, however, made it impossible to obtain that cooperation. The

Chinese, the Indochinese, and the Indonesians could not be persuaded that the "Co-prosperity Sphere" of Asia was anything but a euphemism for the extension of Japanese exploitation.

The "New Order" of Germany was even less palatable to the peoples of Europe. The amount of indiscriminate looting was enormous. The costs of the occupation imposed on defeated countries were notoriously higher than the real charges. While supplies were raked in for shipment to German soldiers and civilians, the subjected countries were rationed even in those goods of which they normally had large surpluses: Holland and Denmark in butter, France in wine and bread, Rumania in bread, and so on.

The political prospects of non-German peoples in the "New Order" were equally dismal. Both allied and subject peoples were to maintain governments sympathetic to Germany and to adopt her policies. There was to be no national autonomy within the "New Order." For the Eastern peoples and for the Jews Germany decreed an especially harsh fate. When the preparations for the invasion of Russia were going forward, the German government made the decision to exterminate racial "inferiors," "unsocial elements," *all* the Jews and gypsies, whether in the east or west, and Communist organizers and political commissars attached to Russian military units. The commissars were to be exterminated in order to make the continuance or revival of a Communist state impossible. The Slav populations were to be shorn of their urban professional and articulate groups; the rest were to supply the "subhuman" slaves of German employers. The task of killing the Communist commissars was accepted by the head of the army, Marshal Keitel; the other tasks devolved upon the SS troops under the command of Heinrich Himmler.

The romantic wandering gypsies were few in number. For centuries they had roamed and camped—repairing copperware, telling fortunes, and foraging informally for their scant cattle—over a few areas of Central Europe. They were rounded up and dispatched to concentration camps, where an estimated 100,000 of them were killed.

The Jews were scattered all over Europe. The success of the Nazis in rooting them out of subject countries varied with the character of the governments. Officials in Denmark and Norway sabotaged the exterminations and gave up only small numbers; few Bulgarian Jews were given up. Under persistent pressure, the Pétain government turned over to the Germans, a quarter of the Jewish population of France, or about 60,000 men, women, and children. The Fascist government of Italy surrendered 20,000 of its 50,000 Jews. In countries that the Nazis administered themselves, such as Holland, Belgium, and Luxembourg, they removed perhaps 80 percent of the Jews. Germany murdered nearly all of the Jewish population that remained after the wholesale exile and escape of the thirties. From all these countries, Jews were pressed into sealed freight cars and shipped to ghettos and concentration camps in Eastern Europe under conditions which destroyed many of the very young, aged, and feeble en route. Most of them were eventually dispatched to extermination camps.

The bulk of Jewry lived in Central and Eastern Europe, with the greatest concentration—three and a half million people—in Poland. Hard upon the heels of the conquering armies that invaded Russia in June 1941, four extermination squads of about 2000 machine gunners pushed into eastern Poland, the Baltic provinces, and western and southern Russia. Speeding from town to town, they rounded up the Jews, stripped them of their belongings, marched them out into nearby forests and fields, compelled them to dig deep ditches, and machine-gunned them into their own graves. This was done with the knowledge of the military commanders and often with the assistance of regular army units.

One third of a million Jews in eastern Poland and western Russia were thus destroyed in four months. The others, together with the hosts exiled from the Western countries and the Balkans, were herded into concentration camps and closed ghettos under conditions of overcrowding, disease, and privation that disposed of many of them. The stronger were exploited as slave labor in the armament factories of the government and by private German employers. From all these groups, batch after batch was extracted, on promise of "resettlement," and done to death.

The Nazi government applied on a large scale a technique developed in 1939 to eliminate the insane in Germany: suffocation by carbon monoxide and other deadly gases. At first people were jammed into sealed vans and suffocated by exhaust gases piped inside. The driver merely pressed the accelerator, and within twenty minutes everyone inside was dead. Then the "final solution" was evolved. A number of camps were equipped with poison-gas chambers, camouflaged as shower rooms, and with crematoria. The larger camps disposed of several thousand lives and bodies a day. It has been estimated that at Auschwitz, in Poland, the most notorious of the camps, nearly a million Jews were done to death; there were days when the rate rose to 12,000 murders a day. By such methods, Germany killed five to six million Jews and several million non-Jews—mainly Poles, other Slavs, and gypsies. Neither women nor infants, neither the old nor the weak, were spared.

There was little resistance. A few isolated groups of rebels were quickly overwhelmed. In 1943 the remnant of Warsaw Jewry, some 40,000 persons, doomed to deportation and extermination, obtained a few light arms and a little ammunition and rose desperately. They were virtually annihilated, and the ghetto was razed.

Hemmed in by an apparently irresistible power, deceived by promises of resettlement or emigration, unable to bring themselves to believe, against mounting evidence, that the government of a civilized country could carry out massacres which the most barbarous governments of the past had not contemplated, rendered fatalistic by centuries of victimization, the majority of Continental Jews were wiped out.

32. *The Victory of the Allies*

The swift victories of the Axis amazed the world. The militarists who engineered them placed their reliance on sudden offensives in the belief that the occupied countries and peoples would not recover from such blows and that the powers still in the field against them would not be able to overcome the advantage that careful preparation had given the Axis. The Axis leaders trusted to the effect of mechanical preparation and speed. They underestimated the importance of economic and moral forces and the resiliency of the societies and polities they had challenged.

The Organization of Victory

The enemies of the Axis were pressed for time, but in the end they not only mobilized greater resources but demonstrated a superior capacity for discipline, organization, and leadership. Partisan politics was adjourned. The Allied governments made popular concessions, each in accordance with its character.

Without abandoning the monopoly of power by the Communist party, the Russian goverment asked the people to support the war on patriotic rather than ideological grounds. It described the war to the population as a war in defense of Russia rather than of Communism. The open contempt of the Nazis for the "inferior" Slavs and their plans to turn Russia into a servile colony made the conflict one of "races" and peoples. Russia had lost, with the conquered areas, more than half her industrial output and much of her agricultural output. Yet her enemy did not gain all she had lost. Before retiring, Soviet armies shipped machines and skilled personnel eastward, in order to supplement industrial potential previously developed in the Ural region and Central Asia. In 1942, tanks, guns, airplanes, small arms, and munitions began to pour out in large quantities. Together with materials obtained from Great Britain and the United States, Russia's industrial output was soon to prove a match for German eqipment on the eastern front. The working day was lengthened, and women were conscripted into industrial and auxiliary fighting services.

No country on either side of the struggle reorganized herself so completely as Great Britain. The various classes of the nation drew more closely together. Three parties—Conservative, Labor, and Liberal—were represented in the coalition cabinet. For the first time Labor leaders shared real power and responsibility in a major war. Increased taxes on the rich and strict and equal rationing of necessaries diminished class distinctions. The evacuation of children from bombed cities to rural homes, the organization of civilian defenses against bombing, and common shelters for rich and poor nurtured a strong sense of community. The government assumed almost complete power over production, allocation of raw materials, and distribution of shipping space for imports and exports. Farm acreage was increased by half. Women as well as men were conscripted for work. Even boys and girls of sixteen were registered for voluntary war jobs or training for the armed forces. At the peak point—September 1943— some two thirds of the adult population was doing full-time war work.

In the United States, the Democratic administration gave members of the Republican party leading positions in the war effort; Republicans headed the Army and Navy Departments. Although war contracts made the rich richer, there were wage increases for the workers. The United States did not organize so "totally" as England, but her resources were greater. Like other countries, she suspended much of the production of consumer goods. She more than made up for the diversion of over twelve million men and women to the fighting forces by drawing into industry country men and women, colored and white alike. In 1942, while Russia and Britain were fighting strenuous campaigns against the Axis, the United States supplied them with food, trucks, and munitions. She shipped large quantities of supplies to Russia along the northern route to the port of Murmansk, despite costly attacks by German submarines and bombers based in Norway, and by way of the Indian Ocean, through the Persian Gulf and across Iran. She supplied Britain both at home and on the North African front. Meanwhile the United States made intensive efforts to convert many of her plants to the production of new weapons. Because it took a year or more to complete the necessary designs and tools for some of these weapons, the superiority of American production was not fully felt until 1943. Thenceforth the results were prodigious. During the whole war, American factories and shipyards turned out twice as much as the Axis: 86,338 tanks, nearly 300,000 planes, 64,500 landing craft, and thousands of other vessels, as well as vast quantities of trucks, synthetic rubber, guns, rifles, and ammunition. Two large armies, navies, and air forces were trained, equipped, and dispatched to the European and Pacific fronts. There were enough ships to launch offensives in the Pacific as early as 1942. The value of goods shipped to the Allies, principally to Great Britain and Russia, under Lend-Lease had reached nearly forty-nine billion dollars by the end of 1945.

The cooperation of the Allies in the political realm was less wholehearted than in the military. From her beginnings in 1917, the Soviet Union had feared that the liberal and capitalist states would combine to destroy her. For their part, these states resented the intimate ties between their Communist parties and the U.S.S.R. There was no love lost between such leaders as Joseph Stalin, who had led the fight against the anti-Bolsheviks in Georgia in 1918-19, and Winston Churchill, who in those years was an energetic advocate of intervention against the Soviet regime. Russia's resentment at being excluded from the Munich conference of 1938 and the shock that the Western countries had suffered when the Soviet-Nazi Pact had laid Poland open to attack and partition lingered in mutual suspicion.

The leaders of the Allied powers, however, swallowed their pride. The Soviet government abolished the Third International, which had coordinated the activities of Communist parties. Under pressure, it acknowledged to its peoples the aid it was receiving from the Western Allies. English and American Communists discovered the virtues of patriotism and even of capitalism. The British and American press and radio depicted Joseph Stalin as a man whose rough exterior concealed a heart of gold. American opinion, both official and popular, became more friendly toward Britain, the former "mother country," than at any time since the American Revolution. Hundreds of thousands of American soldiers trained for battle in Britain, where they were received with cordiality. The eloquent war speeches of Winston Churchill—whose mother was an American—evoked as much admiration in the United States as at home, and Roosevelt's first statue was to rise (immediately after the war) not in Washington but in London.

The Allies compromised their differences on strategy in a series of conferences. Churchill and Roosevelt consulted together regularly. The United States agreed to throw her main weight onto the scales of the European conflict before settling scores with Japan. It was reasoned that Germany might win even if Japan lost, but that Japan could not prevail if Germany were beaten. The United States and Great Britain promised to relieve Russia's military burden by opening a "second front" in Western Europe, although they could not do so as soon as Russia hoped. Stalin promised to join the war against Japan when Germany was defeated.

To Russia the defeat of Nazism was synonymous with the spread of Communism and of Russian influence in Eastern and Central Europe. She therefore kept a jealous control of the war in that part of the world. Great Britain, concerned over her position in the Mediterranean and the Near East, pressed for a decision to start a second front in Italy or the Balkans. England and the United States were agreed on the need to restore liberal institutions in the countries under Nazi rule, but their views of strategy were at variance. The United States was less concerned over Mediterranean questions and more concerned over obtaining Russia's eventual assistance in the war against Japan. Her military leaders agreed with the Russians on the need for opening a major front in France. The English won a minor victory by securing American consent to preliminary invasions of North Africa and Italy.

In their Pacific policies too, the United States and Britain had different views. The defeat of the British in Asia and the allocation of the direction of the war in the Pacific area to the United States tended to replace British with American influence. Australia and New Zealand relied for aid on the United States rather than on the hard-pressed mother country. American opinion became influential in Indian-British relations. The United States was fast outdistancing Britain in naval construction. She demanded a stricter control over neutral trade in wartime than she had been willing to tolerate when Britannia had ruled the waves. It was Great Britain's turn to ask for greater freedom on the seas. On many of these questions a middle way was found, but the balance of strength often determined that it should be the American way. Strategy was brought into alignment by the organization of a U.S.-British Combined Chiefs of Staff. The armies and navies of the two countries fought smoothly under each other's commanders.

The Western Allies gained much support among neutral countries by adopting idealistic war aims. On August 14, 1941, the United States and Great Britain signed the Atlantic Charter, an up-to-date version of Woodrow Wilson's Fourteen Points. In it they renounced territorial aggrandizement and promised to restore self-government to the conquered countries, to allow free access by all nations to raw material and markets, to improve labor standards and social security, to safeguard freedom of the seas, to reduce armaments, and to prevent aggression by establishing "a wider and permanent system of general security." On January 1, 1942, they were joined by Russia and China, and on the next day by 22 other European, American, and Asian states, in the Declaration of the United Nations. The Declaration reaffirmed the principles of the Atlantic Charter and bound its signers to fight together against the Axis and not to make peace separately. A year later, in January 1943, President Roosevelt declared, after a conference with Churchill in Casablanca, French Morocco, that the peace of the world required the "unconditional surrender" of the Axis.

The Defeat of Italy and Germany

The Axis reached the crest of its fortunes in the spring of 1942. In the following twelve months, the tide turned. The Axis was driven on the defensive everywhere, in the Atlantic and in North Africa, in Russia and the Pacific.

In the Atlantic, German submarines had been doing much damage to Allied shipping. The Western Allies developed a many-sided defense: they bombed German and French shipyards and ports, built small vessels on a mass scale to protect convoys, introduced various scientific devices to detect submarines, and used aircraft carriers to enable airplanes to hunt down U-boats in mid-ocean. Within a year, Germany was losing more submarines than she could replace, and the seas were safer for the Allies.

On land, the war took an even more decisive turn. In August 1940 Italy had seized British Somaliland in East Africa and in September she invaded Egypt from Libya. By April 1941 the British had not only turned back the invaders but captured two Italian armies. By the end of the year they had taken Italian East Africa, but since July 1942, a German armored force under Rommel's command had been standing threateningly at El Alamein in Egypt. The British prepared a strong attack, which they launched in October. Rommel's army was defeated and began a long retreat westward, only to face a larger and fresher enemy force. For in November 1942, an American-British armada of 850 warships and transports landed a large army, under the command of the American Lieutenant-General Dwight D. Eisenhower (1890-   ), in French Morocco, Algeria, and Tunisia. There was little opposition by local Vichy officials. The Germans thereupon occupied the portion of France governed by Marshal Pétain. When they sought to seize the French fleet at Toulon, the crews scuttled their ships. The Germans rushed reinforcements to their *Afrika Korps*. In the spring of 1943 they made a stand in Tunisia but were defeated several times. In May the entire Axis force of a quarter million men surrendered. The war for North Africa was over.

A more spectacular contest had meanwhile unfolded on the Volga River. After its failure to take Moscow in December 1941, the German command changed its tactics. In the following spring it concentrated its forces for two offensives in southern Russia alone. One offensive, on the right, was directed toward the Caucasus with the aim of seizing its valuable oil supplies while denying them to the Russians; the other was directed toward Stalingrad, the industrial city on the bend of the Volga, with the double aim of cutting the oil and other supplies moving up the broad river and of carrying out an outflanking movement to the north to envelop the bulk of the Russian armies. In the south, the German armies were only moderately successful: they seized one set of oil fields, but only after the Russians had destroyed their installations. The northern army reached and all but surrounded Stalingrad in September. But Stalingrad proved difficult to take. One of its sides rested on the shore of the river, whence it was supplied and reinforced under cover of darkness. The lines north and south were held by Italian, Rumanian, and Hungarian troops, which crumpled under Russian attacks. While within the city bitter struggles were fought around each house or its ruins, Russian armies were moving to cut off the Germans from their route of supplies to the west. The German commander, General Friedrich von Paulus, with the support of other high officers, counseled a retreat to save his army. But Hitler would not hear of it. By December the besiegers were besieged. Of an army which originally numbered 330,000 men, about 80,000 survived to surrender in January 1943, with a rich array of matériel.

After the victories of Stalingrad and North Africa the Allies accelerated their offensives. In July 1943 the United States, England, and Canada put an army ashore in Sicily. The campaign was a model of clumsiness—roads and civilian centers were bombed unnecessarily—but the Italian armies were captured and the German armies ousted from the island within six weeks. Already discredited, the Mussolini regime could not withstand the shock of the invasion. Two weeks after Allied soldiers set foot in Sicily, the Fascist Grand Council forced the dictator to resign. King Victor Emmanuel III imprisoned Mussolini and installed a cabinet headed by Marshal Pietro Badoglio. The new government dissolved the Fascist party and dismissed many of its leaders from office. Secretly, it asked the Allies for an armistice. The Allies dragged out the negotiations, and the Germans, determined to defend the peninsula, rescued Mussolini from prison. They set up a "republic" for him in the north. The Allies landed in the south in September 1943, but it was not until the following June, after prolonged and costly battles, that they occupied Rome.

The defection of her principal ally, after the surrender of large German armies in North Africa and Stalingrad, faced Germany with critical decisions. Civilian morale had been shaken by "strategic bombing." From the middle of 1942 on, large centers of industry and population had been subjected to increasingly heavy punishment. "Thousand-bomber" raids struck Cologne, Essen, and Bremen. Early in 1943 the Americans and British coordinated their efforts in round-the-clock bombings. City after city was devastated. Thousands lost their lives, and millions their homes. For the first time since the Napoleonic wars, Germany was experiencing on her home front ravages comparable to those that she had often inflicted on other countries.

As Germany's external enemies advanced, a host of "internal" enemies became active. Collaborationist governments and elements in the conquered countries became increasingly unpopular. Patriotic resistance groups formed secret organizations, made contact with the Allies, and engaged in sabotage and guerrilla warfare. In France particularly, an elaborate and hardy organization flourished underground. The Nazis struck back with fury. They shot hostages, exacting dozens and even hundreds of lives for one of their own. In striking at innocent and helpless people they revealed the full measure of their bestiality. When the Protector of Bohemia, Reinhard Heydrich, was assassinated in 1942, the Nazis razed a whole village—Lidice—to the ground and killed 199 of its inhabitants. In June 1944, on the unfounded suspicion that the peaceful French village of Oradour contained a store of arms, a German detachment rounded up the whole population, machine-gunned the adult males, and crowded the women and children into the church, where they burned them alive. Of the 650 victims, two hundred were children. In the death camps, the massacres of Jews were increased as defeat became more imminent. Hitler was determined to snatch a "racial" victory over the Jews from the jaws of military disaster.

Convinced that Germany was losing the war, a few despairing officers attempted to assassinate Hitler by exploding a small time bomb on July 20, 1944, during a conference at his headquarters in East Prussia. The attempt was unsuccessful. Hitler retaliated by putting to death hundreds of officers, bureaucrats, and politicians, many of whom did not have the remotest connection with the plot. Twenty-one officers of high rank were hanged, shot, or compelled to take their own lives.

Hitler's grip on the government and its policy was tightened. The command of the troops stationed at home was transferred from army generals to Gestapo chief Himmler. Hitler pursued the strategy of a desperate gambler. The Allies would not deal with him, and he would neither resign nor retreat. In Eastern Europe, the seat of his principal ambition, he could not bring himself to give up voluntarily a foot of land once he had acquired it, even where military strategy called for retrenchment. German policy lost all semblance of rational direction.

From 1943 on, hard campaigns were fought to reach a foregone conclusion. The Germans tried again to outmatch Russian winter victories with summer triumphs, but their offensive of July 1943 was broken from the beginning. Thousands of American trucks increased the mobility of the Russian armies and enabled them to undertake speedy drives. The Russians relieved Leningrad, took Novgorod, crossed the borders of Poland, and reconquered the Ukraine and Bessarabia in the south.

The climax came in June 1944, when the Soviet Union opened a summer offensive timed to coincide with the most elaborate and spectacular action of the war—the Allied invasion of France under command of General Eisenhower. Landing a large army on a heavily defended coast and supplying and reinforcing it from the sea are regarded as a most hazardous enterprise. The difficulty of such an enterprise was largely responsible for the relative security of Great Britain. The Spanish in the sixteenth century lost a large armada trying to invade Britain; Napoleon assembled an army and a fleet but flinched before the undertaking; so did Hitler, who contemplated it briefly. It was the growth and brilliant employment of industrial potential that enabled the Allies to solve the many problems attending the invasion of Normandy.

For several weeks the Anglo-American air forces weakened German resistance in northern France by destroying airfields, factories, and machines. They immobilized German transportation and supply by destroying rail centers and depots. They isolated the German armies in northwestern France by destroying the road and rail bridges over the Seine and Loire rivers. Finally, they blinded the defense by destroying radar installations.

At dawn on June 6, 1944—"D-Day"—some four thousand ships and landing vessels, accompanied by as many small craft, converged from various points in England on the waters off the French Channel coast. The crucial innovations of the invasion were amphibious tanks and specially constructed craft which could land without the benefit of docks. (It was the shortage of those craft that had been largely responsible for delaying the invasion until 1944.) After a heavy bombardment of beach fortifications and bunkers from the air and from off-shore battleships, hundreds of landing craft carrying troops, tanks, trucks, ammunition, and supplies moved toward the beaches. Upon reaching shallow water, they let down "apron" platforms. Infantrymen, fully armed, waded to shore. Amphibious tanks rolled down the ramps to the beach and beyond. Behind the defenders' lines troops and supplies parachuted down from three thousand airships and gliders. The cost in life was substantial. The foothold was made good during the first day and constantly strengthened by men, tanks, and trucks supplied from small landing craft. The invaders made up for their initial lack of port facilities by sinking sixty blockships offshore and erecting on top of them two huge prefabricated ports, which had been towed from England in

The Normandy landing—D-Day—June 6, 1944. After descending from the ramp of a Coast Guard landing barge, American soldiers are wading toward the fire-swept beach. Their comrades ahead are lying flat under the machine-gun fire of the German defenders. U.S. COAST GUARD

sections. Four pipelines were laid later under the waters of the English Channel and then continued on the land following the advancing armies to supply the thousands of trucks and tanks with fuel.

The operation was brilliantly successful. On the first day, despite heavy German fire, the Allies landed 120,000 men, including paratroops; within a week there were three times as many; by three months after D-Day, the Allies had put ashore a huge army of more than two million men—Americans, British, French, and Canadians—a half million vehicles, and four million tons of supplies. Germany was again confronted by the old nightmare of an active war on two large fronts.

Hitler's strategy made the German defense difficult, if not impossible. German divisions were scattered all along the long French, Belgian, and Dutch coast line. Since the German military leaders expected the invasion but could not predict its direction, they advised that the coast troops be withdrawn and concentrated at a convenient point well within France, there to wait until the invaders had committed themselves and then promptly counterattack. But Hitler was opposed to any withdrawal.

The thinly stretched German armies could not resist a strong invading force and could not assemble quickly to attack it. When they attempted to do so, they met an army with equipment, armor, and air support far in excess of their own. The Allies were better supplied from the sea than the Germans were from land, largely because they controlled the air over both. It was several days before the Germans mounted serious counterattacks, and then it was too late. On August 15, a smaller Allied army landed in the south of France and encountered little resistance. The path of both advances was opened by risings of French partisans. Soon the Allied armies were in control of western France, where they had isolated and captured sizable bodies of enemy troops. They freed Paris and Brussels. By mid-September, they stood on the borders of Germany.

In the east, the Russians had meanwhile made a broad sweep through the Balkans. By October they were masters of Rumania, Bulgaria, and Yugoslavia. Then they moved into Hungary, where Hitler made a determined and futile attempt to save his last source of oil. In the north, Nazi armies were pushed out of the Baltic area and forced to surrender most of Poland.

After the successful landing in France in June 1944, there could be no doubt of the outcome of the war. Yet Hitler could not make peace, and after the bloody purge of July, no German, even a Nazi, dared to question Hitler's decisions. In the spring of 1945, a concentrated air attack and simultaneous advances from east and west finally brought the conflict to an end. The Russians swiftly completed their occupation of Poland, Bohemia, and Austria. The German army in Italy surrendered in April. The Western Allies, who had crossed the Rhine in March, swept through western and southern Germany and on April 25 met the Russian troops on the shore of the Elbe. On April 12, President Roosevelt, who had been re-elected in November 1944 for his fourth term, died of a cerebral hemorrhage. He was succeeded by the Vice President, Harry S. Truman (1884-   ).

On April 28, Mussolini tried to flee from northern Italy to seek asylum in Switzerland. He was caught by Italian partisans, shot, and brought back to Milan, where his body was hanged head down and exhibited before a garage.

In Germany, the "Thousand-Year Reich" immolated itself, twelve years after its birth. On May 1, the official radio announced that Adolf Hitler had committed suicide. Goebbels also took his own life, and so did Himmler, after he had fallen into the hands of the Allies. Goering and a host of political and military leaders were taken into custody. On May 7, General Alfred Jodl (1890-1946) signed the surrender documents. Not only was the surrender unconditional, but Germany ceased, for the moment, to exist as a political entity. For three weeks Hitler's designated successor, Admiral Karl Doenitz (1891-   ), headed the government. On May 23, the Allies superseded this government and placed Doenitz under arrest. All Germany was under foreign occupation. The territory which had been hers in 1937, before Hitler began his conquests, was divided into four zones and placed under the military administration of the Soviet Union, the United States, Britain, and France; the capital city of Berlin was also divided into four sectors.

The War in the Pacific and the Atomic Bomb

Although neither coalition closely coordinated the war in Europe with the war in the Pacific, the continual recession of Japanese power coincided with that of German power. In the summer of 1942, when Germany reached the limit of its offensive power, so did Japan. After six months of unchallenged conquest, the Asian empire sought to protect her gains against future attacks, particularly from the south. In May a task force intent on landing in northern Australia was repelled by American ships in the neighboring waters of the Coral Sea. Three months later the Americans were ready to counterattack. They landed in the Solomon Islands, to the east, and captured a Japanese airfield. Wave after wave of Japanese attacks could not budge them. Far to the northeast, a Japanese fleet was turned back at Midway Island, with the loss of four aircraft carriers. In view of the preponderance of American shipbuilding capacity, this was a serious reduction of Japanese sea power. In the South Pacific the advance that had begun with the attack on Pearl Harbor had been stopped.

After strenuous preparations, the United States mounted a series of massive attacks that gradually increased in intensity. The struggle over strategic islands, ports, and air bases in the Pacific led to some of the bitterest and costliest fighting of the war. In October 1944, the Japanese fleet attempted to prevent the landing of an American army, commanded by General Douglas MacArthur (1880-   ) on Leyte, in the Philippines, and was decisively defeated. Japan's subsequent loss of the Philippines severed communications between Japan and her new-won empire in Indochina. By hard fighting against obstinate defenders, the Americans captured strategic islands, notably Iwo Jima and Okinawa, from which they proceeded to bomb the home islands of Japan. In the spring of 1945 they subjected Japanese cities, industries, and ports to destructive bombing raids. Air attacks, supplemented by an energetic submarine campaign, drove most of the enemy naval and merchant shipping from the seas. Supplies were flown across the "hump" of the Himalayas to assist Chinese forces fighting in the interior of their country. In southeast Asia a British army, assisted by American and Chinese troops, succeeded after a long campaign in destroying three large Japanese armies.

These multiple onslaughts all but overwhelmed Japan. By the spring of 1945, it had become clear that Japan had lost the war, and the imperial government put out feelers for peace. But the Japanese military chiefs refused to surrender. They were brought to heel by an extraordinary advance in scientific warfare. Two developments in theoretical physics since the turn of the twentieth century had prepared the ground for the construction of an "ultimate" weapon that surpassed the fantasies of science fiction. The old Newtonian view of the solidity of matter had been challenged. The theory of relativity, propounded by Albert Einstein in 1905, proceeded from the assumption that matter was energy; inside the atom are positive and negative charges. The other was the isolation by Pierre Curie (1859-1906) and his wife, Marie (1867-1934), of radium, a highly radioactive element, which gave off heat, light, and electricity while disintegrating in the process. By 1939 it was known that uranium atoms could be "split," suddenly releasing much of their energy, and that after "nuclear fission" they bombarded and split other atoms. A chain reaction could simultaneously release much of the enormous energy contained in a few ounces of uranium. The resulting explosion would be thousands of times more powerful than the largest previous detonation of dynamite.

However, the practical use of these theoretical advances presented great technical difficulties. Aware that if Germany succeeded in producing an atomic bomb it might prove impossible to defeat her, the American government launched the elaborate "Manhattan Project" to anticipate her, at a cost of nearly two billion dollars. A galaxy of scientists, seconded by many engineers and technicians, went secretly to work. Some of the scientists were refugees from Germany and Italy, or from occupied countries. They fought, in American laboratories, their own war of retaliation against the common enemy. On July 12, 1945, after nearly six years of effort, the first atomic bomb was exploded in a desert area in New Mexico. The blast was devastating to a degree that surpassed the imagination. It was as powerful as a thousand bomber-loads of ordinary explosives.

The atomic race with Germany had been won, but Germany was already defeated. Japan, however, was still holding out. The American government faced the choice of invading her home islands, at an estimated sacrifice of hundreds of thousands of lives, or using the deadliest weapon ever devised. The sad decision was made, and Japan was warned, on July 26, that unless she surrendered she would be utterly destroyed. There was no reply to the ultimatum, and the tragedy was played out to the end. On August 6 an atomic bomb was dropped on the city of Hiroshima, Japan, from an American plane. The effect

The characteristic mushroom-like billow of smoke from an atomic bomb rises over 20,000 feet above Nagasaki, on August 9, 1945. This bomb, the second dropped by the Americans, killed between 35,000 and 40,000 persons and wounded as many. The next day the Japanese Empire sued for peace. U.S. ARMY AIR FORCE, FROM ACME

was catastrophic. Four square miles were laid waste, about 70,000 inhabitants—a third of the population—were killed, and perhaps 100,000 were wounded or missing. The effects of radiation harmed many of the survivors. No single stroke of man had ever wrought so much death, disease, and destruction. On August 9 a second atomic bomb fell on Nagasaki. The day before, Russia had entered the war against Japan. On August 14, Japan surrendered, saving from the wreckage of militarism and imperialism only the institution of monarchy.

The Losses of the Second World War

The explosion of the atom bomb was a fitting epilogue to the most destructive conflict in modern history. The First World War had been the costliest and bloodiest conflict in history; the Second was thirteen times as expensive and did fifteen times as much damage to property. The governments spent $1,117,000,000,000 for military purposes, and the property damage has been put at twice that figure.

No modern war destroyed so many homes and displaced and transplanted so many people. The enormous uprooting was not, however, due to the fighting itself: much of it resulted from the Nazi racial program, which, from the beginning, shook up the population of the countries that Germany annexed or conquered. Millions of civilians fled from the path of the Nazi armies, and millions more were shifted in order to reshape the ethnic pattern of the Continent in accordance with Nazi views. Before the war broke out, some 400,000 persons, about half of them Jews, fled from Germany. When Hitler occupied Czechoslovakia and Austria, another wave of migrants overflowed the borders. In 1939, following an agreement with Italy, 10,000 Germans were "exchanged" for about 40,000 Italians. Then, by agreement with the Soviet Union, upward of a half million Germans were moved from the Baltic areas and other parts of the Soviet Union, largely to western Poland, which was incorporated into the Reich. At the same time the Communist government transplanted some 400,000 Germanic citizens, regarded as unreliable in case of war with Hitler, from the lower Volga to Siberia. It was part of the Nazi strategy to disorganize the enemy by terrorizing and scattering the civilian population. The *Blitzkrieg* of September 1939 drove 300,000 Poles and Jews eastward to seek refuge in the Soviet Union; the *Blitzkrieg* of 1940 drove several million Frenchmen onto the open roads leading to southern France; the Balkan campaigns of the following year displaced hundreds of thousands of Yugoslavs and Greeks; and the drive into Russia made nearly ten million people homeless. In the course of the war, six and a half million civilians were forcibly moved from one country to another and thirty-three million—nearly a third of them Russians—from one region to another within the same countries. These figures do not include the millions of prisoners of war.

The casualties of the war were twice as heavy as those of the First World War. About fifteen million soldiers lost their lives, and perhaps twenty-six mil-

Burial of victims of Nazi mass murders, in the town of Nordhausen in Germany. Harold Siegman, for the War Picture Pool, FROM ACME

lion were wounded or maimed. Even these figures give no idea of the horror of the Second World War. It was a war—to judge by its consequences—against the civilian population, against women and children, even more than against men in arms. The saying was common that the safest place to be was at the front, so vast was the damage to cities and homes, and so great the losses among their inhabitants, not to mention the losses incident to the forced transplantation of millions of people.

Among those who died in German gas chambers and crematoria, the majority were women and children. They were killed as a deliberate policy, justified by no military necessity, to exterminate whole peoples and classes. It was genocide that gave the Nazi war the aspect of an onslaught against humanity.

33. *Europe and America at the Mid-Century*

The two world wars were acts of a single drama. In both cases European powers and the United States joined forces to arrest Germany's drive for hegemony. Twice Germany took the offensive, won striking initial victories, and went down only after prolonged and bitter fighting. But the meaning of the drama was more than military and imperial. It reached to the roots of the society and civilization of the Western world. The First World War not only led to the collapse of all four Continental empires but precipitated the outbreak of a democratic and then a Communist revolution in Russia. Another revolution—that of the Nazis in 1933—in turn precipitated the Second World War. Although this war destroyed the totalitarian regimes of Germany and Italy, it also provided an opportunity for the expansion of Communism, and it set in motion an irresistible movement against colonialism throughout Asia and Africa.

In effect, therefore, the two world wars amounted to a series of revolutions. They brought to an end the familiar world initiated by the American and French Revolutions and consolidated by the economic achievements of the nineteenth century: a world of increasing liberty, democracy, rationality, and internationalism. They brought into being a world in which dictatorial tendencies are challenging liberty and democracy, in which social pressures are constricting the individual's realm of action and thought, and in which state policy is increasingly impressing itself upon economic life. They accelerated the advance of industry and technology and the application of scientific methods on a large scale, for useful as well as for destructive purposes.

The consequences of the two world wars, particularly of the second, are still being unraveled. The observer of contemporary events lacks the perspective and the materials that enable the historian to analyze past events, discover their drift, and assess their meaning. Developments since 1945 will therefore be sketched here in broad strokes, chiefly with a view to indicating the issues and problems to which they have given rise.

The Eminence of the United States

The wars of the twentieth century upset a balance of power that had existed, in its essentials, for two centuries. Before 1914, Britain, France, Germany (or her predecessor, Prussia), Austria, and Russia had exercised, as great powers, a determining influence in international affairs. After the First World War, Austria disappeared first as an imperial dynasty and then as an independent state, and Russia, now Communist, retreated into diplomatic isolation. The Second World War reduced Germany in size and in prestige, and her fall left a political vacuum in Europe. Great Britain and France, though on the winning side in both wars, were so weakened as to be overshadowed by the Soviet Union and the United States. The Soviet Union became the strongest power on the Continent. The United States, although she had been an influential power for a half century, had previously kept aloof from international commitments and alliances; she seemed now, therefore, to have leaped at one bound to eminence of the first order.

The American government after the Second World War was determined to avoid a repetition of the experience of 1919, when the Republic had withdrawn into isolation. Although isolationism was by no means dead, both major political parties accepted an active role in world affairs. President Roosevelt, profiting from the tragic failure of Woodrow Wilson, had associated opposition leaders with the conduct of foreign affairs and of the war. There was to be no repetition of the repudiation of the peace settlement of 1919. The Republican party, whose chiefs had been instrumental in keeping the United States out of the League of Nations in 1919, supported her membership in a new international organization. The two administrations of Republican Dwight D. Eisenhower, who had commanded the Allied forces in Europe, confirmed the "internationalist" policy of Roosevelt and his Democratic successor, Harry S. Truman. The turn in American foreign policy coincided with the marked increase in the influence of American methods and ideas. In many countries, particularly in Western Europe, "Americanization" has come to mean not only the introduction of advanced industrial and advertising techniques but also the importation of American products, including films and books, and the imitation of American amusements, and even manners.

After the war, the United States responded to her obligations as the richest country in a distracted and impoverished world. She wrote off much of the lend-lease contribution to her allies and supplied the bulk of the funds for the relief and resettlement of refugees. In 1947 General George C. Marshall, Secretary of State, proposed a plan for assisting other countries to reconstruct their economies. The first appropriation authorized under the Foreign Assistance Act of 1948 was 5.3 billion dollars. Disbursements under the Marshall Plan, together with other forms of foreign aid, had reached 68 billion dollars by

1959. American treasure stimulated recovery in many countries, particularly in those of Western Europe. "Underdeveloped" areas in Latin America, Asia, and Africa received special loans and technical assistance.

While the United States assumed an active role in international affairs generally, her relations with Europe became particularly close. Not since the period when the American Republic was born was the mutual influence of Europe and America so penetrating. During the American and French Revolutions, the two continents had reacted sensitively to each other. Later, the bonds between them were weakened by the European reaction against the revolutionary and constitutional movements; while the New World became increasingly democratic, the Old World became more and more conservative. When European liberalism regained its momentum in the middle of the nineteenth century, and when democracy made headway in Western Europe, the consciousness of a common direction burgeoned again. Toward the beginning of the twentieth century, diplomatic relations among the United States, Britain, and France grew increasingly cordial. The United States and France were traditional friends; the United States and Britain, and Britain and France, had not been at war with one another since the time of Napoleon. All three countries felt threatened by the advancing imperialism, and later by the totalitarianism, of Germany. Twice in one generation they fought side by side and prevailed only after great exertions and sacrifices. There emerged, in consequence, a sense of community among them. Thus since the eighteenth century, America had come full circle in her relations with the Old World. But her position had meanwhile risen spectacularly. Once a colony, then a peripheral state, the United States had become a leading power.

The Yalta Conference, Crimea, February 1945, toward the end of the Second World War. Churchill, Roosevelt, and Stalin are seated. Their respective foreign ministers are standing behind them: Anthony Eden, Edward Stettinius, and Vyacheslav Molotov. At the extreme right is Averell Harriman, aide to Roosevelt and later Governor of New York State. UNITED ARTISTS

The Atlantic World and the United Nations

Immediately after the war, Britain, France, and the United States pursued congruent foreign policies. They were intent on preserving and extending the democratic order they had just defended successfully against Nazism, on restoring political stability, and on preventing future aggression. When the war was drawing to an end, President Roosevelt conceived the hope that he could obtain Soviet cooperation in settling the questions bequeathed by the struggle and establishing friendly relations for the future. With that in mind, he had made considerable concessions to the Soviet Union. At conferences held at Yalta, in the Crimea, in February 1945 and, after the death of Roosevelt, at Potsdam, Germany, in the following August, the United States, Britain, and the Soviet Union agreed to destroy the Nazi and Fascist movements, to disband the German General Staff, and, pending a final settlement, to divide Germany into occupation zones. They agreed also to hold free elections and to establish democratic governments in the liberated countries. In compensation for Polish territory retained by the Soviet Union, Poland was to receive certain German areas. Finally, the powers agreed to establish a new international organization to secure peace in the future.

For a brief period, there was cooperation. The Soviet Union joined the Western countries in launching the United Nations Organization in San Francisco on April 25, 1945. The new organization is a somewhat improved version of the League of Nations, which in effect ceased to function in 1939, a victim of the aggression it had been designed to prevent. The future of the League had been bound up with the fortunes of the Versailles settlement of 1919. Its Covenant was part of the Treaty. The United Nations, on the other hand, is an independent creation. Its Charter spells out the power to arrest aggression more clearly than the Covenant had done: the United Nations can invoke "such action by air, sea, or land forces as may be necessary to maintain or restore international peace and security. . . . All members of the United Nations . . . undertake to make available . . . armed forces, assistance, and facilities, including rights of passage." The declaration of Human Rights of the United Nations sums up in contemporary terms, and extends to the world as a whole, the principles enunciated by the American and French declarations of rights of the eighteenth century: "Everyone has the right to life, liberty, and security of person." "Everyone is entitled to all the rights and freedoms set forth in this Declaration, without distinction of any kind, such as race, colour, sex, language, religion, political or other opinion, national or social origin, property, birth or other status."

Like the League, the United Nations has two governing bodies. The General Assembly is a forum of discussion. It makes recommendations for action to preserve peace. All the member states (which by 1960 numbered ninety-nine) are represented in the Assembly. In effect the Assembly is the sounding board of the smaller nations of the world. The more powerful body is the Security Council, which consists of five permanent members—Britain, France, the U.S.S.R., the United States, and China (Taiwan)—and six members elected for two-year terms by the Assembly. It is the Council that bears the principal responsibility for action. The Council acts by majority vote in matters of procedure, but in substantive questions the majority must include all five permanent members. Each great power, in effect, possesses the right to veto Council actions. In addition to the Assembly and the Council, various organizations deal with special problems: the International Court of Justice, which took the place of the old World Court; the Economic and Social Council; the World Health Organization (WHO); the Food and Agriculture Organization (FAO); the United Nations Educational, Scientific, and Cultural Organization (UNESCO); the International Labor Organization (ILO); and several others. The United Nations Relief and Rehabilitation Administration (UNRRA) and the International Refugee Organization (IRO) were established shortly after the war to retrain and resettle the millions of D.P.'s (displaced persons) liberated from camps in Germany, Austria, and Italy.

In addition to cooperating to set up new international agencies, the victorious powers agreed to punish the recent aggressors. They disbanded the totalitarian parties of the Axis countries and called their leadership to account. They conducted a campaign of "denazification" in Germany. Before an International Military Tribunal in Nuremberg in 1945-46, they indicted twenty-four leaders for crimes against peace and humanity. The evidence of extraordinary acts of provocation and aggression, and of plots to carry out atrocities and exterminate whole nations and peoples was spread upon the public record. The tribunal condemned twelve German leaders to death by hanging, acquitted three, and sentenced the others to prison terms. Another International Tribunal, which convened in Tokyo in 1946, condemned to death seven Japanese leaders, including two former premiers, for waging aggressive warfare. Although the charges were not part of recognized international law, the tribunals asserted the principle that political power and national sovereignty do not excuse crime and deliberate aggression.

For a while it seemed that the wartime allies would collaborate on a peace settlement. In 1947, the United States, Great Britain, the Soviet Union, and, later, France and seventeen lesser powers signed treaties with Bulgaria, Finland, Hungary, Rumania, and Italy. These treaties provided for severe limitation of armies and navies. In each case the Soviet Union received reparations while the Western Allies renounced them.

Italy lost her overseas empire. She had played the role of a great power without the resources to sustain that role. In the First World War she had fought against her former allies, and in the Second she fought against both sides in succession. Her monarchical system was so compromised by its association with Fascism that it did not long survive the fall of Mussolini. A plebiscite in 1946 established a democratic republic, and the dream of Mazzini was at last realized.

The Security Council voting unanimously on May 31, 1960, to recommend to the Assembly the admission of a new African state, the Republic of Togo, to membership in the United Nations. At the center of the table, to the right, is Dag Hammarskjöld, Secretary General of the United Nations, who has no vote on the Council. The vote is being taken in the Council chamber at United Nations headquarters in New York. UNITED NATIONS

By a treaty signed in 1951, Japan, like Italy, lost her colonial empire. She was restricted to the four islands from which she had emerged from self-imposed isolation almost a century earlier. She renounced aggression and militarism. Emperor Hirohito in 1946 announced that the "ties between us and our people are not predicated on the false conception that the Emperor is divine and that the Japanese people are superior to other races and fated to rule the world." Japan gained more from defeat than most countries gained from victory, for the American occupation army, under General MacArthur, carried out reforms that amounted to a painless revolution. Large estates were broken up and sold in small lots, at low cost, to land-hungry farmers. While permitting Japan to retain her Emperor—which was a condition of the armistice—the Americans imposed a democratic constitution. They tried to curb monopoly in industry and finance, spurred trade-union organization, and introduced improvements in the public school system.

It proved impossible, however, for the victors to reach agreement on treaties with Germany and Austria. The Soviet Union demanded a share in the control of the industrial district of the Ruhr, and large reparations. Since the United States and Britain were shipping large quantities of food and other supplies into the defeated countries, and payments were to be made partly out of current production, reparations would come indirectly out of their

693

pockets. Negotiations broke down, and the Soviet Union proceeded to requisition large quantities of machinery, livestock, and other movable property from her own zone in Germany. She followed this practice in other Central European countries that she occupied.

The Communist Empire

It soon became apparent that the differences between the two sides went much deeper. The Soviet Union did not share the aims of the Atlantic countries or their vision of the future. The dictatorial party that controlled the country still professed the goal of world revolution. It regarded international relations as the expression of an irrepressible conflict between capitalism and communism, a conflict which would not end until one system or the other prevailed throughout the world. Between the wars, the Soviet Union, persuaded that the "capitalist" states would one day combine to attack her, had remained isolated and suspicious. Although she had carried the victory, with the assistance of the Atlantic countries, she could not forget that a foreign conqueror had invaded and devastated most of her European territory. Since she would not trust her security to treaties with "capitalist" and democratic states or to an international society in which they had a majority, she proceeded to build a wall of dependent states along her western borders.

She soon found an extraordinary opportunity to build such a wall, realizing the expansionist aims of both czarism and Communism. Her armies stood in the middle of Germany, filling the vacuum left by the collapse of Hitler's hegemony in Central Europe and the Balkans. Stalin annexed, without ado, the formerly Russian littoral of the Baltic, including Latvia, Lithuania, and Estonia. Yugoslavia and Albania became communist in 1945, and in 1946-49, by a varying mixture of intimidation, military pressure, and rigged elections, Soviet agents installed Communist governments in Poland, Hungary, Czechoslovakia, Rumania, and Bulgaria. (In Yugoslavia, a communist government came into control of the country under its own steam; under the leadership of Marshal Tito [Josip Broz, 1891-   ] it had conducted vigorous guerrilla warfare against the Nazi occupation.) Thus, without formal annexation, and in defiance of its pledge to the Western powers to hold free elections and to allow the occupied countries to choose their own form of government, the Soviet Union took over effective control of the whole area across which her armies had swept in the last year of the war. The heir of the Romanovs had come into much of the inheritance of the Hohenzollerns and most of that of the Hapsburgs. The Communist dictator had outdone all the conquering czars.

In Asia, Communism had an equally striking triumph. For several decades China had been riven by domestic conflicts. Early in the century a leading reformer, Dr. Sun Yat-sen (1867-1925), organized the Nationalist party, or Kuomintang, with the aim of modernizing the country. In 1911 a revolution broke out, and the last Manchu emperor, Pu-yi, a boy of six, was driven from the throne. China became a Republic and Dr. Sun her first president. It proved difficult to bring the whole country under the authority of the new government. After the Russian Revolution, a Communist wing developed in the Kuomintang. In 1927, Sun Yat-sen's successor as leader of the party, Chiang Kai-shek (1886-   ), who represented the conservative faction, purged the party of Communists. The result was an armed struggle between Nationalists and Communists for control of the country. By 1934 the Communists, led by Mao Tse-tung (1893-   ), were in control of one sixth of China's territory. When Japan invaded China in 1937 the two parties agreed to cooperate against the foreign foe. But they fought the Japanese with separate armies in different sections of the vast country.

Upon the collapse of the Japanese Empire, the Chinese Nationalists and Communists resumed their old conflict. American diplomats made strenuous efforts to bring them together, but without success. The Communists had the advantage in the struggle. They won the support of many of the impoverished peasants by promising them land. They received from the Soviet Union the arms that she had seized from the Japanese. The Nationalist government was rigid and conservative, and its administration was corrupt. Above all, it failed to rise to the task of projecting the reforms necessary for the reconstruction of a country that for so long had been ravaged by domestic and foreign war. By 1950 the followers of Mao were in control of the whole Chinese mainland, and the Nationalist government withdrew with its army to the island of Formosa (Taiwan), which had been yielded by Japan. Thus it came about that the most populous country in Asia—indeed, in the world—joined the ranks of Communism.

These developments exalted the international prestige of the Soviet Union and of its dictator. At home, Stalin tried to consolidate his rule by resuming the repressions of the thirties, which had been relaxed somewhat during the "patriotic war." He again directed purges of suspected or potential critics, and the secret police held unquestioned sway. Millions of people were sent to slave labor camps. Stricter controls than ever were established over literature and other arts; Stalin imposed the practice of "socialist realism," which meant that Soviet life had to be depicted in glowing colors. In the satellite states, he placed in charge despotic bureaucrats obedient to his will. Finally, Stalin sealed his European empire against Western influence. He severed the contacts established during the war and rejected the proffered aid of the Marshall Plan, not only for the Soviet Union, but for her satellite states as well. Winston Churchill observed in a speech at Fulton, Missouri, in 1946 that "an iron curtain has descended across the Continent [from] Stettin, in the Baltic, to Trieste, in the Adriatic. . . . Behind that line lie all the capitals of the ancient states of Central and Eastern Europe—Warsaw, Berlin, Prague, Vienna, Budapest, Belgrade, Bucharest, and Sofia."

The Rise of Asia and Africa

At a moment when the world was being divided into antagonistic halves, a rebellion against Western domination swept Asia and Africa. Since the geographic discoveries of the fifteenth and sixteenth centuries, and especially since the colonial expansion of the eighteenth century, European countries had explored the whole globe and occupied extensive portions of it. Nearly everywhere the native populations had been helpless to resist their penetration. By weakening one another in fierce conflicts, however, the imperial powers had also loosened their hold on the colonies. After the First World War, Germany and Turkey lost their empires. The establishment of the mandate system for some of their former colonies and the assertion of the principle of self-determination in Europe encouraged national movements. In the Second World War, the fighting, which in 1914-18 had been confined for the most part to Europe, spread to North Africa, to large areas in Asia and Oceania, and to the seas and the air around the planet. When it ended, there was a veritable massacre of empires. Italy lost her holdings in Africa, and Japan lost hers in Asia and the Pacific. The losses of the defeated states were not, as in 1918, the gains of the victors. The victorious powers did not acquire the colonies surrendered by Japan and Italy. They lost most of their own—and they had more to lose. The largest of the empires—the British—suffered severely. The Labor government, which came into office in 1945, was determined not to use military force against colonial peoples. Two years later, by agreement with native nationalists, it dismantled the imperial controls in India. The subcontinent was divided between the Dominion of India, with a population of 345 million people, and (since the Moslems did not wish to become part of a predominantly Hindu state) the Dominion of Pakistan, with a population of 74 million. The empire which had originated in Robert Clive's victory at Plassey in 1757 came to an end. Tragically—and ironically—the prime mover of the Indian independence movement, Mohandas Gandhi, was assassinated by a Hindu fanatic in 1948. Gandhi's close colleague, Jawaharlal Nehru (1889-   ), a British-educated socialist, became India's first Prime Minister. The new Dominion started out with liberal parliamentary institutions, its principal task being to blend its heterogeneous provinces, peoples, and tribes into a coherent whole. In 1949-50 the Indian constituent assembly adopted a constitution that made India a federal republic but nevertheless accepted the British Crown as a symbol of the Commonwealth. Pakistan became a republic in 1955 but remained in the Commonwealth. The peaceful withdrawal of British troops from the Indian subcontinent and the maintenance of friendly relations with the new governments were triumphs of British statesmanship.

In 1948 Burma became a republic, leaving the Commonwealth, while

Ceylon became a dominion within it; several African colonies achieved varying degrees of autonomy.

Palestine rose from the status of mandate to statehood. In the thirties, Great Britain, the mandatory power, had restricted Jewish immigration, but Arab nationalists had engaged in sanguinary riots to arrest it altogether and to prevent the sale of land to Zionist organizations. The Second World War brought the issue to a head. The annihilation of two thirds of European Jewry by the Nazis worked a transformation among the survivors. There was a revulsion of feeling against the age-old "exile" and the second-class position into which many countries had forced the Jews. To the thousands of survivors huddled in Displaced Persons' camps, the yearning for Zion became irresistible. The Zionists demanded the establishment of a Jewish state. Arab nationalists in Palestine and in the surrounding countries remained fiercely opposed to both immigration and statehood. In 1947, the United Nations revived, without avail, an old British proposal to partition Palestine into an Arab and a Jewish state. The following year, on May 14, Britain gave up her mandate. On the same day a Jewish provisional government proclaimed the establishment of Israel, the first independent Jewish state in two thousand years. Five neighboring Arab states attacked Israel, which defended herself successfully. The United Nations arranged an armistice but the Arab states maintained a belligerent attitude, refusing to make peace and accept the new state. Despite this uneasy truce, Israel developed rapidly: her population in 1948 stood at 650,000 persons; during the next five years a sweeping "in-gathering of the exiles" more than doubled it.

The second largest colonial empire—that of France—was reduced as drastically as the British. During the war, the Free French had granted independence to the mandated countries of Syria and Lebanon. After the war, Morocco, Tunis, and Indochina secured the same privilege, the last after sharp fighting. The states of Cambodia, Laos, and Vietnam (divided into Communist and non-Communist halves) shared the inheritance of the French empire of Indochina. In Algeria, which has a settlement of more than one million Frenchmen, the demands of Arab nationalists for separation led to the outbreak of a violent and long-drawn-out rebellion in 1954. Meanwhile France, like Britain, has been trying to supplant imperial connections with voluntary cooperation. Her counterpart of the Commonwealth is the French Union, governed by a High Council consisting of the delegates of France and "associated" states and territories. Each member of the Union must have an elective legislature.

Colonial losses and the Algerian civil war precipitated the fall of the Fourth French Republic, established in 1946. The traditional weakness of coalition governments and the multiplicity of parties made a vigorous direction of affairs difficult. In May 1958, the threat of a coup by army officers in Algeria compelled the government to recall to power General Charles de Gaulle, who had headed the Free French and had served as president after the war. The electorate overwhelmingly approved a new constitution which strangthened the

697

executive, and De Gaulle supplanted René Coty as president. A brilliant and daring politician, De Gaulle disavowed dictatorial ambitions and declared his intent to restore French prestige. His colonial policy has been liberal; in 1959 he pledged that Algeria would have an opportunity to choose independence or association with France after the fighting stopped.

Another empire, even older than that of France, crumbled. The Netherlands was constrained in 1949 to grant independence to her East Indian possessions. The new state, the United States of Indonesia, comprised Java, Sumatra, western Borneo, and many smaller islands, with a population of 75 million people.

In Africa, colonies gained their independence with startling rapidity. In 1960, when sixteen new African states were admitted to the United Nations, the number of independent nations in the "Dark Continent" totaled twenty-four, or almost a quarter of the membership of the United Nations.

The defeat of Nazi racialism and the achievement of independence by most of the colored peoples of Africa increased the pressure of the American Negroes for a long-deferred equality with their fellow citizens. The Negroes had fought side by side with white Americans in the Second World War and their aspirations had been encouraged by the liberal attitude of the Roosevelt administration toward minority groups. In 1954 the United States Supreme Court, reversing a decision of 1894, ruled that the practice of segregating the races in the public schools of Southern states was contrary to the Constitution. It called for "desegregation" with "all deliberate speed." There was also agitation against local regulations requiring the separation of races in public places and conveyances. These developments resulted in distinct, though slow, advances in the position of Negroes throughout the country. In addition, the old discrimination against "Orientals" in the rules governing citizenship and naturalization was ended.

In the foundering of European domination overseas the United States played a significant role. During the war she used her influence to advance the cause of self-government and independence throughout the world. She was particularly friendly to the movement for an independent India. In her own sphere, she had anticipated the retreat from imperialism. In the early years of the century, under the so-called Roosevelt Corollary, a broad interpretation of the Monroe Doctrine, she had intervened in several Latin American states, notably in the Caribbean, in order to collect defaulted debts or forestall European intervention. Troops were dispatched on several occasions to obtain control of customs receipts for debt servicing or to support pro-American politicians in disputed elections or domestic disorders. The right of intervention had been written into treaties concluded with Central American and Caribbean states. Beginning in the twenties, however, and continuing through the New Deal years, the United States abated these claims and espoused the policy of the "good neighbor." Gradually troops were withdrawn and intervention rights surrendered in Haiti, Panama, and Cuba. In 1934 the United States, together

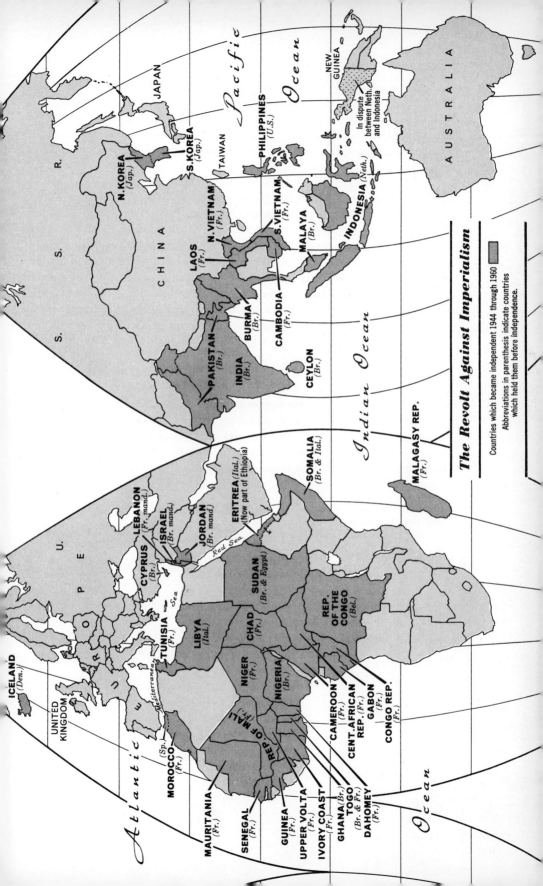

The Revolt Against Imperialism

Countries which became independent 1944 through 1960
Abbreviations in parenthesis indicate countries
which held them before independence.

with other states of the Western Hemisphere, pledged herself not to interfere in the internal affairs of any state. A law enacted in the same year promised the Philippine Islands independence after a transition period, and in 1946 the Republic of the Philippines duly came into being. In 1959, two former territories became members of the federal union. Alaska and Hawaii became the forty-ninth and the fiftieth state, respectively.

The liquidation of empires and the appearance of new states has raised the dignity of non-European peoples. No longer can Westerners assume an attitude of superiority toward other races and nations. In the remaining European colonies, Africans and Asians are demanding equal treatment with Europeans and their descendants. The readjustment of race relations has often been painful. The memory of centuries of domination is living on in a widespread antagonism to Europeans. Nationalist politicians and Communist agitators have exploited this resentment, which has occasionally erupted in violence. The Boer population of the Union of South Africa has reacted against the pressure for racial equality with the extreme policy of *Apartheid,* or segregation of nonwhites into separate areas, occupations, and schools. Nearly everywhere else, the tide is running in the other direction.

In a conference held at Bandung, Indonesia, in 1955, twenty-nine states of Asia and Africa drew up a declaration of rights and brotherly relations, thus emphasizing their sense of distinction from the West. "Asia and Africa," read the report of the conference, "have been the cradle of great religions and civilizations. . . . Unfortunately, cultural contacts among Asian and African countries were interrupted during the past centuries. The peoples of Asia and Africa are now animated by a keen and sincere desire to renew their old cultural contacts and develop new ones in the modern world."

Modern parliamentarianism comes to ancient Africa. Senegalese voters are casting their first ballots in legislative elections in Dakar. FRENCH EM-BASSY PRESS AND INFORMATION DIVISION

It is, however, in the name of Western ideals that Asians and Africans are rebelling against the West. The Bandung Conference condemned colonialism and racialism by invoking the principles of freedom, equality, and national self-determination. The slogans of social reform and democracy which are ringing through the former colonies are echoes of familiar Western programs. Most of the new states are experimenting gingerly with representative institutions, and it is often European- and American-trained natives who have taken the helm of affairs. Nevertheless, dictatorial tendencies are widespread.

Political independence does not mean economic independence. The Asian and African countries are generally little developed economically. Some of them, like India and China, are highly overpopulated and becoming more so with every passing year. All of them feel that they might benefit from the introduction of modern techniques of production both in agriculture and in industry. They need technical and financial help. The Bandung communiqué acknowledged that the assistance given by Western countries had made "a valuable contribution" in the past and appealed for further investment of Western capital.

Economic Recovery and Advance

The fact is that, although Asia accounts for the largest land mass and population of all the continents, the bulk of the economic and political energy in the world is still concentrated in Europe and America. There, across all regional and ideological divisions, a movement to intensify industrial production has been under way. The Second World War redoubled the impulse that the First had given to technological advances. The rationalization of industry through the application of new devices and methods—above all, of scientific discoveries made in the effort to speed and improve the production of weapons— left a deep imprint on the economy. The promotion of industrial development and the coordination of production on a national scale became a policy of state in some countries, particularly those that lacked modern plants and techniques. The example of the Soviet Union inspired other governments to launch three-, four-, even ten-year plans. The Soviet Union herself resumed her Five-Year Plans, with continued emphasis on heavy industry. The fourth Plan, initiated in 1946, was devoted also to the rehabilitation of devastated areas and the repair of internal communications. By the mid-fifties the country was catching up with prewar production and had made sizable advances in heavy industry. The production of consumer goods, though increased, remains modest.

With the help of the Marshall Plan, France, Great Britain, Italy, and West Germany achieved a substantial reconstruction within a decade after the war. Germany again became the most productive country of Western Europe and enjoyed a phenomenal record of employment, exports, and profits. The United States resumed the production of consumer goods on a large scale after the war. Production figures soon surpassed prewar records, and the wide distribution of the new necessities—powerful automobiles, television sets, refined household appliances—made the American consumer the envy of the world. Heavy industry seems to be growing less rapidly than in the Soviet Union, but accurate Russian statistics are not available for comparison. At all events, it remains the Soviet goal to catch up with the wealth, and the living standards, of the United States.

While economic development has tended to ignore existing national and regional divisions, it has had the effect of creating new regions of its own. The Soviet Union has coordinated the activities of new satellite states and tried to mesh them into her industrial plans. Both the British Commonwealth and the French Union have made attempts to promote economic interchange and cooperation among their members. The countries of Western Europe have drawn together. On the initiative of France, the European Coal and Steel Community was formed in 1950 to merge the markets of France, Italy, West Germany, and Benelux (Belgium, the Netherlands, and Luxembourg) and allocate sales among them. In 1953 the Benelux countries agreed to the principle of a common tariff, as did Italy, France, and West Germany. Another free-trade area was formed in 1959 by the so-called Outer Seven—Britain, Norway, Sweden, Denmark, Switzerland, Austria, and Portugal. Thus thirteen countries committed themselves to easier exchanges of goods and held out the hope of abating the policies of economic nationalism that had been adopted in the last decades of the nineteenth century. There was even an attempt to create a United States of (Western) Europe. In a series of conferences held at Strasbourg in 1953, the European Coal and Steel Community drafted the European Political Community Treaty, providing for a loose federal government with a two-chamber legislature. But the member states, though willing to cooperate closely on economic matters, were not yet ready to accept limitations of their sovereignty, and the attempt failed.

Gradually there have emerged two alternative ways of organizing the economy and relating it to political life. One is the Communist system of state control of the principal sources of wealth and production under the dictatorial rule of a single party; the other is the "mixed economy" of private and public enterprises operating within liberal democratic institutions. Communist China and the European satellites of the Soviet Union abolished large-scale property in land, launched ambitious programs of collectivization in agriculture, controlled foreign trade, and, above all, adopted imitations of the Soviet program of intensive and forced industrialization. Yet, within a few years, variations of the official scheme developed. Some of the satellite countries, notably Poland, have modified or slowed down the drive for collectivization or industrialization. China has gone beyond Soviet collectivism, attempting to communize not only agriculture but consumption and even family life. The most extreme forms of Communism have appeared in Asia, becoming diluted as one proceeds westward.

Within the mixed economies of the non-Communist world there is room for greater variation. The Second World War, more distinctly than the First, provided opportunities for an advance in socialization. Great Britain offered the greatest example of such advance. In July 1945 the Labor party won an overwhelming victory and the Conservative Winston Churchill, who had given the country an energetic leadership during the war, was replaced as prime minister by Clement Attlee. The new government passed legislation extending social services and nationalizing the Bank of England, the coal industry, and the basic utilities of gas, electricity, and telephone. In order to prevent too great a concentration of power and expansion of bureaucratic and centralized controls, the nationalized industries were placed under the direction of appointed commissioners who operated under the general rules set up by law but independently of the ministry or party in office. The owners of the nationalized industries were compensated by exchanging their stock for government bonds carrying guaranteed returns over some twenty years. Private ownership and management and corporate organization have remained the rule in most industries and enterprises.

Throughout the Western world, governments are exercising direct or indirect controls over the availability of credit, the value of money, and the flow of foreign trade and are striving to develop cordial relations between capital and labor. The policy of protecting the weak, relieving the unemployed, pensioning the aged, and generally of alleviating the worst consequences of poverty and illness is generally accepted.

The Cold War

The achievements of social reform and economic enterprise stand in sharp contrast to the political and spiritual state of the Western world. The years that followed the worst bloodletting of modern times have been filled with international alarms and portents of total destruction. Much of the tension has been due to the inability of the Atlantic countries and the Soviet Union to agree to a permanent peace settlement and to the expansion and intensification of Communism.

The power of Stalinism reached far beyond the Iron Curtain. Upon the end of the war, Soviet armies outnumbered all the other Continental forces combined. The Communist parties of Italy, France, and other countries grew in strength. Stalin preserved his control over foreign parties as well as satellite states. In 1947, the Soviet dictator revived the International under a new name, the Cominform (Communist Information Bureau). The following year, Marshal Tito of Yugoslavia having refused to accept Soviet interference in the internal affairs of his country, Stalin expelled him and the Yugoslav party from the Cominform.

Like Czarist Russia in the first half of the previous century, the Soviet Union appeared as a threat to Western Europe. This threat brought the United States into play as a defender of the non-Communist countries. In 1947 the Soviet Union abetted a rebellion of Communists against the re-established monarchy of Greece. President Truman promptly announced that the United States   *703* would give military and financial assistance to any country threatened by Communist attack. Aid was sent at once and, after a sharp struggle, the rebels were defeated. Under the Truman Doctrine, aid was at the same time extended to Turkey, whose strategic position on the Dardanelles exposed her to danger. In 1948 Stalin tried, by blockading, to force the Allies out of West Berlin, which consisted of the sectors occupied by the Western countries. He closed the roads leading to West Berlin through the Soviet zone of Germany. American and British planes made several hundred thousand flights to keep the city supplied. They maintained the extraordinary "airlift" for a year and then Stalin abandoned his blockade. In 1949, the Soviet Union established a Communist state in East Germany, under the name of the German Democratic Republic. An election in totalitarian style, with a single list of candidates, sanctioned the new state, which has 17 million inhabitants.

The Western allies then merged their three zones into the German Federal Republic. West Germany has twice the territory and three times the population of East Germany and contains the greater number of the industrial and urban centers. It has adopted a democratic constitution which avoids some of the defects of the Weimar Constitution, particularly the delegation of semidictatorial powers to the president in case of emergency. The powerful Junker class has lost its estates in East Germany, which contains the old provinces of Prussia and Brandenburg, the traditional seats of Junkerdom. Under the circumstances, the opposition to constitutionalism seems weaker than in the Weimar period.

The division of Germany threatens a future revival of nationalism. The reunification of areas committed to divergent social and political systems presents unusual difficulties; but will the Germans accept the permanent division of their country? An older national issue still survives. Hitler had used German minorities abroad to disintegrate and subjugate other states. After the war, in order to avert a repetition of such tactics and reduce domestic tensions, these countries sent "home" more than twelve million Germans from areas where some of them had lived for generations. Eight million persons were repatriated and resettled in West Germany, four million in East Germany, and 150,000 in Berlin. Whether this drastic "solution" of the national question will nurture aggression and revenge in the future depends upon the ability of Europe to attain stable relations among its states.

The next Communist thrust came in the Far East. At the end of the war the United States had occupied the southern part of Korea up to the 38th Parallel, while the Soviet Union occupied the northern part. The two powers had agreed to set up a unified democratic government, but this agreement was never carried out, and the country remained divided even after the occupation forces had been withdrawn. On June 25, 1950, North Korean armies, supplied and assisted by the Soviet Union and Communist China, crossed the Parallel and invaded South Korea. The Soviet Union had momentarily absented herself from the meetings of the Security Council, with whose majority she often disagreed. She was therefore not in a position to interpose a veto when the Council condemned this unprovoked attack and demanded that the invaders withdraw. When they failed to do so, the Council called upon the members of the United Nations to take military action against them. The first international army to enforce peace came into being. Twenty nations sent contingents to assist South Korea, the preponderance of men and weapons being supplied by the United States. On July 27, 1953, an armistice was signed. After protracted fighting and equally protracted negotiations, the boundary of the two Koreas was restored and a demilitarized zone was established on both sides of it to prevent future incidents.

Even before the Korean war, comprehensive alliances to stop Communist aggression had been concluded. In 1949 the United States, Canada, and ten countries of Western and Northern Europe had signed the North Atlantic Treaty. Turkey and Greece adhered to the treaty two years later. The signers declared their determination "to safeguard the freedom, common heritage, and civilization of their peoples, founded on the principles of democracy, individual liberty, and the rule of law." The pact was implemented by the formation of the North Atlantic Treaty Organization (NATO), which pooled military resources contributed by the members and coordinated their strategic planning. In order to preserve the peace in the Pacific regions, a similar organization— the Southeast Asia Treaty Organization (SEATO)—was formed in 1954 by the Western powers, Australia, New Zealand, Pakistan, the Philippines, and Thailand. The United States established, in NATO countries as well as in others, a ring of airfields and bases to contain the Soviet power.

Western Germany has been permitted to rearm. Even though the new German army is small and is integrated into a broad NATO command, its existence has revived fears on both sides of the Iron Curtain that Germany might make a third attempt to win European hegemony and that the other countries might again, as in the thirties, remain divided while she attacks her neighbors in turn. These fears have been deepened by the consideration that, in order to avoid another disastrous war on two fronts, a resurgent Germany might come to an understanding with East or West. In that case, which side would she prefer? For the moment there is, paradoxically, a certain security in the division of Germany. While East Germany is under Soviet control, West Germany has been making determined efforts to reach a lasting understanding with Western countries, above all with France. Might the old enmity of these two countries, which has cost Europe so much blood and wealth, be coming to an end? Will Germany overcome her old opposition to the countries to the west of her?

It is not only Germany that has been affected domestically by the cold war. In Italy and France, the large groups of Communists and "fellow travelers" kept up after the war a continuous opposition to the bonds with Anglo-American countries. In the United States, there developed an agitation against American Communists and later against former party members, fellow travelers, and many persons of advanced social or political views as well. The agitation was occasioned by the infiltration of undeclared Communists into influential positions in government and in professional and labor organizations, *705* and their practice of exploiting their positions for party ends. These organizations had largely eliminated Communist influence when politicians raised the cry of "Red subversion" in public office. Since the American Communist party was subject to the control of the Soviet government, the activities of its members assumed the aspect of treason. Public opinion was alarmed by evidence that Communists had betrayed state secrets, particularly secrets concerning the manufacture of atomic and hydrogen bombs, to the Soviet Union. The federal government instituted "security checks" on its employees and dismissed hundreds of them, often without fair hearing, disclosure of the source of information, or confrontation of accuser and accused. Many states imposed "loyalty oaths" upon public employees and teachers. Under the Smith Act of 1940 Communist leaders were convicted of advocating violent revolution. Congressional investigative committees harried "subversives" and persons suspected of Communist leanings. Senator Joseph R. McCarthy (1909-59) of Wisconsin, charging that Communists had infiltrated the high reaches of the government, especially the State Department, carried on a campaign of intimidation and vilification of liberals as well as "Reds." For several years, the Senator dominated newspaper headlines, in Europe and Asia as in the United States. Gradually, however, Americans became aroused by his highhanded methods and largely unsupported charges. In 1954 the Senate officially censured him. His course was arrested, and the agitation subsided. In a series of decisions, the Supreme Court curbed the abuses of congressional investigative committees and of the security regulations of the government.

Gradually the cold war diminished in intensity. The danger of the war's becoming "hot" was too great to be risked by either side. When Stalin died, at the age of seventy-four, in March 1953, it became apparent that the peoples of the Soviet Union and her satellite states were chafing under martial tensions and the rigors of dictatorship. The struggle for the succession which followed the death of Lenin was now repeated. At first a committee of leaders took over the government. Georgi Malenkov became Premier and Nikita Khrushchev assumed the office of Secretary-General of the Party, the office from which Stalin had risen to supreme power. Khrushchev had been an obedient instrument of Stalin, but he had a greater range of flexibility. He employed similar tactics of maneuver among the various factions to make his way up. In July 1953 he secured the support of other leaders against Lavrenti Beria, who, as chief of the secret police, had accumulated wide functions under Stalin. Beria was charged with being an "enemy of the people" and was swiftly and secretly executed. Two years later Malenkov acknowledged his "incompetence" and resigned. Marshal Nicholas Bulganin, an associate of Khrushchev, became Premier. In 1956 Khrushchev succeeded him in that office and emerged as the unquestioned leader of the Soviet Union. As he felt the need to respond to pressures to ease systematic repression, he strengthened his own position by dissociating himself from Stalin. In a sensational speech before the Twentieth Congress of the Communist Party of the Soviet Union on February 25, 1956, Khrushchev indicted the late dictator as a morbidly suspicious, arbitrary, and vengeful despot who had dispatched untold numbers of people to their death. "Possessing unlimited power, he indulged in great willfulness and choked . . . [people] . . . morally and physically." Khrushchev acknowledged that the confessions at the purge trials had been obtained by informing, fabrication of evidence, and above all by the "application of physical methods of pressuring [the victim], tortures, bringing him to a state of unconsciousness, deprivation of his judgment, taking away his human dignity." After the war, Stalin's "persecution mania reached unbelievable dimensions. . . . Everything was decided by him alone without any consideration for anyone or anything." The Central Committee of the party attempted to exculpate the leaders who had served under the dictator by declaring that the "cult of personality" had so linked the name of Stalin with the achievements of the regime that it was impossible to stop his "lawless deeds." Khrushchev promised to avoid a repetition of Stalin's misdeeds. It was considered a gain that his rivals in the ascent to supreme power lost their positions but not their lives. Many political prisoners held without cause and many inmates of slave labor camps were released. The secret police became less obtrusive and arbitrary. While Khrushchev continued the Five-Year Plans for expanding the industrial plant, he paid somewhat more attention than Stalin had done to the needs of consumers.

Khrushchev's revelations stunned the Communist world. In Western countries, the parties lost many members. The Soviet leadership was subjected to unprecedented public criticism by foreign Communists. In the Soviet Union, there was some evidence of restlessness.

The satellite countries found a vent of protest against Soviet domination as well as against Stalinism. A decade of Communist indoctrination, censorship, and propaganda had not stifled the urge for personal liberty and national autonomy. Three months after Stalin's death, anti-Communist workers and students rioted for three days in East Berlin and fought Soviet tanks in the streets. There were strikes and political demonstrations in Czechoslovakia. In 1956 the people of the Polish industrial center of Poznań rose against economic and political repression. Order was not restored until a week had passed. Dissatisfaction spread through Poland and induced a change in the leadership of the party, Stalinists being replaced by more moderate and flexible Communists under the leadership of Vladislav Gomulka (1905-   ). A rebellion in full style flared up in Budapest and other Hungarian cities. The Communist Imre Nagy assumed control of the government, repudiated one-party rule, and declared in favor of collaboration with non-Communist parties under conditions of political freedom. Nagy searched for a path leading from Communism to democratic socialism. He appealed for aid to the United Nations and the free world, but without success. The Soviet Union promptly rushed in troops. The people of Budapest, and particularly industrial workers and educated youth, battled the tanks in barricaded streets. But the odds were overwhelming and they were crushed without mercy. Before the Soviet Union could seal the borders, 150,000 Hungarians fled their country. The United States accepted and resettled 50,000 refugees.

The Soviet Union re-established her authority, but her behavior in the satellite states became more cautious. Poland, in particular, underwent a quiet change. The government relaxed slightly its controls over speech, writing, and religious practices. Communist dictatorship appeared somewhat less rigid than before. Khrushchev made attempts to diminish the antagonism that Stalin's foreign policy had aroused. He apologized to Marshal Tito of Yugoslavia for his treatment by Stalin, acknowledged that each country might find its own road to socialism, and made many trips abroad to demonstrate that the new leadership was more "human" than the old. While Soviet experiments with ever deadlier nuclear weapons continued, the Premier insisted on his country's peaceful intentions.

These tactics on one side of the Iron Curtain combined with tendencies on the other side to ease international relations. The "neutralist" countries which stood outside the two rival camps became critical of the constant alarms, fearing that their position between the two principal rivals exposed them to the danger of becoming the battleground of another war. In the United States, the Eisenhower administration, intent on reducing the budget, diminished military expenditures, particularly in the field of atomic and missile research and experiment. The Soviet Union soon surpassed the United States in these fields. In 1957 it put the first earth satellite into orbit and two years later placed a rocket on the moon. These feats suggested that it was becoming possible to aim atomic and hydrogen bombs at distant targets and had the effect of equalizing the capacity of the two sides to destroy each other's cities. Peace was becoming necessary for sheer survival.

In 1954 the leaders of France, Britain, the United States, and the Soviet Union had met at Geneva and in informal conferences pledged themselves to peaceful intercourse, although they were unable to settle outstanding differences. The following year they agreed on a treaty with Austria. There were increasing contacts between the two camps, trade exchanges, cultural visits, tourism, and finally visits by high dignitaries.

The Troubled Spirit of Western Man

The spiritual state of the Western world has proved less susceptible than its political and diplomatic condition to adjustment. The horrors of the Second World War stunned the conscience and troubled the spirit of men. The disillusionment that had characterized the aftermath of the First World War had been relieved by a sense of outrage and by moral idealism. It was possible then to blame the tragedy on the monarchs, diplomats, and generals. The mood produced by the second war was more somber and debilitating. Liberals as well as conservatives, Communists and capitalists, pacifists and militarists alike had cause to reproach themselves with the failure to arrest Hitlerism in time. Historians were not called upon to assess the degrees of "war guilt" as they had been in the twenties. The naked aggression of the Nazis and their annihilation of whole classes and nations had no parallel in modern history. The explosion of the atomic bomb and the rapid development of still more destructive weapons dramatized the terrors of "scientific" warfare.

Like the needle of a seismograph that ceases to register too great a shock, literature, otherwise so sensitive to the public temper, shrank from describing and judging such a scene. The fifties did not match the literary revival and energy of the twenties. The new spate of war novels was less impressive and searching than the old.

But it is not only the impact of war that has staggered the faith of Western man and clouded his image of himself. The tide of liberalism that had spread, in widening circles, from its center in the Atlantic world was slowed down in the twenties and then turned back by dictatorship and totalitarianism. Puzzled men are re-examining the ideological premises of Western civilization. Have they not trusted too much to "isms" of one kind or another? Men are becoming concerned over the misuse for political purposes of philosophical and poetic images and scientific theories. They are becoming critical of assumptions that some races and peoples are naturally "superior" to others, that elites have a right to rule by dictatorial means, that the historical process is "inevitable" and so cannot be controlled by man. Scientists have been shocked into an awareness of their role in multiplying man's power to destroy himself and his fellows. They have begun to wonder whether the complexities of modern science and the spirit of specialization have blinded them to the social and moral relevance of their work. The ability of governments, no matter how irresponsible or brutal, to command the services of many a scientist, technician, and professional man, is deeply disturbing. A still larger question has been troubling men. Is not society becoming too highly organized? Is not the individual being sacrificed to the profession, the community, the large industry or corporation, the national trade union, above all to the state, whose power and pervasiveness seem to be growing at a gallop? How far is it desirable that man should conform even to the most beneficent movements or institutions?

Traditionalists would dispose of such questions by restoring a society that would not raise them. Many of them have made efforts to revive and strengthen religious values and practices. Churches have again been crowded, particularly in the United States. Some conservatives and even liberals have traced modern ills to the influence of the masses and harked back to happier times before the rise of modern democracy in the nineteenth century. They have refurbished the doctrines of social discipline and restraint of the old critics of the American and French Revolutions. However, the attempt to find a viable alternative to liberal democracy and to refresh conservatism by original ideas has languished. New political philosophies are not easy to come by.

The dilemma of German conservatives has been particularly painful. Their terrible defeat has touched the pride of Germans to the quick and called into question their view of themselves, of their past, and of their relations to other peoples. The dominant culture of Germany has placed great weight on the

"The Future, as beheld by the Eighteenth, the Nineteenth, and the Twentieth Centuries," by Sir Max Beerbohm. From Observations, *London, 1925.*

importance of continuous historical evolution and on the distinction of the German character. From this viewpoint, Hitlerism appeared as the inevitable result of the whole development of the country and as the latest embodiment of the national "genius," or *Geist.* This conclusion has been naturally unacceptable to German thinking. Yet it has been difficult to abandon old ways of thought which had drawn a line between the German and the Western spirit. The catastrophe has had the effect of dulling rather than stimulating the mind of survivors. There has been a pervasive tendency to treat the experience of Hitlerism as a hiatus in national evolution and to spare the young the knowledge of it. Yet Germans are sensitive to their isolation. For, in the world at large, the old admiration of their country's achievements in science, learning, industry, and strategy has been qualified by the horrors aroused by her recent deeds, especially among the neighboring peoples who have suffered the most from them. Germany is a problem to herself as well as to others.

While conservatives have clung to ancient moorings, others have rejected the very idea of moorings, old or new. Existentialist writers have cut through the supports of ideology, custom, politics, law, and society itself and searched for the root of things in man himself, in his sheer existence. They feel that man confronts alone the ultimate questions of life at every moment, even the most trivial; he cannot stand aside but must commit himself, assume responsibility, and act; and there is no one, and no thing, to help him. His condition is not only tragic but also "absurd": even though his fate is that of his fellows, he is impotent to communicate with them. Existentialism has matched the temper of a time that has gone beyond mere disillusionment.

Between existentialists and conservatives, between those whose world is made up of isolated individuals and those who would ensconce men in a tight

organic community, the advocates of a rational life in a free society have been traveling a lonely road. The attacks upon them have been accumulating for a long time. Throughout the nineteenth century, conservative romantics and Hegelians of the Right fought them in the name of emotion, instinct, custom, and historical evolution. In the twentieth century came fiercer enemies: worshipers of the violent deed and the intemperate will who made men the prey of overwhelming forces and of self-appointed "supermen," first in theory and then in sober fact.

These attacks have placed rationalists on the defensive. Have they not lacked the "tragic sense" that might have forearmed them against the evils lurking in man and society? And if experience has made them more wary, other difficulties seem inherent in the structure and temper of contemporary life. The growth in the scale and complexity of economic and political organizations is inhibiting freedom of choice and rational control. The successes of industrial production and of mechanization have obscured the distinction between the instruments of life and its goals. The absorption with the irrational, with the unconscious, has weakened the view of man as a purposive, moral, and social being.

Yet there is no turning the clock back. The exploration of the dark recesses of the human soul, the intermingling of state and society, the absorption with industrial activities, these are ineluctable accompaniments of contemporary civilization. They have altered beyond recall the atmosphere in which the liberal ideal was born and flourished. There is all the greater need—if man is not to abandon himself to mysterious and mechanical forces—to assert the function of deliberation, to refresh civic energy, and to end the confusion between tools and aims. What other way holds greater hope for physical survival, cultural coherence, and—though the word has fallen under a cloud—progress? And so, although Western men often feel like wanderers

> . . . between two worlds, one dead,
> The other powerless to be born. . . .

they know in their hearts that their fate is bound up with the survival of their values. And not only their own fate. Asians and Africans are appealing to the principles of liberty and equality. And if hypocrisy is the homage that vice pays to virtue, the promise of the Communists to achieve a free society in the future testifies to the excellence of the great ideal.

After much travail and many experiments with violent alternatives, reason and morality, practiced under conditions of freedom, remain, more than ever, man's best hope.

A Reading List

This reading list is highly selective. With few exceptions, it consists of books in the English language, usually in recent editions published in the United States. The titles have been grouped in three sections. Section A contains reference works and general works dealing with the history of Europe and the United States in the last two centuries, with large topics or regions, and with the history of individual countries. Section B lists books on the relations and mutual influences of Europe and America. Section C follows the arrangement of the present work and consists of books pertinent to each of its seven parts. (The subheadings under the parts are general topics and not chapter titles.) In the case of older works which were influential in their own time, the place and year of original publication have been given, as well as the place and date of the latest publication in English, preferably in the United States.

SECTION A

General Works

G. N. Clark et al., eds., *The new Cambridge modern history*, 5 vols. to date (Cambridge, Eng., 1957-)

H. A. L. Fisher, *A history of Europe*, 3 vols. (Boston, 1939)

E. Fueter, *World history, 1815-1920* (New York, 1922)

L. Halphen and P. Sagnac, eds., *Peuples et civilisations*, 20 vols. (Paris, 1926-)

W. L. Langer, ed., *The rise of modern Europe*, 10 vols. (New York, 1934-52)

————, ed., *An encyclopedia of world history* (Boston, 1956)

E. Lavisse and A. Rambaud, eds., *Histoire générale*, 12 vols. (Paris, 1893-1904)

A. W. Ward et al., eds., *Cambridge modern history*, 14 vols. (New York, 1902-11)

Thought, Science, and Art

E. Barker, *Political thought in England from Herbert Spencer to the present day* (New York, 19.15)

L. Barnett, *The universe and Dr. Einstein* (New York, 1957)

M. Beer, *History of British socialism*, 2 vols. (London, 1929)

G. Brandes, *Main currents in nineteenth-century literature*, 6 vols. (New York, 1905-23)

C. Brinton, *Ideas and men* (New York, 1950)

J. Bronowski and B. Mazlish, *The Western intellectual tradition* (New York, 1960)

A. M. Carr-Saunders and P. A. Wilson, *Professions: their organization and place in society* (London, 1928)

C. T. Chase, *The evolution of modern physics* (New York, 1947)

F. W. Coker, *Recent political thought* (New York, 1934)

S. H. Cross, *Slavic civilization through the ages* (Cambridge, Mass., 1948)

F. Delaisi, *Political myths and economic realities* (New York, 1927)

K. Francke, *A history of German literature as determined by social forces* (New York, 1931)

H. Gardner, *Art through the ages*, 4th ed. (New York, 1959)

H. A. R. Gibb, *Mohammedanism* (New York, 1949)

E. H. Gombrich, *The story of art* (New York, 1950)

C. G. Haines, *The revival of natural law concepts* (Cambridge, Mass., 1930)

A. F. Hattersley, *Short history of democracy* (Cambridge, Eng., 1930)

A. Hauser, *The social history of art*, 2 vols. (New York, 1951)

J. A. Hawgood, *Modern constitutions since 1787* (London 1939)

C. J. H. Hayes, *Historical evolution of modern nationalism* (New York, 1931)

F. J. C. Hearnshaw, ed., *The social and political ideas of some representative thinkers of the Victorian age* (London, 1933)

H. Höffding, *A history of modern philosophy*, 2 vols. (New York, 1950)

H. Kohn, *The idea of nationalism* (New York, 1944)

———, *Pan-Slavism* (Notre Dame, Ind., 1953)

H. J. Laski, *The rise of European liberalism* (New York, 1947)

W. E. H. Lecky. *History of the rise and influence of the spirit of rationalism in Europe*, 2 vols. (New York, 1866)

A. O. Lovejoy, *The great chain of being* (New York, 1960)

J. T. Merz, *A history of European thought in the nineteenth century*, 4 vols. (London, 1903-14)

J. H. Randall, *Making of the modern mind* (New York, 1940)

J. M. Robertson, *Short history of free thought*, 2 vols. (London, 1936)

G. de Ruggiero, *The history of European liberalism* (Boston, 1959)

B. Russell, *A history of Western philosophy* (New York, 1945)

G. H. Sabine, *A history of political theory* (New York, 1958)

H. W. Schneider, *A history of American philosophy* (New York, 1946)

H. Semat, *Physics in the modern world* (New York, 1949)

R. H. Soltau, *French political thought in the nineteenth century* (New Haven, Conn., 1931)

D. D. Somervell, *English thought in the nineteenth century* (London, 1948)

F. S. Taylor, *A short history of science and scientific thought* (New York, 1949)

J. A. Thomson, *Modern science* (New York, 1929)

A. N. Whitehead, *Science and the modern world* (New York, 1926)

E. Wilson, *Axel's castle: a study of the imaginative literature of 1870-1930* (New York, 1954)

G. M. Young, *Victorian England* (London, 1954)

Economic and Social Movements

P. W. L. Ashley, *Modern tariff history: Germany, United States, France* (London, 1920)

T. S. Ashton, *The industrial revolution, 1760-1830* (London, 1948)

M. Beard, *A history of the business man* (New York, 1938)

———, *Woman as a force in history: a study in traditions and realities* (New York, 1946)

A. A. Berle, Jr., and G. C. Means, *The modern corporation and private property* (New York, 1932)

W. Bowden, M. Karpovich, and A. P. Usher, *An economic history of Europe since 1750* (New York, 1937)

W. F. Brook, *Social and economic history of Germany from William II to Hitler, 1888-1938* (London, 1938)

D. L. Burn, *Economic history of steel-making, 1867-1939* (New York, 1940)

A. M. Carr-Saunders, *World population: past growth and present trends* (New York, 1936)

J. H. Clapham, *The economic development of France and Germany, 1815-1914*, 3rd ed. (Cambridge, Eng., 1936)

———, *Economic history of modern Britain*, 3 vols. (New York, 1931-32)

W. E. Clark, *The trust problem* (New York, 1929)

G. D. H. Cole, *A short history of the British working class movement*, 3 vols. (London, 1925-27)

M. Dobb, *Studies in the development of capitalism* (New York, 1947)

R. J. Forbes, *Man the maker: a history of technology and engineering* (New York, 1958)

C. E. Gibson, *Story of the ship* (New York, 1958)

C. Gide and C. Rist, *History of economic doctrines* (London, 1948)

S. Giedion, *Mechanization takes command* (New York, 1948)

N. S. B. Gras, *A history of agriculture in Europe and America* (New York, 1940)

———, *Business and capitalism: an introduction to business history* (New York, 1939)

H. Heaton, *Economic history of Europe* (New York, 1948)

J. A. Hobson, *Evolution of modern capitalism* (New York, 1949)

K. Hutchinson, *The decline and fall of British capitalism* (New York, 1950)

L. H. Jenks, *The migration of British capital to 1875* (New York, 1938)

M. M. Knight et al., *Economic history of Europe* (New York, 1928)

L. C. A. Knowles, *The industrial and commercial revolutions in Great Britain during the nineteenth century*, 4th rev. ed. (New York, 1926)

E. M. Kulischer, *Europe on the move: war and population changes, 1917-1947* (New York, 1948)

H. W. Laidler, *Social-economic movements: a historical and comparative survey of socialism, communism, cooperation, utopianism* (New York, 1944)

V. R. Lorwin, *The French labor movement* (Cambridge, Mass., 1955)

N. Mackenzie, *Socialism* (New York, 1950)

P. Mantoux, *The industrial revolution in the eighteenth century* (New York, 1928)

S. T. McCloy, *French inventions of the 18th century* (Lexington, Ky., 1952)

A. Nevins and J. Mirsky, *The world of Eli Whitney* (New York, 1952)

F. L. Nussbaum, *History of the economic institutions of modern Europe* (New York, 1933)

S. Perlman, *Theory of the labor movement* (New York, 1949)

J. E. T. Rogers, *Six centuries of work and wages* (London, 1912)

J. A. Schumpeter, *Capitalism, socialism and democracy* (New York, 1942)

H. E. Sée, *The economic interpretation of history* (New York, 1929)

A. Shadwell, *The socialist movement, 1824-1924* (London, 1925)

G. Stolper, *German economy, 1870-1940* (New York, 1940)

D. R. Taft, *International migrations: the immigrant in the modern world* (New York, 1955)

H. D. Traill and J. S. Mann, eds., *Social England*, 6 vols. (New York, 1909)

A. P. Usher, *A history of mechanical inventions* (Cambridge, Mass., 1954)

T. Veblen, *Imperial Germany and the industrial revolution* (New York, 1939)

S. and B. Webb, *History of trade unionism* (New York, 1920)

W. F. Willcox, ed., *International migrations*, 2 vols. (New York, 1929)

W. S. and E. S. Woytinsky, *World population and production* (New York, 1953)

Diplomacy and Military Affairs

E. M. Earle, ed., *Makers of modern strategy* (Princeton, 1943)

J. F. C. Fuller, *A military history of the Western world*, 3 vols. (New York, 1954-56)

A. T. Mahan, *The influence of sea power upon history, 1660-1783* (Boston, 1890; New York, 1957)

J. A. R. Marriott, *The Eastern question* (New York, 1940)

R. B. Mowat, *A history of European diplomacy, 1815-1932* (New York, 1927)

H. Nicolson, *Diplomacy* (New York, 1950)

E. A. Pratt, *Rise of rail power in war and conquest, 1833-1914* (London, 1915)

R. J. Sontag, *European diplomatic history, 1871-1932* (New York, 1933)

W. O. Stevens and A. Westcott, *A history of sea power* (New York, 1944)

G. B. Turner, ed., *A history of military affairs since the eighteenth century* (New York, 1956)

A. Vagts, *A history of militarism* (New York, 1959)

Encyclopedias, Bibliographies, and Atlases

Catholic encyclopedia, 16 vols. (New York, 1907-14)
Collier's encyclopedia, 20 vols. (New York, 1960)
Columbia encyclopedia (New York, 1950-59)
Dictionary of American biography, 22 vols. (New York, 1928-58)
Dictionary of [British] national biography, 21 vols. and suppl. (New York, 1921-59)
Encyclopedia of American history, R. B. Morris, ed. (New York, 1953)
Encyclopaedia Britannica, 24 vols. (New York, 1960)
Encyclopaedia of Islam, 4 vols. and suppl. (Leyden, 1913-38)
Encyclopaedia of the social sciences, 8 vols. (New York, 1948)
Jewish encyclopedia, 12 vols. (New York, 1901-06)
New international encyclopaedia, 25 vols. (New York, 1925-30)
Webster's biographical dictionary (Springfield, Mass., 1957)
American Universities Field Staff, *A select bibliography on Asia, Africa, Eastern Europe, and Latin America* (New York, 1960)
A. Bullock and A. J. P. Taylor, *Select list of books on European history, 1815-1914* (Oxford, 1957)
E. M. Coulter and M. Gerstenfeld, *Historical bibliographies* (Berkeley, Cal., 1915)
F. C. Dahlmann and G. Waitz, *Quellenkunde der Deutschen Geschichte* (Leipzig, 1931)
G. M. Dutcher et al., *A guide to historical literature* (New York, 1931)
G. P. Gooch, *Bibliography of European history, 1918-1939* (London, 1940)
O. Handlin et al., *Harvard Guide to American history* (Cambridge, Mass., 1955)
International bibliography of the historical sciences (Paris, 1926-   )
R. J. Kerner, *Slavic Europe: a selected bibliography in the Western European languages...* (Cambridge, Mass., 1918)
A. G. Mazour, *An outline of modern Russian historiography* (Berkeley, Cal., 1939)

J. T. Adams, *Atlas of American history* (New York, 1943)
Lippincott's new gazeteer (Philadelphia, 1952)
C. L. and E. H. Lord, *Historical atlas of the United States* (New York, 1953)
Muir's historical atlas: medieval and modern (New York, 1956)
R. R. Palmer, *Atlas of world history* (New York, 1957)
C. O. Paullin, *Atlas of the historical geography of the United States* (New York, 1932)
C. G. Robertson and J. G. Bartholomew, *An historical atlas of modern Europe from 1789 to 1922* (London, 1924)
W. R. Shepherd, *Historical atlas* (New York, 1956)
Webster's geographical dictionary (Springfield, Mass., 1955)
Westermanns Atlas zur Weltgeschichte (Brunswick, West Germany, 1956)

Documents

A. Baltzly and A. W. Salomone, *Readings in twentieth-century European history* (New York, 1950)

F. L. Baumer, *Main currents of Western thought* (New York, 1952)

Columbia University, *Introduction to contemporary civilization in the West*, 2 vols. (New York, 1960)

H. S. Commager, *Documents of American history* (New York, 1958)

A. L. Funk, *Source problems in twentieth-century history* (New York, 1953)

G. H. Knoles and R. K. Snyder, *Readings in Western civilization* (Philadelphia, 1960)

M. R. Konvitz, *Bill of Rights reader* (Ithaca, N. Y., 1960)

W. C. Langsam, *Documents and readings in the history of Europe since 1918* (Philadelphia, 1951)

R. W. Leopold and A. S. Link, *Problems in American history* (New York, 1957)

T. C. Mendenhall et al., *Six problems in historical interpretation* (New York, 1952)

J. F. Scott and A. Baltzly, *Readings in modern and contemporary history* (New York, 1934)

K. M. Setton and H. R. Winkler, *Great problems in European civilization* (New York, 1954)

R. P. Stearns, *Pageant of Europe: sources and selections from the Renaissance to the present day* (New York, 1961)

D. O. Wagner, *Social reformers* (New York, 1934)

European Countries

R. Albrecht-Carrié, *Italy from Napoleon to Mussolini* (New York, 1950)

C. T. Atkinson, *Germany, 1715-1815* (London, 1908)

J. C. Beckett, *A short history of Ireland* (London, 1952)

P. J. Block, *History of the people of the Netherlands*, 5 vols. (New York, 1898-1912)

E. Bourgeois, *History of modern France, 1815-1913*, 2 vols. (Cambridge, Eng., 1919)

C. E. Carrington, *The British overseas: exploits of a nation of shopkeepers* (New York, 1950)

C. U. Clark, *United Roumania* (New York, 1932)

G. D. H. Cole and R. Postgate, *The British people, 1746-1946* (New York, 1947)

G. A. Craig, *The politics of the Prussian army, 1640-1945* (New York, 1955)

B. Croce, *History of Italy, 1871-1915* (Oxford, 1929)

S. M. Dubnow, *History of the Jews in Russia and Poland*, 3 vols. (Philadelphia, 1916-20)

R. Dyboski, *Outlines of Polish history* (London, 1931)

S. B. Fay, *The rise of Brandenburg-Prussia to 1786* (New York, 1937)

R. Flenley, *Modern German history* (New York, 1959)

E. S. Forster, *Short history of modern Greece, 1821-1956* (Hollywood-by-the-Sea, Fla., 1959)

F. A. Golder, *Russian expansion on the Pacific, 1641-1850* (Cleveland, O., 1914)

C. A. Gulick, *Austria from Hapsburg to Hitler*, 2 vols. (Berkeley, Cal., 1948)

E. Halévy, *History of the English people in the nineteenth century*, 5 vols. (London, 1949-52)

C. Hallendorff and A. Schück, *History of Sweden* (New York, 1929)

B. J. Hovde, *Scandinavian countries, 1720-1865*, 2 vols. (Ithaca, N.Y., 1948)

M. M. Karpovich, *Imperial Russia* (New York, 1932)

V. O. Kluchevsky, *A history of Russia*, 5 vols. (London, 1960)

P. Knaplund, *The British empire, 1815-1939* (New York, 1942)

E. J. Knapton, *France since Versailles* (New York, 1952)

H. Kohn, ed., *The mind of modern Russia* (New Brunswick, N. J., 1955)

A. A. Kornilov, *Modern Russian history*, 2 vols. (New York, 1924)

D. G. Kosáry, *A history of Hungary* (New York, 1941)

K. Larsen, *History of Norway* (Princeton, 1948)

E. Lavisse, ed., *Histoire de France contemporaine*, 10 vols. (Paris, 1920-22)

W. E. H. Lecky, *A history of England in the eighteenth century*, 7 vols. (New York, 1892-93)

H. van der Linden, *Belgium* (Oxford, 1920)

J. A. R. Marriott and C. G. Robertson, *The evolution of Prussia* (Oxford, 1946)

T. G. Masaryk, *Spirit of Russia*, 2 vols. (New York, 1955)

J. Mavor, *An economic history of Russia*, 2 vols. (New York, 1925)

P. Miliukov, *Outlines of Russian culture*, 3 vols. (Philadelphia, 1942)

W. Miller, *Ottoman empire and its successors, 1801-1927* (New York, 1936)

W. S. Monroe, *Bulgaria and her people* (Boston, 1914)

F. K. Nielsen, *The history of the papacy in the 19th century*, 2 vols. (London, 1906)

W. Oechsli, *History of Switzerland* (Cambridge, Eng., 1922)

Oxford history of England, 11 vols. (Oxford, 1936-56)

L. von Pastor, *History of the popes*, 40 vols. (London, 1906-53)

W. F. Reddaway et al., *The Cambridge history of Poland*, 2 vols. (Cambridge, 1941-50)

G. T. Robinson, *Rural Russia under the old régime* (New York, 1949)

J. H. Rose et al., eds., *The Cambridge history of the British empire*, 8 vols. (New York, 1929-40)

F. Schevill, *The history of the Balkan peninsula* (New York, 1933)

R. W. Seton-Watson, *A history of the Roumanians* (Cambridge, Eng., 1934)

R. H. Soltau, *French parties and politics* (London, 1930)

A. J. P. Taylor, *The course of German history* (New York, 1946)

——, *The Hapsburg monarchy, 1809-1918* (London, 1948)

H. Temperley, *Serbia* (London, 1917)

G. M. Trevelyan, *British history in the 19th century and after* (London, 1938)

E. R. Turner, *Ireland and England* (New York, 1919)

V. Valentin, *The German people* (New York, 1946)

A. W. Ward, *Germany, 1815-1890*, 3 vols. (Cambridge, Eng., 1916-18)

A. W. Ward and G. P. Gooch, eds., *The Cambridge history of British foreign policy, 1783-1919*, 3 vols. (New York, 1922-23)

A. J. B. White, *The making of modern Italy* (New York, 1944)

A. Yarmolinsky, *Road to revolution: a century of Russian radicalism* (London, 1957)

The Eastern World

D. Bernstein, *The Philippine story* (New York, 1947)

J. K. Fairbank, *The United States and China* (Cambridge, Mass., 1958)

L. Fischer, *The life of Mahatma Gandhi* (New York, 1953)

W. K. Fraser-Tytler, *Afghanistan* (New York, 1950)

L. C. Goodrich, *A short history of the Chinese people* (New York, 1959)

G. A. Grunder and W. E. Livezey, *The Philippines and the United States* (Norman, Okla., 1951)

O. Hardy and G. S. Dumke, *A history of the Pacific in modern times* (Boston, 1949)

B. Harrison, *South-East Asia* (New York, 1954)

H. B. Hulbert, *The history of Korea*, 2 vols. (New York, 1960)

H. M. Hyndman, *Awakening of Asia* (New York, 1919)

D. H. James, *The rise and fall of the Japanese empire* (New York, 1951)

G. E. Kirk, *Short history of the Middle East* (New York, 1955)

H. Kohn, *Nationalism and imperialism in the Hither East* (New York, 1932)

K. S. Latourette, *A history of modern China* (Baltimore, 1954)

————, *The Chinese*, 2 vols. (New York, 1946)

H. G. Rawlinson, *A concise history of the Indian people* (London, 1938)

————, *India* (New York, 1955)

E. O. Reischauer, *Japan: past and present* (New York, 1946)

————, *The United States and Japan* (Cambridge, Mass., 1950)

G. D. Sanderson, *India and British imperialism* (New York, 1951)

G. B. Sansom, *Japan* (New York, 1943)

————, *The Western world and Japan* (New York, 1959)

P. Talbot and S. L. Poplai, *India and America: a study of their relations* (New York, 1958)

G. E. Taylor and F. H. Michael, *The Far East in the modern world* (New York, 1956)

H. M. Vinacke, *A history of the Far East in modern times* (New York, 1959)

B. Vlekke, *The story of the Dutch East Indies* (Cambridge, Mass., 1945)

The United States

C. A. and M. R. Beard, *The rise of American civilization* (New York, 1956)

R. A. Billington, *The Protestant crusade, 1800-1860* (New York, 1938)

————, *The westward movement* (New York, 1949)

J. Bryce, *The American commonwealth*, 2 vols. (London, 1888; New York, 1931-33)

E. Channing, *History of the United States*, 6 vols. (New York, 1927-30)

Chronicles of America, 50 vols. (New Haven, 1918-21)

J. C. Collier, *Indians of the Americas* (New York, 1947)

W. E. B. Du Bois, *The suppression of the African slave trade to the United States of America, 1638-1870* (New York, 1896)

M. Curti, *The growth of American thought* (New York, 1951)

J. Dorfman, *The economic mind in American civilization*, 5 vols. (New York, 1946-59)

H. U. Faulkner, *American economic history* (New York, 1960)

J. H. Franklin, *From slavery to freedom: a history of American Negroes* (New York, 1956)

R. H. Gabriel, *The course of American democratic thought* (New York, 1956)

R. L. Garis, *Immigration restriction* (New York, 1927)

O. Handlin, *The uprooted* (Boston, 1951)

M. L. Hansen, *The Atlantic migration, 1607-1860* (Cambridge, Mass., 1940)

———, *The immigrant in American history* (Cambridge, Mass., 1940)

J. A. Hawgood, *The tragedy of German-America* (New York, 1940)

B. H. Hibbard, *A history of public land policies* (New York, 1939)

J. Higham, *Strangers in the land* (New Brunswick, N. J., 1955)

M. Hillquit, *History of socialism in the United States* (New York, 1910)

H. L. Mencken, *The American language*, 3 vols. (New York, 1936-48)

S. E. Morison and H. S. Commager, *The growth of the American republic*, 2 vols. (New York, 1950)

G. Myrdal, *An American dilemma: the Negro problem and modern deomocracy*, 2 vols. (New York, 1944)

M. Ostrogorskii, *Democracy and the organization of political parties*, 2 vols. (New York, 1908)

V. L. Parrington, *Main currents in American thought*, 3 vols. (New York, 1939)

F. L. Paxson, *A history of the American frontier, 1763-1893* (Boston, 1924)

S. Perlman, *History of trade unionism in the United States* (New York, 1922)

R. B. Perry, *Puritanism and democracy* (New York, 1944)

K. Porter, *A history of suffrage in the United States* (Chicago, 1918)

A. M. Schlesinger and D. R. Fox, eds., *A history of American life*, 13 vols. (New York, 1927-44)

H. E. Stearns, ed., *Civilization in the United States* (New York, 1922)

F. J. Turner, *The frontier in American history* (New York, 1959)

———, *Rise of the new West* (New York, 1959)

W. P. Webb, *The great frontier*, (Boston, 1952)

C. Wittke, *We who built America* (New York, 1939)

L. B. Wright, *The Atlantic frontier: colonial American civilization, 1607-1763* (Ithaca, N.Y., 1959)

SECTION B

Relations Between Europe and America

B. P. Adams, ed., *You Americans* (New York, 1939)

M. Arnold, *Civilization in the United States* (Boston, 1900)

A. M. Babey, *Americans in Russia, 1776-1917* (New York, 1938)

T. A. Bailey, *America faces Russia: Russian-American relations from early times to our day* (Ithaca, N. Y., 1950)

F. C. Barghoorn, *The Soviet image of the United States* (New York, 1950)

M. Berger, *The British traveller in America, 1836-1860* (New York, 1943)

J. B. Botsford, *English society in the eighteenth century as influenced from overseas* (New York, 1924)

P. Bourget, *Outre-Mer: impressions of America* (New York, 1895)

J. B. Brebner, *North Atlantic triangle: the interplay of Canada, the United States, and Great Britain* (New Haven, 1945)

D. W. Brogan, *The American character* (New York, 1950)

J. G. Brooks, *As others see us: a study of progress in the United States* (New York, 1908)

H. C. Bush, *British press and parliamentary opinion about the United States and the Soviet Union, 1946-1950* (Univ. of Chicago thesis, unpublished, 1954)

M. Chevalier, *Lettres sur l'Amérique du Nord* (extracts) (Princeton, 1944)

———, *Society, manners and politics in the United States* (Boston, 1839)

S. L. Clemens, *The innocents abroad* (New York, 1869, 1959)

H. S. Commager, *America in perspective: the United States through foreign eyes* (New York, 1947)

A. Cooke, *One man's America* (New York, 1952)

M. G. Jean de Crèvecœur, *Letters from an American farmer* (London, 1782; New York, 1951)

M. Curti, *Austria and the United States* (Northampton, Mass., 1926)

J. De Onís, *The United States as seen by Spanish-American writers, 1776-1890* (New York, 1952)

C. Dickens, *American notes* (London, 1842; New York, 1957)

G. Duhamel, *America the menace* (New York, 1931)

D. Echeverria, *Mirage in the West: a history of the French image of American society to 1815* (Princeton, 1957)

B. Faÿ, *The American experiment* (New York, 1929)

———, *The revolutionary spirit in France and America* (New York, 1927)

A. Feiler, *America seen through German eyes* (New York, 1928)

Y. Ffrench, ed., *Transatlantic exchanges: cross currents of Anglo-American opinion in the nineteenth century* (New York, 1952)

C. Gohdes, *American literature in nineteenth-century England* (New York, 1944)

G. S. Gordon, *Anglo-American literary relations* (New York, 1942)

O. Handlin, *This was America* (Cambridge, Mass., 1949)

D. Hecht, *Russian radicals look to America, 1825-1894* (Cambridge, Mass., 1947)

R. H. Heindel, *The American impact on Great Britain, 1898-1914: a study of the United States in world history* (Philadelphia, 1940)

H. M. Jones, *America and French culture, 1750-1848* (Chapel Hill, N.C., 1927)

P. Kalm, *The America of 1750* (Stockholm, 1753; New York, 1937)

R. Kipling, *American notes* (Boston, 1899)

A. L. Klinkowström, *America, 1818-1820* (Stockholm, 1824; Evanston, Ill., 1952)

G. H. Knoles, *The jazz age revisited: British criticism of American civilization during the 1920's* (Stanford, Cal., 1955)

H. Koht, *The American spirit in Europe: a survey of transatlantic influences* (Philadelphia, 1949)

M. Kraus, *The Atlantic civilization: eighteenth century origins* (Ithaca, N.Y., 1949)

M. M. Laserson, *The American impact on Russia: diplomatic and ideological, 1784-1917* (New York, 1950)

G. D. Lillibridge, *Beacon of freedom: the impact of American democracy upon Great Britain, 1830-1870* (Philadelphia, 1955)

H. Martineau, *Retrospect of Western travel*, 2 vols. (New York, 1838)

————, *Society in America*, 2 vols. (London, 1837)

J. L. Mesick, *The English traveller in America, 1785-1835* (New York, 1922)

F. Monaghan, *French travellers in the United States, 1765-1932* (New York, 1933)

R. B. Mowat, *Americans in England* (Boston, 1935)

H. Münsterberg, *American traits from the point of view of a German* (Boston, 1902)

A. Nevins, ed., *America through British eyes* (New York, 1948)

R. R. Palmer, *The age of the democratic revolution: a political history of Europe and America, 1760-1800* (Princeton, 1959)

S. Putnam, *Paris was our mistress* (New York, 1947)

P. Rahv, ed., *Discovery of Europe: the story of American experience in the Old World* (New York, 1947)

W. L. Sachse, *The colonial American in Britain* (Madison, Wis., 1956)

G. Santayana, *Character and opinion in the United States* (New York, 1956)

A. Siegfried, *America comes of age* (New York, 1927)

R. E. Spiller, *The American in England during the first half century of independence* (New York, 1926)

W. T. Spoerri, *The Old World and the New: a synopsis of current European ideas on American civilization* (New York, 1937)

W. Stark, *America, ideal and reality: the United States of 1776 in contemporary European philosophy* (London, 1947)

F. Thistlethwaite, *The Anglo-American connection in the early 19th century* (Philadelphia, 1959)

A. de Tocqueville, *Democracy in America*, 2 vols. (Paris, 1835-40; New York, 1954)

F. Trollope, *Domestic manners of the Americans* (London, 1832; New York, 1949)

E. B. White, *American opinion of France* (New York, 1927)

E. Wilson, *Travels in two democracies, 1932-1935* (New York, 1936)

SECTION C

I. The Failure of the Old Regime

THE OLD REGIME

C. M. Andrews, *The colonial period of American history*, 3 vols. (New Haven, 1934-37)

E. G. Barber, *The bourgeoisie in eighteenth-century France* (Princeton, 1955)

G. Beer, *British colonial policy, 1754-1765* (New York, 1933)

W. H. Bruford, *Germany in the 18th century: the social background of the literary revival* (New York, 1935)

A. H. Buffington, *The second Hundred Years' War, 1689-1815* (New York, 1929)

A. M. Davies, *Clive of Plassey* (London, 1939)

H. Dodwell, *Dupleix and Clive: the beginning of empire* (London, 1920)

W. L. Dorn, *Competition for empire, 1740-1763* (New York, 1940)

F. L. Ford, *Robe and sword: the regrouping of the French aristocracy after Louis XIV* (Cambridge, Mass., 1953)

L. Gershoy, *From despotism to revolution, 1763-1789* (New York, 1944)

L. H. Gipson, *The British empire before the American Revolution* (New York, 1958)

A. Goodwin, ed., *The European nobility of the eighteenth century* (London, 1953)

E. F. Heckscher, *Mercantilism*, 2 vols. (New York, 1956)

E. J. Lowell, *Eve of the French Revolution* (New York, 1934)

L. B. Namier, *The structure of politics at the accession of George III*, 2 vols. (New York, 1957)

C. P. Nettels, *The roots of American civilization* (New York, 1938)

S. K. Padover, *The revolutionary emperor: Joseph the Second, 1741-90* (London, 1934)

R. Pares, *War and trade in the West Indies, 1739-1763* (Oxford, 1936)

P. Roberts, *The quest for security, 1715-1740* (New York, 1947)

G. F. von Schmoller, *The mercantile system and its historical significance* (New York, 1897)

H. Sée, *Economic and social conditions in France during the 18th century* (New York, 1927)

A. Small, *The Cameralists* (Chicago, 1909)

A. Sorel, *The Eastern question in the 18th century* (London, 1898)

———, *Europe under the old régime* (Los Angeles, 1947)

A. de Tocqueville, *The old régime* (Paris, 1856; New York, 1947)

THE ENLIGHTENMENT

E. Barker, ed., *Social contract: essays by Locke, Hume, and Rousseau* (New York, 1952)

C. Becker, *The heavenly city of the eighteenth-century philosophers* (New Haven, 1959)

C. Brinton, ed., *The portable Age of Reason* (New York, 1956)

E. Cassirer, *The philosophy of the Enlightenment* (Boston, 1959)

A. Cobban, *Rousseau and the modern state* (London, 1934)

D. Dakin, *Turgot and the ancien régime in France* (London, 1939)

H. N. Fairchild, *The noble savage* (New York, 1928)

P. Hazard, *The European mind* (London, 1953)

————, *European thought in the eighteenth century* (London, 1954)

F. J. C. Hearnshaw, ed., *The social and political ideas of some French thinkers of the Age of Reason* (London, 1930)

H. Higgs, *The Physiocrats* (New York, 1952)

K. Martin, *French liberal thought in the eighteenth century* (London, 1954)

D. Mornet, *French thought in the eighteenth century* (New York, 1929)

R. B. Mowat, *The Age of Reason* (New York, 1934)

P. Smith, *History of modern culture*, 2 vols. (New York, 1930-34)

N. Torrey, *The spirit of Voltaire* (New York, 1938)

THE AMERICAN REVOLUTION AND ITS IMPACT ON EUROPE

J. R. Alden, *The American Revolution, 1775-1783* (New York, 1954)

C. L. Becker, *The Declaration of Independence* (New York, 1942)

M. Beloff, ed., *The debate on the American Revolution* (London, 1959)

S. F. Bemis, *The diplomatic history of the American Revolution* (New York, 1955)

D. M. Clark, *British opinion and the American Revolution* (New Haven, 1930)

E. S. Corwin, *French policy and the American alliance of 1778* (Princeton, 1916)

M. Farrand, ed., *Records of the Federal Convention of 1787*, 4 vols. (New Haven, 1911-37)

————, *The framing of the Constitution of the United States* (New Haven, 1913)

L. H. Gipson, *The coming of the Revolution, 1763-1775* (New York, 1954)

C. S. Graham, *Empire of the North Atlantic: the maritime struggle for North America* (Toronto, 1950)

W. Havighurst, *Land of promise: the story of the Northwest Territory* (New York, 1946)

J. F. Jameson, *The American Revolution considered as a social movement* (Boston, 1956)

M. Jensen, *The new nation* (New York, 1950)

J. Madison, J. Jay, and A. Hamilton, *The Federalist* (New York, 1787-88; various editions)

C. H. McIlwain, *The American Revolution: a constitutional interpretation* (Ithaca, N.Y., 1958)

J. C. Miller, *Origins of the American Revolution* (Stanford, Cal., 1959)

L. B. Namier, *England in the age of the American Revolution* (London, 1930)

A. Nevins, *The American states during and after the Revolution, 1775-1789* (New York, 1924)

C. R. Ritcheson, *British politics and the American Revolution* (Norman, Okla., 1954)

C. Rossiter, *Seedtime of the Republic: the origin of the American tradition of political liberty* (New York, 1953)

M. Savelle, *Seeds of liberty: the genesis of the American mind* (New York, 1948)

R. L. Schuyler, *The constitution of the United States* (New York, 1952)

W. U. Solberg, *The Federal Convention and the formation of the union of American states* (New York, 1958)

G. O. Trevelyan, *History of the American Revolution*, 4 vols. (New York, 1926-29)

C. H. Van Tyne, *Causes of the War of Independence* (Boston, 1922)

G. M. Wrong, *Canada and the American Revolution* (New York, 1935)

———, *The rise and fall of New France*, 2 vols. (New York, 1928)

II. The Revolutionary Alternatives

THE FRENCH REVOLUTION

F. V. A. Aulard, *Christianity and the French Revolution* (London, 1927)

———, *The French Revolution: a political history, 1789-1804*, 4 vols. (London, 1910)

P. A. Brown, *The French Revolution in English history* (London, 1918)

A. Cobban, ed., *The debate on the French Revolution* (London, 1960)

G. P. Gooch, *Germany and the French Revolution* (New York, 1920)

S. E. Harris, *The Assignats* (Cambridge, Mass., 1930)

C. D. Hazen, *Contemporary American opinion of the French Revolution* (Baltimore, 1897)

F. J. C. Hearnshaw, ed., *The social and political ideas of some representative thinkers of the revolutionary era* (London, 1931)

S. Herbert, *The fall of feudalism in France* (London, 1921)

E. L. Higgins, *The French Revolution as told by contemporaries* (New York, 1938)

W. B. Kerr, *The reign of terror* (Toronto, 1927)

W. T. Laprade, *England and the French Revolution, 1789-97* (Baltimore, 1909)

G. Lefebvre, *The coming of the French Revolution* (New York, 1957)

L. Madelin, *The French Revolution* (London, 1936)

A. Mathiez, *After Robespierre: the Thermidorian reaction* (New York, 1931)

———, *The French Revolution* (New York, 1928)

R. R. Palmer, *Twelve who ruled* (Princeton, 1941)

G. Salvemini, *The French Revolution, 1788-1792* (New York, 1954)

J. H. Stewart, *A documentary survey of the French Revolution* (New York, 1951)

J. M. Thompson, *The French Revolution* (New York, 1945)

———, *Robespierre*, 2 vols. (New York, 1936)

———, *Robespierre and the French Revolution* (London, 1953)

A. Young, *Travels in France* (London, 1792, 1929)

THE NAPOLEONIC PERIOD

J. B. Brissaud, *History of French private law* (Boston, 1912)

———, *History of French public law* (Boston, 1915)

H. Cachard, trans., *The French civil code* (Paris, 1930)

P. G. Elgood, *Bonaparte's adventure in Egypt* (New York, 1931)

G. S. Ford, *Stein and the era of reform in Prussia* (Princeton, 1922)

A. Fournier, *Napoleon* (New York, 1930)

P. Geyl, *Napoleon: for and against* (New Haven, 1949)

E. F. Heckscher, *The continental system* (New York, 1922)

F. M. Kircheisen, *Napoleon Bonaparte* (New York, 1932)

A. Lobanov-Rostovsky, *Russia and Europe, 1789-1825* (Durham, N.C., 1947)

A. T. Mahan, *The influence of sea power upon the French Revolution and empire, 1793-1812*, 2 vols. (Boston, 1898)

———, *The life of Nelson* (Boston, 1900)

F. E. Melvin, *Napoleon's navigation system: a study of trade control during the continental blockade* (New York, 1919)

R. W. Phipps, *The armies of the First French Republic and the rise of the marshals of Napoleon I*, 5 vols. (London, 1926-39)

J. H. Rose, *Revolutionary and Napoleonic era* (Cambridge, Eng., 1935)

———, *William Pitt and the national revival* (London, 1911)

———, *William Pitt and the great war* (London, 1911)

J. Seeley, *Life and times of Stein, or Germany and Prussia in the Napoleonic age*, 3 vols. (Cambridge, Eng., 1878)

W. O. Shanahan, *Prussian military reforms, 1786-1813* (New York, 1945)

E. V. Tarlé, *Bonaparte* (New York, 1937)

———, *Napoleon's invasion of Russia* (New York, 1942)

H. H. Walsh, *The Concordat of 1801* (New York, 1933)

S. Zweig, *Joseph Fouché* (New York, 1932)

THE CONGRESS OF VIENNA AND EUROPEAN CONSERVATISM

G. Boas, *French philosophies of the romantic period* (Baltimore, 1925)

C. Brinton, *The political ideas of the English romanticists* (London, 1926)

A. Cobban, *Edmund Burke and the revolt against the 18th century: a study of the political and social thinking of Burke, Wordsworth, Coleridge, and Southey* (London, 1929)

W. P. Cresson, *The Holy Alliance: the European background of the Monroe Doctrine* (New York, 1922)

R. R. Ergang, *Herder and the foundations of German nationalism* (New York, 1931)

F. J. C. Hearnshaw, ed., *The social and political ideas of some representative thinkers of the age of reaction and reconstruction* (London, 1932)

H. G. Nicolson, *Congress of Vienna: a study in allied unity, 1812-1822* (New York, 1946)

H. W. V. Temperley, *The foreign policy of Canning* (London, 1925)

C. K. Webster, *The Congress of Vienna, 1814-15* (London, 1934)

———, *The foreign policy of Castlereagh, 1815-22: Britain and the European alliance* (London, 1934)

E. L. Woodward, *Three studies in European conservatism: Metternich, Guizot, the Catholic Church in the 19th century* (London, 1930)

JEFFERSONIANISM AND THE MONROE DOCTRINE

H. Adams, *History of the United States during the administrations of Thomas Jefferson and James Madison*, 4 vols. (New York, 1930)

C. A. Beard, *Economic origins of Jeffersonian democracy* (New York, 1952)

I. Brant, *James Madison*, 5 vols. (New York, 1941-56)

E. Channing, *The Jeffersonian system* (New York, 1906)

G. Chinard, *Thomas Jefferson* (Ann Arbor, Mich., 1957)

A. C. Clauder, *American commerce as affected by the wars of the French Revolution and Napoleon, 1793-1812* (Philadelphia, 1932)

G. Dangerfield, *The Era of Good Feelings* (New York, 1952)

E. W. Lyon, *Louisiana in French diplomacy* (Norman, Okla., 1934)

S. de Madariaga, *The fall of the Spanish American empire* (London, 1948)

D. Malone, *Jefferson and his time*, 2 vols. (1948-51)

D. Perkins, *A history of the Monroe Doctrine* (Boston, 1955)

A. P. Whitaker, *The United States and the independence of Latin America, 1800-1830* (Baltimore, 1941)

III. The European and American Solutions
AND
IV. The Liberal World

REFORM AND IDEALISM

D. G. Barnes, *A history of the English corn laws* (London, 1930)

J. Blum, *Noble landowners and agriculture in Austria, 1815-1848* (Baltimore, 1948)

G. D. H. Cole, *A history of socialist thought*, 5 vols. (New York, 1953-60)

C. R. Fish, *The rise of the common man, 1830-1850* (New York, 1927)

E. Halévy, *The growth of philosophic radicalism* (New York, 1949)

W. O. Henderson, *The Zollverein* (Cambridge, Eng., 1939)

J. O. Hertzler, *History of utopian thought* (New York, 1926)

M. E. Hirst, *The life of Friedrich List* (New York, 1909)

J. S. Mill, *Autobiography* (London, 1873; New York, 1944)

R. E. Riegel, *Young America, 1830-1840* (Norman, Okla., 1949)

R. L. Schuyler, *The fall of the old colonial system: a study in British free trade, 1770-1870* (New York, 1945)

G. M. Trevelyan, *Lord Grey of the Reform Bill* (New York, 1920)

A. F. Tyler, *Freedom's ferment: phases of American social history, to 1860* (Minneapolis, 1944)

NATIONAL MOVEMENTS AND WARS

O. Aubry, *Second empire* (New York, 1940)

G. F. H. Berkeley, *Italy in the making*, 3 vols. (New York, 1933-40)

H. J. Booras, *Hellenic independence and America's contribution to the cause* (Rutland, Vt., 1934)

E. Eyck, *Bismarck and the German empire* (New York, 1950)

H. Friedjung, *The struggle for supremacy in Germany, 1859-1866* (New York, 1935)

K. R. Greenfield, *Economics and liberalism in the Risorgimento* (Baltimore, 1934)

J. A. R. Marriott and C. G. Robertson, *Evolution of Prussia* (Oxford, 1946)

E. S. Mason, *The Paris Commune* (New York, 1930)

A. G. Mazour, *The first Russian revolution, 1825* (Berkeley, Cal., 1937)

W. A. Phillips, *War of Greek independence, 1821-1833* (New York, 1897)

H. M. Stannard, *Gambetta and the founding of the Third Republic* (London, 1921)

H. von Sybel, *The founding of the German empire by William I*, 7 vols. (New York, 1890-98)

W. R. Thayer, *Life and times of Cavour*, 2 vols. (New York, 1914)

J. M. Thompson, *Louis Napoleon and the second empire* (New York, 1955)

1848 — THE GREAT WATERSHED

F. Fejtö, ed., *The opening of an era: 1848* (London, 1948)

K. Marx and F. Engels, *Revolution and counter-revolution in Germany in 1848* (Stuttgart, 1896; New York, 1919)

A. J. May, *Contemporary American opinion of the mid-[nineteenth] century revolutions in Central Europe* (Philadelphia, 1927)

D. C. McKay, *The national workshops: a study of the French Revolution of 1848* (Cambridge, Mass., 1933)

P. Robertson, *Revolutions of 1848* (New York, 1960)

V. Valentin, *1848: chapters of German history* (New York, 1941)

JACKSONIANISM, CIVIL WAR, AND RECONSTRUCTION

E. D. Adams, *Great Britain and the American Civil War*, 2 vols. (New York, 1958)

Lord Charnwood, *Abraham Lincoln* (New York, 1943)

L. A. Coolidge, *Ulysses S. Grant* (Boston, 1924)

E. M. Coulter, *The South during Reconstruction, 1865-1877* (Baton Rouge, La., 1948)

R. N. Current, *Old Thad Stevens* (Madison, Wis., 1942)

W. E. Dodd, *The cotton kingdom* (New Haven, 1921)

C. Eaton, *A history of the old South* (New York, 1952)

C. R. Fish, *The American Civil War* (New York, 1937)

W. P. Garrison and F. Jackson, *William Lloyd Garrison*, 4 vols. (Boston, 1885-89)

M. James, *Andrew Jackson: the border captain* (New York, 1959)

———, *Andrew Jackson: portrait of a president* (New York, 1937)

J. Macy, *The anti-slavery crusade* (New Haven, 1921)

E. J. Pratt and D. Jordan, *Europe and the American Civil War* (New York, 1931)

F. Pratt, *Ordeal by fire: an informal history of the Civil War* (New York, 1948)

J. G. Randall, *Civil War and reconstruction* (New York, 1953)

K. M. Stampp, *The peculiar institution: slavery in the ante-bellum South* (New York, 1956)

H. C. Syrett, *Andrew Jackson* (Indianapolis, 1953)

F. Tannenbaum, *Slave and citizen: the Negro in the Americas* (New York, 1947)

B. P. Thomas, *Abraham Lincoln* (New York, 1952)
F. J. Turner, *The United States, 1830-1850* (New York, 1950)
C. V. Woodward, *Reunion and reaction* (New York, 1956)
H. A. Wyndham, *The Atlantic and slavery* (London, 1935)

V. Steel, Socialism, and Empire

POLITICAL DEVELOPMENTS

J. Bainville, *The French Republic, 1870-1935* (London, 1940)
D. W. Brogan, *France under the Republic: the development of modern France, 1870-1939* (New York, 1940)
G. Chapman, *The Dreyfus case* (New York, 1956)
E. M. Earle, ed., *Modern France* (Princeton, 1951)
O. Jaszi, *The dissolution of the Hapsburg monarchy* (Chicago, 1929)
R. A. Kann, *The multi-national empire: nationalism and national reform in the Hapsburg monarchy, 1848-1918*, 2 vols. (New York, 1950)
P. W. Massing, *Rehearsal for destruction: a study of political anti-Semitism in imperial Germany* (New York, 1949)
A. J. May, *The Hapsburg monarchy, 1867-1914* (Cambridge, Mass., 1951)
D. C. McKay, ed., *The Dreyfus case* (New Haven, 1937)
A. W. Salomone, *Italian democracy in the making, 1900-1914* (Philadelphia, 1945)
R. W. Seton-Watson, *German, Slav, and Magyar* (London, 1916)
———, *The southern Slav question in the Hapsburg monarchy* (London, 1911)
C. V. Woodward, *Origins of the new South, 1877-1913* (Baton Rouge, La., 1951)

SOCIAL REFORM AND RADICALISM

I. Berlin, *Karl Marx* (New York, 1956)
E. Bernstein, *Evolutionary socialism* (New York, 1912)
S. F. Bloom, *The world of nations: a study of the national implications in the work of Karl Marx* (New York, 1941)
R. E. D. Clark, *Darwin* (London, 1948)
G. D. H. Cole, *The meaning of Marxism* (London, 1948)
W. H. Dawson, *German socialism and Ferdinand Lassalle* (New York, 1899)
———, *Social insurance in Germany, 1883-1911* (New York, 1912)
F. Engels, *Socialism, utopian and scientific* (Paris, 1880; New York, 1935)
P. Gay, *The dilemma of democratic socialism* (New York, 1952)
H. George, *Progress and poverty* (San Francisco, 1879; New York, 1954)
E. F. Goldman, *Rendezvous with destiny* (New York, 1952)
J. D. Hicks, *The populist revolt* (Minneapolis, 1955)
G. Himmelfarb, *Darwin and the Darwinian revolution* (New York, 1959)
R. Hofstadter, *Social Darwinism in American thought, 1860-1915* (New York, 1959)
J. Joll, *The second international, 1889-1914* (New York, 1956)
L. Levine, *Syndicalism in France* (New York, 1914)

A. S. Link, *Woodrow Wilson and the progressive era, 1910-1917* (New York, 1954)

H. D. Lloyd, *Wealth against commonwealth* (New York, 1894; Washington, D. C., 1936)

H. Marcuse, *Reason and revolution: Hegel and the rise of social theory* (Boston, 1950)

Karl Marx, *Capital* (Hamburg, 1867; New York, 1929)

F. Mehring, *Karl Marx* (New York, 1935)

E. R. Pease, *The history of the Fabian Society* (London, 1925)

I. M. Rubinow, *The quest for security* (New York, 1934)

O. Ruhle, *Karl Marx* (New York, 1943)

P. B. Sears, *Charles Darwin* (New York, 1950)

G. Sorel, *Reflections on violence* (Paris, 1908; Glencoe, Ill., 1950)

H. Spencer, *Man versus the state* (New York, 1884; Caldwell, Id., 1940)

L. Steffens, *Autobiography*, 2 vols. (New York, 1936)

G. M. Stekloff, *History of the first international* (New York, 1928)

T. Veblen, *The theory of the leisure class* (New York, 1954)

E. Wilson, *To the Finland Station: a study in the writing and acting of history* (Garden City, N.Y., 1959)

W. Wilson, *The new freedom* (New York, 1914)

IMPERIALISM AND ALLIANCES

H. E. Abend, *Treaty ports* (New York, 1944)

N. Angell, *The great illusion: a study of the relation of military power to national advantage* (New York, 1910, 1933)

M. J. Bau, *Foreign relations of China* (Chicago, 1922)

L. Bauer, *Leopold the unloved: King of the Belgians and of wealth* (Boston, 1935)

E. Brandenburg, *From Bismarck to the World War: a history of German foreign policy, 1870-1914* (New York, 1933)

G. Clark, *A place in the sun* (New York, 1936)

A. R. Colquhoun, *China in transformation* (New York, 1912)

G. L. Dickinson, *The international anarchy, 1904-1914* (New York, 1926)

W. E. B. Du Bois, *The world and Africa: an enquiry into the part which Africa has played in world history* (New York, 1947)

H. Feis, *Europe, the world's banker, 1870-1914: an account of European foreign investment and the connection of world finance with diplomacy before the war* (New Haven, 1930)

R. Y. Gilbert, *The unequal treaties: China and the foreigner* (London, 1956)

O. M. Green, *The foreigner in China* (New York, 1943)

J. A. Hobson, *Imperialism* (New York, 1933)

H. L. Hoskins, *European imperialism in Africa* (New York, 1930)

H. H. Johnston, *A history of the colonization of Africa by alien races* (Cambridge, Eng., 1930)

———, *The opening up of Africa* (New York, 1911)

W. L. Langer, *European alliances and alignments, 1871-1890* (New York, 1931)

———, *European alliances and imperialism, 1890-1902* (New York, 1927)

———, *The Franco-Russian alliance, 1890-1894* (Cambridge, Mass., 1929)   *731*

V. I. Lenin, *Imperialism, the highest stage of capitalism* (New York, 1939)

W. Millis, *The martial spirit: a study of our war with Spain* (New York, 1931)

P. T. Moon, *Imperialism and world politics* (New York, 1939)

T. F. Power, *Jules Ferry and the renaissance of French imperialism* (New York, 1944)

J. T. Pratt, *The expansion of Europe into the Far East* (London, 1947)

J. W. Pratt, *America's colonial experiment* (New York, 1950)

———, *Expansionists of 1898* (Gloucester, Mass., 1952)

J. A. Schumpeter, *Imperialism and social classes* (New York, 1955)

J. B. Scott, *The Hague Peace Conferences of 1899 and 1907*, 2 vols. (Baltimore, 1909)

M. E. Townsend, *European colonial expansion since 1871* (Philadelphia, 1941)

———, *Origins of modern German colonialism, 1871-1885* (New York, 1921)

A. K. Weinberg, *Manifest destiny: a study of nationalist expansionism in American history* (Gloucester, Mass., 1958)

B. Williams, *Cecil Rhodes* (New York, 1921)

E. L. Woodward, *Great Britain and the German navy* (New York, 1935)

VI. War and Revolution

THE FIRST WORLD WAR AND THE VERSAILLES SETTLEMENT

L. Albertini, *The origins of the war of 1914*, vol. I (New York, 1952)

E. H. Buehrig, *Woodrow Wilson and the balance of power* (Bloomington, Ind., 1955)

Carnegie Endowment for International Peace, *The treaties of peace, 1919-1923*, 2 vols. (New York, 1924)

C. R. M. Crutwell, *A history of the Great War, 1914-1918* (Oxford, 1940)

S. B. Fay, *The origins of the World War* (New York, 1938)

H. Folks, *The human costs of the war* (New York, 1920)

K. Kautsky, ed., *Outbreak of the World War: German documents* (New York, 1924)

J. M. Keynes, *The economic consequences of the peace* (New York, 1920)

B. H. Liddell Hart, *A history of the World War, 1914-1918* (London, 1938)

C. A. Macartney, *Hungary and her successors* (New York, 1937)

———, *National states and national minorities* (London, 1934)

E. Mantoux, *The Carthaginian peace: or the economic consequences of Mr. Keynes* (New York, 1952)

F. S. Marston, *The peace conference of 1919* (New York, 1944)

K. F. Nowak, *The collapse of Central Europe* (New York, 1924)

F. L. Paxson, *American democracy and the World War*, 3 vols. (Boston, 1936-48)

A. F. Pribram, *Austrian foreign policy, 1908-1918* (London, 1923)

P. Renouvin, *The immediate origins of the war* (New Haven, 1928)

H. W. V. Temperley, *History of the peace conference at Paris*, 6 vols. (London, 1920-24)

F. P. Walters, *A history of the League of Nations*, 2 vols. (New York, 1952)

J. W. Wheeler-Bennett, *Brest-Litovsk: the forgotten peace* (New York, 1937)

———, *Wreck of reparations* (New York, 1933)

THE RUSSIAN REVOLUTIONS AND COMMUNISM

J. Bunyan and H. H. Fisher, *The Bolshevik revolution: 1917-1918; documents and materials* (Stanford University, 1934)

E. Burns, ed., *A handbook of Marxism* (New York, 1935)

E. H. Carr, *A history of Soviet Russia,* 6 vols. (New York, 1950-59)

W. H. Chamberlin, *History of the Russian Revolution,* 2 vols. (New York, 1935)

I. Deutscher, *The prophet armed: Trotsky, 1879-1921* (New York, 1954)

L. Fischer, *The Soviets in world affairs, 1917-1929,* 2 vols. (Princeton, 1951)

F. A. Golder, ed., *Documents on Russian history, 1914-1917* (New York, 1927)

W. Gurian, *Bolshevism* (New York, 1952)

G. F. Kennan, *Soviet-American relations, 1917-1920,* 2 vols. (Princeton, 1956-58)

L. P. Kirby, *The Russian Revolution* (Boston, 1940)

L. Lawton, *The Russian Revolution, 1917-1926* (London, 1927)

B. Pares, *The fall of the Russian monarchy* (New York, 1939)

A. Rosenberg, *A history of Bolshevism from Marx to the first five-year plan* (New York, 1939)

M. Salvadori, *The rise of modern communism* (New York, 1952)

D. Shub, *Lenin* (Garden City, N.Y., 1951)

L. I. Strakhovsky, *The origins of American intervention in north Russia, 1918* (Princeton, 1937)

L. Trotsky, *The history of the Russian Revolution* (Ann Arbor, Mich., 1957)

C. E. Vulliamy, *The red archives* (London, 1929)

B. D. Wolfe, *Three who made a revolution* (New York, 1948)

ITALIAN FASCISM AND THE WEIMAR REPUBLIC

M. Baumont, *The fall of the Kaiser* (New York, 1931)

A. J. Berlau, *The German Social Democratic Party, 1914-1921* (New York, 1949)

W. Ebenstein, *Fascist Italy* (New York, 1939)

H. Finer, *Mussolini's Italy* (New York, 1935)

S. W. Halperin, *Germany tried democracy: a political history of the Reich from 1918 to 1933* (New York, 1946)

——, *Italy and the Vatican at war* (Chicago, 1939)

R. H. Lutz, *The German revolution, 1918-1919* (Stanford University, 1922)

J. P. Mayer, *Max Weber and German politics: a study in political sociology* (London, 1956)

G. Megaro, *Mussolini in the making* (New York, 1938)

A. Rosenberg, *The birth of the German republic* (New York, 1931)

——, *A history of the German republic* (London, 1936)

H. W. Schneider, *Making the fascist state* (New York, 1929)

H. Stroebel, *The German revolution and after* (New York, 1923)

R. L. G. Waite, *Vanguard of nazism: the free corps movement in postwar Germany, 1918-1923* (Cambridge, Mass., 1952)

THE, TWENTIES IN OTHER COUNTRIES

J. T. Adams, *Our business civilization* (New York, 1929)

H. E. Allen, *The Turkish transformation* (Chicago, 1935)

H. C. Armstrong, *Grey wolf: Kemal Atatürk* (London, 1933)

J. Benda, *The betrayal of the intellectuals* (Boston, 1955)

G. Dangerfield, *The strange death of liberal England* (New York, 1935)

J. Dorfman, *Thorstein Veblen and his America* (New York, 1934)

T. Draper, *The roots of American communism* (New York, 1957)

———, *American communism and Soviet Russia* (New York, 1960)

S. Freud, *An outline of psychoanalysis* (New York, 1949)

R. Graves and A. Hodge, *The long week-end: a social history of Great Britain, 1918-1939* (New York, 1941)

H. Hoover, *American individualism* (Garden City, N.Y., 1922)

L. Infeld, *Albert Einstein* (New York, 1950)

G. L. Lewis, *Turkey* (New York, 1960)

R. S. and H. M. Lynd, *Middletown* (New York, 1937)

E. G. Mears, *Greece to-day* (Stanford University, 1929)

W. A. Phillips, *Revolution in Ireland, 1906-1923* (New York, 1923)

D. J. Saposs, *The labor movement in post-war France* (New York, 1931)

R. W. Seton-Watson, *Twenty-five years of Czechoslovakia* (London, 1945)

J. Swire, *Albania* (London, 1929)

D. E. Webster, *The Turkey of Atatürk* (Philadelphia, 1939)

F. Wittels, *Freud and his time* (New York, 1958)

VII. *The Ordeal of Liberty*

BETWEEN WORLD WARS

F. P. Chambers et al., *This age of conflict* (New York, 1950)

H. W. Ehrmann, *French labor from the popular front to the liberation* (New York, 1947)

G. E. R. Gedye, *Betrayal in Central Europe* (New York, 1939)

———, *Heirs to the Hapsburgs* (Bristol, Eng., 1932)

F. A. von Hayek, *The road to serfdom* (Chicago, 1956)

A. Hutt, *The post-war history of the British working class* (New York, 1938)

O. I. Janowsky, *Nationalities and national minorities* (New York, 1945)

———, *People at bay: the Jewish problem in East Central Europe* (New York, 1938)

J. M. Keynes, *The end of laissez-faire* (London, 1926)

J. A. Leighton, *Social philosophies in conflict* (New York, 1938)

M. Oakeshott, *The social and political doctrines of contemporary Europe* (New York, 1953)

J. S. Roucek, *Contemporary Roumania and her problems* (Stanford University, 1932)

H. Seton-Watson, *Eastern Europe between the wars, 1918-1941* (Cambridge, Eng., 1946)

A. Sturmthal, *The tragedy of European labor, 1918-1939* (New York, 1944)

E. Wiskemann, *Czechs and Germans* (London, 1938)

THE NEW DEAL

D. W. Brogan, *The era of Franklin D. Roosevelt* (New Haven, 1951)
M. Einaudi, *The Roosevelt revolution* (New York, 1959)
P. Einzig, *The world economic crisis, 1929-1931* (New York, 1933)
G. W. Johnson, *Roosevelt* (New York, 1942)
B. Mitchell, *Depression decade* (New York, 1947)
F. Perkins, *The Roosevelt I knew* (New York, 1947)
B. Rauch, *The history of the New Deal, 1933-1938* (New York, 1944)
R. E. Sherwood, *Roosevelt and Hopkins* (New York, 1950)

HITLERISM

R. Andreas-Friedrich, *Berlin underground, 1938-1945* (New York, 1947)
N. H. Baynes, ed., *The speeches of Adolf Hitler: April 1922-August 1939*, 2 vols. (New York, 1942)
A. Bullock, *Hitler: a study in tyranny* (New York, 1952)
R. D. Butler, *The roots of national socialism* (New York, 1942)
E. H. Carr, *German-Soviet relations between two world wars, 1919-1939* (Baltimore, 1951)
G. E. R. Gedye, *Betrayal in Central Europe* (New York, 1939)
K. Heiden, *Der Fuehrer, 1884-1934* (Boston, 1944)
———, *History of national socialism* (New York, 1935)
A. Hitler, *Mein Kampf* (New York, 1939)
E. Kogon, *The theory and practice of hell: the German concentration camps and the system behind them* (New York, 1950)
S. Krieger, ed., *Nazi Germany's war against the Jews* (New York, 1947)
K. Loewenstein, *Hitler's Germany* (New York, 1940)
M. Lowenthal, *The Jews of Germany* (New York, 1936)
F. Meinecke, *The German catastrophe* (Cambridge, Mass., 1950)
C. A. Micaud, *The French Right and Nazi Germany, 1933-1939* (Durham, N.C., 1943)
F. L. Neumann, *Behemoth: the structure and practice of national socialism* (New York, 1942)
L. Poliakov, *Harvest of hate: the Nazi program for the destruction of the Jews of Europe* (Syracuse, N.Y., 1954)
H. Rauschning, *The conservative revolution* (New York, 1941)
———, *Hitler speaks: a series of political conversations with Adolf Hitler . . .* (London, 1940)
———, *The revolution of nihilism* (New York, 1939)
G. Reitlinger, *The final solution: the attempt to exterminate the Jews of Europe, 1939-1945* (London, 1953)
———, *The SS: alibi of a nation, 1922-1945* (London, 1957)
H. Rothfels, *The German opposition to Hitler* (Chicago, 1948)
T. Taylor, *Sword and swastika: generals and Nazis in the Third Reich* (New York, 1952)
H. R. Trevor-Roper, *The last days of Hitler* (New York, 1947)

M. Weinreich, *Hitler's professors: the part of scholarship in Germany's crimes against the Jewish people* (New York, 1946)

J. W. Wheeler-Bennett, *The nemesis of power: the German army in politics, 1918-1945* (New York, 1953)

———, *Wooden titan: Hindenburg in twenty years of German history, 1914-1934* (New York, 1936)

E. Wiskemann, *The Rome-Berlin Axis: a history of the relations between Hitler and Mussolini* (New York, 1949)

STALINISM

A. Baykov, *The development of the Soviet economic system* (New York, 1948)

F. Beck and W. Godin, *Russian purge and the extraction of confession* (New York, 1951)

M. Beloff, *The foreign policy of Soviet Russia, 1929-1941*, 2 vols. (New York, 1949)

F. Borkenau, *The Communist International* (New York, 1939)

E. H. Carr, *The Soviet impact on the Western world* (New York, 1947)

W. P. and Z. Coates, *The second five-year plan of development of the U.S.S.R.* (London, 1934)

J. S. Curtiss, *The Russian church and the Soviet state, 1917-1950* (Boston, 1953)

D. J. Dallin and B. I. Nikolaevsky, *Forced labor in Soviet Russia* (New Haven, 1947)

I. Deutscher, *The prophet unarmed: Trotsky, 1921-1929* (New York, 1959)

———, *Stalin* (New York, 1960)

M. H. Dobb, *Soviet economic development since 1917* (London, 1948)

M. Fainsod, *How Russia is ruled* (Cambridge, Mass., 1953)

M. Farbman, *Piatiletka: Russia's five-year plan* (New York, 1931)

R. Fischer, *Stalin and German communism* (Cambridge, Mass., 1948)

W. Gurian, ed., *The Soviet Union* (Notre Dame, Ind., 1951)

S. N. Harper, *Making Bolsheviks* (Chicago, 1931)

——— and R. Thompson, *Government of the Soviet Union* (New York, 1949)

A. K. Herling, *The Soviet slave empire* (New York, 1951)

R. N. C. Hunt, *The theory and practice of communism* (New York, 1950)

H. Kelsen, *The political theory of Bolshevism* (Berkeley, Cal., 1959)

A. Koestler, *Darkness at noon* (New York, 1954)

H. Kohn, *Nationalism in the Soviet Union* (London, 1933)

R. Magidoff, *The Kremlin vs. the people: the story of the cold civil war in Stalin's Russia* (Garden City, N.Y., 1953)

G. Orwell, *1984* (New York, 1949)

S. M. Schwarz, *Labor in the Soviet Union* (New York, 1951)

———, *Russia's Soviet economy* (New York, 1952)

APPEASEMENT AND THE SPANISH CIVIL WAR

M. Beloff, *The foreign policy of Soviet Russia, 1929-1941*, 2 vols. (New York, 1947-49)

J. A. Brandt, *Toward the new Spain* (Chicago, 1933)

G. Brenan, *The Spanish labyrinth* (New York, 1943)

H. W. Buckley, *Life and death of the Spanish republic* (London, 1940)

R. L. Buell, *Poland: key to Europe* (New York, 1939)

P. Einzig, *Appeasement before, during and after the war* (London, 1942)

H. Feis, *The road to Pearl Harbor* (Princeton, 1950)

G. Freund, *Unholy alliance: Russian-German relations from the treaty of Brest-Litovsk to the treaty of Berlin* (New York, 1957)

H. Gannes and T. Repard, *Spain in revolt* (New York, 1936)

T. J. Hamilton, *Appeasement's child* (New York, 1943)

W. L. Langer and E. Gleason, *The challenge to isolation, 1937-1940* (New York, 1952)

D. E. Lee, *Ten years: the world on its way to war, 1930-1940* (Boston, 1942)

F. E. Manuel, *The politics of modern Spain* (New York, 1938)

W. E. Rappard, *The quest for peace* (Cambridge, Mass., 1940)

B. Rauch, *Roosevelt: from Munich to Pearl Harbor* (New York, 1950)

J. W. Wheeler-Bennett, *Munich: prologue to tragedy* (New York, 1948)

E. Wiskemann, *Prologue to war* (New York, 1940)

A. Wolfers, *Britain and France between two wars* (New York, 1940)

A. M. Young, *Imperial Japan, 1926-1938* (New York, 1938)

THE SECOND WORLD WAR

R. de Belot, *The struggle for the Mediterranean, 1939-1945* (Princeton, 1951)

F. A. Cave et al., *The origins and consequences of World War II* (New York, 1948)

W. Churchill, *Blood, sweat, and tears* (New York, 1941)

———, *The unrelenting struggle* (New York, 1942)

H. S. Commager, ed., *The pocket history of the Second World War* (New York, 1945)

Committee of Records of War Administration, *The United States at war* (Washington, D.C., 1947)

T. Draper, *The six-weeks' war* (New York, 1944)

J. F. C. Fuller, *The Second World War* (London, 1948)

H. W. Gatzke, *Germany's drive to the West* (Baltimore, 1950)

D. L. Gordon and R. J. Dangerfield, *The hidden weapon: the story of economic warfare* (New York, 1947)

J. Hersey, *Hiroshima* (New York, 1956)

E. Janeway, *The struggle for survival: a chronicle of economic mobilization in World War II* (New Haven, 1951)

W. L. Langer, *Our Vichy gamble* (New York, 1947)

——— and E. Gleason, *The undeclared war, 1940-1941* (New York, 1953)

A. J. Liebling, ed., *The republic of silence* (New York, 1947)

A. Maurois, *Why France fell* (London, 1941)

W. H. McNeil, *America, Britain, and Russia, 1941-1946* (New York, 1953)

F. O. Miksche, *Attack: a study of blitzkrieg tactics* (New York, 1942)

S. E. Morison, *History of the United States naval operations in World War II*, 14 vols. (Boston, 1947-60)

THE UNITED NATIONS AND PEACE PROBLEMS

R. Aron, *The century of total war* (Garden City, N.Y., 1954)

N. D. Bentwich, *From Geneva to San Francisco* (London, 1946)

T. Besterman, *UNESCO* (New York, 1951)

H. Finer, *United Nations Economic and Social Council* (Boston, 1946)

S. E. Harris, *The European recovery program* (Cambridge, Mass., 1948)

G. F. Kennan, *American diplomacy, 1900-1950* (Chicago, 1953)

W. Lippmann, *The cold war* (New York, 1947)

P. McGuire, *Experiment in world order* (New York, 1948)

G. Murray, *From the League to the U.N.* (New York, 1948)

W. L. Neumann, *Making the peace, 1941-1945* (Washington, D.C., 1950)

H. L. Roberts, *Russia and America* (New York, 1956)

G. Woodbridge, ed., *UNRRA*, 2 vols. (New York, 1950)

EUROPEAN DEMOCRACIES

V. H. Bernstein, *Final judgment: the story of Nuremberg* (New York, 1947)

R. A. Brady, *Crisis in Britain: plans and achievements of the Labour government* (Berkeley, Cal., 1950)

L. D. Clay, *Decision in Germany* (Garden City, N.Y., 1950)

W. Friedman, *The allied military government of Germany* (London, 1947)

S. Glueck, *The Nuremberg trial and aggressive war* (New York, 1946)

H. Kohn, ed., *German history: some new German views* (Boston, 1954)

H. Luethy, *France against herself* (London, 1955)

E. S. Watkins, *The cautious revolution* (New York, 1951)

F. Williams, *Socialist Britain* (New York, 1949)

G. Wright, *The reshaping of French democracy* (New York, 1948)

COMMUNIST RUSSIA AND CENTRAL EUROPE

G. A. Almond, ed., *The appeals of Communism* (Princeton, 1954)

E. D. Carman, *Soviet imperialism* (Washington, D.C., 1950)

Columbia University, Russian Institute, *The anti-Stalin campaign and international communism: a selection of documents* (New York, 1956)

V. Dedijer, *Tito* (New York, 1953)

G. Fischer, *Soviet opposition to Stalin* (Cambridge, Mass., 1952)

M. J. Lasky, ed., *The Hungarian revolution* (New York, 1957)

S. Mikolajczyk, *The rape of Poland* (New York, 1948)

J. P. Nettl, *The Eastern zone and Soviet policy in Germany, 1945-1950* (New York, 1951)

H. Ripka, *Czechoslovakia enslaved* (London, 1950)

H. L. Roberts, *Rumania* (New Haven, 1951)

J. S. Roucek, *Moscow's European satellites* (Philadelphia, 1950)

H. Seton-Watson, *The East European Revolution* (New York, 1951)

A. B. Ulam, *Titoism and the Cominform* (Cambridge, Mass., 1952)

R. L. Wolff, *The Balkans in our time* (Cambridge, Mass, 1956)

ANTICOLONIALISM IN ASIA AND AFRICA

M. Brecher, *Nehru* (Oxford, 1959)

J. F. Cady, *A history of modern Burma* (Ithaca, N.Y., 1958)

J. Dunner, *Republic of Israel* (New York, 1950)

E. Estorick, *Changing empire: Churchill to Nehru* (New York, 1950)

E. J. Hammer, *The Struggle for Indo-China* (Stanford, Cal., 1954)

J. C. Hurewitz, *The struggle for Palestine* (New York, 1950)

G. McT. Kahin, *Nationalism and revolution in Indonesia* (Ithaca, N.Y., 1952)

W. Z. Laqueur, *Communism and nationalism in the Middle East* (London, 1956)

B. Lasker, *New forces in Asia* (New York, 1950)

L. S. B. Leakey, *Mau Mau and the Kikuyu* (London, 1955)

G. Lenczowski, *The Middle East in world affairs* (Ithaca, N.Y., 1952)

————, *Russia and the West in Iran, 1918-1948* (Ithaca, N.Y., 1949)

R. W. Lindholm, ed., *Viet-Nam: the first five years* (East Lansing, Mich., 1959)

R. Linton, ed., *Most of the world: the peoples of Africa, Latin America, and the East today* (New York, 1949)

B. R. Nanda, *Mahatma Gandhi* (Boston, 1958)

R. C. North, *Moscow and Chinese Communists* (Stanford, Cal., 1953)

E. O. Reischauer, *The United States and Japan* (Cambridge, Mass., 1957)

————, *Wanted: an Asian policy* (New York, 1955)

B. I. Schwartz, *Chinese communism and the rise of Mao* (Cambridge, Mass., 1951)

R. Symonds, *The making of Pakistan* (London, 1950)

P. Tompkins, *American-Russian relations in the Far East* (New York, 1949)

B. Ward, *The interplay of East and West* (New York, 1957)

D. Wehl, *The birth of Indonesia* (London, 1948)

RECENT TRENDS

R. Aron, *The opium of the intellectuals* (Garden City, N.Y., 1957)

R. H. S. Crossman, ed., *The god that failed* (New York, 1950)

M. Djilas, *The new class* (New York, 1957)

H. W. Gatzke, *The present in perspective* (Chicago, 1957)

P. Geyl, *From Ranke to Toynbee* (Northampton, Mass., 1952)

E. Wilson, *Red, black, blond, and olive* (New York, 1956)

A. J. Zurcher, ed., *Constitutions and constitutional trends since World War II* (New York, 1955)

Index